POC
G

AUSTRALIAN COINS AND BANKNOTES

TWENTY THIRD EDITION

INDEPENDENTLY SELF PUBLISHED

Concept, design, layout, financing & marketing are conducted by Jenny & Greg McDonald trading as

Greg McDonald Publishing and Numismatics Pty Ltd

A.B.N. 56 058 911 701

Printed by Ligare Book Printers 138 Bonds Road, Riverwood 2210

PROUDLY PRINTED IN AUSTRALIA

While everyone has a stance on climate change, we just meekly accept that billion dollar companies are free to send jobs and opportunities overseas for short-term profits. If we allow this to continue to happen, who's going to be left to give our grand children and future generations meaningful employment?

Helping to protect Aussie jobs

In purchasing this book you are supporting the Australian Printing Industry and it's employees. Thank you!

Written, designed and privately published by Jenny and Greg McDonald trading as :-

Greg McDonald Publishing & Numismatics Pty Ltd.
Professional Numismatist and Author since 1979.
PO Box 649, LAVINGTON, NSW, 2641, AUSTRALIA

E-mail : gregmcdonaldpublishing@gmail.com

Twenty Third Edition : August 2017
National Library of Australia Card Number. 978-1-875389-06-3
Twenty Second Edition : July 2015
National Library of Australia Card Number. 978 -1-875389-02-5
Twenty First Edition : November 2013
National Library of Australia Card Number. 978-1875389-07-0
Twentieth Edition : November 2012
National Library of Australia Card Number. 978-0-9806936-4-5
Nineteenth Edition : December 2011
National Library of Australia Card Number. 978-0-9806936-2-1
Eighteenth Edition : November 2010
National Library of Australia Card Number. 978-0-9806936-1
Seventeenth Edition : November 2009
National Library of Australia Card Number. 978-0-9806936-0-7
Sixteenth Edition : November 2008
National Library of Australia Card Number. 978-0-9751244-9-9
Fifteenth Edition : November 2007
National Library of Australia Card Number. 978-0-9751244-8-2
Fourteenth Edition : November 2006
National Library of Australia Card Number. 0 9751244 7 1
Thirteenth Edition : November 2005
National Library of Australia Card Number. 0 9751244 5 5
Twelfth Edition : November 2004. Reprinted August 2005
National Library of Australia Card Number. 0 9751244 4 7
Eleventh Edition : November 2003. Reprinted June 2004
National Library of Australia Card Number. 0 9751244 3 9
Tenth Edition : November 2002
National Library of Australia Card Number. 0 9586631 5 7
Ninth Edition : December 2001.
National Library of Australia Card Number. 1 875389 05 9
Eighth Edition : December 2000.
National Library of Australia Card Number. 0 9586631 4 9
Seventh Edition : January 2000.
National Library of Australia Card Number. 0 9586631 2 2
Sixth Edition : November 1998.
National Library of Australia Card Number. 1 875389 04 0
Fifth Edition : August 1997.
National Library of Australia Card Number. 1 875389 02 4
Fourth Edition : July 1996. Reprinted Dec. 1996.
National Library of Australia Card Number. 0 9586631 0 6
Third Edition : June 1995.
National Library of Australia Card Number. 0 646 23249 5
Second Edition : April 1994. Reprinted November 1994
National Library of Australia Card Number. 0 646 18132 7
First Edition : April 1993. Reprinted November 1993
National Library of Australia Card Number. 1 875389 01 6

Also by the same author :-

Rigby's Australian Coin and Banknote Guide
Published : December 1983. Reprinted January 1984
ISBN number 07270 1850 7. (Out of print)

How to Buy and Sell Australian Coins and Banknotes
Published : September 1985.
ISBN number 09589582 03. (Out of print)

The Australian Coin and Banknote Market Guide
Published : November 1987
ISBN number 0 9589582 1 1. (Out of print)

Collecting and Investing In Australian Coins and Banknotes
First Edition : Published : October 1990. Reprinted May 1991
ISBN number 1 875389 00 8. (Out of print)

Second Edition : Published : November 1991
ISBN number 1 875389 00 8. (Out of print)

ADVERTISERS INDEX

ACKNOWLEDGEMENTS

For my wife Jenny and our children, Luke, Lachlan and Lily.

ALSO SPECIAL THANKS TO THE FOLLOWING

Jim Noble; Peter Hiscock, Ken & Kath Downie, Barrie Winsor; Steele Waterman; Eric Eigner; Chris Heath; Jim Johnson, Tony Grant; Klaus Ford; Peter Brooks; Stewart Wright; David L. Allen; Colin Pitchfork; Graeme Petterwood; Roger McNeice OAM; Peter Small; Peter & Seija Strich; John Platts; Mark Freehill; Gerhart Reimann-Basch; David Manning; David Worland; Richard Welling; Bob Climpson Kathryn Harris; Jill Pearson; Alan Flint,; Stephen Fenton; Andrew Crellan; John Mullhall, The Craft family; Paul Hannaford; Trevor Wilkin; Ross MacDiarmid; Ed Harbuz, Peter August, David Miller, Graeme Manning, Peter Hiscock; Fred Lever; Jim Mansell; Bruce Mansfield; Jerry Himelfarb; Mark Nemtsas; Alan Triggett; Shane McCullogh

• A special *'thank you'* to Elizabeth Finniecombe at Ligare Printing. The most dedicated and organised person I have ever met. Thanks Liz, for putting out all the fires that pop up with a project as big as this.

• Special thanks also to Lee McAllister, of Quantum Printing, Albury NSW for her incredible ability to take my pathetically rough pencil drawings and turn them into eye catching front covers.

• Also John O'Connor, gentleman, numismatist, numismatic author and proof reader without equal. Despite his own busy schedule as a cataloguer with Noble Numismatics, John seems to be able to pluck time out of the air to discuss, suggest, read and correct many sections of my books.

VALE MAX STERN

Since the publication of our last book we have lost a true "one off" in the passing of Max Stern. While a light and wiry ball of energy, Max was a true giant amongst those involved in a wide spectrum of life. He was a familiar and much respected figure in many facets of business, sport and family. All roles he obviously did very successfully. Anyone who read his book, My Stamp on Life, couldn't help to be overwhelmed with his zest for life and his refusal to give up despite odds that people living in this generation can hardly imagine. I admired him greatly. Whenever we met, he always had a smile and a kind word. He was always very complimentary of my book and this meant such a lot to me considering his standing in the industry. My son Lachlan and I will never forget the impromptu 90 minutes in his office and behind the scenes tour. A wall full of photographic memories. Pre 'selfie' snaps with virtually every Australian Prime Minister since Malcolm Fraser, pics of world-class soccer hero's that left my son wide-eyed and slack-jawed. His young eyes glossed over images of another face familiar to many. As the camera focused, the man gripped Max's shoulders like only a true friend would. Simon Wiesenthal! We hadn't made an appointment; we were just walking past the Port Phillip Arcade and saw Max behind the counter. I told my then 12 y-o son he was about to meet one of the most remarkable men of the ages. It was supposed to be a quick pit stop, just to say hello. Anyone who encounted Max behind the counter knew that idle chitchat during business hours was not his strong point. What a reception we got when I introduced my son as a keen soccer player. For the next 90 minutes I was just a wallflower as Max pulled out half a century's worth of football memorabilia and Lachlan and he debated the finer points of the 'beautiful game.' I shouldn't complain. My reward for not trying to engage in a sport I knew virtually nothing about was a signed copy of his book, complete with his own Australia Post stamp. Great memories - great bloke! RIP, old mate.

CONTENTS

CONTENTS

CONTENTS

DISCLAIMER

As the title suggests, this book is intended as a *Guide* only, in every sense of the word. While the publisher endeavours to, in good faith, impart useful and helpful information to the reader, the publisher makes no representations or warranties of any kind, express or implied, about the completeness, accuracy, reliability, suitability or availability of any of the information contained herein. Any reliance you place on such information is therefore strictly at your own risk. For further clarification, please turn to page 8 for information on how we collate our data.

If you feel you have scans or information that will improve future editions of the pocketbook, please let us know. Please let us know if any errors or updates. Our email address is back on page One.

As you read through this book, we hope you will notice two things; Firstly we hope you identify a lot of new information previously unavailable in any of our previous books. Careful scrutiny will show that much of this new information goes beyond the most recent new and varied issues from our mints and the Reserve Bank. Keen collectors will see that continual research has added new knowledge to old collecting areas. In some cases, the information within these pages, such as the section on the PNC issues and the very complex series of One Dollar coins, is the most inclusive to be published in any numismatic book anywhere. The other important aspect that must be made clear that all the above improvements are not all my own work. I am very grateful, and indeed, humbled by the many collectors who contact me to advise of an error or typo. Sometimes a simple slip will result in two or three hundred emails from collectors from all over the world saying much the same thing. As I feel compelled to reply to all these notifications, so does the incentive to be more assiduous with my proof reading. Other collectors, who have developed a real passion for some area of the hobby that wasn't even around when I started collecting, willingly offer the results of their laborious research for me to publish and share with other collectors with the same interest. For me, personally, it is a real feeling of satisfaction, when someone writes to say that it was a chance encounter with one of our books that got them started in the hobby. My apologies to the partners of the smitten who might notice smaller portions served up at dinner or start suggestion a camping family holiday close to home rather than the usual five-star oversea resort. Happy Collecting!

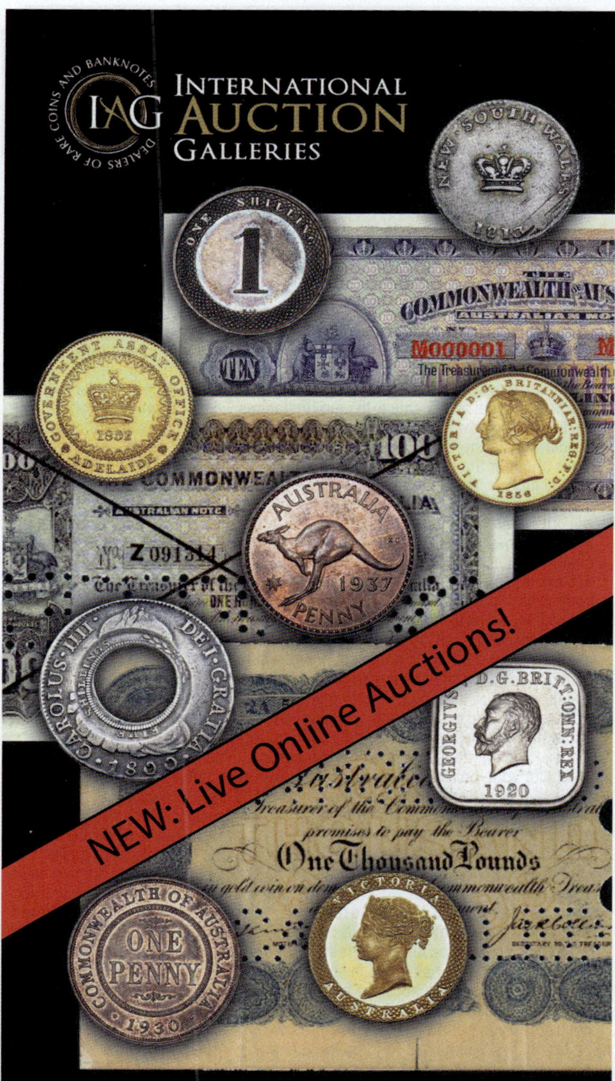

DEALERS OF RARE COINS AND BANKNOTES
IAG
INTERNATIONAL
AUCTION
GALLERIES
NEW: Live Online Auctions!
One Thousand Pounds

NOTE REGARDING PRICING IN THIS GUIDE

PLEASE READ THIS BEFORE GOING TO THE PRICING SECTION

It cannot be stressed strongly enough that the prices listed in this book are only a "guide" - although every effort has been taken to be as accurate as possible at the time of publication. The author acknowledges that the price given in this book for a particular item may vary greatly from similar pieces offered for sale at markets or the internet. The prices listed in this guide are what you might fairly expect to pay as a full retail price from a professional dealer who has to factor in a number of external costs such as shop rent, advertising, GST, company tax, staff wages and insurance to name just a few. Few internet sellers have these added costs that have to be factored into the retail price of a coin or banknote. In most cases most internet sellers also don't have the ability or skill of a professional numismatist. In many instances, coins or banknotes offered on the internet are overgraded or even fake. This is not to suggest that this is done deliberately in the majority of cases, but the result is the same where an item looks cheaper than what other professionals might charge. This doesn't mean that all items offered by dealers or advanced collectors are always correct as any human being is capable of making a mistake. However most professionals will offer a life-time guarantee against any item they sell as being a counterfeit. Many are members of numismatic associations and societies which include a charter of ethical conduct. There are also many other complex reasons for a coin or banknote being attributed a particular price. In some situations (such as very common low grade LSD coins) the price has always reflected the cost of grading, packaging, advertising etc. This will explain the usual shock (maybe outrage) when a collector might be offered just a few cents for a similar coin a dealer might be offering for a dollar. In some instances where the coin has a precious metal content, the price may be tied to the bullion value of the issue rather than price variations brought on by collector interest. This is in fact what has happened with issues made of silver, gold, platinum and palladium. Furthermore the prices quoted are what you might "expect'" to pay for individual items if you were to buy from a dealer or through an auction. The price you would expect to obtain for your collection if you are a seller will naturally be lower to allow the dealer or auctioneer his commercial profit. This is especially so of coins in poor condition where the actual coin is of little interest to many collectors. As mentioned before sellers might feel they are getting a raw deal if offered five cents for a similar coin a dealer might be selling for a dollar. In such cases, the cost represents the time and labour of sorting, grading and packaging such coins. If you have a coin worth $10,000 and the dealer has a likely buyer you might be offered up to 95% of the retail price. In short, any price you are offered when you want to sell will depend on the dealer's own needs. Obviously such a dealer is going to be more interested in a coin another collector wants rather than one he already has ten of in stock. I guess there is no perfect way to put a price against a numismatic item and be completely spot on every time. It is just not possible. Of course, I expect the pricing section to come in for the usual criticism. If you need a coin or banknote for your collection then these prices will be too high; if you have one for sale, the prices will be too low! Of all the coin shows I've attended or taken part in (over 600 starting in 1977) I have yet to see two dealers charge the same price for a simple proof set - so what is a correct price? What I have tried to do is offer prices you might reasonably be expected to pay for a coin or banknote in relationship to its grade. In trying to achieve this I have not only compared auction results but also sometimes more realistic prices achieved through a wide range of dealers' regular pricelists and prices for particular items noted at fairs throughout Australia. On top of this, prices advertised in mediums such as the Australasian Coin and Banknote Magazine (which I co-founded in 1996) are also monitored. However the strongest point regarding our method of arriving at a price involves the utilisation of many independent experts. It is important to remember that the pricing section of this book is not the opinion of one or two people. It is the result of input of over 30 distinguished and respected collectors and professional dealers who collect, buy and sell coins and banknotes every day of the week. With this book you can be guaranteed the most accurate price guide and general information possible.

GLOSSARY OF TERMS

ACCUMULATION : Coins, banknotes or other numismatic items which are unclassified, unsorted and unattributed; in other words, not a pre-planned or organised collection.

ATTRIBUTION : The identification of a numismatic item by characteristics such as the issuing authority, date or period, the denomination or alloy.

AUTHORISED ISSUE : A striking by a government authority or by civilian or military authority in control of an area.

BAG MARKS : Minor abrasions on an otherwise uncirculated coin, caused by handling in mint bags.

BANKNOTE : A promissory note issued by a bank in useful denominations, payable to a bearer and intended to circulate as money.

BASE METAL : Either a pure metal or alloy which has little intrinsic value such as copper and bronze as opposed to gold or silver.

BILLON : A low - grade alloy used for some minor coin issues consisting usually of a mixture of silver and copper, and sometimes covered with a silver wash.

BOURSE : A coin fair or show where collectors and dealers meet to buy, sell or trade numismatic items. From a French word meaning "purse".

BROCKAGE : Due to a striking malfunction the coin will appear to have the same design on both sides. However one side will show a reverse or mirror strike. This is due to a coin not releasing from the die and striking the next coin in the system. The design from the first coin will be imprinted (in reverse) into the second coin.

BULLION : Uncoined precious metal in the form of bars, plates etc. Also the intrinsic value attributed to a worn or very common precious metal coin.

CARBON SPOTS : Not really carbon in the chemical sense but a term used to describe dark spots on the surface of a coin.

CHOICE : A term used to describe a particularly nice example (gem, proof-like etc).

CLASHED DIES : Obverse and reverse dies which have come together in the striking process without a planchet in place. Coins produced from such a pair of dies usually show mirror - image traces of the die on the opposite side.

COIN : Usually a piece of metal, marked with a device, issued by a governing authority and intended to be used as money.

COLLAR : A retaining ring die which encapsulates the blank immediately before striking. The collar may form the edge design such as reeding, milling or lettering.

CONDITION : The state of preservation of a coin or note. The better the condition the more desirable to the collector.

COUNTERFEIT : An object made to imitate a genuine numismatic piece with intent to deceive or defraud, irrespective of whether the intended fraud is primarily monetary or numismatic.

DENOMINATION : The stated face value of a coin or banknote.

DENTICLES : Dots or beads arranged around the edge of many coins, including most pre-decimal coins.

FROSTING : Coins, particularly proof or pattern pieces, may be issued with certain parts of the design slightly dulled. This is accomplished by slight sand blasting or etching that part of the design on the die.

GLOSSARY OF TERMS

GRADE : A carefully constructed series of guidelines to determine the condition and thus the rarity and value of a coin, banknote or another piece of numismatic material.
GEM : A flawless coin struck from normal circulation dies.
HAIRLINES : Almost invisible scratches which appear on some proof surfaces which have been cleaned or mishandled.
INCUSE : Or intaglio. A design which is recessed rather than raised.
INTRINSIC : The meltdown value of the coin rather than its face or numismatic value.
LEGEND : Inscription around the edge of a coin. On Australian coins, the pre - decimal issues included a Latin legend while the decimal issues feature a more simplified English legend.
MASTER DIE : The original die from which working dies are made. New working dies can be taken from the master die as they wear out.
MATTE PROOF : A proof coin or medal with a finely granulated surface. They were mostly produced in the 19th century. Today, most proofs have frosted highlights.
MINT LUSTRE : The "bloom" on the surface of an uncirculated coin or medal resulting from the radial flow of metal caused by striking dies. Mint lustre or "bloom" is somewhat frosty in appearance as opposed to the mirror-like smoothness of the field of a proof.
MINTMARK : A letter or other symbol, sometimes of a privy nature, which indicates the mint of origin.
MINT ROLLS : Usually refers to uncirculated coins wrapped in pre-determined amounts by the issuing authority.
MINT SET : One coin of each denomination or design produced by a given mint in a given year by an issuing authority and usually attractively packaged.
MISPRINT : A banknote error caused by faulty printing.
MIS-STRIKE : An error coin which is usually struck off centre.
MULE : A coin, token or medal whose obverse die is not matched with its official or regular reverse die.
NUMISMATIC : The science, study or collecting of coins, tokens, medals, papermoney, orders, decorations and similar objects.
OBVERSE : The side of a numismatic item which bears the principal design or device, as prescribed by the issuing authority.

OVERDATE : The date made by a mint engraver super -imposing one or more numbers over a previously dated die. In the Australian series the 1922/1 Threepence overdate is the most famous example. Australian overdates can be found in the gold, silver and bronze issues. They carry substantial premiums.
PATINA : Natural colouring acquired by a coin, token or medal with the passing of time. It might also be the result of oxidation produced by certain soils, moisture or impurities in the atmosphere.
PATTERN : A coin submitted to the coin issuing authorities as a proposed issue but not necessarily one which is adopted.
PIEDFORT : A coin of normal design struck on a planchet of at least double the normal thickness.

GLOSSARY OF TERMS

PLANCHET : A blank piece of metal which has been cut to the required shape but yet to be struck into a coin.
PREFIX : Letters or numbers in front of the serial numbers on a banknote.
PRIVY MARK : First used on the coinage of the English King, Edward III, they were originally secret marks showing the period when a coin was struck. Today, the Perth Mint uses them to denote special commemorative issues.
PROOF : A carefully struck coin using special dies with either a mirror - like or matte finish with each individually polished planchet being struck at least twice.
REEDED EDGE : Edge serrations on a coin imposed by a collar die. Now a decorative feature, it was originally put in place to prevent clipping.
RELIEF : The raised lettering on a coin. Opposite to incuse.
RESTRIKE : A coin which is struck at a later date using the original dies.
REVERSE : The "Tails" side of a coin which carries an appropriate design such as the coat of arms of the country.
RIM : A raised area of metal around the edge of a coin or flan. It is intended to protect the rest of the coin from wear. Sometimes within the rim are dots or denticles.
SPECIMEN : A coin or banknote prepared with special care as an example of a given issue.
SUFFIX : Letters appearing after a serial number. Such letters are part of the serial number. See some early pre - decimal Australian banknotes.
SUPERSCRIBED : Wording superimposed over another note to change its value or issuing authority.
TONING : A slow, natural and normal process by which a coin oxidises over a number of years. Blue, yellow, gold and red tonings occur. If attractive in colour, such toning can add appreciable value to an uncirculated coin.
TRIAL PIECE : A test piece struck to examine the efficiency of new or re-worked dies. The test coin may be struck in a metal other than that used for the eventual circulation coins. *(See trial piece at right).*

TYPE : Coins of the same denomination with similar designs. Usually only the date will change.
UNIFACE : A coin struck only on one side.
UPGRADING : Refers to the process whereby a collector progressively improves the overall grade or condition of his or her collection by replacing worn examples with better pieces.
VIGNETTES : The pictorial part of the note as distinguished from the frame or lettering. Vignettes may be portraits, scenes, objects or other features deemed to be the prominent design of the note.
WATERMARK : A section of a note which is specially treated to contain an unobtrusive design which is difficult to see unless held up to the light.
WORKING DIES : Dies taken from the master die to actually do the stamping of coins. These are replaced as they wear out or fracture.
WORKING HUBS : The transfer punch with a relief from which working dies are made.

PROOF : Describes a type of coin, not a condition or grade. Such coins are specially struck collector pieces not intended for circulation. Highly polished dies and blanks are used in their manufacture so that they have a mirror - like finish when struck. They are individually handled during production. Many proof coins have a frosted relief, the design having been treated with acid or sand blasted so that it has a matte finish to make it stand out against the highly polished field surrounding it. Some proof coins have an all over matte finish although this is not usual with Australian coins.

FDC : (FLEUR DE COIN) : This is a French term which literally means: "Flower of the Die". It describes a coin in the highest state of preservation. It can be used with PROOF coins exclusively struck for collectors, or coins produced for normal circulation. The strike should be faultless and well centered. Design details will be razor sharp. The surface of the coin and the rim will not show any Detracting Marks, and full fresh Mint Lustre must be present. There is outstanding Eye Appeal. Silver coins may feature an attractive Patina or Toning (see below). Bronze coins must be virtually fully Brilliant.

GEM UNCIRCULATED : Far more often than not, this will be the highest grade a collector can realistically expect to encounter, as opposed to the above mentioned *"super coins"* referred to as FDC. A "GEM" uncirculated coin will be almost faultless with a strong, but not necessarily absolutely perfect strike. The design may show just a hint of die-wear but such wear should be minimal. Detracting Marks are of a highly insignificant nature. Virtually Full Lustre or Mint Bloom will be evident. Patina or Toning may be present on both silver or bronze coins. Strong Eye Appeal is present. With bronze coins, the degree of Brilliance remaining may have a significant influence on the value of the coin, but not its grade. It is not unusual to find a GEM grade bronze coin that has fully toned. Paradoxically, toning (or lack of Brilliance) is less acceptable to collectors on bronze coins than an attractive tone (Patina) on a GEM grade silver coin. To express the amount of Brilliance remaining on a bronze coin, some dealers will use a "%" as an indicator after the grade. Thus, GEM - 50%B (or 50% Brilliance) refers to a coin retaining half its Brilliance.

CHU : CHOICE UNCIRCULATED : Sometimes abbreviated to CHU. Describes a fairly well struck coin but some weakness in this area is acceptable. A CHU coin will be free of any significant Detracting Marks and still retain a considerable degree of Mint Lustre. Pleasant Eye Appeal is present.

UNC : UNCIRCULATED - TYPICAL : As the name would imply, a coin which has not been circulated in the commercial sense and therefore shows no wear. It may however have been struck from a die nearing the end of its useful life, and not all of the intricate details of the design may be formed fully on the coin. Moderate but not excessive Detracting Marks from the production process may be evident in the fields and on the rim. Fairly attractive Eye Appeal should be present. Footnote. Excessive Detracting Marks or other major imperfections must either be mentioned in addition to the grade, or if reasonable, the grade itself should be lowered into the EF range, to be in keeping with the values given in this guide.

aUNC : ALMOST UNCIRCULATED : Similar to above but with faint traces of wear on the highest points of the design. The coin still shows a reasonable degree of lustre. Coins in aUnc condition might even have more eye appeal than uncirculated coins as they might be a very sharp strike and have minimal bag marks despite showing very minor traces of having been handled or circulated.

EF : EXTREMELY FINE : Generally speaking, this grade describes a coin which shows some slight wear that is barely noticeable to the naked eye. However care should be taken to give due consideration to the striking of the coin in the first place. Be careful not to confuse a soft strike with what might otherwise appear to be wear.

VF : VERY FINE : A coin in this grade will show distinct signs of wear which could not possibly be due to a soft or weak strike. Most of the lustre will have disappeared and the high points of the coin will be completely missing. Some very slight rim damage may be present in the form of tiny indentations (as opposed to significant nicks). Overall though, the coin should still be generally pleasing to the eye with most of the major detail still quite sharp.

F : FINE : By now the coin exhibits extensive evidence of having been circulated. The general design is easy to recognise but most of the significant parts of the design have worn away.

VG : VERY GOOD : A rather misleading term to describe a coin which is anything but in "Very Good" condition. In fact the entire surface of the coin is practically devoid of significant detail although the basic design and the date will still be readable.

PATINA. WHAT IT IS AND WHAT IT'S NOT

DEFINITION : A natural colouring acquired by a coin, token or medal with the passing of time. It may also be the result of oxidation as a consequence of the above being exposed to other influences causing a chemical reaction. From time to time, certain coins appear in the market place fetching quite spectacular record prices at auctions. Such coins are usually scarce types or dates to begin with, and often in a high grade of preservation. Sometimes they have acquired an amazingly attractive patina or toning. Discerning collectors may pay a considerable premium over catalogue for a coin featuring an attractive and original patina with exceptional eye appeal. Conversely, if a coin is unattractively toned and dirty to boot, it will have limited value to a collector. Cleaning or restoring such a coin as closely as possible to its original condition may then be the only way to make it desirable and saleable again.

The issue of cleaning or restoring coins may well be the most contentious one in the context of numismatics. Most of this is due to the damage caused by well - meaning but inexperienced "restorers". The advice generally given by the experts "Don't clean your coins," is indeed, very valid. An undamaged but unattractively toned and dirty coin cleaned with the required expertise can often be restored close to its original condition. This may still not make it as desirable to some as an attractively patinated coin, but the reality of the matter is that it will make such a coin collectable and saleable again. There are many collectors who prefer uncirculated coins in their fully lustrous and brilliant state.

A point of warning to novice collectors : A patinated coin will often hide imperfections like Detracting Marks (such as nicks, scratches and abrasions) in a most effective manner. Never purchase such coins before close inspection with a magnifying glass. Experienced numismatists will not overlook such impediments when the time comes to resell your coins, no matter how "professionally" they might have been graded.

INVESTOR OR COLLECTOR ?

Although only having a relatively short numismatic history, Australia has produced some of the world's rarest and most sought after coins and banknotes. The sale of a proof 1930 Penny by Spink - Noble for $150,000 several years ago made front page news in the US based World Coin News. It still holds the world record as the most expensive 20th century bronze coin. In a London auction room in 1992, a 1920 Sydney Mint sovereign sold for over $260,000. Earlier this year the same coin was knocked down for over $800,000 at the sensational Quartermaster sale where just over 300 lots sold for a total of over $10 million. Despite recessions and other uncertain economic conditions records continue to fall. As well as the possibility of obtaining strong prices for Australian rarities overseas, the Australian market is also well catered for with a network of professional dealers who adhere to a strict code of ethics under the banner of the Australian Numismatic Dealers Association (ANDA) . You would be well advised to deal only with ANDA members or dealers who are members of similar associations which require a high standard of ethics. A portfolio of coins and banknotes has a number of advantages over other more traditional forms of investment if it is not part of a formal superannuation fund. (See previous articles). Firstly, coins are non - taxable while in your possession as they do not produce a profit until sold. Conversely, commerical real estate, shares, bonds, etc produce rents, dividends and interest which are taxable while held. A numismatic portfolio does not require constant supervision. Although regarded as a medium to long term investment, once bought they can be locked away and forgotten about. A fortune in coins could be put into a matchbox. They are also invisible forms of wealth. Only you and the seller know about the transaction. They are a liquid asset and can be sold at a moment's notice. The value of a coin, banknote or other numismatic item is determined by three main factors. These are condition, rarity and popularity of the series. Notice that age does not come into the picture. In fact, there are many ancient Roman bronze coins which can be bought for less than $10. A coin in fresh mint condition is worth many times a similar coin in worn condition. Even the slightest amount of wear can greatly affect value. Working out the demand of a coin or banknote requires some knowledge of the market and the most popular areas. This is why it is of the utmost importance to rely on a reputable dealer tohelp you build up an investment portfolio.

GRADING BANKNOTES

Like coins, banknotes are valued according to their state of preservation. The most common form of grading such notes is as follows.

UNCIRCULATED : A banknote as found in a bundle or section direct from Note Printing Australia. It will have no folds or flickmarks. It might be slightly rippled in the area of the watermark while modern polymer banknotes might show slight buckling from the plastic strapping used to bundle up blocks of notes for transporting. This is normal. Some collectors and dealers refer to such a note as CFU or *(Crisp, Flat, Uncirculated)*. Strictly speaking this is almost impossible to achieve because of the above comments dealing with manufacturing methods.

aUNC : ABOUT UNCIRCULATED : An uncirculated banknote with a teller counting flick or centerfold.

EF : EXTREMELY FINE : Such a note should be clean and crisp with only the slightest amount of folding or creasing. Such a note may have up to three light folds. It should not be stained or faded or impart any other weakness one should expect from a note which has only received marginal handling in circulation.

VF : VERY FINE : A note showing distinct signs of wear although the paper will still be reasonably crisp and not limp. Numerous light folds or even one or two heavy folds will be noticed although the note will be free of heavy soiling or folding.

F : FINE : The note will show soiling and heavy creasing and a number of small tears. Overall the note will still appear to be in a collectable condition although much of the colour and brightness has gone.

VG : VERY GOOD : Such a note is just about at the end of its useful life and is of little value to the collector unless very rare. The note will display major discolouration and staining as well as numerous tears and even pin holes.

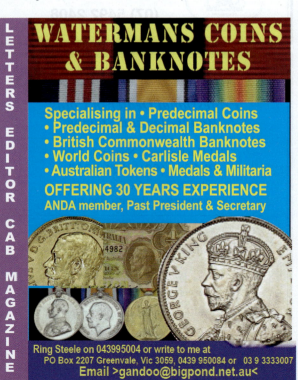

PROCLAMATION COINS

First Coins of the new Colony

The British authorities regarded the new colony of New South Wales as an outdoor prison - a dumping ground for the seemingly endless queue of convicts that paraded through the draconian legal system of the time. All the goods and services required by the band of convicts, guards and administrators that made up the *"First Fleet"* and those that followed, were to be provided by the Government until the new settlement could become self sufficient. Money was originally a low priority. However, as convicts gained their freedom and trading ships brought added luxuries and free settlers looking for a new life, it soon became apparent that some sort of currency was needed. Governor King was to play a decisive part in the future of Australian numismatics when, in 1800, he tried to sort out the economic shambles that threatened the very existence of the colony. What did pass for currency was a hotch-potch of coins from the four corners of the world which traded hands based on their intrinsic value. Naturally no two people could agree exactly on the right value for any given coin. The problem was made worse by the fact that even this meagre supply was continually being syphoned off by visiting traders. Governor King decided to solve both problems with his historic Proclamation of 1800. The proclamation had two aims. He wanted to give the coins circulating an official value, higher than normal, so that the coins would stay in the colony. The theory was that no trader would want them at their inflated value. The coins mentioned in his edict of November 19 are listed below. In most cases the coins illustrated below are only one of a variety of designs issued which could be deemed to be Proclamation coins. The prices quoted are for the most common date, design or mint.

COINS OF THE PROCLAMATION (TABLE OF SPECIE)

Denomination / Country of origin	£.	s.	d.
A gold Guinea / Great Britain	1	2	0
A gold Half - Johanna / Portugal	2	0	0
A gold Mohur / India	1	17	6
A silver Dollar / Spain and her colonies	-	5	0
A gold Johanna / Portugal	4	0	0
A gold Ducat / Netherlands	-	9	6
A gold Pagoda / India	-	8	0
A silver Rupee / India	-	2	6
A silver Guilder / Netherlands	-	2	0
A silver Shilling / Great Britain	-	1	1
A copper Penny (Cartwheel) / Great Britain	-	-	2

GREAT BRITAIN GOLD GUINEA

Coin illustrated : Spade reverse (1787 - 1799) 8.35 grams

Description	Fine	VF	EF	Unc
GEORGE III (Various designs. 1763-1799)	525	950	1,550	2,500

PROCLAMATION COINS

ONE SHILLING (SILVER) GREAT BRITAIN

Coin illustrated : George III one - year issue, 1787

Description	Fine	VF	EF	Unc
Struck in seven provinces as a trade coin	125	195	345	475

ONE PENNY (COPPER) GREAT BRITAIN

Coin illustrated : George III one - year issue, 1797.

Description	Fine	VF	EF	Unc
Struck by Matthew Boulton (Birmingham)	125	295	950	1,800

Although not specifically mentioned in the Proclamation, most collectors include related denominations such as the English sixpence of 1787 as well as the copper halfpenny of 1799 and the bigger twopence piece of 1797.

GUILDER (SILVER) NETHERLANDS

Coin illustrated : West Freisland Province

Description	Fine	VF	EF	Unc
Struck in various provinces.	125	250	550	950

PROCLAMATION COINS

DUCAT (GOLD) NETHERLANDS

Coin illustrated : Province of Holland (1781). 3.5 grams

Description	Fine	VF	EF	Unc
Struck in seven provinces as a trade coin	250	450	650	950

'STAR' PAGODA (GOLD) INDIA

Coin illustrated : Star Pagoda. Circa 1790

Description	Fine	VF	EF	Unc
Various types either milled or hand struck	275	395	650	850

MOHUR (GOLD) INDIA

Coin illustrated : Bengal Presidency (1793). 12.36 grams.

Description	Fine	VF	EF	Unc
Numerous designs - all inscriptional	900	1,350	2,200	3,000

NB : Beware of jeweller's copies

ONE RUPEE (SILVER) INDIA

Coin illustrated : State of Bengal (Sicca Rupee - 1748)

Description	Fine	VF	EF	Unc
Numerous designs - all inscriptional	125	225	300	425

PROCLAMATION COINS

ONE JOHANNA (GOLD) PORTUGAL

Coin illustrated : John V (1722 - 1750). 28.68 grams

Description	Fine	VF	EF	Unc
12,800 Reis or 'Johanna'	4,000	7,250	11,000	14,500

HALF JOHANNA (GOLD) PORTUGAL

Coin illustrated : John V (1722 - 1750). 14.34 grams

Description	Fine	VF	EF	Unc
6,400 Reis or 'Half Johanna'	900	1,850	3,550	5,000

HALF JOHANNA (GOLD) PORTUGAL

Coin illustrated : Joseph I (1750 - 1776). 14.34 grams

AGW: 0.4229oz
Fineness: 0.9170
Weight: 14.3436g

Description	Fine	VF	EF	Unc
6,400 Reis or 'Half Johanna'	850	1,450	2,350	3,500

PROCLAMATION COINS

ONE JOHANNA (GOLD) PORTUGAL

Coin illustrated : Maria & Peter (1777 - 1786). 14.34 grams

Descriptio	Fine	VF	EF	Unc
6,400 Reis or 'Half Johanna'	850	1,350	1,950	2,750

Known as the "Jugate" or twin bust, the obverse shows Maria I and Peter III who jointly ruled Portugal until the death of Peter. See next coin in series.

HALF JOHANNA (GOLD) PORTUGAL

Coin illustrated : Maria (1786 - 1800). 14.34 grams

Description	Fine	VF	EF	Unc
6,400 Reis or 'Half Johanna'	1,000	1,350	2,150	3,000

This subdued portrait type is known as the "Widowed" or "Veiled Head" bust that was adopted immediately after Maria's husband, King Peter III died in 1786.

HALF JOHANNA (GOLD) PORTUGAL

Coin illustrated : Maria (1786 - 1800). 14.34 grams

Description	Fine	VF	EF	Unc
6,400 Reis or 'Half Johanna'	850	1,350	1,950	2,750

This portrait type is known as the "Jewelled Head Dress." Despite the bright clothes and confident, almost smiling portrait, Maria succumbed to insanity in 1799 and the throne was handed over to her son as regent.

PROCLAMATION COINS

DOLLAR (SILVER) SPAIN

Coin illustrated : "Pillar" Dollar type

Description	Fine	VF	EF	Unc
Various Spanish & "New World" mints	325	450	850	1,300

DOLLAR (SILVER) SPAIN

Coin illustrated : "Bust" Dollar type

Description	Fine	VF	EF	Unc
. Various Spanish & "New World" mints	225	350	650	1,150

OTHER BUST DOLLAR PORTRAITS

Not to scale. Other designs exist

Charles IV (IIII)

Ferdinand VII

Ferdinand VII

Description	Fine	VF	EF	Unc
Various Spanish & "New World" mints	225	350	650	1,150

RECOMMENDED FURTHER READING

In 2004, Andrew Crellin, of Currency & Sterling wrote a very readable book titled, *The Coinage of Colonial Australia.* The book offers a lot of historical background as well as useful hints to assist the collector. This book is highly recommended. Only 750 copies were printed. Available from most dealers or direct from Andrew. See *Sterling and Currency* advert.

EVIDENCE MOUNTS THAT TASMANIA HAD IT'S OWN PROCLAMATION COINS

While most collectors are aware of Governor King's Colonial Proclamation of 1800, there is a growing body of evidence to suggest that back in the day when it was known as Van Diemen's Land, Tasmania had its own, stand-alone proclamation. This largely overlooked chapter of our numismatic history was first floated by prolific Tassie author, Roger V. McNeice OAM in his excellent 2013 publication, Colonial Coins of Tasmania. Roger touches on the rag-tag mix of specie that resulted in Governor King having to rework the rule book in 1800. What few Australian collectors realise is that our southern most colony across the Tasman faced the same issues some 20 years later. This is where this book comes into its own, in explaining in detail as to how the successive Governors attempted to solve the monetary crisis with whatever coinage was available at the time. Unfortunately, space here is insufficient to even touch on all that is offered to the reader, but there are fascinating stories that have never been published before. These include the Indian Rupee being shipped from port to port to take advantage of better exchange rates. Another concerns a court case involving the uttering of counterfeit USA dollar coins which the Government had unsuccessfully tried to introduce as legal tender. Amongst all these attempts to use whatever was available, Roger weaves a convincing tale to show that at least two attempts were made to emulate the Holey Dollar and Dump in being uniquely Australian. The first concerns a rather unspectacular delivery of coins from the Royal Mint in London. On May 1, 1827, £2,000 in copper coins was despatched from the Royal Mint to shipping agent W. Lush for shipment to Van Diemen's Land. The manifest comprised of £900 in Pence, £735 in halfpence and £365 in Farthings. At 240 pence to the pound, it amounted to 216,000 pennies. On October 9, 1827, the 448-ton transport ship, Layton, arrived in Hobart Town. Under the command of John H. Luscombe, the "cargo" was certainly diverse. As well as 152 male prisoners from Portsmouth, The Colonial Times recorded "She brings £10,000 of British silver and £2,000 of copper and other stores for the Government here." An unknown number of these copper coins undoubtedly included a number of 1827 pennies, especially struck for exclusive use in Tasmania. As Roger says in his book, "In the face of this growing evidence, I'd suggest that an 1827 penny is essential in any collection of Australian colonial coins".

G41D-040	1826	
G41D-045	1826	PROOF
G41D-050	1826	bronzed PROOF
G41D-055	1827	2

1. Issued in cased proof sets.
2. Struck for circulation in Australia.

On page 574 of the 1997 edition of *Coincraft's Standard Catalogue of English & UK Coins, 1066 to Date,* this short reference to the 1827 George IV penny issue provides irrefutable proof that Roger's assertion that Tasmania can claim it's own "Proclamation Coin," is correct.

THE TASMANIAN RING DOLLAR

The second distinctly Tasmanian issue suggested by Roger was its own version of the Holey Dollar. Although it contains no counter stamp to indicate a date as the 1813 Sydney issue commissioned by Governor Macquarie, it does offer a small clue. The only known example, shown at right, is dated 1820 and therefore a later issue that Roger believes was issued in 1830. Known as the Tasmanian Ring Dollar, evidence of it existence appeared in a letter to the Examiner Newspaper in 1885 when someone involved in the production shared his memories. It states: "I was one of the men who helped to make the "Holey "or "Ring" Dollars in Hobart Town in 1830. The work was done at Kerr's Blacksmith shop in Argyle Street. The Dollars were worth 4s 4d and the portion cut out was called a "dump" and passed into currency at the value of 1s 1d leaving the ring dollar worth 3s 3d". Supporting evidence comes via the above-illustrated ring dollar that passed in trade in Tasmania during the 1830-40 period. It is owned by a Tasmanian family whose ancestors owned stores in Fingal and Mathinna, Northern Tasmania. It has been handed down through the generations and is still in the hands of the original family. Hopefully, this short article will prompt more information to come to life.

1813 COLONIAL HOLEY DOLLAR AND DUMP

When Governor Lachlan Macquarie arrived in Sydney, a lack of coinage saw the infant colony basically a bartering community using rum as its main unit of currency. Macquarie went a long way to solving the problem of what coinage there was being taken by trading ships when he took possession of 40,000 Spanish Dollars which arrived in Port Jackson in 1812. The Spanish Dollar was an international currency with a value of between Four Shillings and Nine Pence and Five Shillings. He made the coins very unattractive to foreign traders by punching the centre out of the coin and giving both parts inflated values over and above the intrinsic value of the silver. *The "Holey Dollar,"* or outer ring, was valued at Five Shillings while the inner plug, known as the *"Dump"* was valued at Fifteen Pence. They were demonetised in 1829 recalled and melted down. Less than 300 Holey Dollars are known to exist and about 1000 Dumps' survive. They are both highly prized possessions among collectors.

FOR MORE INFORMATION REGARDING THE HOLEY DOLLAR & DUMP

For a more detailed analysis of these fascinating coins we recommend you obtain a copy of *The Holey Dollar of NSW* by the late Dr Bill Mira and JIm Noble. Printed in 1988, the book is still available at the offices of co-author Jim Noble at his Noble auction premises at 169 Macquarie Street, Sydney, 02 9223 4578.

1813 DUMP (Fifteen Pence)

Description	Good	VG	Fine	VF	EF
TYPE A/1 : Most common type	3,750	8,000	19,500	55,000	95,000
TYPE D/2 : 2nd most common	4,000	9,500	25,000	60,000	100,000

Types C/4 and E/3 are double A/1 prices for similar grade

IDENTIFYING DUMP OBVERSES

Sydney collector and historian, the late Dr Bill Mira has been at the forefront of research on the Holey Dollar and Dump. In the 1970's he perfected a method of identifying the various die combinations that are now internationally recognised. Mira observed four obverse dies : - A, C, D and E. The reference points identifying the obverses include the following aspects : -

1. The shape of the cross on the crown. *(See line drawings at right).* Two distinct designs exist.
2. The relationship of the cross to the word SOUTH in the legend.
3. The pearls in the band of the crown.

Key to abbreviations : N = N of **N**EW
S = S of WALE**S**
C.B.L.= Crown Base Line
Cross = Cross on top of Crown

Obv A & D

Obv C & E

DUMP OBVERSE MIRA DIE A

Cross Symmetrical

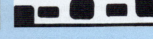

1. A line along the base of the crown (C.B.L.) cuts the "N" and passes above or through the top of the "S".
2. The crown base 6mm across and the height 6mm.
3. The cross points between the "TH" of SOU**TH**.
4. The "3" of 1813 is tilted to the left.
5. All pearls are irregular. The left hand pearl touches the base of the band with the right hand pearl touching the top. The middle pearl is centrally placed with the pearls either side much smaller and elongated.
6. The cross on the crown is symmetrical.

Note : Some pieces which fall into the "A" type category also show a dot above the 3. This is almost certainly due to a pit in the die.

DUMP OBVERSE MIRA DIE AB

NO ILLUSTRATIONS AVAILABLE

1. The Centre Base Line (C.B.L.) passes through the "N" of NEW and "S" of SOUTH.
2. The crown base 6mm across and the height 6mm.
3. The cross points between the "TH" of SOU**TH**.
4. The "3" of 1813 is tilted to the left.

Note : The existence of Obverse AB as a completely separate entity is doubtful, but it is discussed because with Obverse A it fits the criteria of Andrews' 709,712 and 715. It needs the right hand side of the CBL of Obverse A to drop, or seem to drop 0.5mm to convert Obverse A to Obverse AB - all other features of the dies being identical. This small change in angle can occur from the spread of the "S", widening of the right crown base due to wear, a different angle of - or lighter stamping - or of a minor reworking of the die itself. Some specimens of Obverse A do show a thickening, probably due to the die having been adjusted. This is further supported by the fact that Obverse AB only occurs with Reverse 1 - the reverse die associated with Obverse A. The final proof is the presence on several pieces with all characteristics of Obverse AB, and showing the dot above the "3".

DUMP OBVERSE MIRA DIE C

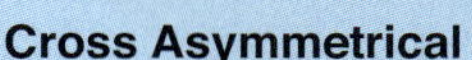

Cross Asymmetrical

1. The Centre Base Line (C.B.L.) passes above the "N" of NEW and "S" of SOUTH.
2. The crown base 6mm across and the height 7mm.
3. The cross points between the "TH" of SOU**TH**.
4. The "3" of 1813 is upright.
5. All pearls irregular and central in the band.
6. The cross on the crown is asymmetrical.

Note : This die shows extensive recutting both in the legend and in the crown whilst the cross is asymmetrical and tilted slightly to the right *(See Obverse E).* This re-engraving has enlarged the crown and dropped the "N" of NEW and "S" of SOUTH to a lower level. It could be a trial die, a poorly engraved die, a reworked Obverse A die, or a separate die altogether. Against it being a reworked Obverse A die or a separate reworked die is the fact that no specimens are known to exist with all the die features except for the reworking. Other possibilities include it being a contemporary forgery or the planchet being reengraved after a hole has been replugged.

Obverse C becomes even more interesting, and controversial, when correlated with the investigations of Philip Spalding in his 1973 book, *The World of the Holey Dollar.* This book analyses the probably development of the reverse dies for the Holey Dollar, and illustrated a sequence of rare dies, heavily recut, which he postulates, result in the final design of the major working dies. Two pieces bearing this obverse die have a peculiar edge. The milling appears to have been applied with a triangular file from each side, and the centre of the rim gives the impression that an attempt was made to "reed" it.

BUTTON DUMP REPLICA

In 1923 Dr. A.W. Yelland began corresponding with Sir William Dixson in the hope he could help him identify what Yelland thought was an unlisted dump. Some of the features were completely different to all known varieties. The lettering of the new piece was of 19th century style while the edge was plain, or not reeded. Two examples known to Dr. Yelland showed a ragged pit in the centre of the reverse while the other had a dot over the N of FIFTEE**N**. It is thought that issue was produced sometime in the mid 1800's for some reason yet to be determined.

DUMP OBVERSE MIRA DIE D

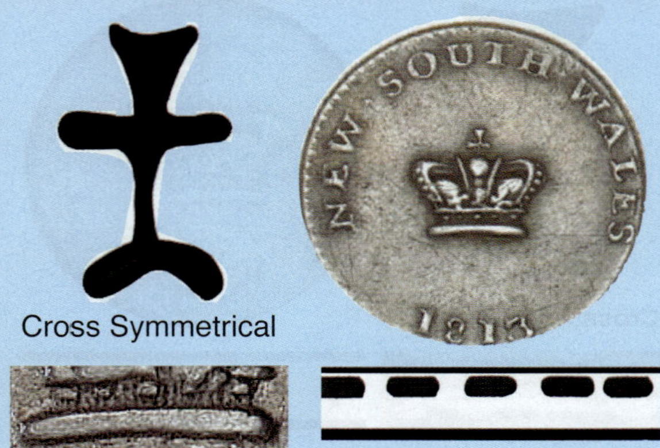

Cross Symmetrical

1. The C.B.L. passes under the "N" and through the "S".
2. The crown base is 5mm across and the height 6mm.
3. The cross points between the "UT" of SO**UT**H.
4. The "3" of 1813 is tilted to the left.
5. All pearls are equal and touch the top of the band.
6. The cross on the crown is symmetrical.

Note : A stop may appear after NEW and SOUTH. The dies apparently had shallow depressions for these stops which seen filled with debris and can be difficult, if not impossible, to identify. This happens even on pieces in better condition.

DUMP OBVERSE MIRA DIE E

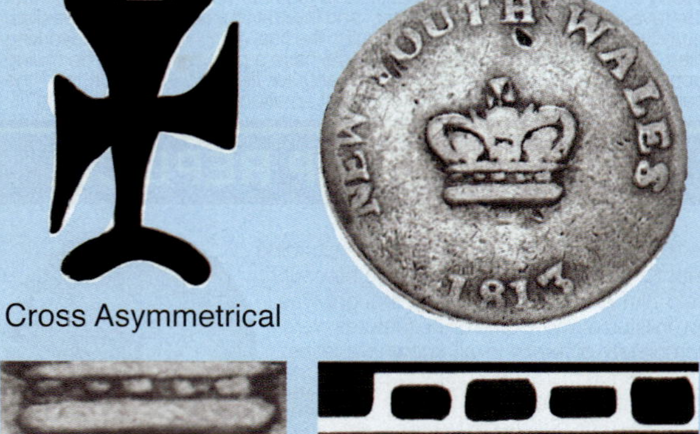

Cross Asymmetrical

1. The C.B.L. passes through the "N" and "S".
2. The crown base 6mm across and the height 6mm.
3. The cross points between the "TH" of SOU**TH**.
4. The "3" of 1813 is tilted to the left.
5. The left hand pearl touches the top of the band.
6. The cross on the crown is asymmetrical.

Note : This die is poorly engraved and appears to be an early effort.

IDENTIFYING DUMP REVERSES

The late Dr Bill Mira also devised a method of identifying the various die combinations which are now internationally recognised. Mira has identified four reverse dies : - 1, 2, 3 and 4. The reference points identifying the reverse include :-

1. The relationship of the first "F" of **F**IFTEEN to "P" of **P**ENCE.
2. The relationship of the "T" of FIF**T**EEN to the "N" of PE**N**CE.
3. High tilted or normal horizontal first ""E" of P**E**NCE.
4. Distance between words FIFTEEN and PENCE.
5. Square stop between "T" of FIF**T**EEN and "N" of PE**N**CE.

Note : In reference to the last point (5) it should be noted that on a few well preserved specimens the square stop has all the characteristics of an "H".

DUMP REVERSE MIRA DIE 1

1. The upright stroke of "P"of **P**ENCE to the right of upright stroke of "F" of **F**IFTEEN.
2. The "T" over "N". The vertical stroke of "T" of FIFTEEN is over the centre of "N" of PE**N**CE
3.High tilted "E".
4. FIFTEEN and PENCE 4.5mm apart.
5. Stop present between FIFTEEN and PENCE.

Note : Even in pieces with well preserved legends it is sometimes still difficult to identify the central stop. This can usually be explained by assuming the stop recess in the die filling with grease or other foreign debris.

DUMP REVERSE MIRA DIE 2

1. 5mm distance between the words FIFTEEN and PENCE.
2. The "T" of FIF**T**EEN is well to the left of "N" of PE**N**CE.
3. The tiny "H" is occasionally, but not generally visible.

Note : Obverse die "D" and Reverse Die 2 accounts for around 25% of the specimens and is crossed referenced as Andrews' 710:711. The tiny "H" is nearly always missing. This is because it was only originally lightly punched into the master die and it quickly filled in as the die was constantly used. The illustration above shows the "H" although it appears to be partially filled in.

DUMP REVERSE MIRA DIE 3

1. Upright stroke of "P" of PENCE to left of upright stroke of "F" of FIFTEEN.
2. "T" OVER "N" . The vertical stroke of "T" is over the left hand vertical stroke of "N" of PENCE.
3. Normal "E".
4. The distance between FIFTEEN and PENCE 3.5 mm apart.
5. Stop present.

Note : This die is poorly engraved with the letters being irregular in height and the word PENCE sloping downwards to the right. The "C" of PENCE is without a serif. This is also absent in Reverse 4. It appears to be an early effort and is found only in combination with Obverse E. Colonial coin expert Dr Bill Mira believes the crudity of this striking suggests that it might have been a trial die. He said the stop was only visible on three or the thirteen specimens he has inspected. He added that on two examples inspected the stop was extremely faint but on the third it looks more like an egg-shaped blob. He further stated this third example was identical to the Spalding Trial Die T.A. for the Holey Dollars and becomes the "H" on the major working punches.

DUMP REVERSE MIRA DIE 4

1. The distance between the words FIFTEEN and PENCE is 4 mm.
2. The "T" of FIF**T**EEN is well to the left of the "N" in PE**N**CE.
3. Normal "E".
4. The upright stroke of "P" of PENCE to right of upright stroke of "F" of **F**IFTEEN.
5. Round punch mark in position of stop.

Note : Writing in the *1974 ANS Yearbook* and in his 1988 book *The Holey Dollars of NSV/* which he co-authored with Jim Noble, Dr Bill Mira made the following obversations on this variety. The legend of this die shows extensive recutting or perhaps uniform poor engraving. Obverse die C and Reverse die 4 are found only in combination and equal Type C/4. Less than ten examples of this type have been seen. He said they majority of examples know are well worn with the circle being hard to distinguish. He said a number showed the arc of another punch close to the full circle, giving the impression of a figure eight. Various possibilities exist for this Obv.C/Rev. 4 combination. They may be trial dies with the punch mark a localising centre point for the engraver during the development of the design. Again they may be comtemporary forgeries on an illegally removed central plug - a profit of three pence being makde for the fabricators. Or could it be that Henshall did not engrave all the dies? Was be assisted by another engraver ' less talented - who produced Obv.C and Rev. 4 and seeing Henshall leave his "H" on his work decided to mark his die for prosperity - with the incuse circle. If this is the case then the similar cross on Obv. E and the cruder work on Rev. 3 would place them as his worl also. The theory that Obv.C/Rev. 4 and Obv.E/ Rev.3 are trial dies would seem to be the most acceptable.

1813, AUSTRALIA'S FIRST EVER COIN

The Holey Dollar was a product of necessity, rather than an example of the die maker's artistry. In fact, the cutting and stamping of the 40,000 imported Spanish dollars was undertaken by a convict, Governor Macquarie noticed had been transported to the colony after being convicted of forging coins. Up until quite recently, numismatists thought the process was done in great haste in an effort to stem the flow of what little specie there was being shipped out in the holds of trading ships. However the collecting world was recently turned on its head when the contents of an old eclectic collection of world coins turned up in a Canadian auction . This astonishing, and previously unpublished trial Holey Dollar, was part of the booty, although it is apparent the previous owner had no clue to the fact that he possessed a true numismatic rarity. It was the only Australian coin in the collection, and was simply described as a *'New South Wales coin'*.

The very first coin struck on Australian soil. Current value in excess of $500.000

The discovery could indicate that the concept of a truly colonial coinage was a well planned exercise and not entirely a rushed project. This trial was struck using a George III British half penny and would indicate that the authorities were keen to see that the workmanship was of a high standard.

The choice of a coin, other than what was envisaged is also of interest. Perhaps, as a trial, there was a concern that the machinery wouldn't work and a silver coin of significant value might be ruined. It could be a case that the dies were being prepared as the shipment of Spanish Dollars were on route from India. The two countermark dies are struck at an upright or zero degrees axis to each other and at an angle of 45 degrees to the upright position of the original coin or matrix. When the unique rarity was first reported in the numismatic press, an overwhelmed scribe said : *"This coin is without parallel as a completely unexpected discovery of the greatest historical significance".* As the very first bespoke coin ever struck on Australian soil, the true value of the find was demonstrated when it was put to auction as lot 1258 in Noble's Sale 84, held in Sydney from March 28-30, 2007. While estimated to bring $40,000, collectors and dealers attending the auction had other ideas. After furious bidding, a private collector took the prize for $200,000 plus commission. The catalogue described the coin thus : *"NEW SOUTH WALES, five shillings or holey dollar, 1813, test strike from dies I/B on a 1799 copper halfpenny. Good very fine, unpublished as a test strike and of the greatest historical significance."*

HOLEY DOLLAR (Five Shillings)

Description	Good	VG	Fine	VF	EF
1813 : Most common type	15,000	25,000	50,000	95,000	225,000

THE COLONIAL HOLEY DOLLAR

STANDARD COUNTERSTAMP DIE COMBINATIONS

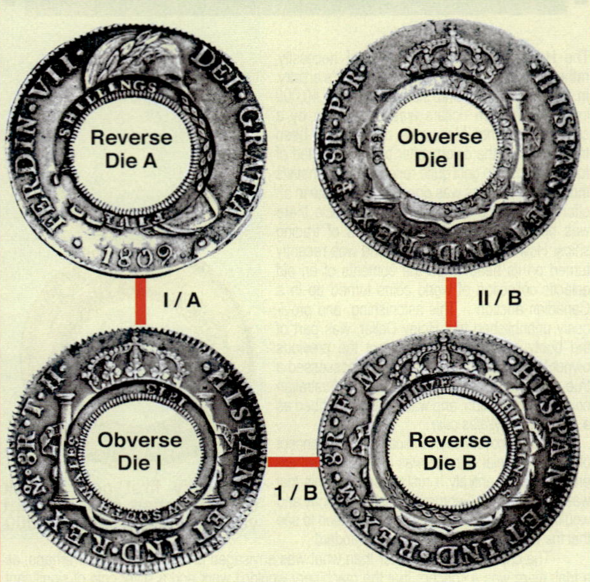

Type I / A : Obverse die I with reverse die A
Type I / B : Obverse die I with reverse die B
Type II / B : Obverse die II with reverse die B

These dies and die combination account for all but five of the known surviving Holey dollars. These are none known with the II/ A combination.

HOLEY DOLLAR MINTMARKS

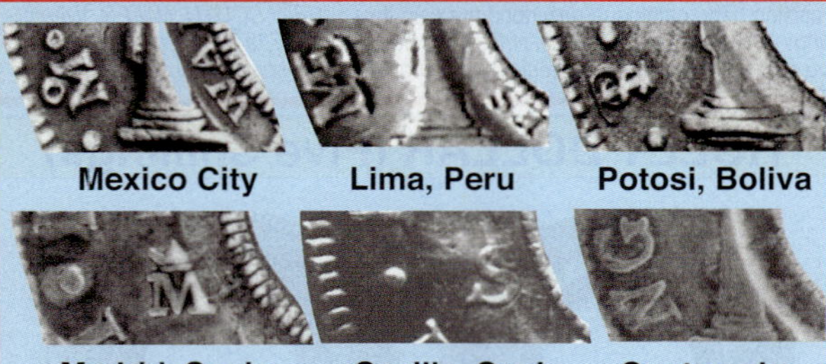

Mexico City — Lima, Peru — Potosi, Boliva

Madrid, Spain — Seville, Spain — Guatemala

Although there is one Holey Dollar that is so worn, it is impossible to identify its mintmark, the surviving 250 plus known examples can be traced to one of six mints. Only six coins were struck in the motherland, with four coming from Madrid and two from Seville. The balance were struck in the "New World" with Mexico City Mint leading the count with over 200 examples. This is followed by Lima [30+]; Potosi [about 30] and one from Guatemala. I have resisted being more specific regarding numbers as several sources show conflicting data. At the time, the best reference was the 1988 Mira/ Noble book mentioned earlier. Since then some 20 previously unknown examples have been discovered. There is always the possibility that more will surface in the future.

HOLEY DOLLAR DIE TYPES

OBVERSE DIE I

1. The "U" of SOUTH is upright and its base sits on the denticles around the central hole.
2. The crossbar of the "T" of SOUTH is horizontal and level with the top of the "H".
3. Two denticles between the "W" of NEW and the "S" of SOUTH.

OBVERSE DIE II

1. The "U" of SOUTH is tilted to the left and its base is absorbed into the denticles around the central hole.
2. The crossbar of the "T" in SOUTH is horizontal and fractionally lower than the top of the "H".
3. Four denticles between the "W" of NEW and the "S" of SOUTH.

REVERSE DIE A

1. A *fleur de lis* between FIVE and SHILLINGS. *(This is the only die to feature the fleur de lis).*
2. There are twenty denticles between FIVE and SHILLINGS

REVERSE DIE B

1. No *fleur de lis* between FIVE and SHILLINGS.
2. Ten denticles between FIVE and SHILLINGS.

HOW THE MARKETPLACE VALUES HOLEY DOLLARS

It is very difficult to give an arbitrary value to any individual Holey Dollar, as there are so many factors to consider. When grading the coin, consideration must be given to both the condition of the host coin, as well as the counterstamp. While condition of the host *(or Dollar itself)* is important, collectors also rate the condition and die combination of the countermark. Added to this, the mintmark and the date is also taken into consideration. Some collectors are willing to pay a premium for coins dated 1788 or 1800. As time goes by. The opportunity for individuals to own a holey dollar diminishes as more and more are purchased for, or on behalf, of museums, thus taking them off the market permanently. The price suggested in various price catalogues - including my own - is what you would pay for a common variety that displays both host coin and counterstamp of similar grading.

AUSTRALIA'S FIRST GOLD ISSUES

PORT PHILLIP 'KANGAROO' ISSUES

William Taylor was a London based die sinker who heard about the gold strike in Australia. Rather than rush to the fields with pick and shovel, he devised a 'suit and tie' approach to make his fortune. He learned that the miners of Victoria's goldfields were selling their nuggets and dust at a substantial discount to the standard price of gold. Taylor saw an opportunity to profit by converting the abundant gold into small ingots or tokens that could be used in daily business. He and his partners purchased a 600-ton ship named the Kangaroo. It departed London in November 1852, and arrived at Hobson's Bay in Victoria on October 23, 1853. On board was the press used by Taylor to strike commemorative medals at London's Crystal Palace Exhibition in 1851. His cargo also included dies that were intended to be used to strike the new token coins. Emigrants to Victoria in the 1850s were greeting by total chaos. Two to three ships were arriving each day at Port Phillip, as many as 300 ships were often anchored in the Bay at any one time. Many of the ships were abandoned as the crews literally jumped ship to join the gold rush. The heavy coining press was impossible to off load in one piece and it took over six months to dismantle and then re-assemble the press at their intended premises on Franklin Street West. In the meantime market conditions had moved significantly against them, specifically the price being paid for gold in Australia had risen by almost 50%. The importation of British sovereigns, ensured that miners could more readily sell their gold much closer to the official price of £4 per ounce. The venture failed and the press was purchased by Stokes who used it to issue many tokens for colonial merchants.

Date	Value	Description	Metal	Weight	Size	Edge	Retail
1853	£8	AS ISSUED	Gold	2 oz	35mm	Reeded	755,000
1853	£4	AS ISSUED	Gold	1 oz	28mm	Reeded	600,000
1853	£2	AS ISSUED	Gold	1/2 oz	22mm	Reeded	450,000
1853	£1	AS ISSUED	Gold	1/4 oz	18mm	Reeded	375,000

The coins listed above are only a small sample of a extensive range of coins commonly referred to as Port Philip,Taylor or Kangaroo Office issues. There are a number of casts, restrikes and off-metal issues. Most of these were later strikes in all mannner of metals. Collectors should also be wary of near perfect fakes produced by the notorious counterfeiter, David Gee back in the 1970's.

1852 ADELAIDE GOLD 'INGOTS'

Type One Ingot

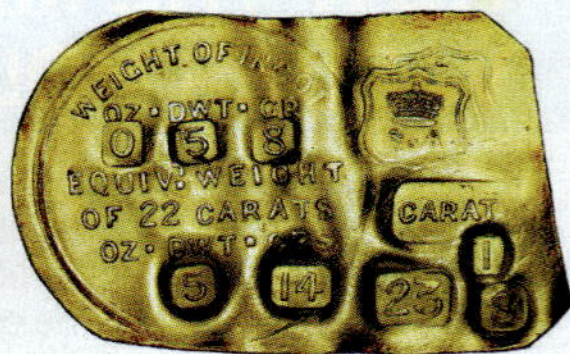

Type Two Ingot

Date	Description				Extremely fine
1852	Type One	—	—	—	1,375,000
1852	Type Two	—	—	—	1,375,000

Several other original examples exist in public institutions. Later electrotypes [Sawtell] are also available to collectors. The above two illustrated pieces are the only examples in private hands.

1852 ADELAIDE POUND

TYPE ONE : CRACKED DIE

GOLD

Position of
Die Crack

Date	Mintage	Fine	VF	EF	aUnc	Unc
1852	Fine reeding	35,000	70,000	95,000	175,000	295,000
1852	Wide reeding	37,500	75,000	95,000	195,000	325,000

1852 ADELAIDE POUND

TYPE TWO : REDESIGNED REVERSE

GOLD

22 carat (916.6 fine)
91.67% Gold & 8.33 Silver.

Type 1 weight 8.69 gms.
Type 2 weight 8.81 gms.
Common size 23 mm.

Date	Mintage	Fine	VF	EF	aUnc	Unc	Ch/Unc
1852	24,648	7,500	15,500	19,500	27,500	47,500	97,500

1852 ADELAIDE FIVE POUND

ONLY PATTERNS EXIST

GOLD

22 carat (916.6 fine)
91.67% Gold & 8.33 Silver.
Weight 43.8 gms. Size 33.1 mm.

Date	Mintage	FDC
1852 Fine reeding	7 surviving restrikes	No recent sales. (see below)

No original strikings from 1852 are thought to have been made. The Melbourne branch of the Royal Mint (London), borrowed the dies for the Five Pound issue in 1919 to strike examples for their own collection and the Royal Mint collection in London. Records indicate that around 12 pieces were struck but five of these were subsequently melted down in 1929 after the Melbourne Mint was not able to sell them to collectors for the value of their gold content. This was about £10 at the time. The Mint had hoped to use the money raised from the sales to fund its acquisition program. One person who did pay the £10 was William Dixson who left his vast collection to the Mitchell Library, in Sydney. His ten pounds was used to obtain the mint's examples of the Sydney Mint 1902 five and two pound pieces. Of the seven remaining restrikes, at least five are known to be in museums or other public institutions. An example, graded as FDC, was sold for $485,300 at the Quartermaster Sale held in Sydney, in June 2009.

EXPERIMENTAL PATTERN ISSUES

[a] 1853 Pattern

Common reverse

[b] 1856 Pattern

PATTERN HALF SOVEREIGNS

McD Ref	Date &	Reverse Type	Type	Very Good	Fine	Very Fine	Extra Fine	aUnc	Unc	Choice Unc	Proof
001	1853	1 / 1	PATTERN	–	–	–	–	–	–	–	350,000
002 a	1855	2 / 3	PATTERN	–	125k	–	–	–	–	–	Not seen
003 b	1856	2 / 3	POSSIBLE PATTERN	–	–	–	–	–	–	–	225,000

1855 and 1856 patterns (002a & 003b) have Type Two portraits - See below. Two of the 1855 patterns circulated. There are three varieties of reverses. *(See Following pages).* Downies auction 309 (lot 601) states that three of the 1856 Type 1 obverse / Type 2 reverse were offered in the 2005 Reserve Bank auction. Another three are in private hands. This makes it one of the rarest coins in the series.

[c]

[d]

[e]

PATTERN FULL SOVEREIGNS

McD Ref	Date &	Reverse Type	Good	Very Good	Fine	Very Fine	Extra Fine	aUnc	Unc	Choice Unc	Proof
101 c	1853	PATTERN	–	–	–	–	*Only one example available to collectors*				575,000
102	1855	PATTERN 2 / 1	–	–	–		*Only one example available to collectors*				395,000
103 e	1856	PATTERN 2 / 1		*Only one example available to collectors. Plain edge. Pattern*							335,000

[c]. This 1853 pattern was adapted for the general circulation issues of 1855-1856. [d]. With subtle differences to the number of berries and ribbon placement, this distinctive reverse design was largely unchanged for the entite life span of the series. [e] This 1856 pattern design was introduced as a circulation coin from 1857.

The discovery of gold in the colony of New South Wales brought with it great economic benefits, including the establishment of a branch of the Royal Mint in Sydney - the first Mint set up outside Britain. The announcement was made in August 1853 - much to the disappointment of the Legislative Councils of Victoria and South Australia who also applied for the honor of having Australia's first official mint. Immediately after the decison was made, the Royal Mint in London set about producing a series of dies to test designs that were intended to be unique for the new mint. The 'Sydney Mint Patterns,' as these coins are now called, are a very important part of Australia's numismatic history. Although the obverse by James Wyon was only slightly different to that used on British minted sovereigns and half sovereigns, the reverse was uniquely Australian. It was the first and last time such licence was ever given to a Royal Mint branch in any of the colonies The reverse was loosely modeled around contemporary reverse designs of the British sixpence and shillings ,with the words "Sydney Mint Australia" and the denomination arranged around a splay of flowers and a crown. Only four sets of the coins were ever produced. Three sets are in museums and just one pair in private hands. Established in a wing of the old Rum Hospital, the mint opened on May 14, 1855 and the first coins were struck on June 23, 1855. The coins broke with tradition several ways in that they bore a stated face value as well as the name of the mint. Like the Adelaide Type I Pound, this issue was also short-lived. In 1857 a new obverse design was incorporated to give the entire coin a completely Australian flavour. The Leonard Charles Wyon obverse gave the still young queen a revised hair style complete with a spray of banksia. Initially, these coins were only intended to circulate in NSW. This was later amended by the British Treasury to include to "Other Colonies of Australasia" but not the United Kingdom. Still hurt by the official rebuff concerning the location of the mint, both Melbourne and Adelaide protested. Charges that the coins were not intrinsically sound resulted in some Victorian merchants discounting them to 19 shillings. Again London had to act; and it did so by making an official assay of the coins in January 1856. The result surprised everyone. It was found the intrinsic value of the Australian coins exceeded that of its British counterpart, due mainly to the fact that the gold was alloyed with silver rather than copper as was the British sovereign. Word spread quickly and those that had not been melted down for the profit were by 1868 being accepted as legal tender as far afield as Newfoundland. India had also adopted the Sydney Mint sovereign as legal tender, in fact they were more popular than their English counterparts because of the yellow colour, (a result of the silver in the alloy) as opposed to the redder colour of London. Ironically, Britain had been accepting the coin since 1863. In fact, this success was the Sydney Sovereigns undoing, and in 1870 it was decided to abolish the distinctive designs.

HALF SOVEREIGN

TYPE ONE : VICTORIA

SYDNEY MINT REVERSE 1855 - 1856

Obverse : James Wyon. **Reverse** : L.C. Wyon
Composition: 91.67% gold; 8.33% silver. Size 19 mm.
(22 carat 916.6 fine). Weight 3.9940 gms. **Pure gold content .1177 oz**

McD Ref	Date &	Reverse Type	Good	Very Good	Fine	Very Fine	Extra Fine	aUnc	Unc	Choice Unc	Proof
002	1855	1/3	19,000	30,000	65,000	97,500	195,000	425,000	Not seen	Not seen	Not seen
003	1856	1/2	500	2,250	5,000	50,000	80,000	120,000	150,000	Not seen	Not seen
003a	1856	1/3	350	1,250	4,250	21,000	15,000	60,000	95,000	Not seen	Not seen

HALF SOVEREIGN

TYPE TWO : VICTORIA

SYDNEY MINT REVERSE 1857 - 1866

Obverse : L.C. Wyon. **Reverse** : L.C. Wyon
Composition: 91.67% gold; 8.33% silver. . Size 19 mm.
(22 carat 916.6 fine). Weight 3.9940 gms. **Pure gold content .1177 oz**

McD Ref	Date &	Reverse Type	Very Good	Fine	Very Fine	Extra Fine	aUnc	Unc	Choice Unc	GEM	Proof
004	1857	2/3	325	450	1,350	8,500	16,000	34,000	60,000	Not seen	Not seen
004a	1857	2/3 PLAIN EDGE		—	—	—	—	—	—	—	145,000
004b	1857/5	OVERDATE		—	—	Extremely Rare. Price yet to be determined					—
005	1858	2/3	300	450	1,350	8,500	16,000	36,000	55,000	110,000	—
005a	1858	SOVRR ERROR	9,500	15,000	—	—	—	—	—	—	—
006	1859	2/3	325	525	2,350	13,500	26,500	42,000	85,000	145,000	—
006a	1859/8	OVERDATE		525	2,900	25,000	52,000	67,000	115,000	160,000	—
007	1860	2/3	750	1,600	4,600	25,500	57,500	75,000	110,000	175,000	—
007a	1860/5	OVERDATE		1,250	4,700	28,000	61,500	88,000	115,000	180,000	—
008	1861	2/3	310	500	1,450	9,500	22,000	42,500	67,500	140,000	—
008a	1861/0	OVERDATE		8,500	14,000	29,000	57,500	80,000	Not seen	Not seen	—
009	1862	2/3	325	525	2,500	13,500	27,000	45,000	75,000	150,000	—
009a	1862	HIGH 6 IN DATE		600	2,500	14,000	32,500	—	—	—	—
010	1863	2/3	325	525	2,550	13,500	27,000	43,500	70,000	145,000	—
011	1864	ARABIC 1	310	500	2,600	13,500	27,000	42,000	67,500	145,000	—
011a	1864	ROMAN 1	4,750	8,000	13,250	29,500	57,500	—	—	—	—
012	1865	2/3	425	800	2,450	14,750	35,000	57,500	92,000	150,000	—
013	1866	2/3	400	625	2,300	13,750	34,000	50,000	95,000	150,000	175,000

005a. Incorrect cut die reads "HALF SOVRREIGN." Discovered in the 1980s, so far six examples have been discovered. One of the best was described as good VF (with obverse scratches) and offered in Downie's Sale 314 held in Melbourne in September 2013. The coin was sold for a new auction record price of $24,465 against an estimate of $15,000. The previous record was also set at a Downie's auction when a coin in similar grade sold for $23,850. It appeared in Downie's sale 309 held in October 2011. The coin was described as being "ex-RBA Sale" and graded as Good / Very Good.
011a. Heyde Sale (Gray Auction, March 23, 1974, lot 138). No other examples seen until 2005 when Winsor & Sons sold one in Extremely Fine condition.
013. Mint records show that in 1867, some 62,000 coins were struck and a further 154,000 were issued in 1869. It would appear that earlier dies were used as no circulation coins bearing these later dates are known. Two proofs/specimens known.

HALF SOVEREIGN OBVERSES RECUT OVERDATE ISSUES

1855 RE-ENTERED DATE : Noble's Sale 84, March 2007 (lot 1285A). Catalogue reads :- *"Clear double entered date. Good Fine (and) amongst the finest of 12 known."* This coin sold for a hammer price of $42,000 against an estimate of $40,000.

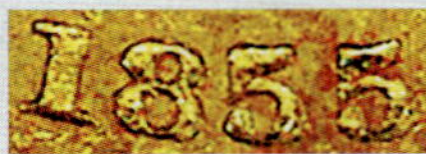

1855 Re-entered Date

1856/5 OVERDATE : This coin has had a change of *'identity.'* Originally described as the *'fat or large 6 type'* it is now thought to be the result of a rather clumsy six being re-entered over a 185**(5)** hub. Gold coin specialist Eric Eigner suggests that about 5% of the total issue displays this variety.

1856/5 Overdate

1857/5 OVERDATE : Described by Spink Australia in their November 1979 auction as *"an interesting specimen which shows that the date has been re-entered, particularly clearly with the last figure of the date, 7, which may have been intended to obliterate a 6 (or 5) thus raising the possibility that a working die dated 1856 (or 1855) had been prepared with the second type bust."* This piece is one of only three 1857/5 overdates on record. The last was included in the 2005 Reserve Bank of Australia sale (lot 553). Regarded as *"excessively rare."*

1857/5 Overdate

1859/8 OVERDATE : This rare overdate was produced when the 8 of 185**(8)** was overstruck with a '9'. An example appeared in Noble's Sale 81, March (lot 1340). Described as having surface marks but otherwise Good Very Fine, it sold for a hammer price of $1,250 against an estimate of $800. According to Eric Eigher, only 30 to 40 examples are known.

1859/8 Overdate

1860/50 OVERDATE. This is the result of another cost cutting measure where the five has been partly obliterated and stamped with a 6.

1860/50 Overdate

1861/0 OVERDATE. Here is the irony. This is arguably the most *'common'* of the overdates and commands high prices simply because it has not been well publicised over the years. Even so, less than 20 examples have been identified, including four lots offered in the 2005 Reserve Bank sale.

1861/60 Overdate

1858 REVERSE LEGEND ERROR

(McD 005a). Incorrect cut die reads "HALF SOV**R**-REIGN." Discovered in the 1980s by the late Sydney dealer, Barry Sparkes. Recently, gold expert Barrie Winsor stated that so far six examples (all in VG condition) have been discovered.

1864 VARIATION IN DATE TYPE FACE

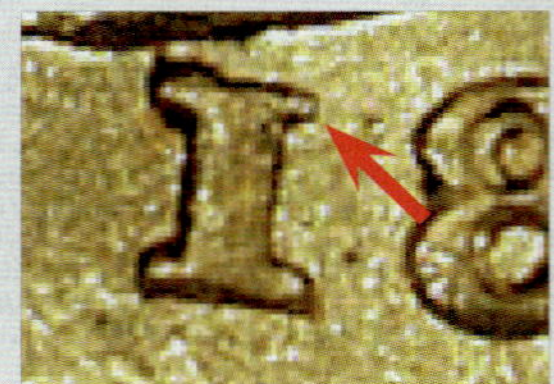

Rare Roman "I" variety

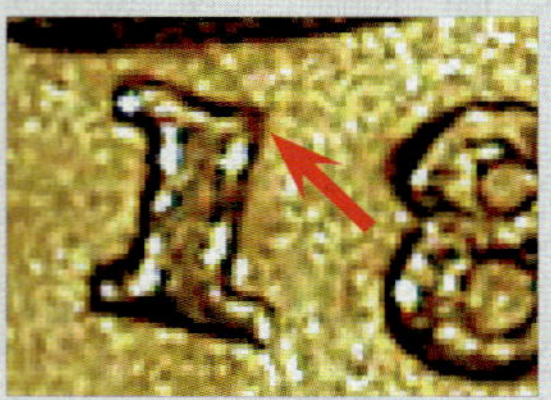

Regular issue Arabic "1"

A rare variation in the numeral "1" has been discovered. Only known in EF condition, the coin features the Roman style "1" (Full serif) rather than the standard Arabic style.

MINTMARK POSITION OF SHIELD REVERSE HALF SOVEREIGNS

YOUNG HEAD OBVERSE SHIELD REVERSE 1871 - 1887

JUBILEE HEAD OBVERSE SHIELD REVERSE 1887 - 1893

Mintmark at the base of the shield.
"S" Mintmark. Sydney Mint.

Mintmark at the base of the shield.
"S" Mintmark. Sydney Mint.

HALF SOVEREIGN REVERSES

Type 1

Type 3

Type 2

There are three distinct dies used in this short series if you include the pattern and proof coins. All variations concern the berries in the wreath on the reverse.

TYPE ONE : (Various dates). Has "L" of HALF plus extra berries (circled)

TYPE TWO : (1856 only). Possibly a reworked pattern die. No dot (berry) above "L" of HALF.

TYPE THREE : (Various dates). Dot above "L" of HALF.

OBVERSE AND REVERSE DIE VARIATIONS ASSOCIATED WITH THE YOUNG HEAD HALF SOVEREIGN

When these coins were struck over 100 years ago, production methods were very different to what we take for granted today. Many of the original dies were cut by hand with no mechanical help. This resulted in each die being slightly different. We welcome feedback from anyone who can add to this list of varieties.

OBVERSE TYPE 1

OBVERSE TYPE 2

OBVERSE TYPE 3

OBVERSE TYPE 1. Date : 1871S only.
Obverse (Type 1) : Short denticles and widely spaced. 117 denticles.

OBVERSE TYPE 2. Date : 1872S only.
Obverse (Type 2) : Legend repositioned. Nose points below "T" in VICTORIA. 123 denticles.

OBVERSE TYPE 3. Dates : 1875S plus 1873M & 1877M
Obverse (Type 3) : Legend repositioned again, nose points below **"T"** in VICTORIA. "I" of DE**I** now above second ribbon. 146 denticles.

OBVERSE TYPE 4. Dates : 1879S plus 1877M & 1882M.
Obverse (Type 4) : Ribbon now narrow. Coins dated 1879S and 1877M have 146 denticles. Coins dated 1882M have 144 denticles.

OBVERSE TYPE 5. Dates : 1880S, 1881S, 1882S & 1883S plus 1881M to 1887M. Low relief, wide head, pony tail close to "G" of **G**RATIA. Wide, coarse border, thicker lettering and date. No front ear lobe. 136 denticles.

OBVERSE TYPE 4

OBVERSE TYPE 5

HALF SOVEREIGN REVERSES

Reverse Type 1

Reverse Type 2

Reverse Type 3

Reverse Type 4

Reverse [Type 1] : Cross on top of shield clear of border. Dot on central vertical line of shield. 120 denticles.
Reverse [Type 2] : Top of cross touches border. Dot missing from central vertical line of shield. Shield redesigned. 122 denticles.
Reverse [Type 3] : As Type 1 but without dot. Cross touches border but with more denticles. 147 in total.
Reverse [Type 4] : Wide coarse border. Top of cross buried in border. Rosettes closer to border. 148 denticles.

DIE VARIETIES ASSOCIATED WITH THE AUSTRALIAN YOUNG HEAD, SHIELD REVERSE HALF SOVEREIGNS : 1871-1887

SYDNEY & MELBOURNE OBVERSE DIE TYPES

DETAILS	TYPE 1	TYPE 2	TYPE 3	TYPE 4	TYPE 5 [A]	TYPE 5 [B]
Date - Sydney	1871S	1872S	1875S	1879S	1880S to 83S	1880S to 87S
Reference	S.3862	S.3862A	S.3862B	S.3862C	S.3862D	S.3862E
Date - Melbourne	—	—	1873M to 77M	1877M to 82M	1881M to 87M	—
Reference	—	—	S.3863 [NB1]	S.3863A [NB1]	S.3863B [NB1]	[NB 2]
Quick Identification	Date + Rev. Dot in shield	Nose points below 'T' in 'VICTORIA'	Wide ribbon	Similar to 3 but narrow ribbon. Double line at front of ear.	No double line at front of ear. Wide border. Hair line square at rear of head	No double line at front of ear. Wide border. Hair line square at rear of head
1. Legend Nose Alignment	Nose points above T of VICTORIA	Legend repositioned. Nose points below T of VICTORIA.	Legend again repositioned Nose points above T of VICTORIA. 'I' in 'DEI' above 2nd ribbon	—	Similar to Type 3	Similar to Type 3
2. Legend. Date Figures / Lettering	Very Thin See point 8.	Thin	Thin	Thin 1877M. Thick 1882M	Very thick See figure 8.	Very thick See figure 8.
3. Ribbon	Wide	Wide	Wide	Narrow	Narrow	Narrow
4. Hair	Coarse	Coarse	Coarse	Medium	Fine	Fine
5. Neck Truncation	Pointed, Normal	Rounded, Normal	Rounded, Normal	Rounded, Normal	Truncation wide at bottom right of neck	Truncation wide at bottom right of neck
6. Denticles	Short & widely spaced. 117 denticles.	Short & widely spaced. 123 denticles	Longer & close spacing. 146 denticles.	Longer & close spacing. 146 [1879S & 77M] & 144 [1882M]	Large square denticles. 136 denticles	Large square denticles. 136 denticles
7. Border Rim	Normal	Normal	Normal	Normal	Wide	Wide
8. Head Ear Lobes	Front of ear 2 lines	Front of ear 2 lines	Front of ear 2 lines	Front of ear 2 lines	* No lines front of ear	No lines front of ear
9. Head Width	Wide	Wide	Wide	Very Wide	Very Wide	Very Wide
10. Head Pony Tail	Further from 'G' of 'GRATIA'	Close to 'G'	Closer to 'G'	Very close to 'G'	Extremely close to 'G'	Extremely close to 'G'
11. Head Alignment	'I' of 'DEI' above rear of head	'I' above rear of head	'I' above 2nd ribbon	'I' above 2nd ribbon	'I' above 2nd ribbon	'I' above 2nd ribbon

SYDNEY & MELBOURNE REVERSE DIE TYPES

DETAILS	TYPE 1	TYPE 2	TYPE 3	TYPE 4
• Cross on top of orb	• Apart from border.	• Touching border • No dot.	• Touching border Shield like Type1	• Top of cross buried in border.
• Shield	• Dot on centre	• Redesigned shield	• without the dot	• Wide rim.
• Denticles	• Verticle line just above centre of shield. • Short & widely	• Short and widely spread. 122 denticles	• 147 denticles	• Denticles close together and large 148 denticles. • Rosettes close

1. Two varieties of both Melbourne dates 1877M, 1882M and two varieties of each four Sydney Mint dates - 1880S, 1881S, 1882S and 1883S are reported. All seen except 1882S 5/3 which is reported but unconfirmed. Viz
[a] 1877M Type 3 wide ribbon. Type 4 narrow ribbon. Type 3 is scarcer.
[b] 1882M Type 4 Obverse [ear]. Type 5 Obverse [ear]. Type 4 scarcer.
[c] 1880S, 1881S, 1882S & 1883S [1882S not verified]. Type 3 Reverse toothed denticles. Type 4 reverse square denticles [Type 3 scarcer].
2. No Melbourne Type 4 reverse has been seen.

HALF SOVEREIGN

YOUNG HEAD SHIELD REVERSE : VICTORIA

SHIELD REVERSE 1871 - 1887

Obverse : William Wyon
Reverse : J.B. Merlen

Specifications : Composition: 91.67% gold; 8.33% copper. Size 21.5 mm. (22 carat 916.6 fine). Weight 7.9881 grams. Pure gold content .2354 oz

McD Ref	Date & M/Mark	Type	Very Good	Fine	Very Fine	Extra Fine	aUnc	Unc	Choice Unc	Gem	Proof
014	1871 S	1/1	295	375	525	3,600	17,750	29,500	45,000	67,500	175,000
015	1872 S	2/2	295	375	600	3,750	18,500	33,000	48,000	70,000	—
016	1873 M	3/3	325	450	650	4,200	19,500	35,500	55,000	78,500	—
017	1875 S	3/3	325	395	650	5,200	19,500	35,500	55,000	78,500	—
018	1877 M	3/3 WR	335	425	775	7,000	21,500	39,000	60,000	72,500	125,000
018a	1877 M	4/3 NR	320	390	700	5,000	19,500	34,000	55,000	78,000	145,000
019	1879 S	4/4	320	390	700	5,000	16,000	29,000	48,000	65,000	—
020	1880 S	5/3	395	675	1,750	16,000	27,500	46,000	67,500	90,000	—
020a	1880 S	5/4	275	295	775	5,750	19,500	41,000	55,000	75,500	135,000
021	1881 S	5/3	345	550	2,600	22,000	43,000	80,000	110,000	Not seen	Not seen
021a	1881 S	5/4	295	475	850	5,750	20,000	38,000	57,500	77,000	—
022	1881 M	5/3	435	750	2,100	16,000	35,000	52,000	75,000	95,000	135,000
023	1882 S	5/3	—	—	—	—	—	—	—	Not seen	—
023a	1882 S	5/4	375	650	1,500	13,750	30,000	52,000	75,000	95,000	—
024	1882 M	4/3	295	350	550	8,000	19,000	38,000	51,000	70,000	—
024a	1882 M	5/3	a	325	550	2,500	9,500	20,000	30,000	41,000	—
025	1883 S	5/3	a	300	1,300	10,500	27,000	46,000	73,500	100,000	—
025a	1883 S	5/4	c	d	395	2,300	8,750	20,000	29,500	43,000	80,000
026	1884 M	5/3	d	475	825	9,000	24,000	41,000	54,000	73,000	85,000
027	1885 M	5/3	325	900	1,850	11,000	28,750	42,000	65,000	87,000	—
028	1886 S	5/4	b	275	425	3,000	11,250	22,000	36,000	56,000	—
029	1886 M	5/3	c	550	1,500	12,500	28,500	46,000	65,000	95,000	85,000
030	1887 S	5/4	c	d	425	2,250	9,000	20,000	30,000	45,000	—
030a	1887 S			69,500		Two examples known		—	Silver Pattern		—
031	1887 M	5/3	320	650	3,650	23,500	46,000	60,000	95,000	145,000	—

Key to mints :- (S) Sydney Mint; (M) Melbourne Mint.
Mintmark position : Below shield on reverse

(1) The proof/specimen issues listed above are extremely rare. In most cases, less than ten examples are known.
(2) All proof issues have reeded edges unless otherwise stated.
(3) There are five obverse portrait varieties and four reverses. Varieties McD 018, McD 020, McD 021, McD 023, McD 024 & McD 025 are scarce varieties.
(4) McD 030a. Only one example of this rare silver piece has been recorded as having been sold through public auction. An example described as "Nearly Very Fine" was sold by Spink (Australia) as lot 392 in November 1979.

IMPORTANT POINTS REGARDING PRICING OF BULLION

Modern rare metal collector issues are very difficult to accurately price on the secondary market. This is because the value of the coins fluctuates with the prevailing metal price and the exchange rate. The prices quoted in this book were taken from the GoldCorp official bullion price guide posted on May 20, 2017. At the time the gold price was USD $1,255.40 or AUD $1,678.94 per ounce. Silver was USD $17.03 or Aust. $22.90. Platinum traded for USD $951.70 or Aust. $1,279.51 and Palladium sold for USD $771.85 or Aust. $1,037.71.

DESIGNER'S INITIALS VARIATIONS

The often ridiculed obverse design of the Jubilee Head obverse design (1887 - 1893) was executed by Sir J.E. Boehm. Although the first year of issue of the half sovereign was a relatively modest 134,000 pieces, there are at least six varieties of the obverse design that portray his initials at the base of the bust of Queen Victoria. Three of the variations appear on the Sydney issued coins with a further three associated with the Melbourne Mint issues.

DESIGNER'S INITIALS VARIATIONS
1887 SYDNEY MINT HALF SOVEREIGN

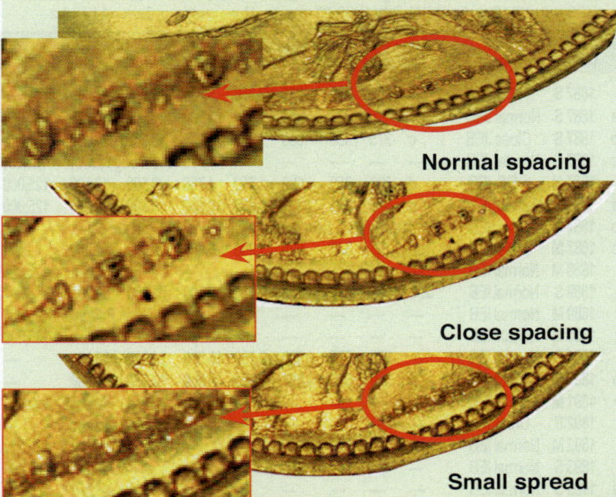

Normal spacing

Close spacing

Small spread

DESIGNER'S INITIALS VARIATIONS
1887 MELBOURNE MINT HALF SOVEREIGN

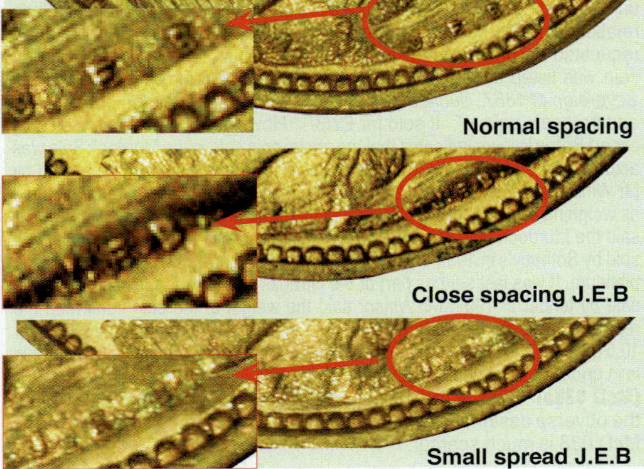

Normal spacing

Close spacing J.E.B

Small spread J.E.B

HALF SOVEREIGN

JUBILEE HEAD : SHIELD REVERSE

SHIELD REVERSE 1887 - 1893

Obverse : Sir J.E. Boehm
Reverse : J.B. Merlen

Specifications: Composition: 91.67% gold; 8.33% copper. Size 19 mm (22 carat 916.6 fine). Weight 3.9940 grams. Pure gold content .1177 oz

McD Ref	Date & M/Mark	Type	Very Good	Fine	Very Fine	Extra Fine	aUnc	Unc	Choice Unc	Gem	Proof
032	1887 S	S.S. JEB	b/v	275	395	975	2,350	5,500	9,500	17,000	—
032a	1887 S	Normal JEB	c	d	325	850	1,750	4,500	7,500	12,500	137,000
032b	1887 S	Close JEB	c	275	395	950	1,950	5,000	8,750	14,000	—
032c	1887 S	Normal JEB	—	—	—	—	—	—	Plain edge proof		125,000
033	1887 M	S.S. IEB	d	325	350	690	1,750	4,750	8,500	13,500	125,000
033a	1887 M	Normal JEB	d	365	495	1,400	5,450	10,500	16,500	22,500	125,000
033b	1887 M	Normal JEB	*Reeded gVF pattern in platinum or silver. Unique?*							—	—
033c	1887 M	Close JEB	d	295	350	925	1,900	5,000	9,000	14,000	—
034	1888 M	Normal IEB	—	—	—	—	—	—	—	Pattern	125,000
035	1889 S	Normal IEB	295	375	950	4,400	9,500	15,500	21,000	32,500	—
036	1889 M	Normal IEB	—	—	—	—	—	—	—	Pattern	125,000
037	1890 M	Normal IEB	—	—	—	—	—	—	—	Pattern	125,000
038	1891 S	Normal IEB	—	375	875	4,500	9,750	16,500	24,000	28,500	—
038a	1891 S	Without IEB	b	300	675	1,950	4,000	8,000	12,500	18,500	—
039	1891 M	Normal IEB	—	—	—	—	—	—		Pattern	110,000
040	1892 S	Unknown	—	—	—	—	—	Unconfirmed pattern			—
041	1892 M	Normal IEB	—	—	—	—	—	—	—	Pattern	125,000
042	1893 S	Normal IEB	—	—	—	—	—	—	—	Pattern	125,000
042a	1893 S	Normal IEB	—	—	—	—	—		Plain edge pattern		125,000
043	1893 M	Normal IEB	b/v	325	375	1,950	4,350	8,500	14,500	20,000	125,000

Key to mints :- (S) Sydney Mint; (M) Melbourne Mint.
Mintmark position : Below shield on reverse.

(McD 033b) The sale of the John G. Murdoch Collection by the London auction house, Sotheby's in March 1903 included what is believed to be a unique Melbourne Mint 1887 half sovereign in silver. Murdoch had a close relat onship with several mint masters and it is accepted that he often requested an off metal striking of various coins. The above mentioned coin was listed as lot 653 in his sale. The catalogue read :- *"Silver Half Sovereign of 1887. Jubilee Head (Melbourne Mint) and edge grained. VF and probably unique".* It sold for £2/3/-. However recent research by gold expert Barrie Winsor indicates that the above coin sold in the Murdoch Sale was actually made of platinum, rather than silver as indicated. The piece, sold by Mr Winsor in early 2003 for $22,500, was in good VF condition and described as weighing 4 grams, being 19.3 mm in diameter and 1.1 mm thick. Mr Winsor said the Murdoch coin was later offered as part of the King Farouk Collection sold by Sotheby's in 1954. As lot 1498, it was then correctly described as being platinum. It was last sold as part of the Strauss Collection that was offered for sale by tender in 1999. Mr Winsor said the weight of the coin confirmed the reported metal content, relative densities are Gold 19.3, Platinum 21.4, Silver 10.5 gms/cm3. A gold half sovereign weighs 3.994 grams. * Only known example is in good VF condition. Current value $85,000.

(McD 038a) Most of the 1891 Sydney issued coins are found without the obverse designer's initials "JEB" (Sir J.E. Boehm). Of the two types, McD 038 is much scarcer.

HALF SOVEREIGN

VEILED OR OLD HEAD TYPE : VICTORIA

ST. GEORGE REVERSE 1893 - 1901

Obverse : Sir Thomas Brock
Reverse : Benedetto Pistrucci
Specifications : Composition: 91.67% gold; 8.33% copper. Size 19 mm (22 carat 916.6 fine). Weight 3.9940 grams. Pure gold content .1177 oz

McD Ref	Date & M/Mark	Type	Very Good	Fine	Very Fine	Extra Fine	aUnc	Unc	Choice Unc	Gem	Proof
044	1893 S		250	295	320	1,000	2,650	5,350	8,750	12,500	115,000
044a	1893 S	PROOF	–	–	–	–	–	–	Plain edge proof		125,000
045	1893 M		175k	Five circ examples including two (VG) pieces in RAM							395,000
046	1894 M	PATTERN	–	–	–	–	–	–	–	–	125,000
047	1895 M	PATTERN	–	–	–	–	–	–	–	–	125,000
048	1896 M		d	250	330	1,300	3,200	6,500	10,000	14,000	125,000
049	1897 S		c	d	280	10	2,600	5,450	9,000	12,750	—
050	1897 M	PATTERN	–	–	–	–	–	–	–	–	125,000
051	1898 M	PATTERN	–	–	–	–	–	–	–	–	125,000
052	1899 M		d	295	425	1,600	4,000	8,750	15,500	23,000	125,000
053	1899 P	PATTERN	–	–	–	–	Only one example known				495,000
054	1900 S		c	265	265	850	2,300	4,450	7,000	10,750	—
055	1900 M		d	300	375	1,350	3,500	7,100	14,500	21,500	125,000
056	1900 P		d	375	550	1,850	5,250	13,000	21,000	28,500	—
057	1901 M	PATTERN	–	–	–	–	–	–	–	–	125,000
058	1901 P	PATTERN	–	–	–	–	–	–	–	–	145,000

IDENTIFYING THE MINT MARKS

Key to mints :- (S) Sydney; (M) Melbourne; (P) Perth.
Mintmark position : Above date on reverse.

(1) In most cases less than ten examples of the proofs are known.
(2) All proof issues have reeded edges unless otherwise stated.
(3) Patterns are coins struck as test pieces but not issued for circulation.
(045) As well as the two examples in the Royal Australian Mint collection in Canberra, there is a total of five examples known. This includes three well circulated coins in private hands. It is possible these rare coins were patterns accidentally released into circulation. Only one proof condition coin is known which is valued at $295,000. An example graded as VG/Fine was purchased by Winsor and Sons Pty Ltd at the RBA sale conducted by Downies in November 2005 for $61,190

FURTHER INFORMATION ON THE ST. GEORGE REVERSE

Most Australian sovereigns and half sovereigns share the famous Benedetto Pistrucci St. George and the Dragon reverse which also appears on British, Canadian, Indian and South African issues. In Australia, St. George reverse gold coins were struck at the Sydney, Melbourne and Perth mints. British coins carry no mintmark. All other "branch" issues carry a mintmark in the area as described above. For Australian coins, look for "S" for Sydney, "M" for Melbourne and "P" for Perth. For other overseas mintmarks look for "C" for Canada (Ottawa), "SA" for South Africa (Pretoria) or "I" for India (Bombay).

HALF SOVEREIGN

EDWARD VII : ST. GEORGE REVERSE

ST. GEORGE REVERSE 1902 - 1910

Obverse : G.W. De Saulles
Reverse : Benedetto Pistrucci

Specifications: Composition: 91.67% gold; 8.33% copper. Size 19 mm (22 carat 916.6 fine). Weight 3.9940 grams. Pure gold content .1177 oz

McD Ref	Date & M/Mark	Type	Very Good	Fine	Very Fine	Extra Fine	aUnc	Unc	Choice Unc	Gem	Proof
059	1902 S	MATTE FINISH	a	b	c	350	600	1,350	1,950	2,750	125,000
059a	1902 S	FROSTED	—	—	—	—	—	—	Brilliant Proof		145,000
060	1903 S		b	c	250	350	800	1,950	3,600	6,750	—
061	1904 P	No BP	d	325	750	3,300	15,500	23,500	33,000	52,000	—
061a	1904 P	BP	—	—	—	—	—	—	Not verified		—
062	1906 S	BP	b	c	d	285	550	1,350	1,950	3,000	—
062a	1906 S	No BP	One uniface (reverse) specimen in Royal Mint (UK) collection								—
063	1906 M	BP	d	325	650	2,250	4,250	8,550	12,500	18,000	—
063a	1906 M	UNIFACE	No BP One uniface (rev) specimen in Royal Mint (UK) collection								—
064	1906 P		One uniface (reverse) specimen in Royal Mint (UK) collection								—
065	1907 M	BP	a	b	250	55	800	2,150	3,850	6,500	—
066	1908 S		a	b	c	260	395	950	1,425	2,500	—
067	1908 M	BP	b	c	d	300	775	1,675	2,950	6,250	—
068	1908 P	BP	d	325	750	3,850	16,500	24,50032	,000	47,500	—
069	1909 M		b	c	d	495	1,250	2,250	4,250	8,550	—
070	1909 P	BP	c	d	525	1,600	5,100	9,250	14,500	23,000	—
071	1910 S		a	b	c	250	400	950	1,520	2,150	—

Key to mints :- (S) Sydney; (M) Melbourne; (P) Perth.
Mintmark position : Above date on reverse.

In most cases less than ten examples of the proof issues are known. All proof issues have reeded edges unless otherwise stated.
(McD 059/McD 059a) Matte proof. There are two types of 1902 proof issues. According to dealer, Barrie Winsor, one is a matte proof while the other has a brilliant proof finish.
(*) The designer's initials "BP" (Benedetto Pistrucci) do not appear on the reverse of any issues dated 1902, 1903 and some 1904 and 1906 pieces.
(061a) A 1904 Perth Mint piece with the "B.P." initials for the designer, Benedetto Pistrucci is thought to exist but yet to be verified.

Key to pricing :-
(a) Bullion value of gold, plus 10%.
(b) Bullion plus 15%.
(c) Bullion plus 20%.
(d) Bullion plus 25%.

At the time of preparing these prices, the bullion price of a Half Sovereign was $240

NOTE : All proof issues have reeded edges unless otherwise stated.

IMPORTANT POINTS REGARDING PRICING OF BULLION

Modern rare metal collector issues are very difficult to accurately price on the secondary market. This is because the value of the coins fluctuates with the prevailing metal price and the exchange rate. The prices quoted in this book were taken from the GoldCorp official bullion price guide posted on May 10, 2015. At the time the gold price was USD $1,179.70. : (AUD $1,529.50) per ounce. Silver was USD $15.87 : (Aust. $20.58; Platinum traded for USD $1,101.20 : (Aust. $1,427.72) and Palladium sold for USD $703 : (Aust. $911.45).

HALF SOVEREIGN

GEORGE V : ST GEORGE REVERSE

ST. GEORGE REVERSE 1911 - 1918

Obverse : Sir E.B. Mackennal
Reverse : Benedetto Pistrucci

Specifications: Composition: 91.67% gold; 8.33% copper. Size 19 mm (22 carat 916.6 fine). Weight 3.9940 grams. Pure gold content .1177 oz

McD Ref	Date & M/Mark	Very Good	Fine	Very Fine	Extra Fine	aUnc	Unc	Choice Unc	Gem	Proof
072	1911 S	b	c	295	330	450	750	1,350	2,200	135,000
073	1911 P	b	c	295	360	450	750	1,200	1,850	—
074	1912 S	a	b	265	295	325	500	750	1,250	—
075	1914 S	a	b	265	295	325	350	425	550	—
076	1915 S	a	b	c	275	300	325	375	495	—
077	1915 M	a	b	265	295	325	395	575	625	—
078	1915 P	b/v	b/v	325	400	675	895	1,450	—	—
079	1916 S	c	d	275	300	325	425	575	775	—
080	1918 P	400	750	1,850	4,350	5,975	8,750	12,000	18,500	—
081	1919 P	–	–	*Dies prepared but no coins known to exist*						—
082	1920 P	–	–	*Dies prepared but no coins known to exist*						—

LOWER GRADE COINS PRICED ON BULLION DEALER ASKING PRICE OF $271.00.

(McD 080) Mintage figures for the 1918 Perth Mint half sovereign could be as low as 200 to 300 pieces. Mint records show that no half sovereigns were struck in 1918. However records indicate half sovereigns were struck in 1919 and 1920 although these were never issued. It is possible these coins were struck using 1918 dies and the majority of the issue being re-melted before being released for circulation. **(McD 081 & McD 082)** In his book, *The Gold Half Sovereign*, author Michael A. Marsh notes that dies dated 1919 and 1920 were prepared but no circulating coins, patterns or proofs are known to exist. Barrie Winsor of Winsor & Son, Jamberoo, advises of an unconfirmed report that a 1919 dated coin had been sighted in London.

1916 SYDNEY MINT DIE VARIETY

Keen sovereign collector, Kevin Parker recently emailed me the following information : "I'm writing about a half sovereign variety in the 1916 Sydney Mint. It appears that the S mintmark makes quite a shift in position in the two varieties. In one type, the S is almost above the 1 in 1916, just slightly to the left. *(See Top)*. In the second variety, the S is pretty much between the 9 and the 1 in 1916. Population wise, (these are only very preliminary and rough estimates based on searches and images online), the S above the 1 type seems to be the most common, where the S in the middle of the 9 and 1 is the least common of the two. For every three or four of the S above the 1, I might see one with the S in the middle (roughly). Other than the mintmark shift, the rest of the coin appears to be identical. This mintmark positioning is not entirely limited to the 1916 coin as other George V half sovs show it also, like the 1911 P [Perth], but none quite to this extreme."

ONE SOVEREIGN

TYPE ONE : PORTRAIT SIMILAR TO UK COINS

SYDNEY MINT REVERSE

1855 - 1856

Obverse : James Wyon
Reverse : L.C. Wyon

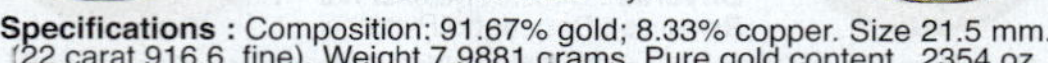

Specifications : Composition: 91.67% gold; 8.33% copper. Size 21.5 mm. (22 carat 916.6 fine). Weight 7.9881 grams. Pure gold content .2354 oz.

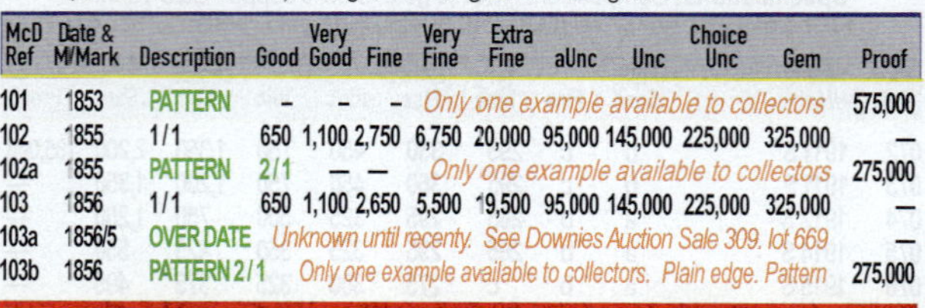

McD Ref	Date & M/Mark	Description	Good	Very Good	Fine	Very Fine	Extra Fine	aUnc	Unc	Choice Unc	Gem	Proof
101	1853	PATTERN	–	–	–	*Only one example available to collectors*						575,000
102	1855	1 / 1	650	1,100	2,750	6,750	20,000	95,000	145,000	225,000	325,000	—
102a	1855	PATTERN 2/1	—	—	*Only one example available to collectors*							275,000
103	1856	1 / 1	650	1,100	2,650	5,500	19,500	95,000	145,000	225,000	325,000	—
103a	1856/5	OVER DATE	*Unknown until recenty. See Downies Auction Sale 309. lot 669*									—
103b	1856	PATTERN 2 / 1	*Only one example available to collectors. Plain edge. Pattern*									275,000

ONE SOVEREIGN

TYPE TWO : PORTRAIT UNIQUE TO AUSTRALIA

SYDNEY MINT REVERSE

1855 - 1856

Obverse : L.C. Wyon
Reverse : L.C. Wyon

Specifications : Composition: 91.67% gold; 8.33% silver. Size 21.5 mm. (22 carat 916.6 fine). Weight 7.9881 grams. Pure gold content .2354 oz.
NB : Some 1868 &1870 coins have 8.33% copper instead of silver.

McD Ref	Date & M/Mark	Description	Good	Very Good	Fine	Very Fine	Extra Fine	aUnc	Unc	Choice Unc	Gem	Proof
104	1357	2 / 1	a	b	550	950	4,250	10,000	20,000	35,000	45,000	295,000
104 a	1357	2 / 1	–	–	*Three available to collectors. Plain edge pattern*							175,000
105	1358	2 / 1	200	400	750	1,500	6,500	22,500	45,000	70,000	105,000	—
106	1359	2 / 1	a	b	525	850	3,000	8,100	16,500	29,500	45,000	—
107	1860	2 / 1	a	600	825	1,900	9,500	22,500	46,000	80,000	100,000	—
107 a	1860/5	O/Date	a	800	1,100	2700	12,250	39,000	52,000	90,000	110,000	—
108	1861	2 / 1	b	d	500	750	2,750	6,250	12,000	21,000	32,000	—
108 a	1861/0	O/Date	b	2,250	3,400	8,100	16,500	34,000	49,000	87,000	120,000	—
109	1862	2 / 1	b	500	600	1,250	5,500	14,500	23,000	38,000	50,000	—
110	1863	2 / 1	c	d	525	825	3,100	7,500	14,000	23,000	39,000	—
111	1864	2 / 1	c	d	500	595	1,450	2,750	6,500	9,000	12,500	—
112	1865	2 / 1	c	d	525	975	3,000	7,250	15,500	26,000	39,000	—
112 a	1865/4	O/Date	a	b	–	11,750	23,000	–	*Two examples known*			—
113	1866	2 / 1	b	d	500	575	1,000	2,150	4,550	8,500	11,250	215,000
114	1867	2 / 1	b	d	500	595	1,100	2,350	5,650	8,500	11,750	—
115	1868	Gold/Silver	b	d	500	550	1,150	2,350	5,650	8,500	11,750	—
115 a	1868	Gold/Copper	b	d	500	525	1,000	2,150	4,750	8,500	11,500	—
116	1869	Unknown	a	b	—	—	—	—	*Issue not verified*			—
117	1870	Gold/Copper	b	d	500	575	950	1,500	3,750	6,500	9,000	225,000

(McD 115a) May have been struck in 1869. *See note below.*
(McD 116) Records show 1,202,000 sovereigns were stuck in 1869 but as none are known to exist, it is thought these coins must have been of an earlier date.

OVERDATE VARIETIES

SYDNEY MINT SOVEREIGNS

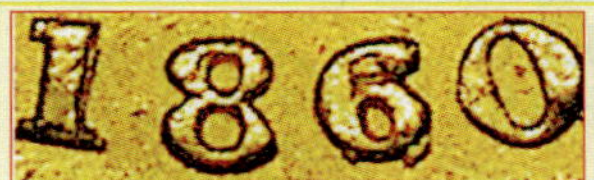

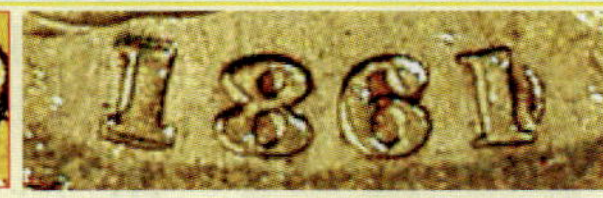

1860/5- OVERDATE : Only one uncirculated example of this overdate is known to exist. It was formed by stamping a "6" over a "5".

1861/0 OVERDATE : This overdate is known in several grades although very rare. It was formed by stamping a "1" over an "0".

1865/4 OVERDATE : Only two examples are known of this overdate which was formed by stamping a "5" over a "4".

PORTRAIT VARIATIONS

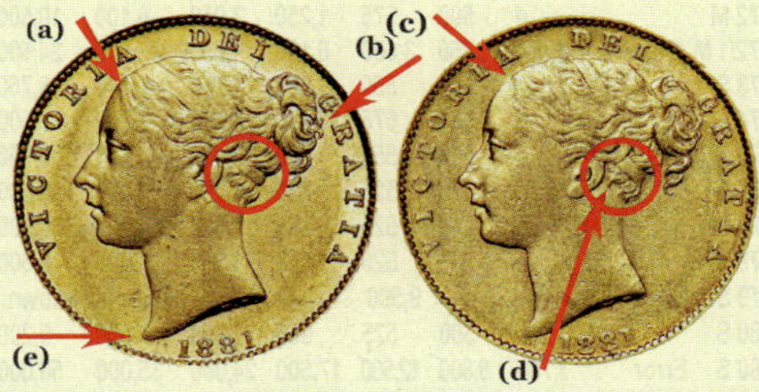

The "low hairline" type (a) also features an extra hair curl at the end of the bob (b). The "high hairline" type (c) also features an extra curl behind the ear and below the ribbon (d). Truncation of neck more rounded an further from the denticals. For more comprehensive details, please refer to page 61 of the 22nd edition of this book.

LEGEND ERRORS

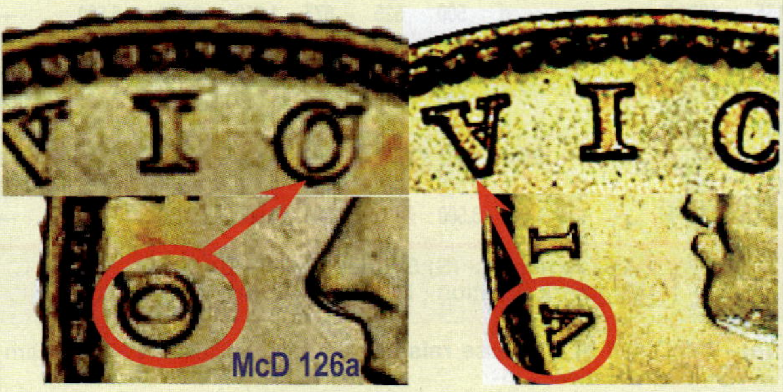

(McD 126a) - Above left. Until recently this die variation was thought to be unique. It concerns an 1879 S Shield Reverse Sovereign variation concerning the word VICTORIA. An "O" was punched into the die and then overstamped with a "C". The first recorded example was graded as *"Good Very Fine."* At Noble's Sale 91 held at Melbourne, 2009, a better example was sold for $12,000 plus commission. The description in the catalogue stated :- "Lot 1354, Minute die breaks on obverse, nearly full mint bloom, Nearly Uncirculated/Uncirculated and extremely rare, only the second we have seen."

McD 127a) - Above right. 1880S. Obverse features an inverted "A" in place of the "V" for Victoria. Only ten examples known. *(See February 1998 issue of Australasian Coin and Banknote Magazine).* A Good Fine example sold for a hammer price of $5,`200 as lot 442 in Noble's Sale 91, held at Melbourne in July 2009. Lot 442.

ONE SOVEREIGN

YOUNG HEAD : SHIELD REVERSE

SHIELD REVERSE 1871 - 1887

Obverse : William Wyon
Reverse : J.B. Merlen

Specifications : Composition: 91.67% gold; 8.33% copper. Size 21.5 mm (22 carat 916.6 fine). Weight 7.9881 grams. Pure gold content .2354 oz

McD Ref	Date & M/Mark	Die Variation	Fine	Very Fine	Extra Fine	aUnc	Unc	Choice Unc	Gem	Proof
118 a	1871 S	WW Raised	d	500	575	875	2,350	4,400	8,000	—
118 b	1871 S	WW Incuse	d	500	575	875	2,350	4,400	8,000	145,000
119	1872 S		d	500	595	1,300	4,600	6,600	11,000	—
120	1872 M		d	500	575	1,250	3,950	6,100	10,500	—
120 c	1872/1 M	O/Date	1,400	2,250	3,600	6,100	9,850	16,500	24,500	—
121	1873 S		d	500	550	1,000	2,750	5,500	8,750	—
122	1874 M		d	525	675	2,000	4,400	7,750	12,500	—
123	1875 S		d	500	550	950	2,450	4,850	8,350	125,000
124	1877 S		c	d	525	750	1,850	4,300	6,500	—
125	1878 S		c	d	525	750	1,850	4,300	6,500	—
126	1879 S		c	d	525	750	1,850	4,300	6,500	125,000
126a d	1879 S	Error	—	—	9,500	—	Two examples known			—
127	1880 S		d	500	525	950	2,350	4,850	8,200	155,000
127a	1880 S	Error	3,750	8,800	12,500	17,500	24,000	35,000	50,000	—
128	1880 M		1,350	3,500	7,000	11,250	17,500	28,500	41,000	—
129	1881 S		d	500	550	950	2,500	4,900	8,000	—
130	1881 M		d	500	750	2,250	4,950	9,000	16,500	—
131	1882 S		d	500	575	1,000	2,950	4,900	8,250	—
132	1882 M		d	500	575	1,000	2,950	4,900	8,250	—
133	1883 S		d	500	535	725	1,850	4,000	5,750	125,000
134 e	1883 M		450	800	1,750	3,500	6,500	9,500	17,500	125,000
135	1884 S		d	500	525	675	1,650	3,750	5,500	—
136	1884 M		d	500	515	675	1,650	3,750	5,500	125,000
137	1885 S		d	500	515	675	1,650	3,850	5,950	Not seen
138	1885 M		d	500	515	675	1,650	3,400	5,750	125,000
139	1886 S		d	500	525	700	1,750	5,150	8,500	Not seen
140	1886 M		5,500	11,500	23,500	38,000	67,500	95,000	130,000	145,000
141	1887 S		c	500	550	1,150	3,750	5,600	8,750	125,000
142	1887 M		1,350	3,500	7,000	11,500	20,000	30,000	45,000	—

Key to mints :- (S) Sydney; (M) Melbourne.
Mintmark position : Below shield on reverse.

(a) - (McD 118 a) Obverse **raised** designer's initials "WW" (William Wyon) on truncation.
(b) - (McD 118 b) Obverse **incuse** designer's initials "WW".
(c) - (McD 120 c) The overdate sovereigns were produced from 1871 dies supplied by the London Mint for a few days in September 1872.
(d) - (McD 126 a) Up until July of this year only one Very Fine example of this variety was known to exist.
(e) - (McD 134 e) - The only known example of this proof is part of the Melbourne Mint archive now housed in the Museum Victoria collection.

ONE SOVEREIGN

YOUNG HEAD : VICTORIA

ST. GEORGE REVERSE 1871 - 1887

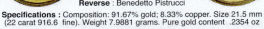

Obverse : William Wyon
Reverse : Benedetto Pistrucci

Specifications : Composition: 91.67% gold; 8.33% copper. Size 21.5 mm (22 carat 916.6 fine). Weight 7.9881 grams. Pure gold content .2354 oz

McD Ref	Date & M/Mark	Die Variation	Very Good	Fine	Very Fine	Extra Fine	aUnc	Unc	Choice Unc	Gem	Proof
143	1871 S	P1/ ST/ Large BP	500	700	750	2,100	5,500	11,000	19,000	35,000	125,000
143a	1871 S	P1/ LT/ Small BP	400	475	650	1,750	5,000	8,500	16,500	26,000	—
144	1872 S	P1 / LT / BP	c	d	450	650	1,100	4,000	6,500	13,000	—
145	1872 M	P1 / LT / BP	350	425	750	3,000	6,750	10,500	24,500	36,000	—
146	1873 S	P1 / LT / BP	b	325	550	750	1,200	4,100	8,500	15,500	—
147	1873 M	P1 / LT / BP	a	300	500	550	950	3,500	6,500	14,000	125,000
148	1874 S	P1 / LT / BP	b	325	550	650	1,100	4,500	8,200	15,500	—
149	1874 M	P1 / LT / BP	a	300	500	575	950	3,500	6,500	13,500	•125,000
150	1875 S	P1 / LT / BP	a	300	500	575	950	4,850	7,500	15,000	—
151a	1875 M	P1 / LT / BP	a	300	500	550	775	2,500	4,600	8,500	•125,000
151b	1875 M	P1 / MT / BP	NEW FIND. One confirmed example in Ted Gibson Collection								
152	1876 S	P1 / LT / BP	a	300	500	550	850	2,750	5,250	8,250	—
153	1876 M	P1 / LT / BP	a	b	475	525	650	1,900	4,100	6,500	—
154	1877 M	P1 / LT / BP	a	b	475	525	650	1,900	4,100	6,500	—
154b	1877 M	P1/MT / BP	NOW VERIFIED. One example in Ted Gibson Collection								
155	1878 M	P1 / LT / BP	a	b	c	525	650	1,900	4,100	6,500	—
156	1879 S	P1 / LT / BP	425	525	600	3,450	5,250	8,750	15,500	32,500	—
157	1879 M	P1 / LT / BP	b	350	450	525	600	1,750	3,300	6,000	—
157a	1879 M	P1 / MT / BP	b	350	450	525	1,000	2,150	4,000	6,100	—
158	1880 S	P1 / LT / BP	a	300	425	500	950	3,100	7,000	8,500	—
158a	1880 S	P1 / ST / No BP	350	500	900	3,500	6,500	9,000	16,250	25,500	—
158b	1880 S	P2 / LT / BP	b	c	d	650	2,000	3,500	5,300	8,350	125,000
158c	1880 S	P2 / LT / No BP	295	425	600	1,250	4,500	7,250	13,000	19,000	—
159	1880 M	P1 / LT / BP	b/v	325	500	525	625	1,825	3,500	6,100	—
159a	1880 M	P1 / MT / BP	b/v	325	500	550	675	1,950	3,700	6,300	—
160	1881 S	P1 / ST / No BP	b/v	350	550	625	975	2,850	5,300	8,250	—
160a	1881 S	P2 / ST / No BP	b/v	325	500	525	800	2,500	4,600	6,900	125,000
161	1881 M	P1 / LT / BP	b/v	325	500	525	625	1,850	4,250	6,300	—
161a	1881 M	P1 / ST / No BP	b/v	325	500	525	725	1,950	4,000	6.750	125,000
161b	1881 M	P1 / MT / BP	c	335	525	550	900	3,150	5,100	7,750	—
162	1882 S	P2 / ST / No BP	b	300	475	500	800	1,550	3,500	5,500	—
162a	1882 S	P2 / ST / BP	b	300	475	500	800	1,550	3,500	5,500	—
163	1882 M	P1 / ST / No BP	b/v	350	550	625	1,000	2,650	5,250	8,000	—
163a	1882 M	P1 / ST / BP	b/v	325	500	525	625	1,850	4,250	6,300	—
163b	1882 M	P2 / ST / BP	395	500	625	750	1,550	3,250	5,800	9,000	—
164	1883 S	P2 / ST / BP	b/v	375	550	1,000	2,250	4,900	7,700	11,500	—
165	1883 M	P1 / ST / No BP	325	450	650	1,300	2,500	5,250	8,250	12,750	—
165a	1883 M	P1 / ST / BP	b/v	375	425	500	550	1,650	2,750	4,000	—
165b	1883 M	P2 / ST / BP	b/v	395	450	600	1,275	2,000	3,100	4,300	125,000
166	1884 S	P2 / ST / BP	b/v	350	425	525	650	1,800	3,500	5,500	—
167	1884 M	P2 / ST / No BP	Now verified. Four confirmed examples in Ted Gibson Collection								
167a	1884 M	P1 / ST / BP	325	395	450	500	950	1,750	4,100	6,300	—

(•) Denotes a specimen issue rather than a proof

ONE SOVEREIGN

YOUNG HEAD : QUEEN VICTORIA

ST. GEORGE REVERSE

1871 - 1887

Obverse : William Wyon.
Reverse : Benedetto Pistrucci.

Specifications : Composition: 91.67% gold; 8.33% copper. Size 21.5 mm. (22 carat 916.6 fine). Weight 7.9881 grams. Pure gold content .2354 oz.

McD Ref	Date & M/Mark	Die Variation	Very Good	Fine	Very Fine	Extra Fine	aUnc	Unc	Choice Unc	Gem	Proof
167b	1884 M	P2/ST/BP	b/v	300	375	495	550	1,550	2,650	4,150	125,000
168	1885 S	P2/ST/BP	325	400	450	525	650	1,650	3,150	4,650	—
169	1885 M	P1/ST/No BP	375	500	650	1,350	4,800	8,000	15,000	22,500	—
169a	1885 M	P1/ST/BP	295	375	500	625	1,150	3,400	6,250	9,500	—
169b	1885 M	P2/ST/No BP	a	295	375	450	500	1,500	2,500	4,000	—
169c	1885 M	P2/ST/BP	a	295	375	450	500	1,500	2,500	4,000	—
170	1886 S	P2/ST/BP	b	310	395	500	600	1,750	3,225	5,200	—
171	1886 M	P2/ST/BP	b	310	395	500	550	1,450	2,300	4,500	125,000
172	1887 S	P2/ST/BP	b	310	395	500	650	1,850	3,800	5,750	—
173	1887 M	P2/ST/BP	b	310	395	500	650	1,850	3,800	5,750	—

(McD 167b) - Noble Numismatic auction house, Jim Noble believes that the only known example of this proof coin is in the British Museum, London.

YOUNG HEAD SOVEREIGN MINTMARK POSITION

YOUNG HEAD OBVERSE
ST. GEORGE REVERSE
1871 - 1887

YOUNG HEAD OBVERSE
SHIELD REVERSE
1871 - 1887

Mintmark at the base of obverse bust.

"S" Mintmark. Sydney Mint.
"M" Mintmark. Melbourne Mint.

Mintmark at the base of the shield.

"S" Mintmark. Sydney Mint.
"M" Mintmark. Melbourne Mint.

Approximate dealer retail prices for common date grade sovereigns

Victoria Young Head : St George Reverse. Bullion value approximately	AUS $435
Victoria Young Head : Shield Reverse. Bullion value approximately	AUS $525
Victoria Jubilee Head : St George Reverse. Bullion value approximately	AUS $430
Victoria Veiled Head : St George Reverse. Bullion value approximately	AUS $430
King Edward VII : St George Reverse. Bullion value approximately	AUS $420
King George V : St George Reverse. Bullion value approximately	AUS $420

SOVEREIGN DIE VARIATIONS

"BP" TYPES

Small BP

No BP

Large BP

1872 MELBOURNE MINT OVERDATE

These overdates (McD 120c) were produced from 1871 dies supplied by the London Mint for a few days in September 1872.

EXTRA PEARL

RARE 12 PEARL NECKLACE

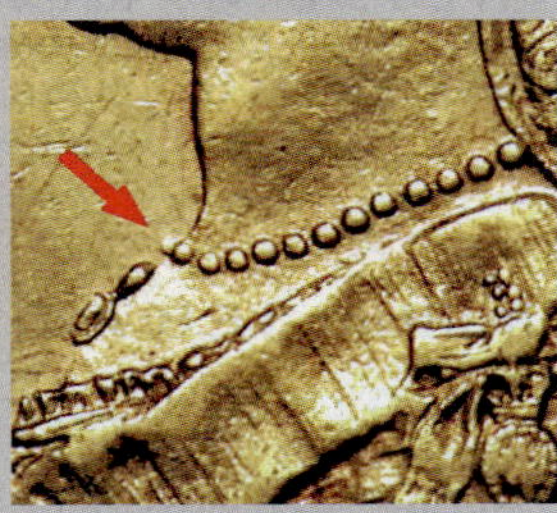

COMMON 13 PEARL NECKLACE

Gold dealer Walter Eigner He states that the variety concerns the necklace on the Jubilee Head half sovereigns of 1889-S and 1893-M. Generally the necklace features 13 pearls *(See above)* The rare type has only 12 pearls and a gap where the 13th pearl should be. (See extreme top).

YOUNG HEAD SOVEREIGNS

TYPE 1 AND TYPE 2 HEAD PORTRAITS

PORTRAIT ONE

TYPE 1 : (First Head).

Designer's initials (WW) are *'buried'* or barely recognisable on the narrow truncation of the bust as shown above at left.

PORTRAIT TWO

TYPE 2 : (Second Head). "WW" complete on broad truncation as shown on boxed coin above at left.

JUBILEE HEAD SOVEREIGNS

TYPE 1 & TYPE 2 LEGEND VARIATIONS

TYPE 1 : "D : G :" further away from crown. Tip of crown overlaps denticles.
TYPE 2 : "D : G :" close to crown and tip of crown barely touches the denticles.

JUBILEE HEAD SOVEREIGNS

NORMAL J.E.B. AND SMALL SPACED J.E.B.

RIGHT : Normal I.E.B.
Reference as in "N IEB".
Normal sized letters and normal spacing. "J" looks more like an "I".

RIGHT : Small spaced J.E.B.
Reference as in "SS JEB".
Wide spacing. "J" is hooked.

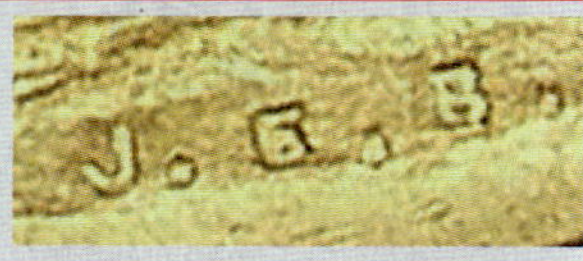

RIGHT : Normal J.E.B.
Reference as in "N JEB".
Normal size letters and spacing. "J" is hooked.

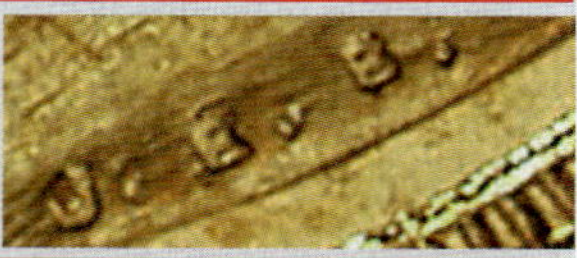

RIGHT : Long J.E.B.
Reference as in "L JEB".
Only found on 1887S.
New variety identified by Eric Eigner of Drake Sterling

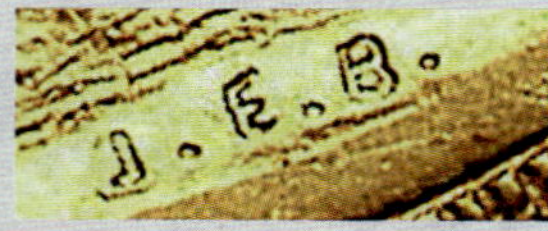

EXPLAINING THE ABBREVIATIONS

Take the example for the Young Head Saint George reverse : -
P1 / LT small BP
On the Obverse >
• The **"P1"** refers to **"Portrait One"** showing "WW" initials buried.
On the Reverse >
• The **"LT"** refers to **"Long Tail."**
• The **"Small BP"** refers to the designer's initials which are smaller than normal. See illustrations listed elsewhere.

SOVEREIGN HORSE TAIL VARIATIONS

EXCLUSIVE TO YOUNG HEAD & JUBILEE ISSUES

LONG TAIL

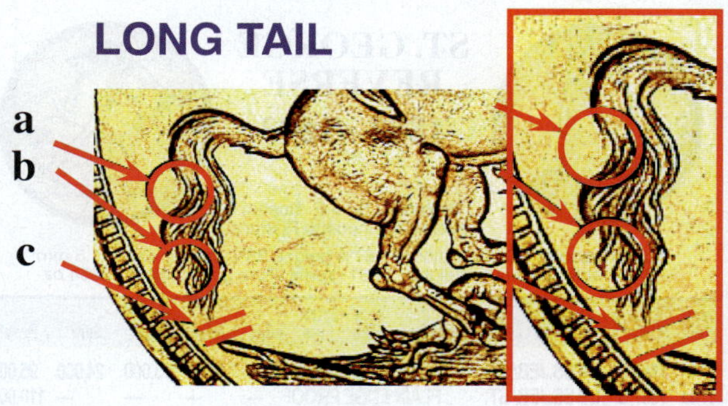

a : One spur. b : Tail points down. c : Gap smaller than both short and medium tails.

MEDIUM TAIL

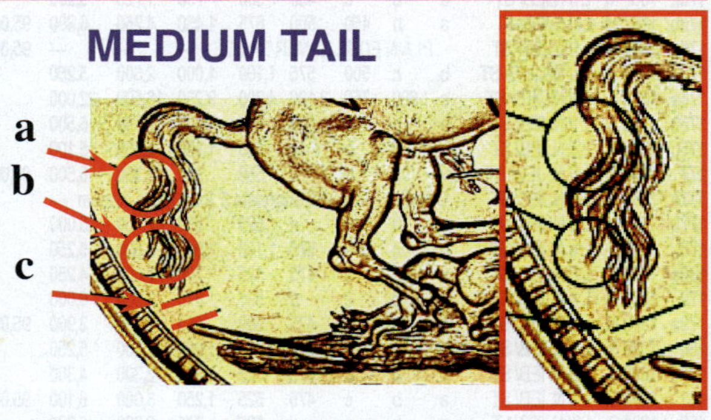

a : No spurs. b : Tail points towards denticles. c : Gap smaller than the short tail but greater than the long tail.

SHORT TAIL

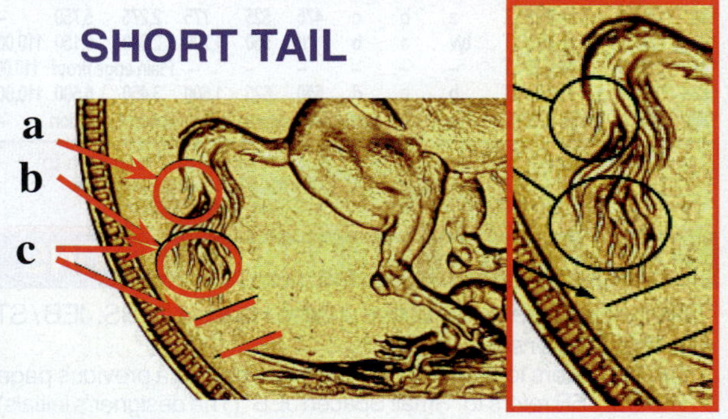

a : Two spurs. b : Different tail. c : Wider gap than the medium and long tail types.

ONE SOVEREIGN

JUBILEE HEAD : QUEEN VICTORIA

ST. GEORGE REVERSE 1887 - 1893

Obverse : Sir J.E. Boehm
Reverse : Benedetto Pistrucci.

Specifications : Composition: 91.67% gold; 8.33% copper. Size 21.5 mm (22 carat 916.6 fine). Weight 7.9881 grams. Pure gold content .2354 oz

McD Ref	Date & M/Mark		Very Good	Fine	Very Fine	Extra Fine	aUnc	Unc	Choice Unc	Gem	Proof
174	1887 S	L1/ SS.JEB/ ST	c	d	550	850	2,300	6,500	13,000	24,000	95,000
174a	1887 S	L1/ SS.JEB/ ST			PLAIN EDGE PROOF		—	—	—	—	110,000
174b	1887 S	L1/ N.JEB/ ST	d	550	1,100	2,850	4,800	10,250	21,500	36,000	—
174c	1887 S	L1/ L.JEB/ ST	d	550	1,100	2,850	4,800	10,250	21,500	36,000	—
175	1887 M	L1/ SS.JEB/ ST	a	b	d	500	650	1,250	2,900	6,250	95,000
175a	1887 M	L1/ N.IEB/ ST	a	b	c	450	500	750	1,725	3,200	—
175b	1887 M	L2/ N.IEB/ ST	a	b	450	500	675	1,450	4,250	6,800	95,000
175c	1887 M	L1/ L.JEB/ ST			PLAIN EDGE SILVER PROOF			—	—	—	95,000
176	1888 S	L1/ SS.JEB/ ST	b	c	500	575	1,100	1,000	2,600	5,250	—
176a	1888 S	L1/ N. JEB/ ST	c	500	750	2,100	4,200	9,250	16,500	22,000	—
176b	1888 S	L1/ N. IEB/ ST	b	c	475	500	900	1,600	2,750	6,500	—
176c	1888 S	L2/ N. IEB/ ST	b/v	a	b	c	550	1,100	2,650	5,100	—
177	1888 M	L1/ N. JEB/ ST	b/v	a	b	c	550	950	2,500	6,500	95,000
177a	1888 M	L1/ N. IEB/ ST	Downies [Sale 310] suggests 5 [not 3] are known —								
177b	1888 M	L2/ N. IEB/ ST	a	b	c	d	525	850	2,150	5,000	—
178	1889 S	L1/ N. IEB/ ST	b	c	500	575	1,100	1,000	2,600	5,250	—
178a	1889 S	L2/ N. IEB/ ST	a	b	c	475	525	700	2,000	4,250	—
179	1889 M	L1/ N. IEB/ ST	a	b	c	d	595	875	2,900	6,000	—
179a	1889 M	L2/ N. IEB/ ST	a	b	d	475	500	550	1,700	3,900	95,000
180	1890 S	L1/ N. IEB/ ST	b	c	500	575	1,100	1,000	2,600	5,250	—
180a	1890 S	L2/ N. IEB/ ST	a	b	c	475	525	975	2,300	4,300	—
181	1890 M	L2/ N. IEB/ ST	a	b	c	475	525	1,250	3,000	6,100	95,000
182	1891 S	L2/ N. IEB/ LT	a	b	c	d	595	875	2,900	6,000	—
183	1891 M	L2/ N. IEB/ ST	b	500	595	900	3,200	5,300	9,250	17,500	—
183a	1891 M	L2/ N. IEB/ LT	b	c	d	495	575	1,100	3,350	6,200	—
184	1892 S	L2/ N. IEB/ LT	a	b	c	475	525	950	2,150	5,250	—
185	1892 M	L2/ N. IEB/ LT	a	b	c	475	525	775	2,275	5,750	—
186	1893 S	L2/ N. IEB/ LT	b/v	a	b	d	550	1,200	2,950	6,150	110,000
187	1893 S	L2/ N. IEB/ LT	–	–	–	–	–	–	Plain edge proof		110,000
188a	1893 M	L2/ N. IEB/ LT	b	c	d	550	625	1,500	3,450	6,500	110,000
188b	1893 M	L2/ N. IEB/ M	a	One confirmed example in Ted Gibson Collection							—

(McD 175c) A Melbourne Mint silver pattern of 1887 is known to exist. A piece graded as FDC sold for $26,500 at a Noble sale (Melbourne) on July 4, 2002, as lot 1232.

EXPLAINING THE ABBREVIATIONS

Take the example for the above Jubilee Head: - L1 / SS. JEB / ST.

On the Obverse :-

- The "L1" refers to "Legend One" as explained on a previous page.
- The SS. JEB refers to "Small Spaced JEB" (The designer's initials).

On the Reverse :-

- The "ST" refers to "Short Tail."

ONE SOVEREIGN

VEILED OR OLD HEAD TYPE : VICTORIA

ST. GEORGE REVERSE 1893 - 1901

Obverse : Sir Thomas Brock
Reverse : Benedetto Pistrucci

Specifications : Composition: 91.67% gold; 8.33% copper. Size 21.5 mm (22 carat 916.6 fine). Weight 7.9881 grams. Pure gold content .2354 oz

McD Ref	Date & M/Mark	Very Good	Fine	Very Fine	Extra Fine	aUnc	Unc	Choice Unc	Gem	Proof
189	1893 S	a	b	c	d	550	1,350	2,350	3,500	95,000
189 a	1893 S	PLAIN EDGE PROOF				–	–	–	–	110,000
190	1893 M	a	b	c	500	675	1,275	2,700	4,500	110,000
191	1894 S	a	b	c	425	525	650	975	1,600	—
192	1894 M	a	b	c	425	525	650	975	1,600	95,000
193	1895 S	b/v	a	b	425	575	800	1,550	2,950	—
194	1895 M	a	b	c	475	525	650	975	1,600	95,000
195	1896 S	a	b	c	525	650	1,300	2,600	4,300	—
196	1896 M	b/v	a	b	475	525	675	1,100	1,750	95,000
197	1897 S	a	b	475	525	675	1,325	2,650	4,650	—
198	1897 M	b/v	a	b	475	525	650	950	1,575	95,000
199	1898 S	b	c	500	575	900	2,500	3,500	5,750	—
200	1898 M	b/v	a	b	425	525	675	1,200	1,600	125,000
201	1899 S	b/v	a	b	425	525	675	1,200	1,600	—
202	1899 M	a	b	c	d	475	575	950	1,500	95,000
203	1899 P	d	450	550	825	2,000	5,300	13,000	28,000	115,000
204	1900 S	b/v	a	b	425	525	675	1,200	1,600	—
205	1900 M	b/v	a	b	425	525	675	1,200	1,600	125,000
206	1900 P	a	b	c	50	550	1,000	1,775	2,850	—
207	1901 S	b/v	a	b	c	425	575	1,100	1,750	—
208	1901 M	b/v	a	b	c	450	550	900	1,750	95,000
209	1901 P	b	c	d	525	675	975	1,950	2,950	95,000

HELMET RIBBON VARIATIONS

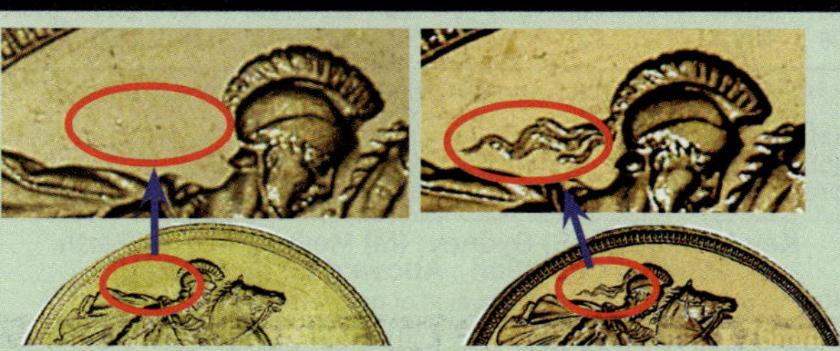

Over the years subtle changes have been made to the famed Benedetto Pistrucci depiction of the St George and the Dragon scene. During the reign of Queen Victoria there was an interesting die change regarding the engraving behind the helmet of the rider. On the Young Head issues struck at both the Melbourne and Sydney mints between 1871 and 1887 there was no ribbon or streamer attached to the back of the helmet. *(See illustration at left).* On all the subsequent issues from the Jubilee Head series to the last George V strikings, a streamer or ribbon can be clearly seen. (See figures at right).

ONE SOVEREIGN

KING EDWARD VII

ST. GEORGE REVERSE 1902 - 1910

Obverse : G.W. De Saulles
Reverse : Benedetto Pistrucci

Specifications : Composition: 91.67% gold; 8.33% copper. Size 21.5 mm (22 carat 916.6 fine). Weight 7.9881 grams. Pure gold content .2354 oz

McD Ref	Date & M/Mark	Very Good	Fine	Very Fine	Extra Fine	aUnc	Unc	Choice Unc	Gem	Proof
210	1902 S	a	b	c	d	450	675	1,200	1,750	85,000
210a	1902 S	FROSTED FINISH PROOF			—	—	—	—	—	95,000
211	1902 M	a	b	c	d	450	675	1,200	1,750	95,000
212	1902 P	b	c	d	450	695	1,350	2,000	2,500	—
213	1903 S	a	b	c	d	450	675	1,200	1,750	—
214	1903 M	a	b	c	d	450	675	1,200	1,750	—
215	1903 P	a	b	c	d	450	675	1,200	1,750	—
216	1904 S	a	b	c	d	450	675	1,200	1,750	—
217	1904 M	a	b	c	d	450	675	1,200	1,750	85,000
218	1904 P	a	b	c	d	450	675	1,200	1,750	—
219	1905 S	a	b	c	d	450	675	1,200	1,750	—
220	1905 M	a	b	c	d	450	675	1,200	1,750	—
221	1905 P	c	d	525	625	850	995	1,350	1,950	—
222	1906 S	b	c	d	525	625	725	1,150	1,600	—
223	1906 M	b	c	d	525	625	725	1,150	1,600	—
224	1906 P	a	b	c	d	450	675	1,200	1,750	—
225	1907 S	b/v	a	b	c	425	650	900	1,400	—
226	1907 M	b/v	a	b	c	425	650	900	1,400	—
227	1907 P	b/v	a	b	425	550	800	1,200	1,825	—
228	1908 S	a	b	c	d	525	750	1,100	1,750	—
229	1908 M	a	b	c	d	525	725	1,000	1,500	—
230	1908 P	b/v	a	b	c	500	575	850	1,250	—
231	1909 S	b/v	a	b	c	450	600	900	1,350	—
232	1909 M	b/v	a	b	c	500	575	800	1,200	—
233	1909 P	c	d	675	750	825	950	1,250	1,850	—
234	1910 S	a	b	c	500	550	650	850	1,350	—
235	1910 M	a	b	c	525	625	700	900	1,325	85,000
236	1910 P	a	b	c	525	625	750	1,250	2,500	—

All proof issues have reeded edges unless otherwise stated.

(a) This proof coin has a matte finish.
(b) This previously unknown proof was discovered in South Africa and was featured in the November 1998 issue of the *Australasian Coin & Banknote Magazine.*

Key to mints :- (S) Sydney; (M) Melbourne; (P) Perth.
Mintmark position : Above date on reverse.

Key to pricing :-
(a) Bullion value of gold, plus 10%.
(b) Bullion plus 15%.
(c) Bullion plus 20%.
(d) Bullion plus 25%.

Approximate dealer retail prices for common date grade sovereigns

Victoria Young Head : St George Reverse. Bullion value approximately	AUS $435
Victoria Young Head : Shield Reverse. Bullion value approximately	AUS $525
Victoria Jubilee Head : St George Reverse. Bullion value approximately	AUS $430
Victoria Veiled Head : St George Reverse. Bullion value approximately	AUS $430
King Edward VII : St George Reverse. Bullion value approximately	AUS $420
King George V : St George Reverse. Bullion value approximately	AUS $420

ONE SOVEREIGN

LARGE HEAD TYPE : GEORGE V

ST. GEORGE REVERSE 1911 - 1928

Obverse : Sir E.B. Mackennal
Reverse : Benedetto Pistrucci

Specifications : Composition: 91.67% gold; 8.33% copper. Size 21.5 mm (22 carat 916.6 fine). Weight 7.9881 grams. Pure gold content .2354 oz

McD Ref	Date & M/ Mark	Very Good	Fine	Very Fine	Extra Fine	aUnc	Unc	Choice Unc	Gem	Proof
237	1911 S	b/v	a	b	c	d	525	625	775	—
238	1911 M	b/v	a	b	c	d	525	650	875	95,000
239	1911 P	b/v	a	b	c	d	525	650	875	—
240	1912 S	b/v	a	b	c	d	500	600	800	—
241	1912 M	b/v	a	b	c	d	525	625	850	—
242	1912 P	b/v	a	b	c	d	525	625	850	—
243	1913 S	b/v	a	b	c	d	525	600	800	—
244	1913 M	b/v	a	b	c	d	525	625	850	—
245	1913 P	b/v	a	b	c	d	550	650	875	—
246	1914 S	b/v	a	b	c	495	525	595	725	95,000
247	1914 M	b/v	a	b	c	495	525	585	750	—
248	1914 P	b/v	a	b	c	495	525	585	750	—
249	1915 S	b/v	a	b	c	495	525	585	750	—
250	1915 M	b/v	a	b	c	495	525	585	750	—
251	1915 P	b	c	650	485	525	550	650	900	—
252	1916 S	b/v	a	b	c	495	535	650	850	—
253	1916 M	a	b	c	485	525	575	675	900	—
254	1916 P	a	b	c	485	525	575	675	900	—
255	1917 S	b/v	a	b	c	495	525	585	750	—
256	1917 M	b/v	a	b	c	d	550	650	875	—
257	1917 P	b/v	a	b	c	d	550	650	875	—
258	1918 S	b/v	a	b	c	495	525	585	750	—
259	1918 M	b/v	a	b	c	495	535	650	850	—
260	1918 P	b/v	a	b	c	495	525	585	750	—
261	1919 S	b/v	a	b	c	495	535	650	850	—
262	1919 M	c	d	650	725	895	1,250	2,150	3,250	—
263	1919 P	a	b	c	d	495	525	600	750	—

ST. GEORGE HALF SOVEREIGN AND SOVEREIGN MINTMARK POSITION

This reverse design by Benedetto Pistrucci was issued during the reign of Queen Victoria, Edward VII and George V.

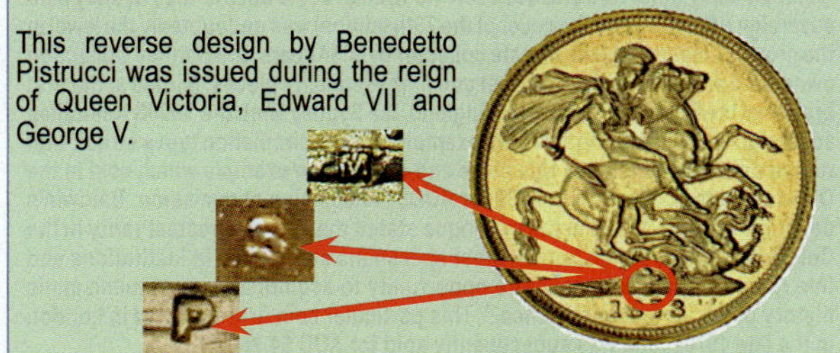

S Mintmark Sydney Mint. **M** Melbourne Mint. **P** Perth Mint.

ONE SOVEREIGN

LARGE HEAD TYPE : GEORGE V

ST. GEORGE REVERSE 1911 - 1928

Obverse : Sir E.B. Mackennal.
Reverse : Benedetto Pistrucci.

Specifications : Composition: 91.67% gold; 8.33% copper. Size 21.5 mm (22 carat 916.6 fine). Weight 7.9881 grams. Pure gold content .2354 oz

McD Ref	Date & M/Mark	Very Good	Fine	Very Fine	Extra Fine	aUnc	Unc	Choice Unc	Gem	Proof
264	1920 S	n/a	n/a	n/a	450k	850k	1.200k	Not seen	Not seen	950,000
265	1920 M	1,350	3,500	6,750	9,250	11,750	14,000	17,000	22,000	—
266	1920 P	b/v	b/v	b/v	b/v	425	550	650	850	—
267	1921 S	500	1,000	1,825	2,575	3,500	4,500	5,750	7,750	—
268	1921 M	9,500	15,000	19,500	28,500	3,000	48,000	60,000	72,000	—
269	1921 P	b/v	b/v	b/v	b/v	b/v	d	675	975	—
270	1922 S	7,500	17,000	24,250	37,50	44,000	53,000	65,000	78,000	• 95,000
271	1922 M	3,000	8,500	12,500	18,500	23,000	26,500	33,000	40,000	—
272	1922 P	b/v	b/v	b/v	b/v	495	525	650	800	—
273	1923 S	6,250	13,500	19,750	24,500	29,000	35,000	45,000	56,000	• 95,000
274	1923 M	b/v	b/v	b/v	495	575	625	750	850	—
275	1923 P	b/v	b/v	b/v	b/v	450	575	700	850	—
276	1924 S	550	1,000	1,750	2,250	3,250	4,250	5,500	7,500	—
277	1924 M	b/v	b/v	b/v	500	575	675	750	900	—
278	1924 P	b/v	b/v	b/v	c	d	800	925	1,100	—
279	1925 S	b/v	b/v	b/v	c	d	550	600	750	—
280	1925 M	b/v	b/v	b/v	b/v	d	525	625	775	—
281	1925 P	b/v	b/v	450	650	850	1,100	1,400	1,900	—
282	1926 S	6,500	15,500	31,750	42,750	49,000	58,000	70,000	84,500	225,000
283	1926 M	b/v	b/v	b/v	c	d	700	825	1,100	—
284	1926 P	550	1,000	2,100	2,750	3,600	5,750	7,000	9,000	—
285	1927 M	NO EXAMPLES KNOWN TO COLLECTORS					—	—	—	—
286	1927 P	b/v	500	595	775	1,000	1,300	1,675	2,100	—
287	1928 M	750	2,100	3,100	4,100	5,250	6,500	7,750	9,750	—
288	1928 P	b/v	b/v	475	550	650	750	875	1,100	—

[•] This dot denotes that the two sovereigns listed are Specimens rather than proofs.

Mc264. A world record price of £780,000 (£650,000 plus 24% buyer's premium) was paid at Baldwin's on September 27, 2012 for a 1920 Sydney Sovereign – one of only three ever offered at auction. Baldwins is one of the largest and longest running numismatic dealers and auction houses in the world and trades in the heart of London. The auction of primarily gold sovereigns known as the Bentley Collection included many other rare and desirable Australian coins but the 1920 Sydney Mint sovereign (illustrated on the cover of the 20th edition) was undoubtedly the jewel in the crown. Amassed by the private collector over 34 years, the Bentley Collection owner had an eye for only the rarest and highest quality pieces. Minted at the first branch of the Royal Mint outside of England, the Sydney Mint, the 1920S Australian sovereign is one of only four known examples. Three circulation types struck with rusted dies which includes this piece and a specimen example which sold in the Quartermaster Collection in 2009 for AUD$800,000 plus commission. Baldwin's description of the 1920S in the catalogue stated that :- "the greatest rarity in the Colonial Gold Sovereign Series, most specimens are housed in institutions and this represents an extremely rare opportunity to acquire a piece of numismatic history of the utmost importance." This particular coin first surfaced in London in the late 1970s. and was subsequently sold for AUD $4,250.

Mc267. Forgeries of the 1921 Sydney Mint sovereigns are known. Most are overweight. Check with a reputable dealer before purchasing on the internet.

ONE SOVEREIGN

SMALL HEAD TYPE : GEORGE V

ST. GEORGE REVERSE 1929 - 1931

Obverse : Sir E.B. Mackennal.
Reverse : Benedetto Pistrucci.

Specifications : Composition: 91.67% gold; 8.33% copper. Size 21.5 mm (22 carat 916.6 fine). Weight 7.9881 grams. Pure gold content .2354 oz

McD Ref	Date & M/Mark	Very Good	Fine	Very Fine	Extra Fine	aUnc	Unc	Choice Unc	Gem	Proof
289	1929 M	1,000	2,150	3,125	4,100	5,200	7,500	8,250	11,000	115,000
290	1929 P	a	b	c	d	550	625	750	975	—
291	1930 M	b	c	d	500	575	750	900	1,250	115,000
292	1930 P	a	b	c	d	500	575	700	875	—
293	1931 M	d	500	775	950	1,275	2,000	2,500	3,500	95,000
294	1931 P	a	b	c	d	500	575	700	875	95,000

(McD 294) Two 1931P proof sovereigns have been identified. One with an American collector who purchased it from Spink & Son, London. Another was acquired some years later by Winsor & Sons, of Jamberoo, NSW.

PATTERN TWO POUNDS

JUBILEE HEAD : VICTORIA

1887

ST. GEORGE REVERSE

SYDNEY MINT

Obverse : Sir J.E. Boehm.

Reverse : Benedetto Pistrucci.

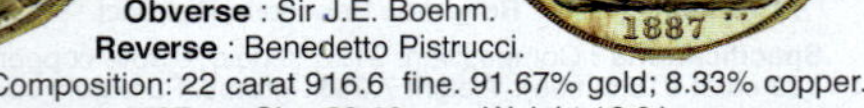

Specifications: Composition: 22 carat 916.6 fine. 91.67% gold; 8.33% copper. Pure gold content .4707 oz. Size 29.18 mm. Weight 16.01 grams.

McD Ref	Date	Mint	Estimated Mintage	Description	Specimen/ Proof
Mc300	1887	Sydney	6 to 8 known	Reeded edged pattern	325,000

A few examples were struck at Sydney for presentation at the time of the Queen's Golden Jubilee. A few were struck subsequently for VIPs right up to the closure of the Sydney Mint in 1926. The known examples in private hands are: (a) A.H.F.Baldwin (probably from Le Souef in 1926) sold in Sale 1 (lot 499), Sale 6 (lot 990), Sale 11 (lot 524) and Quartermaster Sale, June 2009 (lot 121). (b) Spink Australia Sale 3 (lot 296) (from McWhirter and possibly Murdoch, Whetmore, Capt. Vivien Hewitt and Spink London) then Sale 30 (Sharps Pixley Collection, lot 1313) and Sale 89 (lot 402). (c) Allan Sutherland, acquired in New Zealand in 1930s then Sale 9 (lot 1234). (d) Sale 20 (lot 716) possible later striking with 'orange peel' fields. (e) Sale 67 (lot 1248) previously offered in Sothebys Sale November 1997 in London, said to have come from Paris a few years earlier. The latest sale was in the Noble Sale 101 held in November 2012. Lot 1478 was described thus : "Fields scuffed on both sides, underlying brilliance, otherwise nearly unc and extremely rare. It sold for $81,550 against an estimate of $65,000."

PATTERN TWO POUNDS

KING EDWARD VII

1902

ST. GEORGE REVERSE

SYDNEY MINT

bverse : G.W. De Saule

verse : Benedetto Pistru

Specifications: Composition: 22 carat 916.6 fine. 91.67% gold; 8.33% copper. Pure gold content .4707 oz. Size 29.18 mm. Weight 16.01 grams.

McD Ref	Date	Mint	Estimated Mintage	Description	Specimen/ Proof
Mc350	1902	Sydney	5 known	Reeded edged pattern	325,000

An example of the above was offered as lot 943 at the Spink Australia Sale 25 held in July 1988. It was described as :- "One of three struck on the last day of operation of the Sydney Mint." It was described as being FDC. It was passed in after failing to reach its estimate of $20,000. The other two are in the collection of the Museum of Victoria and the Dixson Library. A piece thought to be an original presentation piece was sold as lot 1330 in Spink Australia's Sale 30 held in Nov. 1989. Described as "Nearly FDC" it was passed in after failing to reach its $35,000 estimate. Originally part of the Dangar (lot 233) and S.V. Hagley collections, it was part of a four coin set (half sovereign to £5) sold by Spink to Sharps Pixley in 1979. At the Dangar Sale, Spink & Son Ltd, the set was acquired by David Spink who sold it to the late Sydney Hagley of Adelaide. It is believed that only one other set was issued.

PATTERN FIVE POUNDS

JUBILEE HEAD : VICTORIA

1887

ST. GEORGE REVERSE

SYDNEY MINT

Obv : G.W. De Saules.
Reverse : Benedetto Pistrucci.

Specifications: Composition: 22 carat 916.6 fine. 91.67% gold; 8.33% copper. Pure gold content 1.1771 oz. Size 38 mm. Weight 39.9403 gms.

McD Ref	Date	Mint	Estimated Mintage	Description	Specimen/ Proof
300	1887	Sydney	3 known	Reeded edged pattern	750,000

The first recorded public sale of this coin appears to be the John G. Murdoch example sold by Glendining's auction house in London on July 21, 1903. Offered as lot 613, the catalogue stated : - "Exactly as the English coin of the same date, but with an "S" on the ground under the device of St. George and the Dragon. Brilliant and very rare." The coin sold for £8/15/-. Only three proofs struck. Only two in private hands. The February 1980 issue of the Australian Coin Review carried the following report. "At the recent Australian auction held by Spink & Son Australia Pty Ltd, on Thursday 22, November 1979, a new world record was created for an Australian coin, when a Sydney Mint £5 piece struck in 1887 realised $61,000."

PATTERN FIVE POUNDS

KING EDWARD VII

1902

ST. GEORGE REVERSE

SYDNEY MINT

Obverse : G.W. De Saules.
Reverse : Benedetto Pistrucci.

Specifications: Composition: 22 carat 916.6 fine. 91.67% gold; 8.33% copper. Pure gold content 1.1771 oz. Size 38 mm. Weight 39.9403 gms.

McD Ref	Date	Mint	Estimated Mintage	Description	Specimen or Proof
350	1902	Sydney	3 known	Reeded edged pattern	750,000

Both brilliant frosted and matte proof coins exist. An example thought to be an original presentation piece was offered as lot 1329 in Spink Australia's Sale 30 held in November 1989. Described as "Nearly FDC" it sold for $50,000 against an $80,000 estimate. Originally part of the Dangar (lot 233) and S.V. Hagley collections, the coin was part of a four coin set (half sovereign to £5) sold by Spink to Sharps Pixley in 1979. At the Dangar Sale, which was catalogued by Spink & Son Ltd, the set was acquired by David Spink who sold it to the late Sydney Hagley of Adelaide. There is believed to have been only one other set issued.

HALF PENNY

MINTMARKS AND STATISTICS

GEORGE V MINTMARK POSITIONS

ABOVE : George V Mintmarks : "H" Mintmark (Heaton, England) 1912, 1914, 1915 only. "I" Mintmark (Calcutta, India) 1916, 1917 & 1918 only.

1916 INDIAN "MULE" HALF PENNY

The normal Australian obverse. (Above Left). The Mule obverse of the Indian Quarter Anna. (Above Centre). The common reverse. (Above Right). For more information on this rare mule see the footnotes on the next page.

GEORGE VI MINTMARK POSITIONS

"I" Mintmark (India) 1942 and 1943 only.

Above : Indian independence resulted in reference being deleted from 1948/49 onwards. (See left). Affects all issues.

Dot after "A" (Perth Mint) 1952 & 1953. Dot after "Y" (Perth Mint) 1942, 1943 and 1945 to 1951 inclusive. Letters "PL" after "Y" (London Mint) 1951 only.

DATA AT A GLANCE

ISSUED FROM : 1911-1964. **MINT ROLL** x 60 Coins.
DATES NOT ISSUED : 1937, 1956, 1957, 1958.
KEY DATES : ***Very rare :-*** 1916 (Mule).
Rare :- 1923. ***Scarce :-*** 1915, 1918, 1939 *(Kangaroo Reverse).*

HALF PENNY : George V

***NB* : Prices for Proof/Specimen coins refer only to perfect or *'as struck'* examples. Coins with imperfections must be discounted by as much as 60%.**

1911 - 1936

Copper Alloy

Obv: Sir E.B. Mackennal.
Reverse : W.H.J. Blakemore.
Specifications : Composition: 97% copper; 2.5% zinc; 0.5% tin. Edge plain. Weight 5.67 grams. Size 25.5mm.

Date MM	Mintage (000's)	Very Good	Fine	Very Fine	Extra Fine	aUnc	Unc	Choice Unc	Gem	Proof or Specimen
1911	2,832,000	2	5	15	55	125	375	850	1,750	30,000
1912 H	2,400,000	2.5	6	25	65	195	500	1,150	2,150	30,000
1913	2,160,000	3	8	40	125	325	850	1,750	3,350	—
1914	1,440,000	3	15	60	225	575	1,650	3,500	5,975	—
1914 H	1,200,000	5	15	65	195	495	1,350	3,100	6,250	70,000
1915 H	720,000	45	125	475	1,600	2,950	6,500	12,500	22,500	—
1916 I	3,600,000	1	4	9	50	175	425	850	1,800	30,000
1916 I a	Less than 10	50k	110k	145k	—	MULE	[Unknown in better grade]			—
1917 I	5,760,000	1	3	9	50	175	425	900	1,950	—
1918 I	1,440,000	12	125	725	2,000	4,150	8,250	16,000	—	—
1919	3,326,000	1	3	12	60	165	375	795	1,550	35,000
1920	4,113,000	3	8	30	145	225	625	1,450	3,250	40,000
1920 b	Unknown		–	–	–	–	–	–	Pattern	40,000
1921	5,280,000	1	3	12	60	185	425	875	1,650	—
1922	6,924,000	1	3	12	55	175	495	975	1,850	35,000
1923 c	1,113,000	950	1,750	3,975	12,500	25.000	45,000	85,000	n/s	275,000
1924	68,0001	9	22	65	425	1,000	2,250	4,650	8,250	30,000
1925	1,147,000	3	9	35	195	625	1,450	2,750	4,950	60,000
1926	4,132,000	4	12	20	85	295	750	1,350	2,650	30,000
1927	3,072,000	1	3	8	65	225	450	950	1,825	35,000
1928	2,318,000	2	6	18	85	425	1,250	2,450	4,900	35,000
1929	2,635,000	1	3	9	65	265	575	1,350	2,675	30,000
1930	638,000	5	15	35	125	595	1,450	2,950	6,100	90,000
1931	369,000	3	9	35	125	650	1,850	3,650	7,150	35,000
1932	2,553,000	.50	2	8	45	125	400	850	1,750	35,000
1933	4,608,000	.50	2	6	30	95	325	675	1,250	35,000
1934	3,816,000	.50	2	6	30	125	350	645	1,300	28,000
1935	2,916,000	.50	2	6	30	110	275	600	1,150	24,500
1936	5,577,000	.50	2	4	20	65	135	500	1,100	30,000

Key to mints :- Early dates struck in London. Mintmark "H" for Heaton Mint in Birmingham; "I" for Calcutta in India. All other coins were struck at the Sydney or Melbourne mints and do not have a mintmark.

(a) The obverse die for the Indian Quarter Anna coin was accidentally mixed with the reverse Australian half penny die during production at the Calcutta Mint in India. The legend of this rare "Mule" issue reads : "George V King Emperor". The first of the ten or less known examples was found in June 1965 by Cecil Poole in South Australia. The mules were obviously struck on planchets meant for Australian half pennies. The mules weighed around 5.68 grams which compares favourably with the Australian specifications. By comparison, the Indian quarter Anna weighed 4.76 grams. The error was confirmed as genuine by the RAM. The latest sale of this rarity occurred at the Noble Sale 108 held in March 2015. Lot 1637 and was described as : *Calcutta Mint mule halfpenny, 1916I, struck with the India quarter anna obverse die in error. Pinched planchet or flaw on rim at top, otherwise good very fine and extremely rare, one of the finest known. Ex Spink Australia Sale 11 (lot 827) and Jon Saxton Collection.* It sold for $64,530 (including commission) against an estimate of $60,000.
(b) All circulation coins were struck by the Melbourne Mint. This pattern came from the Sydney Mint which did not issue circulation coins.
(c) Real mintage closer to 15,000. The bulk of the 1,113,600 mintage recorded was made up of 1922 dated coins.

HALF PENNY : George VI

NB : **Prices for Proof/Specimen coins refer only to perfect or *'as struck'* examples. Coins with imperfections must be discounted by as much as 60%.**

1938 - 1939

OLD REVERSE

Copper Alloy

Obverse : Thomas H. Paget.
Reverse : W.H.J. Blakemore.

Specifications : Composition: 97% copper, 2.5% zinc; 0.5% tin.Edge plain. Weight 5.67 grams. Size 25.5mm.

Date MM	Mintage Figures	Very Good	Fine	Very Fine	Extra Fine	aUnc	Unc	Choice Unc	Gem	Proof or Specimen
1938	5,174,000	.40	1	4	18	60	135	265	495	20,000
1939	4,670,000	.40	1	5	20	80	210	475	950	30,000

HALF PENNY : George VI

NB : **Prices for Proof/Specimen coins refer only to perfect or *'as struck'* examples. Coins with imperfections must be discounted by as much as 60%.**

1939 - 1952

KANGAROO REVERSE

Copper Alloy

Obverse : Thomas H. Paget.
Reverse : George Kruger Gray.

Specifications : Composition: 97% copper; 2.5% zinc; 0.5% tin. Edge plain. Weight 5.67 grams. Size 25.5mm.

Date MM	Mintage Figures	Very Good	Fine	Very Fine	Extra Fine	aUnc	Unc	Choice Unc	Gem	Proof or Specimen
1939	782,000	15	30	55	200	550	1,500	3,250	6,250	25,000
1940	1,728,000	1	2	8	35	95	325	650	1,300	35,000
1941	5,304,000	.20	1	5	15	40	175	350	700	35,000
1942	720,000	3	8	20	65	195	475	925	1,850	26,000
1942 Y.	4,334,000	.25	1	6	30	65	195	450	900	26,000
1942 I	6,000,000	.25	1	3	20	45	110	255	520	25,000
1943	41,025,000	.25	1	2	7	22	55	125	260	—
1943 Y.	Pattern	–	–	–	–	–	–	–	–	28,000
1943 I	6,000,000	.20	1	3	8	40	90	185	375	23,000
1944	729,000	3	9	25	95	195	500	1,000	2,150	—
1945	Pattern	–	–	–	–	–	–	–	–	38,000
1945 P	3,494,000	2	5	12	50	100	275	525	1,100	26,000
1945 Y.	Ditto	2	5	14	55	120	395	650	1,300	26,000
1946 Y.	13,372,000	.25	1	3	8	30	80	185	395	26,000
1947 Y.	10,725,000	.20	1	3	12	35	90	220	425	26,000
1948	4,598,000	.20	1	3	9	25	75	225	395	26,000
1948 Y.	25,552,000	.15	.75	2	7	30	65	145	320	26,000
1949	Pattern	–	–	–	–	–	–	–	–	26,000
1949 Y.	20,208,000	.75	2	5	12	25	60	135	295	26,000
1950 Y.	10,515,000	1	2	5	10	35	95	190	365	26,000
1951	29,422,000	.30	2	5	12	20	60	125	260	26,000
1951 Y.	Inc above	.20	1	3	6	15	55	110	235	26,000
1951 PL	6,960,000	.20	1	2	5	10	35	85	160	18,500
1952 A.	1,831,000	1	3	6	15	60	160	325	650	22,000

HALF PENNY : Elizabeth II

***NB :* Prices for Proof/Specimen coins refer only to perfect or *'as struck'* examples. Coins with imperfections must be discounted by as much as 60%.**

1953 - 1964

Copper Alloy

Obverse : Mrs Mary Gillick.
Reverse : George Kruger Gray.
Specifications : Composition: 97% copper; 2.5% zinc; 0.5% tin. Edge plain. Weight 5.67 grams. Size 25.5 mm.

Date MM	Mintage (000's)	Very Good	Fine	Very Fine	Extra Fine	aUnc	Unc	Choice Unc	Gem	Proof or Specimen
1953 A. a	23,967,000	1	2	3	8	25	55	150	250	20,000
1954 Y.	21,962,000	1	2	3	8	20	45	110	225	20,000
1955	9,342,000	1	2	3	8	20	45	95	200	—
1955 Perth	301 *	–	–	–	–	–	–	–	–	8,000
1959	11,193,000	1.50	2	4	7	15	35	85	185	—
1959	1506 *	–	–	–	–	–	–	–	–	900
1960 Y.	16,784,000	.20	.50	1	3	6	15	35	75	—
1960 Y.	1030 *	–	–	–	–	–	–	–	–	875
1961 Y.	24,364,000	.20	.50	1	3	6	15	35	75	—
1961 Y.	1040 *	–	–	–	–	–	–	–	–	875
1962 Y.	16,410,000	.20	.50	1	3	6	15	35	75	—
1962 Y.	1064 *	–	–	–	–	–	–	–	–	875
1963 Y.	16,410,000	.20	.50	1	3	6	15	35	75	—
1963 Y.	1060 *	–	–	–	–	–	–	–	–	950
1964 Y.	18,230	.30	.50	1	2	4	8	25	55	—
1964 Y. b	Unique	–	–	–	–	–	–	–	–	17,500

Key to mints :- Coins with either "A." or "Y." mintmark were struck in Perth. Although it doesn't have a mintmark, the 1955 halfpenny was also struck at the Perth Mint. All other issues were struck at the Melbourne Mint and do not have a mint mark.

* Actual numbers struck, not multiples of "000"

IMPORTANT NOTE REGARDING GRADING AND PRICING

Grading and pricing a bronze coin in UNC or better condition is particularly difficult as the amount of "Brilliance" still visible has a bearing on its condition and value to collectors. Generally speaking, it should be held that a coin graded UNC should retain about 25% Brilliance for the value given in this guide. A "Choice UNC" (CHU) coin should feature about 50% Brilliance, and a GEM coin should show at least 75% Brilliance. A greater or lesser amount of Brilliance remaining for any given grade will influence value by up to 50% either way.

Because the pre-decimal proof coins became more popular during the reign of Elizabeth II, they are dealt with separately in this list with mintage figures included.
(a) Approximately twelve 1953 sets were supplied to the Chase Manhattan Bank for its money museum by the Australian Commonwealth Government. The coins were selected specimens rather than proofs. The silver coins were struck at the Melbourne Mint and the bronze coins were struck at the Perth Mint.
(b) The only known 1964 Y. proof halfpenny was sold by Spink & Son (Sydney) in their March 1987 auction when it and an equally unique penny realised $7,200 for the pair. The half penny was an impaired proof and is believed to have been struck especially for the Mint Master of the time.

ONE PENNY
MINTMARKS AND STATISTICS

GEORGE V MINTMARKS

"H" Mintmark (Heaton, UK) 1912 and 1915 only.
"I" Mintmark (Calcutta, India) 1916, 1917 and 1918 only.
"Dot" below scroll. (Various types - see pricing section).
"Dot" above top scroll and dot above bottom scroll. Both Sydney and Melbourne mints. Which mint depends on the relationship with dots above or below bottom scroll. 1919 and 1920. (See pricing section).

GVI & QEII MINTMARK POSITIONS

(a) Dot after "A" (Perth Mint) 1952 and 1953 only.
(b) Dot between "K" and "G" (Perth Mint) 1940 and 1941 only.
(c) "PL" Mintmark (London Mint) 1951 only.
(d) Dot after "Y" of penny. (Perth Mint). 1941 to 1945, 1947, 1948, 1950, 1951, 1955 to 1964.

DATA AT A GLANCE

ISSUED FROM : 1911-1964. **MINT ROLL** x 60 Coins.
DATES NOT ISSUED : 1937, 1954.
KEY DATES : ***Very rare :-*** 1937 (Pattern).
Rare :- 1930. ***Scarce :-*** 1920 (no dots), 1925, 1946.

JOINING THE DOTS

MINTMARK POSITIONS FOR THE 1919 & 1920 PENNIES

Generally speaking, mintmarks on Australian coins are fairly straight forward to identify. "M" for Melbourne is a given while it takes just a few minutes of research to find the source of other coins that have other letters, such as D, S, PL, H or dots after the A or Y of pennies and halfpennies. However dots used as identification marks attributed to 1919 and 1920 Australian pennies are a different matter. Research helps but good eye sight is better as these dots are minute and to the point that some variations generally accepted as being bonafide varieties may, in reality, be the result of filled dies. These dots, or combination of dots determine whether these coins were struck at the Melbourne or Sydney mints. There are five main, or primary reverse die variations. The postion of the dots can be viewed in conjunction with the images above. The [—] actually refer to the scrolls.

These include 1920 plain or no dots. (May be the result of filled die).

- 1920 dot below bottom scroll
- 1920 dot above bottom scroll. Often shows weak or "crushed" obverse denticles.
- 1920 dot above top scroll and dot below bottom scroll (double dot)
- 1920 dot above top scroll only (this is rare and seldom seen)

Further confusion in identificating the different variations is because there are two different obverse dies to take into consideration. One is referred as the *'Indian obverse'*, and the other the *'London obverse.'* ***See below.*** There doesn't seem to be any logical explanation why one die is referred to by country and the other by capacity. If you add all the accepted dot combinations of the reverse dies and add them to the two obverse dies, there are eight variations. These two dies are similar in that they both feature the crowned bust of George V. The legend reads "GEORGIVS V D.G. BRITT: OMN: REX F.D. IND: IMP:" The legend is the key to identifying the difference between the two dies.

One of the ways to determine the difference between the dies is to compare the alignment of the final stroke of the 'N' in 'OM**N**'.
Indian obverse: Last stroke of 'N' in 'OMN' lines up with outer rim dentical.
London obverse: Last stroke of 'N' in 'OMN' lines up in-between the outer rim denticals.
The London obverse has 177 outer rim denticals while the Indian die has 178 outer rim denticals.

ONE PENNY : George V

NB : **Prices for Proof/Specimen coins refer only to perfect or *'as struck'* examples. Coins with imperfections must be discounted by as much as 60%.**

1911 - 1936

Copper Alloy

Obv : Sir E.B. Mackennal.
Reverse : W.H.J. Blakemore.
Specifications : Composition: 97% copper; 2.5% zinc; 0.5% tin. Edge plain. Weight 9.45 grams. Size 30.8 mm.

Date MM	Mintage Figures	Very Good	Fine	Very Fine	Extra Fine	aUnc	Unc	Choice Unc	Gem	Proof or Specimen
1911	3,768,000	3	8	30	85	275	600	1,300	2,550	50,000
1912 H	3,600,000	3	8	28	85	325	825	1,900	3,750	50,000
1913	2,520,000	4	12	40	175	550	1,450	2,500	4,950	—
1914	720,000	7	25	75	325	1,150	2,950	5,550	10,250	—
1915	960,000	6	20	80	350	1,350	3,500	6,250	10,250	—
1915 H	1,320,000	7	19	65	295	900	2,450	5,250	10,500	—
1916 I	3,324,000	2	6	15	85	250	650	1,650	3,500	80,000
1917 I	6,240,000	1	6	15	75	195	625	1,550	3,250	80,000
1918 I	1,200,000	8	18	65	395	1,100	3,250	6,500	12,500	45,000
1919 No Dots	5,810,000	2	7	20	85	260	675	1,500	3,100	—
1919 =̣	Ditto	2	6	17	85	260	650	1,400	2,750	—
1919 ≑	Ditto	75	195	675	2,500	3,950	6,350	10,150	16,500	80,000
1920 No Dots	9,041,000	35	95	400	2,350	6,550	15,500	35,000	75,000	—
1920 −̇	Ditto	7	16	50	170	425	2,250	4,250	7,600	—
1920 =̣	Ditto	7	19	60	225	650	2,250	3,975	8,200	80,000
1920 ≐	Ditto	250	500	1,350	4,500	10,500	n/s	n/s	n/s	—
1920 ≑	Ditto	55	160	475	1,750	4,000	12,500	n/s	n/s	—
1921	7,438,000	2	7	60	195	550	1,500	3,250	6,000	88,000
1922	12,697,000	3	8	70	245	650	2,250	4,250	8,500	—
1923	3,635,000	3	15	60	125	450	1,150	2,500	4,500	80,000
1924	4,665,000	3	8	40	95	450	1,100	2,500	4,750	50,000
1925	117,000	95	195	295	1,750	6,250	13,000	25,000	50,000	175,000
1926	1,860,000	4	15	60	295	795	2,250	4,600	7,750	50,000
1927	4,920,000	1	4	14	60	220	575	1,250	2,750	55,000
1928	3,086,000	3	8	22	85	420	1,450	2,900	5,250	50,000
1929	2,599,000	2	8	25	85	425	1,800	3,950	6,250	50,000
1930 a	1,200 ?	17	27k	453k	95k	175k	265k	425k	625k	145,000
1931	494,000	4	18	35	250	775	2,250	5,250	8,750	100,000
1932	2,116,000	4	12	20	110	325	775	1,600	3,150	55,000
1933/32	O/Date	35	85	175	400	1,300	2,750	4,950	8,750	—
1933	5,817,000	1	3	15	60	110	325	700	1,300	55,000
1934	5,800,000	1	3	15	60	125	375	750	1,500	35,000
1935	3,724,000	1	3	15	50	120	350	750	1,350	30,000
1936	9,890,000	.50	2	8	30	85	250	500	900	50,000

Key to mints : Early dates struck in London. Mintmark "H" for Heaton Mint in Birmingham; "I" for Calcutta in India. Dot below scroll = Melbourne. Dot above = Sydney.

[a] Estimated mintage figures of 1,200 pieces are based on visitor numbers at the Melbourne Mint in 1930. No accurate figures have yet surfaced.

ONE PENNY : George VI

***NB* : Prices for Proof/Specimen coins refer only to perfect or *'as struck'* examples. Coins with imperfections must be discounted by as much as 60%.**

1938 - 1952

Copper Alloy

Obv: Thomas Humphrey Paget.
Reverse : George Kruger Gray.

Specifications : Composition: 97% copper; 2.5% zinc; 0.5% tin. Edge plain. Weight 9.45 grams. Size 30.8 mm.

Date MM	Mintage (000's)	Very Good	Fine	Very Fine	Extra Fine	aUnc	Unc	Choice Unc	Gem	Proof or Specimen
1937	Pattern	–	–	–	–	–	–	Double sided		275,000
1937	Pattern	–	–	–	–	–	–	'Model' obverse		145,000
1937 a	Pattern	–	–	–	–	Model obverse holed planchet				40,000
1937 b	Pattern	–	–	–	–	–	Uniface obverse in silver			95,000
1938	7,804,000	1	4	12	40	75	130	275	575	28,000
1939	6,924,000	1	4	12	40	80	135	295	595	40,000
1940	4,075,000	2	6	20	60	125	275	550	1,100	—
1940 K.G	1,113,000	9	20	70	295	625	1,350	3,000	6,250	—
1941	1,588,000		4	14	50	110	295	650	1,100	—
1941 K.G	12,794,000	3	8	25	95	175	425	950	2,200	40,000
1941 Y.	Ditto	1	4	14	40	90	225	525	1,100	—
1942 Y.	12,244	1	3	10	35	80	165	325	695	—
1942 I	9,000,000	1	2	6	30	65	125	295	625	30,000
1943	11,107,000	.20	1	5	25	55	125	250	550	—
1943 Y.	33,086,000	.20	1	5	20	50	110	250	495	35,000
1943 I	9,000,000	1	3	9	30	65	195	475	950	32,000
1944	2,450,000	1	4	20	60	225	450	975	2,000	—
1944 Y.	27,830,000	.20	1	5	20	50	145	325	795	35,000
1945	Pattern	–	–	–	–	Only one available to collectors				275,000
1945 Y.	10,125,000	.50	2	8	20	70	210	475	995	35,000
1946	363,000	45	70	125	595	1,250	2,500	5,700	10,500	—
1947	6,759,000	.20	1	6	12	30	75	175	375	—
1947 Y.	4,490,000	2	5	15	70	240	575	1,350	3,950	35,000
1948	26,616,000	.20	1	4	13	30	55	125	250	—
1948 Y.	1,533,000	3	9	40	175	425	1,100	2,750	5,250	40,000
1949	21,412,000	.20	1	3	12	30	65	150	325	45,000
1950	36,358,000	.20	1	3	18	40	95	250	475	—
1950 Y.	21,488,000	.75	3	7	35	90	175	360	725	40,000
1951	45,514,000	.20	1	3	12	25	50	100	210	—
1951 Y.	12,888,000	.20	1	6	20	60	145	310	625	40,000
1951 PL	18,000,000	.20	1	3	8	20	50	100	225	37,000
1952	21,240,000	1	2	4	9	25	75	165	325	30,000
1952 A.	12,408,000	.20	1	2	7	20	60	125	265	30,000

Key to mints : The 1937 patterns and the 1951 "PL" penny were struck in London. All coins with an "I" mintmark were struck in Bombay, India. The Perth Mint simply used a dot to identify its coins. This can be found between the "K" and the "G" on the 1940 and 1941 issues. On other dates there is a dot after the letter "Y" of the word "PENNY" or behind the last "A" of the word "AUSTRALIA." No mintmark for Melbourne issues.

[a] A uniface 1937 penny with the words "Model" replacing the portrait and with a hole drilled through the planchet was sold at the Noble, March 1995 sale, where it realised $2,700 plus 10% buyer's premium. It has since been offered for sale with the hole plugged.
[b] An example of this possibly unique pattern was offered as lot 1206 in Spink (Australia) Sale 17, held in November 1985. It sold for $6,600 plus commission against an estimate of $10,000.

ONE PENNY : Elizabeth II

***NB :* Prices for Proof/Specimen coins refer only to perfect or *'as struck'* examples. Coins with imperfections must be discounted by as much as 60%.**

1953 - 1964

Copper Alloy

Obverse : Mrs Mary Gillick.
Reverse : George Kruger Gray.
Specifications : Composition: 97% copper;

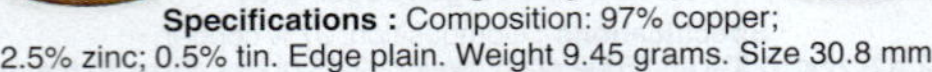

2.5% zinc; 0.5% tin. Edge plain. Weight 9.45 grams. Size 30.8 mm.

Date MM	Mintage (000's)	Very Good	Fine	Very Fine	Extra Fine	aUnc	Unc	Choice Unc	Gem	Proof or Specimen
1953	6,936,000	2	5	9	15	30	65	125	300	30,000
1953 A.	6,202,000	2	5	9	15	30	80	180	350	30,000
1955	6,936,000	3	7	4	9	30	85	220	400	—
1955	1200 *	–	–	–	–	–	–	–	–	950
1955 Y.	6,202,000	.20	1	2	6	20	75	160	325	—
1955 Y.	301 *	–	–	–	–	–	–	–	–	9,500
1956	13,872,000	.15	.50	1	4	18	60	125	260	—
1956	1500 *	–	–	–	–	–	–	–	–	825
1956 Y.	12,121,000	.15	.50	2	4	18	55	120	250	—
1956 Y.	417 *	–	–	–	–	–	–	–	–	8,250
1957 Y.	15,978,000	.15	.50	1	3	12	30	65	150	—
1957 Y. a	1112*	–	–	–	–	–	–	Matte finish		1,750
1957 Y. a	Ditto	–	–	–	–	–	–	Brilliant finish		1,350
1958	10,012,000	.15	.50	1	3	12	30	65	150	—
1958	1506 *	–	–	–	–	–	–	–	–	800
1958 Y.	14,428,000	.20	1	2	4	10	30	75	165	—
1958 Y.	1028 *	–	–	–	–	–	–	–	–	1,150
1959	1,617,000	4	9	15	30	65	175	335	650	—
1959	1506 *	–	–	–	–	–	–	–	–	1,400
1959	Unique	–	–	–	–	Pattern struck in silver				17,500
1959 Y.	14,428,000	.15	.75	1.50	3	7	25	60	135	—
1959 Y.	1030*	–	–	–	–	–	–	–	–	1,350
1960 Y.	20,515,000	.25	1	2	5	12	35	80	175	—
1960 Y.	1030 *	–	–	–	–	–	–	–	–	1,250
1961 Y.	30,607,000	.50	1	2	4	12	35	80	175	—
1961 Y.	1040 *	–	–	–	–	–	–	–	–	1,250
1962 Y.	34,851,000	.50	1	2	4	12	35	85	200	—
1962 Y.	1064 *	–	–	–	–	–	–	–	–	1,250
1963 Y.	10,258,000	.20	.75	2	3	6	18	45	90	—
1963 Y.	1100 *	–	–	–	–	–	–	–	–	1,350
1964	10,000,000	.15	.50	1	2	5	30	70	150	—
1964 Y.	54,590,000	.15	.50	1	2	4	25	65	125	—
1964 Y. b	Unique	–	–	–	–	–	–	–	–	13,000

Key to mints :- Coins with either "A." or "Y." mintmark were struck at the Perth Mint.

[1] Because the pre-decimal proof coins became more popular during the reign of Elizabeth II, they are dealt with separately in this list with mintage figures included.
[a] There are two distinct types of finish associated with the 1957 proof penny. The mint experienced production difficulties which resulted in some orders not being fulfilled until 1959. In the meantime, the quality of finish was substantially improved and the appearance between the coins struck in 1957 and later is very noticeable.
[b] The only known 1964 Y. proof penny was sold by Spink & Son (Sydney) in their March 1987 auction when it and a unique halfpenny realised $7,200 for the pair.

THE THREEPENCE
MINTMARKS AND STATISTICS

GEORGE V MINTMARKS

"M" Mintmark (Melbourne Mint) 1916 to 1921 only. Note : Some 1921 issues were struck at the Sydney Mint and have no mintmark.

GEORGE V OVERDATES

1922/1 Overdate shown at left.

1934/3 Overdate shown at right.

GEORGE VI MINTMARKS

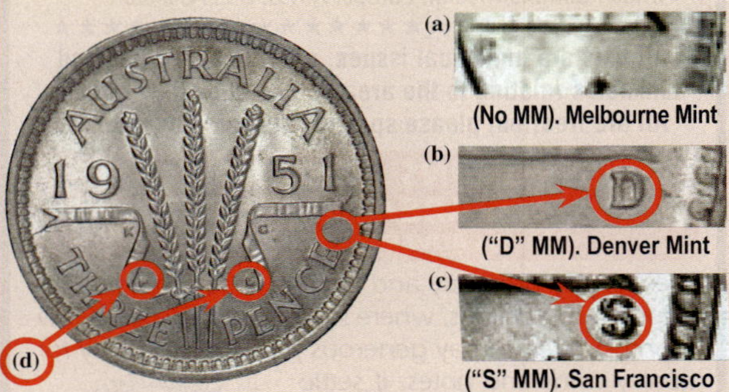

(b) : "S" Mintmark (San Francisco Mint) 1942, 1943, 1944 only.
(c) :"D" Mintmark (Denver Mint) 1942 and 1943 only.
(d) :"PL" Mintmark (London Mint) 1951 only.

DATA AT A GLANCE

ISSUED FROM : 1910-1963. **MINT ROLL** x 40 Coins.
DATES NOT ISSUED : 1913, 29 - 33, 37, 45, 46.
KEY DATES : ***Very rare :-*** 1937 (Pattern). ***Rare:-*** 1922/1 Overdate. ***Scarce :-*** 1912, 1914, 1915, 1923, 1942M.

THREEPENCE : Edward VII

1910 Only

Sterling Silver

Obverse : George W. De Saulles.
Reverse : W.H.J. Blakemore.

Specifications : Composition: 92.5 silver 7.5% copper.Edge plain. Weight 1.41 grams. Size 16 mm.

Date MM	Mintage Figures	Very Good	Fine	Very Fine	Extra Fine	aUnc	Unc	Choice Unc	Gem	Proof or Specimen
1910	4,000,000	3	7	12	35	85	140	250	400	20,000

THREEPENCE : George V

1911 - 1936

Sterling Silver

Obverse : Sir E.B. Mackennal.
Reverse : W.H.J. Blakemore.
Specifications : Composition: 92.5 silver; 7.5% copper. Edge plain. Weight 1.41 grams. Size 16 mm.

Date MM	Mintage (000's)	Very Good	Fine	Very Fine	Extra Fine	aUnc	Unc	Choice Unc	Gem	Proof or Specimen
1911	4,000,000	9	18	65	195	375	695	1,450	3,000	40,000
1911 a	Pattern	–	–	–	–	–	–	Reeded edge		95,000
1912	2,400,000	22	50	145	475	1,150	2,550	4,750	8,750	—
1914	1,600,000	20	45	100	525	1,300	2,750	5,250	9,250	—
1915	800,000	35	95	300	900	1,950	4,250	8,250	15,500	—
1916 M	1,913,000	15	30	90	325	675	1,650	3,250	6,950	24,000
1917 M	3,808,000	5	15	35	110	325	675	1,550	3,250	40,000
1918 M	3,119,000	6	18	40	125	295	625	1,375	2,750	95,000
1919 M	3,201,000	6	18	40	150	325	650	1,375	2,875	40,000
1920 M	4,196,000	5	18	75	295	750	1,550	3,150	6,500	40,000
1921 M	7,378,000	3	7	20	75	185	595	1,100	2,300	40,000
1921	Ditto	7	20	95	395	825	1,750	3,500	6,750	—
1922/ 1	900 *	3k	8k	20k	60k	95k	125k	n/s	n/s	—
1922	5,531,000	4	10	30	175	375	825	1,850	3,950	40,000
1923	815,000	25	55	195	595	1,600	2,600	4,650	7,650	—
1924	2,014,000	5	15	50	275	750	1,500	3,300	7,250	30,000
1925	4,347,000	3	8	25	110	250	525	1,000	2,300	30,000
1926	6,158,000	3	7	20	75	200	425	925	2,150	30,000
1927	6,720,000	2.50	6	20	65	175	375	725	1,500	30,000
1928	5,008,000	2.50	6	20	80	195	395	800	1,700	30,000
1934	2,800,000	5	15	25	70	195	425	850	1,750	15,000
1934/ 3	Ditto	45	95	265	775	1,650	3,250	6,750	14,500	—
1935	2,800,000	3	5	15	55	175	350	725	1,550	30,000
1936	3,600,000	2	3	6	30	95	190	325	675	30,000

Key to mints : 1910 to 1915 struck in London. All other dates struck in Sydney or Melbourne. (M) Melbourne mintmark. No mintmark for Sydney.

(a) : An example of this rarity was offered as lot 1395 in Noble's sale 108 held in March 2015. The description read : GEORGE V, Royal Mint London matt proof or pattern threepence, 1911, with straight grained or milled edge (1.58g). Sharply struck up, FDC and excessively rare. The coin (shown at right) sold for $41,000 (+19.5% commission) against an estimate of $50,000.

(*) 1922/1 overdate. Only 900 coins struck, not 900,000. Most examples of this rare coin are found in very poor condition. This is due to several factors. The strike for this year was quite shallow in order to preserve the working time of the die. Sterling silver also wore very quickly and so, in most cases, this coin is found in lower grades than this catalogue allows for. (eg, Poor or Good). Even in these low grades the coin is still highly sought-after.

THREEPENCE : George VI

***NB :* Prices for Proof/Specimen coins refer only to perfect or *'as struck'* examples. Coins with imperfections must be discounted by as much as 60%.**

1938 - 1952
Silver

Obverse : Thomas H. Paget.
Reverse : George Kruger Gray

Specifications : Composition: (1938 - 1944) 92.5% silver; 7.5% copper. (1947-1952) 50% silver; 40% copper; 5% zinc; 5% nickel. Edge plain. Weight 1.41 gms. Size 16mm

Date MM	Mintage Figure	Very Good	Fine	Very Fine	Extra Fine	aUnc	Unc	Choice Unc	Gem	Proof or Specimen
1937	Pattern	–	–	–	–	–	Uniface (reverse)			115,000
1937 a	Pattern	–	–	–	–	–	–	Double sided		150,000
1938	4,560,000	b/v	2	4	12	35	75	175	350	13,000
1939	3,856,000	b/v	2	5	20	60	100	225	475	—
1940	3,840,000	4	9	19	35	75	155	295	625	—
1941	7,584,000	2	4	7	20	45	95	250	525	—
1942	528,000	10	30	90	650	1,350	3,150	6,750	13,500	—
1942 S	8,000,000	b/v	3	7	12	20	45	125	310	—
1942 D	16,00,0000	b/v	3	7	12	20	30	85	225	—
1943	24,912,000	b/v	3	7	12	20	30	85	195	—
1943 S	8,000,000	2	3	6	9	20	50	130	375	—
1943 D	16,000,000	b/v	3	7	12	20	30	85	225	—
1944 S	32,000,000	b/v	2	3	5	9	20	60	165	—
1947	4,176,000	3	6	10	25	55	135	350	725	—
1948	26,208,000	b/v	2	3	6	15	35	75	150	—
1949	26,400,000	b/v	2	3	5	13	35	75	150	16,000
1950	35,456,000	b/v	1	2	3	10	25	50	110	—
1951	15,856,000	b/v	1	2	6	24	50	100	190	—
1951 PL	40,000,000	b/v	1	2	3	6	15	40	130	16,000
1952	21,560,000	b/v	2	5	9	18	40	85	200	—

Key to mints : The 1937 patterns were struck at the Royal Mint, London. Coins with "S" mintmark were struck at the San Francisco Mint while those with a "D" mintmark were also struck in the USA at the Denver Mint. The 1951 PL threepence was struck at the Royal Mint, London. All other issues were struck at the Melbourne Mint and do not have a mintmark.

(a) The November 1992 edition of the Australian Coin Review reported the sale of a 1937 threepence in a Sotheby's auction in London. A Sydney coin dealer paid $44,700 for the coin described as being tarnished but "Fine to good Fine and excessively rare." It is believed to be the only example in private hands. Another six are thought to be in museums. The abovementioned example was found by a Tasmanian family in change! The coin appeared again as lot 616 in International Auction Galleries sale 78 held in Melbourne in October 2013 and passed in at $200,000.

GENERAL COMMENT : The threepence series features two overdate issues (1922/1 and 1934/3) which are highly sought-after by collectors. Both came into being when the mint decided to re-engrave unused dies from the years 1921 and 1933. Officials from the Melbourne Mint deny this took place and today we are still not sure if their denial is true or an attempt to cover up a pretty poor job of re-engraving an old die. Overdating old dies is a common enough practice. There are a number of such issues in the Australian gold series. Judging by the prices obtained for the above threepence issues, it is evident that collectors have overruled the official denial. The 1922/1 is generally only found in lower grades. Only two or three examples are thought to be Extremely Fine or better.

THREEPENCE : Elizabeth II

***NB* : Prices for Proof/Specimen coins refer only to perfect or *'as struck'* examples. Coins with imperfections must be discounted by as much as 60%.**

1953 - 1964

50% Silver

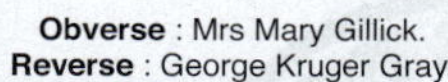

Obverse : Mrs Mary Gillick.
Reverse : George Kruger Gray.

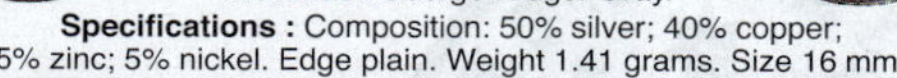

Specifications : Composition: 50% silver; 40% copper; 5% zinc; 5% nickel. Edge plain. Weight 1.41 grams. Size 16 mm.

Date MM	Mintage (000's)	Very Good	Fine	Very Fine	Extra Fine	aUnc	Unc	Choice Unc	Gem	Proof or Specimen
1953	7,664,000	1	2	5	20	40	80	160	350	13,000
1954	2,672,000	3	9	15	25	60	120	240	575	13,000
1955	27,088	1	2	3	6	12	30	70	160	—
1955	1,200 *	–	–	–	–	–	–	–	–	650
1956	14,088,000	b/v	2	3	6	15	45	100	220	—
1956	1,500 *	–	–	–	–	–	–	–	–	200
1957	26,704,000	1	2	3	6	12	30	70	160	—
1957	1256 *	–	–	–	–	–	–	–	–	200
1958	11,248,000	b/v	2	3	6	18	35	70	200	—
1958	1506 *	–	–	–	–	–	–	–	–	200
1959	19,888,000	1	2	3	6	12	30	70	160	—
1959	1509 *	–	–	–	–	–	–	–	–	200
1960	19,600,000	b/v	b/v	1	2	4	8	20	75	—
1960	1509 *	–	–	–	–	–	–	–	–	195
1961	33,840,000	b/v	b/v	1	2	4	8	20	75	—
1961	1506 *	–	–	–	–	–	–	–	–	195
1962	15,968,000	b/v	b/v	1	2	3	12	35	90	—
1962	2016 *	–	–	–	–	–	–	–	–	175
1963	44,016,000	b/v	b/v	2	3	4	9	25	65	—
1963	5042 *	–	–	–	–	–	–	–	–	135
1964	20,320,000	b/v	b/v	b/v	1	2	8	22	55	—

Key to mints :- All above issues were struck at the Melbourne Mint.
* Actual numbers struck, not multiples of "000".

As the pre-decimal proof coins became more popular during the reign of Elizabeth II, they are dealt with separately in this list with mintage figures included.

GENERAL COMMENT : The threepence series enjoys great popularity with collectors who have an eye for detail. The small size of the coin required particular care in the manufacture of the dies. Intricate details needed to be engraved with great care to produce a well struck end - product. Unfortunately, such care was not always forthcoming. This has caused confusion among novice collectors who cannot understand why seemingly "worn" coins are regarded by others as being "Uncirculated". The fact is such coins were weakly struck from a poorly engraved die. In particular, the "Obverse" of the George V issues will often not show a clear set of diamonds and pearls in the crown. Another problem concerning the quality of strike was the result of oil or other foreign material clogging up some of the small engraved cavities in the dies. When these contaminated dies were used to strike the threepence, it resulted in a "weak strike." The wheat stalks on the 1938 to 1964 "reverses" are particularly affected by this problem. However, for the "type" collector, there are certain dates of the series which are generally found in better than average condition for the "quality of strike". These dates include 1911, 1936, 1938, 1951 PL, 1954 and 1956. There is no choice for the 1910 issue, but this coin will turn up well struck, although not regularly.

SIXPENCE
MINTMARKS AND STATISTICS

GEORGE V MINTMARKS

"M" Mintmark (Melbourne Mint)
1916 to 1920 inclusive

GEORGE VI MINTMARKS

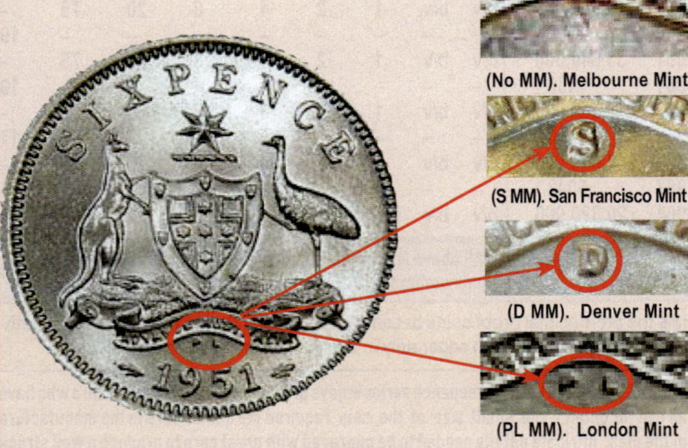

(No MM). Melbourne Mint

(S MM). San Francisco Mint

(D MM). Denver Mint

(PL MM). London Mint

(a) : "S" Mintmark (San Francisco) 1942 to 1944.
(b) : "D" Mintmark (Denver Mint) 1942, 1943 only.
(c) : "PL" Mintmark (Royal Mint, London) 1951 only.

DATA AT A GLANCE

ISSUED FROM : 1910-1963. **MINT ROLL** x 40 Coins.

DATES NOT ISSUED : 1913, 1915, 1929, 1930
1931, 1932, 1933, 1937, 1947, 1949.

KEY DATES : ***Rare :-*** 1918. ***Scarce :-*** 1912, 1922, 1924, 1935, 1939, 1952, 1953.

SIXPENCE : Edward VII

NB **: Prices for Proof/Specimen coins refer only to perfect or *'as struck'* examples. Coins with imperfections must be discounted by as much as 60%.**

TYPE COIN
1910 Only

Sterling Silver

Obverse : George W. De Saulles
Reverse : W.H.J. Blakemore.
Specifications : Composition: 92.5% silver;

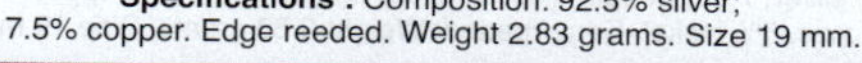

7.5% copper. Edge reeded. Weight 2.83 grams. Size 19 mm.

Date MM	Mintage (000's)	Very Good	Fine	Very Fine	Extra Fine	aUnc	Unc	Choice Unc	Gem	Proof or Specimen
1910	3,046,000	8	18	40	95	215	375	695	1,200	25,000

SIXPENCE : George V

1911 - 1936

Sterling Silver

Obverse : Sir E.B. Mackennal.
Reverse : W.H.J. Blakemore.
Specifications : Composition: 92.5% silver;
7.5% copper. Edge reeded. Weight 2.83 grams. Size 19 mm.

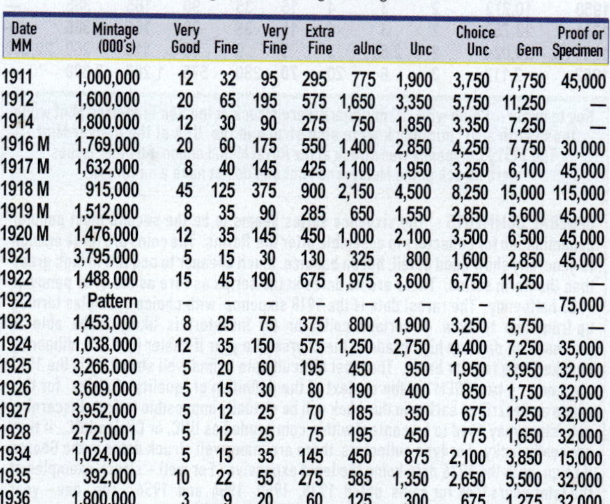

Date MM	Mintage (000's)	Very Good	Fine	Very Fine	Extra Fine	aUnc	Unc	Choice Unc	Gem	Proof or Specimen
1911	1,000,000	12	32	95	295	775	1,900	3,750	7,750	45,000
1912	1,600,000	20	65	195	575	1,650	3,350	5,750	11,250	—
1914	1,800,000	12	30	90	275	750	1,850	3,350	7,250	—
1916 M	1,769,000	20	60	175	550	1,400	2,850	4,250	7,750	30,000
1917 M	1,632,000	8	40	145	425	1,100	1,950	3,250	6,100	45,000
1918 M	915,000	45	125	375	900	2,150	4,500	8,250	15,000	115,000
1919 M	1,512,000	8	35	90	285	650	1,550	2,850	5,600	45,000
1920 M	1,476,000	12	35	145	450	1,000	2,100	3,500	6,500	45,000
1921	3,795,000	5	15	30	130	325	800	1,600	2,850	45,000
1922	1,488,000	15	45	190	675	1,975	3,600	6,750	11,250	—
1922	Pattern					–	–	–	–	75,000
1923	1,453,000	8	25	75	375	800	1,900	3,250	5,750	—
1924	1,038,000	12	35	150	575	1,250	2,750	4,400	7,250	35,000
1925	3,266,000	5	20	60	195	450	950	1,950	3,950	32,000
1926	3,609,000	5	15	30	80	190	400	850	1,750	32,000
1927	3,952,000	5	12	25	70	185	350	675	1,250	32,000
1928	2,72,0001	5	12	25	75	195	450	775	1,650	32,000
1934	1,024,000	5	15	35	145	450	875	2,100	3,850	15,000
1935	392,000	10	22	55	275	585	1,350	2,650	5,500	32,000
1936	1,800,000	3	9	20	60	125	300	675	1,275	32,000

Key to mints : 1910 to 1914 struck in London. All other dates struck in Sydney or Melbourne. (M) Melbourne mintmark. No mintmark for Sydney.

The mintage figures above relate to the normal circulation issues. The mintage for the proof issues is much smaller.

SIXPENCE : George VI

NB : Prices for Proof/Specimen coins refer only to perfect or 'as struck' examples. Coins with imperfections must be discounted by as much as 60%.

1938 - 1952

Silver

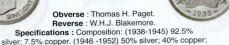

Obverse : Thomas H. Paget.
Reverse : W.H.J. Blakemore.
Specifications : Composition: (1938-1945) 92.5% silver; 7.5% copper. (1946 -1952) 50% silver; 40% copper; 5% zinc, 5% nickel. Edge reeded. Weight 2.83 grams. Size 19 mm.

Date MM	Mintage (000's)	Very Good	Fine	Very Fine	Extra Fine	aUnc	Unc	Choice Unc	Gem	Proof or Specimen
1938	2,864	3	4	8	25	65	125	225	450	16,000
1939	1,600	4	12	20	75	210	475	875	1,550	—
1940	1,600	3	5	17	50	140	315	720	1,500	—
1941	2,912	3	4	9	35	70	145	310	565	—
1942	8,968	3	4	5	15	38	90	200	460	—
1942 S	4,000	3	4	5	12	30	65	195	425	—
1942 D	12,000	3	4	5	7	15	50	125	275	—
1943 S	4,000	3	4	6	12	25	70	195	425	—
1943 D	8,000	3	4	5	9	20	50	135	315	—
1944 S	4,000	3	4	5	12	25	70	195	410	—
1945	10,096	3	4	5	8	25	55	140	360	—
1946	10,024	2	2.5	3	9	25	65	150	375	25,000
1948	1,594	2	2.5	3	12	40	95	235	550	—
1950	10,272	2	3	4	15	35	90	165	385	—
1951	13,750	2	3	4	15	35	90	165	385	—
1951 PL	20,024	2	2.5	3	5	9	35	110	250	20,000
1952	2,112	3	6	20	70	280	575	1,200	2,300	—

Key to mints : Coins with "S" mintmark were struck at the San Francisco Mint while those with a "D" mintmark were also struck in the USA at the Denver Mint. The 1951 PL sixpence was struck at the Royal Mint, London. All other issues were struck at the Melbourne Mint and do not have a mintmark.

GENERAL COMMENTS : The sixpence series seems to be the second most popular denomination for collectors to assemble after the florins. The coins are large enough to generally show good detail, but on balance, much cheaper to acquire in high grade than the florin series. There are no dates in the series as rare as the 1930 penny or 1923 halfpenny. The rarest date is the 1918 sixpence with choice examples turning up from time to time. A serious collector (or investor) is likely to be able to purchase all dates in high grade in the course of a year if dealer lists are diligently checked on a regular basis. The most difficult date to find well struck up is the 1922 sixpence. A true "GEM" in the context of the definition of "quality of strike" for this grade as described earlier in this book will be virtually impossible to find. Discerning collectors may need to be content with a coin graded as UNC, or Choice UNC, if they are really lucky. For type collectors, there are many well struck dates in the George V reign, with the 1936 date being the least expensive. For well - struck examples of the later years look for coins dated 1938, 1950, 1954 and 1956. The one - year type 1910 coin is relatively easy to find in GEM condition.

SPECIAL COMMENT REGARDING PRICING : Some collectors might be a bit surprised that the price of coins graded as VG have almost doubled in price since the last catalogue. This is because of the considerable rise in the silver bullion price in the past year. The price increase merely reflects the fact that coins in such poor grade are worth more "as melt" rather than a collector revival in coins in the lower grades.

SIXPENCE : Elizabeth II

***NB* : Prices for Proof/Specimen coins refer only to perfect or *'as struck'* examples. Coins with imperfections must be discounted by as much as 60%.**

1953 - 1963

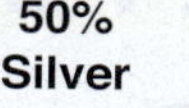

50%
Silver

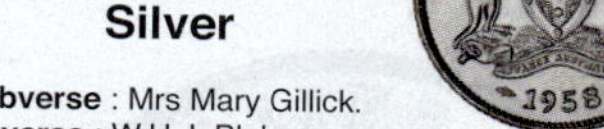

Obverse : Mrs Mary Gillick.
Reverse : W.H.J. Blakemore.
Specifications : Composition: 50% silver; 40% copper; 5% zinc; 5% nickel. Edge reeded. Weight 2.83 grams. Size 19 mm

Date MM	Mintage (000's)	Very Good	Fine	Very Fine	Extra Fine	aUnc	Unc	Choice Unc	Gem	Proof or Specimen
1953	1,152	4	9	20	70	185	375	850	1,850	18,000
1954	7,672	2	2.5	3	4	9	19	60	130	20,000
1955	14,248	2	2.5	3	6	15	40	110	285	—
1955	1200 *	–	–	–	–	–	–	–	–	325
1956	7,904	3	5	9	20	50	100	195	375	—
1956	1500 *	–	–	–	–	–	–	–	–	235
1957	13,752	2	2.5	3	5	9	20	60	165	—
1957	1256 *	–	–	–	–	–	–	–	–	240
1958	17,944	2	2.5	3	5	9	20	60	165	—
1958	1506 *	–	–	–	–	–	–	–	–	225
1959	11,728	2	2.5	3	8	15	40	115	285	—
1959	1506 *	–	–	–	–	–	–	–	–	225
1960	18,592	2	3	4	9	15	45	95	210	—
1960	1509 *	–	–	–	–	–	–	–	–	225
1961	9,152	2	3	4	9	15	45	95	210	—
1961	1506 *	–	–	–	–	–	–	–	–	225
1962	44,816	b/v	b/v	2	3	5	12	45	135	—
1962	2016 *	–	–	–	–	–	–	–	–	200
1963	25,056	b/v	b/v	b/v	2	4	10	40	160	—
1963	5042 *	–	–	–	–	–	–	–	–	160

Key to mints :- All above issues were struck at the Melbourne Mint.
* Actual numbers struck, not multiples of "000".

As the pre-decimal proof coins became more popular during the reign of Elizabeth II, they are dealt with separately in this list with mintage figures included.

GENERAL COMMENT : Top grade Commonwealth coins dated 1938 to 1963 are regarded by many as very desirable acquisitions. Besides the obvious pleasure of owning an uncirculated coin, most dates are financially still well within the reach of the average collector. It would also be reasonable to assume that with many dates, the prospect of further capital gains is excellent. Some might feel that in the case of the 1952 and 1953 sixpences, the horse has already bolted. Yet one should never pass by these dates if they can be purchased in CHU (Choice Uncirculated) or GEM condition. Both years are notorious for weakly struck shields and this is particularly apparent with the 1953 issue. If you can find a sharply struck coin of either date, a reasonable premium which might need to be paid will turn out to be money well spent. The collector should also be on the lookout for other "sleepers." Mintage figures are not always the best indication, as the Mint on occasions had the annoying habit of continuing to use out-of-date dies for some unknown period into the next year. So when the Mint announced the mintage figures for a particular date, a sizable proportion of that date may have been struck with last year's dies. Therefore "hands-on" research and plain experience are the best way to sourcing these "sleepers" or dates which may still be undervalued in high grades.

ONE SHILLING
MINTMARKS AND STATISTICS

GEORGE V MINTMARKS

(a) H" Mintmark (Heaton Mint, Birmingham, UK) 1915 only.
(b) M" Mintmark (Melbourne Mint) 1916, 1917, 1918 and 1920 only.
(c) Star (*) above date (Sydney Mint) 1921 only.

GEORGE VI MINTMARKS

(d) "S" Mintmark (San Francisco Mint, USA) 1942, 1943 and 1944.
(e) (Dot) After star and before "S" in word SHILLING. This was the only pre-decimal silver coin issued by the Perth Mint.

DATA AT A GLANCE

ISSUED FROM : 1910-1963. **MINT ROLL** x 40 Coins.
DATES NOT ISSUED : 1919, 1923, 1929, 1930, 1932, 1937, 1945, 1947, 1949, 1951.

KEY DATES : ***Very rare :-*** 1937 (Pattern).
Rare :- 1915, 1915H, 1921*, 1933.
Scarce :- 1911, 1912, 1913, 1914, 1924, 1939, 1940, 1946 .S

ONE SHILLING : Edward VII

TYPE COIN

1910 Only

Sterling Silver

Obverse : George W. De Saulles.
Reverse : W.H.J. Blakemore.
Specifications : Composition: 92.5 silver; 7.5% copper. Edge reeded. Weight 5.65 grams. Size 23.5 mm.

Date MM	Mintage (000's)	Very Good	Fine	Very Fine	Extra Fine	aUnc	Unc	Choice Unc	Gem	Proof or Specimen
1910	2,536,000	12	25	55	130	245	495	900	2,100	45,000

ONE SHILLING : George V

1911 - 1936

Sterling Silver

Obverse : Sir E.B. Mackennal.
Reverse : W.H.J. Blakemore.
Specifications : Composition: 92.5 silver; 7.5% copper.Edge reeded. Weight 5.65 grams. Size 23.5 mm.

Date MM	Mintage (000's)	Very Good	Fine	Very Fine	Extra Fine	aUnc	Unc	Choice Unc	Gem	Proof or Specimen
1911	1,000	20	45	110	375	825	1,875	3,450	5,750	85,000
1912	1,000	25	75	225	675	2,450	4,550	7,750	12,750	—
1913	1,200	20	65	200	575	1,750	4,500	8,750	13,750	—
1914	3,300	15	30	70	195	500	1,350	2,750	5,750	—
1915	800	45	145	450	1,500	3,000	6,750	12,500	20,000	—
1915 H	500	55	180	525	1,750	5,000	10,000	19,500	30,000	95,500
1916 M	5,141	8	12	35	90	200	475	850	1,650	35,000
1917 M	5,274	8	12	30	90	200	475	850	1,650	70,000
1918 M	3,761	9	18	45	135	325	675	1,200	2,300	—
1918	Pattern	–	–	–	–	Trial pattern in .500 fine				125,000
1919	Pattern	–	–	–	–	Unissued circulation strike				195,000
1920 M	1,642	8	30	100	400	950	3,250	6,250	9,500	70,000
1920 *	Pattern	–	–	–	–	–	–	–	–	175,000
1921 *	522	30	80	260	1,100	2,650	5,250	11,000	18,500	125,000
1922	2,039	8	25	60	240	500	1,750	4,000	7,750	70,000
1924	673	12	40	145	450	2,000	4,000	8,000	14,750	80,000
1925/23	1,449	9	15	35	120	240	750	1,350	2,350	70,000
1926	2,352	9	15	35	120	325	1,100	2,000	3,350	70,000
1927	1,416	8	14	25	90	275	750	1,350	2,350	70,000
1928	664	12	30	80	460	1,150	3,250	6,350	10,500	70,000
1931	1,000	9	12	25	110	295	625	1,150	1,750	70,000
1933	220	95	175	500	2,150	4,500	7,750	12,500	20,500	120,000
1934	480	9	25	75	225	475	995	1,750	2,600	16,000
1935	500	10	17	30	85	275	525	950	1,795	30,000
1936	1,424	b/v	9	20	65	235	450	925	1,650	45,000

Key to mints : 1910 to 1915 issues were struck in London and do not have a mintmark except some 1915 issues carried an "H" mintmark to denote that they were struck at the private Heaton Mint in Birmingham. All other dates were struck in Sydney and Melbourne. Some Melbourne issues have an "M" mintmark.

ONE SHILLING : George VI

NB : Prices for Proof/Specimen coins refer only to perfect or *'as struck'* examples. Coins with imperfections must be discounted by as much as 60%.

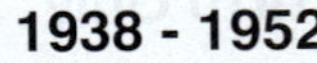

1938 - 1952

Silver

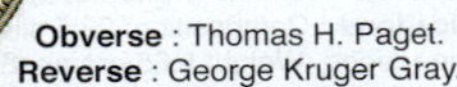

Obverse : Thomas H. Paget.
Reverse : George Kruger Gray.
Specifications : Composition: (1938 - 1945) 92.5% silver; 7.5% copper. (1946 - 1952) 50% silver; 40% copper; 5% zinc; 5% nickel. Edge reeded. Weight 5.65 grams. Size 23.5 mm.

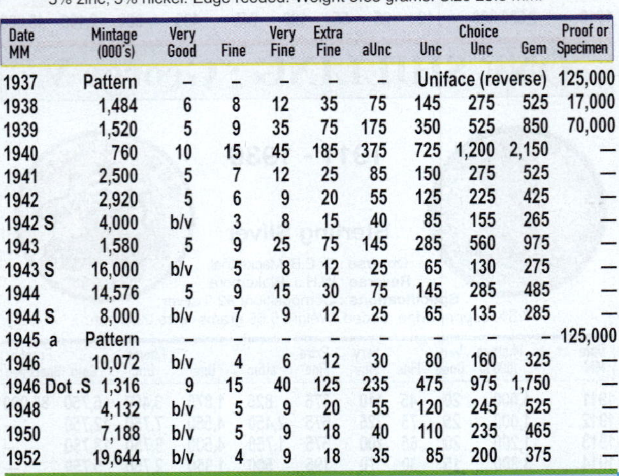

Date MM	Mintage (000's)	Very Good	Fine	Very Fine	Extra Fine	aUnc	Unc	Choice Unc	Gem	Proof or Specimen
1937	Pattern	–	–	–	–	–	Uniface (reverse)			125,000
1938	1,484	6	8	12	35	75	145	275	525	17,000
1939	1,520	5	9	35	75	175	350	525	850	70,000
1940	760	10	15	45	185	375	725	1,200	2,150	—
1941	2,500	5	7	12	25	85	150	275	525	—
1942	2,920	5	6	9	20	55	125	225	425	—
1942 S	4,000	b/v	3	8	15	40	85	155	265	—
1943	1,580	5	9	25	75	145	285	560	975	—
1943 S	16,000	b/v	5	8	12	25	65	130	275	—
1944	14,576	5	9	15	30	75	145	285	485	—
1944 S	8,000	b/v	7	9	12	25	65	135	285	—
1945 a	Pattern	–	–	–	–	–	–	–	–	125,000
1946	10,072	b/v	4	6	12	30	80	160	325	—
1946 Dot .S	1,316	9	15	40	125	235	475	975	1,750	—
1948	4,132	b/v	5	9	20	55	120	245	525	—
1950	7,188	b/v	5	9	18	40	110	235	465	—
1952	19,644	b/v	4	9	18	35	85	200	375	—

KEY TO MINTS :- The 1937 pattern shilling was struck at the Royal Mint, London. Coins with "S" mintmark were struck at the San Francisco Mint, USA. A 1946 shilling with a dot before the "S" of shilling was struck at the Perth Mint. All other issues were struck at the Melbourne Mint and do not have a mintmark.

The mintage figures above relate to the normal circulation issue. The mintage for the proof issues is much smaller.

(a) Three pieces were found during a "stocktake" at the Museum Victoria by the curator, John Sharples, in the late 1970s.

GENERAL COMMENT : The scarcest coins in the George V shilling series are the dates of 1915, 1915 H, 1921 star and 1933. From time to time, the latter two will turn up in high grade, but collectors looking for a top grade 1915 H might have to search a little longer. The 1921 shilling can be regarded as an oddity due to the star above the date. This is the only coin in the whole Commonwealth series, which, because of the star, is clearly identifiable as having been struck by the Sydney Mint. The date of 1925 is another unusual issue, as every coin ever found shows evidence of having been struck from a re-engraved 1923 die. The most likely explanation for this is that the mint had intended to strike coins dated 1923 and prepared dies for that date. However, owing to the relatively high mintage of the 1922 issue, no further shillings were required in 1923. New dies had already been prepared for 1924 and so the first opportunity to use the 1923 dies came in 1925 when they were re-engraved.

ONE SHILLING : Elizabeth II

NB : **Prices for Proof/Specimen coins refer only to perfect or *'as struck'* examples. Coins with imperfections must be discounted by as much as 60%.**

1953 - 1963

50% Silver

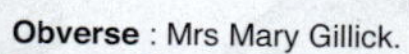

Obverse : Mrs Mary Gillick.
Reverse : George Kruger Gray.
Specifications : Composition: 50% silver; 40% copper; 5% zinc; 5% nickel. Edge reeded. Weight 5.65 grams. Size 23.5 mm.

Date MM	Mintage (000's)	Very Good	Fine	Very Fine	Extra Fine	aUnc	Unc	Choice Unc	Gem	Proof or Specimen
1953	12,204	b/v	3	5	10	30	80	225	450	22,000
1954	16,188	b/v	3	5	10	25	60	125	275	—
1955	7,492	b/v	3	4	15	35	100	225	450	—
1955	1200 *	–	–	–	–	–	–	–	–	425
1956	6,064	3	6	9	25	65	140	275	525	—
1956	1500 *	–	–	–	–	–	–	–	–	350
1957	12,668	2	4	7	12	25	65	150	320	—
1957	1256 *	–	–	–	–	–	–	–	–	390
1958	8,132	3	4	7	12	25	75	195	390	—
1958	1506 *	–	–	–	–	–	–	–	–	350
1959	10,156	b/v	3	6	9	20	60	135	235	—
1959	1506 *	–	–	–	–	–	–	–	–	340
1960	16,408	b/v	3	4	7	12	30	80	160	—
1960	1509 *	–	–	–	–	–	–	–	–	340
1961	10,104	b/v	2	3	5	9	25	60	130	—
1961	1506 *	–	–	–	–	–	–	–	–	340
1962	6,592	b/v	2	3	4	7	20	50	125	—
1962	2016 *	–	–	–	–	–	–	–	–	315
1963	10,072	b/v	b/v	2	3	5	15	40	95	—
1963	5042 *	–	–	–	–	–	–	–	–	255

Key to mints :– All above issues were struck at the Melbourne Mint.
* Actual numbers struck, not multiples of "000".

As the pre-decimal proof coins became more popular during the reign of Elizabeth II, they are dealt with separately in this list with mintage figures included.

GENERAL COMMENT : During the WWII years of 1942, 1943 and 1944, the Australian Government authorized the striking of some of our coinage at the US mints in San Francisco and Denver. Both mints struck threepences and sixpences with the San Francisco Mint also being commissioned to strike shillings and florins. All issues are easily identified by their bold "D" and "S" mintmarks prominently placed in the reverses of the design. For reasons not quite clear, the date of 1922 is notoriously badly struck throughout the silver series in all denominations. By definition, the best grade a collector can expect is UNC and only exceptional "eye appeal" due to an attractive patina may lift this date above the mundane. In the shilling series, the dates of 1924, 1926 and 1927 are also difficult to find well struck up. Type collectors should consider the dates of 1911 or 1936 from the George V series. From the George VI series, select dates from 1938, 1940 , 1943 or 1952. The 1956 issue from the Queen Elizabeth series can be found in exceptionally nice condition. Superbly struck 1910 shillings are reasonably easy to obtain. CHU or GEM grade 1958 and 1962 shillings might be worthwhile acquisitions for the investor on a budget

ONE FLORIN
MINTMARKS AND STATISTICS

GEORGE V MINTMARKS

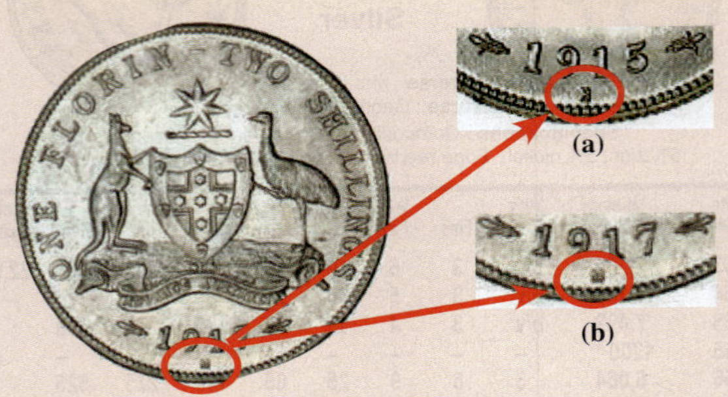

(a) : "H" Mintmark (Heaton, Birmingham, UK) 1914 and 1915 only.
(b) : "M" Mintmark (Melbourne Mint) 1916, 1917, 1918, 1919 only.

GEORGE VI MINTMARKS

(c) : "S" Mintmark (San Francisco Mint). 1942, 1943 and 1944 only.

DATA AT A GLANCE

ISSUED FROM : 1910-1963. MINT ROLL x 20 Coins.

DATES NOT ISSUED : 1920, 1929, 1930, 1937, 1948, 1949, 1950, 1955.

KEY DATES : *Very rare : -* **1937 (Pattern).**

Rare : - **1914H, 1915, 1932.**

Scarce :- **1911, 1912, 1913, 1915 H, 1919M, 1933, 1939.**

ONE FLORIN : Edward VII

TYPE COIN

1910 Only

Sterling Silver

Obv : George W. De Saulles.
Reverse : W.H.J. Blakemore.
Specifications : Composition: 92.5% silver; 7.5% copper. Edge reeded. Weight 11.31 grams. Size 28.5 mm.

Date MM	Mintage (000's)	Very Good	Fine	Very Fine	Extra Fine	aUnc	Unc	Choice Unc	Gem	Proof or Specimen
1910	1,259,000	25	80	265	650	2,000	4,250	8,500	13,000	55,000

ONE FLORIN : George V

1911 - 1936

Sterling Silver

Obv : Sir E.B. Mackennal.
Reverse : W.H.J. Blakemore.

Specifications : Composition: 92.5% silver; 7.5% copper. Edge reeded. Weight 11.31 grams. Size 28.5 mm.

Date MM	Mintage (000's)	Very Good	Fine	Very Fine	Extra Fine	aUnc	Unc	Choice Unc	Gem	Proof or Specimen
1911	1,000	35	95	375	1,475	2,950	6,750	12,750	21,250	90,000
1912	1,000	35	95	375	1,850	5,500	11,250	19,100	28,500	—
1913	1,200	35	95	375	1,950	5,150	12,250	20,500	28,500	90,000
1914	2,300	12	30	100	650	1,350	3,000	7,250	12,250	—
1914 H	500	55	175	650	2,750	5,850	13,200	22,500	35,250	125,000
1915	500	55	175	625	2,850	6,500	15,500	25,200	37,000	—
1915 H	750	40	115	395	1,300	2,750	5,750	11,500	18,500	145,000
1916 M	2,752	15	35	110	450	1,250	2,650	5,125	8,750	50,000
1917 M	4,305	10	30	95	410	875	1,850	3,550	6,750	80,000
1918 M	2,094	15	35	125	550	1,250	2,550	4,750	8,650	80,000
1919 M	1,677	25	65	375	1,450	2,750	5,250	10,250	16,500	90,000
1920	Pattern	–	–	–	–	Unissued circulation strike				400,000
1921	1,247	20	55	350	1,375	2,950	5,850	11,150	18,250	90,000
1922	2,037	15	50	325	1,125	2,275	4,750	10,100	16,500	90,000
1923	1,038	10	45	295	825	1,650	3,250	6,150	9,750	80,000
1924	1,583	10	35	275	750	1,800	3,450	6,100	11,500	70,000
1925	2,960	9	20	75	400	975	2,100	4,150	7,250	75,000
1926	2,487	15	22	80	525	1,175	2,350	5,150	9,150	75,000
1927	1,420	10	15	40	275	775	1,450	3,150	5,000	70,000
1928	1,962	10	15	45	275	625	1,350	2,550	4,550	70,000
1931	3,129	b/v	10	20	65	210	475	875	1,450	85,000
1932	188	225	395	1,150	3,750	6,750	13,500	20,150	32,150	—
1933	488	30	70	395	1,350	3,750	8,750	14,250	21,000	—
1934	1,674	9	12	32	210	575	1,250	3,150	5,150	24,500
1935	915	9	12	45	285	595	1,550	2,650	5,650	75,000
1936	5,054	b/v	9	25	75	210	475	875	1,550	60,000

ONE FLORIN : George VI

***NB :* Prices for Proof/Specimen coins refer only to perfect or *'as struck'* examples. Coins with imperfections must be discounted by as much as 60%.**

1938 - 1952

Silver

Obverse : Thomas H. Paget.
Reverse : George Kruger Gray.
Specifications : Composition: (1938 - 1945) 92.5% silver; 7.5% copper. (1946 - 1952) 50% silver; 40% copper; 5% zinc; 5% nickel. Edge reeded. Weight 11.31 grams. Size 28.5 mm.

Date MM	Mintage (000's)	Very Good	Fine	Very Fine	Extra Fine	aUnc	Unc	Choice Unc	Gem	Proof or Specimen
1937	Pattern	–	–	–	–	–	Uniface [reverse]			125,000
1938	2,990	b/v	10	15	40	95	175	350	625	24,500
1939	630	20	35	95	395	995	2,100	3,600	5,750	—
1940	8,410	b/v	12	18	32	80	165	310	585	—
1941	7,694	b/v	12	18	32	80	160	320	625	—
1942	18,070	b/v	12	18	30	60	130	265	515	—
1942 S	6,000	b/v	12	18	30	75	160	365	775	—
1943	12,562	b/v	8	13	20	55	95	215	410	—
1943 S	11,000	b/v	8	13	22	65	135	315	610	—
1944	22,440	b/v	7	12	20	42	115	235	510	—
1944 S	11,000	b/v	8	13	22	50	125	245	560	—
1945	14,874	b/v	12	19	32	75	210	350	675	—
1946	23,222	b/v	3	6	15	35	85	185	355	34,500
1946 a	Pattern	–	–	–	—	Struck in cupro nickel				70,000
1947	37,482	b/v	3	10	17	45	95	235	465	35,000
1951	10,068	b/v	12	19	30	95	230	510	1,100	—
1952	10,044	b/v	12	19	30	95	230	510	1,100	—

(a) Struck in cupro nickel. Only four coins known. Three are held by the Melbourne Museum and one is in private hands.

Key to mints : The 1937 pattern florin was struck at the Royal Mint, London. Coins with "S" mintmark were struck at the San Francisco Mint, USA. All other issues were produced at the Melbourne Mint and do not have a mintmark.
* Actual numbers struck, not multiples of "000".

GENERAL COMMENT : The florin series is, without doubt, the most collected of all the silver denominations. Being the largest of all the issues - except for the two crowns - it is more avidly collected in all grades than any other type. With the George V dates, again the 1922 is generally a weakly struck coin. Other dates rarely found in better than "CHU" are those of 1914 plain, 1926 and 1927. Well struck examples of the 1924 issue can be found but usually have a "dished" look about them. For many years, the 1932 florin was regarded as the scarcest in the series. This may still hold true for the lower grades, but in top condition, some numismatists now place the 1914H and 1915 florins slightly ahead of the 1932. In recent times, the 1933 florin has made up a lot of ground for value in higher grades. The 1910 florin, relative to the other denominations, is quite difficult to find in UNC. The better grade of CHU is quite scarce, and if a GEM comes your way, don't argue about the price, just buy it if you can afford it. It is rare as such and probably even undervalued in this catalogue.

ONE FLORIN : Elizabeth II

***NB :* Prices for Proof/Specimen coins refer only to perfect or *'as struck'* examples. Coins with imperfections must be discounted by as much as 60%.**

1953 - 1963

50% Silver

Obverse : Mrs Mary Gillick.
Reverse : George Kruger Gray.
Specifications : Composition: 50% silver; 40% copper; 5% zinc; 5% nickel. Edge reeded. Weight 11.31 grams. Size 28.5 mm.

Date MM	Mintage (000's)	Very Good	Fine	Very Fine	Extra Fine	aUnc	Unc	Choice Unc	Gem	Proof or Specimen
1953	13,466	b/v	6	9	15	35	135	275	525	28,000
1954	14,558	b/v	7	10	18	40	145	295	575	70,000
1956	8,090	6	9	15	45	115	225	475	925	—
1956	1500 *	–	–	–	–	–	–	–	–	600
1957	9,692	b/v	5	7	9	19	50	135	295	—
1957	1256 *	–	–	–	–	–	–	–	–	625
1958	8,558	b/v	5	7	9	19	50	135	295	—
1958	1506 *	–	–	–	–	–	–	–	–	600
1959	3,500	b/v	5	8	12	25	60	145	315	—
1959	1506 *	–	–	–	–	–	–	–	–	675
1960	15,760	b/v	b/v	6	8	17	40	115	260	—
1960	1509 *	–	–	–	–	–	–	–	–	600
1961	9,452	b/v	5	7	9	19	50	135	295	—
1961	1506 *	–	–	–	–	–	–	–	–	600
1962	13,748	b/v	b/v	6	8	17	40	115	260	—
1962	2016 *	–	–	–	–	–	–	–	–	575
1963	10,022	b/v	b/v	6	8	17	40	115	260	—
1963	5042 *	–	–	–	–	–	–	–	–	425

Key to mints :- All above issues were struck at the Melbourne Mint.
* Actual numbers struck, not multiples of "000".

At the time of preparing these prices, the bullion value of the Florin was as follows :
Sterling silver .92.5% pure for coins issued from 1910 - 1945 / Pure silver content = Aust. $7.14.
Quaternary silver .50% pure for coins issued from 1946 - 1963 / Pure silver content = Aust. $3.86.

GENERAL COMMENT : Florins between the years 1938 to 1963 are readily available in virtually all dates and grades up to CHU (Choice Uncirculated) condition. The notable exception is the 1939 in high grade. As they are also still quite affordable, many collectors aim for this denomination and range of dates during the early days of their collecting career. If you are looking for quality, a very important aspect to watch out for is "Detracting Marks". These may be bagmarks (scuffs, nicks, scratches etc) inherited by the coin during the manufacturing process or handling marks (scratches) received before actual wear from circulation became an issue. The relatively large and unprotected fields in the design, particularly on the obverse, are highly susceptible to all of these hazards. Opinions are divided if an attractive patina, which may have the effect of hiding otherwise obvious problems, offsets the presence of Detracting Marks. As a rule of thumb, the more common the coin, the more serious are detracting marks, even if they are hiding under an attractive patina. Type collectors looking for generally superbly struck coins should consider the dates of 1919 or 1936, 1938, 1941, 1952, 1954 and 1956. The 1910 florin is the hardest of the type coins to find in top grade with very few GEM coins known.

COMMEMORATIVE FLORINS
1927 PARLIAMENT HOUSE

TYPE COIN

ONE YEAR ISSUE

STERLING SILVER

Obv : Sir Edgar B. Mackennal.
Reverse : George Kruger Gray.
Specifications : Composition: 92.5% silver; 7.5% copper. Edge reeded. Weight 11.31 grams. Size 28.5 mm.

Date & MM	Mintage Figures	Fine	Very Fine	Extra Fine	aUnc	Unc	Choice Unc	Gem	Proof or Specimen
1927	2,000,000	9	18	50	110	225	425	850	40,000
1927 a	Trial	–	–	–	–	Obverse pattern			47,000

Issued on May 9, 1927 to commemorate the opening of Parliament House, Canberra, as the seat of Government.
(a) Canberra florin uniface trial pattern (obverse only) sold by Spink -Noble (Sydney) November 1983 for $7,500.

COMMEMORATIVE FLORINS
1934-35 MELBOURNE CENTENARY

TYPE COIN

ONE YEAR ISSUE

STERLING SILVER

Obverse : Percy Metcalf.
Reverse : George Kruger Gray.
Specifications : Composition: 92.5% silver; 7.5% copper. Edge reeded. Weight 11.31 grams. Size 28.5 mm.

Date & MM	Description	Mintage Figures	Fine	Very Fine	Extra Fine	aUnc	Unc	Choice Unc	Gem	Proof or Specimen
1934/ 35		75,000*	275	325	475	595	850	1,550	3,200	–
1934/ 35	Proof-Like Type One	tba	295	350	550	895	1,950	3,750	7,500	–
1934/ 35	Proof-Like Type Two	tba	295	350	550	895	1,950	3,750	7,500	–
1934/ 35	Pattern specimen Nipple on rider's left breast clearly visible.	tba	7,000	10,000	14,000	19,000	24,000	29,000	35,000	–

Issued to commemorate the anniversary of the founding of Victoria (1834 - 1934) and the establishment of Melbourne (1835 - 1935). Struck at the Melbourne Mint.

(*) These coins were sold for three shillings each to help defray the costs of the Centenary celebrations. Of the 75,000 struck, 21,000 remained unsold and were later returned to the Melbourne Mint to be melted down. This left a nett mintage of just 54,000 coins. Occasionally these coins are found in Foy & Gibson (Melbourne or Perth) bags. The former is scarce while the latter, issued at the Western Australian branch store, is quite rare.

NOTES RELATING TO THE CENTENARY FLORIN

SPECIMEN-PATTERN:- The identifying feature of what has become known as the *SPECIMEN* Centenary Florin is a nipple on the left breast of the rider. Only a handful of coins with a nipple have been observed (less than ten) and it can be regarded as exceedingly rare. While no record has been found to-date to clarify this small mintage, a likely explanation is that (for moral reasons?) the nipple on the rider was removed from the die after only a few strikings. This view is underscored by the fact that the same die that initially struck the "nipple coin" can be observed without the nipple on a fair number of other Centenaries. This then would justify the (nipple) striking that has become known as *SPECIMEN* to be regarded as a *PATTERN* coin. In order to avoid confusion with the well established (if not erroneous) designation of SPECIMEN to this coin, and to assign a more fitting description, it now is listed as a *PATTERN-SPECIMEN*.

PROOF-LIKE Type 1 and Type 2 Centenary Florins:- Recent research has revealed that the Centenary Florin was not produced as a *PROOF* issue. However, it appears that dies were prepared for a *PROOF* striking, but the manufacturing process required for the purpose was never implemented. It seems that these "proof dies" were then nevertheless used in the making of the Centenary Florin, using normal striking procedures which differ from those for proof issues. Two different "proof-like" strikings (from two pairs of dies) of the Centenary have been observed and documented by numismatic researcher Vincent Verheyen in the August 2007 *Coin and Banknote Magazine (CAB)*. The coins can be recognized by die markers, and have been designated as Types 1 and 2. Both types can also be distinguished by their mirror-reflective fields, rather than the cartwheel effect that is found on Centenaries struck from common dies. In addition, the Reverse of a proof like Centenary will feature a square or flat rim, sometimes seen only partly around the circumference of the coin and occasionally characterised by a wire edge. Other Centenaries struck from common dies display a bevelled rim on the Reverse. Proof-like Centenaries have been observed at a ratio of about 1 in 10 at auctions so far in 2008. From a relatively small sample of 101 coins inspected, 5 were of Type 1 and 6 were of Type 2. Generally speaking, auctions do not distinguish between common strikes and proof-like strikes, and the latter has been found in grades as low as VF. A Choice-UNC or Gem-UNC proof-like Centenary is a very beautiful and well struck coin, deserving of acknowledgement in its own right. In the lower grades, the coin's value should be aligned somewhat with the value given to a general issue. Values given for the proof-like Centenaries in this guide are estimates only, and may be subject to adjustment once the coin is recognized by collectors.

THE MELBOURNE CENTENARY FLORIN FOY & GIBSON BAGS

Besides being struck and marketed by the Melbourne Mint, Centenary Florins were sold in 1935 by the Foy and Gibson Department Stores in Melbourne, Adelaide and Perth. There are two types of bags. The first and most common features a mention of the Foy stores in Melbourne, Collingwood, Prahran, Perth and Adelaide at the top of the bag. The second much scarcer bag refers only to the Foy & Gibson store in Perth. Listed below are values for the two types of bags in grades up to EF. For whatever reason, a Foy & Gibson bag has never been observed without having been folded at least once when sold. Therefore (and if we are to borrow grading guidelines from the principles of grading banknotes), an UNC bag does not exist. In fact, a bag in VF condition is quite scarce, as most have been subject to the vagaries of uncaring handling over the years, and are generally found in around Fine condition. When purchasing a Centenary Florin with a Foy & Gibson bag, the value of a bag should be considered in addition to the value of the coin. As most bags will be found in between VG and VF, many will be just a little better or not quite up to the grades for which values are given here. It is therefore reasonable to use designations such as almost VF (aVF) or good Fine (gFine), and allow for this in the value of the bag.

Description	VG	Fine	VF	EF
TYPE ONE. Melbourne, Collingwood, Prahran, Perth, Adelaide in heading				
BAG ONLY : Type One (All stores)	375	595	825	1,800
TYPE TWO. Bag refers only to Perth store				
BAG ONLY : Type Two (Perth only)	495	895	1,600	2,950

MELBOURNE CENTENARY "YOU ARE THE STAR" BOX

Occasionally a Centenary Florin turns up in a presentation box that includes the inscription "You are the Star" on the lid of the box. Inside the lid another inscription states Memento of Melbourne Centenary and The Star *"Who Will It Be?"* contest 1934-1935. The Star was a Melbourne post-Depression era newspaper which ran briefly from October 1933 until its demise in April 1936. The "Who Will It Be" Contest was an immensely popular reader-participation event culminating in a gala presentation night attended by 10,000 people. Major prizes included a cruise and a motor cycle while consolation prizes of various types and values included a silver fox fur, diamond brooch, chocolates and theatre tickets. Although no records are known concerning the boxed Centenary Florins in the event, evidently they were amongst the schedule of prizes though the very small number seen today suggests they were only few in number. Since the above information was first given to me about five years ago, fellow dealer and author, John O'Connor has come up with another variation of the case. In late 2012 John contacted me to say that a vendor showed him another box that was identical in every way except there was no lettering on the lid of the box. No value can be attributed to this case until we can compare similar items coming onto the market.

Description	Slightly Damaged	Slightly Handled	As New Condition
PRESENTATION BOX :	3,250	4,250	6,750

NB : A box, without the coin, that had some of the cover torn off sold for $2,500 plus commission at the July 2010 Noble auction.

COMMEMORATIVE FLORINS

50 YEARS OF FEDERATION. 1901 - 1951

TYPE COIN

ONE YEAR ISSUE

50% SILVER

Obverse : Thomas . Paget.
Reverse : William Leslie Bowles.
Specifications : Composition: 50% silver; 40% copper; 5% zinc; 5% nickel. Edge reeded. Weight 11.31 grams. Size 28.5 mm.

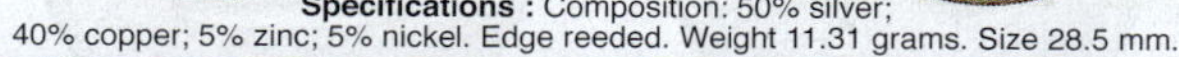

Date & MM	Mintage Figures	Fine	Very Fine	Extra Fine	aUnc	Unc	Choice Unc	Gem	Proof or Specimen
1951	2,000,000	7	8	15	20	60	135	275	—
1951 a	Trial	–	–	–	–	–		Pattern	30,000
1951 b	Trial		–	–	–	–		Pattern	40,000

Issued to mark the 50th anniversary of Federation which was inaugurated in 1901. Struck at the Melbourne Mint.

(a) Cupro - nickel striking. This proof was produced by the Royal Mint, London, utilizing a British Florin planchet that features a very finely reeded edge. The use of base metal is thought to be the result of a silver alloy planchet not being available in London as the mint abandoned the silver standard for the UK general circulation coinage in 1947. There are four examples of this cupro - nickel issue known. One example was purchased by the Museum of Victoria for $4,100 at the Noble Melbourne auction in July 1986.
(b) In early 1994, a unique variation of the above cupro - nickel pattern Federation Florin surfaced. The centre of the obverse had been tooled out in the form of a circle and the word "Pattern" was hand - stamped inside the circle. An illustration of this coin can be found in the introductory pages of this book.

COMMEMORATIVE FLORINS

ROYAL VISIT FLORIN : 1954

TYPE COIN

ONE YEAR ISSUE

50% SILVER

Obverse : Mary Gillick.
Reverse : William Leslie Bowles.
Specifications : Composition: 50% silver; 40% copper; 5% zinc; 5% nickel. Edge reeded. Weight 11.31 grams. Size 28.5 mm.

Date & MM	Mintage Figures	Fine	Very Fine	Extra Fine	aUnc	Unc	Choice Unc	Gem	Proof or Specimen
1954	2,000,000	b/v	5	10	15	55	135	275	35,000

Issued to commemorate the first visit to Australia of Elizabeth II as sovereign the year after her historic live TV coronation in 1953. Struck at the Melbourne Mint.

FIVE SHILLINGS - ONE CROWN

GEORGE VI : 1937 - 1938

Sterling Silver

Obverse : T.H. Paget. **Reverse** : George Kruger Gray.
Specifications : Composition: 92.5% silver; 7.5% copper.
Edge reeded. Weight 28.27 grams. Size 38.5 mm.

Date & MM	Mintage Figures	Fine	Very Fine	Extra Fine	aUnc	Unc	Choice Unc	Gem	Proof or Specimen
1937	1,008	32	40	55	100	200	425	850	—
1937	100 pieces	—	—	—	—	—	—	—	35,000
1937 a	Unique?	Proof. Uniface striking. Reverse only							42,000
1938	101	125	175	275	525	1,100	2,250	3,950	—
1938	250 pieces	—	—	—	—	—	—	—	45,000

Originally issued in 1937 to mark the coronation of George VI. Its commemorative appeal was lost when issued again in 1938.

GENERAL COMMENT : For today's collector, both the 1937 and 1938 crowns represent a particular challenge if they are sought in high grade. The large fields of this coin are notorious for Detracting Marks. Quite often, a small row of what appears to be neatly arranged "tooth marks" are displayed. These were invariably caused by the handling processes of freshly struck coins at the Mint. Trundling along a conveyer belt, they would drop into a collecting bucket. More often than not, the falling coins' reeded edge would heavily "ding" into other coins already resting face up. (Creating a truly genuine "Privy Mark", one might say).

(a) One of the most prolific collectors and authors of Commonwealth coinage, Canadian, Jerome Remick passed away in early 2006 and willed his extensive estate to be auctioned by Spink & Son. London. His collection included a previously unknown uniface 1937 proof crown.

EARLY PROOF / SPECIMEN SETS

Most of the predecimal proof and specimen issues from 1910 to 1953 were simply record coins which were struck in very small numbers. The coins and sets listed below were issued in slightly higher numbers for sale to collectors

Date	Total in set	1/2d	1d	3d	6d	1/-	2/-	5/-	Total
1916 M a	4	—	—	24,000	30,000	35,000	50,000	—	139,000
1927 M b	1	—	—	—	—	—	40,000	—	40,000
1934 M	6	28,000	35,000	15,000	15,000	16,000	25,000	—	134,000
1935 M	2	25,000	30,000	—	—	—	—	—	55,000
1937 M	1	—	—	—	—	—	—	35,000	35,000
1938 M	7	20,000	28,000	12,500	16,500	18,000	20,000	42,000	157,000
1939 M c	1	25,000	—	—	—	—	—	—	25,000
1953 M	6	20,000	30,000	17,500	18,000	25,000	28,000	—	138,500

(a) Assuming set is in original VIP blue box. **(b)** Canberra Florin **(c)** Kangaroo reverse only.

PRE DECIMAL PROOFS
(1955 - 1963)

IMPORTANT. MUST READ = THE PRICES LISTED FOR PROOF AND SPECIMEN ISSUES ARE FOR THOSE IN PERFECT CONDITION. COINS THAT ARE SPOTTED, FINGERPRINTED OR TONED WOULD SELL FOR LESS.

Although proofs, specimens, patterns, trials and record coins go back to the very early gold series, these are extremely rare with only a handful of these special coins being struck for official purposes. (See previous page). By 1955 coin collecting was sufficiently popular for both the Melbourne (M) and Perth (P) mints to issue extra coins for collectors that were struck and sold loose and at the rate of 2/- plus face value. The coins were sold individually rather than as a set and the packaging was no more sophisticated than wrapping them up in cellophane. The Perth Mint only produced and sold bronze pennies and halfpennies while the Melbourne Mint produced all the silver issues and some of the bronze coins. Compared to the modern proof coins, the pre-decimal coins look rather crude and it takes a little knowledge to distinguish them from normal circulation coins. Some of the earlier issues were struck on normal polished dies.

Date	Total in set	Mintage	1/2d	1d	3d	6d	1/-	2/-	Total
1955 M	4	1,200	–	950	650	325	425	–	2,350
1955 P	2	301	8,000	9,500	–	–	–	–	17,500
1956 M	5	1,500	–	825	200	235	350	600	2,210
1956 P	1	417	–	8,250	–	–	–	–	8,250
1957 M	4	1,256	–	–	200	240	390	625	1,455
1957 P a	1	1,112	–	1,750	–	–	–	–	1,750
1957 P b	1	Inc in above	–	1,350	–	–	–	–	1,350
1958 M	5	1,506	–	800	200	225	350	600	2,175
1958 P	1	1,028	–	1,150	–	–	–	–	1,150
1959 M	6	1,506	900	1,400	200	225	340	675	3,740
1959 P	1	1,030	–	1,350	–	–	–	–	1,350
1960 M	4	1,509	–	–	195	225	340	600	1,360
1960 P	2	1,030	875	1,250	–	–	–	–	2,125
1961 M	4	1,506	–	–	195	225	340	600	1,360
1961 P	2	1,040	875	1,250	–	–	–	–	2,125
1962 M	4	2,106	–	–	175	200	315	575	1,265
1962 P	2	1,064	875	1,250	–	–	–	–	2,125
1963 M	4	5,042	–	–	135	160	225	425	945
1963 P	2	1,100	950	1,350	–	–	–	–	1,500

Prices quoted are for coins in unblemished condition. It should however be noted that in particular bronze coins, after having been around for some 50 years, are now quite difficult to find in a fully brilliant state of preservation. This applies in particular to the 1958 and 1959 Melbourne issues, which invariably have acquired a degree of toning. Due to the practice of the Perth Mint to lightly lacquer their pennies and halfpennies they are more often found in fully brilliant condition. While a spotted, stained and unattractive appearance will reduce the value of a bronze coin, similar coins with an even tone will not be discounted so drastically- if at all - if the piece still has eye appeal. It should also be noted that due to the difficulty of assembling a full 1955 to 1963 proof date set in an attractive and high grade of preservation, such a set may well demand a premium.

(a) Matte finish (produced in 1957).

(b) Bright finish (dated 1957 but struck in 1959).

The 1957 Y. mintage of 1112 proof pennies appears to be the combined total output for both the matte and brilliant coins. Unfortunately there does not appear to be any records to indicate how many of each were produced. However by analysing auction catalogues and dealer pricelists, it would appear that about twice as many bright coins seem to be offered in relation to the matte finished type.

KOOKABURRA NICKEL PATTERNS

In 1919 the Commonwealth Government considered replacing the bulky bronze pennies and halfpennies already in circulation with smaller and lighter counterparts. The new nickel penny would weigh an average of 4 grams compared to 9.45 grams for the bronze penny. During the years of 1919, 1920 and 1921, a number of patterns were struck although none officially circulated. All feature a Kookaburra reverse.

All illustrations shown below are larger than actual size.

KOOKABURRA HALF PENNY

1920
TYPE 1

Date	Type	Composition	Size	Weight	Unc
1920	McD1/ R1	Cupro - nickel	14mm	1.97g	225,000

OBVERSE : Portrait by Douglas Richardson. Circular legend. **Legend reads :** GEORGIVS V D.G. BRITT : OMN : REX with date 1920 below with an ornamental stop before and after the date.
REVERSE : Kookaburra of inferior design as a result of being spoilt by the reducing machine. Bird perched on a long thin section of a tree branch. Word "AUSTRALIA" curved above. Words "HALF PENNY" in two lines below. Dies prepared by the Royal Mint, London.The kookaburra has a long, sharp beak.

1921
TYPE 2

Date	Type	Composition	Size	Weight	Unc
1921	McD2/ R2	Cupro - nickel	14mm	1.91g	120,000

OBVERSE : Portrait by Douglas Richardson. Circular legend. **Legend reads** : GEORGIVS V D.G. BRITT : OMN : REX with date 1921 below and a stop before and after the date.
REVERSE : Kookaburra of inferior design as a result of being spoilt by the reducing machine. Bird perched on a short section of a tree branch. Word "AUSTRALIA" curved above. Word "HALFPENNY" in one straight line below. Dies prepared by the Royal Mint, London.

PRICING THE KOOKABURRA SERIES

Unfortunately with this series very few examples come onto the market due to their incredible rarity. Those few coins that have gone to auction in the past two years have sold for prices significantly below what would have been achieved five or six years ago. It should therefore be understood that pricing attributed to those coins that have not been offered for sale in recent years are given a value according to a mathematical formula that compares their rarity to other dates in the series.

KOOKABURRA PENNY : 1919-21

1919 TYPE 3

Date	Type	Composition	Size	Weight	Unc
1919	McD3/ R3	Cupro - nickel	18mm	4.03g	42,500

OBVERSE : Uncrowned effigy of George V within a circular legend. *(Portrait reduced from a medal die supplied by Stokes & Son).* **Legend reads :** GEORGE V D.G. BRITT : OWN : REX with the date 1919 below with an ornamental stop —•— before and after date. **REVERSE :** A small kookaburra with a longer and thinner beak perched on a short section of a tree branch. The word "AUSTRALIA" curved in small lettering above and the words "ONE PENNY" below in two lines.

1919 TYPE 4

Date	Type	Composition	Size	Weight	Unc
1919	McD4/ R4	Cupro - nickel	18mm	3.89g	47,500
1919	McD4a/ R4a	Sterling Silver (.925%)	18mm	4.67g	85,000

OBVERSE : Uncrowned effigy of George V within a circular legend. *(Portrait reduced from a medal die supplied by Stokes & Son).* **Legend reads :** GEORGE V D.G. BRITT : OWN : REX with the date 1919 below with an ornamental stop —•— before and after date. **REVERSE :** Different style of Kookaburra perched on a long section of tree branch. The word "AUSTRALIA" curved in large type above and the words "ONE PENNY" below and in two lines.

1919 TYPE 5

Date	Type	Composition	Size	Weight	Unc
1919	McD5/ R5	Cupro - nickel	18mm	3.89g	45,000
1919	McD5a/ R5a	Sterling Silver (.925%)	18mm	4.67g	85,000

OBVERSE : Obverse design by Douglas Richardson that shows an uncrowned head in lower relief.
Legend reads : GEORGE V D.G. BRITT : OMN : REX with the date 1919 below with an ornament stop —•— before and after the date.
REVERSE : Similar to type four with slightly different design of the kookaburra that appears to be slightly thinner and with a short beak.

KOOKABURRA PENNY : 1919-21

1919
TYPE 6

Date	Type	Composition	Size	Weight	Unc
1919	McD6/ R6	Cupro - nickel	18mm	3.86 g	40,000
1919	McD6a / R6a	Sterling Silver (.925%)	18mm	4.41 g	85,000

OBVERSE : Design by Douglas Richardson which shows an uncrowned head in lower relief within a different circular legend.
Legend reads : GEORGIVS V D.G. BRITT : OMN : REX with the date 1919 below and an ornamental stop —•— before and after date.
REVERSE : A plumper kookaburra with the word "AUSTRALIA" above and "ONE PENNY" below in two lines.

1920
TYPE 7

Date	Type	Composition	Size	Weight	Unc
1920	McD7/ R7	Cupro - nickel	18mm	3.86 g	42,500

OBVERSE : Portrait by Richardson, circular legend.
Legend reads : GEORGIVS V D.G. BRITT : OMN : REX with the date 1919 below, with ornamental stop —•— before and after date.
REVERSE : Kookaburra's plumage is coarse with the word "AUSTRALIA" curved above in larger letters and spaced further apart. The words "ONE PENNY" below in two lines with the word "ONE" further to the right.

1920
TYPE 8

Date	Type	Composition	Size	Weight	Unc
1920	McD8/ R8	Cupro - nickel	18mm	3.79g	47,500

OBVERSE : Portrait by Richardson, circular legend. **Legend reads :** GEORGIVS V D.G. BRITT : OMN : REX and with the date 1920 below and an ornamental stop —•— before and after date.
REVERSE : Plumper kookaburra with a long beak perched on a branch which is slightly curved up. Word "ONE" is almost centred over "PENNY" but still slightly biased to the right.

KOOKABURRA PENNY : 1919-21

1920
TYPE 9

Date	Type	Composition	Size	Weight	Unc
1920	McD9/ R9	Cupro - nickel	18mm	3.89g	80,000

OBVERSE : New bust designed by Douglas Richardson. Legend around and parallel to edge. **Legend reads** : GEORGIVS D.G. BRITT : OMN : REX with the date 1920 below the head.

REVERSE : Kookaburra's plumage is coarser with the word "AUSTRALIA" curved above in larger letters and spaced further apart. The word "ONE" further to the right. Same reverse as Type 7.

1920
TYPE 10

Date	Type	Composition	Size	Weight	Unc
1920	McD10/ R10	Cupro - nickel	18mm	3.88g	150,000

OBVERSE : The only type in the whole series to feature a crowned bust of George V and the only example which does not include the date under the portrait. Bust by Bertram Mackennal with the legend parallel to the rim. **Legend reads :** GEORGIVS V D.G. BRITT : OMN : REX. 1920
REVERSE : Same as type seven and nine.

1920
TYPE 11
Renniks Type 13

Date	Type	Composition	Size	Weight	Unc
1920	McD11/ R13	Cupro - nickel	18mm	3.88g	No sales recorded

This previously unknown type caused a sensation when it was discovered during a stocktake at the Science Museum of Victoria in the 1970s. The two known examples are believed to be the former property of H.M. Le Souef, the late Deputy Master of the Melbourne Mint who left much of his collection to the museum.
OBVERSE : Portrait by Douglas Richardson. Circular legend.
Legend reads : GEORGIVS V D.G. BRITT : OMN : REX with the date 1920 below with ornamental stop —•— before and after the date.
REVERSE : Shows the only known style with the tail feathers of the kookaburra pointing upwards. Designer unknown.

KOOKABURRA PENNY : 1919-21

1921

TYPE 12

Renniks Type 11

Date	Type	Composition	Size	Weight	Unc
1921	McD12/ R11	Cupro - nickel	18mm	3.89g	32,500
1921	McD12a/ R11a	98% Nickel; 2% tin	18mm	4.21g	32,500

OBVERSE : Also by Richardson. Circular legend. **Legend reads :** GEORGIVS V D.G. BRITT : OMN : REX with the date 1921 below and with a dot (.) before and after date.
REVERSE : A larger kookaburra of improved design. The branch appears lower. The word "AUSTRALIA" is similar to earlier types. However the words "ONE PENNY" are in one line below the kookaburra and parallel with the base of the coin.

KOOKABURRA PENNY : 1919-21

1921

TYPE 13

Renniks Type 12

Date	Type	Composition	Size	Weight	Unc
1921	McD13/ R12	Cupro - nickel	18mm	3.86g	32,500

OBVERSE : Head by Bertram Mackennal within a circular legend. **Legend reads :** GEORGIVS V D.G. BRITT : OMN : REX with date 1921 below and with a dot (.) before and after the date. Initals "BM" appear on truncation.
REVERSE : Another well designed kookaburra. Branch is much shorter and thicker. The word "AUSTRALIA" appears in slightly smaller letters and less curved. The words "ONE PENNY" are also slightly smaller.

If you feel you have scans or information that will improve future editions of the pocketbook, please let us know. Please let us know if any errors or updates. Our email address is back on page One.

As you read through this book, we hope you will notice two things; Firstly we hope you identify a lot of new information previously unavailable in any of our previous books. Careful scrutiny will show that much of this new information goes beyond the most recent new and varied issues from our mints and the Reserve Bank. Keen collectors will see that continual research has added new knowledge to old collecting areas. In some cases, the information within these pages, such as the section on the PNC issues and the very complex series of One Dollar coins, is the most inclusive to be published in any numismatic book anywhere. The other important aspect that must be made clear that all the above improvements are not all my own work. I am very grateful, and indeed, humbled by the many collectors who contact me to advise of an error or typo. Other collectors, who have developed a real passion for some area of the hobby that wasn't even around when I started collecting, willingly offer the results of their laborious research for me to publish and share with other collectors with the same interest. For me, personally, it is a real feeling of satisfaction, when someone writes to say that it was a chance encounter with one of our books that got them started in the hobby. My apologies to the partners of the smitten who might notice smaller portions served up at dinner or start suggestion a camping family holiday close to home rather than the usual five-star oversea resort. Happy Collecting!

COCOS KEELING ISLANDS. MEDALS & TOKENS

EMDEN MEDAL
Fashioned by W.R Kerr

Fine	VF	EF
1,200	2,000	3,000

RELICS ASSOCIATED WITH THE SINKING OF THE EMDEN

Common Obverse

Ten Pfennig

Twenty Pfennig

Fifty Pfennig

One Hundred Pfennig

Two Hundred Pfennig

CANTEEN TOKENS CAPTURED FROM THE EMDEN

Description		Metal	Size	Fine	VF	EF
10	Pfennig	Brass	19mm	200	300	750
20	Pfennig	Zinc	n/a	325	500	1,200
50	Pfennig	Brass	24mm	225	350	800
100	Pfennig	Brass	29mm	325	500	1,200
200	Pfennig	Brass	n/a	450	700	1,750

KEELING COCOS ISLANDS 'IVORINE' PLANTATION TOKENS

I am forever grateful when a reader contacts me to update or share new information. You'll find many examples in this book. Now, at last, is a scientific answer to a question that has confused and divided collectors for decades. I am grateful to reader, Doug Spencer for the following email. The material used to manufacture the tokens was a product known at the time as Ivorine, a compound of nitrocellulose and camphor. *Museum Victoria* had previously incorrectly described them as ivory, however at my request they tested one of their examples and now describe them as cellulose nitrate (close enough). Attached is a table showing the highest serial number that I have recorded for each value and the total population of each (to date) that I have recorded from various auctions (Noble's database of past catalogues has been most valuable). In terms of total numbers, the scarcest by far is the C.50, with only 28 recorded by me, none of which are Unc *(2 are aUnc)*. In percentage terms however, the C.5 and C.10 are scarcer - a situation that puzzles me.

Face Value		Declared Mintage	Surviving Examples	Size in mm	Highest Number	Fine	VF	EF	Unc
5	Cents	5,000	46	26x32	4736	210	425	675	850
10	Cents	5,000	44	25mm	4960	175	325	500	750
25	Cents	5,000	110	25x25	4850	65	110	195	450
50	Cents	2,000	28	25x25	1878	275	550	775	1,000
1	Rupee	2,000	56	30x30	1951	90	165	250	425
2	Rupees	1,000	47	31x31	980	110	195	320	450
5	Rupees	1,000	62	32x32	988	110	200	350	550

FOR A MORE DETAILED DESCRIPTION OF THIS SERIES, SEE PP 118-119 OF THE 22ND EDITION

GALLIPOLI - DARDANELLES OVERPRINTS

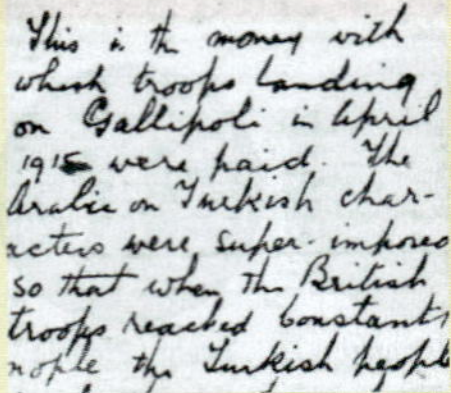
This is the money with which troops landing on Gallipoli in April 1915 were paid. The Arabic or Turkish characters were super-imposed so that when the British troops reached Constantinople the Turkish people

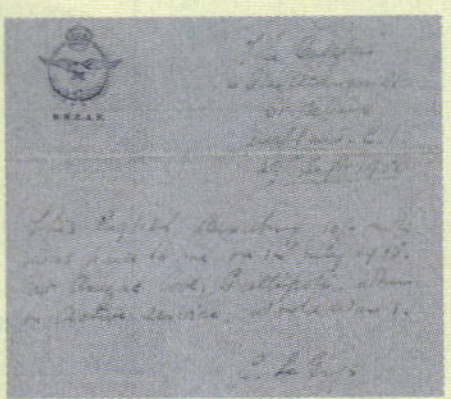

TOP : The above note is a British Ten Shilling second issue of the commonly known "Bradbury" signature issue. The Turkish overprinting indicates that this issue was used by Allied military personnel during the British and Commonwealth occupation of Gallipoli in WWI. Among collectors, this issue is commonly referred to as the "Dardanelles" issue.

ABOVE : Collectors specialising in this hard to research series generally believe that the "Dardanelles" One Pound note is much rarer than the Ten Shilling note. This would help to support the theory that the One Pound note was only issued to officers while the Ten Shilling note was issued to personnel of all ranks.

Description	VF	EF
Ten Shillings	950	1,750
One Pound	2,500	5,000

FOR A MORE DETAILED DESCRIPTION OF THIS SERIES, SEE PP 120-123 OF THE 22ND EDITION

FANNING ISLAND WW2 EMERGENCY ISSUE

Honolulu
Allies Claim
Furious Battle Again Breaks
STORY OF FANNING ISLAND

An interesting and affordable alternative to the rare complete note are the above bisected pieces used as cinema tickets. As well as being cut through the centre, the corners were also clipped to discourage people from trying to redeem the notes for their full One Pound value. Note the left hand segment has been overprinted in (blue) crayon to the value of One Shilling (1/-). The right hand segment of the note has been revalued for Two Shillings.

Description	VF	EF
Full note	1,750	2,950
Half note	140	295

MILITARY MONEY

(WWI) LIVERPOOL NSW INTERNMENT CAMP

The first internment camp in Australia was set up on the outskirts of Liverpool, Sydney, during WWI. It is reported that at least 7000 aliens passed through the camp during the war years. Very little information has come to light about this interesting piece and this is an area which invites further numismatic research. The heraldic eagle is typical of German Empire coinage.

Description			Fine	VF	EF	Unc
No Date	Threepence	Aluminium	1,100	1,850	3,000	4,750
No Date	No denomination	Copper	1,500	2,000	3,500	5,750
No Date	No denomination	Aluminium	1,500	2,000	3,500	5,750

MILITARY MONEY

HAY NSW INTERNMENT CAMP

In April 1941, The Australian Military Board ordered the closure of all civilian owned canteens operating in Internee and POW camps. Up to that point, the Internees had used a bank account in nearby towns to pay for supplies from local civilian outlets. (See details concerning Hay Internment Camp Banknotes in section after pre-decimal banknotes). On April 16,1941, authorities ordered that future purchases were to be made through the Defence Department Canteen Board and not from outside sources. In September of 1941, the following Internment Camp Tokens were introduced in both Australian and New Zealand centres. They were to be used exclusively within the compound and be of no practical help in the event of an escape. Normal Australian coins were prohibited within the camp. Two Victorian firms were commissioned to strike the tokens. H. Arendsen & Sons of Malvern issued the One Penny as well as the Two and Five shilling pieces. Quality control was lax and, although rare, examples missing the central hole or punched off-centre are known. K.G. Luke & Co of Fitzroy produced the Shilling and Threepence issues. They were of a superior quality with sharper cut dies being used. It had always been assumed that error pieces (missing the hole or it being off-centre) also existed. None have surfaced and recent research by Klaus Ford indicates that due to a different manufacturing process, error coins would be all but impossible. The threepence denomination still has one intriguing mystery yet to be fully explored. A Melbourne dealer has what is believed to be a unique example showing the singular word "CAMP" instead of the plural "CAMPS." The majority of surviving threepences clearly show where the die has been re-engraved and an "S" has been added at a later date after the letter "P." Yet another die exists that indicates that the full word "CAMPS" was engraved as a whole and shows no signs of being altered at a later date. All denominations are now highly sought after by collectors. Immediately after the war the tokens were called in and melted as their production, strictly speaking, contravened The Commonwealth Coinage Act. A small number escaped this fate as they were souvenired by prisoners, administrators and guards.

ONE PENNY : BRASS / COPPER

No Date Description	Fine	VF	EF	Unc	CHU
Edge : Plain. 20 mm. Hole in centre (3.6 gms)	125	150	225	325	475
(a) As above but struck in copper (3.3 gms)	265	300	450	625	895
As above but hole punched significantly off - centre	310	500	950	1,350	1,950
As above but with no hole punched in centre	600	950	1,450	1,950	2,500
A Cu/ni pattern sold Spink. (Nov. 1981 for $600)	—	—	—		10,000

Edge : Plain. **Diameter :** 20.32mm. **Manufacturer :** R. Arendeen & Sons
(a). This variety was discovered by collector John Townsend who emailed details to me in April 2007. John said he knows of four examples struck in copper rather than brass.

MILITARY MONEY

HAY NSW INTERNMENT CAMP TOKENS

THREEPENCE : COPPER ALLOY

No Date Description	Fine	VF	EF	Unc	CHU
Hole in centre. Obverse Legend refers to CAMPS	135	185	250	350	450
Hole in centre. Legend shows CAMPS over CAMP	120	155	225	325	400
(a) Obverse die missing "S" in word "CAMPS".	—	—	No sales recorded		

Edge : Plain. **Diameter :** 15.75mm. **Manufacturer** : K.G. Luke & Co Pty Ltd

(a) Recognized expert in this field, Dave Allen,of I.S. Wright reports that he has not seen an example of this coin despite some 45+ years as a dealer. Melbourne's Noble Numismatics representative, Gerhard Reimann - Basch is the only dealer we have found who can confirm the error token exists.

ONE SHILLING : COPPER ALLOY

No Date Description	Fine	VF	EF	Unc	CHU
Hole in centre. Normal issue	325	475	750	1,100	1,500

Edge : Plain. **Diameter :** 18.75 mm. **Manufacturer** : K.G. Luke & Co Pty Ltd

TWO SHILLINGS : COPPER ALLOY

No Date Description	Fine	VF	EF	Unc	CHU
Hole in centre. Normal issue	525	850	1,250	2,250	3,500
As above but hole significantly off - centre	700	1,000	1,650	2,750	4,750
As above but no hole punched in centre	1,200	1,900	2,750	4,250	6,000

Edge : Plain. **Diameter :** 22.85mm . **Manufacturer :** R. Arendeen & Sons

FIVE SHILLINGS : COPPER ALLOY

No Date Description	Fine	VF	EF	Unc	CHU
Hole in centre. Normal issue	2,750	3,850	5,500	7,750	10,000
As above but hole significantly off - centre	3,750	4,750	7,000	10,000	13,500
As above but no hole punched in centre	4,250	6,000	8,750	12,000	17,500

Edge : Plain. **Diameter :** 29.95mm. **Manufacturer :** R. Arendeen & Sons

MILITARY MONEY

HAY INTERNMENT CAMP BANKNOTES

These banknotes were the result of one of the most unfair and scandalous episodes of WWII. Following the evacuation of Dunkirk, British authorities became paranoid about the possibilities of spies now on home soil. Ironically those targeted were already refugees who had fled Nazi Germany or Fascist Italy in the lead up to hostilities. In July, 1940, several thousand of these unfortunate men were taken from their families and shipped to Australia in a barely seaworthy ship, The HMT Dunera. After weighing anchor in Melbourne to off load military POWs, the remaining passengers were off-loaded at Circular Quay on September 7, 1941 and were immediately bundled into a waiting train for their 30 - hour trip to an internment camp in isolated Hay, NSW. Many of these civilian internees were quite wealthy but were prohibited from having actual money in the camps. As Australian legal tender coins and banknotes were prohibited in the camps, this caused problems for internees wishing to purchase goods from the camp canteens. A well organised committee in Camp Seven decided to design its own currency which was subsequently printed by the local newspaper, and printing firm, "The Riverine Grazier." Three banknotes, consisting of a Sixpence, Shilling and Two Shillings denomination were devised by George (or Georg) A. Teltscher, a professional artist who had designed some of the 1934 Austrian banknotes. It was obvious that Teltscher had quite a sense of humour despite the circumstances of his incarceration. The notes are a numismatist's delight for all the cryptic and hidden meanings woven into the designs. The front of the notes feature a coiled barbed wire perimeter fence. Within this design can be seen the repeated wording "We are here because we are here." It has also been suggested that the barbed wire in the fence behind the Coat of Arms is Morse Code. The Coat of Arms is also interesting. The name of the camp leader, W. Eppenstein is written in the fleece of the sheep within the shield. The barbed wire entanglement at the foot of the fencing in the centre of the front of the note contains the wording "HMT (His Majesty's Troopship) Dunera, Liverpool to Hay." The back of the notes features 25 sheep in rows of five. The names of a number of internees are woven into the fleece. The notes only circulated for around three months in 1941 before they were withdrawn and destroyed as they contravened the Australian Currency Act. The only examples available to collectors are those souvenired by the camp inmates and those there to administer or guard the camp.

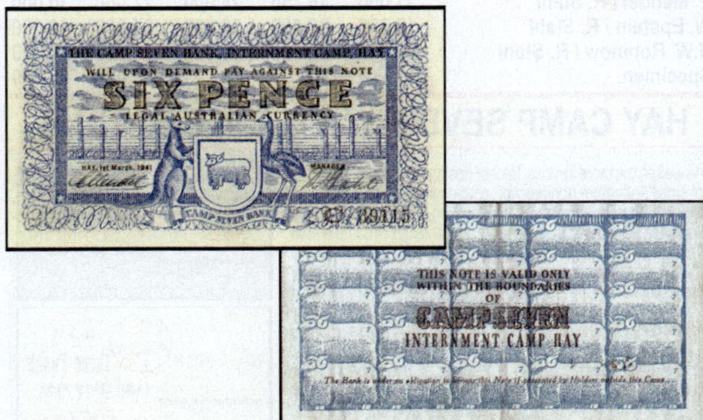

SIXPENCE : ISSUED IN 1941

Black ink on white paper. Blue background (138mm x 76mm)

Signatures	Fine	VF	EF	aUnc	Unc
E. Mendel / R. Stahl	9,000	13,500	17,000	19,500	24,000
W. Epstein / R. Stahl	10,750	16,000	21,500	23,000	29,500
H.W. Robinow / R. Stahl	13,000	20,000	27,000	32,000	37,000
Specimen.	–	–	–	55,000	65,000

MILITARY MONEY

HAY INTERNMENT CAMP BANKNOTES

ONE SHILLING : ISSUED IN 1941

Black ink on white paper. Green background (138mm x 76mm)

Signatures	Fine	VF	EF	aUnc	Unc
E. Mendel / R. Stahl	9,000	14,000	20,000	26,000	33,000
W. Epstein / R. Stahl	11,000	18,500	25,000	35,500	40,000
H.W. Robinow / R. Stahl	8,250	13,500	20,000	26,000	30,000
Specimen	–	–	–	48,000	62,500

TWO SHILLINGS : ISSUED IN 1941

Black ink on white paper. Red background (138mm x 76mm)

Signatures	Fine	VF	EF	aUnc	Unc
E. Mendel / R. Stahl	11,000	16,750	24,000	27,000	30,000
W. Epstein / R. Stahl	15,000	22,500	30,000	34,000	40,000
H.W. Robinow / R. Stahl	15,000	22,500	30,000	34,000	40,000
Specimen.	—	—	—	55,000	65,000

HAY CAMP SEVEN CANTEEN COUPONS

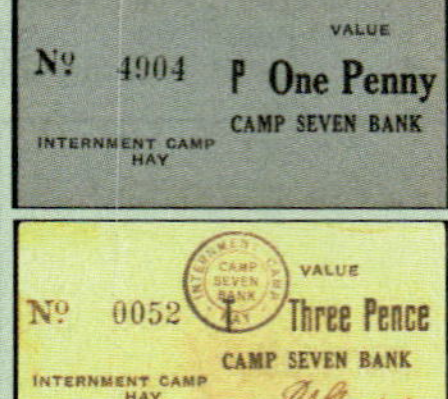

As well as the more famous Telcher designs, there are a number of small and rather nondescript "coupons" of low denomination which are also clearly from Camp Seven. Whether they were issued at the same time as the more ornate issues or came before or after has yet to be established. All we know for sure is that very little information regarding their issue is known to exist. The most comprehensive report on these issues appeared on page 44 of Max Bulluss' very comprehensive treaty on the subject, *"The Hay Internment Camp Notes."* In part he said : *"Also in use in Camp Seven were notes of One Penny and Three Pence value. Just who was responsible for the production of these notes I have been unable to determine; they are very rare and little information seems to exist on them."* Lance Campbell devotes five lines to them in his *"Prisoner of War & Concentration Camp Money,"* while several other writers have diagrams of the notes but little or no information is given on them. These notes, recorded by Lance Campbell as the first series, were made of cardboard and measured 80 mm by 45 mm. The reverse is blank. Some of the Three Pence notes have been rubber stamped within a circle, "INTERNMENT CAMP HAY" around the perimeter, while in the centre, "CAMP SEVEN BANK". Several have been signed, in ink, "R. STAHL". One could only guess that they were an early attempt by Camp Seven to provide themselves with small change for use in their canteen.

Due to the small sample population and the infrequency of sales, these prices have been 'guesstimated' from previous [and outdated] public auction results. Similar issues were produced at various other camps around Australia and we hope to include these in future editions.

DESCRIPTION		Fine	EF
ONE PENNY	11 Known	2,500	5,500
THREEPENCE	4 Known	5,000	8,000

I'd be grateful to hear from any collector who can assist with any further information regarding these fascinating issues.

ONE CENT

FIRST PORTRAIT TYPE

ELIZABETH II
1966 - 1984
COPPER ALLOY
97% Copper;
2.5% Zinc; 0.5% Nickel
Edge plain. Size 17.53 mm

CIRCULATION & NON CIRCULATION (NCLT) ISSUES

Date	TYPE	Mintage Figures	Issuing Mint	Mint Mark	Metal Comp.	Weight in gms	Unc	Choice Unc	Roll or Bagged	Issue Price	Ex Mint Set	Unc	Proof Retail
All mint and proof coins shown in extreme right columns have been broken out of sets													
1966 a	CIRC	146,140,000	Canb	All whiskers pointed		2.59g	5	9	120	–		12	20
1966 b	CIRC	238,990,000	Melb	Blunt 1st whisker		2.59g	6	10	Bag	–		–	–
1966 c	CIRC	26,620,00	Perth	Blunt 2nd whisker		2.59g	20	30	Bag	–		–	–
1967	CIRC	110,055,001	Melb	None	Bronze	2.59g	6	12	135	–		–	–
1968	CIRC	19,930,000	Melb	None	Bronze	2.59g	25	55	1,650	–		–	–
1969	CIRC	87,680,000	Canb	None	Bronze	2.59g	5	9	100	–		–	35
1970	CIRC	72,560,000	Canb	None	Bronze	2.59g	5	9	95	–		–	20
1971	CIRC	102,455,000	Canb	None	Bronze	2.59g	3	9	75	–		–	25
1972	CIRC	82,400,000	Canb	None	Bronze	2.59g	3	9	75	–		–	25
1973	CIRC	140,710,000	Canb	None	Bronze	2.59g	3	9	75	–		–	25
1974	CIRC	131,720,000	Canb	None	Bronze	2.59g	3	9	65	–		–	15
1975	CIRC	134,775,000	Canb	None	Bronze	2.59g	2	5	19	–		–	15
1976	CIRC	172,935,000	Canb	None	Bronze	2.59g	2	5	16	–		–	10
1977	CIRC	153,430,000	Canb	None	Bronze	2.59g	2	5	10	–		–	10
1978	CIRC	97,253,000	Canb	None	Bronze	2.59g	2	5	30	–		–	10
1979	CIRC	130,339,000	Canb	None	Bronze	2.59g	2	5	20	–		–	10
1980	CIRC	137,892,000	Canb	None	Bronze	2.59g	2	4	25	–		–	10
1981	CIRC	183,600,000	Canb	None	Bronze	2.59g	2	4	35	–		–	10
1981	CIRC	40,300,000	Wales	None	Bronze	2.59g	2		Bag	–		–	10
1982	CIRC	134,290,000	Canb	None	Bronze	2.59g	2	4	30	–		–	10
1983	CIRC	205,625,000	Canb	None	Bronze	2.59g	2	4	12	–		–	10
1984	CIRC	74,735,000	Canb	None	Bronze	2.59g	2	4	14	–		–	10

See page 122 for illustrations showing 1966 mintmark positions.

1966 [a] Canberra Mint. All whiskers sharp.
1966 [b] Melbourne Mint. Shows blunted first whisker.
1966 [c] Perth Mint. Features blunted second whisker.

ONE CENT. FINE SILVER

RETRO & PATTERN PORTRAIT ISSUES

[d] Arnold Machin effigy

[e] Ian Rank Broadley effigy.

SEE NEXT PAGE FOR PRICING AND DESCRIPTIONS OF VARIOUS OFF METAL & RESTRIKE ISSUES

[[d] The above is part of the 8 coin 40th anniversary of decimalisation proof set in fine silver that featured the original Arnold Machin effigy of the Queen. This was a unique set as the normal proof and mint sets issued in 2006 carry the current Ian Rank-Broadley obverse. The above coin was not officially issued individually and the complete set is featured in the "off metal" section found elsewhere in this book.
[e] Similar to the six coin set issued to commemorate the 40th anniversary except the obverse features the current Ian Rank Broadley effigy. The unusual mintage figure of 1966 is a reminder that decimal currency was introduced in 1966.

ONE CENT

SECOND PORTRAIT TYPE

ELIZABETH II
1985 - 1991

COPPER ALLOY

97% Copper;
2.5% Zinc; 0.5% Nickel
Edge plain. Size 17.53 mm

Date	TYPE	Mintage Figures	Issuing Mint	Mint Mark	Metal Comp.	Weight in gms	Unc	Choice Unc	Roll or Bagged	Issue Price	Ex Mint Set Unc	Proof Retail
All mint and proof coins shown in extreme right column have been broken out of sets												
1985	CIRC	38,300,000	Canb	None	Bronze	2.59g	3	5	25	–	–	8
1986	EX-SET	180,000	Canb	None	Bronze	Circ coin unique to mint set					9	–
1987	CIRC	122,000,000	Canb	None	Bronze	2.59g	3	5	25	–	5	–
1988	CIRC	105,900,000	Canb	None	Bronze	2.59g	2	4	12	–	–	5
1989	CIRC	168,000,000	Canb	None	Bronze	2.59g	2	4	15	–	–	5
1990	CIRC	52,993,000	Canb	None	Bronze	2.59g	3	5	20	–	–	5

The decision to stop minting one and two cent coins was announced in August 1990. The main reasons included the deminishing purchasing power of the two coins and the rising costs of production which eventually overtook the face value.

NCLT ONE CENT PIECES STRUCK AFTER THEIR WITHDRAWAL

(a) Silver Masterpiece (b&c) Unc & Proof (d) Machin Silver set (e) Rank Broadley (f) Rank mini set

Date	TYPE	Mintage Figures	Metal Comp.	Weight in gms	Description	Issue Price	Unc Retail	Proof Retail
1991	EX-SET	147,700	Bronze	2.60g	Unc coin unique to annual mint set	–	12	–
1991 a	OFF METAL	25,000	Silver	3.01g	Proof M'pieces .925 Stg. 17.65mm	–	–	30
2006 b	EX-SET	84,407	Bronze	2.60g	Unc coin unique to annual mint set	–	10	–
2006 c	EX-SET	45,373	Bronze	2.60g	Proof coin unique to annual set	–	–	15
2006 d	OFF METAL	5,829	Silver	2.93g	Proof. Machin 1st obv. 8 coin set	–	–	45
2006	OFF METAL	300	Gold	5.61g	Proof. Rank Broadley obv. 8 coin set	–	–	400
2011 e	PART PAIR	6,000	Silver	2.93g	Proof 99.9. Paired with 2¢ restrike	–	–	25
2012 f	OFF METAL	2,000	Gold	0.5g	Proof. Mini coins. 99.99 (11.5mm)	–	–	60
2016	OFF METAL	10,000	Bronze	2.60g	Circ. Part of 50th anniv. 1¢ -50¢ set	–	–	10
2016	OFF METAL	5,829	Silver	2.93g	Proof. Current R-Broadley. 8 coin set	–	–	45
2016	OFF METAL	1966	Silver	2.93g	Proof. Part of 50th anniv. 1¢ -50¢ set	–	–	60
2016	OFF METAL	100	Gold	5.61g	Proof. Part of 50th anniv. 1¢ -50¢ set	–	–	400

[a] The 1991 Masterpieces in Silver set consists of Proof Sterling Silver (.925 Fine) versions of all eight of Australia's base metal circulation coins, together with a silver ingot stamped with the Australian Coat of Arms and the issue number of the set.
[b/c] To celebrate the 40th anniversary of decimalisation, the RAM re-introduced the one and two cent coins in the 2006 annual proof and mint sets. This made the bronze pair unique type coins as both featured the current "older" style portrait of QE2 by Ian Rank-Broadley that was introduced in 1999. Neither was officially issued individually or for circulation.
[d] To reflect the style of the original decimal coins when introduced in 1966, this fine silver set included the return of 1 and 2 cent coins and a round 50 cent piece. A special feature was the re-introduction of the original 1966 Arnold Machin portrait of a young Queen. These coins are also a unique type set.
[e] These two fine silver coins celebrate the 21st anniversary of the demise of the bronze 1¢ & 2¢. The pair were sold in a plush hinge lid case for $80. Some of the original coins were recycled in 2000 to produce the bronze Olympic medals.
[f] This eight coin fine gold set featured the addition of the round 50 cent piece, which was only in circulation for one year before it was replaced with the dodecagon shape that is commonly known today. The one and two cent pieces that were respectively discontinued in 1990-92 were also included. Unlike the silver set, the current Rank Broadley portrait featured on all coins. This set also spawned a number of unique issues including the round gold fifty cent and the obvious one and two cent coins.

TWO CENTS

FIRST PORTRAIT TYPE

ELIZABETH II

1966 - 1984

COPPER ALLOY
97% Copper;
2.5% Zinc; 0.5% Nickel
Edge plain. Size 21.59 mm
Obverse : Arnold Machin.
Rev : Stuart Devlin. Frilled Neck Lizard

Date	TYPE	Mintage Figures	Issuing Mint	Mint Mark	Metal Comp.	Weight in gms	Unc	Choice Unc	Roll or Bagged	Issue Price	Ex Mint Set Unc	Proof Retail
All mint and proof coins shown in extreme right column have been broken out of sets												
1966	CIRC	144,880,000	Canb	All claws sharp		5.18g	4	7	100	–	15	25
1966	CIRC	66,575,000	Melb	Blunt left 3rd claw		5.18g	8	12	Bag	–	–	30
1966	CIRC	217,735,000	Perth	Blunt right 1st claw		5.18g	5	8	Bag	–	–	30
1967	CIRC	73,250,000	Perth	None	Bronze	5.18g	12	20	475	–	–	–
1967 a	CIRC	Inc. above	Perth	Missing initals SD		5.18g	130	195	n/a	–	–	–
1968	CIRC	16,995,000	Perth	None	Bronze	5.18g	65	400	2,500	–	–	–
1969	CIRC	12,940,000	Canb	None	Bronze	5.18g	7	9	325	–	–	10
1970	CIRC	39,872,500	Canb	None	Bronze	5.18g	4	6	95	–	–	10
1971	CIRC	60,735,000	Canb	None	Bronze	5.18g	4	6	95	–	–	10
1972	CIRC	77,570,000	Canb	None	Bronze	5.18g	5	4	95	–	–	20
1973	CIRC	68,082,500	Canb	None	Bronze	5.18g	4	7	95	–	–	15
1973 a	CIRC	25,975,000	Perth	None	Bronze	5.18g	4	7	Bag	–	–	–
1974	CIRC	91,732,500	Canb	None	Bronze	5.18g	4	7	75	–	–	35
1974 a	CIRC	85,015,000	Perth	None	Bronze	5.18g	4	7	Bag	–	–	10
1975	CIRC	33,075,000	Canb	None	Bronze	5.18g	2	4	30	–	–	5
1975	CIRC	66,970,000	Perth	None	Bronze	5.18g	2	4	Bag	–	–	–
1976	CIRC	71,882,000	Canb	None	Bronze	5.18g	2	4	60	–	–	7
1976	CIRC	50,000,000	Perth	None	Bronze	5.18g	2	4	Bag	–	–	–
1977	CIRC	72,105,500	Canb	None	Bronze	5.18g	2	4	50	–	–	4
1977	CIRC	30,000,000	Perth	None	Bronze	5.18g	2	4	Bag	–	–	–
1978	CIRC	88,672,500	Canb	None	Bronze	5.18g	2	4	25	–	–	4
1978	CIRC	40,000,000	Perth	None	Bronze	5.18g	2	4	Bag	–	–	–
1979	CIRC	29,705,000	Canb	None	Bronze	5.18g	2	4	20	–	–	4
1979	CIRC	40,000,000	Perth	None	Bronze	5.18g	2	4	Bag	–	–	–
1980	CIRC	105,603,000	Canb	None	Bronze	5.18g	3	5	12	–	–	4
1980	CIRC	40,000,000	Perth	None	Bronze	5.18g	2	4	Bag	–	–	–
1981	CIRC	97,390,000	Canb	None	Bronze	5.18g	2	4	12	–	–	4
1981 a	CIRC	81,064,000	Perth	None	Bronze	5.18g	2	4	Bag	–	–	–
1981 b	CIRC	70,820,000	Wales	None	Bronze	5.18g	2	4	Bag	–	–	–
1982	CIRC	81,324,000	Canb	None	Bronze	5.18g	2	4	25	–	–	4
1982	CIRC	40,446,000	Perth	None	Bronze	5.18g	2	4	Bag	–	–	–
1983	CIRC	156,562,000	Canb	None	Bronze	5.18g	2	4	12	–	–	4
1983	CIRC	20,665,000	Perth	None	Bronze	5.18g	2	4	Bag	–	–	–
1984	CIRC	57,963,500	Canb	None	Bronze	5.18g	2	4	20	–	–	4

Mintmarks : Appear only on the 1966 coins in most denominations although more than one mint was involved in issuing coins in later years. The only exception to this is the 1967 and 1968 two cent coins. With most other dates, it is not possible to determine which mint produced a particular coin.
[a] Designer's initials "SD" on the reverse are missing. Reader Jerry Himelfard said he recently had an examply accepted and graded by PCGS. One proof coin without SD sighted.
[b] The obverse text (or legend) on the Wales issued coins is closer to the rim.

SEE NEXT PAGE FOR PRICING AND DESCRIPTIONS OF VARIOUS OFF METAL & RESTRIKE ISSUES

[c] Arnold Machin effigy

[d] Ian Rank Broadley effigy.

[c] The above is part of the 8 coin 40th anniversary of decimalisation proof set in fine silver that featured the original Arnold Machin effigy of the Queen. This was a unique set as the normal proof and mint sets issued in 2006 carry the current Ian Rank-Broadley obverse. The above coin was not officially issued individually and the complete set is featured in the "off metal" section found elsewhere in this book.
[d] Similar configeration to the 2006 40th anniversary set, except the obverse features the current Ian Rank Broadley effigy. The unusual mintage figure of 1966 is a reminder that decimal currency was introduced in 1966.

TWO CENTS

SECOND PORTRAIT TYPE

ELIZABETH II
1985 - 1991

COPPER ALLOY
97% Copper;
2.5% Zinc; 0.5% Nickel
Edge plain. Size 21.59 mm
Obverse : Raphael Maklouf
Reverse : Stuart Devlin. Frilled Neck Lizard

CIRCULATION & NON CIRCULATION (NCLT) ISSUES

All mint and proof coins shown in extreme right columns have been broken out of sets

Date	TYPE	Mintage Figures	Metal Comp	Weight in gms	Issuing Mint	Unc	Choice Unc	Roll or Bagged	Issue Price	Mint set Retail	Proof Retail
1985	CIRC	34,500,000	Bronze	5.18g	Canb	3	6	25	-	-	-
1986	EX-SET	180,000	Bronze	5.18g	Circ coin unique to mint set				-	10	20
1987	EX-SET	200,000	Bronze	5.18g	Circ coin unique to mint set				-	10	20
1988	CIRC	30,300,000	Bronze	5.18g	Canb	3	6	30	-	-	15
1989	CIRC	43,000,000	Bronze	5.18g	Canb	3	6	12	-	-	15
1990	EX-SET	103,766	Bronze	5.18g	Circ coin unique to mint set				-	50	15
1991	EX-SET	147,700	Bronze	5.18g	Circ coin unique to mint set				-	12	-
1991 a	OFF METAL	25,000	Silver	6.06g	Proof M'pieces .925%. 21.72mm				-	-	45

After the RAM stopped issuing mint rolls, two cent coins were shipped in strong plastic bags containing coins with a total face value of $25.00. Rolls do exist as security companies produced their own.

COMMEMORATIVE OFF METAL, MULES AND PATTERNS

NCLT TWO CENT PIECES STRUCK AFTER OFFICIAL WITHDRAWAL

(a) Silver Masterpiece (b&c) Unc & Proof (d) Machin Silver set (e) Rank Broadley (f) Rank mini set

Date	TYPE	Mintage Figures	Metal Comp.	Weight in gms	Description	Issue Price	Unc Retail	Proof Retail
2006 b	EX-SET	84,407	Bronze	5.20g	Unc coin unique to annual mint set	-	10	20
2006 c	EX-SET	45,373	Bronze	5.20g	Proof coin unique to annual set	-	15	20
2006 d	OFF METAL	5,829	Silver	6.03g	Proof. Machin 1st obv. 8 coin set	-	-	45
2006 e	OFF METAL	300	Gold	11.31g	Proof. Rank Broadley obv. 8 coin set	-	-	400
2011 f	OFF METAL	6,000	Silver	6.03g	Proof 99.9. Paired with 1¢ restrike	-	-	60
2012	OFF METAL	2,000	Gold	0.5g	Proof part mini set. 99.99 Fine. 11.5mm		-	75
2016	EX-SET	10,000	Bronze	5.20g	Circ. Part of 50th anniv. 1¢ -50¢ set	-	-	15
2016	OFF METAL	1,966	Silver	6.03g	Proof. Part of 50th anniv. 1¢ -50¢ set	-	-	60
2016	OFF METAL	100	Gold	11.31g	Proof. Part of 50th anniv. 1¢ -50¢ set	-	-	350

[a] The 1991 Masterpieces in Silver set issued by the Royal Australian Mint consists of Proof Sterling Silver (.925 Fine) versions of all 8 of Australia's base metal circulation coins, together with a silver ingot stamped with the Australian Coat of Arms and the issue number of the set.
[b/c] To celebrate the 40th anniversary of decimalisation, the RAM re-introduced the one and two cent coins in the 2006 annual proof and mint sets. This made the bronze pair unique.
type coins as both featured the current "older" style portrait of QE2 by Ian Rank-Broadley that was introduced in 1999. Neither was officially issued individually or for circulation.
[d] This fine silver set included the return of 1 and 2 cent coins and a round 50 cent piece. A special feature was the re-introduction of the original circa 1966 Arnold Machin portrait of a young queen. These coins are also a unique type set.
[e] This eight coin fine gold set featured several unique features including the addition of the round 50 cent piece, which was only in circulation for one year before it was replaced with the dodecagon shape that is commonly known today. The one and two cent piece have also been included, which were respectively discontinued in 1990-92. Unlike the silver set, the current Rank Broadley portrait was featured on all coins. This set also spawned a number of unique issues including the round gold fifty cent and the obvious one and two cent coins.
[f] These two fine silver coins celebrate the 21st anniversary of the demise of the bronze 1¢ & 2¢. The pair were sold in a plush hinge lid case for $80. Some of the original coins were recycled in 2000 to produce the bronze Olympic medals.

1966 1¢ & 2¢ MINTMARK POSITION

PERTH MINT
Blunted second whisker

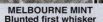

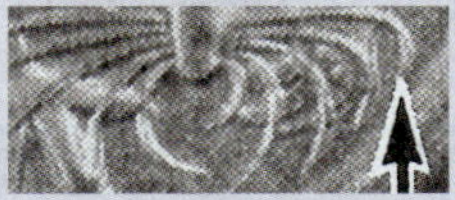

MELBOURNE MINT
Blunted first whisker

TOP : MELBOURNE MINT
Third left claw blunted
ABOVE : PERTH MINT First right claw blunted (1966, 1967 & 1968)
CANBERRA MINT
All claws sharp

FIVE CENT VARIATIONS FOUND IN DESIGNER'S INITIALS

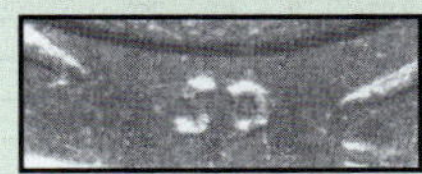

SMALL "SD" INITIALS

LARGE "SD" INITIALS

Research also continues on this aspect of collecting but it is obvious that a number of variations in the size of the designer's initials concerning the reverse of several denominations (all designed by Stuart Devlin) have been noticed. Variations discovered so far (as outlined by decimal researcher Wayne Roberts) are found in the footnotes under each denomination that show the variation.

1966 FIVE CENT MINTMARK POSITION

CANBERRA MINT
Short spine

LONDON MINT
Long spine

No 1966 five cent pieces were struck at the Perth or Melbourne Mints

LARGE AND SMALL ECHIDNA REV DIES

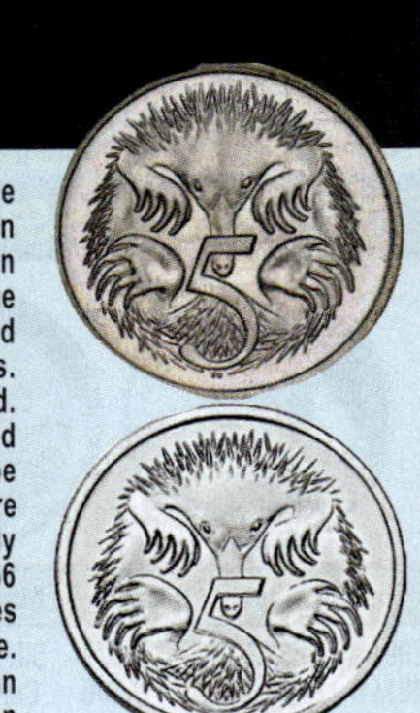

Two different reverse dies for the striking of the 1984 five cent coin was reported in the CAB magazine by the then president of the Metropolitan Coin Club of Sydney, John Cook. A follow-up article a few months later in the same magazine by decimal enthusiast Lindsay Bedogni noted that identical differences were found in the 1986 mint sets. Later, variations in the 1986 proof sets were also noted. Broadly speaking, the Large Reverse Type (Top) is found on all issues from 1966 to 1972. The Small Reverse Type (Bottom) is found from 1973 to 1987 on some issues. There is a Large Head overlap from 1984 to the present. Normally the Large Reverse (Type 1) is found on all issues from 1966 to 1972. The Small Reverse (Type 2) can be found on issues from 1972 to 1987, with coins dated 1987 being very rare. From 1984 to the present, the Large Reverse (Type 2) can be found. Overlaps of Large and Small head occur on coins dated 1972, 1984, 1986 & 1987.

FIVE CENTS

FIRST PORTRAIT TYPE

ELIZABETH II

1966 - 1984

CUPRO NICKEL
75% Copper; 25% Nickel
Edge Reeded. Size 19.41mm
Obverse : Arnold Machin.
Reverse : Stuart Devlin. Echidna

Date	TYPE	Mintage Figures	Issuing Mint	MInt Mark	Metal Comp.	Weight in gms	Unc	Choice Unc	Roll or Bagged	Issue Price	Ex Set	Mint Unc	Proof Retail
All mint and proof coins shown in extreme right columns have been broken out of sets													
1966 a	CIRC	45,384,000	Canb	Short spine		2.83g	7	12	150	–		–	30
1966 b	CIRC	30,000,000	London	Long spine		2.83g	7	12	Bag	–		–	–
1967	CIRC	62,144,000	Canb	None	Cu/ni	2.83g	7	12	250	–		–	–
1968	CIRC	67,336,000	Canb	None	Cu/ni	2.83g	9	12	250	–		–	–
1969	CIRC	38,170,000	Canb	None	Cu/ni	2.83g	7	10	225	–		–	30
1970	CIRC	46,058,000	Canb	None	Cu/ni	2.83g	4	8	125	–		–	25
1971	CIRC	39,516,000	Canb	None	Cu/ni	2.83g	4	8	125	–		–	30
1972	CIRC	8,256,000	Canb	None	Cu/ni	2.83g	35	55	1,100	–		–	40
1973	CIRC	48,816,000	Canb	None	Cu/ni	2.83g	4	8	90	–		–	30
1974	CIRC	64,248,000	Canb	None	Cu/ni	2.83g	3	6	45	–		–	25
1975	CIRC	44,256,000	Canb	None	Cu/ni	2.83g	3	6	100	–		–	10
1976	CIRC	113,180,000	Canb	None	Cu/ni	2.83g	3	6	80	–		–	10
1977	CIRC	108,800,000	Canb	None	Cu/ni	2.83g	2	5	50	–		–	10
1978	CIRC	25,210,000	Canb	None	Cu/ni	2.83g	3	6	35	–		–	10
1979	CIRC	44,533,000	Canb	None	Cu/ni	2.83g	2	3	30	–		–	10
1980	CIRC	115,042,000	Canb	None	Cu/ni	2.83g	2	5	35	–		–	10
1981	CIRC	61,988,000	Canb	None	Cu/ni	2.83g	2	5	40	–		–	10
1981 c	CIRC	50,276,000	Wales	None	Cu/ni	2.83g	2	5	Bag	–		–	–
1981 d	CIRC	50,000,000	Canada	None	Cu/ni	2.83g	2	5	Bag	–		–	–
1982	CIRC	139,468,000	Canb	None	Cu/ni	2.83g	2	5	30	–		–	10
1983	CIRC	131,568,000	Canb	None	Cu/ni	2.83g	2	5	35	–		–	10
1984	CIRC	43,436,000	Canb	None	Cu/ni	2.83g	3	5	20	–		–	10

More on pricing : In some years, prices are given separately for Choice Uncirculated coins and others taken from Mint Sets. This occurs when the coins in the mint sets were of specimen quality or otherwise superior. In other years there does not seem to be any discernable difference.
(a) Canberra Mint. Features a Short Spine on the reverse.
(b) London Mint. Has a Long Spine on the reverse.
(c) Llantrisant, Wales. No distinctive mintmark.
(d) Winnipeg, Canada. Wavy hair curls at the back of the neck on obverse.
Specimen prices : Early vinyl mint set coins were specimen strikes. Some later carded sets also included examples of superior quality.
Proof coin prices : Not issued individually but are often available from damaged proof sets broken up by collectors or dealers. This is a growing segment of the collecting industry.
• From 1966 to 1972 the reverse featured a large echidna design. From 1973 to 1984 the reverse featured a small echidna with some 1984 coins going back to the old larger echidna design.
• Some 1967 issues are missing the designer's initials "SD" (Stuart Devlin) on the reverse.

RETRO ISSUES & UNIQUE DESIGNS

a

b

Date	Type	Mintage	Metal	Weight	Description	Issue	Value
2006 a	RESTRIKE	5,829	Silver	3.24 g	Only available as part of 8 coin set	–	45
2016 b	MINT ROLL	5,000	Cu/ni	2.83 g	Commemorative roll. 20 x Unc coins	–	15
2016 b	EX-SET	n/a	Cu/ni	2.83 g	Specimen. Part of annual 6 coin mint set	–	4
2016 b	EX-SET	n/a	Cu/ni	2.83 g	Proof. Part of annual 6 coin proof set	–	15

FIVE CENTS

SECOND PORTRAIT TYPE

ELIZABETH II

1985 - 1998

CUPRO NICKEL

75% Copper; 25% Nickel
Edge Reeded. Size 19.41 mm

Obverse : Raphael Maklouf. **Reverse :** Stuart Devlin. Echidna

CIRCULATION & NON CIRCULATION (NCLT) ISSUES

Date	TYPE	Mintage Figures	Metal Comp.	Weight in gms	Issuing Mint	Unc	Choice Unc	Roll or Bagged	Issue Price	Mint set Retail	Proof Retail
1985 a	EX-SET	170,000	Cu/ni	2.83g	Unc coin unique to mint set				–	30	30
1986 b	EX-SET	180,000	Cu/ni	2.83g	Unc coin unique to mint set				–	6	10
1987	CIRC	73,500,000	Cu/ni	2.83g	Canb	2	4	40	–	5	9
1988	CIRC	106,423,500	Cu/ni	2.83g	Canb	2	4	35	–	5	9
1989	CIRC	95,753,300	Cu/ni	2.83g	Canb	2	4	18	–	5	9
1990	CIRC	33,252,000	Cu/ni	2.83g	Canb	2	4	22	–	5	15
1991 c	CIRC	29,889,000	Cu/ni	2.83g	Canb	3	6	Bag	–	5	15
1991	OFF METAL	25,000	Silver	3.27g	Proof M'pieces .925 Stg. 19.53mm				–	–	30
1992 c	CIRC	52,558,500	Cu/ni	2.83g	Canb	2	4	Bag	–	5	15
1993 c	CIRC	93,838,000	Cu/ni	2.83g	Canb	2	4	Bag	–	5	15
1994 c	CIRC	146,668,000	Cu/ni	2.83g	Canb	2	4	Bag	–	15	15
1995	CIRC	84,991,000	Cu/ni	2.83g	Canb	2	4	Bag	–	5	15
1996	CIRC	79,212,000	Cu/ni	2.83g	Canb	3	6	Bag	–	10	12
1997 d	CIRC	100,680,000	Cu/ni	2.83g	Canb	2	4	Bag	–	10	12
1998 d	CIRC	88,532,000	Cu/ni	2.83g	Canb	2	4	Bag	–	15	12

(a) Small and large echidna reverse thought to exist. Percentages to be verified. Small echidna design is thought to be most common.
(b) Small and large echidna reverse found in 1986 mint and proof sets. Large echidna reverse used from 1988 onwards. 1987 small reverse is rare.
(c) Normal and large sized designer's initials "SD" (Stuart Devlin) found on reverse of circulation coins. Large SD is rare. Uncirculated examples worth $40.
(d) Normal and small sized designer's initials "SD" (Stuart Devlin) found on reverse of circulation coins. Small SD also found in some early '90's issues.

OFF METAL & UNIQUE ISSUES

While there are a number of interesting and unique off metal issues attributed to the one and two cents coins, the range literally exploded with the addition of even more six coin sets with the lowest denomination being the five cent piece .Below is a variety of special issues but not a complete list. Some sets have been broken up and the coins sold individually to accommodate collectors who specialise in collecting just 50¢, $1 or other denomination. While most of these coins were originally part of sets, from 2013 the mint also issued individually packaged versions of each coin in both silver and gold.

1991 Silver Masterpieces | 2001 Gold Federation set | 2005 End WW2 Silver set | 2005 End WW2 Gold set
2006 Silver Masterpieces | 2006 Gold Decimal 40th | 2007 Gold Lifesaving | 2010 Gold Gottwald Obv

FIVE CENTS

THIRD PORTRAIT
TYPE: 1999 -

CUPRO NICKEL
75% Copper; 25% Nickel
Edge Reeded. Size 19.41 mm
Obverse : Ian Rank Broadley
Reverse : Stuart Devlin. Echidna

Date	TYPE	Mintage Figures	Metal Comp.	Weight in gms	Issuing Mint	Unc	Choice Unc	Roll or Bagged	Issue Price	Mint set Retail	Proof Retail
1999	CIRC	179,016,000	Cu/ni	2.83g	Canb	3	6	Bag	–	–	35
2000 a	CIRC	97,422,000	Cu/ni	2.83g	Canb	2	5	Bag	–	–	40
2001 b	CIRC	174,579,000	Cu/ni	2.83g	Canb	4	8	Bag	–	–	25
2001	OFF METAL	650/ 193	Gold	6.13g	Proof. Part of 6 coin boxed set				–	–	595
2002 a/c	CIRC	148,812,000	Cu/ni	2.83g	Canb	2	4	Bag	–	–	25
2003 a	CIRC	115,100,000	Cu/ni	2.83g	Canb	2	4	Bag	–	–	25
2003	OFF METAL	6,500	Silver	3.24g	Proof. Part of 6 coin boxed set				–	–	45
2004 a	CIRC	145,300,000	Cu/ni	2.83g	Canb	2	4	Bag	–	5	–
2004	OFF METAL	6,500	Silver	3.24g	Proof. Part of 6 coin boxed set				–	–	45
2005 a	CIRC	194,300,000	Cu/ni	2.83g	Canb	2	4	Bag	–	–	25
2005	OFF METAL	6,200	Silver	3.24g	Proof. Part of 6 coin boxed set				–	–	45
2005	OFF METAL	650/ 629	Gold	6.03g	Proof. Part of 6 coin boxed set				–	–	595
2006 a/e	CIRC	306,528,000	Cu/ni	2.83g	Canb	2	4	Bag	–	–	25
2006	OFF METAL	5,829	Silver	3.24g	Proof. A. Machin obv. 8 coin set				–	–	45
2006	OFF METAL	300	Gold	6.03g	Proof. Rank Broadley. 8 coin set				–	–	595
2007	CIRC	59,036,000	Cu/ni	2.83g	Canb	2	4	Bag	–	5	–
2007	OFF METAL	3,475	Silver	3.24g	Proof. Part of 6 coin boxed set				–	–	55
2007	OFF METAL	300	Gold	6.03g	Proof. Part of 6 coin boxed set				–	–	595
2008 d/e	CIRC	200,022,000	Cu/ni	2.83g	Canb	1	3	Bag	–	–	25
2008	OFF METAL	2,600	Silver	3.24g	Proof. Part of 6 coin boxed set				–	–	55
2008	OFF METAL	1,000	Silver	3.24g	Proof. Part of Berlin Expo set				–	–	45
2009 e	CIRC	83,900,000	Cu/ni	2.83g	Canb	2	4	Bag	–	–	25
2009	OFF METAL	2,221	Silver	3.24g	Proof. Part of 6 coin boxed set				–	–	45
2010	CIRC	55,100,000	Cu/ni	2.83g	Canb	2	4	Bag	–	–	25
2010	OFF METAL	2,040	Silver	3.24g	Proof. Part of 6 coin boxed set				–	–	45
2010	OFF METAL	450	Gold	6.03g	Proof. V. Gottwald. 6 coin set				–	–	55
2011	CIRC	44,836,000	Cu/ni	2.83g	Canb	2	4	Bag	–	–	25
2011	OFF METAL	2,072	Silver	3.24g	Proof. Part of 6 coin boxed set				–	–	45
2012	CIRC	68,700,000	Cu/ni	2.83g	Canb	2	4	Bag	–	5	–
2012	OFF METAL	1,400	Silver	3.24g	Proof. Part of 6 coin boxed set				–	–	45
2012	OFF METAL	2,000	Gold	0.5g	Proof. Tiny copies of all 8 coins				–	–	60
2013	CIRC	78,700,000	Cu/ni	2.83g	Canb	2	4	Bag	–	–	25
2013	OFF METAL	1,000	Silver	3.24g	Proof. Individuallly cased coin				35	–	40
2013	OFF METAL	2,000	Silver	3.24g	Proof. Part of 6 coin boxed set				–	–	35
2013	OFF METAL	500	Gold	6.03g	Proof. Individually cased coin				595	–	595
2013	OFF METAL	500	Gold	6.03g	Proof. Part of 6 coin boxed set				–	–	595
2014	CIRC	52,800,000	Cu/ni	2.83g	Canb	2	5	Bag	–	–	25
2014	OFF METAL	1,000	Silver	3.24g	Proof. Individually cased coin				35	–	40
2014	OFF METAL	500	Silver	3.24g	Proof. Part of 6 coin boxed set				–	–	35
2014	OFF METAL	500	Gold	6.03g	Proof. Individually cased coin				595	–	595
2014	OFF METAL	100	Gold	6.03g	Proof. Part of 6 coin boxed set				–	–	595
2015	CIRC	21,200,000	Cu/ni	2.83g	Canb	2	5	Bag	–	–	25
2015	OFF METAL	1,000	Silver	3.24g	Proof. Individually cased coin				45	–	45
2015	OFF METAL	800	Silver	3.24g	Proof. Part of 6 coin boxed set				–	–	35
2015	OFF METAL	500	Gold	6.03g	Proof. Individually cased coin				650	–	650
2015	OFF METAL	50	Gold	6.13g	Proof. Part of 6 coin boxed set				–	–	595
2016	CIRC	n/a	Cu/ni	2.83g	Canb	2	5	Bag	–	–	25
2016	OFF METAL	1,966	Silver	3.24g	Proof. Part of 50th anniv. 1¢-50¢ set				–	–	60
2016	OFF METAL	100	Gold	6.03g	Proof. Part of 50th anniv. 1¢-50¢ set				–	–	650

(a) Both normal and small sized "SD" (Stuart Devlin initals) can be found on rev.
(b) Two distinct obverse dies used for this issue. One is a Large Head type with designer's initials "IRB" spaced. The Smaller Head type shows the "IR" spaced but the "RB" joined :- as "I RB." Both found in Mint and Proof sets.
(c) Smaller Head with "IRB" joined used from 2002 onwards.
(d) New reverse die made in April 2007 that features a tiny sized SD. Wayne Roberts suggests that the new die was used for a small run of circulation coins in May 2007 with the majority of the issue featuring the usual large and small SD die types.
(e) New tiny SD reverse type found on circulation, mint set and proof issues with some set issues also having the old normal or medium SD die type. It is expected the tiny SD type will become the standard as the older dies are used up. There is a new obverse die type also with thicker text, blunted 2 and more elliptical zeros in date.

TEN CENTS

FIRST PORTRAIT TYPE: 1966 - 1984

CUPRO NICKEL

75% Copper; 25% Nickel
Edge Reeded. Size 23.60 mm

Obverse : Arnold Machin.
Reverse : Stuart Devlin. Lyrebird

CIRCULATION & NON CIRCULATION (NCLT) ISSUES

Date	TYPE	Mintage Figures	Issuing Mint	Mint Mark	Metal Comp.	Weight in gms	Unc	Choice Unc	Roll or Bagged	Issue Price	Mint Retail	Proof Retail
1966	CIRC	10,940,000	Canb	4 spikes	Cu/ni	5.66g	8	12	250	–	30	45
1966	CIRC	30,000,000	London	5 spikes	Cu/ni	5.66g	7	10	Bag	–	–	–
1967	CIRC	51,032,000	Canb	None	Cu/ni	5.66g	10	14	200	–	30	–
1968	CIRC	57,206,000	Canb	None	Cu/ni	5.66g	14	20	300	–	30	–
1969	CIRC	22,234,000	Canb	None	Cu/ni	5.66g	9	15	395	–	20	35
1970	CIRC	22,306,000	Canb	None	Cu/ni	5.66g	7	11	120	–	15	70
1971	CIRC	20,726,000	Canb	None	Cu/ni	5.66g	11	17	250	–	20	35
1972	CIRC	12,502,000	Canb	None	Cu/ni	5.66g	20	30	400	–	20	35
1973	CIRC	27,320,000	Canb	None	Cu/ni	5.66g	8	11	150	–	20	35
1974	CIRC	46,550,000	Canb	None	Cu/ni	5.66g	7	9	195	–	15	25
1975	CIRC	50,900,000	Canb	None	Cu/ni	5.66g	3	5	125	–	5	10
1976	CIRC	57,060,000	Canb	None	Cu/ni	5.66g	3	5	70	–	7	12
1977	CIRC	10,940,000	Canb	None	Cu/ni	5.66g	3	5	55	–	4	10
1978	CIRC	48,400,000	Canb	None	Cu/ni	5.66g	3	5	65	–	4	10
1979	CIRC	36,950,000	Canb	None	Cu/ni	5.66g	2	4	45	–	4	19
1980	CIRC	55,084,000	Canb	None	Cu/ni	5.66g	2	4	45	–	4	10
1981	CIRC	76,060,000	Canb	None	Cu/ni	5.66g	2	4	35	–	4	10
1981 a	CIRC	40,000,000	Wales	None	Cu/ni	5.66g	2	4	20	–	–	–
1982	CIRC	61,492,000	Canb	None	Cu/ni	5.66g	2	4	35	–	4	10
1983	CIRC	82,318,000	Canb	None	Cu/ni	5.66g	2	4	40	–	4	10
1984	CIRC	25,728,000	Canb	None	Cu/ni	5.66g	2	4	30	–	4	10

1966 TEN CENT MINTMARK POSITION

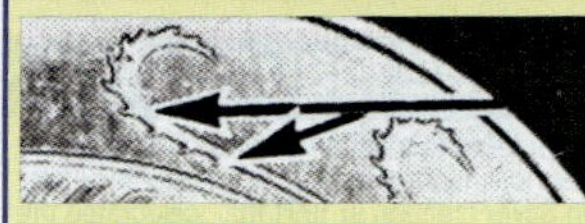

CANBERRA MINT : 4 spikes

LONDON MINT : 5 spikes

[a] Obverse text is closer to the rim than on 1981 Canberra issues.

RETRO ISSUES & UNIQUE DESIGNS

Date	Type	Mintage	Metal	Weight	Description	Issue	Value
2006 b	RESTRIKE	5,829	Silver	3.24 g	Only available as part of 8 coin set	–	45
2016 c	MINT ROLL	5,000	Ci/ni	2.83 g	Commemorative roll. 20 x Unc coins	10	15
2016 c	EX-SET	84,207	Ci/ni	2.83 g	Specimen. Part of 6 coin mint set	–	4
2016 c	EX-SET	n/a	Ci/ni	2.83 g	Proof. Part of 6 coin proof set	–	15

TEN CENTS

SECOND PORTRAIT TYPE

ELIZABETH II

1985 - 1998

CUPRO NICKEL

75% Copper; 25% Nickel
Edge Reeded. Size 23.60 mm

Obverse : Ian Rank-Broadley. **Reverse** : Stuart Devlin. Lyrebird

CIRCULATION & NON CIRCULATION (NCLT) ISSUES

All mint and proof coins shown in extreme right column have been broken out of sets

Date	TYPE	Mintage Figures	Metal Comp	Weight in gms	Issuing Mint	Unc	Choice Unc	Roll or Bagged	Issue Price	Mint set Retail	Proof Retail
1985	CIRC	2,100,000	Cu/ni	5.66g	Canb	9	15	60	–	–	10
1986	EX-SET	180,000	Cu/ni	5.66g	Circ coin unique to mint set				–	10	16
1987	EX-SET	200,000	Cu/ni	5.66g	Circ coin unique to mint set				–	10	15
1988	CIRC	48,083,500	Cu/ni	5.66g	Canb	2	6	25	–	–	10
1989	CIRC	43,510,300	Cu/ni	5.66g	Canb	2	6	20	–	–	10
1990	CIRC	25,038,000	Cu/ni	5.66g	Canb	5	10	Bag	–	–	20
1991	CIRC	4,800,000	Cu/ni	5.66g	Canb	6	12	Bag	–	5	25
1991	OFF METAL	25,000	Silver	6.52g	Proof M'pieces.925 Stg. 28.5mm				–	–	20
1992	CIRC	46,739,500	Cu/ni	5.66g	Canb	5	9	Bag	–	–	15
1993	CIRC	23,093,300	Cu/ni	5.66g	Canb	4	9	Bag	–	–	15
1994	CIRC	43,726,000	Cu/ni	5.66g	Canb	4	9	Bag	–	–	10
1995	EX-SET	71,546	Cu/ni	5.66g	Circ coin unique to mint set				–	15	20
1996	EX-SET	108,773	Cu/ni	5.66g	Circ coin unique to mint set				–	15	20
1997	CIRC	5,699,000	Cu/ni	5.66g	Canb	6	12	Bag	–	–	20
1998	CIRC	47,989,000	Cu/ni	5.66g	Canb	3	7	Bag	–	15	15

Unless stated these mintage figures only refer to general circulation coins. Coins also released in mint sets, baby sets etc have to be added to determine a final total. Off metal issues (such as gold and silver releases) are listed separately. These figures also do not include the Wedding Set which are semi polished specimens.

OFF METAL & UNIQUE ISSUES

For many years, the five and ten cent pieces were there to make up the numbers with the standard cupro nickel alloy being issued in the annual mint and proof sets. A sterling silver [92.5% pure] coin was part of a Masterpieces in Silver creation in 1991 that celebrated the 25th anniversary of the opening of the RAM. It was to be another decade before another off-metal set was issued. This time it was a pure gold ten cent coin that was part of a spectacular six coin set produced to celebrate the centenary of Federation. As you can see from the images below, the list has expanded quite considerably in recent years.

1991 Silver Masterpieces

2001 Gold Federation set

2005 End WW2 Silver set

2005 End WW2 Gold

2006 Silver Masterpieces

2006 Gold Decimal 40th

2007 Gold Life Saving

2010 Gold Gottwald Obv

TEN CENTS

THIRD PORTRAIT TYPE

ELIZABETH II

1998 -

CUPRO NICKEL
75% Copper; 25% Nickel
Edge Reeded. Size 23.60mm
Obverse : Ian Rank Broadley.
Reverse : Stuart Devlin. Lyrebird

Date	TYPE	Mintage Figures	Metal Comp.	Weight in gms	Issuing Mint	Unc	Choice Unc	Roll or Bagged	Issue Price	Mint set Retail	Proof Retail
1998 a	OFF METAL	25,000	Silver	6.57g	Proof. M'pieces in silver .925 Stg				–	–	45
1998	CIRC	47,989,000	Cu/ni	5.66g	Canb	3	5	Bag	–	–	15
1999 b	CIRC	97,016,000	Cu/ni	5.66g	Canb	5	9	25	–	–	15
2000 c	CIRC	51,117,000	Cu/ni	5.66g	Canb	5	9	25	–	–	15
2001c/d	CIRC	109,357,000	Cu/ni	5.66g	Canb	3	5	18	–	–	15
2001	OFF METAL	650/ 193	Gold	12.14g	Proof. Part of 6 coin boxed set				–	–	1,195
2002 e	CIRC	70,329,000	Cu/ni	5.66g	Canb	4	7	18	–	–	5
2003 f	CIRC	53,636,000	Cu/ni	5.66g	Canb	3	6	25	–	–	5
2003	OFF METAL	6,500	Silver	6.57g	Proof. Part of 6 coin boxed set				–	–	45
2004 f	CIRC	89,141,000	Cu/ni	5.66g	Canb	3	6	20	–	–	5
2004	OFF METAL	6,500	Silver	6.57g	Proof. Part of 6 coin boxed set				–	–	45
2005 d/f	CIRC	99,976,000	Cu/ni	5.66g	Canb	3	6	20	–	–	5
2005	OFF METAL	6,200	Silver	6.57g	Proof. Part of 6 coin boxed set				–	–	45
2005	OFF METAL	650/ 629	Gold	12.14g	Proof. Part of 6 coin boxed set				–	–	1,195
2006 d	CIRC	157,078,000	Cu/ni	5.66g	Canb	2	4	n/a	–	–	30
2006	OFF METAL	5,829	Silver	6.57g	Proof. A. Machin obv. 8 coin set				–	–	45
2006	OFF METAL	300	Gold	12.14g	Proof. Rank Broadley. 8 coin set				–	–	2,100
2007 d/f	CIRC	61,096,000	Cu/ni	5.66g	Canb	2	4	tba	–	–	50
2007	OFF METAL	3,475	Silver	6.57g	Proof. Part of 6 coin boxed set				–	–	45
2007	OFF METAL	300	Gold	12.14g	Proof. Part of 6 coin boxed set				–	–	1,195
2008 f	CIRC	136,037,500	Cu/ni	5.66g	Canb	2	4	tba	–	–	n/a
2008	OFF METAL	2,600	Silver	6.57g	Proof. Part of 6 coin boxed set				–	–	45
2008	OFF METAL	1,000	Silver	6.57g	Proof. Berlin Money Show set				–	–	45
2009	CIRC	25,235,000	Cu/ni	5.66g	Canb	3	5	tba	–	–	45
2009	OFF METAL	2,221	Silver	6.57g	Proof. A. Machin obv. 8 coin set				–	–	45
2010	CIRC	104,943,000	Cu/ni	5.66g	Canb	2	4	tba	–	–	45
2010	OFF METAL	2,040	Silver	6.57g	Proof. Part of 6 coin boxed set				–	–	45
2010	OFF METAL	500	Gold	12.14 g	Proof. V. Gottwald Obv. 6 coin set				–	–	65
2011	CIRC	1,750,000	Cu/ni	5.66g	Canb	8	12	tba	–	–	45
2011	OFF METAL	2,072	Silver	6.57g	Proof. Part of 6 coin boxed set				–	–	45
2012	CIRC	53,900,000	Cu/ni	5.66g	Canb	3	5	tba	–	–	45
2012	OFF METAL	1,400	Silver	6.57g	Proof. Part of 6 coin boxed set				–	–	45
2012	OFF METAL	2,000	Gold	0.5g	Proof. Tiny copies of all 8 coins				–	–	60
2013	CIRC	49,200,00	Cu/ni	5.66g	Canb	2	5	Bag	–	–	40
2013	OFF METAL	1,000	Silver	6.57g	Proof. Part of 6 coin boxed set				–	–	45
2013	OFF METAL	500	Gold	12.14g	Proof. Individually cased coin				195	–	195
2014	CIRC	60,700,000	Cu/ni	5.66g	Canb	2	5	Bag`	–	–	20
2014	OFF METAL	1,000	Silver	6.57g	Proof. Individually cased coin				65	–	65
2014	OFF METAL	1,000	Silver	6.57g	Proof. Part of 6 coin boxed set				–	–	65
2014	OFF METAL	500	Gold	12.14g	Proof. Individually cased coin				1,195	–	1,195
2014	OFF METAL	100	Gold	12.14g	Proof. Part of 6 coin boxed set				–	–	1,195
2015	CIRC	14,300,000	Cu/ni	5.66g	Canb	2	5	Bag	–	–	20
2015	OFF METAL	1,000	Silver	6.57g	Proof. Individually cased coin				50	–	50
2015	OFF METAL	800	Silver	6.57g	Proof. Part of 6 coin boxed set				–	–	65
2015	OFF METAL	100	Gold	12.54g	Proof. Individually cased coin				1,250	–	1,250
2015	OFF METAL	50	Gold	12.54g	Proof. Part of 6 coin boxed set				–	–	595
2016	CIRC	tba	Cu/ni	5.66g	Canb	2	5	Bag`	–	–	20
2015	OFF METAL	800	Silver	6.57g	Proof. Part of 6 coin boxed set				–	–	65

[a] Two obverse die varieties. Can be identified by measuring the distance of the lettering in the legend from the rim of the coin. This type shows lettering far from rim. Initials "IRB" spaced.
[b] Reader Jerry Himelfarb reports that he has discovered a 1999 Large Head 10 cent coin. Most are Small Head. Jerry said the coin had been authenticated and graded by PCGS.
[c] Text style different to 1999 issue. Lettering close to rim. IRB spaced.
[d] Two obverse varieties. Large Head / IRB spaced and Smaller Head with initials IRB. showing "IR" spaced and "RB" joined. Text style is different to 1999 and 2000.
[e] From 2002 obverse has smaller head and IRB joined.
[f] Another obverse die features a longer and thicker text with a blunted "2" and elliptical zeros.

TWENTY CENTS

FIRST PORTRAIT

TYPE: 1966 - 1984

CUPRO NICKEL

75% Copper;
25% Nickel
Size 28.52 mm

Obverse : Arnold Machin.
Reverse : Stuart Devlin. Platypus.

Date	TYPE	Mintage Figures	Issuing Mint	MInt Mark	Metal Comp.	Weight in gms	Unc	Choice Unc	Roll or Bagged	Issue Price	Mint Retail	Proof Retail
1966 a	CIRC	28,223,000	Canb	Swirl gap/ head		11.31g	20	35	160	–	–	30
1966 b	CIRC	30,000,000	London	No gap/ head		11.31g	40	50	Bag	–	–	30
1966 c	CIRC	Inc in above	London	Wavy 2 line		11.31g	4,000		Inc	–	–	–
1967	CIRC	83,848,000	Canb	None	Cu/ni	11.31g	35	45	380	–	–	35
1968	CIRC	40,537,000	Canb	None	Cu/ni	11.31g	60	70	n/a	–	–	60
1969	CIRC	16,520,000	Canb	None	Cu/ni	11.31g	35	45	525	–	–	45
1970	CIRC	23,721,000	Canb	None	Cu/ni	11.31g	16	25	395	–	–	40
1971	CIRC	8,947,000	Canb	None	Cu/ni	11.31g	60	95	525	–	–	45
1972	CIRC	16,643,000	Canb	None	Cu/ni	11.31g	20	30	300	–	–	40
1973	CIRC	23,356,000	Canb	None	Cu/ni	11.31g	16	25	230	–	–	40
1974	CIRC	33,548,000	Canb	None	Cu/ni	11.31g	20	25	395	–	–	30
1975	CIRC	53,300,000	Canb	None	Cu/ni	11.31g	6	10	145	–	–	20
1976	CIRC	59,774,000	Canb	None	Cu/ni	11.31g	5	9	85	–	–	20
1977	CIRC	41,272,000	Canb	None	Cu/ni	11.31g	4	6	25	–	–	20
1978	CIRC	37,432,000	Canb	None	Cu/ni	11.31g	2	4	75	–	–	20
1979	CIRC	22,300,000	Canb	None	Cu/ni	11.31g	3	5	65	–	–	20
1980	CIRC	84,357,000	Canb	None	Cu/ni	11.31g	5	9	45	–	–	15
1981	CIRC	65,280,000	Canb	None	Cu/ni	11.31g	5	9	55	–	–	15
1981d/1	CIRC	65,503,000	Wales	None	Cu/ni	11.31g	2	4	Bag	–	–	–
1981d/ 2,3	CIRC	50,000,000	Canada	3.5 claws variety		11.31g	325	550	Bag?	–	–	–
1982	CIRC	76,604,000	Canb	None	Cu/ni	11.31g	5	9	55	–	–	15
1983 e	CIRC	55,113,000	Canb	None	Cu/ni	11.31g	25	40	350	–	–	15
1984 e	CIRC	27,820,000	Canb	None	Cu/ni	11.31g	30	45	375	–	–	15

[a] Canberra Mint. Gap between head of platypus and final point of water ripple.
[b] London Mint. No gap. Tip of water touches platypus's head. Variety common to the mint set.
[c] A small number of London minted 20¢ coins of 1966 display a curious die variety where the top of the baseline of the numeral "2" has a raised or wavy relief rather than a straight surface.
[d/1) No gap. Four claws under 2, large open nostrils. On the obverse, text is rounded and the Queen has strong eyebrow hair lines on unc coin. Coins found in RAM rolls and Mint Sets. On a small number of coins, a dot cud appears above the R in AUSTRALIA. Unc examples sell for around $85.
[d/2] Royal Mint, Llantrisant, Wales. It is possible the London reverse dies were used. Platypus features small nostrils. While most coins have Four Claws, some have a tapering first claw that may appear as half a claw . Some coins may have a die chip to right of O of 20. On the obverse the legend text is rounded and Queen has a weak to no eyebrow hair lines. Coins found in RBA rolls.
[d/3] Royal Canadian Mint, Winnipeg reverse die - Three and Half Claws under 2 with first claw a blunted half claw. Platypus has large open nostrils. On obverse, text is flat, bases are curved on some letters. Queen has strong eyebrow hair lines.
[e] Whilst many millions of twenty cent coins were minted in 1983 and 1984 almost the entire production was later melted down and exported as base metal cupro-nickel bars due to lack of demand. Only one x $200 uncirculated mint roll box of each year has surfaced to date.

RETRO ISSUES & UNIQUE DESIGNS

These special NCLT issues are priced towards the end of the twenty cent section

Date	Type	Mintage	Metal	Weight	Description	Issue	Value
2006 a	RESTRIKE	5,829	Silver	3.24 g	Only available as part of 8 coin set	–	45
2016 b	MINT ROLL	5,000	Ci/ni	2.83 g	Commemorative roll. 20 x Unc coins	10	15
2016 b	EX-SET	n/a	Ci/ni	2.83 g	Specimen. Part of annual 6 coin mint set	–	4
2016 b	EX-SET	n/a	Ci/ni	2.83 g	Proof. Part of annual 6 coin proof set	–	15

1966 ROYAL MINT LONDON PROOF

Although the Royal Mint in London supplied over 30 million 20¢ coins in 1966, this is the only proof available to collectors. The coin was offered for sale as lot 1523 at the Noble Numismatic auction held in Sydney in April 2014. Accompanying the coin was a Royal Australian Mint letter of authenticity, signed R.Gardiner, 19 November 1990 which mentions this coin, matches that held in the Mint Museum in Canberra. Included in the lot is a Canberra Mint proof for comparison, showing two eyelashes instead of one on the London die. The coin was estimated at $50,000 but was passed in.

1966 "WAVY LINE" BASELINE

Raised section on top of horizontal bar on base of "2". Struck at the Royal Mint,UK. A normal version is worth around $900 in Extra Fine grade; $1500 in Uncirculated condition and $2750 in Choice Uncirculated condition.

1966 TWENTY CENT MINTMARK POSITION

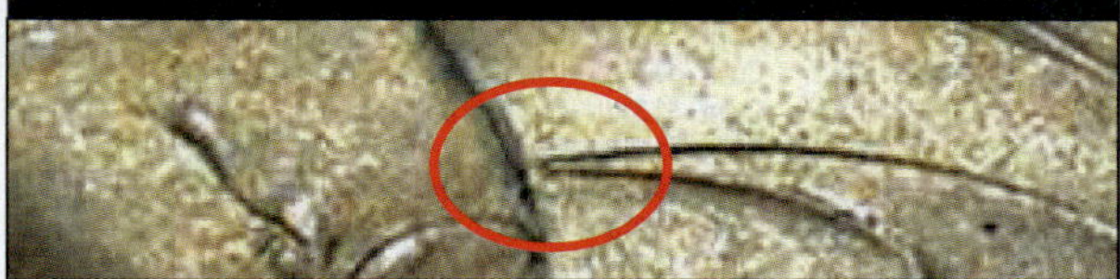

CANBERRA MINT : Gap [Shown above] LONDON MINT : No gap

1978 AUSTRALIA - FIJIAN MULE

Australian obverse with Fijian 20¢ reverse featuring an Abua on a Braided Sennit Cord. Opinions are divided as to whether this curious mule was a genuine error or a bit of sport in the mint's production department. *(There seems to be a lot of spectacular errors from the same era).* It certainly wasn't a concern for collectors attending Noble's Sale 108 in March 2015. Listed as lot 74, this coin was sold for an astonishing $18,000 plus 19.5% commission against an estimate of $3,000.

1981 "SCALLOPED" VARIETY

Struck accidentally on a Hong Kong Two Dollar planchet at the Royal Mint in Llantrisant, Wales. This mint also struck coins for the former British colony. Around six examples have surfaced to date.

THE CURRENT VALUE OF AN EXTREMELY FINE EXAMPLE WOULD BE — $7,500

TWENTY CENTS

SECOND PORTRAIT TYPE

ELIZABETH II

1985 - 1998

CUPRO NICKEL
75% Copper; 25% Nickel
Size 28.52 mm

Obverse : Raphael Maklouf
Reverse : Stuart Devlin. Platypus

CIRCULATION & NON CIRCULATION (NCLT) ISSUES

Date	TYPE	Mintage Figures	Metal Comp.	Weight in gms	Issuing Mint	Unc	Choice Unc	Roll or Bagged	Issue Price	Mint set Retail	Proof Retail
1985	CIRC	2,700,000	Cu/ni	11.31g	Canb	25	35	60	–	–	30
1986	EX-SET	180,000	Cu/ni	11.31g	Circ coin unique to annual mint set				–	12	25
1987	EX-SET	200,000	Cu/ni	11.31g	Circ coin unique to annual mint set				–	11	25
1988 a	CIRC	174,000	Cu/ni	11.31g	Canb	*Not seen*	*Not seen*	*n/a*	–	–	40
1989	EX-SET	150,602	Cu/ni	11.31g	Circ coin unique to annual mint set				–	20	25
1990	EX-SET	103,766	Cu/ni	11.31g	Circ coin unique to annual mint set				–	20	25
1991	EX-SET	169,557	Cu/ni	11.31g	Circ coin unique to annual mint set				–	20	25
1991	OFF METAL	25,000	Silver	13.09g	Proof M'pieces .925 Stg. 28.56mm				–	–	19
1992	EX-SET	118,145	Cu/ni	11.31g	Circ coin unique to annual mint set				–	20	25
1993 b	CIRC	1,490,000 ?	Cu/ni	11.31g	Canb	*Not seen*	*Not seen*	*n/a*	–	–	40
1993	EX-SET	40,255	Cu/ni	11.31g	Circ coin unique to annual mint set				–	25	25
1994	CIRC	14,300,000	Cu/ni	11.31g	Canb	12	20	Bag	–	–	20
1995 c	EX-SET	96,079	Cu/ni	11.31g	Circ coin unique to annual mint set				–	20	25
1996	CIRC	20,595,500	Cu/ni	11.31g	Canb	5	10	Bag	–	–	20
1997	CIRC	16,725,000	Cu/ni	11.31g	Canb	6	25	Bag	–	–	20
1998 d	CIRC	28,831,000	Cu/ni	11.31g	Canb	5	10	Bag	–	–	20

[a] RAM Reports show 174,000 coins were minted for circulation. It is generally thought that those listed were actually of a different date or melted down at a later date. To date, only coins in mint and proof sets are known.
[b] No 1993 twenty cent coins were minted for circulation but the 1993-1994 Annual Report indicates that 1,498,500 coins with pre-1987 dates were issued. These were most likely previously dated coins already on hand at the RAM. Platypus 1993 coins are only available from broken up mint sets.
[c] No circulation platypus 20 cent coins were minted.
[d] The 1998 unc 20¢ coin has the above Raphael Maklouf obverse while the 1998 20¢ in the Masterpieces in Silver set has the Ian Rank-Broadley obverse.

The physical size of the twenty cent piece and the clean uncluttered lines of Stuart Devlin's timeless platypus design combine to give the space for some dramatic effects. The two coins above are among the best of the best. The coloured coin on the left was unique to the 2013 mint set while the superb gold enriched proof coin at right was also a unique coin for that set.

1981 20¢ CANADIAN 3.5 CLAWS MINTMARK

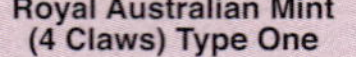
Royal Australian Mint
(4 Claws) Type One

Royal Canadian Mint
(3.5 Claws) Type Two

TWENTY CENTS

THIRD PORTRAIT TYPE

ELIZABETH II

1998 -

CUPRO NICKEL

75% Copper; 25% Nickel
Size 28.52 mm

Obverse : Ian Rank Broadley
Reverse : Stuart Devlin. Platypus

Date	TYPE	Mintage Figures	Metal Comp.	Weight in gms	Issuing Mint	Unc	Choice Unc	Roll or Bagged	Issue Price	Mint set Retail	Proof Retail
1998 a	OFF METAL	25,000	Silver	6.57g	Proof M'pieces in silver .925 Stg				–	–	30
1999	CIRC	64,181,000	Cu/ni	11.31g	Canb	7	12	55	–	–	25
2000	CIRC	35,584,000	Cu/ni	11.31g	Canb	9	16	Bag	–	–	40
2001 b	CIRC	81,967,000	Cu/ni	11.31g	Canb	5	10	25	–	–	40
2001	OFF METAL	650/ 193	Gold	24.36g	Proof. Part of 6 coin boxed set					–	1,650
2002c	CIRC	27,224,000	Cu/ni	11.31g	Canb	5	10	Bag	–	–	20
2004d/e	CIRC	71,609,000	Cu/ni	11.31g	Canb	8	10	Bag	–	–	10
2004 e	VARIETY	400,000	Cu/ni	11.31g	Two types of obverse dies				–	–	10
2004	OFF METAL	6,500	Silver	13.36g	Proof. Part of 6 coin boxed set				–	–	65
2005 f	CIRC	44,600,000	Cu/ni	11.31g	Canb	7	12	Bag	–	–	15
2006	CIRC	102,462,000	Cu/ni	11.31g	Canb	3	7	20	–	–	15
2006	OFF METAL	5,829	Silver	13.36g	Proof. A. Machin obv. 8 coin set				–	–	65
2006 g	OFF METAL	300	Gold	24.36g	Proof. Broadley. 8 coin set				1,650	–	1,650
2007 h	CIRC	42,712,000	Cu/ni	11.31g	Canb	3	7	Bag	–	–	20
2008 i	CIRC	132,870,000	Cu/ni	11.31g	Canb	3	6	Bag	–	–	15
2009	CIRC	49,563,000	Cu/ni	11.31g	Canb	3	6	Bag	–	–	18
2009	OFF METAL	2,221	Silver	13.36g	Proof. Part of 6 coin boxed set				–	–	65
2010	CIRC	59,897,000	Cu/ni	11.31g	Canb	3	6	Bag	–	–	150
2010	OFF METAL	2,040	Silver	13.36g	Proof. Part of 6 coin boxed set				–	–	65
2010	OFF METAL	450	Gold	24.36g	Proof. V. Gottwald. 6 coin set				–	–	55
2011	CIRC	11,575,000	Cu/ni	11.31g	Canb	2	5	Bag	–	–	15
2011	OFF METAL	2,072	Silver	13.36g	Proof. Part of 6 coin boxed set				–	–	65
2012	CIRC	3,600,000	Cu/ni	11.31g	Canb	2	5	Bag	–	–	15
2012	OFF METAL	1,400	Silver	13.36g	Proof. Individually cased coin				55	–	65
2012	OFF METAL	2,000	Gold	0.5g	Proof. Tiny copies all 8 coins				–	–	60
2013	CIRC	43,900,000	Cu/ni	11.31g	Canb	2	5	Bag	–	–	40
2013	EX-MINT	100,000	Cu/ni	11.31g	Coloured 20¢ part of mint set				–	35	–
2013	FAIR SET	1,000	Cu/ni	11.31g	Berlin Money Fair . In mint set				–	15	–
2013	NCLT	50,000	Cu/ni	11.31g	Proof. Unique to set. Gilt rev				–	–	30
2013	OFF METAL	1,000	Silver	13.36g	Proof. Individually cased coin				65	–	65
2013	OFF METAL	2,000	Silver	13.36g	Proof. Part of 6 coin boxed set				–	–	65
2013	OFF METAL	500	Gold	24.36g	Proof. Individually cased coin				1,795	–	1,795
2013	OFF METAL	500	Gold	24.36g	Proof. Part of 6 coin boxed set				–	–	1,795
2014	CIRC	52,300,000	Cu/ni	11.31g	Canb	2	5	Bag	–	–	40
2014	OFF METAL	1,000	Silver	13.36g	Proof. Individually cased coin				65	–	40
2014	OFF METAL	500	Silver	13.36g	Proof. Part of 6 coin boxed set				–		35
2014	OFF METAL	500	Gold	24.36g	Proof. Individually cased coin				1,795	–	1,995
2014	OFF METAL	100	Gold	24.36g	Proof. Part of 6 coin boxed set				–	–	1,795
2015	CIRC	24,400,000	Cu/ni	11.31g	Canb	2	5	Bag	–	–	40
2015	OFF METAL	1,000	Silver	13.36g	Proof. Individually cased coin				65	–	65
2015	OFF METAL	800	Silver	13.36g	Proof. Part of 6 coin boxed set				–	–	65
2015	OFF METAL	500	Gold	24.36g	Proof. Individually cased coin				2,150	–	2,150
2015	OFF METAL	50	Gold	24.36g	Proof. Part of 6 coin boxed set				–	–	2,150
2016	OFF METAL	1,966	Silver	13.36g	Proof. Part of 50th anniv. 1¢-50¢ set					–	n/a
2016	OFF METAL	100	Gold	24.36g	Proof. Part of 50th anniv. 1¢-50¢ set					–	n/a

(a) The 1998 20 cents circulation Mint and Proof sets feature the now obsolete Raphael Maklouf effigy of the Queen while the silver proof 20 cents in the 1998 Masterpieces in Silver Set has the new Ian Rank-Broadley effigy obverse.
(b) Three obverse die varieties - IRB spaced, IR spaced with RB joined and IRB joined. All found in circulation and sets. Spaced variety more common in sets while joined common in circulation. These obverse types can also be found paired with small designer initials "SD" or large "SD" reverse types, the latter large "SD" reverse being most common.
(c) Circulation & mint set issues have "IRB" joined obverse and large "SD" reverse. The 2002 proof set, coins have "IRB" joined obverse and small "SD" reverse.

FOOTNOTES CONTINUED ON NEXT PAGE

2004 LARGE HEAD - SMALL HEAD OBVERSES

The Royal Australian Mint is regarded world-wide as producing among the highest quality collector coins available. In 2004 the mint updated some of its traditional coining machinery with computerised engraving machines and laser scanning technology. To overcome some technical difficulties with dies made out of conventional master tooling during the production of 2004 dated coins, a decision was made to make use of the newly acquired technology. During this technological transition, some design parameters of the new master tooling differed slightly from the original. This resulted in the production of an obverse design that was slightly smaller in size than the original and the font style of the legend was computer generated rather than the hand-cut style. The introduction of the small head obverse occurred after production of both NCLT and circulation coins was well underway. Only the 20¢ and 50¢ issues were affected. The former Controller of the RAM , Vivienne Thom gave a breakdown of the approximate ratio of coins between the two obverse dies. Since then, the following information has been supplied by researcher, Wayne Roberts. He said that both Small and Large 2006 50 cent pieces have been sighted in Uncirculated, Mint and Baby mint sets. Both 50 cent varieties can be found in Silver Proof Year sets with Large Head 20 cent. Most have either small SD or large SD reverse varieties.

2005 PEACE 20¢ WITH PLATYPUS REVERSE

This spectacular error was discovered by an Adelaide collector who bought the set on eBay from a Brisbane collector. The 2005 proof set actually included a 2005 proof 20 cent piece that showed the standard platypus reverse. Apart from this very rare proof set no other combination of this rare mule has appeared to date. Last sale was in 2007 for $3,995.

Current Value $6,000

2001 RARE BIMETAL TWENTY CENT COIN

(a) The above sensational (and possibly unique) bimetal twenty cent piece appeared as lot 323 in Downies Sale 295 held in July 2007. The description read :- "Twenty Cents 2001 bimetal striking, removed from Armaguard security roll and retained by the current purchaser until now. Choice and very rare". It sold for $3600 plus commission against an estimate of $3,500. Further research suggests the planchet has no connection with the Australian market. The weight of this bimetal piece is 10.66 grams. The weight of a normal cupro-nickel Australian 20 cent coin is 11.31 grams. Blanks for our coins are produced in Korea by a firm that produces planchets for many mints world-wide. It's possible that a blank meant for a foreign customer was accidentally mixed with an Australian order. A similar situation occurred in 1981 when a scalloped planchet intended to be struck as a Hong Kong $2 coin was struck as an Australian 20 cent piece.

Current Value (no recent sales) $8,750

FOOTNOTES CONTINUED FROM PREVIOUS PAGE

(d/e) Two obverse die varieties - (d) Large Head type with pointed "A" obverse text and (e) Small Head type with flat top "A" obverse text. Other differences exist. About 400,000 Large Head type went into circulation and is only found in Wedding Sets and Fine Silver Proof sets (Small Head type not sighted to date). Small Head common in circulation. Both types can be found in Mint, Baby and Proof sets. Proof and Silver sets can have small "SD" and large "SD" reverse types. All others have large "SD" type.
(f) Return to large head pointed "A" obverse with text style longer and finer with the zeros in date elliptical. No proof platypus reverse coins were issued in 2005.
(g) Text style thicker and zeros in date more elliptical . Proofs with Small & Large "SD" reverses.
(h) Two obverse 2007 die varieties known. The first is the thin '7' pointed '2' and thick '7' pointed '2'. The thick '7' type is scarcer. Small and Large 'SD' reverse in proof issues and also Unc 2004 10¢ and 50¢. Variations may exist with the 2007 5¢ coin and in the 2008 mint set 5¢.
(i) Has the blunted 2 text style obverse.

TWENTY CENTS

2001 FEDERATION STATE ISSUES

[a] New South Wales

[b] Aust. Capital Territory

[c] Queensland

[d] Victoria

[e] Norfolk Island

[f] Northern Territory

[g] Western Australia

[h] South Australia

[i] Tasmania

CIRCULATION & NON CIRCULATION (NCLT) ISSUES

Date	TYPE	Mintage Figures	Metal Comp.	Weight in gms	Unc	Choice Unc	Roll or Bagged	Proof Retail
2001 a	NSW	3,042,000	Cu/ni	11.31g	2	8	55	20
2001 b	ACT	2,000,000	Cu/ni	11.31g	6	10	60	20
2001 c	Queensland	2,320,000	Cu/ni	11.31g	6	10	60	20
2001 d	Victoria	2,000,010	Cu/ni	11.31g	6	10	60	20
2001 e	Norfolk Island	2,000,000	Cu/ni	11.31g	10	20	90	20
2001 f	Northern Territory	2,000,000	Cu/ni	11.31g	6	12	60	20
2001 g	West Australia	2,400,000	Cu/ni	11.31g	6	12	60	20
2001 h	South Australia	2,400,000	Cu/ni	11.31g	6	12	60	20
2001 i	Tasmania	2,160,006	Cu/ni	11.31g	8	15	60	20

VARIATIONS FOUND IN DESIGNER'S INITIALS

INITIALS "IRB" SPACED

INITIALS WITH "IRB" JOINED

Research continues on this aspect of collecting but it is obvious that a number of obverse designs can be identified by slight variations concerning the spacing of the designer's initials. These seem to be more common with the Ian Rank-Broadley issues which featured the "Mature obverse" of the Queen that was introduced from 1999. Variations (as researched by decimal researcher Wayne Roberts) are found in the footnotes under each denomination.

TWENTY CENTS

1995 [a] United Nations

2001 [b] Sir Donald

2003 [c] Volunteers

2005 [d] Coming Home

2007 [e] Life Saving

2008 [f] Planet Earth

2009 [g] Astronomy

2009 [h] Nursing

(a) 1995 UNITED NATIONS 50th ANNIVERSARY - CIRC

1995	CIRC	4,835,000	Cu/ni	11.31g	Canb	5	10	50	–	15	–
1998	RESTRIKE	25,000	Silver	13.36g	Proof M'pieces .925 Stg. 28.52mm				–	–	40

(b) 2001 SIR DONALD BRADMAN TRIBUTE - CIRC

2001	CIRC	10,000,000	Cu/ni	11.31g	Canb	5	10	30	–	25	–

(c) 2003 AUSTRALIAN VOLUNTEERS

2003	CIRC	7,574,000	Cu/ni	11.31g	Canb	3	6	20	–	–	–
2003	EX-SET	80,512	Cu/ni	11.31g	Unc part of annual mint set				–	6	–
2003	EX-SET	37,748	Cu/ni	11.31g	Unc part of Koala baby set				–	12	–
2003	EX-SET	39,090	Cu/ni	11.31g	Proof coin part of annual set				–	–	20
2003	EX-SET	14,799	Cu/ni	11.31g	Proof part of Koala baby set				–	–	12
2003	OFF METAL	6,500	Silver	13.36g	Proof part 99.9 fine 6 coin set				–	–	25

(d) 2005 "COMING HOME" WWII 60th ANNIVERSARY

2005	CIRC	32,057,000	Cu/ni	11.31g	Canb	5	10	30	–	–	–
2005	EX-SET	71,546	Cu/ni	11.31g	Circ part of annual mint set				–	12	–
2005	EX-SET	28,853	Cu/ni	11.31g	Circ part of Koala baby set				–	12	–
2005	EX-SET	3,627	Cu/ni	11.31g	Fr/unc Coin part of Wedding set				–	15	–
2005	EX-SET	33,520	Cu/ni	11.31g	Proof coin part of annual proof set				–	15	–
2005	OFF METAL	6,200	Silver	13.36g	Proof part of 99.9 fine 6 coin set				–	–	45
2005	OFF METAL	650/629	Gold	24.56g	Proof part of 99.99 fine 6 coin set				–		1,750

(e) 2007 SURF LIFESAVING

2007	EX-SET	66,641	Cu/ni	11.31g	Circ part of annual mint set				–	6	–
2007	FAIR ISSUE	1,500	Cu/ni	11.31g	Circ. 6 coin set. Berlin Money Show				–	12	–
2007	PNC	n/a	Cu/ni	11.31g	Coin & Stamp cover. Priced in PNC section						–
2007	OFF METAL	3,475	Silver	13.36g	Proof. 99.99 fine. Part of 6 coin set				–	–	45
2007	OFF METAL	300	Gold	24.36g	Proof. 99.99 fine. Part of 6 coin set				–		–1,750

(f) 2008 YEAR OF PLANET EARTH

2008	EX-SET	63,234	Cu/ni	11.31g	Circ part of annual mint set				–	6	–
2008	PART PAIR	11,500	Cu/ni	11.31g	Proof paired with Kangaroo $1				–	–	45
2008	OFF METAL	3,475	Silver	13.36g	Proof. 99.99 fine. Part of 6 coin set				–	–	45

(g) 2009 STAR-GAZERS YEAR OF ASTRONOMY

2009	EX-SET	63,652	Cu/ni	11.31g	Circ part of annual mint set				–	6	–
2009	FAIR ISSUE	1,500	Cu/ni	11.31g	Circ ANDA Melb Fair mint set				–	6	–
2009	FAIR ISSUE	1,500	Cu/ni	11.31g	Circ ANDA Sydney Fair mint set				–	6	–
2009	FAIR ISSUE	1,500	Cu/ni	11.31g	Circ ANDA Brisbane Fair mint set				–	6	–
2009	PART PAIR	25,114	Cu/ni	11.31g	Circ paired with $1 Astronomy				–	6	–
2009	PART PAIR	23,257	Cu/ni	11.31g	Proof paired with $1 Astronomy				–	–	20

(h) 2009 AUSTRALIAN SERVICE NURSES - Remembrance Series

2009	NCLT	30,247	Cu/ni	11.31g	Single coin in coloured folder				6.95	25	–

TWENTY CENTS

ONE YEAR COMMEMORATIVE REVERSES

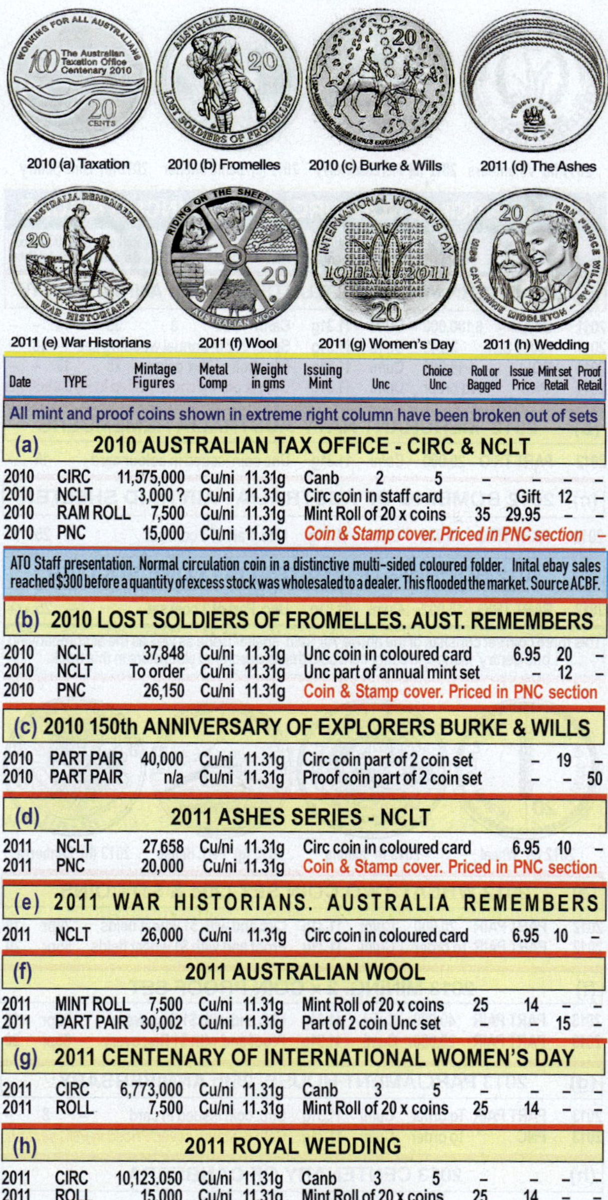

2010 (a) Taxation | 2010 (b) Fromelles | 2010 (c) Burke & Wills | 2011 (d) The Ashes

2011 (e) War Historians | 2011 (f) Wool | 2011 (g) Women's Day | 2011 (h) Wedding

Date	TYPE	Mintage Figures	Metal Comp	Weight in gms	Issuing Mint	Unc	Choice Unc	Roll or Bagged	Issue Price	Mint set Retail	Proof Retail
All mint and proof coins shown in extreme right column have been broken out of sets											
(a)	**2010 AUSTRALIAN TAX OFFICE - CIRC & NCLT**										
2010	CIRC	11,575,000	Cu/ni	11.31g	Canb	2	5	–	–	–	–
2010	NCLT	3,000 ?	Cu/ni	11.31g	Circ coin in staff card			–	Gift	12	–
2010	RAM ROLL	7,500	Cu/ni	11.31g	Mint Roll of 20 x coins			35	29.95	–	–
2010	PNC	15,000	Cu/ni	11.31g	*Coin & Stamp cover. Priced in PNC section*						–
ATO Staff presentation. Normal circulation coin in a distinctive multi-sided coloured folder. Inital ebay sales reached $300 before a quantity of excess stock was wholesaled to a dealer. This flooded the market. Source ACBF.											
(b)	**2010 LOST SOLDIERS OF FROMELLES. AUST. REMEMBERS**										
2010	NCLT	37,848	Cu/ni	11.31g	Unc coin in coloured card				6.95	20	–
2010	NCLT	To order	Cu/ni	11.31g	Unc part of annual mint set				–	12	–
2010	PNC	26,150	Cu/ni	11.31g	Coin & Stamp cover. Priced in PNC section						
(c)	**2010 150th ANNIVERSARY OF EXPLORERS BURKE & WILLS**										
2010	PART PAIR	40,000	Cu/ni	11.31g	Circ coin part of 2 coin set				–	19	–
2010	PART PAIR	n/a	Cu/ni	11.31g	Proof coin part of 2 coin set				–	–	50
(d)	**2011 ASHES SERIES - NCLT**										
2011	NCLT	27,658	Cu/ni	11.31g	Circ coin in coloured card				6.95	10	–
2011	PNC	20,000	Cu/ni	11.31g	Coin & Stamp cover. Priced in PNC section						
(e)	**2011 WAR HISTORIANS. AUSTRALIA REMEMBERS**										
2011	NCLT	26,000	Cu/ni	11.31g	Circ coin in coloured card				6.95	10	–
(f)	**2011 AUSTRALIAN WOOL**										
2011	MINT ROLL	7,500	Cu/ni	11.31g	Mint Roll of 20 x coins			25	14	–	–
2011	PART PAIR	30,002	Cu/ni	11.31g	Part of 2 coin Unc set			–	–	15	–
(g)	**2011 CENTENARY OF INTERNATIONAL WOMEN'S DAY**										
2011	CIRC	6,773,000	Cu/ni	11.31g	Canb	3	5	–	–	–	–
2011	ROLL	7,500	Cu/ni	11.31g	Mint Roll of 20 x coins			25	14	–	–
(h)	**2011 ROYAL WEDDING**										
2011	CIRC	10,123.050	Cu/ni	11.31g	Canb	3	5	–	–	–	–
2011	ROLL	15,000	Cu/ni	11.31g	Mint Roll of 20 x coins			25	14	–	–
2011	CIRC	7,738	Cu/ni	11.31g	Coin Swap. 29/04/2011			–	–	n/a	–
2011	PNC	14,000	Cu/ni	11.31g	Coin & Stamp cover. Priced in PNC section						–

TWENTY CENTS

ONE YEAR COMMEMORATIVE REVERSES

2011 [a] Volunteers

2012 [b] Merchant Navy

2012 [c] Bomb Shelter

2012 [d] Lone Sentry

CIRCULATION & NON CIRCULATION (NCLT) ISSUES

Date	TYPE	Mintage Figures	Metal Comp.	Weight in gms	Issuing Mint	Unc	Choice Unc	Roll or Bagged	Issue Price	Unc Retail	Proof Retail
(a) 2011 INTERNATIONAL VOLUNTEERS. 10th ANNIVERSARY											
2011	CIRC	6,100,000	Cu/ni	11.31g	Canb	1.50	3	35	14	–	–
2011	PART SET	3,249	Cu/ni	11.31g	Spec. 20¢ in annual wedding set				–	18	–
2011	ROLL	10,000	Cu/ni	11.31g	Mint Roll of 20 x coins			25	18	–	–
2011	PNC	To order	Cu/ni	11.31g	Coin & Stamp cover. Priced in PNC section–						
(b) 2012 MERCHANT NAVY. AUSTRALIA REMEMBERS											
2012	PART TRIO	20,000	Cu/ni	11.31g	Unc coin issued in colour card				–	15	–
(c) 2012 BOMBING OF AUSTRALIA - AIR RAID SHELTER											
2012	PART TRIO	18,002	Cu/ni	11.31g	Unc. Part of 3 coin set				–	25	–
(d) 2012 BOMBING OF AUSTRALIA - LONE SOLDIER											
2012	PART TRIO	18,002	Cu/ni	11.31g	Unc. Part of 3 coin set				–	25	–

This three coin set consists of the above 'Air Raid' shelter issue as well as the accompanying 'Lone Sentry' issue and a fifty cent coin that is described elsewhere in this book.

2012 (e) Wheat

2013 (f) Mining

2013 (g) Parl. House

2013 (h) Canberra

Date	TYPE	Mintage Figures	Metal Comp.	Weight in gms	Issuing Mint	Unc	Choice Unc	Roll or Bagged	Issue Price	Unc Retail	Proof Retail
(e) 2012 WHEAT TWO COIN SET (20¢ & $1) COINS											
2012	PART PAIR	20,000	Cu/ni	11.31g	Circ and with $1 wheat fields					20pr	10
2012	PART PAIR	To order	Cu/ni	11.31g	Proof and with $1 wheat fields					55pr	20
(f) 2013 MINING. 2 x COIN PROOF SET											
2013	PART PAIR	40,000	Cu/ni	11.31g	Circ and with $1 Discovery					20pr	10
2013	PART PAIR	25,000	Cu/ni	11.31g	Proof and with $1 Discovery					55pr	20
(g) 2013 PARLIAMENT HOUSE. 25th ANNIVERSARY											
2013	PART PAIR	To order	Cu/ni	11.31g	Circ. coin issued in card				–	8	–
2013	PNC	To order	Cu/ni	11.31g	Coin & Stamp cover. Priced in PNC section						
(h) 2013 CENTENARY OF CANBERRA											
2013	CIRC	6,200,000	Cu/ni	11.31g	Canb	1.50	3	n/a		–	–
2013	PNC	To order	Cu/ni	11.31g	Coin & Stamp cover. Priced in PNC section						

TWENTY CENTS

ONE YEAR COMMEMORATIVE REVERSES

2013 [a] Chaplains

2013 [b] Banknote (T1)

2013 [c] Banknote (T2)

2013 [d] The Ashes

2014 [e] Comfort Fund

2015 [f] ICC Cricket

2015 [g] World Netball

2015 [h] Netball [S] mm

Date	TYPE	Mintage Figures	Metal Comp.	Weight in gms	Description	Issue Price	Unc Retail	Proof Retail
[a]	**2013 ARMY CHAPLAINS. AUSTRALIA REMEMBERS**							
2013	NCLT	To order	Cu/ni	11.31g	Circ coin in coloured card	8	25	–
2013	PNC	300	Cu/ni	11.31g	Coin & Stamp cover. Priced in PNC section			–
[b]	**2013 FIRST COMMONWEALTH BANKNOTE CENTENARY. 1**							
2013	PART TRIO	To order	Cu/ni	11.31g	Circ. Three coin set. $1 & 2 x 50¢		30	–
2013	PNC	To order	Cu/ni	11.31g	Coin & Stamp cover. Priced in PNC section			–
[c]	**2013 FIRST COMMONWEALTH BANKNOTE CENTENARY. 2**							
2013	PART TRIO	To order	Cu/ni	11.31g	Circ. Three coin set. $1 & 2 x 50¢		30	–
2013	PNC	To order	Cu/ni	11.31g	Coin & Stamp cover. Priced in PNC section			–
[d]	**2013 THE ASHES. THE URN RETURNS**							
2013	NCLT	To order	Cu/ni	11.31g	Circ coin in coloured card	–	12	n/a
2013	PNC	7,500	Cu/ni	11.31g	Coin & Stamp cover. Priced in PNC section			–
[e]	**2014 COMFORT FUND. AUSTRALIA REMEMBERS**							
2014	NCLT	To order	Cu/ni	11.31g	Unc coin in coloured card	–	9	–
2014	PART SET	30,000	Cu/ni	11.31g	Unc part of annual mint set	–	12	–
[f]	**2015 ICC CRICKET WORLD CUP**							
2015	NCLT	50,000	Cu/ni	11.31g	Unc coin in coloured card		12	12
2015	PNC	15,000	Cu/ni	11.31g	Coin & Stamp cover. Priced in PNC section			–
[g/h]	**2015 NETBALL WORLD CUP SYDNEY**							
2015	NCLT –	30,000	Cu/ni	11.31g	Circ coin in coloured card	12	12	–
2015	NCLT S	30,000	Cu/ni	11.31g	Unc coin in coloured card	15	12	12
2015	PNC –	15,000	Cu/ni	11.31g	Coin & Stamp cover. Priced in PNC section			

The above 20¢ coin and a silver domed $5 proof coin were issued to mark the third time Australia has hosted the prestigious Netball World Cup since it's inception in 1963. Perth hosted the event in 1967 and Sydney took over the reins for the first time in 1991. The August 2015 competition was not only a winning clean sweep of the three, but the latest meeting was the subject of the two coins mentioned above. The twenty cent coin was also interesting in that there was a plain version and a counterstamped version. This made it the first counterstamped twenty cent coin issued. The non counterstamped version was sold on RAM website for $12. Two versions of the unstamped coin were also included in a PNC issued. The first was the usual generic issue as well as overprinted limited release ANDA show PNCs, which will also be available in a PNC and an overprinted limited release ANDA show PNC. The Mint was onsite from August, 7 to 16, for the entire duration of the games, operating at FanFEST with a mobile press. An "S" countermarked coin could be purchased for $15. Most people had to be at the event to obtain a coin, although RAM Loyalty Legends members could obtain a maximum of five coins over the phone.

TWENTY CENTS

ONE YEAR COMMEMORATIVE REVERSES

2015 [a] Henry Parkes

2015 [b] Magna Carta

2016 [c/d] Dirk Hartog Landing. Obv & Rev

2015 [e] Coo-ee March

2016 [f/g] 50th Year of Decimal Currency

2017 [h] SS Vyner

[a] 2015 800th ANNIVERSARY OF MAGNA CARTA

Date	TYPE	Mint Mark	Mintage Figures	Metal Comp.	Weight in gms	Description	Issue Price	Unc Retail	Proof Retail
2015	NCLT		30,000	Cu/ni	11.31g	Unc coin in coloured card		8	12

Although Magna Carta is primarily a British landmark, it's groundbreaking charter is a foundation stone of Australian constitutional and parliamentary government. In fact one of the four surviving contemporary copies of Magna Carta created in 1297 – the year that Magna Carta was finally enshrined in English law – was purchased by the Australian Government for £12,500 in 1952, and is on display at Parliament House in Canberra. Designed to limit the power of the monarchy, and guarantee justice and freedom for 'the common man', Magna Carta was enforced on the despotic King John by rebellious barons. Signed at Runnymede in June of 1215, Magna Carta played a key part in Britain's journey from absolute to constitutional monarchy.

[b] 2015 HENRY PARKES BIRTHDAY BICENTENNIAL

Date	TYPE	Mint Mark	Mintage Figures	Metal Comp.	Weight in gms	Description	Issue Price	Unc Retail	Proof Retail
2015	NCLT		30,000	Cu/ni	11.31g	Unc coin in coloured folder		8	10

[c/d] 2016 DIRK HARTOG LANDING 400 YEAR ANNIVERSARY

Date	TYPE	Mint Mark	Mintage Figures	Metal Comp.	Weight in gms	Description	Issue Price	Unc Retail	Proof Retail
2016	NCLT		20,000	Cu/ni	11.31g	Circ coin in coloured card	10	12	–

[e] 2015 COO-EE MARCH AUSTRALIA REMEMBERS

Date	TYPE	Mint Mark	Mintage Figures	Metal Comp.	Weight in gms	Description	Issue Price	Unc Retail	Proof Retail
2015	NCLT	–	30,000	Cu/ni	11.31g	Circ coin in coloured card	10	12	–
2015	PNC	–	30,000	Cu/ni	11.31g	Coin & Stamp cover. Priced in PNC section			

[f/g] 2016 DECIMAL CURRENCY 50TH ANNIVERSARY

Date	TYPE	Mint Mark	Mintage Figures	Metal Comp.	Weight in gms	Description	Issue Price	Unc Retail	Proof Retail
2016	NCLT		20,000	Cu/ni	11.31g	Circ coin in coloured card	10	12	–
2016	MINT ROLL		5,000	Cu/ni	11.31g	Mint roll. 20 x Unc coins	10	15	–
2016	EX-SET		40,383	Cu/ni	15.55g	Specimen. Part 6 coin mint set	–	4	–
2016	EX-SET		n/a	Cu/ni	15.55g	Proof. Part of 6 coin proof set	–	–	15

[h] 2017 SINKING OF THE SS VYNER BROOK. 75TH ANNIVERSARY

Date	TYPE	Mint Mark	Mintage Figures	Metal Comp.	Weight in gms	Description	Issue Price	Unc Retail	Proof Retail
2016	NCLT		20,000	Cu/ni	11.31g	Circ coin in coloured card	10	12	–

The SS Vyner Brooke was sunk by Japanese forces on the 14 February 1942 in the course of evacuating nurses and wounded soldiers away from the beleaguered island of Singapore. Some of the survivors made it to Banka Island where they were murdered by Japanese troops. Among the two survivors was Australian nurse Vivian Bullwinkel, who hid in nearby jungle for several days before giving herself up to Japanese troops unaware of the massacre. Bullwinkel spent the rest of the war in Japanese captivity, returning home in 1945.

TWENTY CENTS

A COMBINED RAM & NEWS LTD PROMOTION

2015 WW1 — 2015 Mateship — 2015 Light Horseman — 2015 Home Front — 2015 RAN

2015 Remembrance — 2015 Nurses — 2015 War Horses — 2015 Last Post — 2015 Correspondence

2015 Flying Corps — 2015 AIF — 2015 Unknown Soldier — 2015 Gallipoli

Date	Description	Weight in gms	Type	Metal Content	Size	Mintage Figures	Retail Value
2015 ANZAC REMEMBERED							
2015	Single coin in presentation card	11.3g	Spec	Cu/ni	28.52mm	300,000 avg	Varies
2015 a	Full set of 14 x coins in folder	—	—	—	—	—	55
2015	14 x 20¢ coins plus War Heros $1	—	—	—	—	—	225
2015	14 x 20¢ coins plus War Heros $1	—	—	—	—	—	250

[a] Each NCLT ANZACS 20c design is based on an original WW1 photograph in the AWM.
[b] Both folders have slots for $1 Poppy. New Corp Limited Edition Folder has $1 slot labelled to identify coin. "Normal" folder has slot but no identification labelling.

2016 Afghanistan — 2016 Bomber Command — 2016 Darwin — 2016 Dogs of War — 2016 Fromelles

2016 Korea — 2016 Peace Keepers — 2016 Rats of Tobruk — 2016 Special forces — 2016 Burma Railway

2016 ANZAC TO AFGHANISTAN

Date	Description	Weight in gms	Type	Metal Content	Size	Mintage Figures	Retail Value
2016	Single coin in presentation card	11.3g	Spec	Cu/ni	28.52mm	300,000 avg	Varies
2016	10 x 20¢ coins + 4 x 25¢ coins	—	—	—	—	—	85

TWENTY FIVE CENTS

2015 ANZACS REMEMBERED - News Ltd Issue

2015 Our Legends

2015 Kokoda

2015 Long Tan

2015 Peace

FIFTY CENTS

FIRST PORTRAIT. ONE YEAR TYPE

ELIZABETH II
1966
ONE YEAR TYPE

SILVER ALLOY
80% Silver, 20% Copper
Size 31.5 mm

Obverse : Arnold Machin
Reverse : Stuart Devlin

CIRCULATION & NON CIRCULATION (NCLT) ISSUES

All mint and proof coins shown in extreme right column have been broken out of sets

Date	TYPE	Mintage Figures	Metal Comp.	Weight in gms	Issuing Mint	Unc	Choice Unc	Roll or Bagged	Issue Price	Ex-Mintt Set Retail	Proof Retail
1966 a	CIRC	36,252,000	Silver	13.28g	Canb	18	29	n/a	–	35	–
1966	VARIETY	Inc above	Silver	13.28g	Canb	25	45	Double bar		50	–
1966 b	NCLT	18,054	Silver	13.28g	Canb	Proof coin part of six coin set				–	65

Mintage figures are for normal circulation coins unless otherwise stated.The price for the above 1966 50¢ in less than Unc will depend on the silver bullion price at the time.

The 1966 silver coin is NOT a rare collector piece as many perceive. Unless in uncirculated condition they are traded as bullion. Three coins make a full ounce of silver. When silver peaked at US $50 per ounce during the late 1970s and early 1980s, each coin was worth around Aust $15.00. With silver worth about a third of that today, the bullion value has dropped accordingly. Check with your dealer or an on-line app for the latest silver price.
[a] Fifty cent coins taken from the blue carded mint set deserve a separate pricing note as the coins were of a superior specimen finish compared to circulated issues.
[b] This version appeared in the first of what was to become the first issue of the annual proof set. The six coins were released in two different cases. The first was a dark blue case with a wooden frame. Vapours coming from the wood is thought to have contributed to most of the coins in these sets becoming heavily toned. The more common second case had a metal frame covered in a light blue material. Unless handled or poorly stored, most coins in these sets remained perfect.

1966 PATTERN SILVER FIFTY CENT COIN

In the 18th edition of this book (page 131) a half page article by Andrew Crellin indicated that the coin featured at left had a number of unique features not found on the circulation issue. The recent sale of the London pattern 20¢ coin (see entry in 20¢ section) would give credence to this coin also being a pattern issue. The common link between the two coins concerns the eyebrows that are different between the London and Canberra issues. The Canberra issue has two eyelashes while the London patterns have just one eyelash. Both the London die 20¢ coin and this 50¢ coin share the same attributes... research continues!

DOUBLE BAR VARIETY

A variation known as the "Double Bar" variety has been observed on 50 cent coins dated 1966, 1979 and 1980. While more pronounced on the latter two dates, the common factor was that the "bars" were actually part of the reeding design behind the emu's head. It was a weak spot on the die and caused early fractures. In later strikings the offending part of the design was ground out of the dies.

SILVER PROOF RESTRIKE

2006 ONE YEAR TYPE RETRO PORTRAIT

ELIZABETH II
2006
ONE YEAR TYPE
SILVER ALLOY
Fine Silver .999%
Size 31.5 mm
Obverse : Arnold Machin
Reverse : Stuart Devlin

NCLT. COLLECTOR ISSUES ONLY

Date	TYPE	Mintage Figures	Metal Comp.	Weight in gms	Description	Issue Price	Unc Retail	Proof Retail
2006 40TH ANNIVERSARY OF DECIMAL CURRENCY SET								
2006 b	RESTRIKE	5,829	13.70g	Silver	Decimal currency 40th anniv	–	–	45

(b) : To celebrate the 40th anniversary of decimalisation, the RAM produced a 2006 eight coin fine silver proof set featuring the original Arnold Machin effigy of the Queen. This was a unique issue as the normal proof and mint sets issued in 2006 carry the current Ian Rank-Broadley obverse. For more information refer to the fine silver issues section in the Mint & Proof section of the book.

TWO INTERESTING FIFTY CENT MULES

PICTURED LEFT : 1977 Coat of Arms Reverse : Officially only 50¢ coins with the Royal Jubilee reverse were struck. There are also seven known examples of a 1977 50 cents piece with the coat of arms reverse. An Extremely Fine example would be worth in the region of $8,000.

PICTURED RIGHT : 1988 Coat of Arms Reverse : According to official reports the only 1988 50¢ issue was the commemorative bicentenary design. No normal coat of arms 50 cents were officially produced. It would appear however that some were struck by accident. The above coin appeared as lot 487 in International Auction Galleries Sale 64, held in August 2006. Graded as Uncirculated it sold for $5,400 plus commission. Taking into account the prices similar rare decimal coins sell for at auction the above coin could be worth around $11,000.

1978 50¢ MULE. AUSTRALIA/ FIJI

Just like it's 20¢ counterpart (also the same date) the circumstances concerning the production of this extremely rare mule of an Australian obverse and a Fijian reverse is the subject of hearsay and half truths. It is believed to be unique and the last reference I can find of it selling was at public auction in November 1991. At that time it was lot 409 in Noble Numismatics's sale 37. Described as being Extremely Fine it sold for $900. With no recent sales it is difficult to suggest a current retail. (Any updates on this coin would be appreciated).

FIFTY CENTS

FIRST PORTRAIT TYPE

ELIZABETH II
1969 - 1984

CUPRO NICKEL

75% Copper; 25% Nickel
Size 31.5 mm

Obverse : Arnold Machin
Reverse : Stuart Devlin

CIRCULATION & NON CIRCULATION (NCLT) ISSUES

Date	TYPE	Mintage Figures	Metal Comp.	Weight in gms	Issuing Mint	Unc	Choice Unc	Roll or Bagged	Issue Price	Mint set Retail	Proof Retail
1967	CIRC	Not issued	Patterns exist		London?	–	–	–	–	–	–
1968	CIRC	Not issued	Cu/ni	15.55g	–	–	–	–	–	–	–
1969 a	CIRC	14,015,000	Cu/ni	15.55g	Canb	15	30	–	–	–	90
1971	CIRC	21,056,000	Cu/ni	15.55g	Canb	18	28	300	–	–	60
1972	CIRC	5,586,000	Cu/ni	15.55g	Canb	35	50	600	–	–	60
1973	CIRC	4,009,000	Cu/ni	15.55g	Canb	40	60	1,050	–	–	60
1974	CIRC	8,962,120	Cu/ni	15.55g	Canb	30	45	490	–	–	50
1975	CIRC	19,064,800	Cu/ni	15.55g	Canb	9	15	100	–	–	15
1976	CIRC	27,280,000	Cu/ni	15.55g	Canb	7	10	95	–	–	15
1977	CIRC	7 Known ?	Cu/ni	15.55g	Canb	–	EF	8,000	–	–	–
1978	CIRC	25,765,000	Cu/ni	15.55g	Canb	5	9	50	–	–	10
1979	CIRC	24,886,200	Cu/ni	15.55g	Canb	3	6	50	–	–	10
1979	VARIETY	Ditto	Double Bar		Can	25	35	?	–	–	75
1980	CIRC	38,681,000	Cu/ni	15.55g	Canb	3	6	40	–	–	10
1980	VARIETY	Ditto	Double Bar		Canb	28	40	100	–	–	75
1981	CIRC	24,168,000	Cu/ni	15.55g	Canb	3	6	85	–	–	7
1983	CIRC	48,923,000	Cu/ni	15.55g	Canb	4	7	38	–	–	5
1984	CIRC	26,281,000	Cu/ni	15.55g	Canb	5	9	20	–	–	10

Reference to 'Proof Retail' on far right column refers to coins broken out of proof sets

UNIQUE DIE FOR 1969 OBVERSE

Ongoing research indicates the obverse die for the 1969 50¢ is possibly unique. Compared to the 1970 obverse die, the 1969 issue shows that the hair curls are cut deeper and they are thicker around the crown.

1969 YARRALUMLA PNC

(a) As well as minting some 14 million fifty cent pieces for general circulation, the RAM also struck a small number of specimen coins. Of the 2000 struck, 1650 were produced for a private promotional company. They were housed in a special registered mail envelope that featured two stamps that had been cancelled with a "1969 Yarralumla" postmark. This was one of the first commercial undertakings by the new Mint and has an interesting background. A private firm called Nuphil commissioned the RAM to produce the small run of specimen quality 1969 fifty cent coins for inclusion in a Postal Numismatic Cover. The issue became known as the "Yarralumla Cover" because the stamps were cancelled at this post office. Apparently it was the closest Post Office to the Mint. It is uncertain just how many of these sets were actually sold or have survived. Like the 1930 penny, there are a number of versions of events. One story suggests Nuphil actually ordered the full 2000 coins but could only access 1,650 envelopes. In any event, there were more coins available than needed. The remaining 350 coins were retained by the mint. The RAM sold folders for 50 cents to house the coins the RAM sold at face value at the tourist shop. The unsold coins were eventually dispersed through the tills at the RAM.

Date	TYPE	Mintage Figures	Metal Comp	Weight in gms	Description	Issue Price	Retail Value
1969	PNC	2,000	Cu/ni	15.55g	Specimen coin/Unofficial PNC	n/a	675

FIFTY CENTS

SECOND PORTRAIT TYPE

ELIZABETH II

1985 - 1997

CUPRO NICKEL

75% Copper; 25% Nickel
Size 31.5 mm

Obverse : Raphael Maklouf
Reverse : Stuart Devlin

CIRCULATION & NON CIRCULATION (NCLT) ISSUES

All mint and proof coins shown in extreme right column have been broken out of sets

Date	TYPE	Mintage Figures	Metal Comp.	Weight in gms	Issuing Mint	Unc	Choice Unc	Roll or Bagged	Issue Price	Mint set Retail	Proof Retaill
1985	CIRC	1,000,000	Cu/ni	15.55g	Canb	15	28	60	–	–	30
1986	EX-SET	180,000	Cu/ni	15.55g	Circ. Unique to mint set			–	–	20	25
1987	EX-SET	200,000	Cu/ni	15.55g	Circ. Unique to mint set			–	–	20	25
1989	EX-SET	150,602	Cu/ni	15.55g	Circ. Unique to mint set			–	–	35	40
1990	EX-SET	103,766	Cu/ni	15.55g	Circ. Unique to mint set			–	–	70	75
1992	EX-SET	118,528	Cu/ni	15.55g	Circ. Unique to mint set			–	–	30	40
1993 a	CIRC	982,800	Cu/ni	15.55g	Canb	35	45	Bag	–	15	20
1996	CIRC	19,296,800	Cu/ni	15.55g	Canb	7	12	Bag	–	15	20
1997	CIRC	4,337,200	Cu/ni	15.55g	Canb	30	40	Bag	–	15	20

Reference to 'Proof Retail' on far right column refers to coins broken out of proof sets

[a] Recent research suggests that the actual mintage figure for the 1993 fifty cent coin was not in excess of three million as previously thought but just 982,800. The confusion results from information that appears in the RAM Annual Report for 1993-94. It states that 2,217,200 fifty cent coins were struck for circulation but these were coins "released" during the year from earlier dates that had been stored for several years.

UNDATED UNISSUED PATTERN TRIAL

Whenever a new coin design is being planned, it is not uncommon for various trials to be produced to test out a series of technical and engineering experiments. This coin is of added interest as it is difficult to determine what it was intended to commemorate. The representation of the New Parliament House is similar to the $5 coin issued in 1988. The coat of arms on the other side is identical to that of the ACT Coat of Arms that has appeared on a variety of coins including the 1993 $10 States Series and the 2001 Federation 50¢. Whatever the case, one thing is certain, the coin has shown spectacular capital gains over the years. As far as I know the coin first appeared as lot 488 in the International Auction Galleries Sale 63, held in February 2006. Graded as good Extremely Fine it sold for $2600 plus commission. In sale 108, held by Noble's Numismatics in April 2015, two examples were offered for sale and apart from looking identical there was a small discrepancy in the weight. The first coin (lot 1441) weighed 15.3g. The second (Lot 1442) weighed 15.59g. The nominal weight of a 50¢ piece is 15.88 grams. Both were described as being in "Uncirculated" Condition. The first sold for $12,000 against an estimate of $1,000 and the second, also with an estimate of $1,000 sold for $16,000. Both coins were subject to commission of 19.5%. This meant lot 1441 had a walk away price of $14,340 and the following lot had a final value of $19,120. Value in Uncirculated Grade 22,250

FIFTY CENTS

THIRD PORTRAIT

1999 - Present

CUPRO NICKEL
75% Copper; 25% Nickel
Size 31.5 mm

Obverse : Ian Rank Broadley
Reverse : Stuart Devlin

Date	TYPE	Mintage Figures	Metal Comp.	Weight in gms	Issuing Mint	Unc	Choice Unc	Roll or Bagged	Issue Price	Mint Set Retail	Proof Retail
1999	CIRC	20,300,000	Cu/ni	15.55g	Canb	10	18	Bag	–	–	–
2004 a	EX-SET	80,512	Cu/ni	15.55g	Circ. Unique to annual mint set				–	25	–
2004 b	CIRC	17,918,000	Cu/ni	15.55g	Canb	5	10	Bag	–	25	–
2005	PNC	30,000	Cu/ni	15.55g	*Issued with UK 50p. See PNC issues for details*						–
2006	CIRC	59,455,000	Cu/ni	15.55g	Canb	2	4	Bag	–	20	–
2006 c	EX-SET	84,407	Cu/ni	15.55g	Circ. 8 coin set. 50¢ Broadley obv				–	45	–
2006 d	EX-SET	45,373	Cu/ni	15.55g	Proof. 8 coin set. 50¢ Broadley obv				–	–	45
2006	OFF METAL	5,829	Silver	18.24g	Proof. Part of 6 coin boxed set				–	–	80
2006	OFF METAL	300	Gold	33.63g	Proof. Part of 6 coin boxed set				–	–	2,900
2007	CIRC	19,872,000	Cu/ni	15.55g	Canb	4	8	n/a	–	20	–
2007	OFF METAL	3,475	Silver	18.24g	Proof. Part of 6 coin boxed set				–	–	80
2007	OFF METAL	300	Gold	33.63g	Proof. Part of 6 coin boxed set				–	–	2,800
2008	CIRC	32,518,000	Cu/ni	15.55g	Canb	4	8	n/a	–	20	–
2008	OFF METAL	2,600	Silver	18.24g	Proof. Part of 6 coin boxed set				–	–	80
2009	CIRC	19,031,000	Cu/ni	15.55g	Canb	4	8	n/a	–	20	–
2009	OFF METAL	2,221	Silver	18.24g	Proof. Part of 6 coin boxed set				–	–	80
2010	CIRC	22,200,000	Cu/ni	33.63g	Canb	4	8	n/a	–	25	–
2010	OFF METAL	2,040	Silver	18.24g	Proof. Part of 6 coin boxed set				–	–	80
2010	OFF METAL	300	Gold	33.63g	Proof. Part of 6 coin boxed set				–	–	2,800
2011	CIRC	14,380,000	Cu/ni	15.55g	Canb	4	8	n/a	–	20	–
2011	OFF METAL	2,072	Silver	18.24g	Proof. Part of 6 coin boxed set				–	–	80
2012	CIRC	17,600,000	Cu/ni	15.55g	Canb	4	8	n/a	–	15	–
2012	OFF METAL	1,400	Silver	18.24g	Proof. Part of 6 coin boxed set				–	–	80
2012	OFFMETAL	2,000	Gold	0.5gm	Proof. Tiny copies of all 8 coins				–	–	2,800
2013	CIRC	n/a	Cu/ni	33.63g	Canb	4	8	n/a	–	–	–
2013	OFF METAL	1,000	Silver	18.24g	Proof. Individually cased coin				80	–	80
2013	OFF METAL	2,000	Silver	18.24g	Proof. Part of 6 coin boxed set				–	–	80
2013	OFF METAL	500	Gold	33.63g	Proof. Individually cased coin				2,800	–	2,800
2013	OFF METAL	500	Gold	33.63g	Proof. Part of 6 coin boxed set				–	–	2,800
2014	CIRC	17,743,000	Cu/ni	15.55g	Canb	2	5	Bag	–	–	–
2014	OFF METAL	1,000	Silver	18.24g	Proof. Individually cased coin				85	–	85
2014	OFF METAL	500	Silver	18.24g	Proof. Part of 6 coin boxed set				–	–	80
2014	OFF METAL	100	Gold	33.63g	Proof. Individually cased coin				2,800	–	2,800
2014	OFF METAL	50/ 47	Gold	33.63g	Proof. Part of 6 coin boxed set				–	–	2,800
2015	CIRC	n/a	Cu/ni	15.55g	Canb	2	5	Bag	–	–	–
2015 e	GILT	22,265	Cu/ni	15.55g	Gilt cu/ni 22ct gold plating20				30	–	
2015 f	GILT	Ditto	Gilt	15.55g	Circ. RAM 'Open Day' release				20	45	–
2015 g	PART PAIR	5,000	Cu/ni	15.55g	Circ coin with 'C' mintmark 20				40	–	
2015	OFF METAL	1,000	Silver	18.24g	Proof. Individually cased coin				85	–	85
2015	OFF METAL	800	Silver	18.24g	Proof. Part of 6 coin boxed set				–	–	80
2015	OFF METAL	50	Gold	33.63g	Proof. Individually cased coin				2,950	–	2,950
2015	OFF METAL	50	Gold	33.63g	Proof. Part of 6 coin boxed set				–	–	2,800
2016	CIRC	n/a	Cu/ni	15.55g	Canb	2	5	Bag	–	–	–
2016	EX SET	10,000	Cu/ni	15.55g	Circ. Part of 1¢ -50¢ special mint set				–	25	–
2016	OFF METAL	1,966	Silver	18.24g	Proof. Part of 6 coin boxed set				–	–	80
2016	OFF METAL	100	Gold	33.63g	Proof. Part of 1¢ -50¢ fine gold				2,950	–	2,950

The Ian Rank-Broadley obverse varies between years in the style of the text font, distance of head or text from rim and style of IRB; eg 1999, 2000, 2001, 2004 and 2005.
[a] Obverse has Large Head Type with legend text featuring pointed "A" of AUSTRALIA. No circulation issues of 2004. Exclusive to Mint, Baby Mint, Wedding, Proof, Baby Proof and Fine Silver Proof sets.
[b] Small head and different legend text font with flat top "A." The CofA/ Small Head type is in all 2004 sets. Possibly exclusive in all of the 2004 Student issues.
[c] This mint set included uncirculated the one and two cents coins even though no circulation examples had been produced for around 15 years.
[d] These proof coins were, including the 1¢ & 2¢, also part of the 40th anniversary set. Like the coins listed as (c), they featured the current Rank Broadley obverse.
[e] The first, gold plated cupro nickel 50¢ piece. The unusual mintage figure corresponds with the official opening date of the mint on 22/02/1965.
[f] Some 5,000 of the above were released at a special 'open-day' function on Feb 21, 2015. Packaging was overprinted with the wording 'OPEN DAY 21 February 2015'.
[g] Paired with original 1966 50¢. New 50¢ issue features a "C" mintmark.

FIFTY CENTS

ONE YEAR COMMEMORATIVE REVERSES

The following One Year Type commemoratives include at least one issue that was struck for general circulation. In some instances other NCLT coins were issued in a variety of metals and descriptive folders and cases for the collector market

1970 (a) Captain Cook

1977 (b) Silver Jubilee

1981 (c) Royal Wedding

1982 (d) Brisbane Games

CIRCULATION & NON CIRCULATION (NCLT) ISSUES

(a) 1970 CAPTAIN COOK BICENTENARY

Date	TYPE	Mintage Figures	Metal Comp.	Weight in gms	Issuing Mint	Unc	Choice Unc	Roll or Bagged	Issue Price	Mint set Retail	Proof Retail
1970	CIRC	16,548,100	Cu/ni	15.55g	Canb	8	14	90	–	–	–
1970 a	CASE	556,888	Cu/ni	15.55g	Canb	12	Red plastic case		–	–	–
1970	EX-SET	40,230	Cu/ni	15.55g	Circ included in annual mint set				–	9	–
1970	EX-SET	15,368	Cu/ni	15.55g	Proof included in annual set				–	–	20
1970 b	VIP ISSUE	140	Cu/ni	15.55g	Proof VIP presentation sets				–	–	n/a
1989	RESTRIKE	24,999	Silver	18 g	Proof M'pieces .925 stg.Size 31.65mm				–	–	25

[a] These specimen quality coins were originally issued at 60¢ through the banks and the RAM. They were issued in a red see-both-sides plastic case. The coins were specimen quality but some are toned due to the plastic casing. For more information on this specimen issue, refer to page 89 of the 8th edition of this book.
[b] Just 70 cased sets were produced and contained two proof coins.

DATE VARIATION ON THE CAPTAIN COOK FIFTY CENTS

Normal Date

Tilted Variety

On some of the 1970 Captain Cook 50 cents coins, the "7" appears tilted.

(b) 1977 QEII & PRINCE PHILIP SILVER JUBILEE

Date	TYPE	Mintage Figures	Metal Comp.	Weight in gms	Issuing Mint	Unc	Choice Unc	Roll or Bagged	Issue Price	Mint set Retail	Proof Retail
1977	CIRC	25,067,000	Cu/ni	15.55g	Canb	3	7	120	–	–	–
1977	EX-SET	128,010	Cu/ni	15.55g	Circ included in annual mint set				–	9	–
1977	EX-SET	55,006	Cu/ni	15.55g	Proof included in annual set				–	–	20
1977	VIP ISSUE	4 only	Silver	18 g	Proofs. VIP presentation				Gift	–	tba
1989	RESTRIKE	24,999	Silver	18 g	Proof M'pieces .925 stg. 31.65mm				–	–	45

(c) 1981 ROYAL WEDDING- CHARLES & DIANA

Date	TYPE	Mintage Figures	Metal Comp.	Weight in gms	Issuing Mint	Unc	Choice Unc	Roll or Bagged	Issue Price	Mint set Retail	Proof Retail
1981	CIRC	20,000,000	Cu/ni	15.55g	Canb	4	7	n/a	–	6	–
1989	RESTRIKE	24,999	Silver	18 g	Proof M'pieces .925 stg. 31.65mm				–	–	20

Many collectors are suprised that the above uncirculated coin was the only offering of this important event. Part of the answer is due to the RAM enduring a protracted strike for much of 1981. In fact all of the above 20 million coins were struck by the Royal Mint which was relocated from the Tower of London in 1986 to a state of the art facility in Llantrisant, Mid Glamorgan, Wales, UK.

(d) 1982 COMMONWEALTH GAMES, BRISBANE

Date	TYPE	Mintage Figures	Metal Comp.	Weight in gms	Issuing Mint	Unc	Choice Unc	Roll or Bagged	Issue Price	Mint set Retail	Proof Retail
1982	CIRC	49,610,200	Cu/ni	15.55g	Canb	3	5	n/a	–	–	–
1982	EX-SET	195,950	Cu/ni	15.55g	Circ included in annual mint set				–	9	
1982	EX-SET	100,000	Cu/ni	15.55g	Proof coin included in annual set				–	–	20
1989	RESTRIKE	24,999	Silver	18.00g	Proof M'pieces .925 stg. 31.65mm				–	–	40

FIFTY CENTS

Raphael Maklouf Obv

1988 (a) First Fleet

1991 (b) Decimal Currency

1994 (c) Year of the family

1995 (d) Weary Dunlop

1998 (e) Bass & Flinders

2000 (f) Unc Millennium

2000 (g) Proof Millennium

Date	TYPE	Mintage Figures	Metal Comp.	Weight in gms	Issuing Mint	Unc	Choice Unc	Roll or Bagged	Issue Price	Mint set Retail	Proof Retail
[a]	**1988 FIRST FLEET BICENTENARY**										
1988	CIRC	8,998,800	Cu/ni	15.55g	Canb	14	20	n/a	–	–	–
1988	EX-SET	240,000	Cu/ni	15.55g	Specimen coin in annual mint set				–	30	–
1988	EX-SET	104,518	Cu/ni	15.55g	Proof coin included in annual set				–	–	20
1988	OFF METAL	24,999	Silver	18 g	Proof M'pieces .925 stg.Size 31.65mm				–	–	25
1989	RESTRIKE	24,970	Silver	18 g	Proof M'pieces .925 stg.Size 31.65mm				–	–	25
[b]	**1991 DECIMAL CURRENCY - 25TH ANNIVERSARY**										
1991	CIRC	4,704,400	Cu/ni	15.55g	Canb	9	12	n/a	–	–	–
1991	EX-SET	147,700	Cu/ni	15.55g	Circ coin in annual mint set					9	–
1991	EX-SET	42,490	Cu/ni	15.55g	Proof coin included in annual set				–	–	20
1991	PART SET	24,999	Silver	18 g	Proof M'pieces .925 stg.Size 31.65mm				–	–	40
[c]	**1994 YEAR OF THE FAMILY**										
1994	CIRC	20,8376,100	Cu/ni	15.55g	Canb	18	35	Wide Date variety			
1994	CIRC	Inc in above	Cu/ni	15.55g	Canb	8	15	Narrow Date variety			
1994	EX-SET	91,942	Cu/ni	15.55g	Mint set. Both varieties. Wider date				–	10	–
1994	PROOF	39,004	Cu/ni	15.55g	Proof set. Only narrow date known				–	–	20
1994	EX-SET	39,958	Cu/ni	15.55g	Circ coin part of Koala baby set				–	10	–
1994	PNC	148,393	Cu/ni	15.55g	Coin & Stamp cover. Priced in PNC section						
[d]	**1995 ERNEST EDWARD 'WEARY' DUNLOP**										
1995	CIRC	15,869,200	Cu/ni	15.55g	Canb	9	15	n/a	–	–	–
1995	EX-SET	96,079	Cu/ni	15.55g	Circ part of 6 coin annual mint set				–	9	
1995	EX-SET	48,537	Cu/ni	15.55g	Proof coin included in annual set				–	–	20
1995	EX-SET	36,190	Cu/ni	15.55g	Circ coin part of Koala baby set				–	9	–
1995	EX-SET	6,704	Cu/ni	15.55g	Proof coin part of Koala baby set				–	–	20
1995	PNC	93,915	Cu/ni	15.55g	Coin & Stamp cover. Priced in PNC section						
[e]	**1998 BASS AND FLINDERS**										
1998	CIRC	22,389,200	Cu/ni	15.55g	Canb	10	16	n/a	–	–	–
1998	EX-SET	74,108	Cu/ni	15.55g	Circ coin in annual mint set				–	5	–
1998	EX-SET	31,810	Cu/ni	15.55g	Circ coin part of Koala baby set				–	5	–
1998	EX-SET	32,225	Cu/ni	15.55g	Proof coin included in annual set				–	–	15
1998	EX-SET	5,269	Cu/ni	15.55g	Proof coin part of Koala baby set				–	–	15
1998	PNC	85,004	Cu/ni	15.55g	Coin & Stamp cover. Priced in PNC section						
[f/g]	**2000 MILLENNIUM COMMEMORATION**										
2000 f	CIRC	16,630,000	Cu/ni	15.55g	Canb	12	20	n/a	–	–	–
2000	EX-SET	97,550	Cu/ni	15.55g	Circ coin in annual mint set				–	6	–
2000	EX-SET	27,118	Cu/ni	15.55g	Circ coin part of Koala baby set				–	6	–
2000 g	EX-SET	64,904	Cu/ni	15.55g	Proof [Colour] coin in annual set				–	–	15
2000	EX-SET	15,557	Cu/ni	15.55g	Proof [Colour] in Koala baby set				–	–	15

FIFTY CENTS

UNIQUE OBVERSE COMMEMORATIVE

CIRCULATION & NON CIRCULATION (NCLT) ISSUES

Date	TYPE	Mintage Figures	Metal Comp.	Weight in gms	Issuing Mint	Unc	Choice Unc	Roll or Bagged	Issue Price	Mint set Retail	Proof Retail
[a] 2000 ROYAL VISIT : AUSTRALIAN DESIGN PORTRAIT											
2000 a	CIRC	5,145,000	Cu/ni	15.5g	Canb	5	9	75	–	–	–
2000	NCLT	18,993	Silver	18.24	Cased Proof . 99.9 fine. 31.51mm				45	–	60

[a] The obverse of this issue was short-listed for the new design of Queen Elizabeth II that eventually went to British designer Ian Rank-Broadley. The above design was the work of the RAM's in house artist Vladimir Gottwald. On the eve of the Queen's 13th visit to Australia in early 2000, Royal permission was given for the Gottwald portrait to be used exclusively for this issue. Her first visit, as monarch in 1954, also saw the release of a coin. This was the confusing and controversial Lion and Kangaroo issue
[b] Ten years after the single 50¢ coin, the RAM honoured Mr Gottwald's popular portrait with a six coin release of the prestigious fine gold set. The denominations included images of the normal circulating coins from five cents to two dollars.

For more information on this gold proof set, please turn to page 245.

TWO DIE TYPES USED FOR 2000 UNCIRCULATED COIN

Recent research by Drew Jackson has discovered that two different reverse dies have been used for the circulation issues. The main differences can be found around the area of the "Union Jack". (Illustration supplied by Ken Skinner).

Type [a] : Is the most common. The representation of the crosses of the Union Jack are raised and the Federation star below the flag appears rough.

Type [b] : The RAM provided information that approximately 200,000 circulation coins of this die variation were minted. This incuse variety accounts for just 1 to 2% of the total mintage. The flag appears bigger than shown in Type (a) and the crosses of the Union Jack are incuse rather than raised. The Federation Star is also larger than Type (a) and the field surrounding the star is smoother.

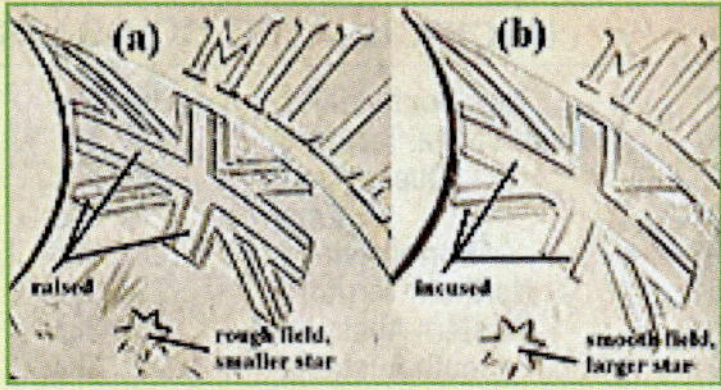

FLAG OR NO FLAG - REAL OR FAKE?

FAR RIGHT : Genuine uncirculated coin with tip of flag touching rim.
CENTRE : Proof coin with pad coloured flag does not touch the edge.
NEAR RIGHT : Occasionally this coin is touted as a circulated "rare error coin" that has been struck without the details showing the Australian flag. In fact, the coin is the proof version with the colour printing having been removed using a solvent.

Considering that examples of this "error" coin have sold for up to $500, it is important that collectors be aware of scams. We are pleased to say that since we included this information in the pocketbook some years ago none of these doubtful coins have appeared in the lists or auction catalogues produced by the more reputable dealers. eBay is still a worry but more and more collectors are doing their homework before buying from a source which is often a mix of blissful ignorance and down-right fraud.

FIFTY CENTS

2001 FEDERATION COMMEMORATIVE ISSUES

Date	Description	Denomination	Mintage Figures	Issue Price	Retail Average
UNCIRCULATED THREE COIN SETS LISTED BELOW					
2001	New South Wales	20¢, 50¢, $1	17,593	16.50	30
2001	Aust. Capital Territory	20¢, 50¢, $1	14,714	16.50	30
2001	Queensland	20¢, 50¢, $1	13,050	16.50	30
2001	Victoria	20¢, 50¢, $1	14,499	16.50	30
2001	Norfolk Island	20¢, 50¢, $1	6,200	16.50	45
2001	Northern Territory	20¢, 50¢, $1	3,970	16.50	45
2001	Western Australia	20¢, 50¢, $1	5,702	16.50	50
2001	South Australia	20¢, 50¢, $1	4,782	16.50	50
2001	Tasmania	20¢, 50¢, $1	4,052	16.50	50
PROOF COINS LISTED BELOW					
2001	New South Wales	20¢, 50¢, $1	9,923	44	65
2001	Aust. Capital Territory	20¢, 50¢, $1	5,516	44	65
2001	Queensland	20¢, 50¢, $1	5,668	44	65
2001	Victoria	20¢, 50¢, $1	5,777	44	65
2001	Norfolk Island	20¢, 50¢, $1	3,750	44	85
2001	Northern Territory	20¢, 50¢, $1	2,985	44	85
2001	Western Australia	20¢, 50¢, $1	3,829	44	95
2001	South Australia	20¢, 50¢, $1	3,625	44	95
2001	Tasmania	20¢, 50¢, $1	2,802	44	95
CASED TWENTY COIN UNC & PROOF COLLECTIONS					
UNCIRCULATED COINS LISTED BELOW					
2001	New South Wales	20¢, 50¢	22,802	6.53	20
2001	Aust. Capital Territory	20¢, 50¢	21,145	6.53	25
2001	Queensland	20¢, 50¢	20,190	6.53	25
2001	Victoria	20¢, 50¢	18,643	6.53	25
2001	Norfolk Island	20¢, 50¢	15,900	6.53	45
2001	Northern Territory	20¢, 50¢	11,852	6.53	40
2001	Western Australia	20¢, 50¢	11,527	6.53	40
2001	South Australia	20¢, 50¢	12,260	6.53	50
2001	Tasmania	20¢, 50¢	11,582	6.53	40
2001	Complete set of 20 Unc coins in folder		21,040	92	280
PROOF COINS LISTED BELOW					
2001	New South Wales	20¢, 50¢	12,492	n/a	60
2001	Aust. Capital Territory	20¢, 50¢	10,244	n/a	65
2001	Queensland	20¢, 50¢	10,242	n/a	65
2001	Victoria	20¢, 50¢	10,147	n/a	65
2001	Norfolk Island	20¢, 50¢	10,024	n/a	85
2001	Northern Territory	20¢, 50¢	10,182	n/a	85
2001	Western Australia	20¢, 50¢	10,199	n/a	85
2001	South Australia	20¢, 50¢	10,179	n/a	85
2001	Tasmania 20¢, 50¢	20¢, 50¢	10,192	n/a	85
2001	Complete set of 20 Proof coins in case		13,000	250	425

Folders and cases were supplied with the NSW coin which was the first in the series. As the coins were released throughout the year, they were sent to pre-paid customers in a protective capsule and a sealed plastic envelope.

FIFTY CENTS

2001 : FEDERATION STATE ISSUES

2001 [a] New Sth Wales 2001 [b] Aust Capital Terr 2001 [c] Queensland 2001 [d] Victoria

2001 [e] Norfolk Island 2001 [f] Nth Territory 2001 [g] West Australia 2001 [h] Sth Australia

2001 [i] Tasmania 2001 Folders for Uncirculated coins 2001 Case for proof

Date	TYPE	Mintage Figure	Metal Comp	Weight in gms	Unc	Choice Unc	Roll/ Bag	Proof Retail
2001 a	NSW	3,042,000	Cu/ni	15.55 g	12	20	110	45
2001 b	ACT	2,000,000	Cu/ni	15.55 g	10	16	95	40
2001 c	Queensland	2,320,000	Cui/ni	15.55 g	20	30	160	50
2001 d	Victoria	2,800,000	Cu/ni	15.55 g	10	16	95	40
2001 e	Norfolk Island	2,000,000	Cu/ni	15.55 g	10	16	95	40
2001 f	Northern Territory	2,080,000	Cu/ni	15.55 g	10	16	95	40
2001 g	West Australia	2,400,000	Cu/ni	15.55 g	10	16	95	40
2001 h	South Australia	2,400,000	Cu/ni	15.55 g	10	16	95	40
2001 i	Tasmania	2,160,006	Cu/ni	15.55 g	10	16	95	40

2001 [a] Federation Circ 2001 [b&c] Proof Federation silver & gold 2002 [d] Year of Outback

[a,b & c] 2001 CENTENARY OF FEDERATION

2001 a	CIRC	43,149,600	Cu/ni	15.55g	Canb	8	15	50	–	–	–
2001	EX-SET	90,822	Cu/ni	15.55g	Circ coin in annual mint set				–	15	–
2001	EX-SET	32,494	Cu/ni	15.55g	Circ coin part of Koala baby set				–	15	–
2001 b	EX-SET	59,569	Cu/ni	15.55g	Proof set with coloured reverse				–	50	–
2001	EX-SET	15,011	Cu/ni	15.55g	Proof coin part of Koala baby set				–	–	30
2001 c	OFF METAL	650/ 193	Gold	33.88g	Proof. 99.99 fine. Federation set				–		–1,750

(d) 2002 YEAR OF THE OUTBACK

2002	CIRC	11,507,000	Cu/ni	15.55g	Canb	6	10	55	–	–	–
2002	EX-SET	68,752	Cu/ni	15.55g	Circ coin in annual mint set				–	15	–
2002	EX-SET	32,479	Cu/ni	15.55g	Circ coin part of Koala baby set				–	15	–
2002	EX-SET	3,322	Cu/ni	15.55g	Spec coin part of Wedding set				–	20	–
2002	EX-SET	39,514	Cu/ni	15.55g	Proof coin part of annual set				–	–	20

FIFTY CENTS

2002 [a] Accession 2003 [b/c] Coronation (Al/Br & Silver) 2003 [d] Volunteers

[a] 2002 ACCESSION. ELIZABETH II. 50th ANNIVERSARY

2002	OFF METAL	13,500	Silver	18.24g	Proof. 99.9 fine. Cased single coin	–	–	80
2002	PART PAIR	1,500	Silver	18.24g	Proof with $100 gold 99.99 fine	–	–	80
2002	PART TRIO	3,000	Silver	18.24g	Part 3 x set with UK & Canada	–	–	80
2002	PNC	32,102	Cu/ni	15.55g	Coin & Stamp cover. Priced in PNC section			–

[b/c] 2003 CORONATION. ELIZABETH II. 50th ANNIVERSARY

2003	OFF METAL	13,500	Silver	18.24g	Proof. 99.9 fine. Cased single coin	–	–	80
2003	PART PAIR	600	Silver	18.24g	Proof with $100 gold 99.99 fine	–	–	80
2003 *i*	PNC	63,003	Al/br	14.09g	Coin & Stamp cover. Priced in PNC section			–

[*i*] The 50¢ coin in the above PNC was the first to be issued in an alum/bronze alloy. (NB) The RAM also produced a four coin set that was displayed in a purpose made presentation case. It contained one of each of the 50¢ and $100 coins.

[d] 2003 AUSTRALIA'S VOLUNTEERS

2003	CIRC	13,927,000	Cu/ni	15.55g	Canb 5 8 36	–	–	–
2003	EX-SET	80,512	Cu/ni	15.55g	Circ coin in annual mint set	–	10	–
2003	EX-SET	37,748	Cu/ni	15.55g	Circ coin also part of baby set	–	10	–
2003	EX-SET	3,249	Cu/ni	15.55g	Spec. part of Wedding set	–	15	–
2003	EX-SET	39,090	Cu/ni	15.55g	Proof coin part of annual set	–	–	20
2003	EX-SET	14,799	Cu/ni	15.55g	Proof coin also part of baby set	–	–	20
2003	OFF METAL	6,500	Silver	18.25g	Proof coin. 99.9 fine. 31.51mm	32	–	40
2003	OFF METAL	620	Gold	33.88g	Proof part of 99.99 fine 6 coin set	–	–	2,000

[e] Primary Student [f] Secondary Student [g / h] Remembrance Silver & Gold

(e) 2004 PRIMARY STUDENT DESIGN

2004	CIRC	10,577,000	Cu/ni	15.55g	Canb 4 9 20	–	–	–
2004	NCLT	36,902	Cu/ni	15.55g	Unc coin in colour folder	4.95	10	–
2004	OFF METAL	8,203	Silver	18.24g	Proof coin. 99.9 fine. 31.51mm	–	–	80

[f] 2005 SECONDARY SCHOOL STUDENT DESIGN

2005	CIRC	20,719,000	Cu/ni	15.55g	Canb 20	–	–	–
2005	NCLT	24,806	Cu/ni	15.55g	Unc coin in colour folder	4.95	10	–
2005	OFF METAL	5,402	Silver	18.24g	Proof coin. 99.9 fine. 31.51mm	80	–	90

[f] While this coin was dated 2005, the design was meant for the Commonwealth Games held in Melbourne the following year. This meant the wording on the presentation card referred to the 2006 games rather than the date on the coin. It is what it is and not an error.

[g/h] 2005 REMEMBRANCE - 60th ANNIVERSARY OF WWII

2005	CIRC	21,033,000	Cu/ni	15.55g	Canb 3 9 20	–	–	–
2005	NCLT	20,000	Cu/ni	15.55g	Circ coin in AP 'New Baby' card	–	4.95	10
2005	EX-SET	71,546	Cu/ni	15.55g	Circ coin in annual mint set	–	15	–
2005	EX-SET	28,853	Cu/ni	15.55g	Circ coin part of Koala baby set	–	15	–
2005	EX-SET	3,627	Cu/ni	15.55g	Fr/Unc coin part of Wedding set	–	18	–
2005	EX-SET	33,520	Cu/ni	15.55g	Proof coin part of annual set	–	–	25
2005	EX-SET	12,884	Cu/ni	15.55g	Proof coin part of Koala baby set	–	–	25
2005	OFF METAL	6,200	Silver	18.24g	Proof part of 99.9 fine 6 coin set	–	–	50
2005	OFF METAL	629	Gold	33.88g	Proof part of 99.99 fine 6 coin set	–	–	2,000

FIFTY CENTS

2006. MELBOURNE GAMES ISSUES

(a) Basketball (b) Hockey (c) Shooting (d) Weightlifting

(e) Badminton (f) Gymnastics (g) Rugby 7's (h) Cycling

(i) Athletics (j) Triathlon (k) Netball (l) Table Tennis

(m) Aquatics (n) Boxing (o) Lawn Bowls (p) Squash

NCLT. COLLECTOR ISSUES ONLY

Date	Description	Mintage Figures	Metal Comp.	Weight	Description	Issue Price	Retail Average
2006 a	Basketball	21,994	Cu/ni	15.55	Unc in card	4.95	8
2006 b	Hockey	21,761	Cu/ni	15.55	Unc in card	4.95	8
2006 c	Shooting	21,070	Cu/ni	15.55	Unc in card	4.95	8
2006 d	Weightlifting	22,332	Cu/ni	15.55	Unc in card	4.95	8
2006 e	Badminton	22,270	Cu/ni	15.55	Unc in card	4.95	8
2006 f	Gymnastics	25,574	Cu/ni	15.55	Unc in card	4.95	75
2006 g	Rugby 7's	24,427	Cu/ni	15.55	Unc in card	4.95	8
2006 h	Cycling	22,861	Cu/ni	15.55	Unc in card	4.95	8
2006 i	Athletics	22,475	Cu/ni	15.55	Unc in card	4.95	8
2006 j	Triathlon	22,302	Cu/ni	15.55	Unc in card	4.95	8
2006 k	Netball	22,432	Cu/ni	15.55	Unc in card	4.95	8
2006 l	Table Tennis	22,502	Cu/ni	15.55	Unc in card	4.95	9
2006 m	Aquatics	31,702	Cu/ni	15.55	Unc in card	4.95	9
2006 n	Boxing	22,602	Cu/ni	15.55	Unc in card	4.95	8
2006 o	Lawn Bowls	22,602	Cu/ni	15.55	Unc in card	4.95	8
2006 p	Squash	21,902	Cu/ni	15.55	Unc in card	4.95	8

The above series featured a different design to highlight each event contested during the Games. The coins were originally promoted as only being available as a NCLT collectable and were sold in a plastic card for $4.95.

FIFTY CENTS

ONE YEAR COMMEMORATIVE REVERSES

2006 [a] 80th Birthday Unc

2006 [b] Birthday Proof

2006 [c] Royal Visit Unc

2006 [d] Royal Visit Gilt

Date	TYPE	Mintage Figures	Metal Comp.	Weight in gms	Description	Issue Price	Unc Retail	Proof Retail
[a/b]	**2006 ELIZABETH II. 80th BIRTHDAY**							
2006	NCLT	28,198	Cu/ni	15.55g	Circ coin in coloured folder	4.95	20	–
2006	PART PAIR	6,098	Silver	18.24g	Proof Gilt with 50¢ Royal Visit	–	–	60
	The above issue and the Royal Visit gilt silver coin below were only available as a two coin set.							
[c/d]	**2006 ELIZABETH II. ROYAL VISIT**							
2006	NCLT	28,593	Cu/ni	15.55g	Circ coin in coloured folder	4.95	35	–
2006	PART PAIR	6,098	Silver	18.24g	Proof Gilt with 50¢ QEII b'day	–	–	60

2006 [e] Fine silver unique original 1966 design

2006 [f] Unique cu/ni round design with current portrait

Date	TYPE	Mintage Figures	Metal Comp.	Weight in gms	Description	Issue Price	Unc Retail	Proof Retail
[e/f]	**2006 ALTERNATIVE 40TH ANNIVERSARY ISSUES**							
2006 e	OFF METAL	5,829	Silver	13.70g	Proof. Part of 8 coin 40th anniv	–	–	75
2006 f	OFF METAL	45,373	Cu/ni	n/a	Proof. Part of 8 coin 40th anniv	–	–	60

[e] This 2006 dated proof version of the original 1966 fifty cent coin was a completely authentic re-creation of the first and only silver circulation decimal coin. This included the original metal mix of 80% silver and 20% copper. For about the last 20 years all silver coins produced at the RAM have been made from .999% fine silver and are collector coins [NCLT] or Non Circulating Legal Tender.
[f] This 2006 fifty cent coin was unique in a number of ways. It was the first round fifty cent piece to be struck as a proof cupro-nickel coin and also the first round example to have the current Rank Broadley obverse. Both sets included the 1¢ & 2¢ cent coins.

2006 [g] Pattern. Part of the fine 8 coin gold set

2007 [h] Diamond Wedding

2008 [i] Scouting

Date	TYPE	Mintage Figures	Metal Comp.	Weight in gms	Description	Issue Price	Unc Retail	Proof Retail
[g]	**2006 ALTERNATIVE 40TH ANNIVERSARY ISSUES**							
2006	OFF METAL	300	Gold	33.63g	Proof. Part of 8 coin 40th anniv	–	–	3,000
[h]	**2007 ELIZABETH II & PHILLIP. DIAMOND WEDDING**							
2007	NCLT	60,030	Cu/ni	15.55g	Unc coin in coloured card	4.95	15	–
[i]	**2008 THE CENTENARY OF SCOUTING**							
2008	NCLT	9,571	Cu/ni	15.55g	Circ coin in coloured folder	4.95	12	–
2008	PNC	33,257	Cu/ni	15.55g	Coin & Stamp cover. Priced in PNC section			–

FIFTY CENTS

ONE YEAR COMMEMORATIVE REVERSES

2008 [a] Australia II   2009 [b] Moon Landing   2009 [c] Gold Private Corporate issue

2010 [d] Australia Day   2010 [e] Australia Day Gilt   2010 [f] Engagement Unc & [g] Gilt Proof

2010 [h] Unique Heritage set round silver issue   2010 [i] Part of Vladimir Gottwald fine gold set

Date	TYPE	Mintage Figures	Metal Comp.	Weight in gms	Description	Issue Price	Unc Retail	Proof Retail
[a]	**2008 AUSTRALIA II AMERICA'S CUP VICTORY**							
2008	NCLT	32,916	Cu/ni	15.55g	Circ coin in coloured folder	7.95	24	–
[b]	**2009 MOON LANDING. 40th ANNIVERSARY**							
2009	NCLT	43,149	Cu/ni	15.55g	Circ coin in coloured card	9.95	40	–
[c]	**2009 GOLD INTERNATIONAL CORPORATE ORDER**							
2009	NCLT	500	Gold	33.63g	Proof in presentation case	tba	–	2,995

2009 Unique Machin obverse gold fifty cent coin. Along with a pure gold $1 coin, the RAM struck 500 proofs of each for an overseas corporate order. They featured the original Arnold Machin portrait that first appeared in 1966. Each was individually cased and numbered. Very few have found their way back to the Australan market.

Date	TYPE	Mintage Figures	Metal Comp.	Weight in gms	Description	Issue Price	Unc Retail	Proof Retail
[d,e]	**2010 AUSTRALIA DAY - JANUARY 26TH**							
2010 d	CIRC	11,452,000	Cu/ni	15.55g	Canb 5 9 40	–	–	7
2010	ROLL	Inc above	Cu/ni	15.55g	Mint roll of 20 Uncirc coins	25	30	–
2010 e	PAIR	10,000	Silver	18.24g	Gilt Proof. Paired with 50¢ wedding	–	–	75
[f,g]	**2010 WILLIAM & CATHERINE ENGAGEMENT ISSUES**							
2010	NCLT	tba	Cu/ni	15.55g	Circ coin in coloured folder	9.95	12	–
2010	OFF METAL	5,000	Silver	18.24g	Proof pair. Cased 99.9 Silver	145	–	165

This and the William & Catherine Royal Wedding coin listed on the next page were only available as a two coin, fine silver and gilt proof set.

Date	TYPE	Mintage Figures	Metal Comp.	Weight in gms	Description	Issue Price	Unc Retail	Proof Retail
[h]	**2010 UNIQUE ROUND ISSUE. PART OF HERITAGE SET**							
2009	NCLT	400	Cu/ni	18.24g	Part of 8 coin Heritage Set	–	–	350

With a mintage of just 400 coins, this is one of the rarest of all the RAM releases with the exception of some of the gold issues. Struck in the original 80% silver, 20% copper alloy, it was part of the 1966 Decimal Heritage Set released in 2010. A similar coin was part of the 2006 Australian proof set which commemorated the 40th anniversary of decimal currency.

Date	TYPE	Mintage Figures	Metal Comp.	Weight in gms	Description	Issue Price	Unc Retail	Proof Retail
[i]	**2010 VLADIMIR GOTTWALD PORTRAIT. GOLD PROOF SET**							
2010	OFF METAL	450	Gold	33.63g	Proof. 6 coin set. Gottwald. obv	–	–	2,995

FIFTY CENTS

ONE YEAR COMMEMORATIVE REVERSES

2010 [a] Melb. Cup. Unc

[b] Melb. Cup. Proof 1

[c] Melb. Cup. Proof 2

2011 [d] National Service

2011 [e] Wedding Unc

2011 [f] Wedding Proof

2011 [g] Triple 000

2012 [h] Kokoda

Date	TYPE	Mintage Figures	Metal Comp.	Weight in gms	Description	Issue Price	Unc / Retail	Proof Value
[a,b,c]	**2010 MELBOURNE CUP 150th ANNIVERSARY**							
2010 a	NCLT	To order	Cu/ni	15.55g	Circ coin in coloured folder	9.95	10	–
2010 b	PNC	16,861	Cu/ni	15.55g	Coin & Stamp cover. Priced in PNC section			–
2010	OFF METAL	5,000	Silver	18.24g	Proof. Cased Silver pair	165	–	275
[d]	**2011 NATIONAL SERVICE 60th ANNIVERSARY**							
2011	NCLT	To order	Cu/ni	15.55g	Circ coin in coloured folder	9.95	10	–
2011	PNC	To order	Cu/ni	15.55g	Coin & Stamp cover. Priced in PNC section			–
[e/f]	**2011 WILLIAM & CATHERINE WEDDING ISSUES**							
2011	NCLT	To order	Cu/ni	15.55g	Circ coin in coloured folder	8.95	10	–
2011	PNC	14,000	Cu/ni	15.55g	Coin & Stamp cover. Priced in PNC section			–
2011	OFF METAL	5000	Silver	18.24g	Proof. Paired. Engagement 50¢	85	–	210
[g]	**2011 "TRIPLE 000" EMERGENCY SERVICE - 50 YEARS**							
2011	NCLT	To order	Cu/ni	15.55g	Circ coin in coloured folder	9.95	30	–
[h]	**2012 KOKODA CAMPAIGN**							
2012	NCLT	To order	Cu/ni	15.55g	Unc coin in coloured folder	9	10	20

[i] Great Britain £5 [i] Australian 50¢ [i] Canadian $20

[i] 2012 COMMONWEALTH MINTS THREE COIN JUBILEE

Date	Value	Country	Weight	Size	Metal	Mintage	Issue	Retail
2012	.50¢	Australlia	18.24	31.5	99.9 silver	4000	522	600
2012	$20	Canada	31.39	38.0	99.99 silver		*Inc in above*	
2012	£ 5	Gt Britain	18.24	38.6	92.5 silver		*Inc in above*	
2012	.50¢	Australlia	33.63	31.5	99.99 gold	375	10,118	12,500
2012	$300	Canada	22.0	25.0	99.999 gold		*Inc in above*	
2012	£ 5	Gt Britain	39.94	38.6	91.67 gold		*Inc in above*	

The above 50 cent coin was part of a three coin "Commonwealth" combined issue that also included contributions from the Canadian and UK mints. The set was commissioned by the Royal Mint (UK) and is not part of the offical numismatic program.

FIFTY CENTS

ONE YEAR COMMEMORATIVE REVERSES

2012 [a] Darwin Bombing

2012 [b] Ballet

2012 [c] Colour. Mint set

2012 [d] Gilt. Proof set

2012 [e] Diamond Jubilee

2013 [f] Bathurst Race

2013 [g] Surfing Australia

2013 [h] Banknotes

NCLT. COLLECTOR ISSUES ONLY

Date	TYPE	Mintage Figures	Metal Comp.	Weight in gms	Description	Issue Price	Unc Retail	Proof Value
[a]			**2012 BOMBING OF AUSTRALIA**					
2012	NCLT	To order	Cu/ni	15.55g	Circ coin in coloured folder	10	10	–
2012	OFF METAL	10,000	Silver	18.24g	Cased Proof. 99.9 fine. 31.51mm	80	–	80
[b]			**2012 50th ANNIVERSARY OF AUSTRALIAN BALLET**					
2012	NCLT	To order	Cu/ni	15.55g	Circ coin in coloured folder	9	10	–
2012	PNC	15,000	Cu/ni	15.55g	Coin & Stamp cover. Priced in PNC section			–
2012	NCLT	10,000	Silver	18.24g	Cased Proof. 99.9 fine. 31.51mm	80	–	80
[c/d]			**2012 COLOURED & GILT COAT OF ARMS**					
2012	EX SET	55,410	Cu/ni	15.55g	Coloured circ. Unique to mint set	–	20	–
2012	EX SET	50,000	Cu/ni	15.55g	Gilt reverse. Unique to proof set	–	–	20
[e]			**2012 ELIZABETH II DIAMOND JUBILEE**					
2012	NCLT	To order	Cu/ni	15.55g	Circ coin in coloured folder	9	10	–
2012	PNC	To order	Cu/ni	15.55g	Coin & Stamp cover. Priced in PNC section			–
2012	NCLT	10,000	Silver	18.24g	Cased Proof. 99.9 fine. 31.51mm	80	–	80
(f)			**2013 50 YEARS OF MOUNT PANAROMA**					
2013	NCLT	To order	Cu/ni	15.55g	Circ coin in coloured folder	9	10	–
2013	PNC	15,000	Cu/ni	15.55g	Coin & Stamp cover. Priced in PNC section			–

The timing of this issue has caused some confusion. The envelope and stamp was post-marked on October 2, 2012 and issued at that time. However the coin itself was dated 2013!

Date	TYPE	Mintage Figures	Metal Comp.	Weight in gms	Description	Issue Price	Unc Retail	Proof Value
(g)			**2013 50 YEARS OF SURFING AUSTRALIA**					
2013	NCLT	To order	Cu/ni	15.55g	Circ coin in coloured folder	9	10	
2013	PNC	15,000	Cu/ni	15.55g	Coin & Stamp cover. Priced in PNC section			–
(h)			**2013 CENTENARY OF COMMONWEALTH BANKNOTES**					
2013	NCLT	To order	Cu/ni	15.55g	Circ coin in coloured folder`	9	10	
2013	PNC	To order	Cu/ni	15.55g	Coin & Stamp cover. Priced in PNC section			

FIFTY CENTS

ONE YEAR COMMEMORATIVE REVERSES

2013 [a] Birth of George

2013 [b] Com'wth Stamps

2013 [c] Coronation

2014 [d] Boer War

CIRCULATION & NON CIRCULATION (NCLT) ISSUES

Date	TYPE	Mintage Figures	Metal Comp.	Weight in gms	Issuing Mint	Unc	Choice Unc	Roll or Bagged	Issue Price	Mint set Retail	Proof Retail
[a]		**2013 BIRTH OF PRINCE GEORGE**									
2013	NCLT	To order	Cu/ni	15.55g	Canb	9	10	Bag	–	–	–
2013	NCLT	10,000	Silver	18.24g	Cased Proof. 99.9 fine. 31.51mm				80	–	80
2013	PNC	14,000	Cu/ni	15.55g	Coin & Stamp cover. Priced in PNC section						–

Date	TYPE	Mintage Figures	Mint Mark	Metal Comp	Weight in gms	Description	Issue Price	Retail Average	
[b]		**2013 CENTENARY OF COMMONWEALTH STAMPS**							
2013	NCLT	To order	M	Cu/ni	15.55g	Circ coin in coloured folder	9	10	–
2013	NCLT	To order	—	Cu/ni	15.55g	Coin & Stamp cover. Priced in PNC section			–

Six variations of the above PNC were issued at the 2013 *World Stamp Expo* held in Melbourne from May 10 to 15th. Each day 1,250 covers were released with a different coloured foil postmark. Unsolds were destroyed on a daily basis. The 50¢ piece featured a mintmark "M" for Melbourne. This was the first 50¢ piece to feature a mintmark.

Date	TYPE	Mintage Figures	Mint Mark	Metal Comp	Weight in gms	Description	Issue Price	Retail Average	
[c]		**2013 QUEEN'S CORONATION. 60th ANNIVERSARY**							
2013	NCLT	To order		Cu/ni	15.55g	Circ coin sold in coloured folder	9	10	–
2013	NCLT	10,000		Silver	18.24g	Cased Proof. 99.9 fine. 31.51mm	80	–	80
[d]		**2014 BOER WAR - AUSTRALIA AT WAR**							
2014	NCLT	50,000		Cu/ni	15.55g	Circ coin in coloured folder	10	13	–

[d] A number of military medal collectors have noticed that the court mounted ribbon colours are around the wrong way. Apparently, the error concerns the complete issue

2014 [e] Cocos Islands

2014 [f] German New Guinea

2014 [g] Aust Flying Corps

2014 [h] Western Front

Date	TYPE	Mintage Figures	Mint Mark	Metal Comp	Weight in gms	Description	Issue Price	Retail Average	
[e]		**2014 COCOS ISLANDS - AUSTRALIA AT WAR**							
2014	NCLT	50,000		Cu/ni	15.55g	Circ coin in coloured folder	10	10	–
2014	PNC	10,000		Cu/ni	15.55g	Coin & Stamp cover. Priced in PNC section			–
[f]		**2014 GERMAN NEW GUINEA - AUSTRALIA AT WAR**							
2014	NCLT	50,000		Cu/ni	15.55g	Circ coin in coloured folder	10	10	–
[g]		**2014 AUSTRALIAN FLYING CORPS - AUST. AT WAR**							
2014	NCLT	50,000		Cu/ni	15.55g	Circ coin in coloured folder	10	10	–
[h]		**2014 THE WESTERN FRONT - AUSTRALIA AT WAR**							
2014	NCLT	50,000		Cu/ni	15.55g	Circ coin in coloured folder	10	10	–

FIFTY CENTS

2014 [a] Circ AIATSIS

2014 [b] Coloured AIATSIS

2014 [c] Gallipoli

2015 [d] El Alamien

[a/b] 2014 AIATSIS - 50TH ANNIVERSARY

2014 a	CIRC	2,000,000	Cu/ni	15.55g	Canb 3 9 45	–	–	–
2014 b	NCLT	30,000	Cu/ni	15.55g	Specimen Colour reverse	13.5	35	–
2014	ROLLS	5,000	Cu/ni	15.55g	Mint rolls of 20 coins	n/a	40	–

[c] 2014 GALLIPOLI CAMPAIGN - AUST. AT WAR

2014	NCLT	50,000	Cu/ni	15.55g	Circ coin in coloured fold	10	13	–
2014	PNC	12,000	Cu/ni	15.55g	Coin & Stamp cover. Priced in PNC section			–

[d] 2015 EL ALAMEIN - AUSTRALIA AT WAR

2015	NCLT	50,000	Cu/ni	15.55g	Circ coin in coloured folder	10	10	13

2015 [e] Greece

2015 [f] Pacific War

2015 (g) Tobruk

2015 [h] Crete

[e] 2015 GREECE - AUSTRALIA AT WAR

2015	NCLT	50,000	Cu/ni	15.55g	Circ coin in coloured folder	10	10	–

[f] 2015 WAR IN THE PACIFIC - AUSTRALIA AT WAR

2015	NCLT	50,000	Cu/ni	15.55g	Circ coin in coloured folder	10	10	–

[g] 2015 TOBRUK - AUSTRALIA AT WAR

2015	NCLT	50,000	Cu/ni	15.55g	Circ coin in coloured folder	10	13	–

[h] 2015 CRETE - AUSTRALIA AT WAR

2015	NCLT	50,000	Cu/ni	15.55g	Circ coin in coloured folder	10	13	–

2015 [i] Royal baby Unc

2015 [j] Royal baby Proof

2015 [k] Longest Reign

2015 [l] Air Training

[i/j] 2015 BIRTH OF THE ROYAL BABY CHARLOTTE

2015 i	NCLT	50,000	Cu/ni	15.55g	Circ coin in coloured folder	10	15	–
2015	PNC	9,000	Cu/ni	15.55g	Coin & Stamp cover. Priced in PNC section			–
2015 j	NCLT	5,000	Silver	18.24g	Proof coin in presentation coin	85	–	100

[k] 2015 LONGEST REIGNING MONARCH

2015 k	NCLT	50,000	Cu/ni	15.55g	Circ coin in coloured folder	10	13	–
2015	PNC	9,000	Cu/ni	15.55g	Coin & Stamp cover. See PNC section			–

[l] 2015 EMPIRE AIR TRAINING SCHEME

2015 l	NCLT	50,000	Cu/ni	15.55g	Circ coin in coloured folder	10	13	–

FIFTY CENTS

ONE YEAR COMMEMORATIVE REVERSES

Common Obverse

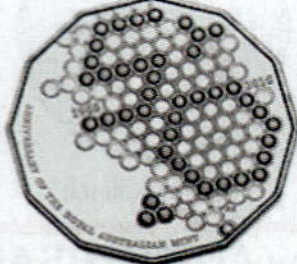
2015 [a] Ex- Mint set

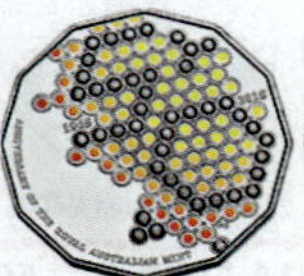
2015 [b] Coloured single

2015 [c] Gold plated. proof

Date	TYPE	Mintage Figures	Metal Comp.	Weight in gm	Description	Issue Price	Unc Retail	Proof Retail
[a,b,c]		**2015 ROYAL AUST. MINT 50TH ANNIVERSARY**						
2015 a	NCLT	100,000	Cu/ni	15.55g	Specimen plain rev in mint set	–	10	–
2015 b	NCLT	30,000	Cu/ni	15.55g	Specimen Colour rev. In card	13.5	15	–
2015 b	NCLT	5,000	Cu/ni	15.55g	Specimen Berlin Fair overprint	19.95	25	–
2015 c	NCLT	To order	Cu/ni	15.55g	Proof. Gilt rev in proof set	–	–	25

2015 [c] 24 carat gold plated 50 years anniversary

2016 [f] Korea

2016 [g] Pozieres

Date	TYPE	Mintage Figures	Metal Comp.	Weight in gm	Description	Issue Price	Unc Retail	Proof Retail
[c/d]		**2015 GOLD PLATED 50 YEARS RAM OPENING**						
2015	NCLT	22,265	Plated	15.55g	Circ. 22ct gilt in Open Day card	n/a	55	–
[f]	**2016**	**KOREA - AUSTRALIA AT WAR**						
2016	NCLT	50,000	Cu/ni	15.55g	Circ coin in coloured folder	10	10	–
[g]	**2016**	**POZIERES - AUSTRALIA AT WAR**						
2016	NCLT	50,000	Cu/ni	15.55g	Circ coin in coloured folder	10	10	–

2016 [h] Fromelles

2016 [i] Vietnam

2016 [j] Malaya

2016 [k] Indonesia

Date	TYPE	Mintage Figures	Metal Comp.	Weight in gm	Description	Issue Price	Unc Retail	Proof Retail
[h]	**2016**	**FROMELLES - AUSTRALIA AT WAR**						
2016	NCLT	50,000	Cu/ni	15.55g	Circ coin in coloured folder	10	10	–
[i]	**2016**	**VIETNAM - AUSTRALIA AT WAR**						
2016	NCLT	50,000	Cu/ni	15.55g	Circ coin in coloured folder	10	10	–
[j]	**2016**	**MALAYAN EMERGENCY - AUST. AT WAR**						
2016	NCLT	50,000	Cu/ni	15.55g	Circ coin in coloured folder	10	10	–
[k]	**2016**	**INDONESIAN CONFRONTATION - AUST. AT WAR**						
2016	NCLT	50,000	Cu/ni	15.55g	Circ coin in coloured folder	10	10	–

FIFTY CENTS

ONE YEAR COMMEMORATIVE REVERSES

2016 [a] Gulf War

2016 [b] Big Ted, Little Ted

2016 [c] Jemima. Play School

2016 [c] Humpty

Date	TYPE	Mintage Figures	Metal Comp	Weight in gms	Description	Issue Price	Retail Average	
[a]	**2016**	**GULF WAR - AUSTRALIA AT WAR**						
2016	NCLT	50,000	Cu/ni	15.55g	Circ coin in coloured folder	10	10	–
[b/c]	**2016**	**FIFTY YEARS OF PLAY SCHOOL. Three coin set**						
2016	NCLT	To order	Cu/ni	15.55g	Specimens in coloured folder	45	45	–
2016 b	PNC	7,500	Cu/ni	15.55g	Big & Little Ted. See PNC section for pricing			
2016 c	PNC	7,500	Cu/ni	15.55g	Jemima & Humpty. See PNC section for pricing			

[b/c] Introduced in 1966, Play School is the longest running children's television show in Australia. Featuring Jemima, Big & Little Ted and Humpty. Sold as a three coin set plus two PNC's

2016 [d] Afghanistan

2016 [e] Gilt Silver

2016 [f/g] Gold plated

2016 [h] Decimal 50th

Date	TYPE	Mintage Figures	Metal Comp	Weight in gms	Description	Issue Price	Retail Average	
[d]	**2016**	**AFGHANISTAN - AUSTRALIA AT WAR**						
2016	NCLT	50,000	Cu/ni	15.55g	Circ coin in coloured folder	10	10	–
[e]	**2016**	**SELECTIVE GOLD PLATED SILVER PROOF**						
2016	NCLT	7,500	Silver	13.70g	Proof. Cased gold plated`	100	–	110
[f/g]	**2016**	**DECIMAL CURRENCY. GOLD PLATED ROUND**						
2016	NCLT	21,966	Cu/ni	15.37g	Circ gold plated Cu/ni in folder	20	30	–
2016 f	NCLT	[10,000]	Cu/ni	15.37g	As above in first day folder.	n/a	40	–
2016 g	NCLT	5,000	Cu/ni	15.37g	Berlin Money Expo. WMF	n/a	45	–

[f] Of the above mintage of 21,966 coins, 10,000 were issued in special Decimal Open Day dated packaging and were released on Saturday 13 February 2016.
[g] These coins have the Berlin special packaging and WMF privy-mark. [See image at right]. The plastic folder was a distinctive burnt orange colour instead of the light blue used in the other issues.

Date	TYPE	Mintage Figures	Metal Comp	Weight in gms	Description	Issue Price	Retail Average	
[g]	**2016**	**DECIMAL CURRENCY 50TH ANNIVERSARY**						
2016	NCLT	95,929	Cu/ni	15.55g	Circ coin in coloured card	10	10	–
2016	ROLL	5,000	Cu/ni	15.55g	Commemorative roll. 20 x Unc coins	10	35	–
2016	BAG	tba	Cu/ni	15.55g	Commemorative bag. 20 x Unc coins	35	40	–
2016	EX-SET	tba	Cu/ni	15.55g	Spec. Part of annual 6 coin mint set	–	10	–
2016	EX-SET	tba	Cu/ni	15.55g	Proof. Part of annual 6 coin proof set	–	–	15

FIFTY CENTS

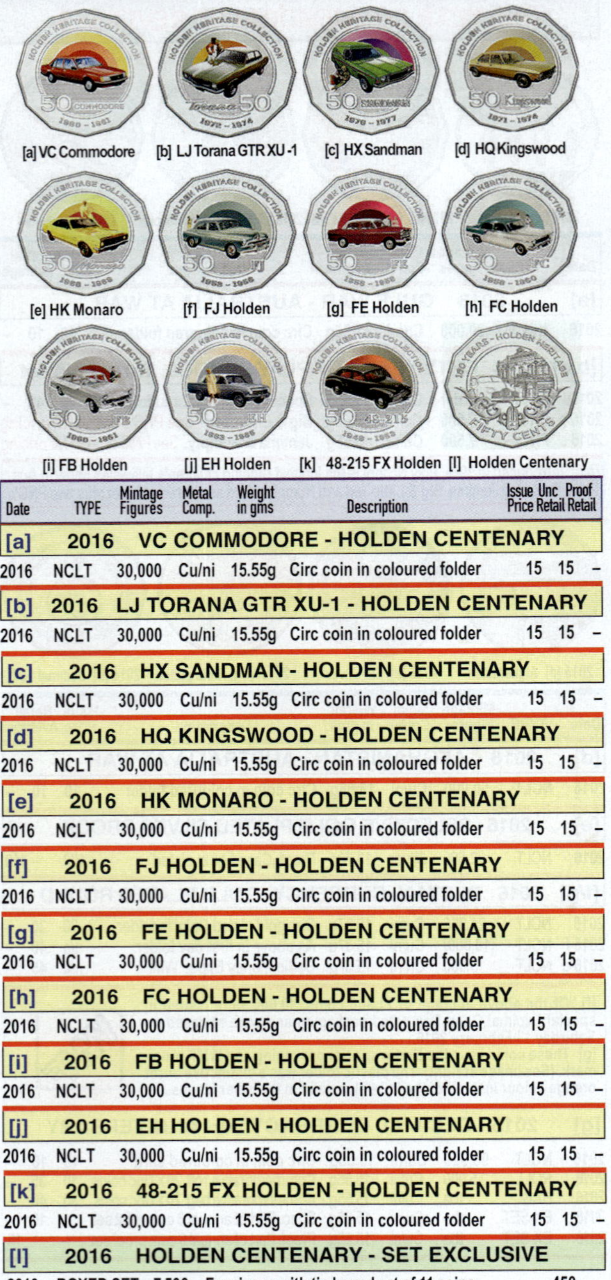

[a] VC Commodore [b] LJ Torana GTR XU-1 [c] HX Sandman [d] HQ Kingswood

[e] HK Monaro [f] FJ Holden [g] FE Holden [h] FC Holden

[i] FB Holden [j] EH Holden [k] 48-215 FX Holden [l] Holden Centenary

Date	TYPE	Mintage Figures	Metal Comp.	Weight in gms	Description	Issue Price	Unc Retail	Proof Retail
[a]	**2016**	**VC COMMODORE - HOLDEN CENTENARY**						
2016	NCLT	30,000	Cu/ni	15.55g	Circ coin in coloured folder	15	15	–
[b]	**2016**	**LJ TORANA GTR XU-1 - HOLDEN CENTENARY**						
2016	NCLT	30,000	Cu/ni	15.55g	Circ coin in coloured folder	15	15	–
[c]	**2016**	**HX SANDMAN - HOLDEN CENTENARY**						
2016	NCLT	30,000	Cu/ni	15.55g	Circ coin in coloured folder	15	15	–
[d]	**2016**	**HQ KINGSWOOD - HOLDEN CENTENARY**						
2016	NCLT	30,000	Cu/ni	15.55g	Circ coin in coloured folder	15	15	–
[e]	**2016**	**HK MONARO - HOLDEN CENTENARY**						
2016	NCLT	30,000	Cu/ni	15.55g	Circ coin in coloured folder	15	15	–
[f]	**2016**	**FJ HOLDEN - HOLDEN CENTENARY**						
2016	NCLT	30,000	Cu/ni	15.55g	Circ coin in coloured folder	15	15	–
[g]	**2016**	**FE HOLDEN - HOLDEN CENTENARY**						
2016	NCLT	30,000	Cu/ni	15.55g	Circ coin in coloured folder	15	15	–
[h]	**2016**	**FC HOLDEN - HOLDEN CENTENARY**						
2016	NCLT	30,000	Cu/ni	15.55g	Circ coin in coloured folder	15	15	–
[i]	**2016**	**FB HOLDEN - HOLDEN CENTENARY**						
2016	NCLT	30,000	Cu/ni	15.55g	Circ coin in coloured folder	15	15	–
[j]	**2016**	**EH HOLDEN - HOLDEN CENTENARY**						
2016	NCLT	30,000	Cu/ni	15.55g	Circ coin in coloured folder	15	15	–
[k]	**2016**	**48-215 FX HOLDEN - HOLDEN CENTENARY**						
2016	NCLT	30,000	Cu/ni	15.55g	Circ coin in coloured folder	15	15	–
[l]	**2016**	**HOLDEN CENTENARY - SET EXCLUSIVE**						
2016	BOXED SET	7,500			Free issue with tin boxed set of 11 coins	–	450	–

50¢ RAM LUNAR ISSUES

FIFTY CENTS TETRADECAGON (14 SIDED)

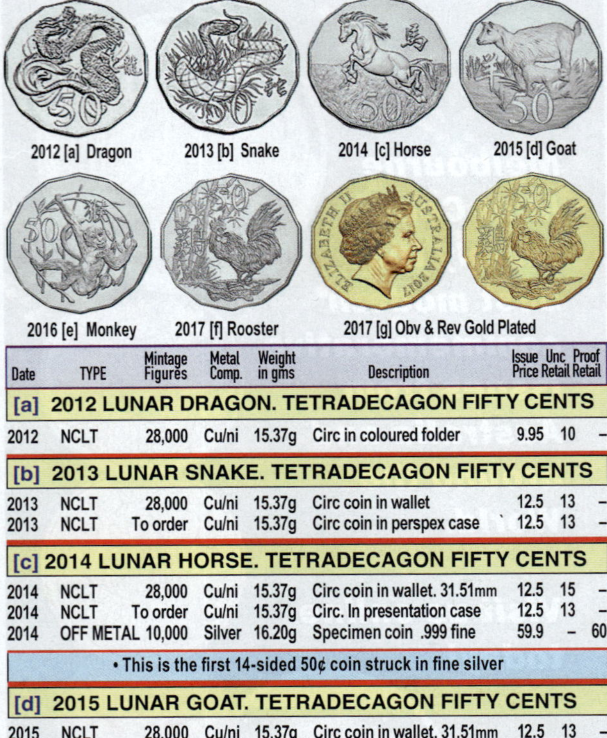

2012 [a] Dragon — 2013 [b] Snake — 2014 [c] Horse — 2015 [d] Goat

2016 [e] Monkey — 2017 [f] Rooster — 2017 [g] Obv & Rev Gold Plated

Date	TYPE	Mintage Figures	Metal Comp.	Weight in gms	Description	Issue Price	Unc Retail	Proof Retail
[a] 2012 LUNAR DRAGON. TETRADECAGON FIFTY CENTS								
2012	NCLT	28,000	Cu/ni	15.37g	Circ in coloured folder	9.95	10	–
[b] 2013 LUNAR SNAKE. TETRADECAGON FIFTY CENTS								
2013	NCLT	28,000	Cu/ni	15.37g	Circ coin in wallet	12.5	13	–
2013	NCLT	To order	Cu/ni	15.37g	Circ coin in perspex case	12.5	13	–
[c] 2014 LUNAR HORSE. TETRADECAGON FIFTY CENTS								
2014	NCLT	28,000	Cu/ni	15.37g	Circ coin in wallet. 31.51mm	12.5	15	–
2014	NCLT	To order	Cu/ni	15.37g	Circ. In presentation case	12.5	13	–
2014	OFF METAL	10,000	Silver	16.20g	Specimen coin .999 fine	59.9	–	60
• This is the first 14-sided 50¢ coin struck in fine silver								
[d] 2015 LUNAR GOAT. TETRADECAGON FIFTY CENTS								
2015	NCLT	28,000	Cu/ni	15.37g	Circ coin in wallet. 31.51mm	12.5	13	–
2015	NCLT	To order	Cu/ni	15.37g	Circ. In box presentation	12.5	13	–
2015	OFF METAL	10,000	Silver	1/2 oz	Specimen coin .999 fine	59.9	–	60
[e] 2016 LUNAR MONKEY. TETRADECAGON FIFTY CENTS								
2016	NCLT	28,000	Cu/ni	15.37g	Circ coin in wallet. 31.51mm	12.5	13	–
2016	NCLT	To order	Cu/ni	15.37g	Circ. In box presentation	12.5	13	–
2016	OFF METAL	10,000	Silver	1/2 oz	Specimen coin .999 fine	59.9	–	60
[f] 2017 LUNAR ROOSTER. TETRADECAGON FIFTY CENTS								
2017	NCLT	28,000	Cu/ni	15.37g	Circ coin in wallet. 31.51mm	12.5	13	–
2017	NCLT	To order	Cu/ni	15.37g	Circ. In box presentation	12.5	13	–
2017 a	NCLT	5,000	Plated	15.37g	Circ. In box presentation	29.95	33	–
2017	OFF METAL	10,000	Silver	1/2 oz	Specimen coin .999 fine	59.9	–	60

[a] This issue broke new ground for a number reasons. It was Australia's first Lunar 50c to be plated in pure 24 carat gold. It is also the first lunar Tetradecagon 50¢ issued for the World Money Fair. The coin is housed in an official WMF pack.

See page 342

UNOFFICIAL ONE DOLLAR

PATTERN DESIGN FOR OUR FIRST ONE DOLLAR

Date	TYPE	Metal Composition	Edge	Size	Weight in gms	Mintage Figures	Issue Price	Retail Average
1967 - SWAN / GOOSE DOLLAR - ACR MAGAZINE COMPETITION								
1967	PROOF	Fine Silver	Plain edge	38mm	28.7 g	750	13.5	2,950
1967	UNC	Fine Silver	Milled edge	38mm	28.7 g	1,500	10	2,250
1967	PROOF	Gold [22 ct]	Plain edge	38mm	40.3 g	10/7	n/a	24,000

Above prices for coins in original case and without marks or hairline scratches

While this coin is not an official issue, it is now part of numismatic history that has attained significant status with collectors. When decimal currency was introduced in 1966, collectors were surprised to learn that a one dollar coin was not considered as part of the new lineup. The Australian Coin Review took up the challenge and conducted a competition among readers. The "Swan Dollar" (more commonly called the Goose Dollar) was the winning entry and the design was forwarded to the relevant Government Department. When the design was rejected, the competition organisers decided to have it privately minted. All coins were issued in a maroon coloured case, with the inscription Australian Pattern "Crown" in three lines inside the lid. The case of the plain edge coin has the designation "PROOF" added as a fourth line.

(a) Two Gold coins were lost in the Victorian Ash Wednesday bushfires in 1983 and another badly mutilated and destroyed. One of the remaining seven gold coins created a new record price when offered as lot 1490 in Nobles sale 103 in August 2013. It was described in the catalogue as : "Unofficial swan pattern dollar, 1967, in gold (22ct, 40.3 gms, 38mm) plain edge by Andor Meszaros for John Pinches. Some edge knocks, contact marks and hairline scratches in fields, otherwise good extremely fine." Against an estimate of $8,000 it was knocked down for $19,000 plus commission.

BEWARE OF REPLICAS. Collector Peter Johnson has advised that fakes of the above silver coins have started to appear on eBay. While Peter says that the seller clearly describes them as 'replicas' there is no such lettering, counterstamp or other identifying mark on the coin itself to indicate this.

2000 ONE DOLLAR / TEN CENTS MULE

Above. The thicker "Mule" edge rim is shown above.

Date	TYPE	Mintage Figures	Mint Mark	Metal Comp	Weight in gms	Fine	Very Fine	Extra Fine	Unc	Proof
2000	CIRC	2,000?	—	Al/Br	9 g	1,250	2,750	6,000	Not seen	n/a

During the production of normal circulation one dollar coins in 2000, it appears that one or more of the obverse dies for the 2000 ten cent coin were mixed up with dollar reverse dies. As the diameter of the ten cents piece is slightly smaller than the one dollar, the resulting mule error can be distinguished by a thicker double rim on the obverse as shown above. Being an error, there are no official figures. However coins being offered for sale by a variety of collectors and dealers quote figures ranging from 500 to 2000. Most examples found so far are well worn [less than very fine]. This would suggest that it took some time for collectors to identify the error.

ONE DOLLAR

FIRST PORTRAIT TYPE

1984 Only

One Year Type Coin

Aluminium bronze

92% copper 6% aluminium; 2% nickel. Size 25 mm

Obverse : Arnold Machin.
Reverse : Stuart Devlin.

CIRCULATION & NON CIRCULATION (NCLT) ISSUES

Date	TYPE	Mintage Figures	Mint Mark	Metal Comp.	Weight in gms	Issuing Mint	Unc	Choice Unc	Roll or Bagged	Issue Price	Mint set Retail	Proof Retail
1984	CIRC	185,985,000	–	Al/br	9 g	Canb	4	6	90	–	–	–
1984 a	NCLT	538,358	–	Al/br	9 g	Circ. Red bubble display card				3.5	10	–
1984 b	NCLT	159,340	–	Al/br	9 g	Proof coin in light blue case				9	–	12
1984 c	RESTRIKE	66,789	–	Al/br	9 g	Circ. Part of 5 x $1 coin set				–	–	20
2009 d	RESTRIKE	1,000	–	Gold	21.5g	Proof. Cased single coin				1,750	–	1,750

[a] Square shaped red Bubble pack.
[b] Cased proof. Sterling silver. 92.5%. First released on May 14, 1984.
[c] In 1992, five previously issued dollar coins were issued in a folder. See table on same page as 1994 issued coins.
[d] 2009 Unique Machin obverse gold dollar : Along with a pure gold 50¢ coin, the RAM stuck 500 proof examples of each for an overseas corporate order. They featured the original Arnold Machin portrait that first appeared in 1966. Each was individually cased and numbered. In Noble's sale 108, a gold $1 with the serial number 241 sold for $1,550 plus 19.5% commission against an estimate of $1,200.

2006 ONE YEAR TYPE RETRO PORTRAIT

2006 Only

One Year Type Coin

99.9 fine silver

Obverse : Arnold Machin.
Reverse : Stuart Devlin.

Date	TYPE	Mintage Figures	Mint Mark	Metal Comp.	Weight in gms	Issuing Mint	Issue Price	Mint set Retail	Proof Retail
2006	EX-SET	5,829	–	Silver	11.66	Proof. Machin obv. 8 coin set	–	–	45

[e] : To celebrate the 40th anniversary of decimalisation, the RAM produced a 2006 eight coin proof set in fine silver. The set featured the original Arnold Machin effigy of the Queen rather than the standard 2006 Ian Rank-Broadley obverse. The above coin was not officially issued individually but part of a complete set.

ONE DOLLAR

1991. FIRST MINT YOUR OWN COIN AT RAM

In 1991, the RAM converted one of its presses to allow visitors to strike their own one dollar coin. The cost was two dollars, including a plastic satchel which changed over the years. Pictured above is the scarce first design. Current Value $45

ONE DOLLAR

SECOND PORTRAIT TYPE

1985-1998

Aluminium bronze
92% copper 6% aluminium; 2% nickel. Size 25 mm
Silver. 92.5% Sterling
Size 25 mm

Obv : Raphael Maklouf. **Rev :** Stuart Devlin

CIRCULATION & NON CIRCULATION (NCLT) ISSUES

Date	TYPE	Mintage Figures	Mint Mark	Metal Comp.	Weight in gms	Issuing Mint	Unc	Choice Unc	Roll or Bagged	Issue Price	Mint set Retail	Proof Retail
1985	CIRC	96,200,000	–	Al/br	9g	Canb	4	7	35		9	15
1985 a	RESTRIKE	66,789	–	Al/br	9g	Circ. Part of 5 x $1 restrike set				–	20	–
1987	EX- SET	200,000	–	Al/br	9g	Circ coin unique to mint set				–	16	–
1989	EX- SET	150,602	–	Al/br	9g	Circ coin unique to mint set				–	12	–
1990	EX- SET	103,766	–	Al/br	9g	Circ coin unique to mint set				–	50	–
1990	OFF METAL	24,999	–	Silver	11.49	Proof M'pieces.925 Stg. 25mm				–	–	25
1991	NCLT	22,500	–	Al/br	9g	RAM. Mint your own coin				2	15	–
1991	EX- SET	147,700	–	Al/br	9g	Circ coin unique to mint set				–	25	–
1991	OFF METAL	25,000	–	Silver	11.49	Proof M'pieces.925 Stg. 25mm				–	–	25
1992 b	CIRC	8,000	–	Al/br	9g	Canb 1,200?		n/a	n/a	n/a	n/a	–
1994	CIRC	47,600,000	–	Al/br	9g	Canb	7	15	125	–	25	–
1995	CIRC	21,422,000	–	Al/br	9g	Canb	5	8	85	–	15	–

[a] In 1992, five previously issued commemoratives were issued in a folder. Although all five issues are "restrikes' produced in 1992, they all feature their original date of issue and are difficult to distinguish them from their original counterparts.
[b] The official RAM report suggests that just 8,000 1992 one dollar coins with the Mob of Roos reverse were struck in aluminium bronze for general circulation. This seems like an impossibly small number of coins that is at odds with other mintages that often run into millions of coins. In 1992, the Barcelona Olympic Games commemorative issue was generally considered to be the only one dollar issue. It appears in a number of collector orientated issues, but again, not released for circulation. Over the years collectors generally agreed that the entry was simply an error. It seemed most likely that the small mintage was somehow connected with "restrikes" of 1984 or 1985 'roo' reverses that were produced for the "Five Dollar Folder" that was released in 1992. However in February 2012, even this plausable explanation was put to the test. In auction sale 310, Downie's Australian Coin Auction offered one of the elusive Roo reverse dollars as lot 2493 with an estimate of $750. The coin was described as being struck on a partially prepared proof blank, as struck and extremely rare. The coin sold for a total of $1,190 including buyer's premium. The author would welcome any new information regarding this intriguing oddity.

2006 ACCIDENTIAL ERROR PROOF MULE

2005 OBVERSE/ 2006 REVERSE

Aluminium bronze

Obverse : Ian Rank-Broadley.
Reverse : Stuart Devlin. Mob of Roos.

Date	TYPE	Mintage Figures	Metal Comp.	Weight in gms	Size	Description	Retail Average
2006	EX-SET	20 to 40?	Al/br	9g	25mm	Unique to proof set	7,750

In a March 2006 press release, leading numismatic dealership Downies offered collectors the following information : "Unprecedented in more than 40 years of the Royal Australian Mint Proof Set series, it has come to light that a tiny number of 2006 Proof Sets comprise a genuine Mule $1. It is amazing enough to find a Proof Set featuring an incorrect dated coin, but when that coin should never actually exist in any form, the importance of the discovery is breathtaking. Destined to be the most valuable issue in the series, we found amongst our original allocation twenty 2006 Proof Sets comprising a 2005-dated Mob of Roos $1." Since then Colonial Coins of Brisbane has also discovered a small number of sets.

ONE DOLLAR

2000 - THIRD PORTRAIT TYPE

2000 -

Aluminium bronze
92% copper 6% aluminium;
2%nickel. Size 25 mm
Silver : Fine 99.9%. Size 25mm
Gold : Fine 99.99%. Size 25mm

Obv : Ian Rank-Broadley
Rev : Stuart Devlin

Date	TYPE	Mintage Figures	Mint Mark	Metal Comp.	Weight in gms	issuing Mint	Unc	Choice Unc	Roll or Bagged	Issue Price	Mint set Retail	Proof Retail
2000	CIRC	7,592,000	–	Al/br	9 g	Canb	35	60	700	–	–	–
2004	CIRC	8,800,000	–	Al/br	9 g	Canb	8	12	90	–	–	–
2004	EX-SET	67,795	–	Al/br	9 g	Spec. part of annual mint set				–	20	–
2004	FAIR ISSUE	2,500	–	Al/br	9 g	Specimen. Berlin Money Fair				10	20	–
2004	EX-SET	31,036	–	Al/br	9 g	Specimen part of baby mint set				–	20	–
2004	EX SET	3,963	–	Al/br	9 g	Specimen part of wedding set				–	25	–
2004 a	EX-SET	50,000	–	Al/br	9 g	Proof hologram in annual set				–	–	35
2004 b	CORPORATE	50,000	–	Al/br	9 g	Proof hologram. Cased single				30	–	45
2004	EX SET	31,036	–	Al/br	9 g	Proof part of Koala Baby set				–	–	25
2004	OFF METAL	2,040	–	Silver	11.56	Proof part of fine silver set				–	–	60
2004 c	ERROR	Unknown	–	Al/br	9 g	Uniface error in baby proof set				–	Rare	–
2004 d	OFF METAL	8,250	–	Silver	1 oz	Proof M'pieces .925 Stg. 40mm				–	–	45
2004	OFF METAL	6,500	–	Silver	11.56	Proof part of cased 6 coin set				–	–	45
2005	CIRC	5,792,000	–	Al/br	9 g	Canb	5	8	55	–	–	45
2006 e	ERROR	40?	–	Al/br	9 g	Proof. 2005 $1 in 2006 proof set				–	Rare	–
2006	CIRC	38,691,000	–	Al/br	9 g	Canb	5	8	n/a	–	–	20
2006	EX-SET	84,407	–	Al/br	9 g	Spec. part of annual mint set				–	20	–
2006	EX-SET	32,095	–	Al/br	9 g	Specimen part of baby mint set				–	20	–
2006	EX-SET	2,752	–	Al/br	9 g	Specimen part of Wedding set				–	20	–
2006	FAIR ISSUE	1,500	–	Al/br	9 g	Specimen. Berlin Money Fair				10	20	–
2006	FAIR ISSUE	1,500	–	Al/br	9 g	Specimen. ANDA Canberra Fair				10	20	–
2006	EX-SET	45,373	–	Al/br	9 g	Proof part of annual 6 coin set				–	–	45
2006	EX-SET	5,829	–	Silver	11.66	Proof. Machin obverse. *See Type 1 section*						
2006	EX-SET	300	–	Gold	21.52	Proof. Rank Broadley. 8 coin set				–		1,795

(a) Australia's first holographic image. For the first time the Proof Year Set contained a coin with a holographic image. The five kangaroos on the $1 coin appear as multi- coloured, iridescent holograms, conveying the impression of colour and movement. The $1 hologram coin was developed by the CSIRO in conjunction with the RAM. This method, called Replica Micro Moulding, uses a high precision elastomer stamp as a means for transferring a complex micro-pattern (the holographic image) onto the surface of the coin. A finely focused electron beam forms a pattern of fine grooves (which is the image that will appear on the reverse of the coin) on a specially prepared elastomer stamp. After striking the coin with the obverse image (effigy of the Queen) in the normal way the coin then goes through a second process where each coin has a resin application and is struck using the elastomer stamp. The fine pattern of grooves applied to the surface of the coin has been specifically designed to give an iridescent image with distinct colours and featuring a movement of the image with tilting of the coin.

(b) Corporate holographic order. A variation of the above hologram $1 as a private international corporate order. While this unique coin shared the same reverse as the proof set issue, the corporate single coin product featured the original 1984 Arnold Machin portrait. It was not sold direct to the public and very few seem to have filtered back to the Australian market.

(c) A possibly unique error uniface obverse 2004 dollar has been found in a 2004 Baby Proof Set. It has a semi-matte surface and is probably a test piece struck prior to die polishing. The reverse is almost blank but on close examination, remnants of the holographic 'mob of roos' design is just visible.

(d) 20 years of the Dollar. This set contained images of three unused dollar patterns as well as representations of three familiar designs. The MOR's issue was an impressive 1oz fine .999 silver piece with a width of 40mm. It was the first time this design was issued as a crown sized coin. The other circulated designs were representations of the 1995 Waltzing Matilda and the 1994 Dollar Decade.

(e) Error 2005/2006 Mule. Some obverse 2005 dies were accidentally mixed with 2006 "Mob of Roos" (MOR) reverses. When discovered it was decided to continue with the mismatched striking to avoid publicity that would be generated from a low mintage mule issue. A similar error occurred the following year when the proof dollar in a few 2006 proof sets included the 2005 dated proof MOR dollar More information and an illustration can be found on the previous page.

ONE DOLLAR

2000 - THIRD PORTRAIT TYPE

2000 -

Aluminium bronze
92% copper 6% aluminium; 2% nickel. Size 25 mm
Silver : Fine 99.9%. Size 25mm
Gold : Fine 99.99%. Size 25mm

Obv : Ian Rank-Broadley
Rev : Stuart Devlin

CIRCULATION & NON CIRCULATION (NCLT) ISSUES

Date	TYPE	Mintage Figures	Mint Mark	Metal Comp.	Weight in gms	Issuing Mint	Unc	Choice Unc	Roll or Bagged	Issue Price	Mint set Retail	Proof Retail
2007	EX- SET	200,000	–	Al/br	9g	Circ unique to annual mint set				–	15	–
2007	PNC	37,100	–	Al/br	9 g	Coin & Stamp cover. Priced in PNC section –						
2008 a	CIRC	30,106,000	–	Al/br	9 g	Canb	4	5	n/a	–	–	20
2008	EX-SET	11,500	–	Al/br	9 g	Paired with 20¢ Planet Earth				–	45	–
2009	CIRC	21,600,000	–	Al/br	9 g	Canb	6	10	60	–	–	60
2009 b	FAIR ISSUE	500	–	Al/br	9 g	Specimen. Berlin Money Fair				–	6	–
2009	NCLT	2,824	–	A/br	9 g	Specimen. Part of Wedding set				–	15	–
2009	PART PAIR	9,599	–	Al/br	9 g	Proof paired with 20¢ astronomy				–	6	–
2009	NCLT	7,700	–	A/br	9 g	Circ Baby keepsake $1. In folder				9	9	–
2009 c	MINT MARK	23,758	C	A/br	9 g	Mintmark C & Roo combo				9.95	15	–
2009 d	MINT MARK	6,500	Cx2	A/br	9 g	Mintmark C & Roo + oval Cmk				12	50	–
2009	EX-SET	2,221	–	Silver	11.56	Proof. Part of 6 coin boxed set				–	–	60
2010	CIRC	20,595,000	–	Al/br	9 g	Canb	3	5	60	–	–	8
2010	EX SET	48,489	–	Al/br	9 g	Specimen part annual mint set				–	15	–
2010	EX SET	2,040	–	Al/br	9 g	Specimen. Berlin Money Fair					15	–
2010	EX SET	18,313	–	Al/br	9 g	Proof included in annual set				–	–	20
2010	EX SET	10,002	–	Al/br	9 g	Proof part of Blinky Bill set				–	–	20
2010	EX SET	2,493	–	Al/br	9 g	Proof part of Wedding set				–	–	20
2010	OFF METAL	2,040	–	Silver	11.56	Proof part of fine silver set				–	–	60
2011	CIRC	17,866,000	–	Al/br	9 g	Canb	3	5	n/a	–	–	20
2011	OFF METAL	2,072	–	Silver	11.56	Proof part of fine silver set				–	–	60
2012	EX- SET	100,000	–	Al/br	9 g	Circ unique to annual mint set				–	15	–
2012	OFF METAL	5,000	–	Silver	11.56	Proof. Individually cased coin				70	–	70
2012	MINI SET	2,000	–	Gold	.5 g	Proof. Part of 6 coin boxed set				–	–	n/a
2013	CIRC	20,850,000	–	Al/br	9 g	Canb	4	5	n/a	–	–	20
2013	EX-SET	8,000	–	Al/br	9 g	Proof included in Baby set				–	–	15
2013	EX-SET	850	–	Al/br	9 g	Proof included Wedding set					–	15
2013	OFF METAL	1,000	–	Silver	11.66	Proof. Individually cased coin				60	–	60
2013	OFF METAL	500	–	Silver	11.66	Proof. Part of 6 coin boxed set					–	60
2013	OFF METAL	500	–	Gold	21.52	Proof. Individually cased coin				1,795	–	1,795
2013	OFF METAL	500	–	Gold	21.52	Proof. Part of 6 coin boxed set				1,795	–	1,795

[a] Obverse modified from 2008 - legend font slightly different to previous issues,blunted "2" and more oval "00" in date. MOR dollar in the 6 coin Mint Set, 2 coin Proof & Baby Proof sets.
[b] 500 Specimen quality coins were offered by the RAM at the World Money Fair in Berlin in February 2009. Participating dealers were offered an allocation.
MASTER MINTMARK : In 2009, the RAM completed a major refurbishment of its production and tourist facilities. It was the most substantial upgrade to its facilities since construction was completed in 1965. The upgrade was celebrated with two versions of a special mintmark. Both featured the letter "C" with a kangaroo passing through it . It was chosen by the mints CEO Janine Murphy from a selection of motifs product by Mint design staff. The Master Mintmark logo is presented in a die-cut packaging that folds into a miniature Mint building.
[c] This mintmark was part of the overall die design and not an additional mintmark added later.
[d] This low mintage issue featured a second privy mark of an incuse C mintmark within an oval that was added by keen collectors attending the re-opening day. This low mintage issue also included the above mintmark but also a second C mintmark was added above the "D" of DOLLAR using the 'mint your own coin' gallery press. This privy mark was similar to the incuse circular mint mark found on coins minted using the mobile press at various off-site shows.

ONE DOLLAR

2000 - THIRD PORTRAIT TYPE

2000 -

Aluminium bronze
92% copper 6% aluminium; 2% nickel. Size 25 mm

Silver : Fine 99.9%. Size 25mm
Gold : Fine 99.99%. Size 25mm

Obv : Ian Rank-Broadley
Rev : Stuart Devlin

CIRCULATION & NON CIRCULATION (NCLT) ISSUES

Date	TYPE	Mintage Figures	Mint Mark	Metal Comp.	Weight in gms	Issuing Mint	Unc	Choice Unc	Roll or Bagged	Issue Price	Mint set Retail	Proof Retail
2014	CIRC	1,052,000	–	Al/br	9 g	Canb	4	5	–	–	20	–
2014	MINT ROLL	5,000	–	Al/br	9 g	Canb. Official RAM issue			150	–	–	–
2014 a	NCLT	5,000	S	Al/br	9 g	Mobile Press. QBE Sydney				10	25	–
2014	EX-SET	36,482	–	Al/br	9 g	Circ colour $1 part of mint set				–	15	–
2014	FAIR ISSUE	1,500	–	Al/br	9 g	Circ. Berlin Fair. $1 coloured				10	40	–
2014	FAIR ISSUE	1,500	–	Al/br	9 g	Circ. Berlin Fair. $1. No Colour				40	–	50
2014 b	OFF METAL	30,000	–	Cu/ni	10.03	Specimen in coloured folder				17	20	–
2014 c	OFF METAL	14,814	–	Cu/ni	10.03	Gilt Proof. Unique to annual set				–	–	45
2014 d	HIGH RELIEF	4,436	–	Silver	1 oz	Proof. Diameter 32mm. Cased				100	–	120
2014	OFF METAL	Ditto	–	Silver	11.66	Proof. Individually cased coin				60	–	60
2014	OFF METAL	1,000	–	Silver	11.66	Proof. Part of 6 coin boxed set				–	–	60
2014	OFF METAL	50	–	Gold	21.52	Proof. Individually cased coin				1,795		1,795
2014	OFF METAL	50/ 47	–	Gold	21.52	Proof. Part of 6 coin boxed set				–	–	1,795

[a] Sydney Mint Mark : This unique "S" mintmarked coin was only available for one day under equally unique circumstances. On Thursday, May 8, 2014 the RAM erected a purpose built "pop-up" tent on the Queen Victoria Building forecourt, between 10am and 4pm. 5,000 coins were sold for $10 each with the purchaser given the opportunity to strike the "S' mintmark themselves on a mobile press.
[b] Cupro nickel first : This issue was the first $1 coin struck in cupro-nickel, an alloy normally associated with the striking of lower denomination Australian coins.
[c] Gilt cupro nickel : A cupro nickel $1 with gold highlights was an exclusive addition to the annual proof set. See image below.
[d] Piedfort first : This Piedfort-sized coin was 32mm in diameter and 6mm thick. It was struck in .999 fine silver. It is the first MOR's piedfort.

2014 ONE DOLLAR SILVER 1oz PIEDFORT

In another first for 2014, the mint produced this impressive one ounce solid silver piedfort coin to commemorate the 40th anniversary of the introduction of the One Dollar coin back in 1984. This Piedfort-sized coin was 32mm in diameter and 6mm thick. It was struck in .999 fine silver. It is the first MOR's piedfort coin to be produced by the mint.

2014 30th ANNIVERSARY OF THE ONE DOLLAR

2014 Common obverse

2014 (a) Cupro Nickel

2014 (b) Al/br colour

2014 (c) Silver Gilt proof

2014 [a] Cupro Nickel in folder : This was the first dollar coin to be struck in Cupro Nickel; a metal that is more familar as the alloy used in five, ten, twenty and fifty cents coin. A frosted unc coin was coloured and sold individually in a distinctive folder. Only 30,000 coins were produced and sold for $17 each.
2014 [b] Aluminium bronze in folder : This coloured coin was struck in the usual aluminium/ bronze alloy and was exclusively produced for the annual mint set.
2014 [c] Cupro Nickel in folder : This proof cupro nickel coin with gold highlights was also unique. It was an exclusive issue for the annual proof set.

ONE DOLLAR

2000 - THIRD PORTRAIT TYPE

2000 -

Aluminium bronze
92% copper 6% aluminium; 2%nickel. Size 25 mm

Silver : Fine 99.9%. Size 25mm
Gold : Fine 99.99%. Size 25mm

Obv : Ian Rank-Broadley
Rev : Stuart Devlin

CIRCULATION & NON CIRCULATION (NCLT) ISSUES

Date	TYPE	Mintage Figures	Mint Mark	Metal Comp.	Weight in gms	Issuing Mint	Unc	Choice Unc	Roll or Bagged	Issue Price	Mint set Retail	Proof Retail
2015	CIRC	22,310,000	–	Al/br	9 g	Canb	2	4	30	–	–	–
2015 a	NCLT	5,000	P	Al/br	9 g	Privymark for ANDA. Perth				10	20	–
2015 b	NCLT	5,000	B	Al/br	9 g	Privymark for ANDA Brisbane				10	22	–
2015 c	NCLT	5,000	M	Al/br	9 g	Privymark for ANDA Melb fair				10	22	–
2015 d	NCLT	5,000	S	Al/br	9 g	Privymark for ANDA. Sydney				10	20	–
2015 e	NCLT	10,000	√	Al/br	9 g	Privymark. Berlin Ampelmann				10	20	–
2015 e	NCLT	1,000	√	Al/br	9 g	Berlin Ampelmann. Mint set				–	20	–
2015	OFF METAL	200	–	Silver	11.66	Proof. Individually cased coin				60	–	60
2015	OFF METAL	800	–	Silver	11.66	Proof. Part of 6 coin boxed set				–	–	60
2015	HIGH RELIEF	10,000	√	Silver	1 oz	Proof. Berlin Ampelmann				100	–	100
2015	OFF METAL	50	–	Gold	21.52	Proof. Individually cased coin				1,900	–	1,900
2015	OFF METAL	50	–	Gold	21.52	Proof. Part of 6 coin boxed set				–	–	1,995
2016	CIRC	tba	–	Al/br	9 g	Canb	2	4	30	–	–	–
2016 f	NCLT	3,000	P	Al/br	9 g	Pre-struck. Perth. Money Expo				19.95	22	–
2016 g	NCLT	5,000	B	Al/br	9 g	Pre-struck. Bris. Money Expo				19.95	22	–
2016 h	NCLT	2,287	M	Al/br	9 g	Pre-struck. Melb. Money Expo				15	22	–
2016 i	NCLT	3,000	S	Al/br	9 g	Pre-struck. Sydney. Money Expo				15	22	–
2016 j	FAIR ISSUE	7,500	#	Al/br	9 g	Pre-struck. Berlin Buddy Bear				19.95	22	–
2017	CIRC	tba	–	Al/br	9 g	Canb	2	4	30	–	–	–
2017 k	FAIR ISSUE	5,000	#	Al/br	9 g	Pre-struck. Berlin WMF Bear				14.95	16	–
2017 l	NCLT	3,000	P	Al/br	9 g	Pre-struck. Perth. Money Expo				19.95	22	–
2017 m	NCLT	3,000	B	Al/br	9 g	Pre-struck. Bris. Money Expo				19.95	22	–

[a] Perth ANDA Fair, held at the Paterson's Stadium, from March 7 - 8th.
[b] Brisbane ANDA fair. Held on May 21-22nd at the Table Tennis Centre, Windsor.
[c] Melbourne ANDA. Melbourne Bayview on the Park, August 22-23, 2015.
[d] Sydney ANDA. Lower Town Hall, Sydney, October 9-10, 2015.
[√ e] Ampelmann privy mark : In recognition of it's 50th anniversary, the RAM was the guest of honour at the Berlin World Money Fair in Germany. To commemorate the event, the RAM produced a single coin in a card and as part of a special mint set. Both issues were released at the fair which is widely regarded as the biggest in the world. The show was held from Jan 30 - Feb 1, 2015. The Ampelmann was a world-first in illuminated pedestrian crossing icons that was designed by traffic psychologist Karl Peglau in 1961. Ampelmann has developed a cult collecting status and is a popular souvenir item in the tourist industry.
[f] Pre-struck privy mark issued at the Perth Domain Stadium Subiaco on March 12-13, 2016
[g] Pre-struck privy mark issued at the Brisbane Table Tennis Centre, Windsor, May 21 - 22, 2016
[h] Melbourne Money Expo issue was available exclusively from the ANDA Stand during the fair. The show was held from August 27-28. The 'M' identification mark was the prestruck 'privy marked' type with the incuse square design.
[i] A pre-struck coin was on offer at the Sydney ANDA Money Expo, held from October 15-16, 2016.
[# j] First appearing in Berlin in 2001 and now recognised by the United Nations, Buddy Bear promotes peace and harmony all around the world.
[# k] Presented in an official WMF card, this coin featured a privymark featuring the Berlin Bear – a symbol used in the Berlin Coat of Arms since 1709.
[l] The first of the pre-struck privy marked $1 coins for 2017 was released at the Perth Money Expo held at the Domain Stadium, Subiaco on February 11-12, 2017.
[m] This pre-struck coin was struck for the 2017 Brisbane Money Expo held on Saturday and Sunday May 13 and 14 at the Royal International Convention Centre, Bowen Hills.

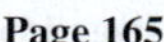

ONE DOLLAR

ONE YEAR COMMEMORATIVE REVERSES

1986 [a] Year of Peace

1988 [b] First Fleet silver & Al/br issues

1992 (c) Barcelona

CIRCULATION & NON CIRCULATION (NCLT) ISSUES

(a) 1986 INTERNATIONAL YEAR OF PEACE

Date	TYPE	Mintage Figures	Mint Mark	Metal Comp.	Weight in gms	Issuing Mint	Unc	Choice Unc	Roll or Bagged	Issue Price	Mint set Retail	Proof Retail
1986	CIRC	25,200,000	–	Al/br	9 g	Canb	4	8	130		–	–
1986	EX SET	180,000	–	Al/br	9 g	Circ part of annual mint set`				–	9	–
1986 a	RESTRIKE	66,789	–	Al/br	9 g	Circ part of five coin $1 set				–	20	–
1986	EX SET	67,000	–	Al/br	9 g	Proof part of annual proof set				–	–	12
1990	PROOF	24,999	–	Silver	11.49	Proof M'pieces .925 Stg. 25.1mm				–	–	25

[a] In 1992, five previously issued commemoratives were issued in a folder. The last of these was the 1992 Olympic issue. See bottom of next page.

(b) 1988 FIRST FLEET BICENTENARY

Date	TYPE	Mintage Figures	Mint Mark	Metal Comp.	Weight in gms	Issuing Mint	Unc	Choice Unc	Roll or Bagged	Issue Price	Mint set Retail	Proof Retail
1988	CIRC	21,600,000	–	Al/br	9 g	Canb	8	12	100	–	–	–
1988	EX SET	250,000	–	Al/br	9 g	Circ part of annual mint set				–	9	–
1988	RESTRIKE	66,789	–	Al/br	9 g	Circ. Part of 5 coin $1 set in folder				–	20	–
1988	EX SET	104,518	–	Al/br	9 g	Proof coin included in annual set				–	–	12
1988	OFF METAL	24,999	–	Silver	11.49	Proof M'pieces .925 Stg. 20.62mm				–	–	35
1990	OFF METAL	24,999	–	Silver	11.49	Proof M'pieces .925 Stg. 25.1mm				–	–	25

(c) 1992 BARCELONA OLYMPIC GAMES

Date	TYPE	Mintage Figures	Mint Mark	Metal Comp.	Weight in gms	Issuing Mint	Unc	Choice Unc	Roll or Bagged	Issue Price	Mint set Retail	Proof Retail
1992 a	NCLT	16,996	–	Al/br	9 g	Mintmark. Gallery. Mint your own				2	55	–
1992 b	CIRC	Inc above	–	Al/br	9 g	Circ coin in RAM plastic satchel				2	45	–
1992 c	CIRC	23,500	–	Al/br	9 g	Syd. Easter Show. Olympic packet				2	85	–
1992 d	CIRC	3,000	–	Al/br	9 g	Circ. As above with entry tab intact				2	120	–
1992	RESTRIKE	66,789	–	Al/br	9 g	Circ. Part of 5 coin $1 set in folder				–	20	–
1992 e	NCLT	2,979	–	Al/br	9 g	Proof. Women in sport. Capsule				32	–	175
1992	EX SET	118,528	–	Al/br	9 g	Circ part of annual mint set				–	45	–
1992	EX SET	56,367	–	Al/br	9 g	Proof part of annual cased set				–	–	12
1992 f	OFF METAL	12,500	–	Silver	11.31	Proof. Cased for general issue				32	–	100
1992 g	OFF METAL	2,500	–	Silver	11.31	Cased Proof .925 Stg. 25.1mm				36	–	210

[a] Sold exclusively at the RAM in a wallet showing Mint Building for $2.
[b] As above but Olympic illustrated wallet. (Replaced above wallet).
[c] Folder with a tear-off competition entry coupon to the Sydney Royal Easter Show.
[d] As above but with entry form coupon still intact.
[e] Women in sport. Proof coin in cylindrical see both sides capsule. See below.
[f] Silver. Interrupted reeding. Square box available through mailing list.
[g] Silver. Issued at March 1992 NAA Coin Fair. Continuous reeding. Long box.

ENCAPSULATED OLYMPIC PROOF ISSUE

This 1992 Barcelona one dollar commemorative issue. Listed as footnote **"e"**, this issue was very short lived and the coin and capsule are now quite scarce.

ONE DOLLAR

ONE YEAR COMMEMORATIVE REVERSES

1993 [a] Landcare Al/br & Proof Silver

1994 [b] Dollar Decade Al/br & Proof Silver

CIRCULATION & NON CIRCULATION (NCLT) ISSUES

Date	TYPE	Mintage Figures	Mint Mark	Metal Comp.	Weight in gms	Issuing Mint	Unc	Choice Unc	Roll or Bagged	Issue Price	Mint set Retail	Proof Retail
(a)	**1993 LANDCARE - WATER CONSERVATION**											
1993 a	CIRC	18,200,000	–	Al/br	9 g	Canb	3	9	20	–	–	–
1993 b	NCLT	228,664	C	Al/br	9 g	Mintmark. Gallery. Mint your own				2	6	–
1993 c	NCLT	119,373	S	Al/br	9 g	Mobile Ctr'stamp. Royal Sydney				2	6	–
1993 d	NCLT	67,185	M	Al/br	9 g	Mobile Counterstamp. Royal Melb				2	6	–
1993 e	NCLT	n/a	–	Al/br	9 g	BBC Hardware Promotion				–	8	–
1993	EX SET	86,068	–	Al/br	9 g	Unc part of annual mint set					9	
1993	EX SET	27,000	–	Al/br	9 g	First commemorative baby set				–	9	–
1993	EX SET	40,255	–	Al/br	9 g	Proof part of annual cased set				–	–	15
1993 f	OFF METAL	20,000	–	Silver	11.56	Proof in case .925 Stg. 25.1mm				32	–	45
1993 g	ERROR	Inc above	–	Silver	11.56	Issued with wrong certificate				32	–	175
1993 h	OFF METAL	5,000	–	Silver	11.56	Proof. Brisbane ANDA Coin Fair				32	–	75

(a) Coins dated 1993 were originally intended as a "C" mintmark *"strike your own coin"* issue at the RAM's tourist gallery. However a shortage of $1 coins in late 1993 forced the Treasury to release a large number of coins into circulation. This became a 'type two' issue as it did not include the 'C' mintmark.
(b) "C" Mintmarked coins as mentioned above. Sold in a special wallet for $2 each.
(c) "S" Countermark. Coins were struck on a mobile press at the Royal Easter Show Sydney.
(d) "M" Countermark. Struck on a mobile press at the Royal Melbourne Show.
(e) Hardware chain BBC commissioned the RAM to produce a coin in promotional folder.
(f) Sterling silver. Similar to (h) below but with interrupted reeding.
(g) Peter and Cathy Craft of Prospect Stamps & Coins discovered an error with the certificate. A small number of mail order coins were despatched with a certificate stating that 24,000 coins were struck. A corrected certificate 20,000 was sent out with the majority of the issue.
(h) NAA Brisbane Fair, May 8 - 9, 1993. 925% silver. Continuous reeding. Certificate 0001 to 5000.

Date	TYPE	Mintage Figures	Mint Mark	Metal Comp.	Weight in gms	Description	Issue Price	Unc Retail	Proof Retail
(b)	**1994 DOLLAR DECADE**								
1994 a	NCLT	105,090	C	Al/br	9 g	Mintmark. Gallery. Mint your own	2	5	–
1994 b	NCLT	74,474	S	Al/br	9 g	Mobile Counterstamp. Royal Syd.	2	5	–
1994 c	NCLT	79,256	M	Al/br	9 g	Mobile Counterstamp. Royal Melb.	2	18	–
1994 d	OFF METAL	5,001	–	Silver	9 g	Proof. Sydney Fair special box	–	–	80
1994 e	OFF METAL	20,000	–	Silver	11.31	Proof in case .925 Stg. 25.1mm	–	–	45

(a) Tourists struck their own coin on a press in the RAM Gallery. Coin in a descriptive folder.
(b) "S" C/M. Only the Al/Br were struck on the mobile press at the Royal Easter Show, Sydney.
(c) "M" C/M. Mobile press. Wording on satchel reads "Special Royal Melbourne Show Issue".
(d) NAA Fair, Sydney, March 26,27, 1994. Continuous reeding. Long box.
(e) Sterling silver and with interrupted reeding, sold through RAM mailing list.

FIVE x ONE DOLLAR COINS IN FOLDER

1984 - 1992 : ALL COINS UNCIRCULATED

Date	Mintage Figures	List of all the coins in the set	Issue Price	Average Price
1984-92	66,789	1984 Arnold Machin Obv. MOR Rev 1985 Raphael Maklouf Obv. MOR Rev 1986 Year of Peace Rev 1988 First Fleet Bicentenary Rev 1992 Barcelona Olympic Games Rev	7.5	45

ONE DOLLAR

ONE YEAR COMMEMORATIVE REVERSES

1995 [a/f] Waltzing Matilda Unc Al/br & Proof Silver   1996 [b/h] Sir Henry Parkes Unc Al/br & Proof Silver

NCLT. COLLECTOR ISSUES ONLY

Date	TYPE	Mintage Figures	Mint Mark	Metal Comp.	Weight in gms	Description	Issue Price	Unc Retail	Proof Retail
(a)						**1995 WALTZING MATILDA CENTENARY**			
1995 a	NCLT	171,709	C	Al/br	9 g	Mintmark. Gallery. Mint your own	2	10	–
1995 b	NCLT	55,391	S	Al/br	9 g	Mobile Counterstamp. Royal Syd	2	20	–
1995 c	NCLT	74,353	B	Al/br	9 g	Mobile Counterstamp. Royal Bris	2	20	–
1995 d	NCLT	76,407	M	Al/br	9 g	Mobile Counterstamp. Royal Melb	2	20	–
1995 e	OFF METAL	2,501	–	Silver	11.49	Proof Sydney NAA . Certificate	32	–	55
1995 f	OFF METAL	20,005	–	Silver	11.49	Proof in case .925 Stg.25.1mm	32	–	35

[a] Visitors could strike their own coin on a specially modified press in the RAM's Tourist Gallery at a modest premium over face value. The coins were generally housed in a brightly coloured souvenir cardboard folder.
[b] "S" Countermark. Mobile press at the Sydney Royal Easter Show.
[c] "B" Countermark. Mobile press at the Brisbane Agricultural Show.
[d] "M" Countermark. Mobile press at the Melbourne Agricultural Show.
[e] Sterling silver (92.5%). Issued at the NAA Sydney Coin Fair on April 1 - 2, 1995. Continuous reeding. Numbered certificate 0001 to 2501.
[f] Sterling Silver. Similar to above but with interrupted reeding.

CIRCULATION & NON CIRCULATION (NCLT) ISSUES

Date	TYPE	Mintage Figures	Mint Mark	Metal Comp.	Weight in gms	Issuing Mint	Unc	Choice Unc	Roll or Bagged	Issue Price	Mint set Retail	Proof Retail
(b)						**1996 SIR HENRY PARKES CENTENARY**						
1996	CIRC	26,200,000	–	Al/br	9 g	Canb	3	9	20	–	–	–
1996 a	NCLT	149,600	C	Al/br	9 g	Mintmark. Gallery. Mint your own				2	12	–
1996 b	NCLT	101,760	C	Al/br	9 g	Privymark. Pre-struck for general retail				2	8	–
1996 c	NCLT	1,500	C	Al/br	9 g	Mobile Counterstamp. Royal Canb				2	10	–
1996 d	NCLT	49,964	S	Al/br	9 g	Mobile Counterstamp. Royal Syd.				2	14	–
1996 e	NCLT	30,000	B	Al/br	9 g	Mobile Counterstamp. Royal Bris				2	5	–
1996 f	NCLT	20,000	A	Al/br	9 g	Mobile Counterstamp. Royal Adel				2	6	–
1996 g	NCLT	20,110	M	Al/br	9 g	Mobile Counterstamp. Royal Melb				2	6	–
1996	EX SET	108,773	–	Al/br	9 g	Circ part of annual mint set				–	9	–
1996	EX SET	25,727	–	Al/br	9 g	Circ in annual Gumnut mint set				–	9	–
1996	EX SET	33,350	–	Al/br	9 g	Proof part of annual cased set				–	–	12
1996	EX SET	3,985	–	Al/br	9 g	Proof in second annual Gumnut set				–	–	12
1996 h	OFF METAL	20,006	–	Silver	11.49	Proof in case .925 Stg. 25.1mm				32	–	45

[a] "C" mintmark appearing as part of the die design. These were distributed to accredited dealers and through the mint's own client list.
[b] Visitors could strike their own coin on a specially modified press in the RAM's Tourist Gallery at a modest premium over face value. The coins were generally housed in a brightly coloured souvenir cardboard folder.
[c] "C" Issued at the Royal Canberra Show in specially printed folder. Same as (a).
[d] "S" Countermark. Struck using a mobile press at the Sydney Royal Easter Show.
[e] "B" Countermark. Struck using a mobile press at the Brisbane Show.
[f] "A" Countermark. Struck using a mobile press at the Adelaide Show.
[g] "M" Countermark. Struck using a mobile press at the Melbourne Show.
[h] Struck in sterling silver (92.5%) with interrupted reeding. No show issue.

ONE DOLLAR

ONE YEAR COMMEMORATIVE REVERSES

1997 [a] K.S. Al/br Circ

1997 [b] K.S.Al/br Circ NCLT

1997 [c] K.S. Silver Proof

1998 [d] Lord Florey

CIRCULATION & NON CIRCULATION (NCLT) ISSUES

Date	TYPE	Mintage Figures	Mint Mark	Metal Comp.	Weight in gms	Issuing Mint	Unc	Choice Unc	Roll or Bagged	Issue Price	Mint set Retail	Proof Retail
(a) 1997 KINGSFORD SMITH - LARGE HEAD Circulated												
1997	CIRC	24,381,000	–	Al/br	9 g	Canb	20	30	60	–	–	–
1997	EX SET	71,022	–	Al/br	9 g	Circ part of annual mint set				–	20	–
1997	EX SET	27,421	–	Al/br	9 g	Circ part of Gumnut/baby set				–	20	–
1997	DUAL SET	50,500	–	Al/br	9 g	Circ paired with other $1 K'Smith				–	60	–
1997	EX SET	32,543	–	Al/br	9 g	Proof coin included in annual set				–	–	30
1997	EX SET	3,617	–	Al/br	9 g	Proof coin included Gumnut set				–	–	30
1997	NPA SET	4,000	–	Silver	11.99	Proof. Coin & $20 note. See NPA section						35

NCLT. COLLECTOR ISSUES ONLY

Date	TYPE	Mintage Figures	Mint Mark	Metal Comp.	Weight in gms	Description	Issue Price	Unc Retail	Proof Retail
(b) 1997 KINGSFORD SMITH - SMALL HEAD Collector only issue									
1997 a	NCLT	102,213	C	Al/br	9 g	Mintmark. Gallery. Mint your own	2	15	–
1997 b	NCLT	50,858	S	Al/br	9 g	Mobile Counterstamp. Royal Sydney	2	25	–
1997 c	NCLT	28,616	B	Al/br	9 g	Mobile Counterstamp. Royal Brisbane	2	25	–
1997 d	NCLT	25,403	A	Al/br	9 g	Mobile Counterstamp. Royal Adelaide	2	25	–
1997 e	NCLT	27,430	M	Al/br	9 g	Mobile Counterstamp. Royal Melbourne	2	25	–
1997 f	OFF METAL	13,611	–	Silver	11.49	Proof in case .925 Stg. 25.1mm	34	–	45
1997 g	DUAL SET	50,500	C	Al/br	9 g	Circ. Twin pack with lge hd K/Smith	3.95	30	–

[a] Visitors could strike their own coin on a specially modified press in the RAM's Tourist Gallery at a modest premium over face value. The coins were generally housed in a brightly coloured souvenir cardboard folder.
[b] Mobile press "S" Countermark at the Sydney Royal Easter Show. Issued in blue folder.
[c] Mobile press "B" Countermark at the Royal Brisbane Show in a dark pink folder.
[d] "A" C/mark. Mobile press striking at the Royal Adelaide Show and sold in a grey/blue folder.
[e] "M" C/mark. Struck using a mobile press at the Royal Melbourne Show and sold in a grey folder.
[f] Struck in fine (99.9%) silver and sold individually in presentation case.
[g] A dual folder pack including uncirculated versions of both Kingsford Smith coins. The "Large Portrait Type" has no mintmark. "Small Portrait Type" with map has the "C" mintmark. All Kingsford Smith issues feature interrupted edge reeding.

Date	TYPE	Mintage Figures	Mint Mark	Metal Comp.	Weight in gms	Description	Issue Price	Unc Retail	Proof Retail
(c) 1998 BIRTH CENTENARY OF LORD HOWARD FLOREY									
1998 a	NCLT	77,035	C	Al/br	9 g	Mintmark. Gallery. Mint your own	2	20	–
1998 b	NCLT	44,080	S	Al/br	9 g	Mobile Counterstamp. Royal Sydney	2	25	–
1998 c	NCLT	29,924	B	Al/br	9 g	Mobile Counterstamp. Royal Brisbane	2	25	–
1998 d	NCLT	21,110	A	Al/br	9 g	Mobile Counterstamp. Royal Adelaide	2	35	–
1998 e	NCLT	21,809	M	Al/br	9 g	Mobile Counterstamp. Royal Melbourne	2	2	–
1998 f	NCLT	11,644	–	Silver	11.66	Proof. 92.5 Stg. Size 25.12 mm	32	–	36

[a] Visitors could strike their own coin on a specially modified press in the RAM's Tourist Gallery at a modest premium over face value. The coins were generally housed in a brightly coloured souvenir cardboard folder.
[b] "S" Countermark. Mint your own. Sydney Royal Easter Show. Grey folder.
[c] "B" Countermark. Mint your own coin. Brisbane Show. Pink folder.
[d] "A" Countermark. Purple folder with overprint :- "ANDA Coin, Note and Stamp Show."
[e] "M" Countermark. Mint your own. Melbourne Show. Pale yellow folder.
[f] This proof issue has the new Ian Rank- Broadley portrait of the Queen.

ONE DOLLAR

ONE YEAR COMMEMORATIVE REVERSES

1999 (a) Older Person

1999 (b) Last ANZACS

2000 (c) Sydney II. Unc

2000 (d) Sydney II. Proof

CIRCULATION & NON CIRCULATION (NCLT) ISSUES

Date	TYPE	Mintage Figures	Mint Mark	Metal Comp.	Weight in gms	Issuing Mint	Unc	Choice Unc	Roll or Bagged	Issue Price	Mint set Retail	Proof Retail
[a]	**1999 YEAR OF THE OLDER PERSON**											
1999	CIRC	29,218,000	–	Al/br	9 g	Canb	4	8	70	–	–	–
1999	EX SET	70,067	–	Al/br	9 g	Circ part of annual mint set				–	9	–
1999	EX SET	35,718	–	Al/br	9 g	Circ part of Koala mint set				–	9	–
1999	EX SET	28,056	–	Al/br	9 g	Proof part of annual 6 coin set				–	–	25
1999	EX SET	6,707	–	Al/br	9 g	Proof part of annual Koala set				–	–	25
1999 a	DUAL SET	33,922	C	Al/br	9 g	Twin Pack with $1 ANZAC				3.95	45	–
1999	PNC	56,065	–	Al/br	9 g	Coin & Stamp cover. Priced in PNC section						–

[a] Dual Set combining the Anzac $1 [with mm] & the Year of the Older Person $1. Presented in a Colour Pack.

NCLT. COLLECTOR ISSUES ONLY

Date	TYPE	Mintage Figures	Mint Mark	Metal Comp.	Weight in gms	Description	Issue Price	Unc Retail	Proof Retail
[b]	**1999 & 2000 - THE LAST ANZACS**								
1999 a	NCLT	126,161	C	Al/br	9 g	Mintmark. Gallery. Mint your own	2	20	–
1999 b	NCLT	53,286	S	Al/br	9 g	Privy. Pre-struck for Syd. Royal Easter	2	25	–
1999 b	NCLT	Ditto	S	Al/br	9 g	Mobile Counterstamp. Syd. Royal Easter	2	25	–
1999 c	NCLT	33,634	B	Al/br	9 g	Privy. Pre-struck for Royal Brisbane	2	25	–
1999 c	NCLT	Ditto	B	Al/br	9 g	Mobile Counterstamp. Royal Brisbane	2	25	–
1999 d	NCLT	28,681	A	Al/br	9 g	Privy. Pre-struck for Royal Adelaide	2	35	–
1999 d	NCLT	Ditto	A	Al/br	9 g	Mobile Counterstamp. Royal Adelaide	2	25	–
1999 e	NCLT	49,841	M	Al/br	9 g	Privy. Pre-struck for Royal Melbourne	2	25	–
1999 e	NCLT	Ditto	M	Al/br	9 g	Mobile Counterstamp. Royal Melbourne	2	25	–
1999	DUAL SET	33,922	–	Al/br	9 g	Twin Pack with Older Person	3.95	40	–
1999 f	NCLT	25,000	–	Silver	11.66	Proof. 92.5 Sterling. Size 25.12 mm	32	–	65
2000 g	PNC	47,830	–	Al/br	9 g	Coin & Stamp cover. Priced in PNC section			–

[a] "C" Countermark. Mint your own coin using a specially prepared press at the RAM.
[b] "S" Countermark. Coins were struck on a mobile press at the Sydney Royal Easter Show.
[c] "B" Countermark. Coins were struck on a mobile press at the Brisbane Show.
[d] "A" Countermark. Coins were struck at the mint and released at the Adelaide Show.
[e] "M" Countermark. Coins were issued at the Australia 99 World Specialised Philatelic Exhibition held in Melbourne between 19-24 March.
[f] Struck in fine 99.9 silver and sold individually in a presentation case.
[g] A similar coin, but dated 2000, appears in the PNC "LAST OF THE ANZACS

Date	TYPE	Mintage Figures	Mint Mark	Metal Comp.	Weight in gms	Description	Issue Price	Unc Retail	Proof Retail
[c/d]	**2000 HMAS SYDNEY II**								
2000 a	NCLT	86,900	C	Al/br	9 g	Mintmark. Gallery. Mint your own	2	10	–
2000 b	NCLT	49,002	S	Al/Br	9 g	Mobile Counterstamp. Royal Easter	2	15	–
2000 c	NCLT	200 - 500?	S	Al/Br	9 g	Counterstamp RAM. HMAS Sydney	2	795	–
2000	NCLT	12,150	–	Silver	11.66	Proof .999 fine. Width 25mm	32	–	65

[a] "C" Countermark. Mint your own coin using a specially prepared press at the visitor's centre.
[b] "S" Sydney dollar coins were struck using the mobile press at the Sydney Royal Easter Show.
[c] Some of the above mentioned "S" issued coins were included in a special folder and given to VIPs attending the launch of the commemorative on its namesake, HMAS Sydney on May 20, 2000. Text inside the folder reads :- *"The HMAS Sydney II coin launch May 2000."* Official mint figures suggest that 2,922 were struck for the launch. In reality, only a small percentage of these coins were actually handed out on the day. General consensus between attendees put the real figure at 200 to 500. The excess were either re-packaged or destroyed.

ONE DOLLAR

ONE YEAR COMMEMORATIVE REVERSES

2000 (a) Victoria Cross

2000 (b) Olymphilex

2001 (c) Federation

2001 (d) Federation

NCLT. COLLECTOR ISSUES ONLY

[a] 2000 VICTORIA CROSS CENTENARY

Date	TYPE	Mintage Figures	Mint Mark	Metal Comp.	Weight in gms	Description	Issue Price	Unc Retail	Proof Retail
2000 a	NCLT	49,979	–	Al/br	9 g	Circ coin in coloured folder	5	195	–
2000	PNC	48,830	–	Al/br	9 g	Coin & Stamp cover. Priced in PNC section			–

[a] Issued in July 2000 to commemorate the centenary of the awarding of Australia's first Victoria Cross. It was awarded on July 24, 1900 to Captain Neville Howse of NSW Medical Staff Corps, Australian Forces. During the action at Vredefort, South Africa, Captain Howse saw a trumpeter fall and went through heavy cross fire to rescue the wounded man. His horse was shot from under him so he continued on foot to dress the man's wounds and then carry him to safety. After a distinguished career he died in 1930.

[b] 2000 OLYMPHILEX COIN AND STAMP TRADE FAIR

Date	TYPE	Mintage Figures	Mint Mark	Metal Comp.	Weight in gms	Description	Issue Price	Unc Retail	Proof Retail
2000 b	NCLT	72,573	–	Al/br	9 g	Canb. Edge inscription re show	2	5	–
2000 b	NCLT	98,567	–	Al/br	9 g	Sydney. Edge inscription re show	2	20	–

[b] The above were struck exclusively at Olymphilex, a Numismatic / Philatelic Trade Fair, held in both Canberra and Sydney from September 15 to 28, 2000 to coincide with the Sydney 2000 Olympic Games. The coin was not released for general circulation. Neither coins show a mintmark but the venue of issue (either Sydney or Canberra) is edge lettered around the coin.

CIRCULATION & NON CIRCULATION (NCLT) ISSUES

[c/d] 2001 THE CENTENARY OF FEDERATION

Date	TYPE	Mintage Figures	Mint Mark	Metal Comp.	Weight in gms	Issuing Mint	Unc	Choice Unc	Roll or Bagged	Issue Price	Mint set Retail	Proof Retail
2001	CIRC	27,905,390	–	Al/br	9 g	Canb	5	10	30	–	–	–
2001	EX-SET	90,822	–	Al/br	9 g	Circ coin part of annual mint set				–	9	–
2001	EX-SET	32,494	–	Al/br	9 g	Circ coin part of Koala mint set				–	9	–
2001	EX-SET	59,569	–	Al/br	9 g	Coloured coin only in proof set				–	–	15
2001	EX-SET	15,011	–	Al/br	9 g	Proof coin part of baby set				–	–	15
2001 c	EX-SET	Varies	–	Al/br	9 g	Circ. Part 3 coin set. $1 plain rev				–	9	–
2001	EX-SET	Varies	–	Al/br	9 g	Proof. Part 3 coin set. $1 coloured				–	–	25
2001	EX-SET	600	–	Silver	13.36	Proof. 20 x coins in grey case				–	–	n/a
2001	EX-SET	650/ 193	–	Gold	33.88	Proof. 99.99 fine. Federation set				–	–	n/a

[c] Part of three coin proof set issued in green case. The Al/br proof $1 coin features a colour pad reverse and the accompanying 20¢ and 50¢ coins are not coloured. Collectors could nominate the state or territory of their choosing. Obviously mintages varied but it is known that the final figures for the Norfolk Island issue was a small 3,750 sets.

DESIGN DIFFERENCES BETWEEN UNC & PROOF FEDERATION $1 COINS

The design of the Uncirculated and Proof one dollar coin varies slightly. The Uncirculated coin has a raised map of Australia while the map on the proof coin is pad inked onto a flat surface. There are two obverse die varieties. On one the initials "IRB" are spaced and are more common on collector sets. The second has the "IRB" joined and is common among circulating issues. There are also two reverse die varieties with one having the spacing of "2001" appearing to be wider.

ONE DOLLAR

ONE YEAR COMMEMORATIVE REVERSES

2001 [a] RAAF

2001 [b] Navy

2001 [c] Army al/br & Proof Silver

Date	TYPE	Mintage Figures	Mint Mark	Metal Comp.	Weight in gms	Description	Issue Price	Unc Retail	Proof Retail
[a]			**2001 RAAF 80th ANNIVERSARY**						
2001 a	NCLT	99,281	–	Al/br	9 g	Circ coin in coloured folder	2	16	–
[b]			**2001 NAVY 90TH ANNIVERSARY**						
2001 b	NCLT	62,429	–	Al/br	9 g	Circ coin in coloured folder	2	45	–
(c)			**2001 CENTENARY OF THE AUSTRALIAN ARMY**						
2001 c	NCLT	125,186	C	Al/br	9 g	Mintmark. Gallery. Mint your own	2	15	–
2001 d	NCLT	Inc above	C	Al/br	9 g	Mintmark. Pre-struck. General sales	2	15	–
2001 e	NCLT	38,095	S	Al/br	9 g	Privymark. Pre-struck for general retail	2	15	–
2001 f	OFF METAL	17,839	–	Silver	11.66	Proof .999 fine. Width 25mm	32	–	60
2001	PNC	27,209	C	Al/br	9 g	*Coin & Stamp cover. Priced in PNC section`*			–

[a] This coin did not carry a mintmark and was not issued for circulation. It was sold ($2.00) at various coin fairs and through the Mint's regular mailing list as well as through coin dealerships.

[b] This coin did not carry a mintmark and was not issued for circulation. It was sold ($2.00) at various coin fairs and through the Mint's regular mailing list as well as through coin dealerships.

[c] Visitors could strike their own coin on a specially modified press in the RAM's Tourist Gallery at a modest premium over face value. The coins were generally housed in a brightly coloured souvenir cardboard folder. This issue can be found with two obverse die varieties; i.e. "IRB" spaced and "IRB" joined.
[d] 'C' mintmark appearing as part of the die design. These were distributed to accredited dealers and through the mint's own client list.
[e] "S" for Sydney countermark. Pre-struck at RAM for Sydney Fair. "IRB" joined only.

2001 ARMY, NAVY & AIR FORCE FOLDER

Date	TYPE	Mintage Figures	Mint Mark	Metal Comp.	Weight in gms	Description	Issue Price	Unc Retail	Proof Retail
2001 g	FOLDER	12,342	C	Al/br	9 g	Above three coins in folder	18.5	65	–

[g] The "C" mintmark only appears on the Army issue in this set.

EXPLAINING THE $1 SPECIAL MINT, PRIVY & COUNTERMARKS

TYPE A
MINTMARK
'C' mm engraved part of design. Indicates coin struck locally.

TYPE B
PRIVY MARK
Incuse mark added at RAM for sale offsite

TYPE C
COUNTER MARK
Incuse mark struck on a mobile press at venue

Mintmarks, privymarks and counterstamps have been around almost as long as coins themselves. These were secret marks known to only a chosen few to pinpoint where a particular coin was struck. These marks often identified the workshops or individual workmen. Their twofold purpose was to keep a strict control on coinage standards and to identify a potential forger. The practice was all but phased out by the 18th century. The RAM revised the practice in 1993 to identify coins struck at Canberra and on a mobile press at selected Agricultural shows. Over the years the issues expanded to include ANDA shows and "pop up" sites. The series became very confusing as the mint in Canberra also struck coins with the privy marks used for shows in various capital cities and then sold them by mail order. A genuinely struck coin at the actual location could only be spotted by the shallower strike produced by the mobile press, which was incapable of producing the high pressure and sharper strikes back in Canberra. In 2008 the RAM introduced three new identification marks to distinguish the origin of different issues around the country. The 'C' identification mark relates to coins struck at the RAM in Canberra and comes in two forms. The first has the identification mark as part of the overall design. The second concerns the mark being added to an already fully struck coin by tourists visiting the mint gallery. Both are correctly called "Mintmarks" as they identify the actual place of manufacture. The images shown at top right illustrate and describes all three varieties.

ONE DOLLAR

ONE YEAR COMMEMORATIVE REVERSES

2001 [a] Volunteers. Unc

2002 [b] Outback. Unc

2002 [c] Outback Unc Colour

2003 [d] Korea Unc

GENERAL CIRCULATION ISSUES ONLY

Date	TYPE	Mintage Figures	Mint Mark	Metal Comp.	Weight in gms	Issuing Mint	Unc	Choice Unc	Roll or Bagged	Issue Price	Mint set Retail	Proof Retail
[a] 2001 INTERNATIONAL YEAR OF THE VOLUNTEER												
2001	CIRC	6,074,000	–	Al/br	9 g	Canb	7	12	100	–	–	–

CIRCULATION & NON CIRCULATION (NCLT) ISSUES

Date	TYPE	Mintage Figures	Mint Mark	Metal Comp.	Weight in gms	Issuing Mint	Unc	Choice Unc	Roll or Bagged	Issue Price	Mint set Retail	Proof Retail
[b/c] 2002 YEAR OF THE OUTBACK												
2002	CIRC	34,074,000	–	Al/br	9 g	Canb	6	10	Bag	–	–	–
2002 a	NCLT	68,447	C	Al/br	9 g	Mintmark. Gallery. Mint your own				2	6	–
2002 b	NCLT	36,931	S	Al/br	9 g	Mobile Counterstamp. ANDA Syd.				2.5	6	–
2002 c	NCLT	32,698	B	Al/br	9 g	Mobile Counterstamp. ANDA Bris				2.5	6	–
2002 d	NCLT	31,694	M	Al/br	9 g	Mobile Counterstamp. ANDA Melb				2.5	6	–
2002	EX-SET	68,752	–	Al/br	9 g	Specimen part of annual mint set				–	3	–
2002	EX-SET	32,479	–	Al/br	9 g	Spec part of Koala baby mint set				–	3	–
2002 e	EX-SET	39,514	–	Al/br	9 g	Coloured $1 annual proof set				–	–	25
2002	EX-SET	13,996	–	Al/br	9 g	Normal $1 in Koala proof set				–	–	25
2002	OFF METAL	12,500		Silver	11.65	Proof .999 fine. Width 25 mm				32	–	55

[a] "C" raised Mintmark. Mint your own coin on a converted press at the RAM's visitor's centre. An undisclosed number of pre-struck coins were also sold through dealers and the mint's own client base.
[b] "S" Countermark incuse rather than raised. Used for the first time by the mobile coin press at the Sydney ANDA Show, April 19-21, 2002.
[c] "B" Incuse countermark. ANDA Brisbane Show from May 24-26.
[d] "M" incuse countermark. ANDA Melbourne Show from October 25-27.
[e] This coloured version was unique to the 2002 proof set.

Date	TYPE	Mintage Figures	Mint Mark	Metal Comp.	Weight in gms	Description	Issue Price	Unc Retail	Proof Retail
[d] 2003 KOREAN WAR 50th ANNIVERSARY									
2003 a	NCLT	93,572	C	Al/br	9 g	[Various] See footnotes for details	2.5	45	–
2003 b	NCLT	36,091	S	Al/br	9 g	Mobile Counterstamp. ANDA Sydney	2.5	6	–
2003 c	NCLT	34,949	B	Al/br	9 g	Mobile Counterstamp. ANDA Brisbane	2.5	15	–
2003 d	NCLT	36,142	M	Al/br	9 g	Mobile Counterstamp. Royal Melb Show	2.5	6	–
2003 e	NCLT	15,000	–	Silver	11.66	Proof. Cased .999 fine. Width 25mm	34	–	55

[a] 'C' mintmark appearing as part of the die design. These were distributed to accredited dealers and through the mint's own customer list.
[a] Visitors could strike their own coin on a specially modified press in the RAM's Tourist Gallery at a modest premium over face value. The coins were generally housed in a brightly coloured souvenir cardboard folder.
[b] "S" incuse countermark. Sydney ANDA Show on April 4, 2003. Extra coins were struck for dealer allocations and the mint's own client list.
[c] "B" incuse countermark. ANDA Brisbane Show on May 23, 2003. Extra coins were struck for dealer allocations and the mint's own client list.
[d] "M" Counterstamp. Released on 15/09/2003 for the Melbourne Royal Ag. Show Sept 18 to 28. Extra coins were struck for dealer allocations and the mint's own client list.
[e] Struck in pure (.999%) silver. The edge of the coin featured interrupted reeding.

ONE DOLLAR

ONE YEAR COMMEMORATIVE REVERSES

2003 (a) Volunteers

2003 (b) Suffrage

2003 (c) Vietnam

2004 (d) Eureka

CIRCULATION & NON CIRCULATION (NCLT) ISSUES

Date	TYPE	Mintage Figures	Mint Mark	Metal Comp.	Weight in gms	Issuing Mint	Unc	Choice Unc	Roll or Bagged	Issue Price	Mint set Retail	Proof Retail
[a]			**2003 AUSTRALIA'S VOLUNTEERS**									
2003	CIRC	4,149,000	–	Al/br	9 g	Canb	12	19	70	–	–	–
2003	EX-SET	80,512	–	Al/br	9 g	Specimen part of annual mint set				–	12	–
2003	EX-SET	37,748	–	Al/br	9 g	Specimen part of Koala mint set				–	12	–
2003	EX-SET	3,249	–	Al/br	9 g	Specimen part of Wedding set				–	20	–
2003 a	NCLT	39,090	–	Al/br	9 g	Coloured $1 part of proof set				–	–	45
2003	EX-SET	14,799	–	Al/br	9 g	Proof. Non-coloured Koala set				–	–	45
2003	OFF-METAL	6,500	–	Silver	13.36	Proof .999 fine silver. In case				–	–	40
[b]			**2003 WOMEN'S SUFFRAGE**									
2003 b	CIRC	10,007,000	–	Al/br	9 g	Canb	4	7	65	–	–	–
2003	NCLT	225	–	Al/br	9 g	Boxed VIP Presentation set				Gift	n/a	–

[b] There are two reverse dies due to the first die cracking. The smaller design is further from the rim and the left prong of the trident is longer.

Date	TYPE	Mintage Figures	Mint Mark	Metal Comp.	Weight in gms	Issuing Mint	Unc	Choice Unc	Roll or Bagged	Issue Price	Mint set Retail	Proof Retail
[c]			**2003 VIETNAM VETERAN'S ISSUE**									
2003	NCLT	57,000	–	Al/br	9 g	Circ coin in coloured folder				7.5	20	–
[d]			**2004 EUREKA STOCKADE - BALLARAT**									
2004 d	NCLT	70,913	C	Al/br	9 g	M'mark. General RAM & dealer retail				2.75	5	–
2004 e	NCLT	No record	C	Al/br	9 g	Mintmark. Gallery. Mint your own coin				2.75	5	–
2004	NCLT	89,276	E	Al/br	9 g	Privymark. Pre-struck for general retail				2.75	5	–
2004 f	NCLT	6,672	E	Al/br	9 g	Mobile C'stamp. Eureka Centre Ballarat				2.75	9	–
2004 g	NCLT	50?	E	Al/br	9 g	Mobile Counterstamp. VIP issue.				2.75	250	–
2004	NCLT	35,483	S	Al/br	9 g	Privymark. Pre-struck for general retail				2.75	5	–
2004 h	NCLT	9,615	S	Al/br	9 g	Mobile Counterstamp. Sydney Royal				2.75	20	–
2004	NCLT	32,142	B	Al/br	9 g	Privymark. Pre-struck for general retail				2.75	5	–
2004 i	NCLT	1,693	B	Al/br	9 g	Mobile Counterstamp. ANDA Brisbane				2.75	45	–
2004	NCLT	28,342	M	Al/br	9 g	Privymark. Pre-struck for general retail				2.75	5	–
2004 j	NCLT	9,184	M	Al/br	9 g	Mobile Counterstamp. Royal Melbourne				2.75	30	–
2004 k	ERROR	3 only	–	Al/br	9 g	Fair coin missing mint mark				2.75	2,500	–
2004 l	OFF METAL	17,697	–	Silver	11.49	Proof .999 fine silver. In case				34	–	45

[d] 'C' mintmark appearing as part of the die design. These were distributed to accredited dealers and through the mint's own client list.
[e] Visitors could strike their own coin on a specially modified press in the RAM's Tourist Gallery at a modest premium over face value. The coins were generally housed in a brightly coloured souvenir cardboard folder.
[f] To mark the 150th anniversary of Australia's most famous rebellion, a mobile press was set up at the Eureka Centre, Ballarat, Victoria on 27 February 2004. Visitors were able to place a circular counterstamp on the specially designed coin.
[g] "E" Mintmark. Mobile press at the Eureka Centre, and presented in a VIP folder that reads: *"Presented at the coin launch, Eureka Centre 27 February 2004."* Mintage is believed to be as low as 50 coins.
[h] "S" Mobile press [shallow strike] at Sydney Royal Easter Show; April 2-15, 2004.
[i] "B" Mobile press [shallow strike] at Brisbane ANDA Show from May 21-23, 2004.
[j] "M" Mobile press [shallow strike] at Royal Melbourne Show, Sept. 16-20, 2004.
[k] Error coin that escaped the mobile press without a mintmark being struck.
[l] Fine Silver Proof Coin in presentation case. No mintmark. Limit of 20,000. 17,697 sold.

ONE DOLLAR

ONE YEAR COMMEMORATIVE REVERSES

2005 [a] End of WW2. Unc [b] WW2 Silver Proof 2005 [c] Gallipoli. Al/Br 2005 [d] Gallipoli. Silver

NCLT. COLLECTOR ISSUES ONLY

Date	TYPE	Mintage Figures	Mint Mark	Metal Comp.	Weight in gms	Description	Issue Price	Unc Retail	Proof Retail
(a/b)						**2005 END OF WWII. 60th ANNIVERSARY**			
2005	EX SET	71,546	–	Al/br	9 g	Circ part of annual mint set	–	9	–
2005	EX SET	28,853	–	Al/br	9 g	Circ included in Koala mint set	–	9	–
2005	EX SET	3,627	–	Al/br	9 g	Spec. coin part of Wedding set	–	15	–
2005	EX SET	33,520	–	Al/br	9 g	Proof part of 6 coin annual set	–	–	25
2005	EX SET	12,884	–	Al/br	9 g	Proof part of Koala baby set	–	–	25
2005	OFF METAL	6,200	–	Silver	11.66	Proof .99.9 fine. Part 6 coin set	–	–	45
2005	OFF METAL	629	–	Gold	21.70	Proof .99.99 fine. Part 6 coin set	–	–	1,600

NCLT. COLLECTOR ISSUES ONLY

Date	TYPE	Mintage Figures	Mint Mark	Metal Comp.	Weight in gms	Description	Issue Price	Unc Retail	Proof Retail
(c/d)						**2005 GALLIPOLI 90th ANNIVERSARY**			
2005 a	NCLT	88,424	C	Al/br	9 g	Mintmark. Gallery. Mint your own	2.75	5	–
2005 b	NCLT	Ditto ?	C	Al/br	9 g	M'Mark. General RAM & dealer retail	2.75	5	–
2005	NCLT	35,782	S	Al/br	9 g	Privymark. Pre-struck for general sale	2.75	5	–
2005 c	NCLT	3,000	S	Al/br	9 g	Mobile Counterstamp. Sydney Expo	2.75	15	–
2005 d	NCLT	2,799	S	Al/br	9 g	Mobile Counterstamp. ANDA Sydney	2.75	15	–
2005	NCLT	35,596	B	Al/br	9 g	Privymark. Pre-struck for general sale	2.75	5	–
2005 e	NCLT	3,792	B	Al/br	9 g	Mobile Counterstamp. AKKA Bris	2.75	27	–
2005 f	NCLT	2,611	B	Al/br	9 g	Mobile Counterstamp. ANDA Bris	2.75	27	–
2005 g	NCLT	30,904	G	Al/br	9 g	Privymark. Pre-struck for general sale	2.75	5	–
2005 h	NCLT	4,548	G	Al/br	9 g	Mobile Counterstamp. Canb AWM	2.75	90	–
2005	NCLT	28,252	M	Al/br	9 g	Privymark. Pre-struck for general sale	2.75	5	–
2005 i	NCLT	10,475	M	Al/br	9 g	Mobile Counterstamp. Royal Melb	2.75	22	–
2005 j	ERROR	2 only	–	Al/br	9 g	Show coin missing mintmark	2.75	1,550	–
2005 k	OFF METAL	17,749	–	Silver	11.66	Proof .999 fine. Width 25mm	38	–	60

[a] Visitors could strike their own coin on a specially modified press in the RAM's Tourist Gallery at a modest premium over face value. The coins were generally housed in a brightly coloured souvenir cardboard folder.
[b] 'C' mintmark appearing as part of the die design. These were distributed to accredited dealers and through the mint's own client list.
[c] "S" privy mark stamped on mobile press at the *Pacific Explorer World Stamp Expo* held in Sydney from April 21-24, 2005 with a mintage of 3,000.
[d] "S" Privy mark stamped on mobile press at the *Sydney ANDA Show* from August 5-7, 2005.
[e] "B" Privymark stamped on mobile press at the *Brisbane Royal National Agricultural Show* from August 11-20, 2005. Mintage of 3,792. Coins show shallower strike
[f] "B" countermarked on mobile press at *Brisbane ANDA Show* from May 20-22, 2005.
[g] "G" Privymark coins struck at the RAM for distribution at a special ceremony at the *Australian War Memorial* (AWM). The official mintage was 40,000 but more likely 30,904.
[h] "G" counterstamp on the mobile press at *The Australian War Memorial,* Canberra on April 18, 2005 with a mintage of 4,548.
[i] "M" Mintmark stamped on mobile press at the Royal Melbourne Show from September 15-25, 2005 with a mintage of 10,475.
[j] Error coin that escaped the mobile press without a mintmark being impressed on the coin.
[k] Fine Silver Proof Coin. No mintmark. Issued in a presentation case.

ONE DOLLAR

ONE YEAR COMMEMORATIVE REVERSES

2006 [a] Melb Games

2006 [b] TV. Proof Silver

2006 [c] TV. Circ Al/br

2007 [d] Polar Circ Al/br

NCLT. COLLECTOR ISSUES ONLY

Date	TYPE	Mintage Figures	Mint Mark	Metal Comp	Weight in gms	Description	Issue Price	Unc Retail	Proof Retail
[a]						**2006 COMMONWEALTH GAMES - MELBOURNE**			
2006	NCLT	58,505	M	Al/br	9 g	Unc coin in coloured folder	2.75	15	–
[b/c]						**2006 50 YEARS OF TELEVISION**			
2006 a	NCLT	135,221	C	Al/br	9 g	Mintmark. Gallery. Mint your own	2.75	5	–
2006 a	NCLT	46,370	TV	Al/br	9 g	Mintmark. Gallery. Mint your own	2.75	12	–
2006	NCLT	37,811	S	Al/br	9 g	Privy. Pre-struck for general sale	2.75	5	–
2006 b	NCLT	10,679	S	Al/br	9 g	Mobile Counterstamp. Royal Syd.	2.75	12	–
2006	NCLT	40,717	B	Al/br	9 g	Privymark. Pre-struck. General sale	2.75	5	–
2006 c	NCLT	6,511	B	Al/br	9 g	Mobile Ctr/stamp. EKKA Brisbane	2.75	20	–
2006 d	ERROR	1 known	B	Al/br	9 g	Mobile Ctr/stamp. EKKA Brisbane	2.75	1,500	–
2006	NCLT	31,364	M	Al/br	9 g	Privymark. Pre-struck. General sale	2.75	10	–
2006 e	NCLT	8,236	M	Al/br	9 g	Mobile Ctr/stamp. Royal Melbourne	2.75	20	–
2006 f	ERROR	4 known	?	Al/br	9 g	MISSING mobile counterstamp	2.75	1,550	–
2006 g	NCLT	1,500	A	Silver	11.7g	Proof. ANDA Canb. Square box	40	–	60
2006 g	NCLT	1,500	A	Silver	11.7g	Proof. ANDA Brisbane Square box	40	–	60
2006 h	NCLT	3,859	A	Silver	11.7g	Proof. ANDA Sydney. Long box	40	–	65
2006 I	NCLT	10,790	–	Silver	11.7g	Proof .999 fine. Width 25mm	38	–	45

[a] For a modest premium over face, Visitors could strike their own coin on a specially modified press in the RAM's Tourist Gallery. The price included a coloured souvenir cardboard folder to house the coin.
[b] Oval counterstamp 'S' struck on a mobile press at the Sydney Royal Easter Show from April 7-20, 2006
[c] Oval counterstamp 'B' struck on a mobile press transported from Canberra to the Brisbane Royal National Agricultural Show held from August 10-19, 2006. Shallow strike.
[d] Error double "B" Mintmark. Twice stamped on mobile press at Brisbane Royal National Agricultural Show from August 10-19, 2006.
[e] Round counterstamp 'M' struck on a mobile press at the Royal Melbourne Show from September 21 to October 1, 2006.
[f] Every issue of this design had a mint, privy or counterstamp marking. Four examples appear to have been sold to fair visitors without the countermark. Two from Brisbane and two from Melbourne are known.
[g] Issued separately at the ANDA Canberra and Brisbane shows, the mintage of just 1,500 coins per venue makes this the lowest issue of any silver proof $1 coin. Featuring an "A" privymark [for ANDA], it was the first time the RAM has the mintmark 'A' stamped on the silver proof coin. Although the original idea was to offer the coin at every coin fair planned throughout the year it was not released at the Melbourne ANDA Show for some reason. The printing on the box holding the Special Release reads :- "This Fine Silver Proof Coin has been minted for exclusive sale at the Australasian Numismatic Dealers Association 2006 shows."
[h] Identical coin to the above but subtle differences to the packaging. The coin is housed in a long rectangular box with a sticker on the outer box reading "Sydney ANDA 4-6 August 2004.
[i] General issue silver proof issue. No mintmark. Issued in a square case.

Date	TYPE	Mintage Figures	Mint Mark	Metal Comp	Weight in gms	Description	Issue Price	Unc Retail	Proof Retail
[d]						**2007 CENTENARY OF POLAR EXPLORATION**			
2007	NCLT	29,893	–	Al/br	9 g	Unc coin in coloured folder	12.95	20	–

ONE DOLLAR

ONE YEAR COMMEMORATIVE REVERSES

2007 [a] Bridge Al/br Unc

[b] Bridge Silver Proof

2007 [c] Lifesaver Al/br

2007 [d] Lifesaver Silver

NCLT. COLLECTOR ISSUES ONLY

[a/b] 2007 SYDNEY HARBOUR BRIDGE

Date	TYPE	Mintage Figures	Mint Mark	Metal Comp.	Weight in gms	Description	Issue Price	Unc Retail	Proof Retail
2007 a	NCLT	187,651	C	Al/br	9 g	M'Mark. General RAM & dealer retail	2.75	6	–
2007 b	NCLT	Inc above	C	Al/br	9 g	Mintmark. Gallery. Mint your own	2.75	5	–
2007 c	NCLT	2,744	C	Al/br	9 g	Mobile Counterstamp. Canb Fair	2.75	27	–
2007	NCLT	55,345	S	Al/br	9 g	P'mark. Pre-struck for general retail	2.75	6	–
2007 d	NCLT	12,355	S	Al/br	9 g	Mobile Counterstamp. Sydney Royal	2.75	12	–
2007	PNC	tba	S	Al/br	9 g	Coin & Stamp cover. Priced in PNC section			–
2007	NCLT	44,593	B	Al/br	9 g	P'mark. Pre-struck for general retail	2.75	6	–
2007 e	NCLT	3,997	B	Al/br	9 g	Mobile Counterstamp. ANDA Brisb	2.75	17	–
2007 f	ERROR	3 only	B	Al/br	9 g	Counterstamp. Struck upside down	2.75	1,500	–
2007 g	NCLT	2,502	B	Al/br	9 g	Berlin Money Fair o'print folder	2.75	90	–
2007	NCLT	40,079	M	Al/br	9 g	P'mark. Pre-struck for general retail	2.75	10	–
2007 h	NCLT	3,935	M	Al/br	9 g	Mobile Counterstamp. ANDA Melb	2.75	17	–
2007 i	ERROR	Unique?	–	Al/br	9 g	MISSING. Mobile Counterstamp.	2.75	1,500	–
2007 j	NCLT	9,500	–	Silver	11.7g	Proof .999 fine. Width 25mm	40	–	45
2007	OFF METAL	629	–	Gold	21.7g	Proof .99.99 fine. Part 6 coin set	–	–	1,600

[a] Struck at the RAM with the 'C' mintmark appearing as part of the complete design. The mm appears raised and not within either a square or oval frame. These were sold through the mint's various retail outlets and to accredited numismatic dealers on a wholesale basis.
[b] For a modest premium over face, Visitors could strike their own coin on a specially modified press in the RAM's Tourist Gallery. The price included a coloured souvenir cardboard folder to house the coin.
[c] Oval counterstamp 'C' struck on a mobile press at the Canberra Collectables Fair in February 2007.
[d] Oval counterstamp 'S' struck on a mobile press at the Sydney Royal Easter Show from April 7-20, 2007.
[e] Oval counterstamp 'B' struck on a mobile press at the Brisbane ANDA Show from May 18-20, 2007.
[f] Error "B" Mintmark stamped upside down on opposite side of reverse using the mobile press at Brisbane ANDA Show from October 12-14, 2007. Only three known.
[g] "B" **Mintmark struck at RAM with folder overprinted "World Money Fair, Berlin."**
[h] Circular counterstamp 'M' struck on a mobile press at the Royal Melbourne Show from October 12-14, 2007.
[i] Error counterstamp coins that escaped the mobile presses without being struck. Three from the mobile press at the Sydney Royal Easter Show are known. Two were offered on eBay with a winning bid of $1,226 on July 14, 2007.
[j] Fine Silver Proof Coin. No mintmark. Issued in a presentation case.

[c/d] 2007 LIFESAVING

Date	TYPE	Mintage Figures	Mint Mark	Metal Comp.	Weight in gms	Description	Issue Price	Unc Retail	Proof Retail
2007	PART SET	30,716	–	Al/br	9 g	Circ. Part of annual mint set	–	12	–
2007	OFF METAL	3,475	–	Silver	11.66g	Proof .999 fine. Width 25mm	–	–	30
2007	OFF METAL	300	–	Gold	21.5g	Proof .9999 fine. Width 25mm	–		1,500

Originally promoted as only being available to collectors as part of the 2007 dated proof set. It was not to be available in either the mint set, either of the Baby Sets or through circulation. However it was later included in the mint set and proof fine Silver and Gold sets.

ONE DOLLAR

ONE YEAR COMMEMORATIVE REVERSES

2007 [a] APEC

2007 [b] Peacekeeping

2007 [c] Norman Lindsay

2008 [d] Coat of Arms

CIRCULATION & NON CIRCULATION (NCLT) ISSUES

All mint and proof coins shown in extreme right columns have been broken out of sets

[a] 2007 SYDNEY APEC MEETING

Date	TYPE	Mintage Figures	Mint Mark	Metal Comp.	Weight in gms	Issuing Mint	Unc	Choice Unc	Roll or Bagged	Issue Price	Ex mint Set Unc	Proof Retail
2007	CIRC	20,108,000	–	Al/br	9 g	Canb	4	7	–	–	–	–
2007 a	NCLT	Ditto	–	Al/br	9 g	Circ coin in VIP case			–	2.95	20	–
2007	ROLL	10,000	–	Al/br	9 g	Mint roll of 20 x $1 coins			40	29.95	–	–

[a] Issued in a special presentation case, these were initally given to APEC delegates. Surplus stocks were later offered to collectors.

[b] 2007 60th ANNIVERSARY OF PEACEKEEPING

Date	TYPE	Mintage Figures	Mint Mark	Metal Comp.	Weight in gms	Issuing Mint	Unc	Choice Unc	Roll or Bagged	Issue Price	Ex mint Set Unc	Proof Retail
2007 b	NCLT	31,028	–	Al/br	9 g	Circ coin in coloured folder				12.95	15	–

[c] 2007-2008 NORMAN LINDSAY - Magic Pudding Mint sets only

Date	TYPE	Mintage Figures	Mint Mark	Metal Comp.	Weight in gms	Issuing Mint	Unc	Choice Unc	Roll or Bagged	Issue Price	Ex mint Set Unc	Proof Retail
2007 c	PART SET	33,693	–	Al/br	9 g	Circ coin unique to baby set				–	7	–
2008 c	PART SET	46,504	–	Al/br	9 g	Circ coin unique to baby set				–	7	–

[c] The above uncirculated coins were available to collectors only in the Magic Pudding Baby Sets dated 2007 and 2008. They were not available in other sets or through circulation.

[d] 2008 COAT OF ARMS CENTENARY

Date	TYPE	Mintage Figures	Mint Mark	Metal Comp.	Weight in gms	Issuing Mint	Unc	Choice Unc	Roll or Bagged	Issue Price	Ex mint Set Unc	Proof Retail
2008 d	NCLT	156,414	C	Al/br	9 g	M'Mark. General RAM & dealer retail				2.75	8	–
2008 e	NCLT	*Inc above*	C	Al/br	9 g	Mintmark. Gallery. Mint your own				3	8	–
2008 f	NCLT	972	C	Al/br	9 g	RAM struck. Special o/print folder				2.75	50	–
2008 g	NCLT	32,529	S	Al/br	9 g	Privymark. Pre-struck for general retail				2.75	9	–
2008 h	NCLT	15,836	S	Al/br	9 g	Mobile Counterstamp. Easter Show				2.75	28	–
2008 i	NCLT	43,133	B	Al/br	9 g	Privymark. Pre-struck for general retail				2.75	9	–
2008 j	NCLT	4,029	B	Al/br	9 g	Mobile Counterstamp. ANDA Bris				2.75	50	–
2008 k	NCLT	1,100	B	Al/br	9 g	RAM struck. Oct. Bris. Fair o/print				2.75	50	–
2008 l	NCLT	42,094	M	Al/br	9 g	Privymark. Pre-struck for general retail				2.75	5	–
2008 m	NCLT	4,004	M	Al/br	9 g	Mobile Counterstamp. ANDA. Melb				2.75	20	–

[d] Struck at the RAM with the 'C' mintmark appearing as part of the complete design. The mm appears raised and not within either a square or oval frame. These were sold through the mint's various retail outlets and to accredited numismatic dealers on a wholesale basis.
[e] For a modest premium over face, Visitors could strike their own coin on a specially modified press in the RAM's Tourist Gallery. The price included a coloured souvenir cardboard folder to house the coin.
[f] 2008 Australian Coat of Arms $1 Uncirculated Coin issued in an overprinted folder with the wording - *'C' Brisbane Coin Fair - February 2008.* Coin has a raised 'C' privymark [not a B for Brisbane]. A "B" countermark was later released at the October ANDA fair.
[g] Incuse square 'S' counterstamp for the Sydney Royal Easter Show. Pre-struck at the RAM for general sale at the show.
[h] Coins feature "S" counterstamp and struck at the Sydney Royal Easter Show.
[i] Incuse square "B" counterstamp. Pre-struck at RAM for general sale.
[j] Coins feature "B" counterstamp and were struck at the Brisbane ANDA Show.
[k] As for (f), but Folder overprinted with "Brisbane Coin Fair, October 2008."
[l] Incuse square 'M' counterstamp for Melbourne. Pre-struck at RAM for general sale.
[m] Coins feature M" counterstamp and struck at the Melbourne ANDA Show.
[n] For the first time the fine Silver Proof coin contained a raised "C" Mintmark.

ONE DOLLAR

ONE YEAR COMMEMORATIVE REVERSES

2008 [a] Quarantine 2008 [b] Planet Earth 2008 [c] St Mary McKillop 2008 [d] Rugby League

2008 [e] Scouting 2009 [f] Australia Post 2009 [g] Aged Pension [h] Aged Pension Mint Roll

NCLT. COLLECTOR ISSUES ONLY

Date	TYPE	Mintage Figures	Mint Mark	Metal Comp.	Weight in gms	Description	Issue Price	Unc Retail	Proof Retail
[a]	**2008 CENTENARY OF QUARANTINE**								
2008	NCLT	30,094	–	Al/br	9 g	Circ. Paired with 20¢ in case	15	20	–
2008	PNC	21,600	–	Al/br	9 g	Coin & Stamp cover. Priced in PNC section			–
(b)	**2008 INTERNATIONAL YEAR OF PLANET EARTH**								
2008 b	PART SET	28,399	–	Al/br	9 g	Circ. Part of 2 coin cased set	15	15	–
2008 b	PART SET	28,569	–	Al/br	9 g	Proof. Part of 6 coin set	–	–	20
2008	NCLT	2,600	–	Silver	11.6	Proof .999 fine. Width 25mm	45	–	50
2008	PART SET	1,000	–	Silver	11.6	Proof. Berlin Money Fair	45	–	50

[b] The two coin Mint Set, two coin Proof Set and six coin Proof Set mentioned above included the standard 20 cents and commemorative $1 issues.

Date	TYPE	Mintage Figures	Mint Mark	Metal Comp.	Weight in gms	Description	Issue Price	Unc Retail	Proof Retail
[c]	**2008 SAINT MARY MACKILLOP**								
2008	NCLT	29,802		Al/br	9 g	Circ coin in coloured folder	12.95	75	–
[d]	**2008 CENTENARY OF RUGBY LEAGUE**								
2008	NCLT	35,280	–	Al/br	9 g	Circ coin in coloured folder	12.95	20	–
2008	NCLT	26,109	–	Al/br	9 g	AP Prestige Stamp Booklet`	n/a	25	–

CIRCULATION & NON CIRCULATION (NCLT) ISSUES

Date	TYPE	Mintage Figures	Mint Mark	Metal Comp.	Weight in gms	Issuing Mint	Unc	Choice Unc	Roll or Bagged	Issue Price	Mint set Retail	Proof Retail
[e]	**2008 CENTENARY OF SCOUTING**											
2008	CIRC	17,157,000	–	Al/br	9 g	Canb	4	7	–	–	–	–
2008	NCLT	500	–	Al/br	9 g	Circ launch issue @ function				29.95	n/a	-
2008	ROLL	10,000	–	Al/br	9 g	Mint roll of 20 x $1 coins				29.95	40	–
[f]	**2009 BICENTENARY OF AUSTRALIA POST**											
2009	EX-SET	10,000	–	Al/br	9 g	Paired with $5 coin featuring PO				–	–	35
2009	PNC	32,300	–	Al/br	9 g	Coin & Stamp cover. Priced in PNC section						–
[g/h]	**2009 CENTENARY OF THE AGED PENSION**											
2009 g	CIRC	10,167,950	–	Al/br	9 g	Canb	4	7	–	–	–	–
2009 h	ROLL	7,950	–	Al/br	9 g	Mint roll of 20 x $1 coins				29.95	40	–

ONE DOLLAR

ONE YEAR COMMEMORATIVE REVERSES

Common obverse 2009 [a] Astronomy Al/Br 2009 [b] Citizens Al/br Unc & Silver Proof

(a) 2009 YEAR OF ASTRONOMY

Date	TYPE	Mintage Figures	Mint Mark	Metal Comp.	Weight in gms	Description	Issue Price	Unc Retail	Proof Retail
2009	EX-SET	63,652	–	Al/br	9 g	Circ part of annual set	–	15	–
2009	EX-SET	23,257	–	Al/br	9 g	Proof part of annual set	–	–	18
2009	EX-SET	25,114	–	Al/br	9 g	Circ $1 & 20¢ pair in folder	–	7	–
2009	EX-SET	10,500	–	Al/br	9 g	Proof $1 & 20¢ pair in case	–	–	45

(b) 2009 60 YEARS OF AUSTRALIAN CITIZENSHIP

Date	TYPE	Mintage Figures	Mint Mark	Metal Comp.	Weight in gms	Description	Issue Price	Unc Retail	Proof Retail
2009 a	NCLT	86,207	C	Al/br	9 g	M'Mark. General RAM & dealer retail	3	5	–
2009 b	NCLT	67,896	C	Al/br	9 g	Mintmark. Gallery. Mint your own	3	5	–
2009 c	NCLT	1,493	C	Al/br	9 g	Mintmark with overprint folder	3	10	–
2009 d	NCLT	38,202	S	Al/br	9 g	Privymark. Pre-struck for general retail	3	5	–
2009 `	NCLT	34,354	B	Al/br	9 g	Privymark. Pre-struck for general retail	3	5	–
2009 e	NCLT	1,493	B	Al/br	9 g	P'mk. Folder overprint. ANDA Bris	3	10	–
2009	NCLT	36,763	M	Al/br	9 g	Privymark. Pre-struck for general retail	3	5	–
2009 f	OFF METAL	7,050	C	Silver	11.6g	Proof .999 fine. Width 25mm	40	–	45

[a] 'C' mintmark appearing as part of the die design. These were distributed to accredited dealers and through the mint's own client list.
[b] Visitors could strike their own coin on a specially modified press in the RAM's Tourist Gallery. The coins were generally housed in a brightly coloured souvenir cardboard folder.
[c] Similar to (a) but folder overprinted with "Brisbane Coin Fair February 2009." These overprints were privately produced by local dealership, VP coins. Although unofficial they are Included here as collectors value the innovative issue as part of the overall series.
[d] Incuse square 'S' privymark for Sydney. Pre-struck at the RAM for general sale.
[e] Similar to (a) but prestruck with a 'B' privymark and overprinted by dealership VP Coins.
[f] Fine Silver (99.9%) Proof coin with raised "C" MM. Interrupted reeding.

2009 (c) Dorothy Wall 2009 (d) Steve Irwin 2010 (e) Fred Hollows 2010 (f) Girl Guides

(c) 2009 - DOROTHY WALL - Blinky Bill Baby Sets only

Date	TYPE	Mintage Figures	Mint Mark	Metal Comp.	Weight in gms	Description	Issue Price	Unc Retail	Proof Retail
2009	EX-SET	34,179	–	Al/br	9 g	Circ only in Blinky Bill mint set	–	8	–
2010	EX-SET	33,131	–	Al/br	9 g	Circ only in Blinky Bill mint set	–	8	–
2011	EX-SET	27,168	–	Al/br	9 g	Circ only in Blinky Bill mint set	–	8	–

(d) 2009 STEVE IRWIN. INSPIRATIONAL AUSTRALIANS

Date	TYPE	Mintage Figures	Mint Mark	Metal Comp.	Weight in gms	Description	Issue Price	Unc Retail	Proof Retail
2009	NCLT	35,058	–	Al/br	9 g	Circ coin in coloured folder	12.95	30	–

(e) 2010 FRED HOLLOWS INSPIRATIONAL AUSTRALIANS

Date	TYPE	Mintage Figures	Mint Mark	Metal Comp.	Weight in gms	Description	Issue Price	Unc Retail	Proof Retail
2010	NCLT	32,649	–	Al/br	9 g	Circ coin in coloured folder	12.95	20	–

(f) 2010 CENTENARY OF GIRL GUIDES AUSTRALIA

Date	TYPE	Mintage Figures	Mint Mark	Metal Comp.	Weight in gms	Description	Issue Price	Unc Retail	Proof Retail
2010	CIRC	12,585,000	–	Al/br	9 g	Canb 5 9 –	–	–	–
2010	ROLL	7,499	–	Al/br	9 g	RAM mint roll 20 x $1 coins	40	29.95	– –
2010	PNC	23,000	–	Al/br	9 g	Coin & Stamp cover. Priced in PNC section			–

ONE DOLLAR

ONE YEAR COMMEMORATIVE REVERSES

2010 [a] Burke & Wills

2011 [b] CHOGM

2011 [c] Census

2011 [d] Dame Joan

2011 [e] Wool Industry

2012 [f] Co-Operatives

2012 [g] Mawson

2012 [h] Fields of Gold

CIRCULATION & NON CIRCULATION (NCLT) ISSUES

Date	TYPE	Mintage Figures	Mint Mark	Metal Comp.	Weight in gms	Issuing Mint	Unc	Choice Unc	Roll or Bagged	Issue Price	Mint set Retail	Proof Retail
[a]	**2010 150th ANNIVERSARY OF BURKE & WILLS**											
2010	EX SET	40,000	–	Al/br	9 g	Circ 20¢ & $1 pair in folder				15	20	–
2010	EX SET	9,995	–	Al/br	9 g	Proof 20¢ & $1 pair in case				45	–	50
[b]	**2011 CHOGM (PERTH OCTOBER 28/30)**											
2011	CIRC	9,397,000	–	Al/br	9 g	Canb	5	9	–	–	–	–
2011	ROLL	10,000	–	Al/br	9 g	RAM mint roll 20 x $1 coins				29.95	40	–

NCLT. COLLECTOR ISSUES ONLY

Date	TYPE	Mintage Figures	Mint Mark	Metal Comp.	Weight in gms	Description	Issue Price	Unc Retail	Proof Retail
[c]	**2011 CENTENARY OF NATIONAL CENSUS**								
2011	NCLT	15,024	–	Al/br	9 g	Circ coin in coloured folder	12.95	15	–
[d]	**2011 DAME JOAN SUTHERLAND**								
2011	NCLT	24,951	–	Al/br	9 g	Circ coin in coloured folder	12.95	15	–
[e]	**2011 AUSTRALIAN WOOL INDUSTRY**								
2011	NCLT	30,002	–	Al/br	9 g	Circ $1 & 20¢ pair in folder	15	15	–
2011	NCLT	10,500	–	Al/br	9 g	Proof $1 & 20¢ pair in case	45	–	45
[f]	**2012 INTERNATIONAL YEAR OF CO-OPERATIVES**								
2012	NCLT	20,463	–	Al/br	9 g	Circ coin in coloured folder	12.5	14	–
2012	NCLT	15,000	–	Al/br	9 g	Coin & Stamp cover. Priced in PNC section			
[g]	**2012 DOUGLAS MAWSON**								
2012	NCLT	24,951	–	Al/br	9 g	Circ coin in coloured folder	12.95	15	–
2012	PNC	19,980	–	Al/br	9 g	Coin & Stamp cover. Priced in PNC section			
[h]	**2012 FIELDS OF GOLD. TWO COIN SET (20¢ & $1)**								
2012	PART SET	20,000	–	Al/br	9 g	Circ $1 & 20¢ pair in folder	15	35	–
2012	PART SET	7,502	–	Silver	11.66	Proof $1 & 20¢ pair in case	53	–	60

ONE DOLLAR

ONE YEAR COMMEMORATIVE REVERSES

2012 [a] Women's Tennis

2012 [b] Men's Tennis

2012 [c] Ethel C. Pedley

2012 [d] The Farmer

2012 [e] AFL Unnamed

2012 [f] AFL Named

2012 [g] AFL Silver

2013 [h] Benevolent

Date	TYPE	Mintage Figures	Mint Mark	Metal Comp.	Weight in gms	Description	Issue Price	Unc Retail	Proof Retail
[a]	**2012 AUSTRALIAN WOMEN'S OPEN TENNIS**								
2012	NCLT	12,004	–	Al/br	9 g	Circ coin in coloured folder	15	15	–
2012	PNC	15,000	–	Al/br	9 g	Coin & Stamp cover. Priced in PNC section			–
[b]	**2012 AUSTRALIAN MEN'S OPEN TENNIS**								
2012	NCLT	12,044	–	Al/br	9 g	Circ coin in coloured folder	15	15	–
2012 b	PNC	15,000	–	Al/br	9 g	Coin & Stamp cover. Priced in PNC section			–
[b] This is the first official 2 x coin PNC issue and included both above coins.									
[c]	**2012 - ETHEL C. PEDLEY - Dot & The Kangaroo Baby Sets**								
2012	EX SET	23,084	–	Al/br	9 g	Circ exclusive to annual Baby Set	–	20	–
2013	EX SET	21,001	–	Al/br	9 g	Circ exclusive to annual Baby Set	–	20	–
2014	EX SET	16,611	–	Al/br	9 g	Circ exclusive to annual Baby Set	–	20	–
[d]	**2012 AUSTRALIAN YEAR OF THE FARMER**								
2012	NCLT	23,084	–	Al/Br	9 g	Circ coin in coloured folder	12.95	15	–
[e/f/g]	**2012 AFL PREMIERS - SYDNEY SWANS**								
2012 a	PNC	15,000	–	Al/br	9 g	*Coin & Stamp cover. Priced in PNC section*			–
2012 b	NCLT	88,424	–	Al/br	9 g	Circ coin in coloured folder	19.95	25	–
2012 c	OFF METAL	1,500	–	Silver	1 oz	Proof 999. Single cased coin	115	–	115
2012 d	CASED SET	5,000		Silver & Cu/ni		Proof $1+ replica cup & Medal	295	–	300
2012 e	DUAL SET	5,000	–	Silver	9 g	Proof Silver & Unc $1+ signed card	–	–	70
2012 f	CORPORATE	n/a	–	Al/br	9 g	Circ. Corporate AFL promotion	–	–	n/a

(a) This PNC features the first of two die variations. The PNC design is the same type used for the coin toss before the final was played at the MCG on September 29th 2012. Due to the timing, the PNC coin does not have the winner's name as part of the design. The legends read "2012 AFL Premiers" on the reverse above the cup and "One Dollar" below the cup. The obverse is standard. However the envelope features the Sydney Swans as the AFL Premiership winners.
(b) This "Type 2" Al/Br Unc coin comes in a folder featuring the names of all the premiership winning players. Both the obverse and reverse designs show subtle changes. The legend reads "2012 AFL Premiers" with "Sydney Swans" written below the same Premiership Cup. The obverse features the words "1 Dollar" and the Ian Rank-Broadley portrait of Queen Elizabeth II has been reduced in size to fit the extra text.
(c) The silver 1oz proof coin included the type Two Design.
(d) Packaged in a mahogany box with a replica of the Premiership Medallion and Premiership Cup.
(e) This set included the 2012 $1 Silver Proof Premiership Coin; the 2012 $1 Uncirculated AFL Premiership Coin, and a souvenir card autographed by a Sydney Swans star player.
(f) The AFL used a Type Two dollar coin in exclusive packaging as gifts for VIPs at AFL corporate functions. Similar to the publically available PNC, this corporate issue featured a small card in a sealed bag.

Date	TYPE	Mintage Figures	Mint Mark	Metal Comp.	Weight in gms	Description	Issue Price	Unc Retail	Proof Retail
[h]	**2013 BENEVOLENT SOCIETY**								
2013	NCLT	16,002?	–	Al/br	9 g	Unc coin in coloured folder	13.95	15	–

ONE DOLLAR

ONE YEAR COMMEMORATIVE REVERSES

2013 [a] Mining/ Gold

2013 [b/c] Opera House Al/br & Proof Silver

2013 [d] Slim Dusty

NCLT. COLLECTOR ISSUES ONLY

Date	TYPE	Mintage Figures	Mint Mark	Metal Comp.	Weight in gms	Description	Issue Price	Unc Retail	Proof Retail
[a]	**2013 AUSTRALIAN MINING. DISCOVERY OF GOLD**								
2013	PART PAIR	40,000	–	Al/br	9 g	Circ 20¢ & $1 cased as a pair	15	15	–
2013	OFF METAL	25,000	–	Silver	11.65	Proof 20¢ & $1 cased as a pair	53	–	60
[b/c]	**2013 SYDNEY OPERA HOUSE 40th ANNIVERSARY**								
2013	NCLT	To order	–	Al/br	9 g	Circ coin in coloured folder	13.5	16	–
2013	NCLT	10,000	–	Silver	1 oz	Proof. 99.9 fine. Width 40mm	100	–	100
[d]	**2013 SLIM DUSTY. COUNTRY MUSIC ICON**								
2013	NCLT	15,278?	–	Al/br	9 g	Circ coin in coloured folder	12.95	25	–

2013 [e] AFL Circ Al/br

2013 [f] AFL Proof Silver

2013 [g] Korea Al/br

2014 [h] Medi-Mazing

Date	TYPE	Mintage Figures	Mint Mark	Metal Comp.	Weight in gms	Description	Issue Price	Unc Retail	Proof Retail
[e/f]	**2013 AFL PREMIERS - HAWTHORN HAWKS**								
2013 e	NCLT	tba	–	Al/br	9 g	Circ coin in coloured folder	19.5	20	–
2013	PNC	15,000	–	Al/br	9 g	Coin & Stamp cover. Priced in PNC section –			
2013	OFF METAL	tba	–	Silver	1 oz	Proof in plush case 40mm	129	–	145
2013 f	PART SET	5,000	–	Silver	11.65	Proof $1+ replica cup & Medal	295	–	295

(e) Coin comes in folder featuring the names of all the premiership winning players.
(f) This two coin set included the 2013 $1 Silver Proof & Al/br Unc Premiership coin as well as a souvenir card autographed by a Sydney Swans star player.

Date	TYPE	Mintage Figures	Mint Mark	Metal Comp.	Weight in gms	Description	Issue Price	Unc Retail	Proof Retail
[g]	**2013 KOREAN WAR 60th ANNIVERSARY**								
2013	NCLT	13,102?	–	Al/br	9 g	Circ coin in coloured folder	13.5	n/a	–
2013	NCLT	5000/ n/a	–	Silver	11.65	Proof .999 fine. Width 25mm	55	–	95
[h]	**2014 CLEVER AUSTRALIA. MEDI-MAZING**								
2014	NCLT	30,000	–	Al/br	9 g	Circ coin in coloured folder	13.5	15	–

[h] This is the first of a series that celebrates the scientific achievements of often little-known Australians. These include the pacemaker, penicillin, IVF embryo freezing and spray-on skin for burns' victims. This first issue has been released to coincide with the International Year of Crystallography that celebrates the work of Lawrence Bragg. In 1912 Bragg derived the equation for how to use x-rays to determine the atomic structure of crystals. This work revolutionised the medical profession, with a technique that gave a wealth of insight into the structure of matter. In 1915, Bragg and his father William were awarded the Nobel Prize in Physics for their collaboration on this research.

ONE DOLLAR

ONE YEAR COMMEMORATIVE REVERSES

2014 [a] AFL Hawthorn

2014 [b] G for George

2014 [c] ANZAC

2015 [d] WW1 News Corp

[a] 2014 AFL PREMIERS - HAWTHORN HAWKS

2014 a	NCLT	To order	–	Al/br	9 g	Circ coin in coloured folder	19.5	20	–
2014	PNC	15,000	–	Al/br	9 g	*Coin & Stamp cover. Priced in PNC section*			–
2014	OFF METAL	tba	–	Silver	1 oz	Proof in plush case 40mm	129	–	145
2014 b	CASED SET	5,000	–	Silver	11.65	Proof $1+ replica cup & Medal	295	–	295

[a] Coin comes in folder featuring the names of all the premiership winning players.
[b] This three piece timber cased set included the silver Premiership proof coin, a silver Premiership medallion and a 2D replica 2014 Premiership Cup

[b] 2014 G FOR GEORGE. WW2 BOMBER

2014	NCLT	30,000	–	Al/br	9 g	Circ coin in coloured folder	13.5	15	–

[c] 2014 - [2018] ANZAC. THE SPIRIT LIVES ON

2014	CIRC	21,830,500	–	Al/br	9 g	Canb	4	7	Bagged	–	–	–
2014	NCLT	To order	–	Al/br	9 g	Circ coin in colour folder				6.95	7	–
2014 a	NCLT	14,913	AL	Al/br	9 g	Mobile Counterstamp. Albany				19.95	30	–
2014 b	NCLT	11,292	M	Al/br	9 g	Mobile Counterstamp. Shrine				10	25	–
2014	PNC	14,500	–	Al/br	9 g	*Coin & Stamp cover. Priced in PNC section*						–
2015	CIRC	1,300,000	–	Al/br	9 g	Canb	4	7	Bagged	–	–	–
2015 c	NCLT	tba	Map	Al/br	9 g	Circ. Changeover regional tour				10	65	–
2016	CIRC	1,800,000	–	Al/br	9 g	Canb	4	7	Bagged	–	–	–
2016 c	NCLT	tba	Map	Al/br	9 g	Circ. Changeover tour				10	45	–
2016 c	NCLT	tba	–	Al/br	9 g	Circ coin in colour folder				10	25	–
2017 c	NCLT	tba	–	Al/br	9 g	Circ coin in colour folder				10	17	–

[a] This coin was issued in Albany WA between October 30 & November 2, 2014 during a series of ceremonies held to highlight the 100th anniversary of the departure of the first troops to leave Australian shores at the beginning of WWI.
[b] Released at the Melbourne Shrine on Remembrance Day, November 11, 2014.
[c/d] In 2015, members of the RAM staff hit the road with a popup tent, the mobile press and loads of uncirculated ANZAC, The Spirit Lives On, $1 coins. For many people in country areas, it was the first experience of seeing the mobile press in action. The countermark was a distinctive map of Australia, which was in keeping with the theme of the tour. Dubbed the Changeover Tour it included Albury, Bendigo, Ballarat, Melbourne, Launceston and Hobart. The success of the venture led to a similar tour operating over a wide section of Victoria, South Australia, Western Australia, Tasmania, Queensland and the Northern Territory. Again collectors had the opportunity to purchase a 2016 counterstamped map of Australia.

[d] 2015 WORLD WAR I - NEWS CORP RELEASE

2015	NCLT	13,543	–	Al/Br	9 g	UNC coin in coloured folder	13.5	175	–

This One Dollar coin, part of a fifteen piece ANZAC collection was designed and produced by the RAM and distributed nationally through News Corp Australia. The set was made available to the general public when purchasing News Corp publications from participating retail outlets from 11 – 26 April 2015. The final issue was a 2015 $1 coloured frosted uncirculated coin, previously only available to News Corp subscribers, was later offered for sale at the RAM mint shop and through selected dealers.

ONE DOLLAR

ONE YEAR COMMEMORATIVE REVERSES

[a] Circ Al/bronze [d] Frosted Silver [e] Colour Silver [f] Gold plated Circ

2015 AFL - CUSTODIANS OF THE GAME

2015 a	NCLT	3,907	M	Al/br	9 g	Circ. Mobile press at Grand final	15	20	–
2015 b	NCLT	500	–	Al/br	9 g	Circ. Coloured. Ballot only	–	200	–
2015 c	PNC	3,000	–	Al/br	9 g	*Coin & Stamp cover. Priced in PNC section*			–
2015 d	NCLT	4,433		Silver	11.66	Circ. Frosted finish	120	n/a	–
2015 e	NCLT	500		Silver	11.66	Spec. Winning club colours. Ballot	120	–	
2015 f	NCLT	67		Gilt Silver	11.66	Circ. Gold plated Ballot	120	–	

Common obverse [g] Circ Al/bronze [h] Colour Al/br [i] Frosted Silver

2015 NRL - MOMENTS THAT MATTER

2015 g	NCLT	3,481	S	Al/br	9 g	Circ. Mobile press at Grand final	15	20	–
2015 h	NCLT	500	–	Al/br	9 g	Circ. Coloured. Ballot only	–	350	–
2015 i	PNC	3,000	–	Al/br	9 g	*Coin & Stamp cover. Priced in PNC section*			–
2015 j	NCLT	4,433		Silver	11.66	Circ. Frosted finish	120	n/a	–
2015 k	NCLT	500		Silver	11.66	Spec. Winning club colours. Ballot	200	–	
2015 l	NCLT	67		Gilt Silver	11.66	Circ. Gold plated Ballot	120	–	

In a sports-mad country, the grand finals of two of our favourite footy codes ranks just behind the running of the Melbourne Cup. The NRL and AFL deciders are held on the same weekend and just a month or so before the running of 'The Cup.' In 2015, the RAM raised the bar a notch or two in the skilful marketing of several coin options available for both codes. Mint your own coin opportunities, coupled with ballot only issues, added some real excitement to the whole sport + collectables anticipation. The mint set up mobile presses in both Melbourne and Sydney to allow fans to strike a countermark $1 coin with either a M or S.

[a] The RAM mobile press was part of a 'pop-up' site operating outside the MCG in the leadup to the grand final , October 2, 2015.

[b] Each set includes an exclusive fine silver coin, pack of 10 officially licensed trading cards and maxicard (themed postcard and stamp).

[c/i] The PNC issues were unique as they did not include a counterstamp.

[g] The RAM set up its second mobile press at NRL Nation in Darling Harbour from October 1 - 3, 2015 to allow fans to countermark the special NRL al/br $1 coin with the 'S' for Sydney emblem. These two venues were the only way to obtain one of the counterstamped coins. The issue price of $15 also included an entry form to go into the draw to win one of 500 coins with the finalists team colours. Multiple coin purchases resulted in an equal number of entry forms. The prize was one of 500 coins with the finalists team colours as well as one of the following that were randomly added to each set. Some of these were sold separately after the ballot as shown above.

1 in 75 sets includes a gilt-plated silver coin!
1 in 25 sets includes a signature pack of ten officially licensed trading cards!
1 in 10 sets includes a Coloured Silver Coin featuring the Premiership winning team's colours!
1 in 10 sets includes a maxicard with gold postmark!

With special thanks to Kathryn & Mark from the Purple Penny for their assistance in updating the mintage figures of many of the recent issues. Also a special thanks to Brett Stokes from WA who has turned the collecting and study of the $1 coin into a science.

ONE DOLLAR

ONE YEAR COMMEMORATIVE REVERSES

2015 (a) Standard reverse

2015 (b) Silver. 1 of 26

2016 (c) Silver. 1 of 26

2017 (c) Silver. 1 of 26

Date	Description	Type	Metal Content	Weight	Size	Mintage Figures	Issue Price	Retail Value
[a,b,c,d] THEME : 2015 ALPHABET SINGLE COIN BABY ISSUE								
2015 a	Standard mint set coin	Fr/unc	Alum/ br	9 g	25 mm	To order	15	15
2015	Alphabet letter choice	Fr/unc	Alum/ br	9 g	25 mm	To order	15	15
2015	Alphabet letter choice	Fr/unc	.999 Silver	11.66g	25 mm	5,000	50	50
2016 b	Standard mint set coin	Fr/unc	Alum/ br	9 g	25 mm	To order	15	15
2016	Alphabet letter choice	Fr/unc	Alum/ br	9 g	25 mm	To order	15	15
2016	Alphabet letter choice	Fr/unc	.999 Silver	11.66g	25 mm	5,000	50	50
2017 c	Standard mint set coin	Fr/unc	Alum/ br	9 g	25 mm	To order	15	15
2017	Alphabet letter choice	Fr/unc	Alum/ br	9 g	25 mm	To order	15	15
2017	Alphabet letter choice	Fr/unc	.999 Silver	11.66g	25 mm	5,000	50	50

Collectors have a number of options to obtain the above coins. They could be purchased individually, as a set, or have a coin with a particular letter included in the annual proof set. This is possible as the proof set displays the coins in individual capsules rather than as a sealed case. Each year all 26 letters of the alphabet have subtle differences in the design appearing between the silver and aluminium/bronze coins. An added feature of the designs that will appeal to all children [and most adults] is the sort of "Where's Wally" theme, where the longer you stare at each design, the more items beginning with that letter will come into view. How to present these coins, in this book, is something I am still grappling with. The designs by Bronwyn King are both beautiful and wimsical but with 26 coins x 2 each year in a book this size, creates a logistical nightmare. Prices listed above are generic at this stage. A separate price listing to distinguish movements in the market for individual coins will be included when the need arises.

2016 [d] Decimal Currency 50th anniversary

2016 [e] Lighthouse

2016 [f] Brazil Olympics

[d] 2016 DECIMAL CURRENCY 50TH ANNIVERSARY

2016	NCLT	95,929	Cu/ni	15.55g	Circ coin in coloured card	10	10	–
2016	ROLL	5,000	Cu/ni	15.55g	Commemorative roll. 20 x Unc coins	50	95	–
2016	BAG	tba	Cu/ni	15.55g	Commemorative bag. 10 x Unc coins	35	40	–
2016	EX-SET	tba	Cu/ni	15.55g	Spec. Part of annual 6 coin mint set	4	2	–
2016	EX-SET	tba	Cu/ni	15.55g	Proof. Part of annual 6 coin proof set	–	–	15

The Royal Australian Mint took the mobile press to Parliament House Canberra during March for the Enlighten Festival. A "C" for Canberra counterstamp was struck on the obverse of the 50th anniversary of Decimal Currency $1 coin. It was the first time a coin was struck on the obverse of a coin.

[e] 2016 AUSTRALIAN LIGHTHOUSE

2016	NCLT	30,000	–	Al/br	9 g	CIRC coin in coloured folder	13.5	15	–
2016	PNC	9,000	–	Al/br	9 g	Coin & Stamp cover. Priced in PNC section			–

[f] 2016 AUSTRALIAN OLYMPIC TEAM PROGRAM

2016	Basketball	tba	Al/br	9 g	CIRC. Folder honours Patrick Mills	15	15	–
2016	Athletics	tba	Al/br	9 g	CIRC. Folder honours Melissa Breen	15	15	–
2016	Swimming	tba	Al/br	9 g	CIRC. Folder Thomas Fraser Holmes	15	15	–

VARIOUS DENOMINATIONS

MULTIPLE ISSUES - SINGLE THEME

Beginning with the 2007 Ashes series, coins featuring the same theme were struck in base metal, silver and gold in denominations of one, five and ten dollars. While the coins were sold individually, they did reflect the same theme so it was decided to list the issues as a "set" in this position and then list the individual higher denominations in their respective sections.

$1 [a] Al/br Unc

$5 [b] Silver Obv

$5 [b] Silver Proof

$10 [c] Gold Proof

NCLT. COLLECTOR ISSUES ONLY

THEME : 2007 THE ASHES

Date	Face Value	TYPE	Mintage Figures	Mint Mark	Metal Comp.	Weight in gms	Description	Issue Price	Unc Retail	Proof Retail
2007a	1	NCLT	41,438	–	Al/br	9 g	General RAM retail & dealer sales	2	4	–
2007	1	PNC	8,000	–	Al/br	9 g	Coin & Stamp cover. Priced in PNC section			–
2007b	5	NCLT	7,750	C	Silver	33.	Proof .999 fine. Width 25mm	65	–	70
2007c	10	NCLT	2,315	C	Gold	3.1 g	Proof. 99.99 fine. Size 17.5mm	175	–	280

$1 [a] Al/br Unc

Reverse mint mark position

$5 [b] Silver Proof

NCLT. COLLECTOR ISSUES ONLY

THEME : 2010 CENTENARY OF AUSTRALIAN COINAGE

Date	Face Value	TYPE	Mintage Figures	Mint Mark	Metal Comp.	Weight in gms	Description	Issue Price	Unc Retail	Proof Retail
2010	1	NCLT	tba	C	Al/br	9 g	M'Mark. General RAM & dealer retail	3	5	–
2010	1	NCLT	tba	C	Al/br	9 g	Mintmark. Gallery. Mint your own	10	20	–
2010	1	NCLT	4,970	C	Al/br	9 g	Mobile Counterstamp. ANDA Canb	5	10	–
2010	1x4	NCLT	30,990	C,S,B,M		9 g	Mint & countermarks in colour folder	14.95	15	–
2010	1x4	NCLT	600	C,S,B,M		9 g	Mint & countermarks . Bris fair	14.95	15	–
2010	1x4	NCLT	20,001	H,A,D,P		9 g	Mint & countermarks in colour folder	15	20	–
2010	1	PNC	25,600	C	Al/br	9 g	Coin & Stamp cover. Priced in PNC section			–
2010	1	NCLT	2,000	C	Silver	11.31	MASTER Privymark. ANDA Canberra	45	–	60
2010	1	NCLT	1,248	S	Silver	11.31	MASTER Privymark. ANDA Sydney	45	–	60
2010	1	NCLT	1,228	B	Silver	11.31	MASTER Privymark. ANDA Brisbane	45	–	60
2010	1	NCLT	1,350	M	Silver	11.31	MASTER Privymark. ANDA Melbourne	45	–	60
2010	1	NCLT	1,713	P	Silver	11.31	MASTER Privymark. ANDA Perth	45	–	60
2010	1	NCLT	9,046	C	Silver	11.31	Proof .999 fine. Interrupted reeding	38	–	40

Each of the above Master privymarked coins was restricted to just 2,000 units per show. The RAM had a strict 'meltdown policy'. Every coin not sold during the ANDA Shows to either the public or to dealers were melted down.

VARIOUS DENOMINATIONS

MULTIPLE ISSUES - SINGLE THEME

2011 Al/Br Obverse 2011 [a] Al/br Circulation 2011 [b] Obverse & reverse Silver Proof

2011 [c] $1. Gilt Silver 2011 [d] $1. Gilt Silver 2011 [e] Obv & Rev of $25. 1/4 oz. Fine Gold

NCLT. COLLECTOR ISSUES ONLY

Date	Face Value	TYPE	Mintage Figures	Mint Mark	Metal Comp.	Weight in gms	Description	Issue Price	Unc Retail	Proof Retail
THEME : 2011 THE PRESIDENTS CUP										
2011 a	1	NCLT	15,000	–	Al/br	9 g	Circ in coloured card. 25mm	14.85	20	–
2011	1	PNC	15,025	–	Al/br	9 g	Coin & Stamp cover. Priced in PNC section			–
2011 b	1	NCLT	2,997	–	Silver	11.66	Proof. 99.9 fine silver. Size 25mm	66	–	70
2011 c	1	NCLT	7,500	–	Gilt	1 oz	Proof. Gilt/Silver 99.9 fine. 40mm	99	–	110
2011 d	10	NCLT	1,500	–	Gilt	5 oz	Proof. Gilt/Silver 99.9 fine. Priced in $10 section			–
2011 e	25	NCLT	1,500	–	Gold	1/4 oz	Proof. 99.99. 17.5mm. Priced in the $25 section			–

Common Obverse 2011 [a] Al/br Unc 2011 [b] Silver Proof 2011 [c] Gold Proof

NCLT. COLLECTOR ISSUES ONLY

Date	Face Value	TYPE	Mintage Figures	Mint Mark	Metal Comp.	Weight in gms	Description	Issue Price	Mint Set Retail	Proof Retail
THEME : 2011 RAM'S HEAD ISSUE										
2011	1	NCLT	tba	C	Al/br	9 g	Mintmark. Gallery. Mint your own	n/a	n/a	–
2011	1 x 4	NCLT	24,996	C,S,B,M		9 g	Mint & countermarks in colour folder	4.95	15	–
2011	1 x 4	NCLT	14,998	H,A,D,P		9 g	Mint & countermarks in colour folder	14.95	19	–
2011 a	1	NCLT	5,100	P	Al/br	9 g	Mobile Counterstamp. ANDA Perth	10	25	–
2011 b	1	NCLT	5,000	B	Al/br	9 g	Mobile Counterstamp. ANDA Brisb	15	20	–
2011 c	1	NCLT	4,997	M	Al/br	9 g	Mobile Counterstamp. ANDA Melb.	10	20	–
2011 d	1	NCLT	5,000	S	Al/br	9 g	Mobile Counterstamp. ANDA Syd.	10	19	–
2011 e	1	NCLT	5,002	A	Al/br	9 g	Mobile Counterstamp. ANDA Adel.	10	20	–
2011	1	NCLT	9,038	C	Silver	11.31	Proof .999 fine. Cased. 25mm	45	–	45
2011	10	NCLT	2,500	C	Gold	1/10oz	Proof. 99.99 fine. Size 17.5mm	320	–	350

[a] Issued at the Perth ANDA show. [b] Issued at the Brisbane ANDA show. [c] Issued at the Melbourne ANDA show. [d] Issued at the Sydney ANDA show. [e] Issued at the Adelaide ANDA show.

VARIOUS DENOMINATIONS

MULTIPLE ISSUES - SINGLE THEME

Bluebell Privymark

THEME : 2012 WHEAT SHEAF ISSUES

2012	1	CIRC	tba	C	Al/br	9 g	Mintmark. Gallery. Mint your own	4.75	9	–
2012 a	1	NCLT	6,050	√	Al/br	9 g	Mintmark pre-strike . ACT. Bluebell	12	22	–
2012 b	1	NCLT	5,000	P	Al/br	9 g	Mobile Counterstamp. ANDA Perth	10	20	–
2012 c	1	NCLT	5,000	B	Al/br	9 g	Mobile Counterstamp. ANDA Brisb	10	20	–
2012 d	1	NCLT	5,004	M	Al/br	9 g	Mobile Counterstamp. ANDA Melb	10	20	–
2012 e	1	NCLT	5,000	S	Al/br	9 g	Mobile Counterstamp. ANDA Sydney	10	15	–
2012	4 x 1	NCLT	24,996	C,S,B,M		9 g	Counter m'k & Privy marks in folder	14.95	15	–
2012	1	NCLT	12,500	C	Silver	11.66	Proof . 999 fine. Width 25mm	40	–	55
2012	10	NCLT	2,500	C	Gold	1/10oz	Proof. 99.99 fine. Size 17.5mm	360	–	360

(a) [√] This mintmark was used to commemorate the autumn 'Enlighten' Canberra Festival held during March 2012. The Bluebell is the ACT's floral emblem. Indicated by [√] in above table.
(b) Although distributed at the Perth ANDA Fair on March 3 & 4, the 'P' min mark was struck in Canberra as the mobile press was being used at the Enlighten Festival in Canberra.
(c) Two "B" Mintmarks exist. The Square version is included in the four coin mintmark set. The circular mintmark was struck on the mobile press at the Brisbane ANDA Fair on May 26 - 27.
(d) Two "M" Mintmarks exist. The Square version is included in the four coin mintmark set. The circular mintmark was struck on the mobile press at the Melbourne ANDA Fair on July 7 & 8.
(e) Two "S" Mintmarks exist. The Square version is included in the four coin mintmark set. The circular mintmark was struck on the mobile press at the Sydney ANDA Fair on August 18 & 19.

[f] Al/Br PNC. No colour

[g] Al/Br Colour

[h] 1oz Silver Proof

[i] 1oz Cook Islands

THEME : 2013 BLACK CAVIAR

2013 f	1	PNC	15,025	–	Al/br	9 g	Coin & Stamp cover. Priced in PNC section			–
2013 g	1	NCLT	19,278	–	Al/br	9 g	Specimen. Colour coin in card	16.95	25	–
2013 h	1	NCLT	2,500?	–	Silver	1 oz	Cased proof .999. 40mm	115	–	195
2013 h/i	1	PAIR	2,500	–	Silver	1 oz	Aust & Cook Island pair	250	–	265
2013 j	1	CORP	1,000	Framed		–	Framed 2 x silver & 2 x Albr	795	–	795

(f) The Al/br PNC $1 coin was not coloured.
(g) Packaged in a folder, this $1 coin featured the colours of Black Caviar's jockey silks. coins were launched at the 2013 World Stamp Expo in Melbourne on Saturday May 11 with all of the champion's trophies on display. Black Caviar broke all records with an unbeaten 25 consecutive wins.
(h) This silver proof coin was individually sold in a presentation case. This coin might be scarcer than the 2,500 suggested mintage figure. *[See notation (e) for more information].*
(i) This two-coin set included a Cook Islands $1 coin struck at the Royal MInt in Wales. The silver coin celebrated Black Caviar winning the 2012 Queens Diamond Jubilee at Royal Ascot. It was paired with the above mentioned Australian silver proof. There were 5,000 coins issued by the RAM and 40,000 made by The Royal Mint, however only 2,500 of each coin was released in this pack.
(j) This attractive montage contained all four above mentioned coins. There was some concern among some collectors that the RAM produced an "extra" 1,000 coins after the official low issue of 5,000 coins was sold out. However it appears that the Black Caviar licensing company purchased 1,000 of the single packaged coins to make up the framed sets on the secondary market.

MULTIPLE ISSUES - SINGLE THEME

Common Obverse

2013 [a] Al/br Unc

2013 [b] Silver Proof

2013 [c] Gold Proof

THEME : 2013 HOLEY DOLLAR & DUMP

Date	Face Value	TYPE	Mintage Figures	Mint Mark	Metal Comp.	Weight in gms	Description	Issue Price	Mint Set Retail	Proof Retail
2013	1	CIRC	tba	C	Al/br	9 g	Mintmark. Gallery. Mint your own	3	14	–
2013 a	1	NCLT	5,000	P	Al/br	9 g	Mobile Counterstamp. ANDA Perth	10	22	–
2013 b	1	NCLT	12,592	S	Al/br	9 g	Mobile Counterstamp. Royal Easter	10	20	–
2013 c	1	NCLT	2,403	B	Al/br	9 g	Mobile Counterstamp. ANDA Bris	9	12	–
2013 d	1	NCLT	3,704	M	Al/br	9 g	Mobile Counterstamp. ANDA Melb	10	20	–
2013	1x4	NCLT	12,195	C,S,B,M		9 g	Mint & countermarks in folder	22.5	25	–
2013	1	PNC	To order	C	Al/br	9 g	Coin & Stamp cover. Priced in PNC section			–
2013	1	NCLT	12,500	C	Silver	11.66	Proof .999 fine. Width 25mm	55	–	55
2013	10	NCLT	2,500	C	Gold	3.1 g	Proof. 99.99 fine. 17.53mm	320	–	350

[a] This counterstamped was pre-struck at the Canberra Mint except for a P for Perth privymark. It was released for sale at the Perth ANDA Coin & Banknote fair.
[b] The Sydney Royal Easter Show was held between 21st March and 3rd April 2013 during this time this counterstamp coin was produced at the Sydney Royal Easter Show. The 'S' Counterstamp coin was available to customers of the show as a special show souvenir where visitors could stamp and produce their own coin.
[c] The Brisbane Show (EKKA) was held between 8th and 17th August 2013. Patrons were able to strike their own coin which carried a 'B' privymark.
[d] The Melbourne International Coin show was held in Melbourne for the first time and over the weekend of the 18th - 20th October. Although the advertised mintage was set at 7,500 it is thought that only 3,714 patrons took up the offer.

2014 [a] $1 Al/br Uncirc

2014 [b] $1 Proof Silver

2014 $10 gold obverse

2014 [c] $10 Proof Gold

THEME : 2014 TERRA AUSTRALIS

Date	Face Value	TYPE	Mintage Figures	Mint Mark	Metal Comp.	Weight in gms	Description	Issue Price	Unc Retail	Proof Retail
2014	1	CIRC	53,000	C	Al/br	9 g	Mintmark. Gallery. Mint your own	3	12	–
2014	1x4	NCLT	11,738	C,S,B,M		9 g	Mint & countermarks in folder	22.5	24	–
2014 a	1	NCLT	3,052	P	Al/br	9 g	Mobile Counterstamp. ANDA Perth	10	20	–
2014 b	1	NCLT	8,571	S	Al/br	9 g	Mobile Counterstamp. Royal Easter	5	20	–
2014	1	NCLT	*Ditto*	S	Al/br	9 g	Mobile Counterstamp. ANDA Syd	10	20	–
2014 c	1	NCLT	8,360	B	Al/br	9 g	Mobile Counterstamp. ANDA Brisb	10	20	–
2014	1	NCLT	3,926	M	Al/br	9 g	Mobile Counterstamp. Royal Melb	5	15	–
2014 d	1	NCLT	*Ditto*	M	Al/br	9 g	Mobile Counterstamp. ANDA Melb.	10	20	–
2014	1	NCLT	12,500	C	Silver	11.66	Proof .999 fine. Width 25mm	55	–	55
2014	10	NCLT	2,500	C	Gold	1/10oz	Proof .9999 fine. Size 17.53mm	See $10 section		

This three coin series celebrates the bicentenary of one of the most significant publications in exploration history. Matthew Flinders' A Voyage to Terra Australis was published in July 1814, four years after the completion of his pioneering circumnavigation of Australia and long journey home to England.
[a] Perth ANDA Fair. Although $1 coins featuring a 'P' mintmark were offered at the fair they were pre-struck in Canberra to save on the cost of shipping the press across Australia.
[b] Sydney Royal Easter Show. The RAM took a stand to strike 'S' mintmarks on a mobile press. The show was held between 10th - 23rd April 2014.
[c] Brisbane ANDA Show. The Mint had a booth at the Ekka show where mobile press was used to strike a 'B' mintmark.
[d] Melbourne ANDA Show. One Dollar coins with an 'M' mintmark were pre-struck at the RAN for the Melbourne ANDA Show on 8-9 August 2014.

VARIOUS DENOMINATIONS

MULTIPLE ISSUES - SINGLE THEME

Common Obverse

2015 Al/br ANZAC

2015 Silver ANZAC

2015 Gold ANZAC

Date	Face Value	TYPE	Mintage Figures	Mint Mark	Metal Comp.	Weight in gms	Description	Issue Price	Unc Retail	Proof Retail
THEME : 2015 ANZAC CENTENARY										
2015	1	CIRC	56,654	C	Al/br	9 g	Mintmark. Gallery. Mint your own	3	10	–
2015	4x1	NCLT	17,229	C,S,B,M		9 g	Mintmark & countermarks in folder	22.5	30	–
2015 a	1	CIRC	9,973	S	Al/br	9 g	Mobile Counterstamp. Syd. REShow	5	18	–
2015 b	1	CIRC	5,813	B	Al/br	9 g	Mobile Counterstamp. Bris. EKKA	5	10	–
2015 c	1	CIRC	5,790	M	Al/br	9 g	Mobile Counterstamp. Royal Melb	5	10	–
2015	1	NCLT	6,055	C	Silver	11.66	Proof .999 fine. Boxed. Width 2550	–	60	
2015	10	NCLT	2,500	C	Gold	3.1g	Proof. 99.99 fine. Size 17.5m See $10 section			–

a] This carded uncirculated $1 coin was issued at the Sydney Royal Easter Show, from March 26 to April 7, 2015. Patrons could counterstamp the round 'S' themselves using the mobile press. This process entailed striking an 'S' on a RAM pre-struck coin.
[b] This issue features the round B countermark used exclusively to denote that the coin was struck using the mobile press set up at a stand at the annual EKKA show held in Brisbane.
[c] The RAM set up its mobile press for collectors to strike their own distinctive 'M' countermark in a booth at the Royal Melbourne Showgrounds from September 19 to 29, 2015.

2016 First Mint Silver Proof

2016 First Mint Gold Proof

2017 Trains Silver Proof

2017 Trains Gold Proof

Date	Face Value	TYPE	Mintage Figures	Mint Mark	Metal Comp.	Weight in gms	Description	Issue Price	Unc Retail	Proof Retail
THEME : 2016 AUSTRALIA'S FIRST MINTS										
2016	1	CIRC	tba	C	Al/br	9 g	Mintmark. Gallery. Mint your own	4.75	9	–
2016	4 x 1	NCLT	25,000	C,S,B,M		9 g	Mint & countermarks in folder	25	25	–
2016 a	1	NCLT	5,000	S	Al/br	9 g	Mobile Counterstamp. Syd Royal	10	12	–
2016 b	1	NCLT	Ditto	M	Al/br	9 g	Mobile Counterstamp. Melb	10	12	–
2016 c	1	NCLT	Ditto	B	Al/br	9 g	Mobile Counterstamp. Bris	10	12	–
2016	1	NCLT	5,000	C	Silver	11.66	Proof .999 fine. Width 25mm	50	–	55
2016	10	NCLT	5,000	C	Gold	3.1g	Proof. 99.99 fine. Size 17.5mm See $10 section			–

Australia's first official mint opened in Sydney in 1855, with Melbourne following in 1872. These were followed by Perth in 1899 and Canberra's RAM in 1965.
[a] This al/br $1 uncirculated 'S' Sydney counterstamp was struck for the Royal Agricultural Easter Show, Sydney Olympic Park 17th - 30th March 2016.
[b] Struck for the Royal Melbourne (Agricultural) Show from 23rd September to the 3rd October 2016.
[c] Issued at the Brisbane ANDA/ APTA fair held at the Brisbane Tennis Centre, Windsor on May 21-22nd.

Date	Face Value	TYPE	Mintage Figures	Mint Mark	Metal Comp.	Weight in gms	Description	Issue Price	Unc Retail	Proof Retail
THEME : 2017 AUSTRALIAN RAILWAYS										
2017	1	CIRC	tba	C	Al/br	9 g	Mintmark. Gallery. Mint your own	4.75	7	–
2017	4x1	NCLT	15,000	C,S,B,M		9 g	Mint & countermarks in folder	22.5	25	–
2017	1	NCLT	4,500	C	Silver	11.66	Proof .999 fine. Width 25mm	50	–	50
2017	10	NCLT	1,000	C	Gold	3.1g	Proof. 99.99 fine. Size 17.5mm See $10 section			–

VARIOUS DENOMINATIONS

MULTIPLE ISSUES - RAM LUNAR ISSUES

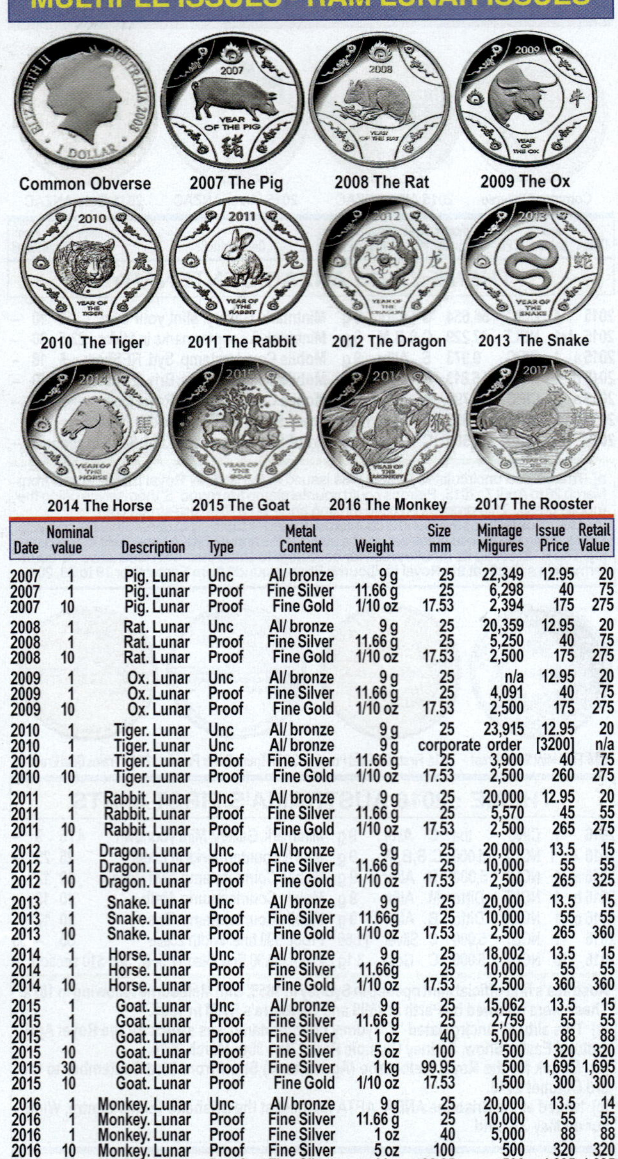

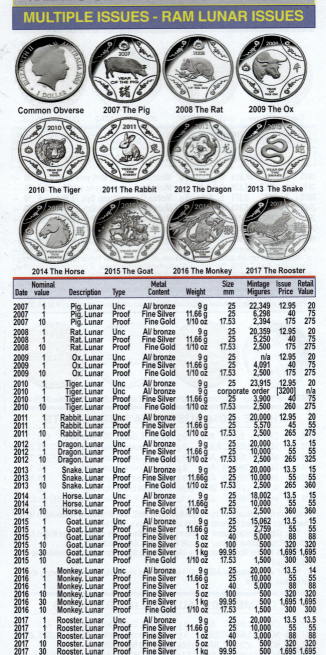

Common Obverse — 2007 The Pig — 2008 The Rat — 2009 The Ox

2010 The Tiger — 2011 The Rabbit — 2012 The Dragon — 2013 The Snake

2014 The Horse — 2015 The Goat — 2016 The Monkey — 2017 The Rooster

Date	Nominal value	Description	Type	Metal Content	Weight	Size mm	Mintage Migures	Issue Price	Retail Value
2007	1	Pig. Lunar	Unc	Al/ bronze	9 g	25	22,349	12.95	20
2007	1	Pig. Lunar	Proof	Fine Silver	11.66 g	25	6,298	40	75
2007	10	Pig. Lunar	Proof	Fine Gold	1/10 oz	17.53	2,394	175	275
2008	1	Rat. Lunar	Unc	Al/ bronze	9 g	25	20,359	12.95	20
2008	1	Rat. Lunar	Proof	Fine Silver	11.66 g	25	5,250	40	75
2008	10	Rat. Lunar	Proof	Fine Gold	1/10 oz	17.53	2,500	175	275
2009	1	Ox. Lunar	Unc	Al/ bronze	9 g	25	n/a	12.95	20
2009	1	Ox. Lunar	Proof	Fine Silver	11.66 g	25	4,091	40	75
2009	10	Ox. Lunar	Proof	Fine Gold	1/10 oz	17.53	2,500	175	275
2010	1	Tiger. Lunar	Unc	Al/ bronze	9 g	25	23,915	12.95	20
2010	1	Tiger. Lunar	Unc	Al/ bronze	9 g	corporate	order	[3200]	n/a
2010	1	Tiger. Lunar	Proof	Fine Silver	11.66 g	25	3,900	40	75
2010	10	Tiger. Lunar	Proof	Fine Gold	1/10 oz	17.53	2,500	260	275
2011	1	Rabbit. Lunar	Unc	Al/ bronze	9 g	25	20,000	12.95	20
2011	1	Rabbit. Lunar	Proof	Fine Silver	11.66 g	25	5,570	45	55
2011	10	Rabbit. Lunar	Proof	Fine Gold	1/10 oz	17.53	2,500	265	275
2012	1	Dragon. Lunar	Unc	Al/ bronze	9 g	25	20,000	13.5	15
2012	1	Dragon. Lunar	Proof	Fine Silver	11.66 g	25	10,000	55	55
2012	10	Dragon. Lunar	Proof	Fine Gold	1/10 oz	17.53	2,500	265	325
2013	1	Snake. Lunar	Unc	Al/ bronze	9 g	25	20,000	13.5	15
2013	1	Snake. Lunar	Proof	Fine Silver	11.66g	25	10,000	55	55
2013	10	Snake. Lunar	Proof	Fine Gold	1/10 oz	17.53	2,500	265	360
2014	1	Horse. Lunar	Unc	Al/ bronze	9 g	25	18,002	13.5	15
2014	1	Horse. Lunar	Proof	Fine Silver	11.66g	25	10,000	55	55
2014	10	Horse. Lunar	Proof	Fine Gold	1/10 oz	17.53	2,500	360	360
2015	1	Goat. Lunar	Unc	Al/ bronze	9 g	25	15,062	13.5	15
2015	1	Goat. Lunar	Proof	Fine Silver	11.66 g	25	2,759	55	55
2015	1	Goat. Lunar	Proof	Fine Silver	1 oz	40	5,000	88	88
2015	10	Goat. Lunar	Proof	Fine Silver	5 oz	100	500	320	320
2015	30	Goat. Lunar	Proof	Fine Silver	1 kg	99.95	500	1,695	1,695
2015	10	Goat. Lunar	Proof	Fine Gold	1/10 oz	17.53	1,500	300	300
2016	1	Monkey. Lunar	Unc	Al/ bronze	9 g	25	20,000	13.5	14
2016	1	Monkey. Lunar	Proof	Fine Silver	11.66 g	25	10,000	55	55
2016	1	Monkey. Lunar	Proof	Fine Silver	1 oz	40	5,000	88	88
2016	10	Monkey. Lunar	Proof	Fine Silver	5 oz	100	500	320	320
2016	30	Monkey. Lunar	Proof	Fine Silver	1 kg	99.95	500	1,695	1,695
2016	10	Monkey. Lunar	Proof	Fine Gold	1/10 oz	17.53	1,500	300	300
2017	1	Rooster. Lunar	Unc	Al/ bronze	9 g	25	20,000	13.5	13.5
2017	1	Rooster. Lunar	Proof	Fine Silver	11.66 g	25	10,000	55	55
2017	1	Rooster. Lunar	Proof	Fine Silver	1 oz	40	3,000	88	88
2017	10	Rooster. Lunar	Proof	Fine Silver	5 oz	100	500	320	320
2017	30	Rooster. Lunar	Proof	Fine Silver	1 kg	99.95	500	1,695	1,695
2017	10	Rooster. Lunar	Proof	Fine Gold	1/10 oz	17.53	1,500	300	300

RAM LUNAR ISSUES

PRESTIGE LUNAR COIN SERIES

2013 (a) Silver Snake

2013 (b) Gold Snake

2014 (c) Silver Horse

2014 (d) Gold Horse

[a & b] 2013 YEAR OF THE SNAKE - PROOF-LIKE

2013	1 kg	3,000	Fr/unc	Gold. 99.99	75 mm	100/ n/a	79,750	73,945
2013	5 oz	500	Fr/unc	Gold. 99.99	60 mm	1,000/ n/a	13,200	11,450
2013	1 oz	100	Fr/unc	Gold. 99.99	38.7 mm	1,500/n/a	2,475	2,475
2013	1 kg	30	Fr/unc	Silver. 99.9	100 mm	1,500/ 356	1,815	1,900
2013	5 oz	10	Fr/unc	Silver. 99.9	65 mm	5,000/ 1,174	357.5	320
2013	1 oz	1	Fr/unc	Silver. 99.9	40 mm	10,000/ 2,500	88	90

[c & d] 2014 YEAR OF THE HORSE - PROOF-LIKE

2014	1 kg	3,000	Fr/unc	Gold. 99.99	75 mm	100/ n/a	73,945	b/v
2014	5 oz	500	Fr/unc	Gold. 99.99	60 mm	1,000/ n/a	11,450	b/v
2014	1 oz	100	Fr/unc	Gold. 99.99	38.7 mm	1,500/ 148	2,475	2,475
2014	1 kg	30	Fr/unc	Silver. 99.9	100 mm	1,500/ 89	1,695	1,695
2014	5 oz	10	Fr/unc	Silver. 99.9	60 mm	5,000/ 688	320	320
2014	1 oz	1	Fr/unc	Silver. 99.9	40 mm	10,000/ 2,988	80	80

2015 YEAR OF THE GOAT - PROOF-LIKE

2015	1 kg	3,000	Fr/unc	Gold. 99.99	75 mm	100/ n/a	73,945	60,000
2015	5 oz	500	Fr/unc	Gold. 99.99	60 mm	1,000/ n/a	11,450	b/v
2015	1 oz	100	Fr/unc	Gold. 99.99	38.7 mm	1,500/n/a	2,275	b/v
2015 d	1 kg	30	Fr/unc	Silver. 99.9	100 mm	1,500/ n/a	1,695	1,695
2015	5 oz	10	Fr/unc	Silver. 99.9	60 mm	5,000/ n/a	300	300
2015 c	1 oz	1	Fr/unc	Silver. 99.9	40mm	10,000/ n/a	80	80

$5 Undated Obverse

$100 Undated Obverse

2016 [f] Monkey Rev

2017 [g] Rooster Rev

[f] 2016 YEAR OF THE MONKEY - UNC GOLD

2016	1/20 oz	5	Uncirc	Gold	99.99	14.06	To order/ tba	345	b/v
2016	1/10 oz	15	Uncirc	Gold	99.99	17.53	To order/ tba	345	325
2016	1/4 oz	25	Uncirc	Gold	99.99	21.69	To order/ tba	345	b/v
2016	1/2 oz	50	Uncirc	Gold	99.99	30mm	To order/ tba	1,750	1,750
2016	1 oz	100	Uncirc	Gold	99.99	34mm	To order/ tba	1,750	1,750

Issued by the RAM and exclusively distributed by the European bullion company, Produits Artistiques Métaux Précieux that is based in Switzerland and has a world-wide presence.

[g] 2017 YEAR OF THE ROOSTER - UNC GOLD

2017	1/20 oz	5	Uncirc	Gold	99.99	14.06	To order/ tba	345	b/v
2017	1/10 oz	15	Uncirc	Gold	99.99	17.53	To order/ tba	345	b/v
2017	1/4 oz	25	Uncirc	Gold	99.99	21.69	To order/ tba	345	b/v
2017	1/2 oz	50	Uncirc	Gold	99.99	30mm	To order/ tba	1,750	1,750
2017	1 oz	100	Uncirc	Gold	99.99	34mm	To order/ tba	1,750	1,750

This section is incomplete. Other coins associated with the above series will be included in the next edition [24th].

VARIOUS DENOMINATIONS

2006 (a) Clown Fish 2006 (b) Dolphin 2007 (c) Biscuit Fish 2007 (d) Bannerfish 2007 (e) Shark 2007 (f) Seahorse

Date	Description	Mint Mark	Weight in gms	Type	Metal Content	Mintage Figures	Issue Price	Retail Value
2006 - 2007 OCEAN SERIES. FROSTED UNC								
2006 a	Clown Fish	—	9 g	Specimen	Al/br	29,743	14.95	20
2006 b	Bottlenose Dolphin	—	9 g	Specimen	Al/br	29,949	14.95	20
2007 c	BIscuit Star Fish	—	9 g	Specimen	Al/br	25,093	14.95	20
2007 d	Longfin Bannerfish	—	9 g	Specimen	Al/br	25,088	14.95	20
2007 e	White Shark	—	9 g	Specimen	Al/br	30,416	14.95	20
2007 f	Bigbelly Seahorse	—	9 g	Specimen	Al/br	24,666	14.95	20

2008 (g) Koala 2008 (h) Wombat 2008 (i) Echidna 2008 (j) Wallaby 2009 (k) Lizard 2009 (l) Bilby

Date	Description	Mint Mark	Weight in gms	Type	Metal Content	Mintage Figures	Issue Price	Retail Value
2008 - 2009 LAND SERIES. FROSTED UNC								
2008 g	Koala	—	9 g	Spec	Al/br	28,445	14.95	22
2008 h	Wombat	—	9 g	Spec	Al/br	23,995	14.95	17
2008 i	Echidna	—	9 g	Spec	Al/br	21,889	14.95	17
2008 j	Rock Wallaby	—	9 g	Spec	Al/br	25,163	14.95	25
2009 k	Frilled Neck Lizard	—	9 g	Spec	Al/br	22,690	14.95	17
2009 l	Bilby	—	9 g	Spec	Al/br	17,950	14.95	17

2011 [m] Cockatoo 2011 [n] Kingfisher 2011 [o] Kookaburra 2011 [p] Rosella 2011 [q] Butterfly 2011 [r] Flying Fox

Date	Description	Mint Mark	Weight in gms	Type	Metal Content	Mintage Figures	Issue Price	Retail Value
2011 AIR SERIES. FROSTED UNC								
2011 m	Major Mitchell	—	9 g	Spec	Al/br	28,445	14.95	16
2011 n	Sacred Kingfisher	—	9 g	Spec	Al/br	23,995	14.95	16
2011 o	Kookaburra	—	9 g	Spec	Al/br	21,889	14.95	16
2011 p	Crimson Rosella	—	9 g	Spec	Al/br	25,163	14.95	16
2011 q	Birdwing Butterfly	—	9 g	Spec	Al/br	17.502	14.95	16
2011 r	Flying Fox	—	9 g	Spec	Al/br	17,950	14.95	16

2012 [s] Frog 2012 [t] Tree Kangaroo 2012 [u] Elephant 2012 [v] Orang-utan 2012 [w] Gorilla 2012 [x/y] Tiger

Date	Description	Mint Mark	Weight in gms	Type	Metal Content	Mintage Figures	Issue Price	Retail Value
2011 ZOO SERIES. FROSTED UNC								
2012 s	Corroboree Frog	—	9 g	Spec	Al/br	15,000	15	16
2012 t	Tree Kangaroo	—	9 g	Spec	Al/br	15,014	15	16
2012 u	Asian Elephant	—	9 g	Spec	Al/br	15,002	15	16
2012 v	Orang-utan	—	9 g	Spec	Al/br	15,000	15	16
2012 w	Lowland Gorilla	—	9 g	Spec	Al/br	15,000	15	16
2012 x	Sumatran Tiger	—	9 g	Spec	Al/br	15,990	14.95	16
2012 y	Sumatran Tiger	—	9 g	Coin & Stamp cover - Priced in PNC section				–

ONE DOLLAR

PAD COLOURED THEMES

2013 [a] Penguin 2013 [b] Polar Bear 2013 [c] Walrus 2013 [d] Weddell Seal 2013 [e] Atlantic Puffin 2013 [f] Humpback Whale

Date	Description	Mint Mark	Weight in gms	Type	Metal Content	Mintage Figures	Issue Price	Retail Value
2013 POLAR ANIMALS SERIES. FROSTED UNC								
2013 a	Rockhopper Penguin	—	9 g	Spec	Al/br	11,000	15	16
2013 b	Polar Bear	—	9 g	Spec	Al/br	11,000	15	16
2013 c	Walrus	—	9 g	Spec	Al/br	10,002	15	16
2013 d	Weddell Seal	—	9 g	Spec	Al/br	10,002	15	16
2013 e	Atlantic Puffin	—	9 g	Spec	Al/br	10,002	15	16
2013 f	Humpback Whale	—	9 g	Spec	Al/br	10,002	15	16

2014 (g) Blow Fly 2014 (h) Butterfly 2014 (i) Beetle 2014 (j) Cuckoo Wasp 2014 (k) Bull Ant 2014 (l) Grasshopper

Date	Description	Mint Mark	Weight in gms	Type	Metal Content	Mintage Figures	Issue Price	Retail Value
2014 BRIGHT BUG SERIES. FROSTED UNC								
2014 g	Blow Fly	—	9 g	Spec	Al/br	10,002	15	16
2014 h	Ulysses Butterfly	—	9 g	Spec	Al/br	13,220	15	16
2014 i	Stag Beetle	—	9 g	Spec	Al/br	20,081	15	16
2014 j	Cuckoo Wasp	—	9 g	Spec	Al/br	10,588	15	16
2014 k	Red Bull Ant	—	9 g	Spec	Al/br	11,000	15	16
2014 l	Grasshopper	—	9 g	Spec	Al/br	10,002	15	16

[a] *Murphy*. Donkey [b] Ship's cat [c] Shake. Roo [d] Horrie. Dog [e] Sandy. Horse [f] Blue Cock

Date	Description	Finish	Size	Metal	Weight in oz's	Mintage Max/ Actual	Issue Price	Retail Average
2015 UNLIKELY HEROES. ANIMALS AT WAR								
2015 a	'Murphy' the Donkey	Fr/Unc	Al/br	9 g	25mm	30,000/ 10,080	15	15
2015 a	PNC Murphy. Donkey	Fr/Unc	Al/br	9 g	Coin & Stamp cover. See PNC section			–
2015 b	Cat HMAS Encounter	Fr/Unc	Al/br	9 g	25mm	30,000/ 10,002	15	16
2015 c	Shake the Kangaroo	Fr/Unc	Al/br	9 g	25mm	30,000/ 9,135	15	16
2015 d	Horrie the Dog	Fr/Unc	Al/br	9 g	25mm	30,000/ 10,002	15	16
2015 e	Sandy the War Horse	Fr/Unc	Al/br	9 g	25mm	30,000/ tba	15	16
2015 f	Blue Chequered Cock	Fr/Unc	Al/br	9 g	25mm	30,000/ tba	15	16

ONE DOLLAR

FINE SILVER KANGAROO SERIES

1993 (a) Silver only

1994 (b) Silver only

1995 (c) Silver only

1996 (d) Silver only

1997 (e) Silver only

1998 (f) Silver only

1999 (g) Silver only

2000 (h) Silver only

2001 (i) Silver only

2002 (j) Silver only

2003 (k) Silver Gilt

2004 (l) Silver Gilt

Date	Nominal Value	Description	Metal Type	Metal Content	Mint Mark	Weight	Size	Mintage Figures	Issue Price	Retail Value
1993 a	1	Carded coin	Fr/Unc	Silver	C	1 oz	40mm	150,000/ 78,031	15	60
1993 b	1	Fair issue	Fr/Unc	Silver	C	1 oz	40mm	5,000/ All sold	17.5	95
1994	1	Carded coin	Fr/Unc	Silver	C	1 oz	40mm	75,000/ 45,542	15	60
1994 c	1	Fair issue	Fr/Unc	Silver	C	1 oz	40mm	2,500/ All sold	17.5	95
1995	1	Carded coin	Fr/Unc	Silver	C	1 oz	40mm	To order/ 72,850	17.5	60
1995 d	1	Fair issue	Fr/Unc	Silver	C	1 oz	40mm	2,500/ All sold	36	95
1996	1	Carded coin	Fr/Unc	Silver	C	1 oz	40mm	To order/ 49,398	17.5	60
1997	1	Carded coin	Fr/Unc	Silver	C	1 oz	40mm	To order/ 43,797	17.5	60
1998	1	Carded coin	Fr/Unc	Silver	C	1 oz	40mm	To order/ 49,398	19.75	60
1998	1	First proof	Proof	Silver	C	1 oz	40mm	To order/ 7,645	44	95
1999	1	Carded coin	Fr/Unc	Silver	C	1 oz	40mm	To order/ 30,185	19.75	60
1999	1	Cased coin	Proof	Silver	C	1 oz	40mm	To order/ 11,250	44	95
2000	1	Carded coin	Fr/Unc	Silver	—	1 oz	40mm	To order/ 35,426	19.75	60
2000	1	Cased coin	Proof	Silver	—	1 oz	40mm	To order/ 9,972	44	95
2001	1	Carded coin	Fr/Unc	Silver	—	1 oz	40mm	To order/ 45,562	19.75	60
2001	1	Cased coin	Proof	Silver	—	1 oz	40mm	To order/ 10,292	44	95
2002	1	Carded coin	Fr/Unc	Silver	—	1 oz	40mm	To order/ 32,376	22	40
2002	1	Cased coin	Proof	Silver	—	1 oz	40mm	To order/ 7,813	48	60
2003	1	Carded coin	Fr/Unc	Silver	—	1 oz	40mm	To order/ 35,230	22	60
2003	1	Gilt Kangaroo	Fr/Unc	Silver	—	1 oz	40mm	10,000/ 7,450	67.5	90
2003	1	Cased coin	Proof	Silver	—	1 oz	40mm	10,000/ n/a	48	80
2004	1	Carded coin	Fr/Unc	Silver	—	1 oz	40mm	To order/ 19,324	24.6	70
2004	1	Gilt Kangaroo	Fr/Unc	Silver	—	1 oz	40mm	12,500/ 11,750	74.5	100

[a] This first fine silver (.999) one ounce coin featured a "Specimen" finish which was half way between a proof and an uncirculated finish.
[b] Issued at the NAA Coin and Banknote Fair held in Sydney on November 20 - 21,1993. The coin has interrupted edge reeding.
[c] Issued at the NAA Fair in Sydney on November 19-20, 1994.
[d] Issued at the NAA Coin and Banknote Fair held in Sydney on November 25 - 26, 1995. The last of the RAM coin fair issues.

ONE & TEN DOLLARS

FINE SILVER KANGAROO SERIES

2005 Gilt Silver

2006 Gilt Silver

2007 Gilt Silver

2008 Gilt Silver

2009 Gilt Silver

2010 Proof Silver

2011 Proof Silver

2012 Proof Silver

2013 Proof Silver

2009 Three coin set. Colour reverses by Rolf Harris, Reg Mombassa and Ken Done. The coins were sold as a set.

Date	Nominal Value	Description	Metal Type	Metal Content	Mint Mark	Weight	Size	Mintage Figures	Issue Price	Retail Value
2005	1	Carded coin	Fr/Unc	Silver	–	1 oz	40mm	To order/ 16,446	24.6	70
2005	1	Gilt Kangaroo	Fr/Unc	Silver	–	1 oz	40mm	12,500/ 8,123	74.5	100
2005	1	Cased coin	Proof	Silver	–	1 oz	40mm	12,500/ 8,300	54	85
2006	1	Carded coin	Fr/Unc	Silver	–	1 oz	40mm	To order/ 18,925	24.6	70
2006	1	Gilt Kangaroo	Fr/Unc	Silver	–	1 oz	40mm	7,500/ 6,150	74.5	100
2006	1	Cased coin	Proof	Silver	–	1 oz	40mm	12,500/ 7,382	54	85
2007	1	Cupro/ Nickel	Fr/Unc	Cu/Ni	–	1 oz	40mm	To order/ 12,002	24.6	35
2007	1	Gilt Kangaroo	Fr/Unc	Silver	–	1 oz	40mm	12,500/ 5,516	74.5	100
2007	1	Cased coin	Proof	Silver	–	1 oz	40mm	12,500/ 10,352	65	120
2007	1	Carded coin	Fr/Unc	Silver	–	1 oz	40mm	5,000/ 4,000	48	70
2007	10	Cased coin	Proof	Gold	–	1/10oz	17.53mm	1,000/ All sold	175	300
2008	1	Cupro/ Nickel	Fr/Unc	Cu/Ni	–	1 oz	40mm	20,000/ 9,234	24.6	25
2008	1	Gilt Kangaroo	Fr/Unc	Silver	–	1 oz	40mm	12,500/ 5,463	74.5	95
2008	1	Cased coin	Proof	Silver	–	1 oz	40mm	20,000/ 7,500	65	80
2008	1	Carded coin	Fr/Unc	Silver	–	1 oz	40mm	20,000/10,000	50	70
2008	10	Cased coin	Proof	Gold	–	1/10oz	17.53mm	1,500/ All sold	175	350
2009	1	Cupro/ Nickel	Fr/Unc	Cu/Ni	–	1 oz	40mm	20,000/ 7,522	24.6	25
2009	1	Gilt Kangaroo	Fr/Unc	Silver	–	1 oz	40mm	12,500/ 5,997	74.5	95
2009	1	Cased coin	Proof	Silver	–	1 oz	40mm	12,500/ 7,476	65	85
2009	1	Carded coin	Fr/Unc	Silver	–	1 oz	40mm	20,000/ 6,320	50	80
2009	10	Cased coin	Proof	Gold	–	1/10oz	17.53mm	1,500/ n/a	235	310
2009	3 x 1	Cased Set	Proof & Coloured set. Famous artists					1,500/ 1,499	235	310
2010	1	Carded coin	Fr/Unc	Silver	–	1 oz	40mm	To order/ n/a	50	80
2010	1	Cased coin	Proof	Silver	–	1 oz	40mm	20,000/ 5,999	65	85
2010	10	Cased coin	Proof	Gold	–	1/10oz	17.53mm	1,500/ All sold	235	310
2011	1	Carded coin	Fr/Unc	Silver	–	1 oz	40mm	25,019/ n/a	70	75
2011	1	Cased coin	Proof	Silver	–	1 oz	40mm	20,000/ n/a	80	80
2011	10	Cased coin	Proof	Gold	–	1/10oz	17.53mm	1,500/ n/a	295	310
2012	1	Carded coin	Fr/Unc	Silver	–	1 oz	40mm	To order/ n/a	87	87
2012	1	Cased coin	Proof	Silver	–	1 oz	40mm	20,000/ n/a	100	100
2012	10	Cased coin	Proof	Gold		1/10oz	17.53mm	1,500/ n/a	365	365
2013	1	Carded coin	Fr/Unc	Silver	–	1 oz	40mm	20,000/ n/a	80	80
2013	1	Cased coin	Proof	Silver	–	1 oz	40mm	5,000/ n/a	100	100
2013	10	Cased coin	Proof	Gold	–	1/10oz	17.53mm	5,000/ n/a	365	365

ONE & TEN DOLLARS

FINE SILVER KANGAROO SERIES

2013 (a) Frosted Unc

2013 (b) Silver proof

2017 (c) Silver proof

Sunset series

Date	Face Value	Finish	Weight in oz's	Metal	Size	Mintage Max/ Actual	Issue Price	Retail Average
2013 a	1	Fr/unc	1 oz	Silver. 999 fine	40mm	20,000/ n/a	80	80
2013	1	Proof	1 oz	Silver. 999 fine	40mm	20,000/ n/a	100	100
2013	10	Proof	1/10 oz	Gold. 9999 fine	7.53mm	1,500/ n/a	360	360
2014	1	Fr/unc	1 oz	Silver. 999 fine	40mm	20,000/ n/a	80	80
2014	1	Proof	1 oz	Silver. 999 fine	40mm	10,000/ n/a	100	100
2014	10	Proof	1/10 oz	Gold. 9999 fine	17.53mm	1,500/ n/a	360	360
2015	1	Fr/unc	1 oz	Silver. 999 fine	40mm	20,000/ n/a	80	80
2015	1	Proof	1 oz	Silver. 999 fine	40mm	20,000/ n/a	100	100
2015	10	Proof	1/10 oz	Gold. 9999 fine	17.53mm	1,500/ n/a	*See $10 section*	
2016	1	Fr/unc	1 oz	Silver. 999 fine	40mm	10,000/ n/a	80	80
2016	1	Proof	1 oz	Silver. 999 fine	40mm	20,000/ n/a	100	100
2016	10	Proof	1/10 oz	Gold. 9999 fine	17.53mm	1,500/ n/a	*See $10 section*	
2017	1	Fr/unc	1 oz	Silver. 999 fine	40mm	20,000/ n/a	80	80
2017 c	1	Proof	1 oz	Silver. 999 fine	40mm	20,000/ n/a	100	100
2017	10	Proof	1/10 oz	Gold. 9999 fine	17.53mm	1,500/ n/a	*See $10 section*	

[d] SILVER KANGAROO AT SUNSET SERIES

Date	Face Value	Finish	Weight in oz's	Metal	Size	Mintage Max/ Actual	Issue Price	Retail Average
2009	1.00	Unc	1 oz	Silver .999 fine	40mm	To order / 7,100	80	80
2009	1.00	Proof	1 oz	Silver .999 fine	40mm	To order/ 4,366	100	100
2010	1.00	Unc	1 oz	Silver .999 fine	40mm	7,000/ 2,500	80	80
2010	1.00	Proof	1 oz	Silver .999 fine	40mm	1,500 / 1,500	100	100
2011	1.00	Unc	1 oz	Silver .999 fine	40mm	7,000 / 2,500	80	80
2011	1.00	Proof	1 oz	Silver .999 fine	40mm	1,500 / 1,500	100	100
2012	1.00	Unc	1 oz	Silver .999 fine	40mm	7,000/ 2,500	80	80
2012	1.00	Proof	1 oz	Silver .999 fine	40mm	1,500/ 1,500	100	100
2013	1.00	Unc	1 oz	Silver .999 fine	40mm	7,000/ 2,500	80	80
2013	1.00	Proof	1 oz	Silver .999 fine	40mm	1,500 / tba	65	n/a
2014	1.00	Unc	1 oz	Silver .999 fine	40mm	7,000 / tba	80	80
2014	1.00	Proof	1 oz	Silver .999 fine	40mm	5,000 / tba	100	100
2015 d	1.00	Unc	1 oz	Silver .999 fine	40mm	7,000 / tba	80	80
2015	1.00	Proof	1 oz	Silver .999 fine	40mm	5,000 / tba	60	60
2016	1.00	Proof	1 oz	Silver .999 fine	40mm	5,000 / tba	60	60
2017	1.00	Proof	1 oz	Silver .999 fine	40mm	5,000 / tba	60	60

(e) Narrows Bridge

(f) Story Bridge

(g) Princes Bridge

(h) Pyrmont Bridge

(i) Derrick VC Bridge

ANDA FAIR ONE DOLLAR BRIDGE SERIES

Date	Description	Finish	Metal	Weight oz's	Fair location	Issue Mintage	Retail Price	Price Average
2011 e	Narrows Bridge	Proof	Silver	1oz	Perth ANDA Fair	1,386	65	75
2011 f	Story Bridge	Proof	Silver	1oz	Brisbane ANDA Fair	1,203	65	75
2011 g	Princes Bridge	Proof	Silver	1oz	Melbourne ANDA Fair	1,046	85	75
2011 h	Pyrmont Bridge	Proof	Silver	1oz	Sydney ANDA Fair	2,000	85	75
2011 i	'Diver' Derrick Br	Proof	Silver	1oz	Adelaide ANDA Fair	2,000	85	75

ONE DOLLAR

SUBSCRIPTION SILVER PROOF ISSUES

1996 (a) Decimal Currency

1997 (b) Old Parliment

1998 (c) New Parliament

1999 (d) Majestic Images

2000 (e) Proc. Penny

2002 (f) Melb Mint

2003 (g) Holey Dollar

2004 (h) Last Penny

2005 (i) Sydney Mint

2006 (j) Spanish Dollar

2007 (k) Proclamation Johanna (Obv & Rev)

2008 (l) Kooka Pattern

2009 (m) Adelaide Ingot

2010 (n) Aust. Currency

2011 (o) Zuytdorp Wreck

Date	Description	Metal Type	Content	Weight	Size	Mintage Figures	Issue Price	Retail Value
1996 a	Decimal Currency	Proof	.999 Silver	1 oz	40	19,927	45	80
1997 b	Old P'ment House	Proof	.999 Silver	1 oz	40	21,791	45	60
1998 c	New P'ment House	Proof	.999 Silver	1 oz	40	17,096	45	60
1999 d	Majestic Images	Proof	.999 Silver	1 oz	40	16,829	47.5	60
2000 e	Proclamation Coins	Proof	.999 Silver	1 oz	40	18,457	47.5	60
2001	No Subscription Coin Issued					—	—	—
2002 f	Melbourne Mint	Proof	Gilt silver	31.6	40	13,329	65	80
2003 g	Holey Dollar 190TH	Proof	.999 Silver	54.3	50	14,203	85	95
2004 h	Last Penny Issue	Proof	Copper/ Silver	56.45	50	16,437	77	95
2005 i	Sydney Mint 150TH	Proof	Gilt silver	60.46	50	11,845	77	95
2006 j	Spanish Pillar Dollar	Proof	Antique Silver	60.46	50	9,846	88	100
2007 k	Portuguese Johanna	Proof	Gilt silver	60.46	50	6,949	88	125
2008 l	Kookaburra Penny	Proof	.999 Silver	60.46	50	6,592	95	110
2009 m	Adelaide Ingot	Proof	Gilt silver	1 oz	40	5,894	85	125
2010 n	Currency Centenary	Proof	.999 Silver	1 oz	40.6	4,975	75	140
2011 o	Zuytdorp Wreck	Proof	.999 Silver	1 oz	40.6	2,948	75	110

End of the series

The "Subscription Issue" was a special series in which the Mint allowed the collector a limited amount of time to order. The offer was strictly limited to one coin per order. A small allocation was made available to selected dealers.

ONE DOLLAR

VARIOUS SILVER THEMED SERIES

2013 [a] 1oz Bindi Spec

2013 [b] 1oz Bindi Proof

2014 [c] 1oz Graham Spec

2014 [d] 1oz Graham Proof

2015 [e] 1oz Agro Jnr Spec

2015 [f] 1oz $5 Agro Jnr Proof

2016 [g] 1oz Monty Spec

2016 [h] 1oz Monty Proof

Date	TYPE	Face Value	Mintage Figures	Size	Weight in oz	Metal comp.	Description	Issue Price	Retail Average
SALTWATER CROCODILE 1oz SILVER SERIES									
2013a	Bindi	1.00	10,000	40mm	1 oz	Silver	Spec .999 fine	80	80
2013b	Bindi	1.00	5,000	40mm	1 oz	Silver	Proof. Coloured	110	110
2014c	Graham	1.00	10,000	40mm	1 oz	Silver	Proof .999 fine	80	80
2014d	Graham	1.00	5,000	40mm	1 oz	Silver	Proof. Coloured	110	110
2014e	Graham	1.00	10,000	40mm	1 oz	Silver	Spec .999 fine	80	80
2015 f	Argo Jnr.	5.00	10,000	40mm	1 oz	Silver	Proof.999 fine	See $5 section	
2016e	Monty	1.00	5,000	40mm	1 oz	Silver	Spec .999 fine	80	80
2016f	High relief	5.00	1,500	40mm	1 oz	Silver	Spec .999 fine	See $5 section	

Common Obverse

2013 (a) Fr/unc Kangaroo

2014 (b) Fr/unc Koala

2015 (c) Fr/unc Emu

Date	TYPE	Face Value	Mintage Figures	Size	Weight in oz	Metal comp.	Description	Issue Price	Retail Average
2013 KANGAROO ROAD SIGNS SERIES									
2013	Kangaroo	1	40,000	40mm	1 oz	Silver	Spec .999	88	88
2013	Kangaroo	10	5,000	65.1mm	5 oz	Silver	Spec..999	375.5	375
2013	Kangaroo	30	1,500	99.95mm	1 kg	Silver	Spec. .999	1,815	1,815
2013	Kangaroo	100	5,000	38.74mm	1 oz	Gold	Spec..9999	2,475	2,475
2013	Kangaroo	500	500	59.8mm	5 oz	Gold	Spec .9999	13,200	b/v
2013	Kangaroo	3,000	100	74.77mm	1 kg	Gold	Spec..9999	79,750	b/v
2014 KOALA ROAD SIGNS SERIES									
2014	Koala Sign	1	40,000	40mm	1 oz	Silver	Spec. .999	80	80
2014	Koala Sign	10	5,000	65.1mm	5 oz	Silver	Spec. .999	320	350
2014	Koala Sign	30	1,500	99.95mm	1 kg	Silver	Spec. .999	Struck to order	
2014	Koala Sign	100	5,000	38.74mm	1 oz	Gold	Spec. .9999	2,275	2,275
2014	Koala Sign	500	500	59.8mm	5 oz	Gold	Spec. .9999	11,250	b/v
2014	Koala Sign	3,000	100	74.77mm	1 kg	Gold	Spec. .9999	Struck to order	
2015 EMU ROAD SIGNS SERIES									
2015	Emu Sign	1	40,000	40mm	1 oz	Silver	Spec. .999	80	80
2015	Emu Sign	10	5,000	65.1mm	5 oz	Silver	Spec. .999	320	350
2015	Emu Sign	30	1,500	99.95mm	1 kg	Silver	Spec. .999	1,695	b/v
2015	Emu Sign	100	5,000	38.74mm	1 oz	Gold	Spec. .9999	2,275	b/v
2015	Emu Sign	500	500	59.8mm	5 oz	Gold	Spec. .9999	11,450	b/v
2015	Emu Sign	3,000	100	74.77mm	1 kg	Gold	Spec. .9999	Struck to order	

ONE DOLLAR

NON CIRCULATING ISSUES

2013 [a] The $1 Australian Silver Proof issue — 2013 [b] Polish 20 Zloty Proof Issue

2013 - KANGAROOS OF THE WORLD

2013 a/b	$1 & 20 Zloty pair	1 oz	Silver	Proof	40mm	10,000/ tba	190	190

[b] The coin produced by Norowdy Bank Polski features a coloured image of their rare Albino Kangaroo, a Red-necked Wallaby, which was born in captivity. The contribution by the RAM features an Eastern Grey Kangaroo with its joey.

2013 [c] Holey Dollar three coin set — 2014 [d] Albany AIF — 2014 [e] UNESCO

Date	Nominal F/Value	Weight in oz's	Diameter	Description	Mintage Figures	Issue Price	Current Retail
2013 BICENTENARY - HOLEY DOLLAR & DUMP							
2013 c	1.00	18.65g	40mm	Holey Dollar. 99.9 fine silver	5,000/ n/a	200	220
2013 c	25¢	5.8 g	19mm	Dump. 99.9 fine silver	Three coin cased set		
2013 c	10 eu	27 g	40mm	Mexico. 8 Reales. 92.5 silver	Three coin cased set		

2014 - CENTENARY OF THE FIRST AIF CONVOY

2014	1	First AIF Convoy	1 oz	Silver	Proof	40mm	10,000 / tba	100	100
2014d	10	First AIF Convoy	1/10 oz	Gold	Proof	17.51	1,500 / tba	*See $10's*	

2014 - BARRIER REEF. UNESCO SERIES

2014 e	1	Reef. UNESCO	1 oz	Silver	Proof	40mm	1,500 / tba	110	110
2014	25	Reef. UNESCO	1/4 oz	Gold	Proof	21.69	1,500 / tba	*See $10's*	

2014 [f] New Year — 2015 [g] New Year — 2016 [h] New Year — 2017 [i] New Year

Date		Description	Weight in oz's	Metal	Finish	Size	Mintage Max/ Actual	Issue Price	Retail Average
2014 - 2017 NEW YEAR'S EVE SERIES									
2014 f	1	Shine	1 oz	Silver	Proof	40.7	15,000/ tba	120	110
2015 g	1	Inspire	1/2oz	Silver	Fr/unc	35.89	15,000/ tba	60	60
2016 h	1	City of Colour	1/2oz	Silver	Fr/unc	35.89	15,000/ tba	60	60
2017 i	1	Sydney NYE	1/2oz	Silver	Fr/unc	35.8	5,000/ tba	60	60

ONE DOLLAR

VARIOUS SILVER THEMED SERIES

Common Obverse

2016 [a] Gaol Bird

[b] Remember Me

[c] Forget Me Not

Date	TYPE	Face Value	Mintage Figures	Size	Weight in oz	Metal comp.	Description	Issue Price	Retail Average
2016 HONOURING CONVICT LOVE									
2016 a	Gaol Bird	1.00	30,000	33mm	14.3g	Copper	Antique Uncirc	24.95	24.95
2016 b	Remember Me	1.00	30,000	33mm	14.3g	Copper	Antique Uncirc	24.95	24.95
2016 c	Forget Me Not	1.00	30,000	33mm	14.3g	Copper	Antique Uncirc	24.95	24.95

[a] This token has special significance for me. I originally unearthed this piece while attending a coin fair at the Cumberland Hotel in London back in the 1990's. I sold the piece to a client back in Australia. It was later consigned to a Noble Auction where it was purchased on behalf of Sydney Mint Museum.

AUSTRALIAN DECIMAL EFFIGIES SERIES 2012 - 2104

The above two imagines are from a short series of coins struck as a loyality program

Date	Face Value	Description	Metal Weight	Metal	Size	Mintage Figures	Issue Price	Retail Average
2012 - FIRST PORTRAIT. 1966 MACHIN								
2012	1	Specimen. 99.9%	11.6 g	Silver	25mm	100 / All sold	100	500
2012	1	Proof. 99.9%	11.6 g	Silver	25mm	100 / All sold	200	550

Obv: Legend reads 2012, 1 Dollar with portrait of QEII by Ian Rank Broadley. Rev: "Australian Decimal Currency Effigies Machin-1966." Design features Arnold Machin portrait of QE2.

Date	Face Value	Description	Metal Weight	Metal	Size	Mintage Figures	Issue Price	Retail Average
2013 - SECOND PORTRAIT. 1985 MAKLOUF								
2013	1	Specimen. 99.9%	11.6 g	Silver	25mm	330 / All sold	100	335
2013	1	Proof. 99.9%	11.6 g	Silver	25mm	310 / All sold	200	tba

Obv: Rank Broadley portrait of QE2. Rev: Legend reads : "Australian Decimal Currency Effigies 1966-2014 Maklouf-1985." Unfortunately, the much acclaimed Vladimar Gottwald portrait was omitted.

Date	Face Value	Description	Metal Weight	Metal	Size	Mintage Figures	Issue Price	Retail Average
2014 - DECIMAL EFFIGIES - ELIZABETH II. 1966-2014								
2014	1	Specimen. 99.9%	11.6 g	Silver	25mm	750 / All sold	75	150
2014	1	Proof. 99.9%	11.6 g	Silver	25mm	1,000 / All sold	99	150

Obv: Rank Broadley portrait of QE2.Rev: Legend reads :"Australian Decimal Currency Effigies 1966-2014" and image of three official portraits in profile. Unfortunately, the much acclaimed Vladimar Gottwald portrait was omitted.

As the above issue of coins was produced for an in-house loyality program within the RAM, it received very little publicity among general collectors. With the help of a few dedicated collectors, I have been able to pass on the information shown above. It is not complete and what is published, may need to be verified.

TWO DOLLARS

ELIZABETH II

1988 - 1998

Aluminium
Bronze & Silver

Obverse : Raphael Maklouf.
Reverse : Horst Hahne. Aboriginal Elder.
Specifications : Composition 92% copper; 6% aluminium; 2% nickel. Interrupted reeding. Weight 6.60 grams. Size 20.62 mm. Proof. Sterling silver (92.5% pure); 7.5% copper. Weight 8.35 grams

CIRCULATION & NON CIRCULATION (NCLT) ISSUES

Date	TYPE	Mintage Figures	Metal Comp.	Weight in gms	Issuing Mint	Unc	Choice Unc	Roll or Bagged	Issue Price	Mint set Retail	Proof Retail
1988	CIRC	160,852,000	Al/br	6.6 g	Canb	8	9	80	–	–	–
1988 a	OFF METAL	24,970	Silver	8.35g	Proof M'pieces .925 Stg. 20.62mm				–	–	35
1988 b	OFF METAL	25,000	Silver	8.35g	Proof 3 coin & Banknote album				–	–	30
1989	CIRC	31,637,800	Al/br	6.6 g	Canb	5	9	Bag	–	–	20
1990	CIRC	10,338,500	Al/br	6.6 g	Canb	8	12	Bag	–	–	25
1991	EX-SET	147,900	Al/br	6.6 g	Circ coin exclusive to mint set				–	20	–
1991	OFF METAL	25,000	Silver	8.43g	Proof M'pieces .925 Stg. 20.62mm				–	–	40
1992	CIRC	15,504,000	Al/br	6.6 g	Canb	10	15	Bag	–	–	25
1993	CIRC	4,873,500	Al/br	6.6 g	Canb	18	25	Bag	–	–	40
1994	CIRC	22,143,000	Al/br	6.6 g	Canb	6	10	Bag	–	–	35
1995	CIRC	15,528,500	Al/br	6.6 g	Canb	8	15	Bag	–	–	25
1996	CIRC	13,909,000	Al/br	6.6 g	Canb	8	15	Bag	–	–	25
1997	CIRC	19,039,000	Al/br	6.6 g	Canb	6	10	Bag	–	–	35
1998	CIRC	8,719,000	Al/br	6.6 g	Canb	8	15	Bag	–	–	25

[a & b] Other proof versions were struck for a number of special packages including the Three Coin, Three Banknote set and the Masterpieces in Silver. The reverse carried the "HH" initials for the designer Horst Hahne from 1988 to 1989 and deleted in later years. The 1988 issue was the first silver proof $2 coin. Made from sterling silver (92.5% silver and 7.5% copper. It weighed 8.35 gms and had the standard dimensions of 20.62 mm.

c d

Date	TYPE	Mintage Figures	Weight	Metal comp.	Metal	Description	Issue Price	Retail Average
2006 SILVER PORTRAIT RETRO PORTRAIT								
2006 c	RESTRIKE	5,829	8.55gm	Silver	99.9 fine	Decimal currency 40th	–	30

[a] To celebrate the 40th anniversary of decimalisation, the RAM produced a 2006 eight coin proof set in fine silver that featured the original Arnold Machin effigy of the Queen. This was a unique set as the normal proof and mint sets issued in 2006 carry the current Ian Rank-Broadley obverse. Issued individually and the complete set is featured in the "off metal" section found elsewhere in this book.

2015 DECIMALISATION 50 YEARS - PART OF SET

Date	TYPE	Mintage	Metal	Weight	Description	Issue Price	Retail
2016 d	MINT ROLL	5,000	Al/br	6.6 g	Commemorative roll. 20 x Unc coins	–	15
2016 d	MINT BAG	tba	Al/br	6.6 g	Commemorative bag. 5 x Unc	10	10
2016 d	EX-SET	n/a	Al/br	6.6 g	Specimen. In annual 6 coin mint set	4	–
2016 d	EX-SET	n/a	Al/br	6.6 g	Proof. Part of annual 6 coin proof set	–	15

TWO DOLLARS

ELIZABETH II

1999 -

Aluminium
Bronze & Silver

Obverse : Ian Rank - Broadley. **Reverse :** Horst Hahne. Aboriginal Elder.

CIRCULATION & NON CIRCULATION (NCLT) ISSUES

Date	TYPE	Mintage Figures	Mint Mark	Metal Comp.	Weight in gms	Issuing Mint	Unc	Choice Unc	Roll or Bagged	Issue Price	Mint set Retail	Proof Retail
1999 a	CIRC	27,718,000	–	Al/br	6.6g	Canb	11	18	Bag	–	–	–
2000	CIRC	5,706,000	–	Al/br	6.6g	Canb	25	35	Bag	–	–	–
2001a/b	CIRC	35,650,000	–	Al/br	6.6g	Canb	3	7	Bag	–	–	–
2001	OFF METAL	193	–	Gold	16.03	Proof. 99.99 fine. Federation set					–	950
2002	CIRC	29,689,000	–	Al/br	6.6g	Canb	8	13	Bag	–	–	–
2003 d	CIRC	13,656,000	–	Al/br	6.6g	Canb	3	6	Bag	–	–	–
2004 d	CIRC	20,084,000	–	Al/br	6.6g	Canb	3	6	Bag	–	–	–
2005 c/d	CIRC	45,875,000	–	Al/br	6.6g	Canb	9	18	Bag	–	–	–
2005	OFF METAL	1,600	–	Silver	8.58g	Proof .999. 20.5mm. Part set				–	–	60
2005	OFF METAL	650/ 629	–	Gold	15.88g	Proof .9999. 11.5mm. Part set				–	–	950
2006	CIRC	40,487,000	–	Al/br	6.6g	Canb	3	5	Bag	–	–	–
2006	OFF METAL	5,829	–	Silver	13.26g	Proof. Machin obv 8 coin set				–	–	45
2006	OFF METAL	300	–	Gold	15.88g	Proof. Broadley obv 8 coin set				–	–	950
2007c/d	CIRC	25,002,000	–	Al/br	6.6g	Canb	7	12	Bag	–	–	–
2007	OFF METAL	300	–	Gold	15.88g	Proof .9999. 11.5mm. Part set				–	–	950
2008 d	CIRC	46,956,000	–	Al/br	6.6g	Canb	12	17	Bag	–	–	–
2009 d	CIRC	74, 500,000	–	Al/br	6.6g	Canb	12	17	Bag	–	–	–
2010c/d	CIRC	36,379,000	–	Al/br	6.6g	Canb	8	13	Bag	–	–	–
2010	OFF METAL	1,600	–	Silver	8.55g	Proof .999. 20.5mm. Part set				–	–	60
2010	OFF METAL	500	–	Gold	15.88g	Proof. Gottwald obv in set				–	–	950
2011 d	CIRC	17,800,000	–	Al/br	6.6g	Canb	8	13	Bag	–	–	–
2011	OFF METAL	2,072	–	Silver	8.55g	Proof .999. 20.5mm. Part set				–	–	60
2012 d	CIRC	5,900,000	–	Al/br	6.6g	Canb	n/a	n/a	Bag	–	–	–
2012	OFF METAL	6,000	–	Silver	8.55g	Proof .999. 20.5mm. Part set				–	–	40
2012	OFF METAL	2,000	–	Gold	0.5g	Proof .9999. 11.5mm. Part set				–	–	60
2013	CIRC	35,100,000	–	Al/br	6.6g	Canb	2	5	Bag	–	–	-
2013	OFF METAL	1,000	–	Silver	8.55g	Proof. Single coin cased				65	–	65
2013	OFF METAL	1,000	–	Silver	8.55g	Proof. Part of boxed set				–	–	65
2013	OFF METAL	500	–	Gold	15.88g	Proof. Single coin cased				1,395	–	1,395
2013	OFF METAL	500	–	Gold	15.88g	Proof. Part of boxed set				–	–	750
2014	CIRC	39,900,000	–	Cu/ni	6.6g	Canb	2	5	Bag	–	–	–
2014	OFF METAL	1,000	–	Silver	8.55g	Proof. Single coin cased				65	–	65
2014	OFF METAL	1,000	–	Silver	8.55g	Proof. Part of boxed set				–	–	65
2014	OFF METAL	500	–	Gold	15.88g	Proof. Single coin cased				1,395	–	1,395
2014	OFF METAL	500	–	Gold	15.88g	Proof. Part of boxed set				–	–	750
2015	CIRC	21,800,000	–	Al/br	6.6g	Canb	2	5	Bag	–	–	–
2015	OFF METAL	1,000	–	Silver	8.55g	Proof. Part of boxed set				–	–	55
2015	OFF METAL	1,000	–	Silver	8.55g	Proof. Single coin cased				55	–	55
2015	OFF METAL	500	–	Gold	15.88g	Proof. Single coin cased				1,395	–	1,395
2016	OFF METAL	1,000	–	Silver	8.55g	Proof. Single coin cased				55	–	55
2016	OFF METAL	500	–	Gold	15.88g	Proof. Single coin cased				1,395	–	1,395

[a] Two obverse die varieties. Identify by measuring the distance of the lettering in the legend from the rim of the coin. This type shows lettering far from rim. Initials "IRB" spaced.
[b] Text style different to 1999 issue. Lettering close to rim. IRB spaced.
[c] Two obverse varieties. Large Head / IRB spaced and Smaller Head with initials IRB showing "IR" spaced and "RB" joined. Text style is different to 1999 and 2000.

TWO DOLLARS

MISCELLANEOUS ISSUES

2012 (a) Men's Open 2012 (b&c) Remembrance. Plain & Coloured 2013 (d) Coronation

CIRCULATION & NON CIRCULATION (NCLT) ISSUES

[a] 2012 MENS' TENNIS OPEN CENTENARY

Date	TYPE	Mintage Figures	Mint Mark	Metal Comp.	Weight in gms	Issuing Mint	Unc	Choice Unc	Roll or Bagged	Issue Price	Mint set Retail	Proof Retail
2012	OFF-METAL	3,000	–	Silver	20 g	Proof. Gold plated centre				95	–	95

[b / c] 2012 REMEMBRANCE DAY - POPPY REVERSE

Date	TYPE	Mintage Figures	Mint Mark	Metal Comp.	Weight in gms	Issuing Mint	Unc	Choice Unc	Roll or Bagged	Issue Price	Mint set Retail	Proof Retail
2012	CIRC	5,799.000	–	Al/br	6.6 g	Canb	4	8	–	–	–	–
2012 a	NCLT	503,000	–	Al/br	6.6 g	Unc. Red poppy. RSL charity			250	10	35	–
2012	NCLT	41,000	C	Al/br	6.6 g	Unc coloured red poppy				13	50	–

[a] This was the second coin in the world to be be released with a coloured microtext reverse.Canada was the first. The coin featured a red coloured poppy in the centre of the reverse. These coins were distributed through the RSL Poppy Appeal from Friday Oct 26 to Nov 11. The RSL asked for a $10 donation for each of the coins. A $10 certificate of donation was issued by the RSL with each coin. The coin is normally found in a small plastic pack stapled to the donation certificate. Examples exist where over-zealous RSL club volunteers have directly glued the obverse of the coin to the certificate.

[d] 2013 CORONATION 60TH - ST EDWARD'S CROWN

Date	TYPE	Mintage Figures	Mint Mark	Metal Comp.	Weight in gms	Issuing Mint	Unc	Choice Unc	Roll or Bagged	Issue Price	Mint set Retail	Proof Retail
2013	CIRC	995,753	–	Al/br	6.6 g	Canb	12	20	–	–	–	–
2013	NCLT	35,000	C	Al/br	6.6 g	Circ. Purple colour. Folder				12.95	13	–

2013 (e) Lizard 2014 (f) Platypus 2014 (g) Remembrance 2015 (h) Lest We Forget

(e) 2013 NATURE OF AUSTRALIA FRILLED NECK LIZARD

Date	TYPE	Mintage Figures	Mint Mark	Metal Comp.	Weight in gms	Issuing Mint	Unc	Choice Unc	Roll or Bagged	Issue Price	Mint set Retail	Proof Retail
2013	NCLT	7,500	–	Gold	0.5 g	Proof. 99.99 fine. Wide 11mm				65	–	65

(f) 2014 NATURE OF AUSTRALIA PLATYPUS

Date	TYPE	Mintage Figures	Mint Mark	Metal Comp.	Weight in gms	Issuing Mint	Unc	Choice Unc	Roll or Bagged	Issue Price	Mint set Retail	Proof Retail
2014	NCLT	7,500	–	Gold	0.5 g	Proof. 99.99 fine. Wide 11mm				65	–	65

(g) 2014 REMEMBRANCE DAY - GREEN DOVE

Date	TYPE	Mintage Figures	Mint Mark	Metal Comp.	Weight in gms	Issuing Mint	Unc	Choice Unc	Roll or Bagged	Issue Price	Mint set Retail	Proof Retail
2014	CIRC	1,856,000	–	Al/br	6.6 g	Canb	10	17	Roll	–	–	–
2014	NCLT	27,500	C	Al/br	6.6 g	Circ. Green colour in folder				12.9	25	–

(h) 2015 ANZAC DAY - LEST WE FORGET

Date	TYPE	Mintage Figures	Mint Mark	Metal Comp.	Weight in gms	Issuing Mint	Unc	Choice Unc	Roll or Bagged	Issue Price	Mint set Retail	Proof Retail
2015	CIRC	1,476,000	–	Al/br	6.6 g	Canb	4	8	120	–	–	–
2015	NCLT	50,000	Poppy	Al/br	6.6 g	Circ. Red colour in folder			–	12.50	13	–

TWO DOLLARS

2015 [a] Remembrance   2016 [b]/c Decimal Coinage 50th Anniversary   [d] Paralympics . Week 6

[e] Week 1 : 19/07/2016   [f] Week 2 : 25/07/2016   [g] Week 3 : 01/08/2016   [h] Week 4 : 8/08/2016

[i] Week 5 : 15/08/2016   2017 [k] Remembrance   2017 [l] With 'C' Mintmark

[a] 2015 REMEMBRANCE DAY ORANGE

2015	CIRC	1,500,000	–	Al/br	6.6 g	Canb	4	7	–	–
2015	ROLL	10,000	–	Al/br	6.6 g	Mint roll of 25 coins`		–	150	–
2015 a	NCLT	50,000	C	Al/br	6.6 g	Circ. Orange colour in folder		–	12.95	–

[b/c] 2016 DECIMAL CURRENCY ANNIVERSARY

2016 b	EX-SET	n/a	–	Al/br	6.6 g	Specimen. Part of mint set	–	4	–
2016 b	EX-SET	n/a	–	Al/br	6.6 g	Proof. Part of 6 coin proof set	–	–	15
2016 b	MINT ROLL	5,000	–	Al/br	6.6 g	Contains 25 x Unc coins	n/a	110	–
2016 b	MINT BAG	50,000	–	Al/br	6.6 g	Circ. 20 x Unc coins		12.5	13
2006 b	RESTRIKE	5,829	–	Silver	3.24 g	Exclusive as part of 8 coin set		–	45

To celebrate the Rio Olympic Games, the RAM engaged with partner Woolworths to launch a series of limited edition Australian Olympic and Paralympic $2 coins. The issue was exclusive to the retail giant and some 12 million coins were randomly doled out in change. The accompanying Paralympic coin was Australia's first ever multi-coloured $2 coin. The different coloured coins were released a week apart with the first issue, the blue reverse, being added to Wollie's cash registers on Tuesday, July 19, 2016. Others followed in sequence : Week 2: Monday 25 July 2016 - Black; Week 3: Monday 1 Aug. 2016 - Red; Week 4: Monday 8 Aug. 2016 - Yellow; Week 5: Monday 15 Aug. 2016 - Green; Week 6: Monday 22 Aug. 2016 - Australian Paralympic Team. Each coin was also issued in a brightly coloured folder. The five Olympic coins sold for $15 each. The Paralympic coin was available for $3. All coin were available from both Woolworths outlets and the RAM.

[d] 2016 PARALYMPICS - MULTIPLE COLOURS

2016 d	NCLT	2,000,000	—	Al/br	6.6 g	Circ. Olympic in wheel chair	3	13	–

[f/i] 2016 OLYMPIC COLOURED FIVE COIN SET

2016 e	NCLT	2,000,000	–	Al/br	6.6 g	Circ. Olympic. Blue ring	–	7	–
2016 f	NCLT	2,000,000	–	Al/br	6.6 g	Circ. Olympic. Black ring	–	7	–
2016 g	NCLT	2,000,000	–	Al/br	6.6 g	Circ. Olympic. Red ring	–	7	–
2016 h	NCLT	2,000,000	–	Al/br	6.6 g	Circ. Olympic. Yellow ring	–	7	–
2016 i	NCLT	2,000,000	–	Al/br	6.6 g	Circ. Olympic. Green ring	–	7	–

[j] 2017 REMEMBRANCE - MULTIPLE COLOURS

2017	NCLT	tba	–	Al/br	6.6 g	Circ. Lest we forget folder	12.95	13	–
2017	NCLT	40,000	C	Al/br	6.6 g	Circ. Special museum folder	15	15	–
2017	ROLL	5,000	–	Al/br	6.6 g	Mint roll of 25 coins`	tba	125	–
2017	BAG	10,000	C	Al/br	6.6 g	Satchel of 5 x coloured coins	10	10	–

FIVE DOLLARS

MIXED METAL COMMEMORATIVES

1988

Aluminium - Bronze
Obv : Raphael Maklouf.
Reverse : Stuart Devlin
Specifications : Composition 92% copper, 6% aluminium; 2% nickel. Edge reeded. Weight 28 grams. Size 38.74 mm.

1988 : NEW PARLIAMENT HOUSE OPENING

Date	Mintage Figures	TYPE	DESCRIPTION	Issue Price	Current Retail
1988 a	3,001,127	Circ/ NCLT	CBA Promo. Circ.	5	14
1988 b	Unknown	Circ/ NCLT	Omomatic Promo. Circ.	5	16
1988 c	124,804	Proof	Cased Proof Issue	28	20
1988 c	25,000	Proof	Three coin & banknote set	120	125
1988 c	24,970	Proof	Masterpieces in Silver	95	75

[a] The RAM report (1987/ 88) states that the CBA commissioned over three million coins to be issued in a sealed cellophane satchel that featured their logo. These were sold at face value through the bank's branches. It was also issued in two other packets. One is a normal double-sided plastic coin flip-style satchel with a 48mm wide CBA card in the opposite side. The other is a similar style of satchel but with an extra coin space at the side, half the width of the main holder, and the CBA card in the opposite side is the full 70mm wide. The 48mm card differs from the 70mm card which is in the cello pack and the wider satchel. The difference is that it has the words "Manufactured by the Royal Australian Mint" at the bottom reverse.
[b] OMO is a popular laundry detergent made by Unilever. Launched in the Netherlands in 1952 and other countries, including Australia and New Zealand, in 1954. I have yet to find any information regarding the mintage figures or even the reasoning behind this one-off issue by the multinational behemoth.
[c] Other proof versions of this coin were also struck for a number of special packages including the Three Coin, Three Banknote set and the Masterpieces in Silver.

FIVE DOLLARS

1990 : 75th ANZAC ANNIVERSARY

Obverse : Raphael Maklouf. **Reverse :** Horst Hahne (New Zealand design at left). Wojciech Pietranik (Australian design at right). **Specifications :** Composition 92% copper, 6% aluminium; 2% nickel. Edge reeded. Weight 28 grams. Size 38.74 mm.

Date	Mintage Figures	Mint	Type	Issue Price	Current Retail
1990	1,000,050	Canb	Circ/ NCLT	5	8
1990 a	40,000	Canb	Proof	75	65
1990 b	3,061	Canb	Proof	Presented	650

(a) In an historic dual venture, the New Zealand proof was included and offered to collectors as a packaged pair. (Pictured left).
(b) Presented to all surviving Gallipoli veterans. In metal case with special letter and certificate signed by the then Prime Minister, R.J. (Bob) Hawke.

FIVE DOLLARS

1992 [a,b & c] Al/br Proof. Year of Space 1994 [d] Bimetal Unc 1994 [e] Al/br Proof

Date	Description	Type	Metal	Weight	Size	Mintage	Issue Price	Retail Aveage
[a/b/c]	**1992 YEAR OF SPACE**							
1992	Coin in flip satchel	Circ	Al/br	28g	38.9mm	239,555	5	6
1992	Coin in printed card	Circ	Al/br	28g	38.9mm	*Inc above*	5	6
1992 a	Normal reverse	Proof	Al/br	28g	38.9mm	25,000	25	20
1992 b	Matte reverse	Proof	Al/br	28g	38.9mm	*Inc above*	25	250
1992 c	Sterling .925 silver	Proof	Al/br	35.79g	38.9mm	2,500	50	75

[a] The standard proof features a matte surface on the map of Australia and a coarse finish across the flag.
[b] Rare variety has an even matte surface over both the flag and the map.
[c] These sterling silver proof coins were only available at the NAA Coin Fair held in Adelaide on September 5 & 6, 1992.

[d/e] 1994 WOMEN'S ENFRANCHISEMENT

Date	Description	Type	Metal	Weight	Size	Mintage	Issue Price	Retail Aveage
1994 d	Coin in plastic card	Circ	Bimetal	10.6 g	28.12mm	250,328	5	10
1994 e	Presentation case	Proof	Al/br	28 g	38.9mm	20,006	26	25

[d] This was Australia's first bi-metal coin and was struck as a tribute to Mary Lee, the leading South Australian suffragist who was part of the movement to establish the Enfranchisement of Women in South Australia. The coin was made of two parts. Outer Ring: Austenitic Stainless Steel. Inner Ring: Aluminium Bronze: 92% Copper, 6% Aluminium, 2% Nickel.
Sold in credit-card like plastic folder. Commemorates the centenary of the historic achievement of South Australian suffragists
[e] Cased proof available through RAM mailing list and selected dealers.
[e] Cased proof issued at the NAA Perth Coin Fair on August 20-21, 1994.

1996/ 97 (f) Bimetal 1996 (g) Bronze Proof 1998 (h) Bimetal 1998 (i) Bronze Proof

[f/g] 1996/ 97 SIR DONALD BRADMAN TRIBUTE

Date	Description	Type	Metal	Weight	Size	Mintage	Issue Price	Retail Aveage
1996 f	Coin in green card	Circ	Bimetal	10.6 g	28.12mm	237,728	5	7
1996 f1	Westpac promotion	Circ	Bimetal	10.6 g	28.12mm	310,213	5	7
1997 f2	PNC coin & stamps	Circ	Bimetal	10.6 g	28.12mm	Priced in PNC's section		
1996 g	Presentation case	Proof	Al/br	28 g	38.9mm	22,523	30	75

[f] Sold in credit-card like plastic folder. Reverse design different from proof design.
[f1] Sold through Westpac Bank with a special outer case sleeve.
[2i] Similar to original 1996 bi-metal coin but dated 1997. Encased in a special (PNC) Philatelic and Numismatic Cover (dated January 23, 1997) with two 45¢ stamps.
[g] Cased proof available through RAM mailing list and selected dealers. A number of the proof coins were donated to the Bradman Foundation. They were Number 1; number 999 (representing his test average of 99.94); number 452 (Bradman's highest score - not out when playing for NSW against QLD in 1930); Number 334 (Bradman's highest first class score scored against England in a game at Leeds).

[h/i] 1998 FLYING DOCTOR SERVICE - 70 YEARS

Date	Description	Type	Metal	Weight	Size	Mintage	Issue Price	Retail Aveage
1998 h	Coin & Phonecard	Unc	Bimetal	10.6 g	28mm	49,556	9.95	40
1998 i	Presentation case	Proof	Al/br	28 g	38.74mm	15,158	30	30

FIVE DOLLARS

MIXED METAL COMMEMORATIVES

2000 (a) Bimetal

2000 (b) Bronze Proof

2002 (c) Bimetal

2002 (d) Bronze Proof

Date	Description	Type	Metal	Weight	Size	Mintage	Issue Price	Retail Aveage
2000 PHAR LAP RACE HORSE								
2000 a	Phar Lap. Head	Unc	Bimetal	10.6g	28mm	97,804	5	10
2000 b	Phar Lap. Full horse	Proof	Al/br	28g	38.74mm	18,804	30	25
2002 BATTLE OF SUNDA STRAIT. 60TH ANNIVERSARY								
2002 c	HMAS Perth. In card	Unc	Bimetal	10.6g	28mm	40,983	5	10
2002 c	USS Houston. In card	Unc	Bimetal	10.6g	28mm	*Ditto*	5	10
2002 d	Coins in plush case	Proof	Al/br	28g	38.74mm	10,400	35	45

2001 (e) Finale Centenary of Federation

2002 (f) Year of the Outback

2003 (g) Australia's Volunteers

Date	Description	Type	Metal	Weight	Size	Mintage	Issue Price	Retail Aveage
2001, 02, 03 MILLENNIUM HOLOGRAM ISSUES								
2001 e	Federation Cent.	Proof	Silver .999	36.31g	38.74	10,001	79.5	395
2002 f	Year of Outback	Proof	Silver .999	36.31g	38.74	15,001	79.5	160
2003 g	Aust's Volunteers	Proof	Silver .999	36.31g	38.74	15,001	79.5	85

2002 (h) Queen Mother

2002 (i) Games Silver

2002 (j) Games Al/br Three coin set

Date	Description	Type	Metal	Weight	Size	Mintage	Issue Price	Retail Aveage
2002 QUEEN MOTHER COMMEMORATIVE								
2002 h	Coin in plush case	Proof	Silver	36.31g	40mm	19,982	45	45
2002 MANCHESTER COMMONWEALTH GAMES								
2002 i	Coin in plush case	Proof	Silver	36.31g	38.74mm	7,581	60	60
2002 MANCHESTER COMMONWEALTH GAMES TRIO								
2002 j	Coin in plush case	Proof	Silver	20g	38.74mm	11,145	n/a	40

FIVE DOLLARS

MIXED METAL COMMEMORATIVES

2003 [a] World Cup

2003 [b] World Cup

2004 [c] Al/br Games

2004 [d] Silver Games

Date	Metal Comp	Type	Weight gms or oz	Size	Mintage Figures	Description	Issue Price	Retail Value
2003 RUGBY WORLD CUP ISSUES								
2003 a	Al/br	Unc	20 g	38.744	43,802	Unc coin in folder	14.95	10
2003 b	Silver	Proof	1 oz	40mm	20,501	Gilt 99.9 fine silver	77	50

Rugby World Cup is now widely regarded as the third biggest international sporting event after the Olympics and Soccer World Cup. The tournament was contested by 20 nations who played 48 matches over 44 days in 10 cities across Australia.

2004 SYDNEY TO ATHENS PAIR

Date	Metal Comp	Type	Weight	Size	Mintage	Description	Issue Price	Retail Value
2004 c	Al/br	Unc	20 g	38.744	24,376	Unc. Coloured flag	14.95	10
2004 d	Silver	Proof	36.1 g	40mm	14,350	Gilt .999 fine silver	77	50

[c] This was one of the first issues to feature colour (ink pad) printing as part of the design. Shortly after its release a number of "error" coins started to appear on ebay. Hailed as a major error because the coloured flag is missing, these coins were selling for highly inflated prices. The mystery was solved when a dealer was shown one of the coins at an ANDA fair the following year. The dealer immediately realised this error was 'created' by dipping the coin in acetone or nail polish. This caused the ink on the flag's coloured surface to disintegrate. Similar 'errors' dealing with the flag of the 2000 Millennium 50¢ have been foisted on unsuspecting collectors.

2004 (e) Tasmania

2004 (f) AFL Centenary

2004 (g) 150 Years Steam

2004 (h) Adelaide to Darwin

2004 TASMANIAN BICENTENNIAL

Date	Metal Comp	Type	Weight	Size	Mintage	Description	Issue Price	Retail Value
2004	Al/br	Circ	20 g	38,74	21,402	RAM struck H m'mark	20	22
2004	Al/br	Circ	20 g	38.74	Inc above	Mobile press H at show	20	30
2004 e	Silver	Proof	36.3 g	38.74	7,500	Cased 99.9 fine silver	79.5	80

NOTES ON THE TASMANIAN BICENTENNIAL : While most of the uncirculated coins were struck on presses at the RAM, some had the mintmark struck on them at the same time. However at a special launch in Hobart, Tasmania, a number of coins were struck using the mobile press. These coins will show a slightly different mintmark font to the RAM issues and show a shallower strike due to the reduced pressure from the mobile press. (e) "H" mm total mintage includes coins struck at RAM and on mobile press at Hobar Fair.

2004 AFL AUSTRALIA'S OWN GAME

Date	Metal Comp	Type	Weight	Size	Mintage	Description	Issue Price	Retail Value
2004 f	Gilt/ Cu/ni	Proof	27.25 g	38.74mm	14,350	24ct gold overlay	77	50

2004 150 YEARS OF STEAM

Date	Metal Comp	Type	Weight	Size	Mintage	Description	Issue Price	Retail Value
2004 g	Silver	Proof	31.6 g	40mm	14,070	In case of issue	68.5	60

2004 ADELAIDE TO DARWIN TRAIN SERVICE

Date	Metal Comp	Type	Weight	Size	Mintage	Description	Issue Price	Retail Value
2004 h	Silver	Proof	31.6 g	40mm	12,500	In case of issue	68.5	80

FIVE DOLLARS

MIXED METAL COMMEMORATIVES

2006 (a) Queen's Baton Relay

2006 (b) Melbourne Games

2006 (c) Melb. City of Sport

Date	Metal Type	Type	Weight gms	Mintage Size	Figures	Description	Issue Price	Retail Value
(a)				**2006 QUEEN'S BATON RELAY**				
2006	Al/br	Circ	20 g	38.74	23,375	Unc coin in folder	12.95	10
2006 *i*	Al/br	Circ	20 g	38.74	15,000	Part of complete album	n/a	n/a
2006	Al/br	PNC	20 g	38.74	22,002	*Coin & Stamp cover - See PNC section*		
2006 a	Silver	Proof	36.31 g	38.74	9,100	Coin in plush case	68.50	70

(i) Above figure also includes coins used in Commonwealth Games Folder Collection that is featured elsewhere in this book.

Date	Metal Type	Type	Weight gms	Mintage Size	Figures	Description	Issue Price	Retail Value
(b)				**2006 COMMONWEALTH GAMES MELBOURNE**				
2006 b	Al/br	Circ	20 g	38.74	9,100	Circ coin in folder	12.95	10
2006	Al/br	PNC	20 g	38.74	22,552	*Coin & Stamp cover - See PNC section*		
(c)				**2006 MELBOURNE CITY OF SPORT**				
2006 c	Silver	Proof	36.3 g	38.74	5,054	Presentation case	68.5	50

(c) The above figure includes 2,063 coins issued as part of a Three Coin Games Set.

2006 (d) Aust $1 Al/br

2006 (e) Aust $5 Silver

2006 (f) Dutch 5 euros

(d) 1606 - 2006 DUYFKEN - VOYAGE OF DISCOVERY

2006 d	Australia. Ship full sail	Circ	Al/br	20g	38.74mm	17,110	12.95	10
2006 e	Australia. Ship full sail .999	Proof	Silver	36.31g	38.74mm	n/a	135	135
2006 f	Dutch. Globe. 5 Euro .925	Proof	Silver	11.9g	29mm	328	650	750
2006	Pair. Silver $5 & 5 euro	Proof	Silver	Inc	As above	3,999	135	140

2006 (g) Aust $5 Al/br

2006 (h) Dutch 5 euro Silver

2006 (i) Gold $10

2006 (j) Gold 10 Euros

FOUR COIN PRESTIGE GOLD PROOF AUSTRALIAN & DUTCH SET

2006 g	Aust.Sailing ship	.999	Proof	Silver	36.31 g	38.74mm	328	*Part of set*	
2006 h	Dutch globe. 5 Eu	.925	Proof	Silver	11.9 g	29mm	328	*Part of set*	
2006 i	Aust. ship. $10	.999	Proof	Gold	5 g	20mm	328	*Part of set*	
2006 j	Dutch globe. 10 Eu	.999	Proof	Gold	6.72 g	22.5mm	328	650	750

[i/j] The two gold coins listed above are unique to this set.

FIVE DOLLARS

MIXED METAL COMMEMORATIVES

2006 (a) 150 years of State Govt. NSW. (1857-2006)

2006 (b) 150 years of State Govt. TAS. (1857-2006)

2006 (c) 150 years of State Govt. VIC. (1857-2006)

2007 (d) 150 years of State Government. SA. (1858-2007)

2008 (e) 30 years of the Northern Territory. (1978-2008)

2009 (f) 150 years of State Government. QLD. (1859-2009)

Date	Description	Type	Metal	Weight	Size	Mintage	Issue Price	Retail Aveage
2006/ 2009 ANNIVERSARY OF STATE GOVERNMENT								
2006 a	NSW	Proof	Silver .999	36.31g	38.74mm	3,514	65	60
2006 b	TAS	Proof	Silver .999	36.31g	38.74mm	3,162	65	60
2006 c	VIC	Proof	Silver .999	36.31g	38.74mm	3,102	65	60
2007 d	SA	Proof	Silver .999	36.31g	38.74mm	2,500	65	60
2008 e	NT	Proof	Silver .999	36.31g	38.74mm	2,717	65	60
2009 f	QLD	Proof	Silver .999	36.31g	38.74mm	2,902	65	60

Common obverse

2007 (g) Lifesaver

2007 (h) Harbour Bridge

2008 (i) Scouting

2008 (j) Rugby League

2008 (k) Bradman

2009 (l) Meteorite

2009 (m) Post Office

MISCELLANEOUS FIVE DOLLAR COMMEMORATIVES

Date	Description	Type	Metal	Weight	Size	Mintage	Issue Price	Retail Aveage
2007 g	Year of Lifesaver	Proof	Silver .999	36.31g	38.74mm	5,064	65	65
2007 h	Sydney Harbour Br	Proof	Silver .999	36.31g	38.74mm	8,996	65	65
2008 i	Year of the Scout	Proof	Silver .999	36.31g	38.74mm	5,000	65	90
2008 j	Rugby League	Proof	Silver .999	36.31g	38.74mm	5,002	65	65
2008 k	Birth of Bradman	Proof	Alum/ Bronze	20g	38.74mm	30,604	18.75	20
2009 l	Meteorite	Proof	Silver .999	36.31g	38.74mm	10,000	155	160
2009 m	Cased with Unc PO $1	Proof	Silver .999	36.31g	38.74mm	7,200	120	120

(m) The design on this coin depicts Isaac Nichol's Sydney house where he became Australia's first Postmaster in 1809 – a position he held until 1819. The artwork on the coin is taken from a photograph in "History of the Post Office in New South Wales" by Andrew Houison, Sydney, 1890.

FIVE DOLLARS

MIXED METAL COMMEMORATIVES

2008 (a) Bilby

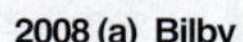

2008 (b) Koala

2009 (c) Lizard

2009 (d) Platypus

2010 (e) Cockatoo

2010 (f) Tas. Devil

2008/ 2010 : LITTLE DINKUM CARTOON SERIES

Date	Description	Weight	Metal	Type	Size	Mintage Limit / Actual	Issue Price	Retail Average
2008 a	Bilby	1/25 oz	Gold	Proof	14mm	10,000/ 4,399	95	99
2008 b	Koala	1/25 oz	Gold	Proof	14mm	10,000/ 4,000	95	99
2009 c	Lizard	1/25 oz	Gold	Proof	14mm	10,000/ 1,924	95	99
2009 d	Platypus	1/25 oz	Gold	Proof	14mm	10,000/ 1,985	95	99
2010 e	Cockatoo	1/25 oz	Gold	Proof	14mm	10,000/ 1,302#	95	99
2010 f	Tas. Devil	1/25 oz	Gold	Proof	14mm	10,000/ 1,300#	95	99

(g) Skua in Flight

(h) Three Explorers

(I) Gold corporate

(j) Aurora Australis

2008/ 2009 : INTERNATIONAL POLAR YEAR SERIES

Date	Description	Type	Metal Type	Weight in gms	Size	Mintage Figures	Issue Price	Retail Value
2008 g	Skua in Flight	Proof	Silver .999	36.31g	38.74mm	5,111	65	65
2009 h	Three Explorers	Proof	Silver .999	36.31g	38.74mm	5,508	65	65
2009 i	Explorers (Gilt)	Proof	Silver .999	36.31g	38.74mm	500?	*Gift*	200
2009 j	Aurora Australis	Proof	Silver .999	36.31g	38.74mm	8,504	95	90

[i] Lot 334 of Noble Numismatic's 100th sale in Sydney (July 2012) featured an interesting version of the 2008 issued Three Explorers fine silver proof coin. This coin was a special commission by the Royal Society of Victoria in 2009 to celebrate the centenary of the first party to locate the South Magnetic Pole. This special edition was gold plated and limited to only 500 being struck. This coin, numbered 83 of 500, sold for $300 against an estimate of $200.

FIVE DOLLARS

[a] Remembrance

[b] Hyde Park

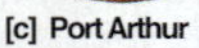

[c] Port Arthur

[d] Female Factory

[e] Fremantle Prison

[f] Coal Mines

[g] Govt. House

[h] Royal Visit

[a] 2011 REMEMBRANCE DAY

2011 a	Red Poppy	Unc	All/br	20g	38.74mm	20,284	25	25

(a) In 2011, Remembrance Day fell on the significant date of 11.11.11. The principal design element was a bright red poppy. A sign of hope and renewal, it was among the first plants to spring up in the devastated battlefields of Europe.

[b/g] 2011 CONVICT LANDMARKS 6 COIN SET

2011	Six proof coins sold as a complete set	3,000/ n/a	720	720

[h] 2011 QUEEN'S ROYAL VISIT

2011 h	Frosted finish	Unc	Al/br	20g	38.74mm	21,144	20	20

2012 (i) Crux 2013 (j) Pavo 2014 (k) Orion 2016 (l) Cassiopela 2016 [m] Ursa Major

[i/m] SOUTHERN & NORTHERN SKY CURVED PLANCHET

2012 i	Crux	Silver	1oz	Proof	33.92mm	10,000/ n/a	110	120
2013 j	Pavo	Silver	1oz	Proof	33.92mm	10,000/ n/a	110	120
2014 k	Orion	Silver	1oz	Proof	33.92mm	10,000/ n/a	110	120
2016 l	Cassiopela	Silver	1oz	Proof	33.92mm	10,000/ n/a	110	120
2016 m	Ursa Major	Silver	1oz	Proof	33.92mm	10,000/ n/a	110	120

[n] Parliament [o] Lest We Forget [p] ANZAC [q] The Fallen [r] Devotion

[n/q] COMMEMORATIVE TRIANGULAR COINS

2013 n	Parliament's 25th	Proof	Silver .999	33.92mm	22.23g	10,000	90	90
2014 o	Lest We Forget	Proof	Silver .999	33.92mm	22.23g	10,000	90	90
2015 p	ANZAC Centenary	Proof	Silver .999	33.92mm	22.23g	10,000	90	90
2015 p	ANZAC Aust & NZ pair	Proof	Silver .999	33.92mm	22.23g	1,500	825	pair
2016 q	Remember Our Fallen	Proof	Silver .999	33.92mm	22.23g	10,000	85	90
2017 r	Devotion. Nursing	Proof	Silver .999	33.92mm	22.23g	10,000	85	90

[p] Cased pair includes 2015 $5 coloured fine silver proof triangular coin from Australia and 2015 50c coloured fine silver proof coin from New Zealand. $5 coin: 22.23 grams pure silver. 50c coin: 1 oz pure silver

FIVE DOLLARS

MIXED METAL COMMEMORATIVES

[a] Perth

[b] Brisbane

[c] Melbourne

[d] Sydney

Date	Description	Type	Metal Content	Weight in gms	Size in mm	Mintage Figures	Issue Price	Retail Value
2012 a	Perth Town Hall	Unc	Al/br/zn	20 g	38.74mm	2,000	55	55
2012 b	Brisbane Town Hall	Unc	Al/br/zn	20 g	38.74mm	2,000	55	55
2012 c	Mellb. Town Hall	Unc	Al/br/zn	20 g	38.74mm	2,000	55	55
2012 d	Sydney Town Hall	Unc	Al/br/zn	20 g	38.74mm	2,000	55	55

The above four coins were exclusive ANDA issues distributed at the four national shows held throughout Australia in 2009. After the conclusion of each show, left over coins were offered through the RAM's web site for a ten day period. Any unsolds were melted down.

2012 [e] Tennis Open

2013 [f] Canberra

2014 [g] Victoria Cross

2015 [h] Agro Jnr

Date	Description	Type	Metal Content	Weight in gms	Size in mm	Mintage Figures	Issue Price	Retail Value
[e] 2012 CENTENARY OF MEN'S TENNIS OPEN								
2012	Postcard display	Unc	Al/br/zn	50g	38.74mm	10,000	25	25
2012	First $5 PNC	Unc	Al/br/zn	50g	8.74mm	10.000	*See PNC section*	
[f] 2013 THE CENTENARY OF CANBERRA								
2013	In plush case	Proof	Silver	36.31g	38.74mm	10,000	110	130
[g] 2014 THE VICTORIA CROSS FOR AUSTRALIA								
2014	**Victoria Cross**	**Spec**	**Silver**	**1 oz**	**40mm**	**14,850**	**70**	**90**
[h] 2015 AGRO JNR. CROCODILE								
2015	Cased High Relief	Unc	Silver	1 oz	32mm	1,500	100	100

2015-16 [i] Eternal Love proof silver obv & rev

2015 [j] ICC Cricket proof silver obv & rev

Date	Description	Type	Metal Content	Weight in gms	Size in mm	Mintage Figures	Issue Price	Retail Value
[i] 2015 - HEART SHAPED ETERNAL LOVE								
2015	First coin this shape	Proof	Silver	1 oz	42.9 x 39.5	15,000/ n/a	100	100
2016	Second in a series	Proof	Silver	1 oz	42.9 x 39.5	7,500/ n/a	100	100
[j] 2015 ICC CRICKET WORLD CUP DOMED COIN								
2015	Coin in case	Proof	Silver	1 oz	39.62mm	5,000/ n/a	125	175

FIVE DOLLARS

MIXED METAL COMMEMORATIVES

2015 (a/b) Gold Cross of Valour. Obv & rev 2015 (c) Distinctly Aust. 2015 (d) Landing

(a & b) 2015 AUSTRALIAN BRAVERY

2015	Gold plated	Spec	Silver	1 oz	40mm	5,000	120	120

(c) 2015 DISTINCTLY AUSTRALIAN

2015	Multicultural scene	Spec	Al/br/zn	20 g	38.74mm	30,000	50	50

(d) 2015 CENTENARY OF GALLIPOLI LANDING

2015	Gallipoli Landing	Proof	Silver	1 oz	40mm	10,000	100	100

2015 (e) Australia. $5. Obv & rev

2015 (f) Turkey. 20 Lira. Obv & Rev.

2015 (g) Great Britain. £5. Obv & rev

2015 (h) New Zealand. $1. Obv & Rev.

(e & h) 2015 GALLIPOLI LANDING FOUR COIN PROOF SET

2015 e	Australian $5	Proof	Silver .999	1 oz	40mm	10,000/ n/a	495	500
2015 f	Turkey 20 Lira	Proof	Silver .925	1 oz	38.61mm	5,000/ n/a	*ditto*	*ditto*
2015 g	British £5	Proof	Silver .925	28.8	38.61mm	5,000/ n/a	*ditto*	*ditto*
2015 h	New Zealand $1	Proof	Silver .999	1 oz	40mm	5,000/ n/a	*ditto*	*ditto*

[e] This part of a four coin set. The price of $495 was the issue price for all four coins.

2015 Australian Obv

Australian Proof Silver

Canadian Proof Silver

British Proof Silver

(i) 2015 ELIZABETH II LONGEST REIGNING

2015	Individual coin	Proof	Silver	1 oz	40mm	5,000/ n/a	120	100
2015	Part of three coin set	Proof	Silver	1 oz	40mm	5,000/ n/a	100	100

[i] This coin was available in two forms. It was issued as a stand alone individually cased pure silver coin and also as part of the following three coin set. In the section listing $100 coins, a gold version of this design is also available as part of the three coin set.

FIVE DOLLARS

MIXED METAL COMMEMORATIVES

[a] Netball Obv. Domed planchet [b] Netball Rev. [c] Magna Carta Obv & Rev

Date	Description	Type	Metal Content	Weight in gms	Size in mm	Mintage Figures	Issue Price	Retail Value
[a/b] 2015 NETBALL WORLD CUP - SYDNEY								
2015	Netball & globe	Proof	Silver	1 oz	39.62mm	5,000/ n/a	125	125
[c] 2015 MAGNA CARTA - 800TH ANNIVERSARY								
2015	Antique Silver	Proof	—	1 oz	40x28mm	10,000/ n/a	120	120

2015 [d] VOC Batavia 2015 [e] Lighthouse 2015 [f] West Aust 2016 [g] Monty

Date	Description	Type	Metal Content	Weight in gms	Size in mm	Mintage Figures	Issue Price	Retail Value
[d] 2015 THE STORY OF THE V.O.C. BATAVIA								
2015	Ship under sail	Proof	Silver	1 oz	40mm	5,000/ n/a	100	100
[e] 2015 CENTENARY LIGHTHOUSE LEGISLATION								
2015	Light beams	Proof	Silver	1 oz	40mm	5,000/ n/a	80	80
[f] 2015 WESTERN AUSTRALIA - 125 YEARS								
2015	WA Highlighted	Proof	Silver	36.31g	38.74mm	12.500/ n/a	115	115
[g] 2016 MONTY CROCODILE								
2015	Crocodile. Monty	Proof	Silver	1 oz	40mm	5,000/ n/a	100	100

[h] Long Tan [i] Olympic 1oz Gilt Silver [j] Olympic 1kg Silver [k] Olympic 1kg Gold

Date		Description	Type	Metal Content	Weight in gms	Size in mm	Mintage Figures	Issue Price	Retail Value
[h] 2016 BATTLE OF LONG TAN									
2016		Cross & Trees	Unc	Al/br	20g	38.74mm	15,000/ n/a	100	100
[I] 2016 AUSTRALIAN OLYMPIC TEAM									
2016	1	Gilt reverse	Proof	Silver	1 oz	40mm	15,000/ n/a	130	140
2016	30	Cased	Proof	Silver	1 kg	99.95	50/ n/a	2,016	2,100
2016	3,000	Cased	Proof	Gold	1 kg	74.77	5/ n/a	80,000	80,000

TEN DOLLARS

MIXED METAL COMMEMORATIVES

1982 [a] Obv & Rev Commonwealth Games

Common Obverse

1985 [b] Victoria

1986 [c] South Aust

1987 [d] NSW

1988 [e] Bicentenary

1989 [f] Queensland

1990 [g] West Aust

1991 [h] Tasmania

1992 [i] Northern Territory

1993 [j] ACT

1982 BRISBANE COMMMONWEALTH GAMES

Date	Description	Metal Alloy	Type	Weight in gms	Size in mm	Mintage Figures	Issue Price	Retail Value
1982	In red vinyl satchel	.925% Stg Silver	Unc	20g	34 mm	125,700	44	30
1982 a	Red plush case	.925% Stg Silver	Proof	20g	34 mm	85,142	45	40

[a] Due to an industrial strike at the RAM in late 1981, sub contracts were offered to mints and private companies to produce coins. The firm of Stokes & Son of Melbourne was commissioned to strike some of the above proof coins from dies provided by the RAM. The Stokes' issues feature the firm's name printed inside the presentation box. Stokes produced 10,048 coins while the RAM struck 75,094 pieces. Hard to suggest a price on a box as the coins are the same.

1985 - 1993 AUSTRALIAN STATES & TERRITORIES

Date	Description	Metal Alloy	Type	Weight in gms	Size in mm	Mintage Figures	Issue Price	Retail Value
1985 b	Victoria	Silver .925%	Unc	20g	34 mm	81,751	15.5	30
1985 b	Victoria	Silver .925%	Proof	20g	34 mm	55,806	35	30
1986 c	South Australia	Silver .925%	Unc	20g	34 mm	78,100	17.5	30
1986 c	South Australia	Silver .925%	Proof	20g	34 mm	52,150	37	30
1987 d	New South Wales	Silver .925%	Unc	20g	34 mm	55,000	20.5	30
1987 d	New South Wales	Silver .925%	Proof	20g	34 mm	50,500	40	30
1988 e	Bicentenary	Silver .925%	Unc	20g	34 mm	111,497	20.5	30
1988 e/1	Bicentenary	Silver .925%	Proof	20g	34 mm	50,099	40	30
1989 f	Queensland	Silver .925%	Unc	20g	34 mm	48,929	20.5	30
1989 f	Queensland	Silver .925%	Proof	20g	34 mm	48,573	40	30
1990 g	Western Australia	Silver .925%	Unc	20g	34 mm	28,133	22	30
1990 g	Western Australia	Silver .925%	Proof	20g	34 mm	29,089	40	30
1991 h	Tasmania	Silver .925%	Unc	20g	34 mm	26,150	22	30
1991 h	Tasmania	Silver .925%	Proof	20g	34 mm	27,664	43	30
1991 h/2	Coin Fair Issue	Silver .925%	Proof	20g	34 mm	1,000	43	30
1992 i	Northern Territory	Silver .925%	Unc	20g	34 mm	24,164	22	30
1992 i	Northern Territory	Silver .925%	Proof	20g	34 mm	25,404	44	30
1993 j	Aust. Capital Territory	Silver .925%	Unc	20g	34 mm	19,288	22	30
1993 j	Aust. Capital Territory	Silver .925%	Unc	20g	34 mm	21,183	44	35

[e/1] Also see Three Coins, Three Banknotes Set.
[h/a] The first coin fair version of the $10 state series was released at the Tasmanian International Coin Fair held in Hobart from May 11 - 12, 1991. Only 1000 proof coins were released and can be distinguished by a special coin fair certificate.

TEN DOLLARS

Common Obverse

1989 [a] Kookaburra

1990 [b] White Cockatoo

1991 [c] Jabiru

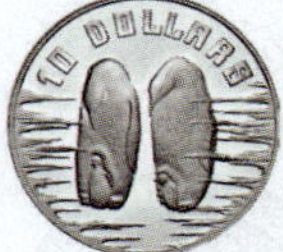

1992 [d] Penguin

1993 [e] Cockatoo

1993 [e/1] UNEP Special

1994 [f] Eagle

1989 - 1994 RARE BIRD SILVER PROOF SERIES

Date	Description	Nominal value	Type	Weight in gms	Size in mm	Mintage Figures	Issue Price	Retail Value
1989 a	Kookaburra	Standard	Proof	20g	34.1mm	50,000	42	30
1989 a	Kookaburra	Piedfort	Proof	40g	34.1mm	11,000	85	50
1989 a	Kookaburra	Piedfort. Fair	Proof	40g	34.1mm	4,000	85	55
1990 b	Cockatoo	Standard	Proof	20g	34.1mm	49,801	43	30
1990 b	Cockatoo	Standard. Fair	Proof	20g	34.1mm	2,000	53	32
1990 b	Cockatoo	Piedfort	Proof	40g	34.1mm	13,794	86	50
1990 b	Cockatoo	Piedfort. Fair	Proof	40g	34.1mm	1,000	96	55
1991 c	Jabiru	Standard	Proof	20g	34.1mm	32,446	43	30
1991 c	Jabiru	Standard. Fair	Proof	20g	34.1mm	1,000	45	32
1991 c	Jabiru	Piedfort	Proof	40g	34.1mm	13,980	86	50
1991 c	Jabiru	Piedfort. Fair	Proof	40g	34.1mm	1,000	90	55
1992 d	Penguin	Standard	Proof	20g	34.1mm	25,319	44	30
1992 d	Penguin	Standard. Fair	Proof	20g	34.1mm	1,000	45	32
1992 d	Penguin	Piedfort	Proof	40g	34.1mm	13,782	86	50
1992 d	Penguin	Piedfort. Fair	Proof	40g	34.1mm	1,000	90	55
1993 e	Cockatoo	Standard	Proof	20g	34.1mm	22,172	43	30
1993 e	Cockatoo	Standard. Fair	Proof	20g	34.1mm	1,000	53	32
1993 e	Cockatoo	Piedfort	Proof	40g	34.1mm	13,706	86	50
1993 e/1a	Cockatoo	Piedfort. UNEP	Proof	40g	34.1mm	1,000	96	55
1994 f	Eagle	Standard	Proof	20g	34.1mm	23,326	43	30
1994 f	Eagle	Standard. Fair	Proof	20g	34.1mm	1,000	45	32
1994 f	Eagle	Piedfort	Proof	40g	34.1mm	13,134	88	50
1994 f	Eagle	Piedfort. Fair	Proof	40g	34.1mm	1,000	90	55

[E/1a] This interesting variation appeared as lot 1045 in Downie's special Masterpieces auction 219a held in late May 2015. The description in the catalogue picks the story."1993 $10 Silver Proof Bird Series UNEP Cockatoo FDC. This coin has rarely been seen and was struck as part of the United Nations Environment Programme. Little is known about this release but it should be noted that on this production unit the strike is noticeably weaker than the standard and piedfort versions, and as a result appears to be missing feathers. It sold for $360 plus commission on an estimate of $250."

1995 [g] Numbat

1996 [h] Right Whale

1997 [i] Black Cockatoo

1998 [j] Wombat

TEN DOLLARS ENDANGERED SPECIES (1995-1998)

Date	Description	Nominal value	Type	Weight in gms	Size in mm	Mintage Figures	Issue Price	Retail Value
1995 g	Numbat	Standard	Proof	20g	34.1mm	24,000	44	30
1995 g	Numbat	Standard. Fair	Proof	20g	34.1mm	1,000	44	32
1995 g	Numbat	Piedfort	Proof	40g	34.1mm	14,000	88	50
1995 g	Numbat	Piedfort. Fair	Proof	40g	34.1mm	1,000	88	50
1996 h	Right Whale	Standard	Proof	20g	34.1mm	24,000	44	35
1996 h	Right Whale	Piedfort	Proof	40g	34.1mm	14,000	88	50
1997 i	Cockatoo	Standard	Proof	20g	34.1mm	24,000	44	30
1997 i	Cockatoo	Piedfort	Proof	40g	34.1mm	14,000	88	50
1998 j	Wombat	Standard	Proof	20g	34.1mm	24,000	44	30
1998 j	Wombat	Piedfort	Proof	40g	34.1mm	14,000	88	50

TEN DOLLARS

LIVING LEGEND SERIES

1994 Edwin Flack

1995 Dawn Fraser

1996 Betty Cuthbert

1994 Sarah Durack

1995 Murray Rose

1996 Shirley Strickland

Composition 99.9% silver. Edge reeded. Weight 20 .77grams. Size 34.1 mm. Specimen finish.

Date	Mintage Figures	Cased	Description	Issue Price	Current Retail
1994	21,484	Pair	Edwin Flack / Sarah Durack	62	60
1995	30,000	Pair	Dawn Fraser / Murray Rose	56	60
1996	15,300	Pair	Betty Cuthbert / Shirley Strickland	56	90
1996	n/a	---	Set of six coins in case	n/a	195

TEN DOLLARS LANDMARK SERIES

1997 Opera House

1998 Melbourne Trams

1999 Snowy Mtn Tunnel

1997 Harbour Bridge

1998 M.C.G

1999 Snowy Mtn Dam

Specifications : Composition 99.9% silver. Edge reeded.
Weight 20 .77grams. Size 34 mm. Specimen finish.

Date	Mintage Figures	Cased	Description	Issue Price	Current Retail
1997	20,000	Pair	Opera House / Harbour Bridge	65	85
1998	20,000	Pair	Melbourne Trams / M.C.G.	65	95
1999	20,000	Pair	Snowy Mountains Scheme	65	110

TEN DOLLARS

MIXED METAL COMMEMORATIVES

1999 [a] The Past 2000 [b] The Present 2001 [c] The Future

The Past : Composition. Outer ring : .999 fine silver. Centre .999 copper.
The Present : Outer ring : 24ct plated .9999 gold. Centre .999 fine silver
The Future : Composition. Outer ring : .999 copper. Centre .999 silver with 24ct gold plating. Common Weight 33.15 grams. Size 38.74 mm. Edge reeded.

Date	Description	Nominal value	Type	Weight in gms	Size in mm	Mintage Figures	Issue Price	Retail Value
[a/b/c] 1999/2001 THE MILLENNIUM TRIO OF COINS								
1999 a	The Past	Bimetal	Proof	33.15g	38.74	20,000/ 19,250	49.5	125
2000 b	The Present	Bimetal	Proof	33.15g	38.74	20,000/ All sold	56.5	125
2001 c	The Future	Bimetal	Proof	33.15g	38.74	20,000/ All sold	56.5	125
1999/2001	Set of above three coins in special presentation case					To order	—	375

Although not sold as a set, the RAM did provide the same serial number and a presentation case for collectors who committed to buy all three. Later a box to house all three coins was also offered to customers. The three coins in a box and with matching certificates carry a premium of around ten percent.

2002 (d) Adelaide Pound 2003 (e) 1853 Pattern Sovereign

Obverse : Ian Rank-Broadley. **Reverse :** Wojciech Pietranik.
Specifications : Composition. Outer ring : .999 fine silver. Centre gilt silver

Date	Description	Nominal value	Type	Weight in gms	Size in mm	Mintage Figures	Issue Price	Retail Value
[d] 1852 ADELAIDE POUND BIMETAL GILT SILVER								
2002 d	Adelaide Pound	Bimetal	Proof	60.5g	50mm	10k/ All sold	85	165

Obverse : Vladimir Gottwald. **Reverse :** Vladimir Gottwald.
Specifications : Composition. Outer ring : .999.fine silver. Centre Gilt silver

Date	Description	Nominal value	Type	Weight in gms	Size in mm	Mintage Figures	Issue Price	Retail Value
[e] 1853 PATTERN SOVEREIGN GOLD SYDNEY MINT								
2003 e	Pattern Sovereign	Bimetal	Proof	60.5g	50mm	10k/ All sold	85	95

[d] The RAM scanned a genuine Adelaide Pound coin as well as a restrike from its archives. The reduction punch was then cut directly by the Mint's recently acquired computer engraving machine.
[e] The reverse and obverse gold plated designs within a host silver coin, are based on images of an original Sovereign Pattern that is featured on electrotypes housed in the Mint's National Coin Collection. For more information on the original issue see the gold section at the beginning of this book.

TEN DOLLARS

MIXED METAL COMMEMORATIVES

2005 [a] Syd. Mint. Obv 2005 [b] Syd. Mint. Rev 2006 [c] Aust. Duyfken 2006 [d] Dutch Duyfken

Date	Description			Type	Weight in gms	Size in mm	Mintage Figures	Issue Price	Retail Value
[a/b]	**(1855- 2005) SYDNEY MINT SOVEREIGN SESQUICENTENARY**								
2005	24ct. gold inlay on silver host			Proof	60.5g	50mm	10,000/ 5,078	95	95
[c/d]	**2006 DUYFKEN TWO COIN PRESTIGE SET**								
2006 c	Australian issue	Gold	99.99	Proof	5g	20mm	1,000/ 328	700	795
2006 d	Dutch 10 euros	Gold	.90 fine	Proof	6.72g	22.5mm	Part of above set		

The above two gold coins were part of a four coin cased set that included the two silver coins listed elsewhere in this book.

2007 (e) The Ashes 2008 (f) AFL Cent 2008 (g) Scouts 2011 (h) RAM

Date	Description			Type	Weight	Size	Mintage Figures	Issue Price	Retail Value
[e]	**2007 THE ASHES**								
2007	Coin has C mm	Gold	99.99	Proof	1/10oz	17.5mm	1,500/ n/a	175	295
[f]	**2008 CENTENARY OF RUGBY LEAGUE**								
2008	Coin has C mm	Gold	99.99	Proof	1/10oz	17.5mm	3,000/ n/a	210	250
[g]	**2011 CENTENARY OF SCOUTING**								
2008	Coin has C mm	Gold	99.99	Proof	1/10oz	17.5mm	2,500/ n/a	210	250
[h]	**2011 RAM'S HEAD ISSUE**								
2011	Coin has C mm	Gold	99.99	Proof	1/10oz	17.5mm	2,500/ n/a	320	350

2011 (i) Gilt. Golf 2012 (j) Wheat Sheaf 2013 (k) Obv & Rev Gold Holey Dollar

Date	Description			Type	Weight	Size	Mintage Figures	Issue Price	Retail Value
[i]	**2011 THE PRESIDENTS CUP. GOLF**								
2011	24ct. gold inlay on silver host			Proof	5 oz	65mm	1,500/ n/a	550	750
[j]	**2012 WHEAT SHEAF ISSUES**								
2012	Coin with C mm	Gold	99.99	Proof	1/10oz	17.5mm	2,500/ n/a	360	350
[k]	**2013 HOLEY DOLLAR & DUMP**								
2013	Coin with C mm	Gold	99.99	Proof	1/10oz	17.5mm	2,500/ n/a	320	350

TEN DOLLARS

MIXED METAL COMMEMORATIVES

2013 (a) Blue Mtns 2014 (b) Terra Australis 2014 (c) From Albany 2014 (d) Victoria Cross

Date	Description	Metal	Purity	Type	Weight in gms	Size in mm	Mintage Figures	Issue Price	Retail Value
(a)	**2013 BICENTENARY BLUE MOUNTAINS CROSSING**								
2013	Mountain views	Silver	99.9	Proof	60.5g	50mm	5,000/ n/a	175	175
(b)	**2014 TERRA AUSTRALIS**								
2014	Coin has C mm	Gold	99.99	Proof	1/10oz	17.5mm	2,500/ n/a	320	350
(c)	**2014 AIF CENTENARY. FROM ALBANY TO EGYPT**								
2014	Soldier on horse	Gold	99.99	Proof	1/10oz	17.53mm	1,500/ n/a	360	360
(d)	**2015 VICTORIA CROSS**								
2014	Similar to $5 design	Antique Copper		Proof	82.25g	57mm	5,000/ All sold	10	#

This coin was put to a ballot which attracted 13,000 entries for the 5,000 coins made available. A silver $5 issue with a similar design was also issued at the same time as the above. On Saturday 26 April 2014, the RAM had the four surviving Australian recipients of the Victoria Cross strike one of the coins. These specially were added to the final mintage but without any way to identify their uniqueness.
This is one of the very few coins in this book that we have not priced. Obviously with 8,000 people missing out on such an emotive coin, the secondary market has gone off the radar. Prices.recently researched have varied from $700 to close to $2,000. We will revisit this coin in the next edition.

2015 Common obverse 2015 [e] Bravery 100th 2015 [f] Gallipoli Landing 2016 [g] First Mints

Date	Description	Metal	Metal Purity	Metal Content	Weight in gms	Size in mm	Mintage Figures	Issue Price	Retail Average
[e]	**2015 AUSTRALIAN BRAVERY**								
2015	Canb 'C'	Gold	99.99	Proof	1/10oz	17.53mm	2,500/ n/a	300	330
[f]	**2015 CENTENARY OF THE GALLIPOLI LANDING**								
2015	Lone Pine	Gold	99.99	Proof	1/10oz	17.53mm	1,500/ n/a	360	360
[g]	**2016 AUSTRALIA'S FIRST MINTS - GROWTH FROM GOLD**								
2016	Canb 'C'	Gold	99.99	Proof	1/10oz	17.53mm	1,000/ n/a	300	300

$25 & $30 PROOF ISSUES

MIXED METAL COMMEMORATIVES

2007- (a) Sunset rev 2011 (b) Presidents Cup 2014 (c) Barrier Reef 2006 (d) Melb. Games

(a) 2007 - $25. GOLD KANGAROO AT SUNSET PROOF

2007	Cased	Gold	99.99	Proof	6.22g	1/5oz	21.69mm	1,000/ 998	365	1,600
2008	Cased	Gold	99.99	Proof	6.22g	1/5oz	21.69mm	1,000/ tba	365	1,100
2009	Cased	Gold	99.99	Proof	6.22g	1/5oz	21.69mm	1,000/ tba	395	1,100
2010	Cased	Gold	99.99	Proof	6.22g	1/5oz	21.69mm	1,000/ tba	420	1,000
2011	Cased	Gold	99.99	Proof	6.22g	1/5oz	21.69mm	1,000/ tba	460	950
2012	Cased	Gold	99.99	Proof	6.22g	1/5oz	21.69mm	1,000/ tba	620	900
2013	Cased	Gold	99.99	Proof	6.22g	1/5oz	21.69mm	1,000/ tba	650	850
2014	Cased	Gold	99.99	Proof	6.22g	1/5oz	21.69mm	1,000/ tba	665	850
2015	Cased	Gold	99.99	Proof	6.22g	1/5oz	21.69mm	1,000/ tba	650	850
2016	Cased	Gold	99.99	Proof	6.22g	1/5oz	21.69mm	1,000/ tba	650	850
2017	Cased	Gold	99.99	Proof	6.22g	1/5oz	21.69mm	1,000/ tba	650	850

(b) 2011 - $25. THE PRESIDENTS CUP

2011	Cased	Gold	99.99	Proof	6.22g	1/4oz	21.69mm	1,500/ n/a	695	750

(c) 2014 - $25. UNESCO SERIES

2014	Cased	Gold	99.99	Proof	6.22g	1/4oz	21.69mm	1,500/ n/a	695	750

(d) 2006 - $30. COMMONWEALTH GAMES PROOF

2006	Cased	Silver	99.9	Proof	1000g	1 kg	100 mm	500/ n/a	880	750

HERITAGE COINS & PATTERNS

After the Australian Government announced in 1963 that it would introduce a decimal currency system, six artists were commissioned to produce coins for the new 1c, 2c, 5c, 10c, and 20c coins. Initial sketches were submitted by the artists and those that were approved by the Advisory Panel were made into plaster sculptures known as 'plasters'. Many of the entries followed themes of native Australian flora and fauna. But it was Stuart Devlin's now familiar designs that were chosen to feature reverse side of the new decimal coins. The 1966 Decimal Currency Heritage set contained proof versions of the original coin designs as well as replica 'resins' of some alternative designs by recommissioned artists in 1963. The set includes 10 resin replicas of some of the designs submitted in the competition. These resins are approximately 70mm in diameter. The Devlin decimal coins includes the current effigy by Ian Rank- Broadley and all are dated 2010. The low mintage makes the 50¢, 2¢ and 1¢ among the lowest issues in the entire decimal series. Only 400 sets were produced and even at the issue price of $695, were an instant sellout. Very few sets come onto the market but a starting retail figure would at least be in the $1,800 region.

METAL	CUPRO NICKEL					80% SILVER	AL/BRONZE	
Denomination	1¢	2¢	5¢	10¢	20¢	50¢	$1	$2
Mass in grams	2.60	5.20	2.83	5.65	11.30	13.28	9.00	6.60
Diameter (mm)	17.63	21.59	19.41	23.60	28.52	31.51	25.00	20.50

$50 & $100 PROOF ISSUES

2002 [a] Manchester Rev 2004 [b] Sydney to Athens 2006 [c] Melbourne Games. Obverse & Reverse

Date	Description		Type	Weight in gms	Size in mm	Mintage Figures	Issue Price	Retail Value
[a&b] 2002 - $50 TRIMETAL. MANCHESTER GAMES								
2002	Trimetal	Gold, Silver, Copper	Proof	36.51g	38.74mm	5,000/2,497	435	475
[c] 2004 - $50 TRIMETAL. AUSTRALIA TO ATHENS								
2004	Trimetal	Gold, Silver, Copper	Proof	36.51g	38.74mm	2,500/2,063	600	500

The above coin was only available as part of a three coin set that included the two $5 coins shown in the section on $5 coins. Both of the $5 coins were also available individually.

Date	Description		Type	Weight in gms	Size in mm	Mintage Figures	Issue Price	Retail Value
[d] 2006 - $50 TRIMETAL. MELBOURNE GAMES								
2006	Trimetal	Gold, Silver, Copper	Proof	36.51g	38.74mm	2,500/n/a	385	425

ONE HUNDRED DOLLARS

2002 (e) Accession 2003 (f) Coronation 2016 [g] Kangaroo 2016 [h] Sunset Decade

Date	Description			Type	Weight	Size	Mintage Figures	Issue Price	Retail Value
[e] 2002 - $100. QEII ACCESSION									
2002	With special 50¢	Gold	99.99	Proof	1 oz	34mm	2,002/1,500	1,295	1,550
[f] 2003 - $100. QEII CORONATION									
2003	With special 50¢	Gold	99.99	Proof	1 oz	34mm	2,003/660	1,295	1,550
[g] 2013 -$100. THE KANGAROO 20TH ANNIVERSARY									
2016	Original Design	Gold	99.99	Proof	1 oz	34mm	500/n/a	2,600	3,000
[h] 2016 -$100. THE KANGAROO AT SUNSET DECADE									
2016	First $100 issue	Gold	99.99	Proof	1 oz	34mm	500/n/a	2,600	3,000

2016 [i] Longest reigning monarch Obv & Rev 2016 [j] Southern Sky 2016 [k] 1oz bullion

Date	Description			Type	Weight	Size	Mintage Figures	Issue Price	Retail Value
[i] 2016 -$100. LONGEST REIGNING MONARCH									
2016	Part 3 coin set	Gold	99.99	Proof	1 oz	38.7mm	100/n/a	2,600	3,000
[j] 2016 -$100. CELESTIAL DOME - SOUTHERN SKY									
2016	Concave planchet	Gold	99.99	Unc	1 oz	38.5mm	750/n/a	2,600	3,000
[k] 2016 -$100. AUSTRALIAN BULLION GOLD ISSUE									
2016	Struck for O/S market	Gold	99.99	Unc	1 oz	38.5mm	To order	b/v	b/v

$100 & $150 GOLD ISSUES

1995 [a] NSW. Waratah

1996 [b] TAS. Blue Gum

1997 [c] WA. Mangle's K'roo

1998 [d] SA. Desert Pea

1999 [e] VIC. Common Heath

2000 [f] QLD Orchid

2001 [g] WA. Golden Wattle

2002 [h] NT. Desert Rose

2003 [i] ACT. Blue Bell

2004 [j] Cassowary

2005 [k] Mallee Fowl

2006 [l] Cockatoo

Date	Description	State	Face Value	Type	Weight gms	Size	Mintage Figures	Issue Price	Retail Value
GOLD FLORAL EMBLEM SERIES									
1995 a	Waratah	NSW	100	Unc	10.37g	25mm	3,000/ 2,803	260	530
1995 a	Waratah	NSW	100	Proof	10.37g	25mm	2,500/ 2,506	350	585
1995 a	Waratah	NSW	150	Proof	15.16g	30mm	1,500/ 1,506	580	875
1996 b	Blue Gum	TAS	100	Unc	10.37g	25mm	3,000/ 2,057	260	530
1996 b	Blue Gum	TAS	100	Proof	10.37g	25mm	2,500/ 2,254	350	585
1996 b	Blue Gum	TAS	150	Proof	15.16g	30mm	1,500/ 1,503	580	825
1997 c	Mangles Roo	WA	100	Unc	10.37g	25mm	3,000/ 1,800	260	530
1997 c	Mangles Roo	WA	100	Proof	10.37g	25mm	2,500/ 2,003	350	585
1997 c	Mangles Roo	WA	150	Proof	15.16g	30mm	1,500/ 1,503	580	825
1998 d	Desert Pea	SA	100	Unc	10.37g	25mm	3,000/ 1,501	260	530
1998 d	Desert Pea	SA	100	Proof	10.37g	25mm	2,500/ 1,866	350	585
1998 d	Desert Pea	SA	150	Proof	15.16g	30mm	1,500/ 1,501	580	825
1999 e	Common Heath	VIC	100	Unc	10.37g	25mm	3,000/ 1,034	260	530
1999 e	Common Heath	VIC	100	Proof	10.37g	25mm	2,500/ 1,684	350	585
1999 e	Common Heath	VIC	150	Proof	15.16g	30mm	1,500/ 1,370	580	825
2000 f	C'town Orchid	QLD	100	Unc	10.37g	25mm	3,000/ 1,060	260	530
2000 f	C'town Orchid	QLD	100	Proof	10.37g	25mm	2,500/ 1,064	350	585
2000 f	C'town Orchid	QLD	150	Proof	15.16g	30mm	1,500/ 1,236	580	825
2001 g	Golden Wattle	CWH	100	Unc	10.37g	25mm	3,000/ 1,425	260	530
2001 g	Golden Wattle	CWH	100	Proof	10.37g	25mm	2,500/ 913	350	585
2001 g	Golden Wattle	CWH	150	Proof	15.16g	30mm	1,500/ 1,124	580	825
2002 h	Desert Rose	NT	100	Unc	10.37g	25mm	3,000/ 900	260	530
2002 h	Desert Rose	NT	100	Proof	10.37g	25mm	2,500/ 1,417	350	585
2002 h	Desert Rose	NT	150	Proof	15.16g	30mm	1,500/ 1,154	580	825
2003 i	Royal Blue Bell	ACT	100	Unc	10.37g	25mm	3,000/ 852	285	530
2003 i	Royal Blue Bell	ACT	100	Proof	10.37g	25mm	2,500/ 1,417	350	585
2003 i	Royal Blue Bell	ACT	150	Proof	15.16g	30mm	1,500/ 1,154	580	825
RARE AUSTRALIAN BIRDS - PROOF GOLD									
2004 j	Cassowary		150	Unc	10.37g	25mm	2,500/ 1,017	450	585
2004 j	Cassowary		200	Proof	15.16g	30mm	2,500/ 987	350	850
2005 k	Mallee Fowl		150	Unc	10.37g	25mm	3,000/ 2,057	260	585
2005 k	Mallee Fowl		200	Proof	15.16g	30mm	2,500/ 2,254	350	850
2006 l	Red Tailed Cockatoo		150	Unc	10.37g	25mm	3,000/ 1,800	260	585
2006 l	Red Tailed Cockatoo		200	Proof	15.16g	30mm	2,500/ 2,003	350	850

Obverse : Ian Rank - Broadley. **Reverse :** Wojciech Pietranik.
Specifications : Proof $100. Composition. 99.99% fine gold. Edge reeded. Weight 10.367 grams (1/3 troy ounce). Size 25mm. **Proof $150.** Composition. 99.99% fine gold. Edge reeded. Weight 15.51 grams (1/2 troy ounce). Size 30mm.

TWO HUNDRED DOLLARS

Machin Obv. 1980-84 Maklouf Obv.1985-86 Koala reverse 1981 [a] Wedding 1982 [b] Games

1987 [c] Departure 1988 [d] First Fleet 1989 [e] F'Neck Lizard 1990 [f] Platypus

1991 [g] Emu 1992 [h] Echidna 1993 [i] Squirrel Glider 1994 [j] Tasmanian Devil

1980-1986 $200 GOLD KOALA REVERSES

1980	200	Koala in tree	Unc	Gold	10 g	24mm	207,500	240	550
1980	200	Koala in tree	Proof	Gold	10 g	24mm	50,007	310	575
1983	200	Koala in tree	Unc	Gold	10 g	24mm	88,000	210	550
1983	200	Koala in tree	Proof	Gold	10 g	24mm	15,889	320	575
1984	200	Koala in tree	Unc	Gold	10 g	24mm	49,200	210	550
1984	200	Koala in tree	Proof	Gold	10 g	24mm	12,584	320	575
1985	200	Koala in tree	Unc	Gold	10 g	24mm	29,186	205	550
1985	200	Koala in tree	Proof	Gold	10 g	24mm	16,691	260	575
1986	200	Koala in tree	Unc	Gold	10 g	24mm	15,298	239	550
1986	200	Koala in tree	Proof	Gold	10 g	24mm	16,654	295	575

COMMEMORATIVE TWO HUNDRED DOLLARS ISSUES

1981 a	Charles & Di Wedding	Uncirc	10 gm	24mm	77,890	240	550
1981 a/1	Charles & Di Wedding	As abv	10 gm	24mm	As above	240	550
1982 b	Bris. C/weath Games	Uncirc	10 gm	24mm	77,206	210	550
1982 b	Bris. C/weath Games	Proof	10 gm	24mm	30,032	350	575
1987 c	First Fleet Departure	Uncirc	10 gm	24mm	20,800	239	550
1987 c	First Fleet Departure	Proof	10 gm	24mm	20,000	295	575
1988 d	First Fleet Arrival 1788	Uncirc	10 gm	24mm	11,000	239	550
1988 d	First Fleet Arrival 1788	Proof	10 gm	24mm	20,000	295	575
1989 e	Frilled Neck Lizard	Uncirc	10 gm	24mm	10,020	242	550
1989 e	Frilled Neck Lizard	Proof	10 gm	24mm	30,032	298	575
1990 f	Platypus	Uncirc	10 gm	24mm	8,340	242	550
1990 f	Platypus	Proof	10 gm	24mm	14,616	298	575
1991 g	Emu	Uncirc	10 gm	24mm	6,879	242	550
1991 g	Emu	Proof	10 gm	24mm	9,560	298	575
1992 h	Echidna	Uncirc	10 gm	24mm	3,935	242	550
1992 h	Echidna	Proof	10 gm	24mm	5,921	298	575
1993 i	Squirrel Glider	Uncirc	10 gm	24mm	3,014	242	550
1993 i	Squirrel Glider	Proof	10 gm	24mm	5,000	298	575
1994 j	Tasmanian Devil	Uncirc	10 gm	24mm	4,000	242	550
1994 j	Tasmanian Devil	Proof	10 gm	24mm	5,000	298	575

Specifications : Composition 91.67% gold; 8.33% copper. Edge reeded. Weight 10 grams. Size 24 mm.

[a/1] There are two distinct varieties concerning the blue vinyl satchel housing this coin that was only struck in Uncirculated form. One variety had large gold lettering while the second type shows much smaller lettering. They seem to be similar rarity.

MASTERPIECES IN SILVER

1988 BICENTENNIAL ISSUE

Reference #	**MS/Mc 01**
Mintage	19,999/ All sold
Silver Weight	2.19 oz Fine
Issue Price	95.00
Retail Average	75.00
Reference #	**P/Mc 01/a**
Special edition	Coin Fair Issue
Mintage	5,000/ All sold
Issue Price	135.00
Retail Average	60.00

All coins sterling silver (92.5% fine); 7.5% copper.

Consisting of four proof sterling silver versions of the normal base metal 1988 commemorative issues. Of the 25,000 issued, 5000 were released at the Sydney Coin Fair on November 12 - 13, 1988. The Coin Fair issue includes a specially printed ribbon wrap-around.

ERROR ISSUE - 1988 BICENTENNIAL ISSUE

Reference #	**MS/Mc 02**
Description 3.	Standard Issue Wrong date on box
Mintage	Unknown. Rare ?
Issue Price	95.00
Retail Average	TBA

Collector David Nestor reported a 1988 set with the lid of the box dated 1989. The RAM confirmed that the original intention was to use the same shaped box for the 1989 issue. However the decision to produce a six piece silver set caused a rethink. The RAM correspondent told Mr Nestor that an unknown number of cases were made up with the 1989 lettering and accidently mixed up with the packaging of the 1988 issue.

1989 FIFTY CENT COLLECTION

Reference #	**MS/Mc 03a**
Description 1.	Standard Issue
Mintage	22,499/ 22,499
Silver Weight	3.37 oz Fine
Issue Price	125.00
Retail Average	95.00
Reference #	**P/Mc 03b**
Description 2.	Coin Fair Issue
Mintage	2,500/ All sold
Issue Price	135.00

All coins sterling silver (92.5% fine); 7.5% copper.

Consisting of five proof sterling silver dated "copies" of Australia's five commemorative fifty cent pieces from 1970 to 1988 and a silver numbered ingot. All five coins are dated 1989. A limited number were released at the Sydney Coin Fair on November 18 & 19, 1989.

1990 ONE DOLLAR COLLECTION

Reference #	**MS/Mc 04a**
Mintage	22,499/ 22,499
Silver Weight	2.23 oz Fine
Issue Price	130.00
Retail Average	65.00
Reference #	**P/Mc 04b**
Description 2.	Coin Fair Issue
Mintage	2,500/ 2,500
Issue Price	135.00
Retail Average	70.00

Consisting of three proof sterling silver versions of the normal base metal One Dollar reverses struck since its inception in 1984. The set also contains an individually numbered ingot of sterling silver fashioned in the shape of the dollar note. Of the 25,000 sets issued, 2500 (1 to 2500) were sold at the Sydney International Coin Fair on November 17 - 18, 1990.

MASTERPIECES IN SILVER

1991 CIRCULATION COINS

Reference #	**MS/Mc 05a**
Description 1.	Standard Issue
Mintage	24,000/ 24,000
Silver Weight	2.56 oz Fine
Issue Price	140.00
Retail Average	95.00
Reference #	**MS/Mc 05b**
Description 2.	Coin Fair Issue
Mintage	1,000/ All sold
Issue Price	110.00

THIS IS THE LAST OF THE YEARLY COIN FAIR ISSUES

All coins sterling silver (92.5% fine); 7.5% copper.

Consisting of proof quality sterling silver versions of all eight base metal circulation coins plus an individually numbered silver ingot featuring the Australian Coat of Arms. It was also a farewell set for the one and two cent pieces that were deleted from the coinage in 1991. 1000 sets were issued at the Sydney Coin Fair on November 16 - 17, 1991.

1992 THE ROYAL LADIES

TWENTY FIVE DOLLARS ISSUE	
Reference #	**MS/Mc 06a**
Mintage	To order/ 11,611
Silver Weight	5.50 oz Fine
Issue Price	135.00
Retail Average	175.00

$250 DOLLARS ISSUE	
Reference #	**MS/Mc 06b**
Mintage	To order/ 1,045
Gold Weight	2.9981 oz Fine
Issue Price	2,240.00
Retail Average	4,500.00

Issued to commemorate the 40th anniversary of the accession of Queen Elizabeth II (1952 - 1992). The reverses, designed by Stuart Devlin, portray the Queen Mother (the wife of the late George VI); the late Princess Diana and the Princess Royal Anne facing to the right and the late Princess Margaret facing left. The set was offered in pure gold and pure silver versions.

TWENTY FIVE DOLLARS - PROOF STERLING SILVER

Sterling silver (92.5% fine). Contains four proof silver crowns plus a silver Royal Medallion.

ADDITIONAL SPECIFICATIONS

F/Value	Diameter	Thickness	Weight	Edge
$25.00	38.90 mm	3.10 mm	33.63 gms	Reeded
Medallion	45.00 mm	3.50 mm	50.44 gms	Plain

$250 DOLLARS - PROOF GOLD

22 Carat gold (91.67 fine). Contains four proof gold coins plus a silver Royal Medallion.

ADDITIONAL SPECIFICATIONS

F/Value	Diameter	Thickness	Weight	Edge
$250.00	28.12 mm	2.10 mm	16.95 gms	Reeded
Medallion	34.00 mm	2.50 mm	33.93 gms	Plain

In 2010, a possibly unique pattern turned up that gave gravitas to a long assumed theory that the set offered to collectors was actually *'Try Two'* as the Palace went into meltdown when it was proposed that the original set included the perennial broke Sarah Ferguson. A number of widely published photographs at the time showed that while Fergie had a somewhat soiled past she had impeccably clean toes! The recently discovered rejected Pattern shows the portrait of the far more saintly Diana. While coins in the set released for collectors measure 28mm and have a denomination of $250, the Pattern measures 18mm and has a denomination of $25. Patterns, struck and forwarded to the Queen for her approval were rejected. The RAM completely revamped the collection at the request of Buckingham Palace. The collection finally approved and released in 1992 comprised four 28mm gold $250 coins and a gold medal. Any future reference to Fergie was confined to the tabloids.

MASTERPIECES IN SILVER

1993 THE EXPLORERS - PART ONE

Reference #	**MS/Mc 07**
Description 1.	Standard Issue
Mintage	20,000/ 12,349
Silver Weight	5.32 oz Fine
Issue Price	135.00
Retail Average	175.00

All coins sterling silver (92.5% pure); 7.5% copper

The 1993 Masterpieces in Silver was the first in a new series paying tribute to the people who pioneered the development of Australia. Each collection consists of five sterling silver proof coins that have a nominal face value of five dollars. With a diameter of 38.90 mm, they are among the largest coins struck by the Royal Australian Mint. The 1993 designs pay tribute to our original inhabitants, the Aborigines as well as explorers Abel Tasman, James Cook, Matthew Flinders, Gregory Blaxland, William Lawson and William Charles Wentworth.

1994 THE EXPLORERS - PART TWO

Reference #	**MS/Mc 08**
Description 1.	Standard Issue
Mintage	20,000/ 18,364
Silver Weight	5.32 oz Fine
Issue Price	135.00
Retail Average	125.00

All coins sterling silver (92.5% pure); 7.5% copper

The 1994 Masterpieces in Silver was the second release of the Explorers Series that paid tribute to Australia's first human inhabitants; the early sea - faring explorers and the pioneers who followed. This second series acknowledges the contributions of John McDouall Stuart; Sir Douglas Mawson; Charles Sturt; Ludwig Leichhardt and Sir John Forrest.

1995 COLONIAL AUSTRALIA

Reference #	**MS/Mc 09**
Description 1.	Standard Issue
Mintage	20,000/ 14,000
Silver Weight	5.32 oz Fine
Issue Price	140.00
Retail Average	175.00

All coins sterling silver

The 1995 Masterpieces in Silver, titled "Colonial Australia", commemorates the people, places and events that collectively changed Australia from a struggling penal settlement into a wealthy young nation. This set of five coins celebrates the major advancements in our primary industry, communications, transport and economy. Specifically the coins pay tribute to Elizabeth Macarthur's involvement in the wool export industry; the founding and planning of Adelaide by Colonel William Light; the economic impetus of the gold rush and the opening up of transport and communications networks by Cobb & Co and Charles Todd's overland telegraph.

HOW VALUES ARE DETERMINED

The introduction of the internet and third party grading or "slabbing" services, are the latest phases in the evolution of this ever changing hobby. This has added an extra complexity in pricing up a guide like this and the expectations some people might expect when selling. We strongly suggest you read our pricing procedure as outlined on Page 8.

MASTERPIECES IN SILVER

1996 NATIONAL IDENTITY

Reference #	**MS/Mc 10**
Description 1.	Standard Issue
Mintage	20,000/ 9,031
Silver Weight	5.32 oz Fine
Issue Price	140.00
Retail Average	175.00

All coins .925 sterling silver

The 1996 Masterpieces in Silver, titled "Shaping a National Identity", pays tribute to the people and events that have had a major influence in making us uniquely Australian. From Tom Robert's passion as an impressionist painter, Henry Lawson's push for 'realism' in literature, Dame Nellie Melba's dazzling voice and flamboyant lifestyle through to the stockman who embodied tenacity and personified the image of the hard working Australian and horse racing, the one sport that, even today, stops the entire nation with the running of the now world famous "Melbourne Cup" at Flemington racecourse each November.

1997 THE OPENING OF A CONTINENT

Reference #	**MS/Mc 11**
Mintage	10,000/ All sold
Silver Weight	5.32 oz Fine
Issue Price	140.00
Retail Average	175.00

All coins .925 sterling silver

"The Opening Of The Continent" commemorates the many forms of early transport, from camels to steam trains, which opened up this vast continent. In the mid - 19th century the Victorian Government imported 24 camels from India as well as their Afghan cameleers. As the wool industry grew in the 1860s, steam boats were relied upon to carry the wool to coastal destinations. The very first Australian railway line was a mere two and a half miles and travelled from the Melbourne port of Sandridge to the city centre. It was the first working link from a commercial centre in the world. The united strength of Australia's bullock teams was a familiar sight in the country and inspired Susannah Prichard to write the novel "Working Bullocks". The first steam engine was imported into Australia in 1813 to work in the Sydney flour mill.

1998 THE COMMEMORATIVE SET

Reference #	**MS/Mc 12**
Mintage	15,000/ All sold
Silver Weight	4.60 oz Fine
Issue Price	165.00
Retail Average	175.00

All coins .999 fine Silver

This sets commemorates the various reverse designs for the twenty cent - sized coins including the normal platypus reverse; the UN coin of 1995 and the pre-decimal issues which includes the 1910 and 1938 normal reverse issues. Also included is the commemorative florins issued for 1927 Canberra; 1934/35 Melbourne Centenary; 1951 Federation florin and 1954 Royal Visit. The large five shilling piece of 1937 completes the series.

MASTERPIECES IN SILVER

1999 CIRCULATION COINS

Reference #	**MS/Mc 13**
Mintage	15,000/ All sold
Silver Weight	1.29 oz Fine
Issue Price	125.00
Retail Average	135.00

The 1999 Masterpieces in silver continued the theme of featuring pre-decimal coinage issues which made the 1998 masterpieces such a success and the fastest product sellout in recent history. The 1999 set of six coins featured the dates of rare coins in each of the main denominations. These included the 1930 penny; the 1920 (Sydney Mint) sovereign; the 1940 shilling; 1918 sixpence and the 1939 (kangaroo reverse) halfpenny. Although pre-decimal coins, each of the pure silver masterpieces had a decimal value as per the table below. Each of the coins carried the then new obverse design by Ian Rank - Broadley.

Date	Description	Value	Diameter	Weight
1939	Halfpenny	Five cents	25.00 mm	5.53 gms
1930	Penny	Ten cents	30.00 mm	8.36 gms
1942	Threepence	Twenty cents	17.53 mm	2.99 gms
1918	Sixpence	Fifty cents	19.41 mm	3.24 gms
1940	Shilling	One dollar	23.60 mm	6.57 gms
1920	Sovereign	Two dollars	28.52 mm	13.36 gms

2000 TWENTIETH CENTURY MONARCHS

Reference #	**MS/Mc 14**
Mintage	15,000/ 10,412
Silver Weight	3.68 oz Fine
Issue Price	125.00
Retail Average	95.00

All coins .999 fine Silver

This set features the actual portraits of all the monarchs who have appeared on 20th century coinage. The portrait of Queen Victoria appeared only on the gold sovereign and half sovereign as no silver or bronze coins were struck in Australia during her reign. Those that did circulate were struck in the UK. It is interesting to note that the portraits of the Kings that followed - Edward VII and George V - were different on the gold coinage where they were both shown uncrowned. The four remaining designs shown here were used on all Commonwealth of Australia silver and bronze issues.

ADDITIONAL SPECIFICATIONS

Monarch	Value	Diameter	Weight
King Edward VII	Twenty cents	28.52 mm	13.36 gms
King George V	Twenty cents	28.52 mm	13.36 gms
Queen Elizabeth II	Twenty cents	28.52 mm	13.36 gms
King George VI	Fifty cents	38.74 mm	36.31 gms
Queen Victoria	Two dollars	20.50 mm	8.55 gms
Plaque	Fine Silver (99.9%)	54 x 35 mm	29.50 gms

MASTERPIECES IN SILVER

2001 FEDERATION (1901 - 2001)

Reference #	**MS/Mc 15**
Mintage	5,000/ All sold
Silver Weight	7.00 oz Fine
Issue Price	250.00
Retail Average	175.00

All coins .999 fine Silver

This set celebrates the dedicated group of Australians who played a fundamental role in shaping our Constitution and the creation of Federation. Each coin shows people grouped according to the nature of their contribution to the development of Australia. A detailed biography of each pioneer is included in a 28-page booklet.

2002 VOYAGES INTO HISTORY

Reference #	**MS/Mc 16**
Mintage	10,000/ 9,096
Silver Weight	4.67 oz Fine
Issue Price	165.00
Retail Average	195.00

All coins .999 fine Silver

Featuring four of the European vessels that were amongst the first to sail the waters of the *"Great South Land"* long before the days of steam.

DUYFKEN : Under the command of Willem Janszoon, the 17th century Dutch square-rigger, the Duyfken, *(Little Dove)* is regarded as the first European vessel to record the sighting of the Australian land mass (Cape Yorke Peninsula).

HMB ENDEAVOUR : Without doubt the best known vessel of the 18th century. This humble refitted Whitby collier sailed into history during 1769-1771 when Capt. James Cook took the tiny craft around the world on a voyage of discovery.

HMS SIRIUS : This was the flagship of the First Fleet which landed in Botany Bay and then Port Jackson (Sydney Harbour) in 1788. It was commanded by Captain Arthur Phillip who was to be the colony's first Governor.

HMS INVESTIGATOR : In 1801-03 Matthew Flinders sailed this ship around Australia for the first time. His charts were so accurate that many were used well into the 20th century.

2003 PORT PHILLIP PATTERNS

Reference #	**MS/Mc 17**
Mintage	10,000/ 7,489
Silver Weight	3.99 oz Fine
Issue Price	160.00
Retail Average	185.00

All coins .999 fine Silver

The 2003 Masterpieces in Silver celebrates the 150th anniversary of the establishment of the Port Phillip/Kangaroo Office. Also known as the Taylor Patterns after the entrepreneur who devised the scheme that was supposed to make him a wealthy man. The venture failed after a sucessession of unforeseen setbacks.

Face Value	Value	Diameter	Weight
Quarter Ounce	One Dollar	28.52 mm	13.36 gms
Half Ounce	Two Dollars	32.50 mm	18.22 gms
One Ounce	Five Dollars	38.74 mm	36.31 gms
Two Ounces	Ten Dollars	38.74 mm	36.31 gms
Plaque	Fine silver	Rectangular	19.90 gms

MASTERPIECES IN SILVER

2004 20 YEARS OF THE ONE DOLLAR

Reference #	**MS/Mc 18**
Mintage	18,000/ 8,250
Silver Weight	2.51 oz Fine
Issue Price	195.00
Retail Average	225.00

All coins .999 fine Silver

One area of numismatics most collectors find fascinating in the small and select series of *patterns*. In general these are the coins and banknotes that didn't get much further than the drawing board. Some of the dies and p atterns shown above are on display at the tourist gallery of the Royal Australian Mint These unusual pieces are extremely rare and cost about the same amount as an average sized house when they do come onto the market. In celebrating the 20th anniversary of the introduction of the $1 coin, the RAM has included three previously unseen patterns to the mix.

THERE WAS NO 2005 MASTERPIECES IN SILVER

2006 TWENTIETH CENTURY ART

Reference #	**MS/Mc 19**
Mintage	10,000/ 6,018
Silver Weight	4.67 oz Fine
Issue Price	195.00
Retail Average	125.00

All coins .999 fine Silver

BRETT WHITELEY (1939 - 1991) :- *SELF PORTRAIT IN THE STUDIO* (1976). Born in Sydney, Whiteley matured as an artist in Europe and London and established an international reputation.
JEFFREY SMART (1921-) :- *KESWICK SIDING* (1945). Born in Adelaide, Smart received formal academic training and at the same time experienced his first modernistic influence and this shaped his direction as a realist painter.
RUSSELL DRYSDALE (1912- 1981) :- *THE DROVER'S WIFE* (1945). Drysdale was the first Australian artist to take as his primary subject the complex relationships between the landscape and inhabitants of inland Australia. He achieved international attention for this distinctly 'Australian' character in his work.
SIDNEY NOLAN (1917- 1992) :- *BURKE and WILLS EXPEDITION* (1948). Sidney Nolan was born in Melbourne where he painted his most famous series based on the outlaw Ned Kelly in 1946-1947.

2007 TWENTIETH CENTURY ART

Reference #	**MS/Mc 20**
Mintage	10,000/ 3,975
Silver Weight	4.67 oz Fine
Issue Price	195.00
Retail Average	210.00

All coins .999 fine Silver

.GRACE COSSINGTON (1892 - 1984) :- *CURVE OF THE BRIDGE.* She used great sunlight and wonderful patterns of vibrant colour with cool colours added to shadows, giving them a sense of energy.
CLIFFORD POSSUM TJAPALTJARRI (1934 - 2002) :- *YUELAMU HONEY ANT DREAMING.* Clifford was the most famous of the Aboriginal artists when the "dot art" painting style began.
WILLIAM DOBELL (1899 - 1970) :- *MARGARET OLLEY.* Born in Newcastle, Sir William Dobell was one of the world's leading modern portraitists. His best portraits reveal extraordinary psychological insight.
MARGARET PRESTON (1875 - 1963) :- *IMPLEMENT BLUE.* Well known for her decorative still lifes, she was also a skilful wood engraver and linocut printer.

MASTERPIECES IN SILVER

2008 FLYING THROUGH TIME

Avro 504K	(a) Part of dual set
Reference #	MS/Mc 21a
Mintage	7,000/ 1,903
Silver Weight	2.33 oz Fine
Airbus A380	**(b) Part of dual set**
Reference #	P/Mc 21b
Issue Price	105.00
Retail Average	75.00

All coins .999 fine Silver

2008 (a) Avro 504K 2008 (b) Airbus A 380

2009 FLYING THROUGH TIME

De Havilland DH 86	(c) Part of dual set
Reference #	MS/Mc 21c
Mintage	7,000/ 1,590
Silver Weight	2.33 oz Fine
Constellation L749	**(d) Part of dual set**
Reference #	P/Mc 21d
Issue Price	105.00
Retail Average	75.00

All coins fine .999 Silver

2009 (c) De Havilland DH 86 2009 (d) Constellation L749

2010 FLYING THROUGH TIME

Boeing 747	(e) Part of dual set
Reference #	MS/Mc 21e
Mintage	7,000/ 1,300
Silver Weight	2.33 oz Fine
S 25 Sandringham	**(f) Part of dual set**
Reference #	MS/Mc 21f
Issue Price	105.00
Retail Average	75.00

All coins .999 fine Silver

2010 (e) Boeing 747 2010 (f) S 25 Sandringham

2011 ROYAL AUSTRALIAN NAVY

Reference #	MS/Mc 22
Mintage	5,000/ TBA
Silver Weight	3.91 oz Fine
Issue Price	195.00
Retail Average	210.00

All coins .999 fine Silver

HMAS AE2, one of the very first of the Royal Australian Navy's submarines, commissioned in 1914 following the outbreak of World War I.
HMAS Australia II, a county class heavy cruiser commissioned in 1928.
HMAS Hobart II, an Adams class guided missile destroyer ordered for the Royal Australian Navy in the 1960s.
HMAS Yarra III, a modified type 12 frigate, commissioned in 1961.
HMAS Sydney III, a veteran of two tours of duty during the Korean War and completed 24 round trips between Australia and Vung Tau during the Vietnam War.
HMAS Armidale II, a boarder protection patrol boat commissioned in 2005.

AUSTRALIAN MINT SETS

Date	Description	One Year Special Issues			Mintage	Issue Price	Current Retail
1966	Six circulation coins in blue card	—	—	—	77,250	24.5	135
1966	Blue vinyl wallet	—	—	—	15,809	1.50	160
1966 a	Reserve Bank coloured wallet	—	—	—	12,260	1.00	180
1966 b	VIP presentation wallet	—	—	—	520	Gift	700
1966 c	Operation "Fastbuck" wallet	—	—	—	70	Gift	1,800
1966	1¢ & 2¢ "Green" card	—	—	—	43,100	.05	110
1969	Red wallet	—	—	—	16,825	1.5	125
1969	Blue wallet	—	—	—	14,351	1.5	145
1970	Captain Cook Bicentenary	—	50¢	—	40,230	1.5	50
1971		—	—	—	28,572	1.5	110
1972		—	—	—	39,065	1.5	110
1973		—	—	—	30,928	1.7	110
1974		—	—	—	25,475	1.7	85
1975		—	—	—	30,121	1.7	40
1976		—	—	—	40,004	1.8	60
1977	QE II 25th Anniversary Jubilee	—	50¢	—	128,010	1.8	25
1978		—	—	—	70,006	2	25
1979		—	—	—	70,006	2	25
1980		—	—	—	100,000	2.2	19
1981		—	—	—	120,000	3	18
1982	XII C'wealth Games (Bris.)	—	50¢	—	195,950	3	15
1983		—	—	—	155,700	3	35

(a) Approximately 12,260 red, blue, green and black Reserve Bank wallets were sold through the RAM. Covers feature the wording. "Australian Decimal Currency First Issue 1966" along with a map of Australia. More might have been sold through the Reserve Bank and other outlets. Accurate records are difficult to source.

(b) Dark blue wallet with gold printing of coat of arms including date "14th February, 1966".

(c) The logistics of ensuring that virtually every bank in Australia had adequate supplies of coins and banknotes on February 14, 1966 was a monumental task that went off without any serious problems being reported. Amazingly there wasn't a single robbery despite the fact that around 600 million coins and 150 million banknotes were involved. In appreciation for their efforts, around 70 T.N.T drivers were presented with a special 1966 mint set *(see illustration at right)* as a memento of their participation in "Operation Fastbuck". This was the code - name for the highly confidential pre-release distribution of decimal currency around Australia. The name of each driver was impressed on the cover of the wallet. The full inscription read " Presented by the / Reserve Bank of Australia / to / ... *(name of driver)*... / as a memento of / his participation in / "Operation Fastbuck" / Nov. 1965 - Feb. 1966". This wallet was followed by a series of similar issues prepared for official gifts and others for the general collector. Both the Royal Australian Mint and the Reserve Bank produced plastic wallets to house the full set of decimal coins from one cent to fifty cents. The issues are easily distinguished by their distinctive covers. The RAM issue carried the Australian Coat of Arms while the Reserve Bank issue featured a map of Australia. The 1966 RAM wallet was blue while those from the Reserve Bank are known in red, blue, green and black. All above wallets are considered scarce. The RAM produced two wallets. One had the title "Australian Decimal Coins 14th February, 1966" and was a VIP issue. Only 520 were distributed. The normal 1966 blue wallet has the coat of arms and a shortened legend that simply reads : "Royal Australian Mint." The vinyl wallet was used until 1983. It was not particularly successful as the plastic was of poor quality and the method of packaging meant the coin was not sealed in an airtight environment. It is normal for the coins to show toning.

1966 Operation Fastbuck. Only 70 issued. Current Value .$1,800

AUSTRALIAN MINT SETS

Date	Description	One Year Special Issues			Mintage	Issue Price	Current Retail
BUBBLE PACK INTRODUCED							
1984 a	Clear plastic insert	—	—	—	150,014	3.2	65
1984 a/1	Yellow coloured plastic covering	—	—	—	Ditto	3.2	35
1985	All coins have regular reverses	—	—	—	170,000	4.2	60
1985 a/1	Yellow coloured plastic covering	—	—	—	Ditto	3.2	45
1986	International Year of Peace	—	—	$1	180,000	4.5	20
1987	All coins have regular reverses	—	—	—	200,000	9.7	25
1988	First Fleet Bicentenary	—	50¢	$1	240,000	12	20
1988 b	Coin Fair issue	—	—	—	10,000	13	25
1989	All coins have regular reverses	—	—	—	150,602	13.5	45
1990	All coins have regular reverses	—	—	—	103,766	15	100
1991	Decimal Currency 25th Anniv.	—	50¢	—	147,700	15	35
1991 c	Singapore Coin Fair issue	—	—	—	200	12.75	70
1992	Barcelona Olympic Games	—	—	$1	118,528	15	75
1993	Landcare. Water conservation	—	—	$1	86,068	15	55
1994	International Year of the Family	—	50¢	—	91,942	15	35
1994 d	As above but with 50¢ wide date	—	50¢	—	Ditto	15	50
1995	End WWII. 50th Anniversary	—	50¢	—	96,079	15	60
1996	Sir Henry Parkes Centenary	—	—	$1	108,773	18.75	70
1997	Sir Charles Kingsford - Smith	—	—	$1	71,022	18.75	85
1998	Bass and Flinders Anniversary	—	50¢	—	74,108	18.75	35
1999	International Year of Older Persons	—	—	$1	70,067	19.95	45
2000	Millennium Celebration. Plain 50¢ flag	—	50¢	—	97,550	19.95	100
2001	Centenary of Federation	—	50¢	$1	90,822	22.7	55
2002	Year of the Outback	—	50¢	$1	68,752	22.7	45
2003	Australia's Volunteers	20¢	50¢	$1	80,512	22.7	35
2004 e	All coins have regular reverses	—	—	—	67,795	23.5	50
2005	End of WWII 60th Anniversary	20¢	50¢	$1	71,546	23.5	55
2006 f	40 Years of Decimals (inc 1¢ & 2¢)	—	—	—	84,407	23.5	45
2006 g	*Berlin World Money Fair. 1st issue*	—	—	—	1,500	25	80
2006 h	ANDA Canberra Coin Fair	—	—	—	1,500	35	80
2007 i	Lifesaver with exclusive 20¢ coin	20¢	—	$1	66,641	23	35
2007	*Berlin World Money Fair. 2nd issue*	20¢	—	$1	1,500	25	70
2008 j	International Year of Planet Earth	20¢	—	—	63,734	26	25

(a) Two types of folder have been sighted. Both light and blue folders are known.
(a/1) During the packaging stage an unknown quantity of sets were produced with a yellow coloured laminate covering the obverse side of the coins. This detracts from the value of the set as the coins are hard to see.
(b) Outer packet contained sticker relating to being a coin fair issue.
(c) Outer pocket has a yellow sticker, with the wording : *"1 in 200! This set is one of only two hundred specially packed for the 1991 Singapore Coin Convention by the Royal Australian Mint."* Set also contains a special certificate.
(d) About 20% of 1994 mint sets contain 50¢ with wide date.
(e) 2004 Mint Sets show a variety of 20¢ & 50¢ "Large Head" & "Small Head" types.
(f) This issue also included examples of the now obsolete one and two cent coins.
(g) Issued in February 2006 by the RAM for release at the Berlin World Money Fair. The eight coin set has a special circular overprint on the outer sleeve.
(h) On the weekend of February 11 & 12, 2006, ANDA conducted its inaugural Fair at the Canberra Rydges Lakeside Hotel. To commemorate the event, the RAM had the outer sleeve of 1500 2006 mint sets overprinted with the ANDA logo.
(i) 6 coin set celebrating the Year of the Surf Lifesaver with commemorative 20 cents.
(j) 6 coin International Year of Planet Earth set with commemorative $1 and 20 cents.

ERROR SETS

Date	Description	Mintage	Issue Price	Current Retail
1986	Contains 10¢ coin dated 1985	Unknown	4.5	350
1989 •	10¢ coin facing the wrong way	Unknown	n/a	225
1991 •	Contains 5¢ coin dated 1990	Unknown	n/a	200
1991	All coins upside down	Unique?	15	700
1994	Contains $2 coin dated 1993	Unknown	15	300
1995	$2 coin facing wrong way	Unique?	15	600
1995	5¢ coin facing wrong way	Unique?	15	600
2001	Contains $2 coin dated 2000	Unique?	22.5	550
2007	Has Royal Diamond Wedding 50¢	Unique?	n/a	n/a

• The above two errors are recent discoveries reported by John O'Connor while preparing the catalogue for Noble Auctions Sale 108 in July 2015.

AUSTRALIAN MINT SETS

Date	Description	One Year Special Issues			Mintage	Issue Price	Current Retail
2009 l	International Year of Astronomy	20¢	—	—	50,957	35	45
2009	*Berlin World Money Fair. 3rd issue*	20¢	—	—	1,500	26.5	50
2009 m	Brisbane ANDA Fair. (Feb 5 & 6)	20¢	—	—	1,500	35	40
2009 m	Sydney ANDA Fair. (Aug 13 & 14)	20¢	—	—	1,498	35	40
2009 m	Melbourne ANDA Fair. (July 2 & 3)	20¢	—	—	1,497	35	40
2010	All coins have regular reverses	—	—	—	48,489	30	40
2010	*Berlin World Money Fair. 4th issue*	—	—	—	1,500	26	60
2010 n	Boston ANA Fair (USA) overprint	—	—	—	2,500	35	5
2011	All coins have regular reverses	—	—	—	40,383	30	85
2011	*Berlin World Money Fair. 5th issue*	—	—	—	1,500	40	85
2012	Featuring hyper-metallic printed 50¢	—	50¢	—	57.054	32.5	95
2012	Boston ANA Fair (USA) overprint	—	50¢	—	2.500	40	45
2012	*Berlin World Money Fair. 6th issue*	—	50¢	—	1,500	40	60
2013	Featuring hyper-metallic printed 20¢	20¢	—	—	44,750	32.5	75
2013	*Berlin World Money Fair. 7th issue*	20¢	—	—	1,500	49.95	85
2014	All six coins with coloured $1	—	—	$1	42,277	32.5	75
2014	*Berlin World Money Fair. 8th issue*	—	—	$1	1,500	49.95	50
2015	RAM. 50th Anniversary Six coin set	—	50¢	—	48,682	25	35
2015	*Berlin World Money Fair. 9th issue*	—	50¢	—	1,000	2.5	160
2016	50th Anniversary of Decimal Currency				61,468	30	35
2016 o	*Berlin World Money Fair. 10th issue*	—	50¢	—	1,250	25	60
2016	In Come the Dollars [1¢ to 50¢]	*Listed & illustrated on page 243*					
2017	Effigy of an Era. Ian Rank Broadley	—	—	—	n/a	25	25
2017 p	*Berlin World Money Fair. 10th issue*	—	—	—	1,250	25	65

(l) The ANDA special issues have an overprint on the outer packaging.
(m) The six coin set celebrating the *International Year of Astronomy* with commemorative 20 cents with the normal $1.
(n) This issue was released at the Boston Numismatic Society Coin Fair to celebrate the 25th anniversary of the sister city relationship between Boston, USA and Melbourne, Australia. The set was contained in its own specially printed packaging that featured the skylines of both cities
(o) Released at the Berlin Money Expo, this set had a bespoke cover promoting the WLF.

WEDDING SET

Coins included in this series were specimen finish until 2009. In 2010 proof quality coins were introduced. Sets issued in their own distinctive cream coloured case reading :- "Australian Wedding Coin Collection." The set features a nickel-silver inscription plaque on which the names of the couple or a special message can be engraved. The cover of the case features two silver Brolgas in a courtship dance. Known for their life-long commitment to the same partnership, these majestic natives of the Australian wetlands also feature on the accompanying gift card.

Date	Description	Mintage	Issue Price	Current Retail
	FOLLOWING COINS ARE ALL SPECIMEN QUALITY			
2002	Wedding set with nickel silver plaque	3,322	69.5	100
2003	Wedding set with nickel silver plaque	3,249	69.5	110
2004	Wedding set with nickel silver plaque	3,963	73	120
2005	Wedding set with nickel silver plaque	3,627	77	100
2006	Wedding set with nickel silver plaque	2,752	77	90
2007	Wedding set with nickel silver plaque	2,629	77	99
2008	Wedding set with nickel silver plaque	3,278	77	99
2009	Wedding set with new design presentation	2,824	95	95
	FOLLOWING COINS ARE ALL PROOF QUALITY			
2010	Wedding set with updated design	2,493	120	120
2011	Wedding set with updated design	2,506	120	120
2012	Wedding set with normal 50¢ reverse	2,027	125	145
2013	Wedding set with normal 20¢ reverse	n/a	145	145
2014	Wedding set with normal $1 reverse	n/a	145	145

AUSTRALIAN PROOF SETS

Prices are for official RAM issues and reflect the value for sets with perfect unblemished coins. Coins that are spotted or enclosed in cracked or scratched cases should also be heavily discounted. Sets missing packaging and certificates are also of lesser value.

The iconic 1966 proof set was a one year type that was issued in two distinct cases. Although all the coins were dated 1966, records show it took well into 1967 to fulfil all orders. The first presentation case had a timber frame, which over the years, exuded organic fumes that toned the coins. When the original allocation of cases were exhausted, a new shipment of cases arrived from South Africa. These were made from pressed metal. In general, coins issued in the metal case show less toning or carbon spots.
a. 1966 hinged lid case showing coins were not protected. b. Timber framed case. c. Metal pressed case. When the production of proof sets resumed with the 1969 issue of the 50¢ coin, the proof coins were encased in plastic and ultrasonically sealed. While packaging has changed over the years, this form of packaging has remained largely unchanged. The concept remains popular as the coins are protected and can still be seen both sides.

Date	Description	One Year Special Issues	Mintage	Issue Price	Current Retail
1966	Light or dark blue case	— — —	18,054	12.5	425
1966	Toned coins	— — —	Ditto	12.5	150
1966 a	In sealed 1969 case	— — —	12	—	500
1969	All coins have regular reverses	— — —	13,056	10	350
1969	Toned coins	— — —	Ditto	10	150
1970	Captain Cook Bicentenary	— 50¢ —	15,368	10	195
1971	All coins have regular reverses	— — —	10,066	10	220
1972	All coins have regular reverses	— — —	10,272	10.5	220
1973	All coins have regular reverses	— — —	10,090	11	230
1974	All coins have regular reverses	— — —	10,918	11	170
1975	All coins have regular reverses	— — —	23,021	12	45
1976	All coins have regular reverses	— — —	21,200	13.5	60
1977	QE II 25th Anniversary Jubilee	— 50¢ —	55,006	13.5	30
1978	All coins have regular reverses	— — —	38,519	16.5	35
1979	All coins have regular reverses	— — —	36,006	16.5	40
1979	(50¢) Double bar variety	— — —	Ditto	16.5	130
1980	All coins have regular reverses	— — —	68,000	18	20
1981	All coins have regular reverses	— — —	86,100	35	30
1981b	Missing 4th claw,left paw from 20¢	— — —	Ditto	35	100
1981	Blue Casing. Export Issue	— — —	Ditto	35	50
1982	XII C'wealth Games (Bris.)	— 50¢ —	100,000	38	30
1982	Blue Casing. Export Issue	— — —	Ditto	35	50
1983	All coins have regular reverses	— — —	80,000	38	30
1983	Blue Casing. Export Issue	— — —	Ditto	35	50
1984	All coins have regular reverses	— — —	61,000	38.5	35
1984	Blue Casing. Export Issue	— — —	Ditto	35	50

(a) All 1966 proof sets were issued in an unsealed hinged-lid presentation case. Just 12 sets of 1966 coins were later used in an experimental sealed plastic case. This case was later used from 1969 to 1984.
(b) 1981 was a difficult year for the RAM with a long strike that required many of the circulation coins of that year being struck at other Royal mints in Wales and Canada. Already we have found a variety in the 1981 Canadian circulation 20 cent piece where there is a 3.5 claw variation. It appears that the RAM also has a similar variation with a small number of 1981 proof sets. In this case the fourth claw on the left paw of the 20 cent coin is missing. Research continues.

AUSTRALIAN PROOF SETS

A (—) Indicates standard reverse. A numeral (20¢, 50¢ or $1) signifies a special design or shape. A coloured denomination (20¢, 50¢ or $1) indicates that the coin is gilded, plated, coloured etc.

Date	Description	20¢	50¢	$1	Mintage	Issue Price	Current Retail
NEW ONE DOLLAR COIN INCLUDED AND NEW STYLE PACKAGING							
1985	All coins have regular reverses	—	—	—	74,089	45	50
1986	International Year of Peace	—	—	$1	67,000	49	40
1987	All coins have regular reverses	—	—	—	69,684	49	40
TWO DOLLAR COIN INCLUDED							
1988	First Fleet Bicentenary ($2)	—	50¢	$1	101,518	55	50
1988	Coin Fair issue	—	50¢	$1	3,000	60	60
1989	All coins have regular reverses	—	—	—	67,618	55	45
1989	Coin Fair issue	—	—	—	5,000	60	60
1990	All coins have regular reverses	—	—	—	51,015	60	95
1990	Coin Fair issue	—	—	—	1,985	60	100
1991	Decimal Currency 25th Anniv	—	50¢	—	41,490	60	90
1991 a	Singapore Coin Fair issue	—	50¢	—	1,000	51	295
ONE AND TWO CENT COINS DELETED							
1992	Barcelona Olympic Games	—	—	$1	56,367	60	65
1993	Landcare. Water Conservation	—	—	$1	40,255	60	75
1994	Year of the Family	—	50¢	—	39,004	60	65
1995	End of WWII. 'Weary' Dunlop	—	50¢	—	48,537	60	80
1996	Sir Henry Parkes Centenary	—	—	$1	33,350	60	135
1997	Sir Charles Kingsford-Smith	—	—	$1	32,543	60	125
1998	Explorers Bass & Flinders	—	50¢	—	32,225	60	125
1999	Year of Older Persons	—	—	$1	28,056	64.75	135
2000	Millennium (Coloured 50¢ Flag)	—	50¢	—	64,904	64.75	175
2000 b	Federation. VIP release	—	50¢	—	100	Gift	500
2001	Centenary of Federation	—	50¢	$1	59,569	70.25	165
2002	Year of the Outback	—	50¢	$1	39,514	73.5	110
2003	Australia's Volunteers	20¢	50¢	$1	39,090	73.5	75
2004 c	Come Alive. ($1 in colour)	—	—	$1	50,000	80	110
2005	60 years. End of WWII	20¢	50¢	$1	33,520	80	95
2006 d	Decimal Currency (inc 1¢ & 2¢)	—	50¢	—	45,373	80	100
2007	Year of the Surf Lifesaver	20¢	—	$1	30,516	80	95
2008 e	Year of Planet Earth	—	—	$1	28,569	95	100
2009 f	Year of Astronomy	—	—	$1	23,257	115	100
2010	All regular circulation issues	—	—	—	18,753	120	150
2011	All regular circulation issues	—	—	—	15,597	120	150
2012	Normal designs + gold plated	—	50¢	—	20,175	120	130
2013	Normal designs + gold plated	20¢	—	—	50,000	130	160
2014	Normal + $1 Cu/ni gold plated	—	—	$1	14,814	130	135
2015	Six coin set inc "honeycomb" 50¢	—	50¢	—	19,720	100	110
2016 g	Decimal 50th. All commemorative revs	20¢	50¢	$1	20,852	100	110
2017	Effigy on an Era. Ian Rank Broadley	—	—	—	n/a	100	100

[a] Outer box has a yellow sticker with the wording "One in 1000". A total of 10 sets were produced for the Singapore International Convention. Set also contains a special certificate.
[b] To celebrate the centenary of the passing by the British Parliament of the Commonwealth of Australia Constitution Act on July 5, 1900 (which became operative on January 1, 1901), the mint issued 100 especially labelled proof sets. Each set included a specially numbered certificate signed by the then Mint Controller, Graeme Moffatt.
[c] Approximately 50% of the 20¢ and 50¢ coins are "Large Head" types with the balance being "Small Head" types. (See 20 cent section for more information).
[d] This issue also included examples of the now obsolete one and two cent coins.
[e] Normal 20 cent coin but with special $1 coin celebrating the Year of Planet Earth.
[f] Six coin set for International Year of Astronomy with commemorative $1.
[g] Set included 5¢ to $2. All have commemorative pre-decimal coin image on reverse,

ERROR SETS

Date	Description	Mintage	Issue Price	Current Retail
1991	Contains 10¢ coin dated 1990	Unknown	60	500
1996	Contains 5¢ coin dated 1995	Unknown	60	400
2006	Contains Mob of Roos dated 2005	Unknown	80	3,500
2006	Contains Platypus 20¢ dated 2005	Unknown	80	3,900

THIS IS NOT A COMPLETE LIST OF ERROR SETS. THE ABOVE HAVE BEEN VERIFIED.
BEWARE OF FAKES. CHECK THAT THE COVERS HAVE NOT BEEN REGLUED OR TAMPERED

THEMED BABY SETS

Gumnut Design Koala Design

GUMNUT MINT SETS 1993 - 1997

92.5% Sterling Silver medallion 45mm included in set

1993 a	Landcare. Incorrect artwork	—	50¢	$1	16,000	15	150
1993 b	Landcare. Revised artwork	—	50¢	$1	11,000	15	115
1994	Family Year. 50¢ Narrow date	—	50¢	—	39,958	15	35
1994 c	Family Year. 50¢ wide date	—	50¢	—	Inc above	15	85
1994 Error	Set with $2 dated 1993	—	—	??	Unknown	15	350
1995	End of WWII. 'Weary' Dunlop	—	50¢	—	36,190	19.5	75
1996	Sir Henry Parkes	—	—	$1	25,727	24.5	235
1996 d	As above. (Type Two)	—	—	—	Inc above	24.5	195
1997	Sir Charles Kingsford-Smith	—	—	$1	27,421	24.5	400

(a) Two versions of the Gumnut special baby set exist. The wording on the first set reads. "A special gift for your new baby from the Royal Australian Mint." This set was withdrawn mid - year after it was found to contain artwork not attributed to the "Gumnut" creator May Gibbs.
(b) Wording changed to "Marking a special day with a gift to last forever."
(c) About 20 percent of 1994 mint sets contain 50¢ with wide date.
(d) Wording on cover smaller and back of outer folder has a barcode.

GUMNUT PROOF SETS 1995 - 1997

92.5% Sterling Silver medallion 45mm included in set

1995	End of WWII. 'Weary' Dunlop	—	50¢	—	6,704	75	185
1996	Sir Henry Parkes Centenary	—	—	$1	3,985	75	535
1997	Sir Charles Kingsford-Smith	—	—	$1	3,617	75	995

KOALA MINT SETS 1998 - 2005

92.5% Sterling Silver medallion 45mm included in set

1998	Bass & Flinders	—	50¢	—	31,810	24.5	200
1999	Year of Older Persons	—	—	$1	35,718	24.5	125
2000	Millennium (50¢ non-coloured Flag)	—	50¢	—	27,118	24.5	90
2001	Centenary of Federation	—	50¢	$1	32,494	26.5	160
2002	Year Outback (Non-coloured $1)	—	50¢	$1	32,479	29.3	110
2003	Australia's Volunteers	20¢	50¢	$1	37,748	29.3	75
	A bronze medallion was added to the 2004 set						
2004	Come Alive. ($1 not coloured)	—	—	—	31,036	30.5	75
	A cupro-nickel medallion was added to the set from this year onwards						
2005	60 years. End of WWII	20¢	50¢	$1	28,853	30.5	135

KOALA PROOF SETS 1998 - 2005

Includes 92.5% sterling silver medallion. Width 45 mm. Mass 43g. Thickness 3mm

1998	Bass & Flinders	—	50¢	—	5,269	75	495
1999	Year of Older Persons	—	—	$1	6,707	75	375
2000	Millennium (50¢ Coloured Flag)	—	50¢	—	15,557	75	235
2001	Centenary of Federation	—	50¢	$1	15,011	85	210
2002	Year of the Outback	—	50¢	$1	13,996	89.5	200
2003	Australia's Volunteers	20¢	50¢	$1	14,799	89.5	210
2004	Come Alive. ($1 not coloured)	—	—	—	16,000	95	195

THEMED BABY SETS

Magic Pudding Norman Lindsay $1 mint set

Blinky Bill Dorothy Wall $1 mint set

MAGIC PUDDING MINT SETS 2006 - 2008

Mint set features exclusive Norman Lindsay One Dollar coin

2006	With exclusive Lindsay $1 coin	—	—	—	15,127	30.5	65
2007	With exclusive Lindsay $1 coin	—	—	$1	33,693	30.5	70
2008	With exclusive Lindsay $1 coin	—	—	$1	46,504	30.5	40

MAGIC PUDDING PROOF SETS 2006 - 2008

Includes 92.5% sterling silver medallion. Width 45 mm. Mass 43g. Thickness 3mm

2006	All reverses are normal issue	—	—	—	32,095	30.5	125
2007	All reverses are normal issue	—	—	—	12,417	95	195
2008	All reverses are normal issue	—	—	—	15,500	95	100

BLINKY BILL MINT SETS 2009 - 2011

Mint set features exclusive Norman Lindsay One Dollar coin

2009	Exclusive Dorothy Wall $1 coin	—	—	$1	34,179	35	65
2010	Exclusive Dorothy Wall $1 coin	—	—	$1	33,131	35	45
2011	Exclusive Dorothy Wall $1 coin	—	—	$1	27,168	35	60

BLINKY BILL PROOF SETS 2009 - 2011

Includes 92.5% sterling silver medallion. Width 45 mm. Mass 43g. Thickness 3mm

2009	All reverses are normal issue	—	—	—	12,307	120	165
2010	All reverses are normal issue	—	—	—	10,002	120	225
2011	All reverses are normal issue	—	—	—	8,008	145	175

DOT & KANGAROO MINT SETS 2012 - 2014

Mint set features exclusive Ethel Pedley One Dollar coin

2012	Exclusive Ethel Pedley $1 coin	—	—	$1	23,084	45	50
2013	Exclusive Ethel Pedley $1 coin	—	—	$1	21,001	45	60
2014	Exclusive Ethel Pedley $1 coin	—	—	$1	18,088	45	95

DOT & KANGAROO PROOF SETS 2012 - 2014

Includes 92.5% sterling silver medallion. Width 45 mm. Mass 43g. Thickness 3mm

2012	All reverses are normal issue	—	—	—	9,270	125	145
2013	All reverses are normal issue	—	—	—	8,000	125	145
2014	All reverses are normal issue	—	—	—	6,650	125	130

THEMED BABY SETS

ALPHABET BABY MINT SETS 2015 -

Mint baby sets contain normal reverse designs. Set also includes "A,B,C" medallion

2015 a	All reverses share A,B,C token	—	—	18,500	45	50
2016 a	All reverses share A,B,C token	—	—	To order	45	50
2017 a	All reverses share A,B,C token	—	—	To order	45	45

In future issues of the pocketbook, this extensive issue will be listed individually

[a] The mint set didn't allow for an individual letter of the alphabet to be included in the set. Each contained the usual six denominations from the 5¢ to $2 coin. The set also included an added bonus of a cupro-nickel medallion that featured coloured representations of A,B,C surrounded by a number of native Australian animals.

ALPHABET BABY PROOF SETS 2015 -

Medallion not included. Packaging redesigned to include photo frame

2015 b	All reverses have standard designs	6,552	125	145
2015 c	Five coins plus choice of alphabet $1	To order	125	145
2016 b	All reverses have standard designs	To order	125	135
2016 c	Five coins plus choice of alphabet $1	To order	125	135
2017 b	All reverses have standard designs	To order	125	125
2017 c	Five coins plus choice of alphabet $1	To order	125	125

[a] All coins except the $1 coin are standard proof. The $1 coin is cupro nickel and features the regular "Mob of Kangaroo's" reverse.
[b] This second alternative gave the purchaser the option to personalise the proof set by replacing the standard MOR's reverse $1 coin with one of the individually produced 26 designs to feature each letter of the alphabet.

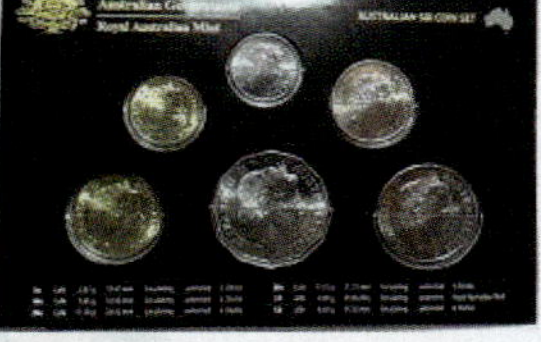

NCLT. COLLECTOR ISSUES ONLY

Date	Description. Mint Set. Original six denominations	Mintage	Issue Price	Current Retail
2016 IN COME THE DOLLARS, IN COME THE CENTS				
2016 c	Mint set 1¢ to 50¢. The 50¢ similar to original round type	10,000	66	130
2016 RAM LEGEND MEMBERS EXCLUSIVE MINT SET				
2016 d	Mint set 5¢ to $2. Includes C mm on First Mint's $1 coin	1,200	tba	150

[c] While featuring the six original denominations and metal shapes, all six coins carry the current Rank Broadley obverse design. The 50 cent is struck in the original alloy of 80% silver and 20% copper.
[d] This low mintage set was only available to registered RAM Legend members drawn on ballot. The set features the 2016 "First Mint's issue Unc $1 'C' MM which is normally only available through the Gallery Press in Canberra and not available for sale through the mint's eShop or Mint Issue catalogues.

SILVER OFF METAL SETS

COMMEMORATIVE SILVER PROOF SETS

The table below shows the denomination if it's a commemorative. A dash (–) indicates a regular Stuart Devlin reverse while a dot (•) indicates that the denomination was not part of this issue.

Date	Description	1¢	2¢	5¢	10¢	20¢	50¢	$1	$2	Mint-age	Issue Price	Current Average
WHERE POSSIBLE, THE ACTUAL MINTAGES HAVE BEEN LISTED RATHER THAN THE ESTIMATE												
2003	Volunteers	•	•	—	—	20¢	50¢	$1	—	6,500	185	195
2004	Standard Rev	•	•	—	—	—	—	—	—	6,500	220	225
2005	End of WWII	•	•	—	—	20¢	50¢	$1	—	6,200	220	225
2006 a	Machin Obv	—	—	—	—	—	—	—	—	5,829	230	275
2007	Surf Lifesaver	•	•	—	—	20¢	—	$1	—	3,475	195	275
2008	Planet Earth	•	•	—	—	20¢	—	$1	—	2,600	225	280
2008	Planet Earth/ Berlin Fair			—	—	20¢	—	$1	—	1,000	280	295
2009	Astronomy Year	–	–	—	—	—	—	—	—	2,231	295	335
2009	Planet Earth/ Berlin Fair			—	—	20¢	—	$1	—	1,000	290	295
2010	Standard rev	•	•	—	—	—	—	—	—	2,040	295	220
2011	Standard rev	•	•	—	—	—	—	—	—	2,072	295	295
2012	Standard rev	•	•	—	—	—	—	—	—	1,400	305	325
2013	Standard rev	•	•	—	—	—	—	—	—	2,000	325	325
2014	Standard rev	•	•	—	—	—	—	—	—	500	325	325
2015	Standard rev	•	•	—	—	—	—	—	—	800	350	395
2016 b	Original designs	1¢	2¢	—	—	—	50¢	•	•	1,966	350	350
2017	Standard rev	•	•	—	—	—	—	—	—	1,000	350	350

[a] Commemorating the 40th anniversary of Australia's first decimal coins, the Royal Australian Mint struck a 1c and 2c for inclusion in the year sets – the last time this occurred was in 1991. The set also included a round silver 50 cent with the original Arnold Machin obverse. This was the first time a round silver 50c coin was produced in 40 years!

[b] Similar to the six coin set issued to commemorate the 40th anniversary except the obverse features the current Ian Rank Broadley effigy. Set contains 1¢ & 2¢ coins and round 50 cent coin but no $1 or $2. The mintage figure was significant in that 1,966 coincided with the year of decimal currency.

DUAL ISSUE COIN SETS

Date	Description	Type	First Coin	Second Coin	MIntage	Issue	Retail
2008	Year of Planet Earth	Proof	20¢. Cu/ni	$1 Al/br. MOR	11,500	45	50
2008	Year of Planet Earth	Unc	20¢. Cu/ni	$1 Al/br. MOR	30,449	15	25
2009	Year of Astronomy	Proof	20¢. Cu/ni	$1 Al/br. Telescope	9,599	45	50
2009	Year of Astronomy	Unc	20¢. Cu/ni	$1 Al/br. Telescope	25,114	15	25
2010	Burke & Wills	Proof	20¢. Cu/ni	$1 Al/br. Dig Tree	9,995	45	50
2010	Burke & Wills	Unc	20¢. Cu/ni	$1 Al/br. Dig Tree	40,000	15	20
2011	Australian Wool pair	Proof	20¢. Cu/ni	$1. Al/br. Shearing	10,500	45	50
2011	Australian Wool pair	Proof	20¢. Cu/ni	$1. Al/br. Shearing	30,002	15	15
2012	Wheat. Fields of Gold	Proof	20¢. Cu/ni	$1. Al/br. Harvester	7,502	53	55
2012	Wheat. Fields of Gold	Unc	20¢. Cu/ni	$1. Al/br. Harvester	20,000	19	25
2013	Gold discovery. Mining	Proof	20¢. Cu/ni	$1. Al/br. Panning	6,220	55	60
2013	Gold discovery. Mining	Unc	20¢. Cu/ni	$1. Al/br. Panning	14,889	20	19
2015	Original Unc silver 50¢	Proof	50¢. Cu/ni	Restrike C'mm	5,000	50	50

GOLD OFF METAL SETS

COMMEMORATIVE GOLD SETS

The table below shows the denomination if it's a commemorative; ie, a coloured 50¢, $1 etc indicates that the issue has a special reverse design. A dash (–) indicates a regular Devlin reverse while a dot (•) indicates that there was no issue that year.

Date	Description	1¢	2¢	5¢	10¢	20¢	50¢	$1	$2	Mint-age	Issue Price	Current Average
2001	Federation	•	•	—	—	—	50¢	$1	—	193	3,200	7,500
2005	End of WWII	•	•	—	—	20¢	50¢	$1	—	629	3,740	6,750
2006	Decimal 40th	—	—	—	—	—	—	—	—	300	3,890	8,500
2007	Surf Lifesaver	•	•	—	—	20¢	—	$1	—	300	4,350	7,250
2010	Gottwald Obv	•	•	—	—	—	—	—	—	450	6,995	6,500
2012	Mini Gold Set	—	—	—	—	—	—	—	—	2,000	590	550
2014	Standard rev	•	•	—	—	—	—	—	—	50/47	9,500	11,000
2015	Standard rev	•	•	—	—	—	—	—	—	50/47	9,995	10,000
2016	Decimal 50th	1¢	2¢	5¢	10¢	20¢	50¢	•	•	100	9,995	10,000

WHERE POSSIBLE, THE ACTUAL MINTAGES HAVE BEEN LISTED RATHER THAN THE ESTIMATE

2001. Federation. (6 coin set) Perhaps it was the plethora of issues that celebrated the Centenary of Federation, but this handsome cased set of pure .9999 gold coins did not sell to expectations. 650 sets were produced but only 193 were sold. There are now significantly less full sets as dealers broken them up to sell the coins individually. Today complete sets, still in their Tasmanian Myrtle presentation box, command a substantial premium over the bullion value. The full set of six coins contains a total of 114.59 grams or 3.68 troy ounces of pure gold.

2005. End of WW2. (6 coin set) Issued in a She-Oak and Jarrah display case, this set contains a total of 113.56 gms or 3.65 troy ounces of fine .9999 gold.

2006. Decimal Currency 40th. (8 coin set) This impressive eight coin set included the one and two cent issues struck in gold for the first time. Another feature was the inclusion of the Gold 50¢ piece in its original 1966 round form.

2010. Gottwald Obverse set. (6 coin set) The reverse designs were all the normal circulation issues, the obverses were very special. All six featured the RAM's Vladimir Gottwald distinctive design that was featured and not used since the 2000 Royal Visit 50¢.

2012. Mini Gold Set. (8 coin set) This set features the "round" fifty cent coin which has been issued as a NCLT issue since its first appearance as Australia's only circulation silver coin in 1966. Each coin in this set is the same size and weight (0.5grams). Each coin were individually encapsulated within a foam surround. The complete set was then housed in a bespoke timber presentation case.

2013- Single coin and sets. Beginning in 2013, the RAM changed direction in its packaging of both its fine silver and gold coins. As well as selling the coins in sets, as in the past, the mint is also offering each of the six coins in individual presentation cases. More information on each of the above coins can be found in the earlier part of the book under each coin's denomination. There you will find extra information not listed above

2016. Decimal Currency 50th. (6 coin set) Just 100 sets were produced to commemorate the half century anniversary of decimal coins. Unlike the 40th anniversay set, this issue did not include the one or two dollar coins. The highlight of the set is the inclusion of a round 'fifty cent' coin.' While the reverse was a faithful reproduction, the obverse included the current 'mature' Rank-Broadley obverse. The obverses for both the one and two cent coins also carried this portrait even though both coins had been phased out before this obvers had been introduced

ACTUAL GOLD WEIGHT

DATE	NO OF COINS	TOTAL AGW .9999 FINE
2001	6 = 5¢ / 50¢	3.654 oz
2005	6 = 5¢ / 50¢	3.654 oz
2006	8 = 1¢ / $2	4.195 oz
2007	6 = 5¢ / 50¢	3.654 oz
2010	6 = 5¢ / 50¢	3.654 oz
2012	8 = 1¢ / $2	0.414 oz
2015	6 = 5¢ / 50¢	3.654 oz
2016	6 = 5¢ / 50¢	3.654 oz

PNC : PHILATELIC NUMISMATIC COVERS

1994 INTERNATIONAL YEAR OF THE FAMILY

Reference #	Mc94/ 01
Issuing Mint	RAM
Face Value	.50¢
Mintage	148,393
Date issued	14/ 04/ 1994
Issue Price	See below
Retail Average	See below

• Available in other issues

Mc 94/01	1994	50¢	Wider 7 mm date :	Common PNC	Type 1	3.95	40
Mc 94/01a	1994	50¢	Narrow 6 mm date :	Rare Type PNC	Type 2	3.95	95

This issue polarised collectors. The love it or loathe it reverse was only one aspect of the issue that continues to interest collectors decades later. The date 1994 features *"wide"* and *"narrow"* types. An excellent explanation on how to tell the difference can be found on *http://wiki.australian-coins.net/wiki/au...varieties.* According to collector Dennis Hughes, the narrow date is much scarcer in the PNC, as well as the mint &baby mint sets. Surprisingly the Narrow Date type is the most common circulation type and also almost exclusive to proof sets.

1995 AUSTRALIA REMEMBERS - WEARY DUNLOP

Reference #	Mc 95/ 01
Issuing Mint	RAM
Face Value	.50¢
Mintage	154,641
Date issued	20/ 04/ 1995
Issue Price	3.95
Retail Average	28.00

• Available in other issues

1997 AUSTRALIAN LEGENDS SIR DONALD BRADMAN

Reference #	Mc 97/ 01
Issuing Mint	RAM
Face Value	$5.00
Mintage	275,000
Date issued	23/ 01/ 1997
Issue Price	9.95
Retail Average	25.00

• Available in other issues

Above Bradman coin dated 1997. Uncirculated coins in folders were dated

1998 BASS AND FLINDERS COMMEMORATIVE

Reference #	Mc 98/ 01
Issuing Mint	RAM
Face Value	.50¢
Mintage	*See below*
Date issued	*See below*
Issue Price	*See below*
Retail Average	*See below*

• Available in other issues

Mc 98/01a	1998	.50¢	82,004	General issue Sept 10 1998	3.95	30
Mc 98/01b	1998	.50¢	1,000	Sydney ANDA Oct. 30 1998	n/a	110
Mc 98/01c	1998	.50¢	1,000	Sydney ANDA Oct. 31 1998	n/a	110
Mc 98/01d	1998	.50¢	1,000	Sydney ANDA Nov. 01 1998	n/a	175

1999 YEAR OF THE OLDER PERSONS

Reference #	Mc 99/ 01
Issuing Mint	RAM
Face Value	$1.00
Mintage	56,065
Date issued	11/ 02/ 1999
Issue Price	3.95
Retail Average	14.00

• Available in other issues

PNC : PHILATELIC NUMISMATIC COVERS

RESTRICTED TO OFFICIAL ISSUES FEATURING COINS - NO MEDALLIONS

2000 AUSTRALIAN LEGENDS. THE LAST ANZACS

Reference #	Mc 00/ 01
Issuing Mint	'C' mm/ RAM
Face Value	$1.00
Mintage	47,830
Date issued	21/ 01/ 2000
Issue Price	7.90
Retail Average	70.00

• Exclusive to PNC issues

The above coin could arguably be called a re-strike. The coin was first struck in 1999 in both al/br and fine silver. Examples also appeared as countermarks, privy and mintmarks in a number of national shows and expos. It was also issued as part of a dual set with the Year of the Older Persons $1. The 2000 $1 release was only issued in the above PNC.

2000 FOR VALOUR. VICTORIA CROSS

Reference #	Mc 00/ 02
Issuing Mint	RAM
Face Value	$1.00
Mintage	48,830
Date issued	24/ 07/ 2000
Issue Price	9.85
Retail Average	225.00

• Available in other issues

2000 AQUATICS : SYDNEY OLYMPIC GAMES / TYPE 1

Reference #	Mc 00/ 03
Issuing Mint	RAM
Face Value	$5.00
Mintage	30,000
Date issued	17/ 08/ 2000
Issue Price	10.85
Average	95.00

• Available in other issues

2000 ATHLETICS : SYDNEY OLYMPIC GAMES / TYPE 2

Reference #	Mc 00 /04
Issuing Mint	RAM
Face Value	$5.00
Mintage	30,000
Date issued	17/ 08/ 2000
Issue Price	10.85
Retail Average	95.00

• Available in other issues

2001 CENTENARY OF AUSTRALIAN ARMY

Reference #	Mc 01/ 01
Issuing Mint	C mm RAM
Face Value	$1.00
Mintage	27,209
Date issued	15/ 02/ 2001
Issue Price	17.85
Retail Average	140.00

• Available in other issues

2002 QE2 GOLDEN JUBILEE/ ACCESSION

Reference #	Mc 02 /01
Issuing Mint	RAM
Face Value	.50¢
Mintage	32,102
Date issued	06/ 02/ 2002
Issue Price	9.95
Retail Average	175.00

• Cu/ni coin exclusive to PNC. Silver NCLT proof in other sets

PNC : PHILATELIC NUMISMATIC COVERS

RESTRICTED TO OFFICIAL ISSUES FEATURING COINS - NO MEDALLIONS

2003 QE2 GOLDEN JUBILEE/ CORONATION

Reference #	Mc03/ 01
Issuing Mint	RAM
Face Value	.50¢
Mintage	63,003
Date issued	02/ 06/ 2003
Issue Price	11.90
Retail Average	40.00

• Exclusive to PNC issues

The above PNC features Australia's only Aluminium / Bronze 50 cent piece. Many of the sets have been broken up by fifty cent collectors needing the unique off-metal coin to complete their sets.

2004 EUREKA STOCKADE

Reference #	Mc03/ 01
Issuing Mint	Perth
Face Value	$5.00
Mintage	62,250
Date issued	29/ 06/ 2004
Issue Price	14.85
Retail Average	28.00

• Available in other issues

2005 ROOSTER : NEW YEAR THEME

Reference #	Mc 05/ 01
Issuing Mint	Perth
Face Value	.50¢
Mintage	To Order
Date issued	04/ 01/ 2005
Issue Price	11.95
Retail Average	25.00

• Exclusive to PNC issues

2005 CENTENARY AUSTRALIAN TENNIS OPEN

Reference #	Mc 05/ 02
Issuing Mint	RAM
Face Value	$5.00
Mintage	62,556
Date issued	11/ 01/ 2005
Issue Price	14.95
Retail Average	28.00

• Exclusive to PNC issues

PNC : PHILATELIC NUMISMATIC COVERS

2005 WORLD HERITAGE SITES

Reference #	Mc 05/03
Issuing Mint	RAM/ RM
Face Value	50¢/ 50p
Mintage	30,000
Date issued	21/ 04/ 2005
Issue Price	39.60
Retail Average	110.00

• Australian 50¢ exclusive to PNC

This PNC was advertised in the July 2005 RAM retail booklet, *Mint Issue (Number 62)*. Some 5000 sets (out of a world-wide issue of 30,000) were allocated for sale in Australia. The set contains four stamps as well as an Australian 50 cent piece and a British 50 pence. The set features the only release of the 2005 Coat of Arms 50 cents piece. In an email sent to me, Jeffrey Atkinson stated :- *" The only way you can get a 2005 50 cents Coat of Arms issue is by buying this PNC. This may be the lowest mintage 50 cents Coat of Arms ever produced".* The British 50 pence coin was issued for general circulation.

Mc 05/ 03a	ERROR 'Stamps Affixed Upside Down	Unique?	39.60	tba

[a] Advanced PNC collector and pocketbook contributer Jim Mansell has in his collection a possibly unique error version of the above Australian/ UK folder. Jim advises that his example [#17977] shows that the left-hand, top two stamps are upside down. Jim is interested in hearing from any other collectors with a similar error set. I will pass on any information you send to me via my email >*gregmcdonaldpublishing@gmail.com*<

2005 GAMES QUEEN'S BATON RELAY

Reference #	Mc 05/ 04
Issuing Mint	RAM
Face Value	$5.00
Mintage	22,002
Date issued	28/ 10/ 2005
Issue Price	14.95
Retail Average	26.00

• Exclusive to PNC issue

2006 DOG : NEW YEAR THEME

Reference #	Mc 06/ 01
Issuing Mint	Perth
Face Value	.50¢
Mintage	To order
Date issued	05/ 01/ 2006
Issue Price	11.95
Retail Average	25.00

• Exclusive to PNC issue

2006 MELBOURNE COMMONWEALTH GAMES

Reference #	Mc 06/ 02
Issuing Mint	RAM
Face Value	$5.00
Mintage	22,552
Date issued	12/ 01/ 2006
Issue Price	14.95
Retail Average	28.00

• Available in other issues

PNC : PHILATELIC NUMISMATIC COVERS

2006 QE2's 80th BIRTHDAY

Reference #	Mc 06/ 03
Issuing Mint	Perth
Face Value	.50¢
Mintage	n/a
Date issued	19/ 04/ 2006
Issue Price	14.95
Retail Average	26.00

• Exclusive to PNC issue

2006 DAME EDNA aka BARRY HUMPHRIES

Reference #	Mc 06/ 04
Issuing Mint	Perth
Face Value	.50¢
Mintage	To order
Date issued	24/ 10/ 2006
Issue Price	14.95
Retail Average	26.00

• Exclusive to PNC issue

2007 PIG : NEW YEAR THEME

Reference #	Mc 07 /01
Issuing Mint	Perth
Face Value	.50¢
Mintage	To order
Date issued	09/ 01/ 2007
Issue Price	11.95
Retail Average	15.00

• Exclusive to PNC issue

2007 "HOWZAT" AUSTRALIA WINS ASHES

Reference #	Mc 07/ 02
Issuing Mint	RAM
Face Value	$1.00
Mintage	8,000
Date issued	16/ 01/ 2007
Issue Price	19.95
Retail Average	195.00

• Individually numbered

2007 YEAR OF THE SURF LIFESAVER

Reference #	Mc 07/ 03
Issuing Mint	RAM
Face Value	.20¢
Mintage	To order
Date issued	06/ 03/ 2007
Issue Price	14.95
Retail Average	22.00

• Available in other issues

2007 SYDNEY HARBOUR BRIDGE 75 YEARS

Reference #	Mc 07/ 04
Issuing Mint	'S' mk RAM
Face Value	$1.00
Mintage	*See below*
Date issued	*See below*
Issue Price	*See below*
Retail Average	*See below*

• Available in other issues

Mc 07/ 04	2010	$1	'S'	PM/ AP	25,600	June 15, 2007	14.95	18
Mc 07/ 04a	2010	$1	'S'	Sydney	250	June 15, 2007	n/a	200

[a] 250 specially overprinted folders.were released at the Sydney Stamp Expo held from June 15-17, 2007. It was one of the few issues to feature a coin with a mintmark [S]. The issue also sported a silver overprint highlighting the Expo connection.

PNC : PHILATELIC NUMISMATIC COVERS

2007 50th ANNIVERSARY OF THE SAS

Reference #	Mc 07/ 05
Issuing Mint	Perth
Face Value	$1.00
Mintage	n/a
Date issued	04/ 09/ 2007
Issue Price	14.95
Retail Average	32.00

• This issue features a larger 30.2mm diameter coin weighing 13.8 gms.

2007 AUSTRALIAN SAS FOLDER

Reference #	Mc 07/ 06
Issuing Mint	Perth
Face Value	$1.00
Mintage	2,000
Date issued	n/a
Issue Price	79.95
Retail Average	250.00

• Same details as above

2007 BOUNDING KANGAROOS

Reference #	Mc 07/ 07
Issuing Mint	RAM
Face Value	$1.00
Mintage	37,100
Date issued	03/ 12/ 2007
Issue Price	19.95
Retail Average	42.00

• Available in other issues

2008 RAT : LUNAR NEW YEAR THEME

Reference #	Mc 08/ 01
Issuing Mint	Perth
Face Value	$1.00
Mintage	To order
Date issued	08/ 01/ 2008
Issue Price	14.95
Retail Average	20.00

• Coin exclusive to PNC

2008 CENTENARY OF SCOUTING

Reference #	Mc 08/ 02
Issuing Mint	RAM
Face Value	.50¢
Mintage	33,002
Date issued	19/ 02/ 2008
Issue Price	14.95
Retail Average	See below

• Available in other issues

Mc 08/01	2008	.50¢	RAM/ AP	33,002	February 19,2008	14.95	20
Mc 08/01a	2008	.50¢	Canb	250	March 14-16,2008	18	25

[a] This special issue is essentially the same as the original issue with the exception of a 24 carat gold stamp overprint. Just 250 covers were issued and sold at the Canberra Stampshow held between March 14-16, 2008.

2008 WORLD YOUTH DAY

Reference #	Mc 08/ 03
Issuing Mint	Perth
Face Value	$1.00
Mintage	500,000
Date issued	04/ 03/ 2008
Issue Price	14.95
Retail Average	28.00

• Available in other issues

PNC : PHILATELIC NUMISMATIC COVERS

RESTRICTED TO OFFICIAL ISSUES FEATURING COINS - NO MEDALLIONS

2008 BEIJING OLYMPIC GAMES

Reference #	Mc 08/ 04
Issuing Mint	Perth
Face Value	$1.00
Mintage	To order
Date issued	24/ 06/ 2008
Issue Price	16.95
Retail Average	28.00

• Available in other issues

2008 CENTENARY OF QUARANTINE

Reference #	Mc 08/ 05
Issuing Mint	RAM
Face Value	$1.00
Mintage	21,600
Date issued	15/ 07/ 2008
Issue Price	14.95
Retail Average	24.00

• Available in other issues

2008 150 YEARS OF AUSTRALIAN FOOTBALL

Reference #	Mc 08/ 06
Issuing Mint	Perth
Face Value	$1.00
Mintage	26,109
Date issued	29/ 07/ 2008
Issue Price	14.95
Retail Average	22.00

• Available in other issues

2008 LEST WE FORGET END OF WWI. 90TH ANNIVERSARY

Reference #	Mc 08/ 07
Issuing Mint	Perth
Face Value	$1.00
Mintage	To order
Date issued	*See below*
Issue Price	*See below*
Retail Average	*See below*

• Larger 32.2mm size

Mc 08/07	2008	$1	PM/ AP	tba	Nov 3, 2008	14.95	35
Mc 08/ 07a	2008	$1	PM/ AP	1,111	Nov 11, 2008	35	250

[a] This low volume issue can be recognised by a subtle change to the design as well as an exclusive post mark. On the flap of the envelope, and on the cardboard inset, a representation of the *"Rising Sun"* Army emblem has been printed. It features a gold leaf poppy postmark and each is individually numbered in a block under the stamps.

2009 OX : LUNAR NEW YEAR THEME

Reference #	Mc 09/ 01
Issuing Mint	Perth
Face Value	$1.00
Mintage	*See below*
Date issued	*See below*
Issue Price	*See below*
Retail Average	*See below*

• Exclusive to PNC issue

Mc 09/ 01	2009	$1	PM/ AP	tba	January 8, 2009	14.95	22
Mc 09/ 01a	2009	$1	Melb	250	July 23-26, 2009	n/a	200

[a] 250 specially overprinted folders were a feature of the Melbourne Stamp Show held from July 23 - 26, 2009. Gold foil was used as part of the overprint.

PNC : PHILATELIC NUMISMATIC COVERS

RESTRICTED TO OFFICIAL ISSUES FEATURING COINS - NO MEDALLIONS

2009 AUSTRALIA 200 YEARS OF POSTAL SERVICE

Reference #	Mc 09/ 02
Issuing Mint	Perth
Face Value	$1.00
Mintage	32,200
Date issued	25/ 03/ 2009
Issue Price	17.95
Retail Average	20.00

• Exclusive to PNC issue

2009 AUSTRALIA POST BICENTENARY

Reference #	Mc 09/ 03
Issuing Mint	RAM
Face Value	$1.00
Mintage	32,300
Date issued	*See below*
Issue Price	*See below*
Retail Average	*See below*

• Al/br coin exclusive to PNC. Silver NCLT proof in other sets

Mc 09/ 03	2009	$1	RAM/ AP	32,000	June 26, 2009	14.95	16
Mc 09/ 03 a	2009	$1	Melb/ Gold	300	July 23-26, 2009	45	155

[a] 32,300 of these PNC's were issued by Australia Post with 300 overprinted with gold lettering and sold at the Melbourne Stamp Show in 2009, that was held at the Rod Laver Arena, National Tennis Centre from July 23-26. Each PNC was individually numbered and overprinted in gold leaf.

GENERAL COMMENTS : To celebrate the bicentential of the Australian postal in service, the dollar coin was released by the Royal Australian Mint. This uncirculated coin was also released in a two coin set as well as the above PNC. There is a growing trend for third parties to overprint, stamp, add postmarks or similar to officially produced items to add value or commemorate a particular occasion, in this case the stamp show.

2009 STAR GAZING

Reference #	Mc 09/ 04
Issuing Mint	Perth
Face Value	$1.00
MintageT	To order
Date issued	25/ 08/ 2009
Issue Price	14.95
Retail Average	27.00

• Exclusive to PNC issue

2010 TIGER : LUNAR NEW YEAR THEME

Reference #	Mc 10/ 01
Issuing Mint	Perth
Face Value	$1.00
Mintage	15,000
Date issued	12/ 01/ 2010
Issue Price	14.95
Retail Average	15.00

• Exclusive to PNC issue

2010 LACHLAN MACQUARIE BICENTENARY

Reference #	Mc 10/ 02
Issuing Mint	Perth
Face Value	$1.00
Mintage	15,000
Date issued	16/ 02/ 2010
Issue Price	19.95
Retail Average	60.00

• Exclusive to PNC issue

2010 CENTENARY OF COMMONWEALTH COINAGE

Reference #	Mc 10/ 03
Issuing Mint	"C"mm RAM
Face Value	$1.00
Mintage	25,100
Date issued	*See below*
Issue Price	*See below*
Retail Average	*See below*

• Available in other issues

Mc 10/03	2010	$1	C	RAM/AP	25,100	February 23, 2010	14.95	32
Mc 10/03 a	2010	$1		Canberra	250	March 12-14, 2010	n/a	n/a
Mc 10/03 b	2010	$1		Melbourne	300	April 17, 2010	45	n/a
Mc 10/03 c	2010	$1		Richmond	50	April 24, 2010	50	150
Mc 10/03 c	2010	$1		Richmond. Rare	5	Members Only	50	250
Mc 10/03 d	2010	$1		Adelaide/ Green	tba	August 20, 2010	30	n/a
Mc 10/03 d	2010	$1		Adelaide/ Black	tba	August 21, 2010	30	n/a
Mc 10/03 d	2010	$1		Adel/aide/ Red	tba	August 22, 2010	30	n/a
Mc 10/03 d	2010	$1		Adelaide/ Logo	tba	August 20-22, 2010	30	n/a
Mc 10/03 e	2010	$1		Mandurah	300	Nov 19-21, 2010	35	n/a

[a] This Canberra fair issue had an unusual overprint of a WW1 era biplane as its logo. The bourse was held from March 12-14, 2010. Gold leaf was used to imprint the logo and show details. The above was released exclusively on the Sunday admission. A special overprint of the Centenary of Powered Flight was released on Friday, March 12 and a show release for the Centenary of Girl Guides PNC was released on the Saturday, March 13 trading day. The one dollar coin included in all three variations have a mint mark 'C'.
[b] This PNC has the honour of being the first souvenir fair issue offered by the Royal Philatelic Society of Victoria at its fourth annual one-day bourse held on Saturday, April 17, 2010, at Purves House, 303 High Street, Ashburton Vic. Just 300 PNC's were overprinted in gold foil with a representation of Queen Victoria, in profile, being part of the overprint.
[c] A special overprint was produced for a stamp & coin fair for The St Monica's Church Hall Corner of Windsor Street and Bourke Street, Richmond, NSW. Ann, a spokesperson for the club, emailed information that there were 50 gold overprints that featured the wording *"RICHMOND STAMP & COIN SHOW, 24th APRIL 2010,* and a bust of Lachlan Macquarie, numbered 1 to 50." Ann also mentioned there was a printers error and "we ended up with an extra gold overprint which was unnumbered." There was also 5 silver overprints. The description was the same as above plus bust of Lachlan Macquarie, no number, but printed "MEMBERS ONLY."
[d] This three day STAMPEX Adelaide fair was held at the A Drill Hall, King William Rd, Adelaide from August 20-22, 2010. A different coloured postmark was released for each day of the fair.
[e] 300 specially gold overprinted covers were produced for the National One Frame Philatelic Numismatic & Postcard Fair held in Mandurah, WA on Nov. 19-21, 2010.

2010 CENTENARY OF POWERED FLIGHT

Reference #	Mc 10/ 04
Issuing Mint	Perth
Face Value	$1.00
Date issued	*See below*
Issue Price	*See below*
Retail Average	*See below*

• Exclusive to PNC issue

Mc 10/04	2010	$1	PM/ AP	tba	March 9- 10 2010	14.95	30
Mc 10/04a	2010	$1	London	tba	March 9- 10 2010	n/a	95
Mc 10/04b	2010	$1	Canberra	250	March 12- 14 2010	30	65
Mc 10/04c	2010	$1	Mandurah	25	October 31 2010	30	65
Mc 10/04d	2010	$1	Perth	300	January 3 2011	30	50

[a] This intriging London overprint? appeared as lot 2010 in The ACE Stamp Auction Number 9. The brief auction description stated (9th March Cent of Powered Flight overprinted with London 2010 & logo in red. No 87 of only 500." ***[Any information regarding this issue would be appreciated.***
[b] Held from March 12 - 14, 2010, the Canberra Stampshow issued 250 overprinted covers. The distinctive gold post mark was in the shape of an early plane design.
[c] As below, but overprinted *"Flown by Capt. Rod Edwards Serpentine to Murrayfield 31st October 2010"* & pilot signed. Only 25 flown & signed. Arranged by the Mandurah Stamp Fair group. This may be the first flown PNC.
[d] 300 black overprinted covers were produced by the Philatelic Society of WA Open Day to celebrate the Centenary of Powered Flight in WA by JJ Hammond in a Bristol Boxkite 3rd January 1911" in black. Issue limited to 300.

PNC : PHILATELIC NUMISMATIC COVERS

RESTRICTED TO OFFICIAL ISSUES FEATURING COINS - NO MEDALLIONS

2010 SHANGHAI WORLD EXPO

Reference #	Mc 10/ 05
Issuing Mint	Perth
Face Value	$1.00
Mintage	To order
Date issued	18/ 05/ 2010
Issue Price	14.95
Retail Average	32.00

• Exclusive to PNC issue

2010 WWI LOST SOLDIERS OF FROMELLES

Reference #	Mc 10/ 06
Issuing Mint	RAM
Face Value	.20¢
Mintage	26,150
Date issued	*See below*
Issue Price	*See below*
Retail Average	*See below*

• Available in other issues

Mc 10/ 06	2010	.20¢	RAM/ AP	26,150	July 19, 2010	14.95	26
Mc 10/ 06 a	2010	.20¢	Melb. APTA	200	Nov 13-14, 2010	39.95	40

[a] A gold foil overprint of 200 covers was released at the APTA Stamp, Coin & Collectables Fair held in Melbourne on November 13th & 14th, 2010. Each was individually numbered.

2010 CENTENARY OF AUSTRALIAN TAX OFFICE

Reference #	Mc 10/ 07
Issuing Mint	RAM
Face Value	.20¢
Mintage	15,000
Date issued	27/ 07/ 2010
Issue Price	19.95
Retail Average	32.00

• This is the only NCLT issue. Coin also circulated

2010 BURKE & WILLS. 150TH ANNIVERSARY

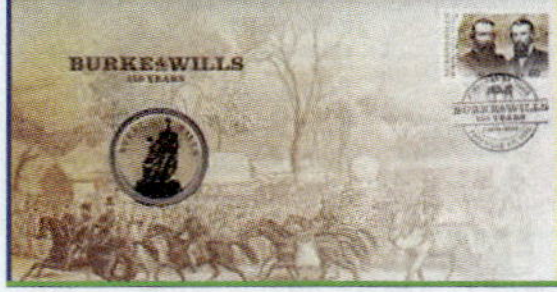

Reference #	Mc 10/ 08
Issuing Mint	Perth
Face Value	$1.00
Mintage	56,065
Date issued	03/ 08/ 2010
Issue Price	14.95
Retail Average	26.00

• Exclusive to PNC issue

2010 GIRL GUIDES CENTENARY

Reference #	Mc 10/ 09
Issuing Mint	RAM
Face Value	$1.00
Mintage	23,000
Date issued	31/ 08/ 2010
Issue Price	14.95
Retail Average	26.00

• Available in other issues

POINTS CONCERNING THE PRICING OF PNC ISSUES

The pricing of this section provided many challenges. While it is clear that rare or popular issues have improved, or maintained their position, it is also obvious that some dealers have over ordered on some releases. I am very grateful to PNC enthusiast Peter Hiscocks who allowed me access to his spreadsheet that lists sales for all issues that have appeared on ebay, dealer lists and auction results over the years. In examining Peter's spreadsheet prices from the lowest to the highest for the same item sold about the same time varied by as much as 250%. Some of these sales included offers of bundles of ten or more PNC's. This made the unit cost of some offers well below issue price. As a result I am sure that collectors will have their own opinion of the prices listed which have largely been determined by averaging out the prices as listed by Peter. As well as the sterling effort displayed by Peter, I would also like to acknowledge the input of fellow enthusiasts Bruce Mansfield, Jim Mansell and David Miller. Thanks also to John O'Connor for his expertise.

2010 NATIONAL SERVICE MEMORIAL

Reference #	Mc 10/ 10
Issuing Mint	RAM
Face Value	.50¢
Mintage	To order
Date issued	*See below*
Issue Price	*See below*
Retail Average	*See below*

• Available in other issues

Mc 10/ 10	2010	50¢	RAM/ AP	tba	September 8, 2010	14.95	30
Mc 10/ 10 a	2010	50¢	Canberra	tba	September 8, 2010	tba	40
Mc 10/ 10 b	2010	50¢	Mandurah	300	Nov. 19-21, 2010	30	45
Mc 10/ 10 c	2010	50¢	Malvern	200	Feb. 12-13, 2011	30	65

[a] Cover overprinted "Naming of Canberra May 12th 1913 Commencement Stone Laid by King O'Malley MP" in red. More information required.
[b] 300 overprints issued at the Mandurah Fair, held on November 19th to 20th, in the pretty WA seaside city. The gold overprint depicted dolphin & bird emblems.
[c] An overprint of 200 covers were released at the APTA Stamp, Coin & Collectables Fair at the Malvern Town Hall on February 12th - 13th, 2011. The covers were numbered. There may also be a "Supporters Club" issue of 100 covers. Any advice would be appreciated.
Note : Like the Bathurst PNC, this issue featured a coin with a different postmarked envelope.

2010 MELBOURNE CUP 150th ANNIVERSARY

Reference #	Mc 10/ 10
Issuing Mint	RAM
Face Value	.50¢
Mintage	*See below*
Date issued	*See below*
Issue Price	*See below*
Retail Average	*See below*

• Available in other issues

Mc 10/ 11	2010	50¢	RAM/ AP	15,000	November 1, 2010	14.95	35
Mc 10/ 11a	2010	50¢	Ballot/ AP	1,861	November 2, 2010	19.95	295

[a] A limited release of 1,861 coin and stamp covers *(The Melbourne Cup has been run annually since 1861)*. These PNC's feature a gold postmark of a jockey's helmet cancelled 2 November 2010 at Flemington, Vic. They are individually numbered on the front and were released for $19.95 each. These were only available from Australia Post by mail order.

2011 RABBIT : LUNAR NEW YEAR THEME

Reference #	Mc 11/ 01
Issuing Mint	Perth
Face Value	$1.00
Mintage	*See below*
Date issued	*See below*
Issue Price	*See below*
Retail Average	*See below*

• Exclusive to PNC issue

Mc 11/ 01	2011	$1	PM/ AP	tba	January 11, 2011	15.95	20
Mc 11/ 01a	2011	$1	Sydney	200	Mar 31-Apr 03, 2011	n/a	30
Mc 11/ 01b	2011	$1	Melb	250	April 16, 2011	50	n/a

[a] A special fair release of just 200 overprint covers were released at the APTA Sydney National Stamp Expo held at the Randwick Racecourse from March 31 to April 3, 2011.
[b] Issued by the Royal Philatelic Society of Victoria at its 5th annual one-day bourse on April 16 2010, at Purves House, 303 High Street, Ashburton Vic. Just 250 PNC's were overprinted in gold foil. Part of the overprint includes the logo of the RPSV and a represenation of Queen Victoria, in profile.

2011 QUEEN'S 85th BIRTHDAY CELEBRATION

Reference #	Mc 11/ 02
Issuing Mint	Perth
Face Value	$1.00
Mintage	*See below*
Date issued	*See below*
Issue Price	*See below*
Retail Average	*See below*

• Exclusive to PNC issue

Mc 11/ 02	2011	$1	PM/ AP	tba	April 5, 2011	15.95	35
Mc 11/ 02 a	2011	$1	Geelong	150	August 5-7, 2011	n/a	40

[a] 150 gold foil covers were produced for the *National Frame Victorian Philatelic Club Geepex80 Fair* held at the Geelong West Town Hall, Geelong West, from August 5-7, 2011.

2011 DAME NELLIE MELBA. 1861-1931

Reference #	Mc 11/ 03
Issuing Mint	Perth
Face Value	$1.00
Mintage	*See below*
Date issued	*See below*
Issue Price	*See below*
Retail Average	*See below*

• Exclusive to PNC issue

Mc 11/03	2011	$1	PM/ AP	tba	May 10, 2011	15.95	35
Mc 11/03 a	2011	$1	Melb. APTA	150	Nov. 12-13, 2011	n/a	45

[a] An overprint issue of 150 covers were released at the APTA Stamp, Coin &Collectables Fair held at the Lower Town Hall, Box Hill on November 12th & 13th, 2011.

2011 THE ROYAL WEDDING - WILLIAM & KATE

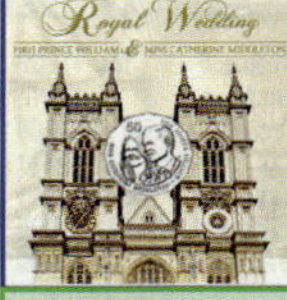

Reference #	Mc 11/ 04
Issuing Mint	RAM
Face Value	.50¢
Mintage	*See below*
Date issued	*See below*
Issue Price	*See below*
Retail Average	*See below*

• Available in other issues

Mc 11/ 04	2011	.50¢	RAM/ AP	14,000	May 20, 2011	15.95	17
Mc 11/ 04 a	2011	.50¢	Melb. APTA	150	July 23-24, 2011	n/a	25

[a] A gold overprint of 150 covers were released at the APTA Stamp, Coin & Collectables Fair held at Malvern Town Hall on July 23th - 24th, 2011. Covers are individually numbered.

2011 ROYAL AUSTRALIAN NAVY CENTENARY

Reference #	Mc 11/ 05
Issuing Mint	Perth
Face Value	$1.00
Mintage	*See below*
Date issued	*See below*
Issue Price	*See below*
Retail Average	*See below*

• Exclusive to PNC issue

Mc 11/ 05	2011	$1	PM/ AP	tba	June 14, 2011	15.95	35
Mc 11/ 05 a	2011	$1	Bris. APTA	150	Oct. 01- 02, 2011	n/a	40

[a] An overprint of 150 covers were released at the APTA Stamp, Coin & Collectables Fair held at the Brisbane Table Centre in Windsor on October 1st - 2nd, 2011.

2011 DUNTROON CENTENARY

Reference #	Mc 11/ 06
Issuing Mint	Perth
Face Value	$1.00
Mintage	*See below*
Date issued	*See below*
Issue Price	*See below*
Retail Average	*See below*

• Exclusive to PNC issue

Mc 11/ 06	2011	$1	PM/ AP	tba	June 27, 2011	15.95	35
Mc 11/ 06 a	2011	$1	Canb. APTA	125	March 16-18, 2012	n/a	n/a
Mc 11/ 06 b	2011	$1	Canb. Mawson	250	March 16-18, 2012	n/a	75

[a] An overprint of 125 covers were released at the Canberra Stamp show 2012 held at the Hellenic Club of Canberra, Matilda St, Phillip (Woden), ACT from March 16-18, 2012.
[b] Commemorating the anniversary the establishment of Mawson's Antarctic base. It featured a overprint in the shape of the ACT reading *"Mawson 100 Years Canberra Stamp Show 2012.*

2011 KOALA : BUSH BABIES THEME

Reference #	Mc 11/ 07
Issuing Mint	Perth
Face Value	$1.00
Mintage	To order
Date issued	01/ 07/ 2011
Issue Price	15.95
Retail Average	20.00

• Exclusive to PNC issue

PNC : PHILATELIC NUMISMATIC COVERS

RESTRICTED TO OFFICIAL ISSUES FEATURING COINS - NO MEDALLIONS

2011 DINGO : BUSH BABIES THEME

Reference #	Mc 11/ 08
Issuing Mint	Perth
Face Value	$1.00
Mintage	To order
Date issued	02/ 08/ 2011
Issue Price	15.95
Retail Average	20.00

• Exclusive to PNC issue

2011 BILBY : BUSH BABIES THEME

Reference #	Mc 11/ 09
Issuing Mint	Perth
Face Value	$1.00
Mintage	To order
Date issued	06/ 09/ 2011
Issue Price	15.95
Retail Average	20.00

• Exclusive to PNC issue

2011 SUGAR GLIDERS : BUSH BABIES THEME

Reference #	Mc 11/ 10
Issuing Mint	Perth
Face Value	$1.00
Mintage	To Order
Date issued	04/ 10/ 2011
Issue Price	15.95
Retail Average	20.00

• Exclusive to PNC issue

2011 CHRISTMAS THEME

Reference #	Mc 11/ 11
Issuing Mint	Perth
Face Value	$1.00
Mintage	To Order
Date issued	31/ 10/ 2011
Issue Price	15.95
Retail Average	30.00

• Exclusive to PNC issue

2011 KANGAROO : BUSH BABIES THEME

Reference #	Mc 11/ 12
Issuing Mint	Perth
Face Value	1.00
Mintage	To Order
Date issued	02/ 11/ 2011
Issue Price	15.95
Retail Average	20.00

• Exclusive to PNC issue

2011 INTERNATIONAL YEAR - VOLUNTEERS

Reference #	Mc 11/ 13
Issuing Mint	RAM
Face Value	.20¢
Mintage	20,000
Date issued	02/ 11/ 2011
Issue Price	15.95
Retail Average	35.00

• Coin also circulated

This PNC marks the 10th anniversary of the UN proclaimed International Year of Volunteers (2001). The RAM released a commemorative 20c which was released for circulation. This PNC was released jointly with the RAM and Australia Post. Each PNC up to 20,000 is individually numbered on the back with an Australia Post authentic merchandise sticker.

PNC : PHILATELIC NUMISMATIC COVERS

RESTRICTED TO OFFICIAL ISSUES FEATURING COINS - NO MEDALLIONS

2011 REMEMBRANCE DAY

Reference #	Mc 11/ 14
Issuing Mint	RAM
Face Value	$5.00
Mintage	*See below*
Date issued	*See below*
Issue Price	*See below*
Retail Average	*See below*

Mc 11/ 14	2011	$5	RAM/ AP	15,000	November 2, 2011	29.95	55
Mc 11/ 14 a	2011	$5	RAM/ AP	1,111	November 30, 2011	39.95	950

[a] This coin was struck on a scalloped hendecagonal shaped blank, a round edged 11 sided planchet! The reverse design is by Aaron Baggio. The obverse depicts a central portrait of Queen Elizabeth II by Ian Rank-Broadley with "Remembrance Day 11.11.11 Five Dollars" around the legends. Struck onto a 38.74mm 20 gram planchet made from Aluminium Zinc and Bronze, it has a frosted uncirculated finish. Australia Post also issued a limited edition of 1,111 PNC's with a red foil postmark for $39.95 where customers had to place an order over the phone from noon on Wednesday, November 30.

2011 GOLF. THE PRESIDENTS CUP

Reference #	Mc 11/ 15
Issuing Mint	RAM
Face Value	$1.00
Mintage	15,025
Date issued	02/ 11/ 2011
Issue Price	15.95
Retail Average	33.00

• Available in other issues

2011/2013 THE ASHES. AUSTRALIA vs ENGLAND

Reference #	Mc 11/ 16
Issuing Mint	RAM
Face Value	.20¢
Mintage	20,000
Date Produced	25/ 11/ 2010
Date issued	05/ 01/ 2011
Issue Price	19.95
Retail Average	48.00

Mc 11/ 16 a	2011	.20¢	RAM/ AP	20,000	November 25, 2011	19.95	18
Mc 11/ 16 b	2011	.20¢	RAM/ AP	200	May 10 - 15, 2013	n/a	n/a

[a] Postmarked at Woolloongabba QLD on 25th November 2010 where the first match of this series was held. The release date was held over to January 5, 2011.
[b] Issued as an overprint almost two years after its original release, this PNC was issued on *May 10 - 15, 2013* to commemorative the centenary of the Kangaroo Stamp. The jury is still out on finding a common link to connect cricket and a stamp issue. Help!

2012 AUSTRALIAN CENTENARY MEN'S OPEN

Reference #	Mc 12/ 01
Issuing Mint	RAM
Face Value	$5.00
Mintage	10,000
Date issued	10/ 01/ 2012
Issue Price	29.95
Retail Average	52.00

• Available in other issues

The four Grand Slam ® tournaments; Australian Open, French Open, Wimbledon and US Open, represent the zenith of world tennis competition. Wimbledon was the first of these tournaments and commenced in 1877, with the Australian Open, originally the Australasian Championships, starting in 1905. Since then, the Australian Open has been contested each year except during the two world wars and in 1986, when the tournament shifted from mid-December to mid-January. The 2012 Australian Open Men's Singles Final winner was the tournament's 100th Australian Open Men's Champion. This $5 uncirculated coin is a representation of the medal that was presented to the 100th Australian Open Men's Champion, Novak Djokovic who battled for a record breaking six hours to finally beat Rafael Nadal to take the title.

2012 DRAGON : NEW YEAR THEME

Reference #	Mc 12/ 02
Issuing Mint	Perth
Face Value	$1.00
Mintage	*See below*
Date issued	*See below*
Issue Price	*See below*
Retail Average	*See below*

• Exclusive to PNC issue

Mc 12/ 02	2012	$1	PM/ AP	10,000	January 10, 2012	15.95	20
Mc 12/ 02 a	2012	$1	Melb.APTA	150	Feb. 11-12, 2012	n/a	45
Mc 12/ 02 b	2012	$1	Canb	250	Mar. 16-18, 2012	n/a	45

[a] An overprint issue of 150 covers were released at the APTA Stamp, Coin & Collectables Fair held in Malvern from February 11th & 12th, 2012.
[b] Commemorating the anniversary the establishment of Mawson's Antarctic base. It featured a overprint in the shape of the ACT reading "Mawson 100 Years Canberra Stampshow 2012.

2012 AUSTRALIAN TENNIS OPEN

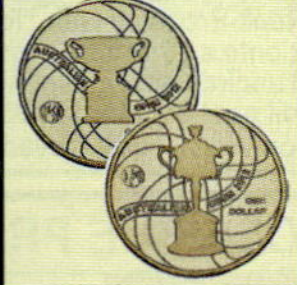

Reference #	Mc 12/ 03
Issuing Mint	RAM
Face Value	$1.00 x 2
Mintage	15,000
Date issued	16/ 01/ 2012
Issue Price	29.95
Retail Average	35.00

• Available in other issues

This was the first offical PNC to contain two different coins. The women's singles Memorial Cup [lower top] was named after Australian Daphne Akhurst, who won five titles between 1925 and 1930. The men's Norman Brookes Challenge Cup, is named in honour of the Australian who claimed singles and doubles titles in the Australia, US and Wimbledon championships between 1907 and 1924. All are individually numbered.

2012 YEAR OF THE CO-OPERATIVES

Reference #	Mc 12/ 04
Issuing Mint	RAM
Face Value	$1.00
Mintage	15,000
Date issued	14/ 02/ 2012
Issue Price	19.95
Retail Average	35.00

• Available in other issues

2012 QUEEN ELIZABETH II DIAMOND JUBILEE

Reference #	Mc 12/ 05
Issuing Mint	RAM
Face Value	.50¢
Mintage	To order
Date issued	03/ 04/ 2012
Issue Price	15.95
Retail Average	28.00

• Available in other issues

2012 ANZAC DAY - LEST WE FORGET

Reference #	Mc 12/ 06
Issuing Mint	Perth
Face Value	$1.00
Mintage	*See below*
Date issued	*See below*
Issue Price	*See below*
Retail Average	*See below*

Mc 12/ 06	2012	$1	PM/ AP	tba	April 17, 2012	15.95	25
Mc 12/ 06a	2012	$1	Melbourne	250	April 21, 20112	50	n/a
Mc 12/ 06b	2012	$1	Brisbane	125	Sept. 1 - 2, 2012	n/a	70
Mc 12/ 06c	2012	$1	Perth	100	Oct. 6 - 7, 2012	35	70

[a] Issued by the Royal Philatelic Society of Victoria at its 6th annual one-day bourse on April 21 2012, at Purves House, 303 High Street, Ashburton. 250 PNC's were overprinted in gold foil.
[b] An overprint of 125 covers were released at the APTA Stamp, Coin & Collectables Fair held in Brisbane's Table Tennis Centre, Windsor from September 1st & 2nd, 2012.
[c] Just 100 individually numbered covers were released at the Perth Stamp & Coin Fair held at the University of WA, Crawley. The gold leaf overprint read : "APTA Proudly supporting the PERTH STAMP & COIN SHOW 6th-7th October 2012"

PNC : PHILATELIC NUMISMATIC COVERS

2012 OLYMPIC TEAM MASCOT & THE ROAD TO LONDON

Reference #	Mc 12/ 07
Issuing Mint	Perth
Face Value	$1.00
Mintage	*See below*
Date issued	*See below*
Issue Price	*See below*
Retail Average	*See below*

Mc 12/ 07	2012	$1	PM/ AP	20,000	May 6, 2012	15.95	32.00
Mc 12/ 07a	2012	$1	Melb.APTA	125	July 21-22, 2012	n/a	n/a

[a] An overprint of 125 covers were released at the APTA Stamp, Coin & Collectables Fair held at the Malvern Town Hall, Melbourne from July 21st & 22nd, 2012.

2012 LONDON OLYMPICS - 3 COIN SET

Reference #	Mc 12/ 08
Issuing Mint	Perth
Face Value	$1 x 3
Mintage	10,000
Date issued	17/ 07/ 2012
Issue Price	34.95
Retail Average	50.00

2012 GOLD MEDALIST. FREESTYLE WOMEN'S 4x100m

Reference #	Mc 12/ 09
Issuing Mint	Perth
Face Value	$1.00
Mintage	1,000
Date issued	01/ 08/ 2012
Issue Price	1 of 7 in folder
Retail Average	20.00

Alicia Coutts, Cate Campbell, Brittany Elmslie & Melanie Schlanger set new world record of 3.33.15.

2012 GOLD MEDALIST. SAILING. MEN'S LASER

Reference #	Mc 12/ 10
Issuing Mint	Perth
Face Value	$1.00
Mintage	1,000
Date issued	09/ 08/ 2012
Issue Price	1 of 7 in folder
Retail Average	20.00

Olympic gold medallist Tom Slingsby also won the 34th America's Cup as the strategist in Oracle. Team USA.

2012 GOLD MEDALIST. CYCLING : WOMEN'S SPRINT

Reference #	Mc 12/ 11
Issuing Mint	Perth
Face Value	$1.00
Mintage	1,000
Date issued	01/ 08/ 2012
Issue Price	1 of 7 in folder
Retail Average	20.00

As well as winning gold, Anna Meare also won a bronze medal with Kaarle McCulloch in the team sprint.

2012 GOLD MEDALIST. ATHLETICS : 100m HURDLES

Reference #	Mc 12/ 12
Issuing Mint	Perth
Face Value	$1.00
Mintage	1,000
Date issued	01/ 08/ 2012
Issue Price	1 of 7 in folder
Retail Average	20.00

Sally Pearson won gold in London with a new Olympic record time of 12.35s (Wind (m/s): -0.2)

2012 GOLD MEDALIST. SAILING : MEN'S 49er CLASS

Reference #	Mc 12/ 13
Issuing Mint	Perth
Face Value	$1.00
Mintage	1,000
Date issued	13/ 08/ 2012
Issue Price	1 of 7 in folder
Retail Average	20.00

Iain Jensen & Nathan Outteridge won the 2009 and 2011 49er World Championships as long as gold in the 2012 Summer Olympics.

2012 GOLD MEDALIST. CANOE / KAYAK : MEN'S K4 1000m

Reference #	Mc 12/ 14
Issuing Mint	Perth
Face Value	$1.00
Mintage	1,000
Date issued	13/ 08/ 2012
Issue Price	1 of 7 in folder
Retail Average	20.00

Team members were Jacob Clear David SmithTate Smith and Murray Stewart

2012 GOLD MEDALIST. SAILING. MEN'S 470 CLASS

Reference #	Mc 12/ 15
Issuing Mint	Perth
Face Value	$1.00
Mintage	1,000
Date issued	13/ 08/ 2012
Issue Price	1 of 7 in folder
Retail Average	20.00

Mathew Belcher & Malcolm Page have a string of world championship wins as well as a London gold medal

2012 SIR DOUGLAS MAWSON CENTENARY

Reference #	Mc 12/ 16
Issuing Mint	RAM
Face Value	$1.00
Mintage	15,000
Date issued	04/ 09/ 2012
Issue Price	15.95
Retail Average	18.00

• Available in other issues

2012 AUSTRALIAN ZOO - SUMATRAN TIGER

Reference #	Mc 12/ 17
Issuing Mint	RAM
Face Value	$1.00
Mintage	*See below*
Date issued	*See below*
Issue Price	*See below*
Retail Average	*See below*

• Available in other issues

Mc 12/ 17	2012	$1	RAM/ AP	tba	September 28, 2012	15.95	32
Mc 12/ 17 a	2013	$1	Melb. AFTA	125	Feb. 09 -10, 2013	32	33

[a] An overprint of 125 covers were released at the APTA Stamp, Coin & Collectables Fair held at the Malvern Town Hall from February 9 - 10, 2013.

2012/2013 BATHURST. RACING ENDURANCE

Reference #	Mc 12/ 18
Issuing Mint	RAM
Face Value	.50¢
Mintage	*See below*
Date issued	*See below*
Issue Price	*See below*
Retail Average	*See below*

• PNC 2012. Coin dated 2013

Mc 12/ 18	2012	.50¢	RAM/ AP	15,000	October 2, 2012	19.95	34
Mc 12/ 18 a	2012	.50¢	Melb. APTA	125	Nov 10-11, 2012	30	70

[a] An overprint of 125 covers were released at the APTA Stamp, Coin & Collectables Fair held at the Box Hill Lower Town Hall, Melbourne on February 10 - 11, 2012.

2012 FIFTY YEARS OF AUSTRALIAN BALLET

Reference #	Mc 12/ 19
Issuing Mint	RAM
Face Value	.50¢
Mintage	15,000
Date issued	16/ 10/ 2012
Issue Price	19.95
Retail Average	35.00

• *Available in other issues*

2012 AFL PREMIERS SYDNEY SWANS

Reference #	Mc 12/ 20
Issuing Mint	RAM
Face Value	$1.00
Mintage	15,000
Date issued	26/ 10/ 2012
Issue Price	19.95
Retail Average	45.00

• *Covers are numbered*

A coin similar to the above was used for the grand final toss before the grand final was played out on September 29, 2012. Obviously no one knew the winner, so the reverse of the coin was generic. This same unspecified coin was used in the PNC that came out about three weeks after the game was played out. Later, another coin heralding the Sydney Swans as the champions was struck for several other asociated issues. All 15,000 covers were individually numbered.

2012 REMEMBRANCE DAY COLOURED

Reference #	Mc 12/ 21
Issuing Mint	RAM
Face Value	"C" mm $2.00
Mintage	20,000
Date issued	01/ 11/ 2012
Issue Price	19.95
Retail Average	38.00

• *Available in other issues*

2012 MERRY CHRISTMAS THEME

Reference #	Mc 12/ 22
Issuing Mint	Perth
Face Value	$1.00
Mintage	To order
Date issued	01/ 11/ 2012
Issue Price	15.95
Retail Average	30.00

• *Exclusive to PNC issue*

2013 LUNAR. YEAR OF THE SNAKE

Reference #	Mc13/ 01
Issuing Mint	Perth
Face Value	$1.00
Mintage	*See below*
Date issued	*See below*
Issue Price	*See below*
Retail Average	*See below*

• *Exclusive to PNC issue*

Mc 13/ 01	2013	$1	RAM/ AP	28,205	January 8, 2013	15.95	18.00
Mc 13/ 01 a	2013	$1	Brisbane	100	March 14-16, 2013	n/a	70.00

[a] An overprint of 100 covers were released at the APTA Stamp, Coin & Collectables Fair held in Brisbane from March 13th & 14th, 2013. The wording "100 Club 2013" was part of the overprint on the overprint.

See their advertisement on page 21

PNC : PHILATELIC NUMISMATIC COVERS

RESTRICTED TO OFFICIAL ISSUES FEATURING COINS - NO MEDALLIONS

2013 SURFING AUSTRALIA

Reference #	Mc13/ 02
Issuing Mint	RAM
Face Value	.50¢
Mintage	See below
Date issued	*See below*
Issue Price	*See below*
Retail Average	*See below*

• Available in other issues

Mc 13/ 02	2013	50¢	RAM/ AP	15,000	February 12, 2013	15.95	25
Mc 13/ 02 a	2013	50¢	Brisbane	130	Sept. 21-22, 2013	36	40

[a] Issued by the APTA Stamp, Coin & Collectables Fair held at the Table Tennis Centre at Downey Park, Winsor, Brisbane from September 21-22, 2013. Red foil op.

2013 CENTENARY OF CANBERRA

Reference #	Mc13/ 03
Issuing Mint	RAM
Face Value	.20¢
Mintage	To order
Date issued	05/ 03/ 2013
Issue Price	15.95
Retail Average	28.00

• Available in other issues

Mc 13/ 03	2013	20¢	RAM/ AP	tba	March 5, 2013	15.95	30
Mc 13/ 03 a	2013	20¢	Melb.RPSV	100	April 20, 2013	40	n/a

[a] A gold overprint limited edition of just 100 covers was produced by the Royal Philatelic Society of Victoria at its 7th annual one-day bourse held on April 20, 2013

2013 KOOKABURRA BUSH BABIES II

Reference #	Mc 13/ 04
Issuing Mint	Perth
Face Value	$1.00
Mintage	*See below*
Date issued	*See below*
Issue Price	*See below*
Retail Average	*See below*

• Exclusive to PNC issue

Mc 13/ 04	2013	$1	PM/ AP	tba	April 2, 2013	15.95	25
Mc 13/ 04 a	2013.	$1	Melb/RPSV	100	April 20, 2013	50	n/a
Mc 13/ 04 b	2013	$1	Melb/ APTA	130	July 20 - 21, 2013	36	55

2013 QUEEN'S CORONATION JUBILEE

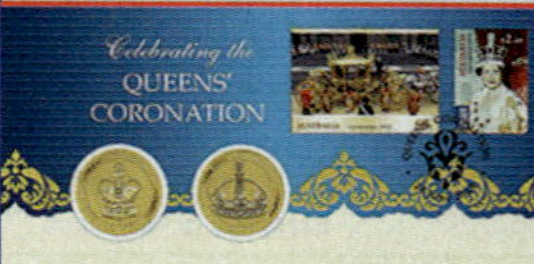

Reference #	Mc13/ 05
Issuing Mint	Perth
Face Value	$1.00 x 2
Mintage	To order
Date issued	09/ 04/ 2013
Issue Price	24.95
Retail Average	35.00

• Exclusive to PNC issue

2013 POSSUM BUSH BABIES II

Reference #	Mc13/ 06
Issuing Mint	Perth
Face Value	$1.00
Mintage	To order
Date issued	07/ 05/ 2013
Issue Price	15.95
Retail Average	25.00

• Exclusive to PNC issue

PNC : PHILATELIC NUMISMATIC COVERS

2013 COMMONWEALTH STAMPS CENTENARY

Reference #	Mc13/ 07
Issuing Mint	RAM
Face Value	.50¢
Mintage	*See below*
Date issued	*See below*
Issue Price	*See below*
Retail Average	*See below*

• Available in other issues

Mc 13/ 07	2013	$1	RAM/ AP	tba	May 10, 2013	15.95	25
Mc 13/ 07 a	2013	$1	Melb/ Expo	150	May 10-58, 2013	40	45

This gold leaf overprint postmark commemorated the 2013 *World Stamp Expo* held in Melbourne Exhibition Hall between May 10 - 15, 2013.

2013 BLACK CAVIAR RACE HORSE

Reference #	Mc13/ 08
Issuing Mint	RAM
Face Value	$1.00
Mintage	*See below*
Date issued	*See below*
Issue Price	*See below*
Retail Average	*See below*

• No colour $1. Unique to PNC

Mc 13/ 08	2013	$1	RAM/ AP	56,065	May 10, 2013	19.95	30
Mc 13/ 08 a	2013	$1	Perth	150	August 17-18, 2013	40	n/a

[a] Black Caviar PNC overprinted *"PERTH STAMP & COIN SHOW 17th-18th August 2013 Proudly supported by APTA"* with both the PS&CS & APTA logos. Limited to only 150 and each individually numbered.The fair was held at the Guild Function Centre, Nedlands.

2013 CENTENARY OF KANGAROO STAMP

Reference #	Mc13/ 09
Issuing Mint	'M' mm RAM
Face Value	.50¢
Mintage	*See below*
Date issued	*See below*
Issue Price	*See below*
Retail Average	*See below*

• Available in other issues

Mc 13/ 09	2013	50¢	RAM/AP	56,065	May 10, 2013	19.95	45
Mc 13/ 09 a	2013	50¢	Green o/p	1,250	May 10, 2013	30	95
Mc 13/ 09 b	2013	50¢	Silver o/p	1,250	May 11, 2013	30	95
Mc 13/ 09 c	2013	.50¢	Blue o/p	1,250	May 12, 2013	30	95
Mc 13/ 09 d	2013	.50¢	Mauve o/p	1,250	May 13, 2013	30	95
Mc 13/ 09 e	2013	.50¢	Black o/p	1,250	May 14, 2013	30	95
Mc 13/ 09 f	2013	.50¢	Red o/p	1,250	May 15, 2013	30	95

[a] May 10, 2013 [b] May 11, 2013 [c] May 12, 2013 [d] May 13, 2013 [e] May 14, 2013 [f] May 15, 2013

Issued at the 2013 *World Stamp Expo* held in Melbourne between May 10 - 15th. Each day a different coloured foil postmark was used to cancel a maximum of 1,250 covers per day. Any leftovers were destroyed. This was the first fifty cent piece to feature a mintmark, an 'M' for Melbourne.

2013 AUSTRALIA'S FIRST BANKNOTE

Reference #	Mc13/ 10
Issuing Mint	Perth & RAM
Face Value	$1 & .20¢
Mintage	15,000
Date issued	11/ 05/ 2013
Issue Price	29.95
Retail Average	39.95

• Available in other issues

2013 PLATYPUS BUSH BABIES II

Reference #	Mc13/ 12
Issuing Mint	Perth
Face Value	$1.00
Mintage	To order
Date issued	04/ 06/ 2013
Issue Price	15.95
Retail Average	25.00

• Exclusive to PNC issue

2013 PARLIAMENT HOUSE

Reference #	Mc13/ 13
Issuing Mint	RAM
Face Value	.20¢
Mintage	15,000
Date issued	02/ 07/2013
Issue Price	15.95
Retail Average	25.00

• Available in other issues

2013 ECHIDNA BUSH BABIES II

Reference #	Mc13/ 14
Issuing Mint	Perth
Face Value	$1.00
Mintage	To order
Date issued	02/ 07/ 2013
Issue Price	15.95
Retail Average	25.00

• Exclusive to PNC issue

2013 WOMBAT BUSH BABIES II

Reference #	Mc13/ 15
Issuing Mint	Perth
Face Value	$1.00
Mintage	To order
Date issued	06/ 08/ 2013
Issue Price	11.95
Retail Average	25.00

• Exclusive to PNC issue

2013 LEICHHART. AUST/ GERMANY JOINT ISSUE

Reference #	Mc13/ 16
Issuing Mint	Perth
Face Value	$1.00
Mintage	14,000
Date issued	08/ 10/ 2013
Issue Price	15.95
Retail Average	28.00

• Exclusive to PNC issue

2013 BIRTH OF PRINCE GEORGE

Reference #	Mc13/ 17
Issuing Mint	Perth
Face Value	$1.00
Mintage	*See below*
Date issued	*See below*
Issue Price	*See below*
Retail Average	*See below*

Mc 13/ 17	2013	$1	RM/ AP	12,000	October 18, 2013	15.95	25
Mc 13/ 17 a	2013	$1	Melb.	300	Oct.18 - 19, 2013	n/a	60

[a] 300 gold leaf cancelled pnc's were released at the World Stamp Expo held in Melbourne at the Ethad Stadium from October 18th and 19th.

PNC : PHILATELIC NUMISMATIC COVERS

RESTRICTED TO OFFICIAL ISSUES FEATURING COINS - NO MEDALLIONS

2013 HOLEY DOLLAR & DUMP BICENTENARY

Reference #	Mc13/ 18
Issuing Mint	RAM
Face Value	'C'mm $1.00
Mintage	*See below*
Date issued	*See below*
Issue Price	*See below*
Retail Average	*See below*

- *Coin has 'C' mintmark*

Mc 13/ 18	2013	$1	RAM/ AP	15,000	October 22, 2013	15.95	20
Mc 13/ 18 a	2013	$1	Melb/ APTA	130	Nov. 9 -10, 2013	36	55

[a] An overprint issue of 130 covers were released at the APTA/ ANDA Stamp, Coin & Collectables Fair held at the Box Hill Main Town Hall, 1022 Whitehorse Road, Box Hill from Nov 9-10, 2013

2013 MERRY CHRISTMAS

Reference #	Mc13/ 19
Issuing Mint	Perth
Face Value	$1.00
Mintage	12,000
Date issued	01/ 11/ 2013
Issue Price	15.95
Retail Average	27.00

- *Exclusive to PNC issue*

2013 BLACK CAVIAR SPECIAL EDITION

Reference #	Mc 13/ 20
Issuing Mint	RAM/ RM [UK]
Face Value. Each coin	$1.00
Proof Silver	99.9% fine silver
Diameter. Each coin	40mm
Mintage. For this issue	100
Date issued	01/ 11/ 2013
Issue Price	250.00
Retail Average	375.00

(*) The PNC is a large size with decorative foiling and a commemorative postmark in a special leather-look wallet. The stamps were produced at the May 2013 World Stamp Expo in Melbourne and cancelled on November 1, 2013.

2013 ARMY CHAPLAINS

Reference #	Mc 13/ 21
Issuing Mint	RAM
Face Value	.20¢
Mintage	300
Date issued	01/ 11/ 2013
Issue Price	29.95
Retail Average	450.00

- *Available in other issues*

2013 AFL PREMIERS HAWTHORN

Reference #	Mc13/ 22
Issuing Mint	RAM
Face Value	$1.00
Mintage	13,000
Date issued	03/ 12/ 2013
Issue Price	24.95
Retail Average	20.00

- *Available in other issues*

PNC : PHILATELIC NUMISMATIC COVERS

RESTRICTED TO OFFICIAL ISSUES FEATURING COINS - NO MEDALLIONS

2014 LUNAR ISSUE. THE YEAR OF THE HORSE

Reference #	Mc14/ 01
Issuing Mint	Perth
Face Value	$1.00
Mintage	15,000
Date issued	07/ 01/ 2014
Issue Price	15.95
Retail Average	25.00

• Exclusive to PNC issue

2014 ROYAL CHRISTENING - PRINCE GEORGE

Reference #	Mc14/ 02
Issuing Mint	RAM
Face Value	.50¢
Mintage	*See below*
Date issued	*See below*
Issue Price	*See below*
Retail Average	*See below*

• Available in other issues

Mc 14/ 02	2014	.50¢	RAM/ AP	14,000	January 07, 2014	15.95	20
Mc 14/ 02a	2014	.50¢	Melb/APTA	130	February 8-9, 2014	36	50
Mc 14/ 02b	2014	.50¢	Melb/RPSV	100	April 12, 2014	50	n/a

[a] An overprint issue of 130 covers were released at the APTA Stamp, Coin & Collectables Fair held at the Malvern Town Hall, Melbourne,/l;k/ from February 8-9, 2014.
[b] An overprint issue of 100 covers were released at the Royal Philatelic Society of Victoria Inc on 8th Annual Bourse (12 April 2014)

2014 THE URN RETURNS

Reference #	Mc14/ 03
Issuing Mint	RAM
Face Value	.20¢
Mintage	7,500
Date issued	20/ 01/ 2014
Issue Price	24.95
Retail Average	55.00

• Coin is dated 2013

2014 THE CENTENARY OF ANZAC - OUR BOYS

Reference #	Mc14/ 04
Issuing Mint	RAM
Face Value	$1.00
Mintage	*See below*
Date issued	*See below*
Issue Price	*See below*
Retail Average	*See below*

Mc 14/ 04	2014	$1	RAM/ AP	12,000	April 22, 2014	15.95	42
Mc 14/ 04 a	2014	$1	Brisbane	130	May 24-25, 2014	36.00	50

[a] Just 130 specially covers were sold at the ANDA/ APTA Brisbane Fair held at the Brisbane Table Tennis Centre on May 24-25, 2014.

2014 ANZAC - DECLARATION OF WWI

Reference #	Mc14/ 05
Issuing Mint	Perth
Face Value	$1.00
Mintage	To order
Date issued	22/ 04/ 2014
Issue Price	15.95
Retail Average	20.00

• Exclusive to PNC issue

PNC : PHILATELIC NUMISMATIC COVERS

2014 THE CENTENARY OF RED CROSS

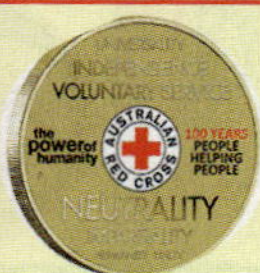

Reference #	Mc14/ 06
Issuing Mint	Perth
Face Value	$1.00
Mintage	*See below*
Date issued	*See below*
Issue Price	*See below*
Retail Average	*See below*

• Exclusive to PNC issue

Mc 14/ 06	2014	$1	PM/ AP	10,000	May 6, 2014	15.95	26
Mc 14/ 06 a	2014	$1	Melb/ APTA	125	Nov 8-9, 2014	36	50

[a] At the APTA & ANDA Melbourne Stamp, Coin & Collectables Fair held at the Malvern Town Hall on November 8-9, there was a release of 125 overprinted and gold foil cancelled covers.

2014 BANJO PATERSON - BUSH BALLADS

Reference #	Mc 14/ 07
Issuing Mint	Perth
Face Value	$1.00
Mintage	*See below*
Date issued	*See below*
Issue Price	*See below*
Retail Average	*See below*

• Exclusive to PNC issue

Mc 14/ 07	2014	$1	PM/ AP	12,000	May 13, 2014	15.95	28
Mc 14/ 07 a	2014	$1	Melb/ APTA	130	July 19-20, 2014	36	50

[a] 130 overprinted and foil cancelled covers were available at the APTA & ANDA Melbourne Fair held at the Malvern Town Hall on July 19-20, 2014.

2014 AVIATION & SUBMARINES CENTENARY

Reference #	Mc 14/ 08
Issuing Mint	Perth
Face Value	$1.00 x 2
Mintage	*See below*
Date issued	*See below*
Issue Price	*See below*
Retail Average	*See below*

• Exclusive to PNC issue

Mc 14/ 08	2014	$1x2	PM/ AP	10,000	August 5, 2014	24.95	30
Mc 14/ 08 a	2014	$1x2	Perth	150	Aug. 16-17, 2014	40	45

[a] One of the few multi-coin PNC's to be issued. It was also one of the few two-coin fair issues. Just 150 covers were issued for the Perth Stamp & Coin Show held at the University of WA, Guild Function Centre, Crawley, WA from August 16-17th.

2014 THINGS THAT STING - THE BULL ANT

Reference #	Mc 14/ 09
Issuing Mint	RAM
Face Value	$1.00
Mintage	11,000
Date issued	23/ 09/ 2014
Issue Price	15.95
Retail Average	18.00

• Available in other issues

2014 SYDNEY/ EMDEN - KEELING COCOS

Reference #	Mc 14/ 10
Issuing Mint	RAM
Face Value	.50¢
Mintage	10,000
Date issued	14/ 10/ 2014
Issue Price	15.95
Retail Average	35.00

• Available in other issues

PNC : PHILATELIC NUMISMATIC COVERS

2014 MERRY CHRISTMAS

Reference #	Mc14/ 11
Issuing Mint	Perth
Face Value	$1.00
Mintage	*See below*
Date issued	*See below*
Issue Price	*See below*
Retail Average	*See below*

• Exclusive to PNC issue

Mc 14/ 11	2014	$1	PM/ AP	9,700	Oct 31, 2014	15.95	30
Mc 14/ 11 a	2014	$1	ERROR	Unique?	Oct 31, 2014	15.95	350
Mc 14/ 11 b	2014	$1	Melb	300	July 23-26, 2009	n/a	200

[a] There is at least one example of an error associated with this issue. As can be seen from the image at the right, there is a double layer of stamps adhered to the envelope. The fact that the cancellation stamp is over the stamp would have to help determine that the PNC is genuine. The price given above may change if more errors are found.
[b] 250 specially overprinted, and individually numbered, folders were a feature of the Melbourne Stamp Show held from July 23 - 26, 2009.

2014 REMEMBRANCE DAY. SINGLE COIN ISSUE

Reference #	Mc14/ 12
Issuing Mint	RAM
Face Value	$2.00
Mintage	14,500
Date issued	02/ 11/ 2014
Issue Price	19.95
Retail Average	30.00

• Available in other issues

2014 REMEMBRANCE DAY. TWO COIN ISSUE

Reference #	Mc14/ 13
Issuing Mint 'C' mm	RAM
Face Value	$2 pair
Mintage	1,111
Date issued	11/ 11/ 2014
Issue Price	59.95
Retail Average	195.00

• Available in other issues

This unusual offering is more than a low numbered variation of an established variation. Two coin issues are rare and this one breaks new ground with one of the coins being two years old. The 2012 $2 Remembrance coin featured the 'C' for Canberra mintmark. The 2014 $2 Remembrance coin is also the coloured variety but does not include any mintmark. The special cancellation partly reads *"11am, 11/11/14."*

2014 AFL PREMIERS HAWTHORN

Reference #	Mc14/ 14
Issuing Mint	RAM
Face Value	$1.00
Mintage	5,000
Date issued	08/ 12/ 2014
Issue Price	24.95
Retail Average	25.00

2015 CHINESE NEW YEAR - LION DANCE

Reference #	Mc15/ 01
Issuing Mint	Perth
Face Value	$1.00
Mintage	8,888
Date issued	08/ 01/ 2015
Issue Price	19.95
Retail Average	16.00

• Exclusive to PNC issue

PNC : PHILATELIC NUMISMATIC COVERS

RESTRICTED TO OFFICIAL ISSUES FEATURING COINS - NO MEDALLIONS

2015 YEAR OF THE GOAT

Reference #	Mc15/02
Issuing Mint	Perth
Face Value	$1.00
Mintage	*See below*
Date issued	*See below*
Issue Price	*See below*
Retail Average	*See below*

• Exclusive to PNC issue

Mc 15/02	2015	$1	PM/ AP	15,000	January 8, 2015	15.95	22
Mc 15/02 a	2015	$1	Perth	200	March 7-8, 2015	n/a	50
Mc 15/02 b	2015	$1	Brisbane	125	May 23-24, 2015	n/a	50
Mc 15/02 c	2015	$1	Punchbowl	100	May 23-24, 2015	n/a	50

[a] An overprint of 200 covers were released at the ANDA Stamp & Coin Fair held in Perth on March 7th & 8th, 2015.
[b] An overprint of 125 covers were released at the ANDA/APTA Stamp, Coin & Collectables Fair held in Brisbane on May 23th & 24th, 2015
[c] First Day Cover overprinted "Overprint Booklets Collectors Club Stamp Fair 2015 Punchbowl Stamp & Coin Fair" with OPBCC logo. No.....of only 100.

2015 ICC WORLD CRICKET CUP

Reference #	Mc15/03
Issuing Mint	RAM
Face Value	.20¢
Mintage	8,500
Date issued	03/02/2015
Issue Price	19.95
Retail Average	35.00

• Available in other issues

2015 ON YOUR WEDDING DAY

Reference #	Mc15/04
Issuing Mint	Perth
Face Value	$1.00
Mintage	5,000
Date issued	10/03/2015
Issue Price	15.95
Retail Average	30.00

• Exclusive to PNC issues

2015 GALLIPOLI - LANDING CENTENARY

Reference #	Mc15/05
Issuing Mint	RAM
Face Value	.50¢
Mintage	*See below*
Date issued	*See below*
Issue Price	*See below*
Retail Average	*See below*

• Available in other issues

Mc 15/05	2015	.50¢	RAM/ AP	12,000	April 14, 2015	15.95	30
Mc 15/05 a	2015	.50¢	Syd/ ANDA	250	April 16-19th, 2015	50	50
Mc 15/05 b	2015	.50¢	Perth	75	August 1-2nd, 2015	50	50

[a] This overprinted Stamp and Coin cover was produced by ANDA for the Sydney Stamp Show that was held from April 16 - 19th, 2015. Cover overprinted "ANDA at SSE15 ANZAC Centenary 16th-19th April 2015" with ANDA logo. No.... of 250. Sold out at the event.
[b] Cover overprinted "Perth Stamp & Coin Show 2015 1st & 2nd August 2015 Proudly Sponsored by Ace Stamp Auctions" with Ace & show logos. Issue was limited to just 75 covers.

PNC : PHILATELIC NUMISMATIC COVERS

RESTRICTED TO OFFICIAL ISSUES FEATURING COINS - NO MEDALLIONS

2015 GALLIPOLI - SIMPSON & HIS DONKEY

Reference #	Mc15/ 06
Issuing Mint	Perth
Face Value	$1.00
Mintage	See below
Date issued	See below
Issue Price	See below
Retail Average	See below

Exclusive to PNC issue

Mc 15/ 06	2015	$1	PM/ AP	11,000	April 14, 2015	15.95	28
Mc 15/ 06 a	2015	$1	Sydney	250	April 16-19, 2015	15.95	50
Mc 15/ 06 b	2015	$1	Perth	75	August 1-2, 2015	35	50

[a]. This overprinted Stamp and Coin cover was produced by ANDA for the Sydney Stamp Show which was held from April 16 - 19th, 2015. The coin features a representation of Private John Simpson Kirkpatrick who enlisted in the AIF as John Simpson, and was drafted into the 3rd Ambulance of the Australian Medical Corps. Soon after landing at Gallipoli, he rescued a donkey (possibly more than one) to help him carry the wounded. Considering his enduring legend status, it is surprising to learn he was killed by a Turkish sniper just three weeks after beginning his life saving work.

[b]. PNC overprinted "PERTH STAMP & COIN SHOW 2015 Perth, Western Australia 1st & 2nd August 2015 Proudly Sponsored by Ace Stamp Auctions" overprinted with both PS&CS & Ace Stamp Auctions logos. Limited to only 75 and each individually numbered by hand.

2015 MAGNA CARTA. 800 YEARS

Reference #	Mc15/ 07
Issuing Mint	RAM
Face Value	.20¢
Mintage	7,500
Date issued	02/ 07/ 2015
Issue Price	15.95
Retail Average	35.

• Individually numbered

2015 CENTENARY OF LIGHTHOUSES [RAM]

Reference #	Mc15/ 08
Issuing Mint	RAM
Face Value	$1.00
Mintage	9,000
Date issued	07/ 07/ 2015
Issue Price	15.95
Retail Average	32.00

• Exclusive to PNC issue

2015 CENTENARY OF LIGHTHOUSES [PM]

Reference #	Mc15/ 09
Issuing Mint	Perth
Face Value	$1.00
Mintage	See below
Date issued	See below
Issue Price	See below
Retail Average	See below

• Exclusive to PNC issue

Mc15/09	2015	$1	PM/ AP	10,000	July 7, 2015	15.95	25
Mc15/09a	2015	$1	Perth/ APTA	100	August 1-2, 2015	n/a	55

[a] 100 specially overprinted covers were produced by the 100 Club and released at the APTA Perth Coin & Stamp Fair held on August 1st & 2nd, 2015.

There is nothing that collectors hate more than a series they have been building up, suddenly stops or is rebranded. In recent years there have been some rearranging of issues that were starting to look like a regular yearly staple. The annual footie grand final PNC's for 2016 retired hurt while Santa took his long running Christmas issue off shore and reinvented itself as a Tuvalu issue.

PNC : PHILATELIC NUMISMATIC COVERS

2015 NETBALL WORLD CUP

Reference #	Mc15/ 10
Issuing Mint	RAM
Face Value	.20¢
Mintage	*See below*
Date issued	*See below*
Issue Price	*See below*
Retail Average	*See below*

• Available in other issues

Mc15/10	2015	.20¢	RAM/ AP	9,000	August 4, 2015	19.95	22
Mc15/10a	2015	.20¢	Melb. ANDA	250	Aug 22 - 23, 2015	n/a	45
Mc15/10b	2015	.20¢	Sydney ANDA	150	October 9-10, 2015	n/a	50

Australia hosted - and won - the world's pinnacle netball championship in August 2015 . Held every four years since its inception in 1963, Australia previously hosted the Netball World Cup on two occasions, in Perth in 1967 and in Sydney in 1991.
[a] A limited edition of 250 gold foil covers were released at the ANDA Melbourne Show held on August 22nd & 23rd. Each PNC was individually numbered.
[b] At the APTA/ ANDA Sydney Show held from October 9th & 10th, a total of just 150 covers were issued. Each PNC was individually numbered with a gold overprint with wording *"ANDA/ APTA congratulates the Australian Diamonds Winners 2015."*

2015 WELCOME PRINCESS CHARLOTTE

Reference #	Mc15/ 11
Issuing Mint	RAM
Face Value	.50¢
Mintage	*See below*
Date issued	*See below*
Issue Price	*See below*
Retail Average	*See below*

• Exclusive to PNC issue

Mc15/11	2015	.50¢	RAM/ AP	9,000	August 25, 2015	15.95	22
Mc15/11a	2015	.50¢	Sydney	150	Oct 9 -10, 2015	33	135

[a] A limited edition of 150 covers was released at the APTA/ ANDA Sydney Show held from October 9th-10th. The overprint read *"ANDA/APTA Sydney Show 9th-10th October 2015"* in gold with APTA logo. Each PNC was individually numbered in gold foil.

2015 BIRTH OF PRINCESS CHARLOTTE

Reference #	Mc15/ 12
Issuing Mint	Perth
Face Value	$1.00
Mintage	*See below*
Date issued	*See below*
Issue Price	*See below*
Retail Average	*See below*

• Exclusive to PNC issue

Mc15/12	2015	$1	PM/ AP	9,000	August 25, 2015	15.95	17.50
Mc15/12 a	2015	$1	Perth Show	250	Aug 22 - 23, 2015	39.95	45

[a] A limited edition of 250 covers was released at the ANDA Melbourne Show held from August 22nd & 23rd. Each PNC was individually numbered.

2015 LONG MAY SHE REIGN. JOINT ISSUE WITH UK

Reference #	Mc15/ 13
Issuing Mint	RAM
Face Value	.50¢
Mintage	250
Date issued	9/ 09/ 2015
Issue Price	149.95
Retail Average	250.00

• Oversized envelope

The above is a combined RAM – UK issue. The RAM coin is the .50¢ also issued as part of a three-coin set. The British contribution was a commemorative One Crown coin.

PNC : PHILATELIC NUMISMATIC COVERS

2015 LONG MAY SHE REIGN - PERTH MINT

Reference #	Mc15/ 14
Issuing Mint	Perth
Face Value	$1.00
Mintage	9,000
Date issued	09/ 09/ 2015
Issue Price	15.95
Retail Average	36.00

• Exclusive to PNC issue

2015 LONGEST REIGNING COMMONWEALTH MONARCH

Reference #	Mc15/ 15
Issuing Mint	RAM
Face Value	.50¢
Mintage	9,000
Date issued	09/ 09/ 2015
Issue Price	15.95
Retail Average	48.00

• Available in other issues

2015 UNLIKELY HEROS - ANIMALS AT WAR

Reference #	Mc15/ 16
Issuing Mint	RAM
Face Value	$1.00
Mintage	*See below*
Date issued	*See below*
Issue Price	*See below*

• Available in other issues

Mc 15/ 16	2015	$1	RAM/ AP	10,805	October 27, 2015	15.95	25
Mc 15/ 16 b	2015	$1	Melb	150	Nov. 7 - 9, 2015	33.00	45
Mc 15/ 16 a	2015	$1	Canb	100	March 18-20, 2016	39.95	45

[a] Released at the APTA/ ANDA Melbourne Show held from November 7th-9th.
[b] Issued at the Canberra Philatelic Fair held from March 18 - 20, 2016. Each cover was individually numbered. Issue was a sellout.

2015 REMEMBRANCE DAY

Reference #	Mc15/ 17
Issuing Mint	RAM
Face Value	$2.00
Mintage	11,000
Date issued	27/ 10/ 2015
Issue Price	19.95
Retail Average	20.00

• Available in other issues

2015 MERRY CHRISTMAS

Reference #	Mc15/ 18
Issuing Mint	Perth
Face Value	$1.00
Mintage	8,000
Date issued	30/ 10/ 2015
Issue Price	15.95
Retail Average	40.00

• An overprint and exists & will be listed in the 24th ed.

2015 LIGHTHOUSES [PM] : LIMITED EDITION

Reference #	Mc15/ 19
Issuing Mint	Perth
Face Value	$1.00
Mintage	200
Date issued	02/ 11/ 2015
Issue Price	69.95
Retail Average	$195.00

• Exclusive to PNC issue

PNC : PHILATELIC NUMISMATIC COVERS

RESTRICTED TO OFFICIAL ISSUES FEATURING COINS - NO MEDALLIONS

2015 NORTH QLD COWBOYS NRL PREMIERS

Reference #	Mc15/ 20
Issuing Mint	RAM
Face Value	$1.00
Mintage	3,000
Date issued	09/ 11/ 2015
Issue Price	24.95
Retail Average	30.00

• *Available in other issues*

Scores:	Half-time	Full-time
North Queensland Cowboys	12	16
Brisbane Broncos	14	17
Tries:		

This PNC will be remembered for more than being the first ever NRL themed coin and stamp cover. Shortly after the covers were printed, it was discovered a very embarrassing error had occured in the recording of the full time scores. The final whistle indicated that the Brisbane Broncos 17, had a one point result over the North Queensland Cowboys [16]. However the PNC cover clearly showed the Cowboys holding the cup and it was soon realised that the scores were the wrong way around. The complete allocation of 3,000 covers was reprinted but it is thought that about 15 or so of the originals escaped into the market or 'souvenired' once the error was discovered. Several have been offered on ebay with prices ranging from $350 to $750.

2015 UNLIKELY HEROS. LIMITED EDITION

Reference #	Mc15/ 21
Issuing Mint	RAM
Face Value	$1.00
Mintage	300
Date issued	11/ 11/ 2015
Issue Price	39.95
Retail Average	450.00

• Individually numbereD

2015 THE HISTORY OF THE VICTORIA CROSS

Reference #	Mc15/ 22
Issuing Mint	RAM
Face Value	$5.00
Mintage	150
Date issued	11/ 11/ 2015
Issue Price	149.95
Retail Average	750.00

• Silver $5. Dated 2014

2015 HAWTHORN AFL PREMIERS

Reference #	Mc15/ 23
Issuing Mint	RAM
Face Value	$1.00
Mintage	3,000
Date issued	09/ 11/ 2015
Issue Price	24.95
Retail Average	42.00

• *Available in other issues*

2015 REMEMBRANCE DAY. LIMITED EDITION

Reference #	Mc15/ 24
Issuing Mint	RAM
Face Value	$2.00
Mintage	*See below*
Date issued	*See below*
Issue Price	*See below*
Retail Average	*See below*

• Individually numbered

Mc15/24	2015	$2	RAM/ AP	1,111	November 11, 2015	49.95	75.00

This issue differs in a number of ways from the more common general release. This low volume issue also featured two stamps rather than one and red foil is used to cancel the stamp. The representation of the poppies is also different. The PNC was not issued at a show. Collectors had to order by phone using a 'hot line' until the allocation was exhausted.

PNC : PHILATELIC NUMISMATIC COVERS

2016 ON YOUR WEDDING DAY

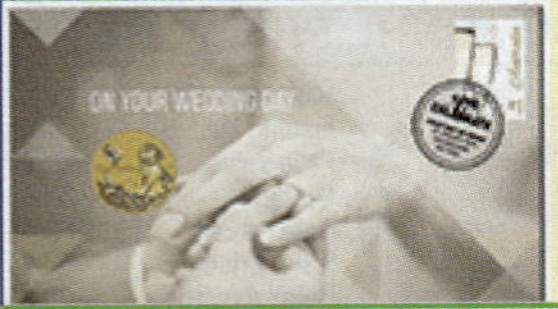

Reference #	Mc16/ 01
Issuing Mint	Perth
Face Value	$1.00
Mintage	3,500
Date issued	25/ 01/ 2016
Issue Price	19.95
Retail Average	20.00

• Exclusive to PNC issue

2016 YEAR OF THE MONKEY

Reference #	Mc16/ 02
Issuing Mint	Perth
Face Value	$1.00
Mintage	*See below*
Date issued	*See below*
Issue Price	*See below*
Retail Average	*See below*

• Exclusive to PNC issue

Mc16/02	2016	$1	PM/ AP	11,000	February 3, 2016	17.95	18
Mc16/02a	2016	$1	Perth	500	Feb 27-28, 2016	30	45

[a] A total of 500 Lunar PNC's were overprinted to mark the 2016 Perth ANDA Money Expo held on February 27th and 28th, 2016. As well as the overprinting, the covers also featured a gold foil cancellation.

2016 DECIMAL CURRENCY 1966-2016 - $1 COIN

Reference #	Mc16/ 03
Issuing Mint	RAM
Face Value	$1.00
Mintage	9,000
Date issued	09/ 02/ 2016
Issue Price	17.95
Retail Average	20.00

• Available in other issues

2016 DECIMAL CURRENCY 1966-2016 - $2 COIN

Reference #	Mc16/ 04
Issuing Mint	RAM
Face Value	$2.00
Mintage	9,000
Date issued	09/ 02/ 2016
Issue Price	19.95
Retail Average	22.00

• Available in other issues

2016 FAIR DINKUM. QLD. 'Q' FOR QUOKKA

Reference #	Mc16/ 05
Issuing Mint	RAM
Face Value	$1.00
Mintage	7,500
Date issued	01/ 03/ 2016
Issue Price	17.95
Retail Average	20.00

• Available in other issues

2016 FAIR DINKUM. WA 'W' FOR WOMBAT

Reference #	Mc16/ 06
Issuing Mint	RAM
Face Value	$1.00
Mintage	7,500
Date issued	01/ 03/ 2016
Issue Price	17.95
Retail Average	19.00

• Available in other issues

PNC : PHILATELIC NUMISMATIC COVERS

RESTRICTED TO OFFICIAL ISSUES FEATURING COINS - NO MEDALLIONS

2016 DECIMAL CURRENCY 1966-2016. $1 COIN

UNIQUE COVER COLOUR FOR CANBERRA COIN FAIR

Reference #	Mc16/ 07
Issuing Mint	RAM
Face Value	$1.00
Mintage	225
Date issued	18/ 03/ 2016
Issue Price	n/a
Retail Average	125.00

• Available in other issues

[a] The above was one of a number of special coin fair issues released at the three-day Canberra Coin & Stamp fair from March 18, 2016. This and the following $2 special overprint issue were limited to a total of 225 units with only 75 $1 PNCs and 75 $2 PNCs being released per day. Then, a different cancellation stamp was used as shown at right.

2016 DECIMAL CURRENCY 1966-2016. $2 COIN

UNIQUE COVER COLOUR FOR CANBERRA COIN FAIR

Reference #	Mc16/ 08
Issuing Mint	RAM
Face Value	$2.00
Mintage	225
Date issued	18/ 03/ 2016
Issue Price	n/a
Retail Average	125.00

• Exclusive to PNC issue

[a] Like the above mentioned One Dollar issue, the accompanying Two Dollar PNC also received a colour make-over to distinguish it from the general issue. THe postmarks were the same as the $1 issue. The main difference is that the envelope featured two $1 stamps.

2016 GUMNUT CENTENARY

Reference #	Mc16/ 09
Issuing Mint	Perth
Face Value	$1.00
Mintage	5,000
Date issued	29/ 03/ 2016
Issue Price	19.95
Retail Average	23.00

• Exclusive to PNC issue

2016 90TH BIRTHDAY QEII

Reference #	Mc16/ 10
Issuing Mint	Perth
Face Value	$1.00
Mintage	*See below*
Date issued	*See below*
Issue Price	*See below*
Retail Average	*See below*

• Exclusive to PNC issue

Mc16/10	2016	$1	PM/ AP	8,540	April 10, 2016	17.95	25
Mc16/10	2016	$1	Perth Show	100	August 1-2, 2016	n/a	n/a

PNC : PHILATELIC NUMISMATIC COVERS

RESTRICTED TO OFFICIAL ISSUES FEATURING COINS - NO MEDALLIONS

2016 LETTERS FROM THE FRONT

Reference #	Mc16/ 11
Issuing Mint	Perth
Face Value	$1.00
Mintage	*See below*
Date issued	*See below*
Issue Price	*See below*
Retail Average	*See below*

• Exclusive to PNC issue

Mc16/11	2016	$1	PM/ AP	10,000	April 12, 2016	17.95	17.95
Mc16/11a	2016	$1	Melb APTA	150	April 30, 2016	35.	60.00
Mc16/11a	2016	$1	Perth APTA	100	August 1-2, 2015	35	50.00

[a] A limited issue of 150 individually numbered covers were produced for the Melbourne APTA Coin , banknote & Stamp Show held on April 30, 2016.
[b] 100 specially covers were produced by the 100 Club and released at the Perth Coin & Stamp Fair held on August 1st & 2nd, 2015.

2016 BIRDWING BUTTERFLY

Reference #	Mc16/ 12
Issuing Mint	Perth
Face Value	$1.00
Mintage	7,500
Date issued	03/ 05/ 2016
Issue Price	17.95
Retail Average	18.00

• Available in other issues

2016 90TH BIRTHDAY QEII - ANDA BRISBANE FAIR

UNIQUE COVER COLOUR FOR ANDA MONEY EXPO

Reference #	Mc16/ 13
Issuing Mint	Perth
Face Value	$1.00
Mintage	600
Date issued	21/ 05/ 2016
Issue Price	35.00
Retail Average	65.00

• Exclusive to PNC issue

The 2016 Queen's 90th Birthday overprinted Stamp & Coin cover was produced by ANDA exclusively for the Brisbane ANDA Expo and features a different main colour to the regular issue. The ANDA logo and the Brisbane Money Expo date was overprinted in gold foil and individually numbered. This overprint was limited to only 600 covers and was sold out before show ended.

2016 FAIR DINKUM. ANDA BRISBANE FAIR

UNIQUE COVER COLOUR FOR STAMP & COIN FAIR

Reference #	Mc16/ 14
Issuing Mint	RAM
Face Value	$1.00
Mintage	500
Date issued	21-22/ 05/ 2016
Issue Price	35.00
Retail Average	50.00

• Only cover is exclusive

The above PNC was produced exclusively for ANDA's Brisbane fair held from May 21, 22nd 2016. The original general issue was blue in colour so this is a very distinctive issue. The ANDA logo appears in gold leaf under the 'Q' $1 coin as well as the wording *"ANDA The Brisbane Money Expo, May 21-22 2016."* Each of the 500 issued were individually numbered in gold foil.

PNC : PHILATELIC NUMISMATIC COVERS

2016 RSL CENTENARY. 1916-2016

Reference #	Mc16/ 15
Issuing Mint	Perth
Face Value	$1.00
Mintage	7,500
Date issued	31/ 05/ 2016
Issue Price	17.95
Retail Average	20.00

• Exclusive to PNC issue

2016 BIG TED/LITTLE TED. PLAY SCHOOL

Reference #	Mc16/ 16
Issuing Mint	RAM
Face Value	.50¢
Mintage	7,500
Date issued	26/ 07/ 2016
Issue Price	24.95
Retail Average	27.00

• Available in other issues

2016 JEMMA & HUMPTY. 50 YRS PLAY SCHOOL

Reference #	Mc16/ 17
Issuing Mint	RAM
Face Value	.2 x 50¢
Mintage	5,000
Date issued	26/ 07/ 2016
Issue Price	29.95
Retail Average	30.00

• Available in other issues

2016 DECIMAL CURRENCY. PERTH COIN

Reference #	Mc16/ 18
Issuing Mint	RAM
Face Value	$1.00
Mintage	100
Date issued	12-13/ 08/ 2016
Issue Price	40.00
Retail Average	60.00

• Available in other issues

2016 50th Anniversary of Decimal Currency PNC overprinted "PERTH STAMP & COIN SHOW Perth, Western Australia 12th & 13th August 2016 Proudly Sponsored by Ace Stamp Auctions" overprinted with both PS&CS & Ace Stamp Auctions logos. Also for the first time each cover has been individually autographed. It has been signed by Melinda Coombes, the $1 stamp and cover designer. Limited to only 100 and each individually numbered by hand

2016 FAIR DINKUM. ALPHABET PART 2 -'T'

Reference #	Mc16/ 19
Issuing Mint	RAM
Face Value	$1.00
Mintage	7,500
Date issued	16/ 08/ 2016
Issue Price	17.95
Retail Average	19.00

• Available in other issues

2016 FJ HOLDEN. GENERAL ISSUE. RED COVER

Reference #	Mc16/ 20
Issuing Mint	RAM
Face Value	.50¢
Mintage	8,000
Date issued	23/ 08/ 2016
Issue Price	24.95
Retail Average	29.95

• Available in other issues

PNC : PHILATELIC NUMISMATIC COVERS

RESTRICTED TO OFFICIAL ISSUES FEATURING COINS - NO MEDALLIONS

2016 MONARO. GENERAL ISSUE. BLACK COVER

Reference #	Mc16/ 21
Issuing Mint	RAM
Face Value	.50¢
Mintage	8,000
Date issued	23/ 08/ 2016
Issue Price	24.95
Retail Average	30.00

• Black main print

QUEEN'S 90TH BIRTHDAY. MACHIN PORTRAIT. 1966 - 1984

Reference #	Mc16/ 22
Issuing Mint	RAM
Face Value	.20¢
Mintage	9,000
Date issued	26/ 08/ 2016
Issue Price	17.95
Retail Average	16.00

• Available in other issues

QUEEN'S 90TH BIRTHDAY. MAKLOUF PORTRAIT. 1985 - 1998

Reference #	Mc16/ 23
Issuing Mint	RAM
Face Value	.20¢
Mintage	9,000
Date issued	26/ 08/ 2016
Issue Price	17.95
Retail Average	16.00

• Available in other issues

QUEEN'S 90TH BIRTHDAY. RANK BROADLEY PORTRAIT. 1998 -

Reference #	Mc16/ 24
Issuing Mint	RAM
Face Value	.50¢
Mintage	9,000
Date issued	26/ 08/ 2016
Issue Price	17.95
Retail Average	16.00

• Available in other issues

COIN FAIR ISSUES : As well as the above three PNC's issued to commemorate the Queen's 90th birthday, a similar set, but with different coloured covers, were issued for the Sydney ANDA fair. These are listed as Mc16/30, Mc16/31 & Mc16/.32

2016 FAIR DINKUM. ALPHABET 'T'

UNIQUE COVER COLOUR FOR COIN FAIR

Reference #	Mc16/ 25
Issuing Mint	RAM
Face Value	$1.00
Mintage	*See below*
Date issued	*See below*
Issue Price	*See below*
Retail Average	*See bel*

• Available in other issues

Mc16/25	2016	$1	Melb/ Day 1	200	August 27, 2016	35	70
Mc16/25a	2016	$1	Melb/ Day 2	200	August 28, 2016	35	70

[a] The above PNC was produced exclusively for ANDA's Melbourne fair held from August 27, 28th 2016. The original general issue was blue in colour so this is a very distinctive issue. The ANDA logo appears in gold leaf under the 'T' $1 coin as well as the wording *"The Melbourne Money Expo, August 27-28, 2016."* Each of the 200 issued were individually numbered in gold leaf.

PNC : PHILATELIC NUMISMATIC COVERS

2016 FJ HOLDEN 1953 - ANDA FAIR ISSUE

UNIQUE BLACK COVER COLOUR FOR COIN FAIR

Reference #	Mc16/ 26
Issuing Mint	RAM
Face Value	.50¢
Mintage	750
Date issued	27-28/ 08/16
Issue Price	45.00
Retail Average	80.00

• Available in other issues

750 exclusively coloured envelopes were produced for the ANDA Melbourne Money Expo held from August 27 28, 2016. The main print was in black ink. The more common general issue was predominately red. A silent auction was conducted for the sale of PNC's 1 to 10. There were no details concerning successful bids at the time of going to press.

2016 MONARO. ANDA EXPO. RED COVER

UNIQUE RED COVER COLOUR FOR COIN FAIR

Reference #	Mc16/ 27
Issuing Mint	RAM
Face Value	.50¢
Mintage	750
Date issued	27-28/ 08/16
Issue Price	35.00
Retail Average	80.00

• Available in other issues

750 exclusively coloured envelopes were produced for the ANDA Melbourne Money Expo held from August 27 - 28, 2016. The main print was in red ink. The more common general issue was predominately black. A silent auction was conducted for the sale of PNC's 1 to 10. There were no details concerning successful bids at the time of going to press

2016 DIRK HARTOG. 400TH ANNIVERSARY

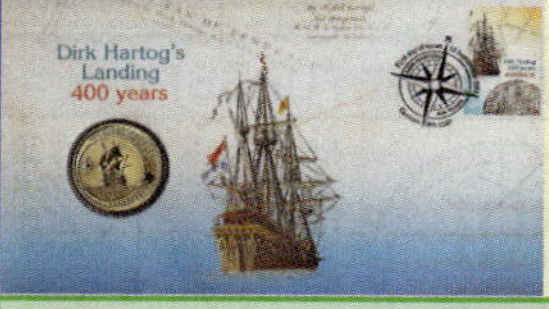

Reference #	Mc16/ 28
Issuing Mint	Perth
Face Value	$1.00
Mintage	7,501
Date issued	13/ 09/ 16
Issue Price	17.95
Retail Average	19.95

• Exclusive to PNC issue

Mc16/28	2016	$1	PM/ AP	7,501	Sept. 13, 2016	19.95	20
Mc16/28a	2016	$1	Mandurah	100	November 3, 2016	35	45
Mc16/28b	2016	$1	Mandurah	100	November 4, 2016	35	45
Mc16/28c	2016	$1	Mandurah	100	November 5, 2016	35	45

[a/b/c] Issued at the Mandurah Stamp/Coin Fair held from Nov. 3 to 5th, this offering consisted of just 100 envelopes being released on each of the three days. Each cover featured a different postmark and local emblem that were unique to each day,

2016 VIETNAM WAR. 1962-1975

Reference #	Mc16/ 29
Issuing Mint	RAM
Face Value	$1.00
Mintage	*See below*
Date issued	*See below*
Issue Price	*See below*
Retail Average	*See below*

• Available in other issues

Mc16/29	2016	.50¢	RAM/ AP	8,000	October 11 2016	17.95	18
Mc16/29a	2016	.50¢	Syd. ANDA	600	October 15-16	50	50
Mc16/29b	2016	.50¢	Mandurah	100	November 3-5	50	50

[a] Released for the ANDA Sydney Money Expo held on the weekend of 15th - 16th October 2016. The set has been altered from the original issue to make it an exclusive issue for the ANDA Expo. Just 600 covers were produced.
[b] Issued at the Perth Coin and Stamp Fair at Mandurah on November 3-5, 2016 featured just 100 covers with a unique gold leaf overprint.

PNC : PHILATELIC NUMISMATIC COVERS

QUEEN'S 90TH BIRTHDAY. MACHIN PORTRAIT. 1966 - 1984

2016 DIFFERENT COLOUR SYDNEY ANDA MONEY EXPO

Reference #	Mc16/ 30
Issuing Mint	RAM
Face Value	.20¢
Mintage	750
Date issued	15-16/ 10/ 2016
Issue Price	Part x 3 set
Retail Average	30.00

• Gold foil ANDA overprint

QUEEN'S 90TH BIRTHDAY. MAKLOUF PORTRAIT. 1985 - 1998

2016 DIFFERENT COLOUR SYDNEY ANDA MONEY EXPO

Reference #	Mc16/ 31
Issuing Mint	RAM
Face Value	.20¢
Mintage	750
Date issued	15-16/ 10/ 2016
Issue Price	Part x 3 set
Retail Average	30.00

• Gold foil ANDA overprint

QUEEN'S 90TH BIRTHDAY. RANK BROADLEY PORTRAIT. 1998 -

2016 DIFFERENT COLOUR SYDNEY ANDA MONEY EXPO

Reference #	Mc16/ 32
Issuing Mint	RAM
Face Value	.50¢
Mintage	750
Date issued	15-16/ 10/ 2016
Issue Price	Part x 3 set
Retail Average	40.00

• Gold foil ANDA overprint

2016 REMEMBRANCE. LEST WE FORGET

Reference #	Mc16/ 33
Issuing Mint	RAM
Face Value	$1.00
Mintage	9,000
Date issued	02/ 11/ 2016
Issue Price	17.95
Retail Average	30.00

• Available in other issues

2016 90TH BIRTHDAY HER MAJESTY. PRESTIGE PNC

Reference #	Mc16/ 34
Issuing Mint	RAM
Face Value	3 x Various
Mintage	1,926
Date issued	2/ 11/2016
Issue Price	59.95
Retail Average	75.00

• Three RAM coins. Individually numbered covers with foiled Postmark. Exclusive digitally printed minisheet & an embossed presentation folder.

2016 DISTINCTLY AUSTRALIAN

Reference #	Mc16/ 35
Issuing Mint	RAM
Face Value	$5.00
Mintage	150
Date issued	02/11/ 2016
Issue Price	149.95
Retail Average	250.00

• Ballot. Limited edition Coin dated 2015

PNC : PHILATELIC NUMISMATIC COVERS

2016 REMEMBRANCE DAY. LEST WE FORGET

Reference #	Mc16/ 36
Issuing Mint	RAM
Face Value	$1.00
Mintage	1,111
Date issued	11/11/ 2016
Issue Price	49.95
Retail Average	125.00

• *Ballot. Limited edition*

2016 DIRK HARTOG - LIMITED EDITION

Reference #	Mc16/ 37
Issuing Mint	Perth
Face Value	$1.00
Mintage	100
Date issued	25/10/ 2016
Issue Price	149.95
Retail Average	375.00

Contains a 1oz Silver Perth Mint coin. Oversized envelope opens into a folder with numbered minisheet.

2017 ROOSTER : LUNAR NEW YEAR THEME

Reference #	Mc17/ 01
Issuing Mint	RAM
Face Value	$1.00
Mintage	150
Date issued	10/10/ 2017
Issue Price	17.95
Retail Average	18

• *Ballot. Limited edition*

2017 ROOSTER : LUNAR NEW YEAR THEME

UNIQUE GREEN COVER COLOUR FOR COIN FAIR

Reference #	Mc17/ 02
Issuing Mint	Perth
Face Value	$1.00
Mintage	750
Date issued	11/02 /17
Issue Price	30.00
Retail Average	30.00

• *Individually numbered*

750 exclusively green coloured envelopes were produced for the ANDA Perth Money Expo held from February 11-12, 2017. Each envelope was individually numbered.

THIS INTERESTING INSIGHT INTO THE NUMBERING SYSTEM WAS PART OF A LONGER EMAIL SENT TO ME WITH SOME OVERALL COMMENTS ABOUT PNC's.

The following observations were sent to me by Jim Mansell. "Over the years there were PNCs which didn't receive a number at all, and even instances where two different PNCs received the same number, presumably by accident. Sometimes a single digit number was listed as such, e.g., "6", and sometimes like this "06". This year, 2016, has been the year where I would say they have had the most successfully accurate numbering of PNCs, without mistakes, or not giving a PNC a number. That having been said, the sequence of the numbering does not necessarily match up with the dates the PNCs actually get released. In 2008 was the commencement of numbering PNCs for the year sequentially. Some missed out on a number however. In 2011 the ROYAL AUSTRALIAN NAVY PNC was "2011 Issue 05" and the Dame Nellie Melba PNC was "2011 Issue 5." The BUSH BABIES red kangaroo was "2011 Issue 14" and the INTERNATIONAL YEAR OF VOLUNTEERS PNC was also "2011 Issue 14"/ When they first started issuing PNCs they didn't have a number on the back. Later on they started numbering them throughout the year, and most, if not all, had a sequential number on them. On occasions, they seem to slip up and use the same number for two PNCs, e.g., in 2013, it was the BUSH BABIES POSSUM PNC and the CENTENARY OF COMMONWEALTH STAMPS PNC that both had on the back "2013 Issue 5."

1993 OLYMPIC GAMES ISSUE

Date	Description	Size	Weight	Mintage Figures	Issue Price	Current Retail
1993 TWENTY DOLLARS. PROOF STERLING [92.5%] SILVER						
1993	Friendship Theme/ Swimmers	40mm	33.63g	13,647	54	60
1993	Fair play/ Athletes on dias	40mm	33.63g	13,073	54	60
1993	Above two silver proof coins as boxed pair			5,699	108	120
1993	NAA Sydney Coin fair. Two silver coins. Boxed set			500	108	120
1993 TWO HUNDRED DOLLARS. PROOF 22ct GOLD						
1993	Individual Participation Perth	28mm	16.97g	4,066	492	875
1993	Three coin boxed set			7,642	600	975

The Royal Australian Mint was one of five partner mints selected by the IOC to participate in a landmark program that celebrated the first 100 years of the modern Olympic Games. The other mints included Canada 1992; France 1994; Austria 1995 and Greece 1996. Each mint contributed a gold coin and two sterling silver coins of uniform size and weight but with different denominations and designs. The Olympic motto of "Faster, Higher, Stronger" (Citius, Altius, Fortius) is edge lettered around each coin. This was the first time an Australian coin has been so inscribed.

1997 - 2000 SYDNEY OLYMPIC COIN DESIGNS

ONE HUNDRED DOLLARS

[a] The Journey Begin

[b] Dedication (1)

[c] Dedication (2)

[d] Preparation (1)

[e] Preparation (2)

[f] Achievement (Stadium)

[g] Achievement (Athlete)

[h] Achievement \(Torch)

Date	Description	Mint	Size	Weight	Mintage Figures	Issue Price	Current Retail
2000 a	The Journey Begin	Perth	25mm	10g	100,000/n/a	380	775
2000 b	Dedication (1)	Perth	25mm	10g	100,000/n/a	380	450
2000 c	Dedication (2)	Perth	25mm	10g	100,000/n/a	380	450
2000 d	Preparation (1)	Perth	25mm	10g	100,000/n/a	380	450
2000 e	Preparation (2)	Perth	25mm	10g	100,000/n/a	380	450
2000 f	Achievement (Stadium)	Perth	25mm	10g	100,000/n/a	380	450
2000 g	Achievement (Athlete)	Perth	25mm	10g	100,000/n/a	380	450

1997 - 2000 SYDNEY OLYMPIC COIN DESIGNS

FIVE DOLLARS ISSUE

[a] Dreaming Festival [b] Kangaroo & Grasstrees [c] Sea Change (1) [d] White Shark & Coral

[e] Sea Change (2) [f] Frilled Neck Lizard [g] Reaching the World (1) [h] Emu &Wattle

[i] Reaching the World (2) [j] Koala & Flowering Gum [k] Harbour of Life (Water) [l]. Platypus & Water Lily

[m] Harbour of Life (Land) [n] Echidna & Tea Tree [o] Harbour of Life (Air) [p] Kookarurra &Waratah

Date		Mintage Figures	Mint	Description	Issue Price	Current Retail
2000	a	100,000	Perth	Festival of the Dreaming	54	70
2000	b	100,000	Perth	Kangaroo & Grasstrees	54	85
2000	c	100,000	Canb	A Sea Change (1)	54	70
2000	d	100,000	Canb	Great White Shark & Coral	54	70
2000	e	100,000	Perth	A Sea Change (2)	54	70
2000	f	100,000	Perth	Frilled Neck Lizard	54	70
2000	g	100,000	Canb	Reaching the World (1)	54	70
2000	h	100,000	Canb	Emu and Wattle	54	70
2000	i	100,000	Perth	Reaching the World (2)	54	70
2000	j	100,000	Perth	Koala & Flowering Gum	54	70
2000	k	100,000	Canb	Harbour of Life (Water)	54	70
2000	l	100,000	Canb	Platypus & Water Lily	54	70
2000	m	100,000	Perth	Harbour of Life (Land)	54	70
2000	n	100,000	Perth	Echidna & Tea Tree	54	70
2000	o	100,000	Canb	Harbour of Life (Air)	54	70
2000	p	100,000	Canb	Kookaburra & Waratah	54	70

Eight of the 16 silver coins celebrate Australia's unique fauna and flora, and the other eight depict aspects of the nation's cultural development. The Royal Australian Mint and the Perth Mint shared production of the silver coins. Each is surrounded by a rich border of Australian flora. All of the coins were designed by Stuart Devlin, who based two of the cultural series designs, Festival of the Dreaming and A Sea Change 1, on original sketches by Aboriginal athlete and artist, Nova Peris-Kneebone.

FIVE DOLLARS ISSUE

SYDNEY 2000 OLYMPIC GAMES

The Sydney 2000 Olympic Coin Collection is the first Olympic numismatic program to dedicate a coin to each of the sports represented at an Olympic Games. These are depicted on the 28 "sports" bronze coins.

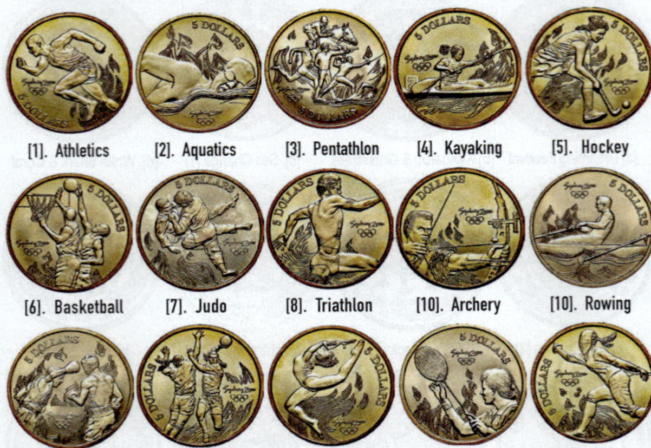

[1]. Athletics [2]. Aquatics [3]. Pentathlon [4]. Kayaking [5]. Hockey

[6]. Basketball [7]. Judo [8]. Triathlon [10]. Archery [10]. Rowing

[11]. Boxing [12]. Netball [13]. Gymnastics [14]. Badminton [15]. Fencing

Date	Sport	Mint	Size	Description	Mintage Figures	Issue Price	Current Retail
2000 01	Athletics	Canb	Al/br	In plastic card	100,000	8.95	15
2000 Mc00/ 02	Athletics	Canb	Al/br	*Coin & Stamp cover. Priced in PNC section*			
2000 02	Aquatics	Canb	Al/br	In plastic card	100,000	8.95	15
2000 Mc00/ 03	Aquatics	Canb	Al/br	*Coin & Stamp cover. Priced in PNC section*			
2000 03	Pentathlon.	Canb	Al/br	In plastic card	100,000	8.95	15
2000 04	Kayaking.	Canb	Al/br	In plastic card	100,000	8.95	15
2000 05	Hockey.	Canb	Al/br	In plastic card	100,000	8.95	15
2000 06	Basketball	Canb	Al/br	In plastic card	100,000	8.95	15
2000 07	Judo	Canb	Al/br	In plastic card	100,000	8.95	15
2000 08	Triathlon	Canb	Al/br	In plastic card	100,000	8.95	15
2000 09	Archery	Canb	Al/br	In plastic card	100,000	8.95	15
2000 10	Rowing	Canb	Al/br	In plastic card	100,000	8.95	15
2000 11	Boxing	Canb	Al/br	In plastic card	100,000	8.95	15
2000 12	Netball	Canb	Al/br	In plastic card	100,000	8.95	15
2000 13	Gymnastics	Canb	Al/br	In plastic card	100,000	8.95	15
2000 14	Badminton	Canb	Al/br	In plastic card	100,000	8.95	15
2000 15	Fencing.	Canb	Al/br	In plastic card	100,000	8.95	15

2000 FINE $30 PROOF SILVER KILOGRAM

Date	Mintage Figures	Mint	Type	Issue Price	Current Retail
2000	20,000	Perth	Complete Olympic Sports theme	855	950

FIVE DOLLARS ISSUE

SYDNEY 2000 OLYMPIC GAMES

The Sydney 2000 Olympic Coin Collection is the first Olympic numismatic program to dedicate a coin to each of the sports represented at an Olympic Games. These are depicted on the 28 "sports" bronze coins.

[16]. Softball

[17]. Sailing

[18]. Volleyball

[19]. Taekwondo

[20]. Football

[21]. Weightlifting

[22]. Equestrian

[23]. Table tennis

[24]. Wrestling

[25]. Cycling

[26]. Shooting

[27]. Baseball

[28]. Tennis

Date	Sport	Mint	Size	Description	Mintage Figures	Issue Price	Current Retail
2000 16	Softball.	Canb	Al/br	In plastic card	100,000	8.95	15
2000 17	Sailing.	Canb	Al/br	In plastic card	100,000	8.95	15
2000 18	Volleyball	Canb	A/br	In plastic card	100,000	8.95	15
2000 19	Taekwondo	Canb	Al/br	In plastic card	100,000	8.95	15
2000 20	Football	Canb	Al/br	In plastic card	100,000	8.95	15
2000 21	Weightlifting	Canb	Al/br	In plastic card	100,000	8.95	15
2000 22	Equestrian	Canb	Al/br	In plastic card	100,000	8.95	15
2000 23	Table Tennis	Canb	Al/br	In plastic card	100,000	8.95	15
2000 24	Wrestling	Canb	Al/br	In plastic card	100,000	8.95	15
2000 25	Cycling	Canb	Al/br	In plastic card	100,000	8.95	15
2000 26	Shooting	Canb	Al/br	In plastic card	100,000	8.95	15
2000 27	Baseball	Canb	Al/br	In plastic card	100,000	8.95	15
2000 28	Tennis	Canb	Al/br	In plastic card	100,000	8.95	15
2000	Complete set	Canb	Al/br	28 coins in official album		290.3	295

SYDNEY 2000 PARALYMPIC GAMES

TEN DOLLARS PROOF : 10oz. 99.9% SILVER

Date	Mintage Figures	Mint	Type	Issue Price	Current Retail
2000	3,000	Perth	Individual coin in jarrah box	495	45

THEME : MULTIPLE COIN DESIGNS

2000 - SYDNEY PARALYMPIC GAMES

(a) $1. Proof finish Fine Silver

(b) $5. Specimen finish Aluminium Bronze

(c) $5. Proof finish Fine Silver

(d) $100. Proof finish 99.99% Fine Gold

Date	Mintage Figures	Mint	Value	Description	Issue Price	Current Retail
2000 a	n/a	Canb	1	Silver Proof Issue	45	85
2000 b	14,920	Canb	5	Alum/ Bronze Specimen	10.95	20
2000 c	15,000	Perth	5	Silver Proof Issue	55	85
2000 d	7,500	Canb	100	Gold Proof Issue	380	550
2000	2,000	Perth		One of each above coins in case	445.95	625

ADDITIONAL SPECIFICATIONS

F/Value	Diameter	Weight	Edge
1.00 a	38.74 mm	20 gms	Reeded
5.00 b	40.50 mm	31.635 gms	Reeded
5.00 c	38.74 mm	20 gms	Reeded
100.00 d	25.00 mm	10.00 gms	Reeded

THEME : MULTIPLE COIN DESIGNS

2008 - AUSTRALIAN OLYMPIC TEAM. BEIJING

a. Aluminium bronze

b. Fine Silver Proof

c. Fine Gold Proof

Date	Mint	Mintage Max/ Actual	Weight in oz's	Metal	Description	Issue Price	Average Retail
2008 a	Perth	8,000/ n/a	1/2 oz	Al/Br	Specimen	See PNC section	
2008 b	Perth	8,808/ 4,758	1 oz	Silver	Proof	95	95
2008 c	Perth	2,008/ 401	10 gm	Gold	Proof	795	795
2008	Perth	500/ 497	1/2 oz	Silver	Stamp/ Proof	89.95	130
				THREE COIN CASED SET			
Proof c	Above three coins in case				888/ 589	890	950

[a] The aluminium bronze Boxing Kangaroo $1 was also available in the PNC and is priced elsewhere in this book.
[b] The coloured silver proof 50¢ resembles the stamps issued to mark the Beijing Olympics and came in a presentation case along with the stamp.
[c] The coins for the cased set come from the individual coins listed above.

THEME : MULTIPLE COIN DESIGNS

2012 - AUSTRALIAN OLYMPIC TEAM. LONDON

(a) Gold (b) Silver (c) Bronze (d) Stamp

Date	Face Value	Description	Weight in oz's	Metal	Finish	Size mm	Mintage Max/ Actual	Issue Price	Average Retail
2012 a	50	Victory	10g	Gold	Proof	25	2,012/ All sold	1,350	1,200
2012 b	1	Hurdles	1/2 oz	Silver	Proof	38.74	5,000/ 4,561	104	135
2012 c	1	Boxing	1 oz	Silver	Proof	40.6	5,000/ All sold	104	135
2012	—	Cased set	1 oz	Silver	Proof	40.6	750/ n/a	1,445	1,200
2012 d	60¢	Stamp	1/2 oz	Silver	Proof	n/a	8,000/ n/a	99.95	8.5

2012 - OLYMPIC TEAM. SET OF FIVE COINS

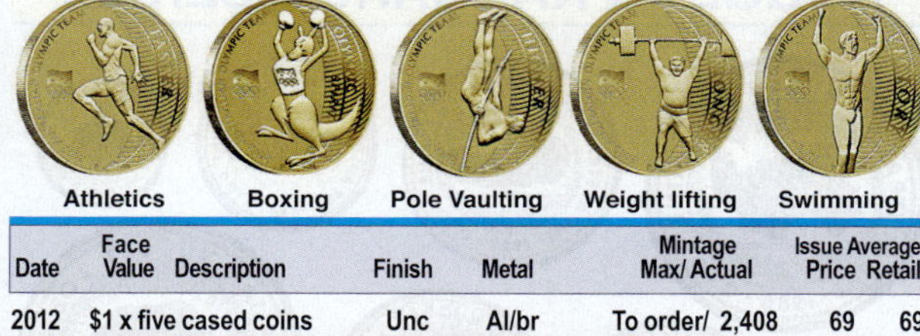

Athletics Boxing Pole Vaulting Weight lifting Swimming

Date	Face Value	Description	Finish	Metal	Mintage Max/ Actual	Issue Price	Average Retail
2012	$1 x five cased coins		Unc	Al/br	To order/ 2,408	69	69

PALLADIUM : MULTIPLE DATES

EMU PROOF & SPECIMEN

THREE YEAR SERIES - 1995 TO 1997

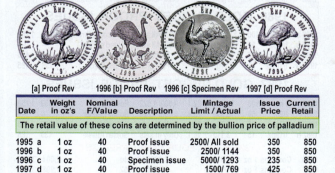

[a] Proof Rev 1996 [b] Proof Rev 1996 [c] Specimen Rev 1997 [d] Proof Rev

Date	Weight in oz's	Nominal F/Value	Description	Mintage Limit / Actual	Issue Price	Current Retail
The retail value of these coins are determined by the bullion price of palladium						
1995 a	1 oz	40	Proof issue	2500/ All sold	350	850
1996 b	1 oz	40	Proof issue	2500/ 1144	350	850
1996 c	1 oz	40	Specimen issue	5000/ 1293	235	850
1997 d	1 oz	40	Proof issue	1500/ 769	425	850

THEME : MULTIPLE COIN DESIGNS

2001 - SIR DONALD BRADMAN TRIBUTE

[a] Al/Br Reverse [b] Silver Proof [c] Obv & Rev. Bi-metal Gold & Silver

Date	Face Value	Weight	Finish	Type	Metal	Mintage Max/ Actual	Description	Issue Price	Average Retail
2001 a	5	20 gm	38.74	Unc	bronze	245,000	Green card	12.95	20
2001 b	5	1 oz	40.5	Proof	Silver	20,227	Cased	55	85
2001 c	20	1 oz	32.1	Proof	Bi-metal	7,155	Cased	380	400

ONE OF EACH ABOVE COINS IN CASED PRESENTATION CASE

2001	SET OF THREE	5,000/1,434	447.95	450

[a] Bi-metal : Gold centrepiece .27oz Fine. Silver outer ring .161 oz Fine

GOLD : MULTIPLE DATES

NUGGET & KANGAROO SERIES

Date	Weight in oz's	Face Value	Weight in gms	Size mm	Mintage Max/ Actual	Reverse Description	Issue Price	Average Retail
1986 GOLD NUGGET PROOF ISSUES								
1986 a	1 oz	100	131.1g	32.1	3,000/ All sold	Welcome Stranger	1,039	1,750
1986 b	1/2 oz	50	15.55g	25.1	3,000/ All sold	Hand of Faith	—	—
1986 c	1/4 oz	25	7.78g	20.1	Part of set	Golden Eagle	352	450
1986 d	1/10 oz	15	3.11g	16.16	Part of set	Little Hero	139	185
1987 GOLD NUGGET PROOF ISSUES								
1987 e	1 oz	100	131.1g	32.1	3,000/ 1,522	Poseidon	1,039	1,750
1987 f	1/2oz	50	15.55g	25.1	3,000/ 1,220	Bobby Dazzler	—	—
1987 g	1/4oz	25	7.78g	20.1	Only in sets	Father's Day	352	450
1987 h	1/10oz	15	3.11g	16.1	Only in sets	Golden Aussie	139	185

1986 & 1987 FOUR COIN CASED SET

1986	Contains 1 oz to 1/10 oz.	12,000/ All sold	2,004	3,250
1987	Contains 1 oz to 1/10 oz.	12,000/ 11,002	1,998	3,250

1986 & 1987 TWO COIN CASED SET

1986	Contains 1/4 oz and 1/10 oz.	3,000 / All sold	423	650
1987	Contains 1/4 oz and 1/10 oz.	3,000 / 2,690	423	650

GOLD : MULTIPLE DATES

NUGGET & KANGAROO SERIES

Pride of Australia
(a) 1 oz

Welcome
(b) 1/2 oz

Ruby Well
(c) 1/4 oz

Jubilee
(d) 1/10 oz

Date	Weight in oz's	Face Value	Weight in gms	Size mm	Mintage Max/ Actual	Reverse Description	Issue Price	Average Retail
1988 GOLD NUGGET PROOF ISSUES								
1988 a	1 oz	100	131.1g	32.1	1,000/ 679	Pride of Australia	1,039	1,750
1988 b	1/2 oz	50	15.55g	25.1	3,000/ 540	Welcome	558	900
1988 c	1/4 oz	25	7.78g	20.1	Only in sets	Ruby Well	—	—
1988 d	1/10 oz	15	3.11g	16.1	Only in sets	Jubilee	—	—
FOUR COIN CASED SET								
1988	Contains 1 oz to 1/10 oz.				9,000 / 8,180		1,998	3250
TWO COIN CASED SET								
Contains 1/4 oz and 1/10 oz.					3000 / 1,276		790	650

Common obverse for all iisues

1989 Proof bounding kangaroo

Date	Weight in oz's	Face Value	Weight in gms	Size mm	Mintage Max/ Actual	Reverse Description	Issue Price	Average Retail
1989 GOLD NUGGET PROOF ISSUES								
1989	1 oz	100	131.1g	32.1	3,000/ 1,522	Standard reverse	1,039	1,750
1989	1/2 oz	50	15.55g	25.1	3,000/ 1,224	Standard reverse	—	—
1989	1/4 oz	25	7.78g	20.1	n/a/ 3,480	Standard reverse	231	450
1989	1/10 oz	15	3.11g	16.1	n/a/ 7,725	Standard reverse	92.5	185
1989	1/20 oz	5	1.55g	14.1	n/a/ 20,340	Standard reverse	49.5	95
FIVE COIN CASED SET								
1989	Contains 1 oz to 1/20 oz.*				8,000 / 6,246		1,998	3,350

* This set was produced to commemorate the 90th anniversary of the Perth Mint. As well as the five gold coins, the set also included a quarter-ounce 9 carat (20.8 gms) gold medallion which was inscribed : *"The Perth Mint / 1899-1999 / 90th / Anniversary / Mintage 8000 / .375".*

NUGGET & KANGAROO SERIES

1990 Proof Reverse

1990 Specimen

1991 Proof 1/20oz

Date	Weight in oz's	Face Value	Size	mm	Mintage Max/ Actual	Reverse Feature	Issue Price	Average Retail
1990 GOLD NUGGET/ KANGAROO PROOFS								
1990	1 oz	100	131.1 g	32.1	2,000/ 519	Standard reverse	945	1,750
1990	1/2 oz	50	15.55 g	25.1	Only in set	Standard reverse	—	—
1990	1/4 oz	25	7.78 g	20.1	n/a/ 1,193	Standard reverse	231	450
1990	1/10 oz	15	3.11 g	16.1	n/a / 2,007	Standard reverse	92.5	185
1990	1/20 oz	5	1.55 g	14.1	n/a / 6,589	Standard reverse	49.5	95
FIVE COIN CASED SET								
1990	Contains 1 oz to 1/20 oz.				5,000 / 2,248		1,998	3,350
THREE COIN CASED SET								
	Contains 1/4 oz; 1/10 oz; 1/20 oz.				2,000 / 1,119		435	730
1991 GOLD NUGGET/ KANGAROO PROOFS								
1991	1 kg	10,000	1000.4g	75.3	100/ 100	Standard reverse	22,110	52,000
1991	10 oz	2,500	311.32g	60.3	500/ 500	Standard reverse	7,115	17,500
1991	2 oz	500	62.26g	40.6	500/ 500	Standard reverse	1,565	3,500
Above three coins feature the Red Kangaroo reverse								
1991	1 oz	100	131g	32.1	1,000/ 198	Standard reverse	945	1,750
1991	1/2 oz	50	15.55g	25.1	Part of set	Standard reverse	—	—
1991	1/4 oz	25	7.78g	20.1	1,000/ 202	Standard reverse	231	450
1991	1/10 oz	15	3.11g	16.1	5,000/ 526	Standard reverse	92.5	185
1991	1/20 oz	5	1.55g	14.1	10,000/ 2,076	Standard reverse	49.5	95
1991 a	1/20 oz	5	1.55g	14.1	1,000/ 568	Fair issue	65	10
Above six coins feature the Common Wallaroo reverse								
FIVE COIN CASED SET								
1991	Contains 1 oz to 1/20 oz				2,000 / 1,096		1,998	3,350
1991 : THREE COIN CASED SET								
1991	Contains 1/4 oz; 1/10 oz; 1/20 oz.				1,000 / 353		435	730

[a] Issued at the Melbourne Coin Fair on July 13 -14, 1991.

SOME POINTERS ON BUYING GOLD BULLION COINS

As a general rule most one ounce gold bullion coins are made available to world bullion dealers at a 3% premium over the current gold fix, so that after distribution costs, the coins would be available to investors in quantity at about 6% to 7% over intrinsic gold values, and sometimes as much as 12% premium for single pieces. By weight, the smaller the denomination *(fractional sizes such as 1/2oz. 1/4oz etc)* the higher the premium. These are generally sold to bullion dealers at a premium of between 5% and 9% respectively. The fractional coins have never been as popular as the full one ounce coins and are usually only purchased as singles by budget minded collectors or to be incorporated in a piece of jewellery. As such the premium over spot gold would usually be 10% to 25% premium for the half and quarter ounce, and from 20% to 35% premium for the tenth ounce.

GOLD : MULTIPLE DATES

NUGGET & KANGAROO SERIES

1992 Nailtailed Wallaby

1992 Wallaby Specimen

1993 Whiptail Wallaby

Date	Weight in oz's	Face Value	Weight in gms	Size mm	Mintage Max/ Actual	Reverse Description	Issue Price	Average Retail
1992 GOLD NUGGET/ KANGAROO PROOFS								
1992	1 kg	3,000	1000.4g	75.3	100/ 25	Standard reverse	22,110	52,000
1992	10 oz	1,000	311.32g	60.3	250/ 40	Standard reverse	7,115	17,500
1992	2 oz	200	62.26g	40.6	500/ 152	Standard reverse	1,565	3,500
1992	1 oz	100	131.1g	32.1	1,000/ 156	Standard reverse	785	1,750
1992	1/2 oz	50	15.55g	25.1	Part of set	Standard reverse	—	—
1992	1/4 oz	25	7.78g	20.1	1,000/ 201	Standard reverse	228.5	450
1992	1/4 oz	25	7.78g	20.1	n/a/ n/a	Eagle Privy	—	—
1992	1/10 oz	15	3.11g	16.1	2,000/ 467	Standard reverse	92.5	185
1992	1/20 oz	5	1.55g	14.1	5,000/ 1,160	Standard reverse	49.5	95

FIVE COIN CASED SET

	Mintage	Issue Price	Average Retail
Contains 1 oz to 1/20 oz.	2,000 / 628	1,653	3,350

THREE COIN CASED SET

	Mintage	Issue Price	Average Retail
Contains 1/4 oz; 1/10 oz; 1/20 oz.	1,000 / 264	393	730

USA EAGLE PRIVY MARK CASED SET

Date	Description	Mintage	Issue Price	Average Retail
1992 a	USA Eagle privy mark	500	1,184.65	1,500

[a] This set contains a one-ounce ($1) proof Kookaburra silver coin; a gold proof 1/4 ounce ($25) Kangaroo nugget and a 1/4 ounce ($25) platinum koala.

Date	Weight in oz's	Face Value	Weight in gms	Size mm	Mintage Max/ Actual	Reverse Description	Issue Price	Average Retail
1993 GOLD NUGGET/ KANGAROO PROOFS								
1993	1 kg	3,000	1000.4g	7 5.3	100/ 16	Standard reverse	22,240	52,000
1993	10 oz	1,000	311.32g	60.3	250/ 21	Standard reverse	7,158	17,500
1993	2 oz	200	62.26g	40.6	500/ 113	Standard reverse	1,574	3,500
1993	1 oz	100	131.1g	32.1	1,000/ 122	Standard reverse	789	1,750
1993	1/2 oz	50	15.55g	25.1	Only in set	Standard reverse	—	—
1993	1/4 oz	25	7.78g	20.1	1,000 / 210	Standard reverse	229.5	450
1993 a	1/4 oz	25	7.78g	20.1	Only in set	Standard reverse	—	—
1993	1/10 oz	15	3.11g	16.1	2,000/ 602	Standard reverse	93	185
1993	1/20 oz	5	1.55g	14.1	5,000/ 988	Standard reverse	49	95

FIVE COIN CASED SET

Date	Description	Mintage	Issue Price	Average Retail
1993	Contains 1 oz to 1/20 oz.	2000 / 430	1,661	3,350

1993 : THREE COIN CASED SET

Date	Description	Mintage	Issue Price	Average Retail
1993	Contains 1/4 oz; 1/10 oz; 1/20 oz.	1000 / 203	395	750

1993 CHINESE "FOK" PROSPERITY PRIVY MARK

Date	Face Value	Weight	Mintage	Issue Price	Average Retail
1993	100	1 oz	150 / 150	900	1,750
1993	25	1/4 oz	200 / 200	275	450

1993 : FIVE COIN CASED SET

	Mintage	Issue Price	Average Retail
Contains 1 oz to 1/20 oz.	350 / 350	1,872	3,350

[a] Eagle Privy mark. Part of three metal cased set.

GOLD : MULTIPLE DATES

NUGGET & KANGAROO SERIES

1994 Proof Red Kangaroo

1995 Proof Kangaroo & Joey

1995 Specimen. 2 oz issue

Date	Weight in oz's	Face Value	Weight in gms	Size mm	Mintage Max/ Actual	Reverse Description	Issue Price	Average Retail
1994 GOLD NUGGET/ KANGAROO PROOFS								
1994	2 oz	200	62.21gm	40.4	75/ All sold	Standard reverse	1,697	3,500
1994	1 oz	100	31.1gm	32.1	Sets only	Standard reverse	—	—
1994	1/2 oz	50	15.55gm	25.1	Sets only	Standard reverse	—	—
1994	1/4 oz	25	7.78gm	20.1	250/ All sold	Standard reverse	245	450
1994	1/10 oz	15	3.11gm	16.1	500/ All sold	Standard reverse	99	185
1994	1/20 oz	5	1.55gm	14.1	Sets only	Standard reverse	—	—
FIVE COIN CASED SET								
1994	Contains 1 oz to 1/20 oz plus medallion					250 / 250	1,778	3,350
1995 GOLD NUGGET/ KANGAROO PROOFS								
1995	2 oz	200	62.21gm	40.4	100/ 100	Standard reverse	1,697	3,500
1995	1 oz	100	131.1gm	32.1	Only in set	Standard reverse	—	—
1995 a	1 oz	100	131.1gm	32.1	300 / 300	Peace Privy	857	1,75
1995	1 oz	100	131.1gm	32.1	Part of set	Standard reverse	825	1,75
1995	1/2 oz	50	15.55gm	25.1	Part of set	Standard reverse	—	—
1995	1/4 oz	25	7.78gm	20.1	350/ 350	Standard reverse	245	450
1995 b	1/4 oz	25	7.78gm	20.1	7,500/ 4,624	Standard reverse	239	450
1995	1/10 oz	15	3.11gm	16.1	600/ 600	Carnation Privy	99	185
1995	1/20 oz	5	1.55gm	14.1	Only in set	Standard reverse	—	—
FIVE COIN CASED SET								
Contains 1 oz to 1/20 oz plus medallion					300 / 300		1778	3350

[a] 50 Years Beyond World War II (Peace) Privy Mark.
[b] Carnation Privy Mark. See elsewhere for more details on above issues.

GOLD : MULTIPLE DATES

NUGGET & KANGAROO SERIES

1996 Proof Reverse

1996 Specimen issue

1986-1996 Prospector

Date	Weight in oz's	Face Value	Weight in gms	Size mm	Mintage Max/ Actual	Reverse Description	Issue Price	Average Retail
1996 GOLD NUGGET PROOF ISSUES								
1996	2 oz	200	62.21g	40.4	125/ All sold	Standard reverse	1,685	3,500
1996	1 oz	100	131.1g	32.1	Only in set	Standard reverse	—	—
1996	1/2 oz	50	15.55g	25.1	Only in set	Standard reverse	—	—
1996	1/4 oz	25	7.78g	20.1	400/ All sold	Standard reverse	245	450
1996	1/10 oz	15	3.11g	16.1	700/ All sold	Standard reverse	100	185
1996	1/20 oz	5	1.55g	14.1	Only in set	Standard reverse	—	—

FIVE COIN CASED SET

1996	Contains 1 oz to 1/20 oz plus medallion	350/ 350	1,767	3,350

The reverse of the medallion states : "Australian / Nugget / 1996 proof Issue / Maximum Mintage / 350 Sets."

1996 PROOF 10TH ANNIVERSARY OF NUGGET

Contains 1/2 oz, 1/4 oz, 1/10 oz + medal.	400/ 400	800	1,650

To commemorate the tenth anniversary of the Nugget set, the Perth Mint struck a three - coin set, consisting of a proof 1/2 oz, 1/4 oz and 1/10 oz nugget. Each coin had a privy mark featuring a prospector panning for gold. The set also contained a 1 oz gold - plated 99.9 fine silver medallion that depicted a prospector.

1996 SPECIMEN GOLD NUGGETS

THREE STAR GODS PRIVY MARKS

1995	Fortune	50	1/2 oz	5,000/ All sold	325	900

FIVE COIN CASED SET

Contains 1 oz to 1/20 oz.	5,000/ 5,000	1,125	3,350

Only the 1/2 oz coin features the fortune privy mark in the five coin set

1996 SPECIMEN FOUNDATION STONE CENTENARY

1996	50	1/2 oz	500/ 500	335	950

The Perth Mint foundation stone was laid on September 23, 1896. To commemorate the centenary, silver and gold edge - numbered and edge - dated *"Specimen"* quality bullion coins were issued. The edge number matches the certificate number.

GOLD : MULTIPLE DATES

NUGGET & KANGAROO SERIES

1997 Proof Obverse

1997 Proof Reverse

1997 Specimen Reverse

1997 Large bullion reverse

1997 GOLD NUGGET/ KANGAROO PROOFS

Date	Weight in oz's	Face Value	Weight in gms	Size mm	Mintage Max/ Actual	Reverse Description	Issue Price	Average Retail
1997	2 oz	200	62.21gm	40.4	150/ All sold	Standard reverse	1,535	3,500
1997	1 oz	100	131.1gm	32.1	Only in set	Standard reverse	—	—
1997	1/2 oz	50	15.55gm	25.1	Only in set	Standard reverse	—	—
1997	1/4 oz	25	7.78gm	20.1	425/ 414	Standard reverse	225	450
1997	1/10 oz	15	3.11gm	16.1	725/ 582	Standard reverse	92	185
1997	1/20 oz	5	1.55gm	14.1	Only in set	Standard reverse	—	—
					FIVE COIN CASED SET			
1997	Contains 1 oz to 1/20 oz plus medallion				375 / 375		1,625	3,350
					1997 : SPECIMEN THREE STAR GODS PRIVY MARKS			
Fok	Prosperity	50	1/2 oz		10,000 / n/a		335	500
Shu	Longevity	50	1/2 oz		10,000 / n/a		335	500
Luk	Success	50	1/2 oz		Part of set		—	—

1998 Proof Reverse

1998 Specimen Obverse

1998 Specimen Reverse

1998 GOLD NUGGET/ KANGAROO PROOFS

Date	Weight in oz's	Face Value	Weight in gms	Size mm	Mintage Max/ Actual	Reverse Description	Issue Price	Average Retail
1998	2 oz	200	62.21gm	40.4	250/ 149	Standard reverse	1,535	3,500
1998	1 oz	100	131.1gm	32.1	Only in set	Standard reverse	—	—
1998 a	1/2 oz	50	15.55gm	25.1	435 / n/a	Standard reverse	550	910
1998	1/2 oz	50	15.55gm	25.1	Only in set	Standard reverse	—	—
1998	1/4 oz	25	7.78gm	20.1	425 / 322	Standard reverse	225	450
1998	1/10 oz	15	3.11gm	16.1	725 / 521	Standard reverse	92	185
1998	1/20 oz	5	1.55gm	14.1	Only in set	Standard reverse	—	—
1998 b	1/20 oz	5	1.55gm	14.1	15k/ 4,370	Standard reverse	80	110
					FIVE COIN CASED SET			
1998	Contains 1 oz to 1/20 oz plus medallion.				375/ 375		1,625	3,350
					1998 : SPECIMEN THREE STAR GODS PRIVY MARKS			
Fok	Prosperity	50	1/2 oz		200 / n/a		320	910
Shu	Longevity	50	1/2 oz		10,000 / n/a		320	910
Luk	Success	50	1/2 oz		Part of set		—	—
					1998 : SPECIMEN THREE COIN CASED SET			
One of each of the above coins in a case.					200 / n/a		925	2,950

[a] This new issue comprises a 99.99% fine 1/2 oz 1998 proof nugget gold coin and a natural alluvial gold nugget weighing between 1.09 and 1.39 grams.
[b] Colour folder containing a natural nugget and a 1/20 oz proof coin.

GOLD : MULTIPLE DATES

NUGGET & KANGAROO SERIES

1999 Proof Reverse

1999 Specimen Reverse

Date	Weight in oz's	Face Value	Weight in gms	Size mm	Mintage Max/ Actual	Reverse Description	Issue Price	Average Retail
1999 GOLD NUGGET/ KANGAROO PROOFS								
1999	1 oz	100	131.1gm	32.1	Only in set	Standard reverse	—	—
1999	1/2 oz	50	15.55gm	25.1	Only in set	Standard reverse	—	—
1999 a	1/2 oz	50	15.55gm	25.1	500/ 415	Twin Set	775	1,750
1999	1/4 oz	25	7.78gm	20.1	450/ 216	Standard reverse	229	450
1999 b	1/4 oz	25	7.78gm	20.1	255/ 225	Heritage set	1,195	1,200
1999	1/10 oz	15	3.11gm	16.1	750/ 379	Standard reverse	93	185
1999	1/20 oz	5	1.55gm	14.1	Only in set	Standard reverse	—	—
FIVE COIN CASED SET								
Contains 1 oz to 1/20 oz plus medallion.					400 / 400		1,653	3,350

[a] Limited to 500 sets and comprised of a 1999 1/2 oz Proof and a Specimen Nugget gold coin. They both carry the "P100" mintmark.
[b] 100 Year Heritage Set issued to mark the Perth Mint Centenary. Set included a natural nugget of approximately 1/4 oz weight; an original 1899 Perth Mint Sovereign and a 1999 1/4 oz Australian Nugget gold proof coin.

2000 Proof Reverse

2000 Specimen Reverse

2000 1 Kilo Specimen

Date	Weight in oz's	Face Value	Weight in gms	Size mm	Mintage Max/ Actual	Reverse Description	Issue Price	Average Retail
2000 GOLD NUGGET/ KANGAROO PROOFS								
2000	2 oz	200	131.1gm	32.1	275/ 265	Standard reverse	1,580	3,500
2000	1 oz	100	131.1gm	32.1	Only in set	Standard reverse	—	—
2000	1/2 oz	50	15.55gm	25.1	Only in set	Standard reverse	—	—
2000	1/4 oz	25	7.78gm	20.1	450/ 309	Standard reverse	229	450
2000	1/10 oz	15	3.11gm	16.1	750/ 478	Standard reverse	93	185
2000 c	1/20 oz	5	1.55gm	14.1	10,000/ 748	Standard reverse	—	—
FIVE COIN CASED SET								
Contains 1 oz to 1/20 oz plus medallion.					600 / 574		1,653	3,350
2000 SPECIMEN GOLD NUGGETS PRIVY MARKS								
2000 d	1/4oz	25			Basler Stab Privy	500/ 100	200	350
2000 e	1/4oz	25			Hanover Expo Privy	500/ 100	210	35

[c] 1/20 oz and Olympic pin featuring the "Millennium Man" logo.
[d] Issued in Januaray 2000 to commemorate the Year 2000 Basel Coin Fair. The Basler Stab is the emblem of the City of Basel, Switzerland.
[e] Issued to commemorate the Hanover, Germany Exhibition (June & October 2000)

GOLD : MULTIPLE DATES

NUGGET & KANGAROO SERIES

2001 Proof Reverse

2001 1oz Prospector Rev.

2001 Specimen Reverse

Date	Weight in ozs	Face Value	Weight gms	Size in mm	Mintage Max/ Actual	Reverse Feature	Issue Price	Retail Average
2001 GOLD NUGGET/ KANGAROO PROOFS								
2001	2 oz	200	62.21gm	40.4	300/ 276	Standard reverse	1,699	3,500
2001	1 oz	100	131.1gm	32.1	1500/ 577	Prospector	—	—
2001	1/2 oz	50	15.55gm	25.1	Part of set	Standard reverse	—	—
2001	1/4 oz	25	7.78gm	20.1	500/ 340	Standard reverse	259	450
2001	1/10 oz	15	3.11gm	16.1	800/ 415	Standard reverse	108.5	185
2001	1/20 oz	5	1.55gm	14.1	10,000/ 1,608	Standard reverse	79	95
FIVE COIN CASED SET								
Contains 1 oz to 1/20 oz plus medallion					650/ 419		1,795	3,500
2001 : GOLD "PROSPECTOR" SINGLE COIN AND SETS								
2001	1 oz	100	Coloured 1 oz gold coin		1,500/ 577		950	1,750
2001	1 oz	100	1oz coin and nugget		150/ 107		1,350	1,750
2001	1 oz	100	Coin / nugget / Sovereign		250/ 220		1,590	2,350
2001	1/20 oz	5	1/20 oz coin & nugget		n/a		99	99

2002 Proof Reverse

2002 1oz Dry Blowing Rev.

2002 Liberty Bell Privy

Date	Weight in oz's	Face Value	Weight in gms	Size mm	Mintage Max/ Actual	Reverse Description	Issue Price	Average Retail
1999 GOLD NUGGET/ KANGAROO PROOFS								
2002	2 oz	200	62.21gm	40.4	300/ 166	Standard reverse	2,275	3,500
2002	1 oz	100	131.1gm	32.1	1,500/ 204	Dry Blowing	—	—
2002	1/2 oz	50	15.55gm	25.1	Only in set	Standard reverse	—	—
2002	1/4 oz	25	7.78gm	20.1	500/ 246	Standard reverse	305	450
2002	1/10 oz	15	3.11gm	16.1	800/ 474	Standard reverse	120	185
FIVE COIN CASED SET								
Contains 1 oz to 1/20 oz plus medallion					650/ 515		1,795	3,500

2002 : "DRY BLOWING" SINGLE PROOF COIN

Date		Description	Mintage	Issue Price	Average Retail
2002	Single coin	1 oz Coloured Dry Blowing	1,500	1,062	1,750
2002	coin pair	1 oz Silver & 1/2 oz nugget	999	650	1,200
2002	Gold trio	Coin / Nugget / Sovereign	150/ 110	1,690	2,400
2002	Gold pair	1 oz Gold coin & nugget	150/ 111	1,450	2,200

2002 : "TRIBUTE TO FREEDOM" SINGLE COIN AND SETS

Date	Weight in oz's	Face Value	Weight in gms	Size mm	Mintage Max/ Actual	Reverse Description	Issue Price	Average Retail
2002	1/4 oz	25	7.78g	20.1	500/ 246	Standard reverse	305	450
2002	1 oz	100	131.1g	32.1	Only in set	Liberty Bell Privy	—	—
2002	1/2 oz	50	15.55g	25.1		Liberty Bell Privy	—	—
Contains 1 oz Silver and two Nuggets				—	499/ n/a		1,650	1,900
Contains 1 oz Silver and 1/2 oz nugget				—	999/ n/a		650	925

GOLD : MULTIPLE DATES

NUGGET & KANGAROO SERIES

2003 : Proof Reverse

2003 : 1oz Canvas Town

2003 : Specimen Reverse

2003 GOLD NUGGET/ KANGAROO PROOFS

Date	Weight in oz's	Face Value	Weight in gms	Size mm	Mintage Max/ Actual	Reverse Description	Issue Price	Average Retail
2003	2 oz	200	62.21gm	40.4	200/ 200	Standard reverse	2,394	3,500
2003	1 oz	100	131.1gm	32.1	See below	Canvas Town	—	—
2003	1/2 oz	50	15.55gm	25.1	Only in set	Standard reverse	—	—
2003	1/4 oz	25	7.78gm	20.1	250/ 236	Standard reverse	352	450
2003	1/10 oz	15	3.11gm	16.1	500/ 500	Standard reverse	139	185

FIVE COIN CASED SET

2003	Contains 1 oz to 1/20 oz plus medallion	500/ 336	2,473	3500

PROOF ONE OUNCE "CANVAS TOWN" REVERSE

2003	100.00	1 oz	Coloured coin	1500 / 160	1,189	1,850

"CANVAS TOWN" PROOF COIN & NUGGET SET

2003	Contains 1 oz proof coin and 1/4 oz nugget	150 / 96	1,595	2200

"CANVAS TOWN" THREE PIECE GOLD COLLECTION

2003	Contains 1 oz coin, 1/4 oz nugget and sovereign	150/ 66	1,996	2450

2004 : Proof Reverse

2004: 1 oz Eureka

2004 : Specimen Reverse

2004 GOLD NUGGET/ KANGAROO PROOFS

Date	Weight in oz's	Face Value	Weight in gms	Size mm	Mintage Max/ Actual	Reverse Description	Issue Price	Average Retail
2004	2 oz	200	62.21g	40.4	200/ 168	Standard reverse	2,629	3,500
2004	1 oz	100	131.1g	32.1	See below	Eureka Stockade	—	—
2004	1/2 oz	50	15.55g	25.1	Only in set	Standard reverse	—	—
2004	1/4 oz	25	7.78g	20.1	250 / 250	Standard reverse	385.5	450
2004	1/10 oz	15	3.11g	16.1	500/ 452	Standard reverse	151	185

FIVE COIN CASED SET

Contains 1 oz to 1/20 oz plus medallion	500/ 336	2,473	3,500

PROOF ONE OUNCE "EUREKA STOCKADE" REVERSE

2004	1 oz	100	Coloured coin	1500/ 160	1,302	1,850

"EUREKA STOCKADE" PROOF COIN & NUGGET SET

2004	Contains 1 oz proof coin and 1/4 oz nugget	150/ 84	1,727	2,200

"EUREKA STOCKADE" THREE PIECE GOLD COLLECTION

2004	Contains 1 oz, 1/4 oz nugget and sovereign	150/ 99	1,996	2,300

NUGGET & KANGAROO SERIES

Proof Obverse

Proof Reverse

Welcome Stranger

2005 : Specimen Rev

Date	Weight in oz's	Face Value	Weight in gms	Size mm	Mintage Max/ Actual	Reverse Description	Issue Price	Average Retail

2005 GOLD NUGGET/ KANGAROO PROOFS

Date	Weight in oz's	Face Value	Weight in gms	Size mm	Mintage Max/ Actual	Reverse Description	Issue Price	Average Retail
2005	2 oz	200	62.21g	40.4	200/ All sold	Standard reverse	2,629	3,500
2005	1 oz	100	131.1g	32.1	Only in set	Welcome Stranger	—	—
2005	1/2 oz	50	15.55g	25.1	Part of set	Standard reverse	—	—
2005	1/4 oz	25	7.78g	20.1	250 / All sold	Standard reverse	385.5	450
2005	1/10 oz	15	3.11g	16.1	500 / All sold	Standard reverse	151	185
2005	1/125 oz	4			10,000/ All sold	Standard reverse	n/a	n/a

2005 : FIVE COIN CASED SET

Description	Mintage	Issue Price	Average Retail
Contains 1 oz to 1/20 oz plus medallion	500/ All sold	2,715.5	3,350

"WELCOME STRANGER" ONE OUNCE PROOF COIN

Date	Face Value	Weight	Description	Mintage	Issue Price	Average Retail
2005	100.00	1 oz	Gold 1 oz coin	1500/ 265	1,302	1,750

"WELCOME STRANGER" PROOF COIN & NUGGET SET

Description	Mintage	Issue Price	Average Retail
Contains 1 oz proof coin and natural nugget	150/ 108	1,799	2,250

"WELCOME STRANGER" THREE PIECE GOLD COLLECTION

Description	Mintage	Issue Price	Average Retail
Contains 1 oz coin, nugget and sovereign	150/ 77	2100	2250

PROSPECTOR TEN COIN COMPANION SERIES - BOXED SET

Description	Mintage	Issue Price	Average Retail
Contains 1 oz & 1/25 oz coins from 2001-2005	100/ 68	7,750	2,950

PROOF LUNAR SERIES ONE

FIRST ISSUE 1996 - LAST ISSUE 2007

Obverse $100 1oz

1996 Proof Mouse

Obverse $15 1/10oz

1997 Proof Ox

1996 : YEAR OF THE MOUSE - GOLD PROOF

Date	Weight in oz's	Face Value	Size mm	Mintage Max/ Actual	Reverse Feature	Issue Price	Average Retail
1996	1 oz	100	32.1	3,800 / 2,886	Standard reverse		*Part of set*
1996	1/4 oz	25	20.1	3,800 / 2,886	Standard reverse		*Part of set*
1996	1/10 oz	15	16.1	3,800 / 2,886	Standard reverse		*Part of set*

MOUSE : THREE COIN CASED PROOF GOLD SET

Date	Weights	Mintage	Reverse Feature	Issue Price	Average Retail
1996	1 oz, 1/4 oz, 1/0 oz	3,800 / 2,886	Jarrah case	1,157	2,390

1997 : YEAR OF THE OX - GOLD PROOF

Date	Weight in oz's	Face Value	Size mm	Mintage Max/ Actual	Reverse Feature	Issue Price	Average Retail
1997	1 oz	100	32.1	3,000/ 842	Standard reverse		*Part of set*
1997	1/4 oz	25	20.1	5,000/ 842	Standard reverse	235	455
1997	1/10 oz	15	16.1	3,000/ 1,067	Standard reverse	95	185

OX : THREE COIN CASED PROOF GOLD SET

Date	Weights	Mintage	Reverse Feature	Issue Price	Average Retail
1997	1 oz, 1/4 oz, 1/0 oz	3,888/ 3146	Jarrah case	1,157	2,390

GOLD ISSUES : MULTIPLE DATES

PROOF LUNAR SERIES ONE

FIRST ISSUE 1996 - LAST ISSUE 2007

1998 (a) Tiger

1999 (b) Rabbit

2000 (c) Dragon

2001 (d) Snake

Date	Weight in oz's	Face Value	Size mm	Mintage Max/ Actual	Reverse Feature	Issue Price	Average Retail
1998 : YEAR OF THE TIGER - GOLD PROOF							
1998	1 oz	100	32.1	3,000/ 916	Standard reverse	*Part of set*	
1998	1/4 oz	25	20.1	3,000/ 916	Standard reverse	230	625
1998	1/10 oz	15	16.1	3,000/ 1,123	Standard reverse	94	245
TIGER : THREE COIN CASED PROOF GOLD SET							
1998	1 oz, 1/4 oz, 1/0 oz			3,888/ 1,918	Jarrah case	1,110	2,390
1999 : YEAR OF THE RABBIT - GOLD PROOF							
1999	1 oz	100	32.1	3,000/ 747	Standard reverse	*Part of set*	
1999	1/4 oz	25	20.1	3,000/ 747	Standard reverse	230	625
1999	1/10 oz	15	16.1	3,000/ 1,443	Standard reverse	94	245
RABBIT : THREE COIN CASED PROOF GOLD SET							
1999	1 oz, 1/4 oz, 1/0 oz			3,800/ 1,634	Jarrah case	1,100	2,390
2000 : YEAR OF THE DRAGON - GOLD PROOF							
2000	1 oz	100	32.1	3,000/ 2,008	Standard reverse	*Part of set*	
2000	1/4 oz	25	20.1	5,000/ 2,008	Standard reverse	242	625
2000	1/10 oz	15	16.1	5,000/ 3,841	Standard reverse	99	245
2000a	1/10 oz	15	16.1	To order/ n/a	Baby pack	99	245
GOLD DRAGONS - EAST MEETS WEST							
2000	Sovereign & 1/4 oz Dragon. Jarrah box			1,000/ 191		480	995
DRAGON YEAR : GOLD AND SILVER SET							
2000	1oz Gold Dragon & 1/2oz Silver Dragon			2,000/ 749		860	2,650
DRAGON : THREE COIN CASED PROOF GOLD SET							
2000	1 oz, 1/4 oz, 1/0 oz			2,000/ Sold out		1,175	2,390

(a) "Baby pack" contains a 1/10 oz gold proof Dragon coin complete with a printed folder with blank areas to record the baby's personal details.

Date	Weight in oz's	Face Value	Size mm	Mintage Max/ Actual	Reverse Feature	Issue Price	Average Retail
2001 : YEAR OF THE SNAKE - GOLD PROOF							
2001	1 oz	100	32.1	3,000/ 1,487	Standard reverse	*Part of set*	
2001	1/4 oz	25	20.1	7,000/ 1,487	Standard reverse	247.5	45
2001	1/10 oz	15	16.1	7,000/ 1,860	Standard reverse	101	185
SNAKE : THREE COIN CASED PROOF GOLD SET							
2001	1 oz, 1/4 oz, 1/0 oz			3,000/ 1,223	Jarrah case	1,197	2,390

GOLD ISSUES : MULTIPLE DATES

PROOF LUNAR SERIES ONE

FIRST ISSUE 1996 - LAST ISSUE 2007

2002 [a] Horse 2003 [b] Goat 2004 [c] Monkey 2005 [d] Rooster 2006 [d] Dog 2007 [e] Pig

Date	Weight in oz's	Face Value	Size mm	Mintage Max/ Actual	Reverse Feature	Issue Price	Average Retail
2002 : YEAR OF THE HORSE - GOLD PROOF							
2002	1 oz	100	32.1	3,000/ 1,471	Standard reverse	*Part of set*	
2002	1/4 oz	25	20.1	7,000/ 724	Standard reverse	283	455
2002	1/10 oz	15	16.1	7,000/ 1,341	Standard reverse	118	185
HORSE : THREE COIN CASED PROOF GOLD SET							
2002	1 oz, 1/4 oz, 1/0 oz			3,000/ 1,471	Jarrah case	1,376	2,390
2003 : YEAR OF THE GOAT - GOLD PROOF							
2003	1 oz	100	32.1	3,000/ 1,187	Standard reverse	*Part of set*	
2003	1/4 oz	25	20.1	7,000/ 782	Standard reverse	314.5	455
2003	1/10 oz	15	16.1	7,000/ 1,816	Standard reverse	124.8	185
GOAT : THREE COIN CASED PROOF GOLD SET							
2003	1 oz, 1/4 oz, 1/0 oz			3,000/ 1,187	Jarrah case	1,490	2,390
2004 : YEAR OF THE MONKEY - GOLD PROOF							
2004	1 oz	100	32.1	3,000/ 999	Standard reverse	*Part of set*	
2004	1/4 oz	25	20.1	7,000/ 402	Standard reverse	386.5	455
2004	1/10 oz	15	16.1	7,000/ 967	Standard reverse	152.5	185
MONKEY : THREE COIN CASED PROOF GOLD SET							
2004	1 oz, 1/4 oz, 1/0 oz			3,000/ 999	Jarrah case	1,752	2,390
2005 : YEAR OF THE ROOSTER - GOLD PROOF							
2005	1 oz	100	32.1	3,000 / 1,388	Standard reverse	*Part of sets*	
2005	1/4 oz	25	20.1	7,000/ 573	Standard reverse	386.5	445
2005	1/10 oz	15	16.1	7,000/ 1,152	Standard reverse	152.5	185
ROOSTER : THREE COIN CASED PROOF GOLD SET							
2005	1 oz, 1/4 oz, 1/0 oz			3,000 / 1,388	Jarrah case	1,752	2,390
2006 : YEAR OF THE DOG - GOLD PROOF							
2006	1 oz	100	32.1	3,000 / 1,274	Standard reverse	*Part of set*	
2006	1/4 oz	25	20.1	7,000/ 777	Standard reverse	433	445
2006	1/10 oz	15	16.1	7,000/ 1,620	Standard reverse	169.5	185
DOG : THREE COIN CASED PROOF GOLD SET							
2005	1 oz, 1/4 oz, 1/0 oz			3,000 / 1,274	Jarrah case	1,995	2,390
2007 : YEAR OF THE PIG - GOLD PROOF							
2007	1 oz	100	32.1	3,000/ 1,556	Standard reverse	*Part of set*	
2007	1/4 oz	25	20.1	7,000/ 650	Standard reverse	465	455
2007	1/10 oz	15	16.1	7,000/ 1,474	Standard reverse	179	185
PIG : THREE COIN CASED PROOF GOLD SET							
2005	1 oz, 1/4 oz, 1/0 oz			3,000 / 1,274	Jarrah case	2,390	2,450

GOLD ISSUES : MULTIPLE DATES

SPECIMEN LUNAR SERIES ONE

FIRST ISSUE 1996 - LAST ISSUE 2007

1996 Specimen Mouse

1997 Specimen Ox

1998 Specimen Tiger

Date	Weight in oz's	Face Value	Size mm	Mintage Max/ Actual	Reverse Feature	Issue Price	Average Retail
1996 : YEAR OF THE MOUSE - GOLD SPECIMEN							
1996	1 oz	100	39.34	30,000/ 16,593	Standard reverse	473.60	1,750
1996	1/4 oz	25	22.60	60,000/ 1,390	Standard reverse	152.14	445
1996	1/10 oz	15	18.60	80,000/ 3,792	Standard reverse	71.23	185
1996	1/20 oz	5	14.60	100,000/ 7,405	Standard reverse	39	95
1997 : YEAR OF THE OX - GOLD SPECIMEN							
1997	1 oz	100	39.34	30,000/ 13,709	Standard reverse	473.6	1,750
1997	1/4 oz	25	22.60	60,000/ 2,904	Standard reverse	152.14	445
1997	1/10 oz	15	18.60	80,000/ 4,960	Standard reverse	71.23	185
1997	1/20 oz	5	14.60	100,000/ 7,131	Standard reverse	39	95
1998 : YEAR OF THE TIGER - GOLD SPECIMEN							
1998	1 oz	100	39.34	30,000/ 16,907	Standard reverse	473.6	1,750
1998	1/4 oz	25	22.60	60,000/ 5,683	Standard reverse	152.14	445
1998	1/10 oz	15	18.10	80,000/ 9,085	Standard reverse	71.23	185
1998	1/20 oz	5	14.60	100,000 /10,427	Standard reverse	45	95

Common obverse

1999 Specimen Rabbit

2000 Specimen Dragon

Date	Weight in oz's	Face Value	Size mm	Mintage Max/ Actual	Reverse Feature	Issue Price	Average Retail
1999 : YEAR OF THE RABBIT - GOLD SPECIMEN							
1999	1 oz	100	39.34	30,000/ 18,261	Standard reverse	530	1,750
1999	1/4 oz	25	22.6	60,000/ 5,893	Standard reverse	165	445
1999	1/10 oz	15	18.6	80,000 / 8,799	Standard reverse	78	185
1999	1/20 oz	5	14.6	100,000 / 9,642	Standard reverse	56	95
2000 : YEAR OF THE DRAGON - GOLD SPECIMEN							
2000	1 kg	3,000	100.6	30,000/ 227	Standard reverse	58,000	58,000
2000	10 oz	1,000	75.6	60,000/ 214	Standard reverse	b/v	18,500
2000	2 oz	200	41.1	80,000/ 2,342	Standard reverse	b/v	3,500
2000	1 oz	100	39.34	30,000/ All sold	Standard reverse	458	1,750
2000	1/4 oz	25	22.6	60,000/ 20,148	Standard reverse	143	455
2000	1/10 oz	15	18.6	80,000/ 23,706	Standard reverse	67	185
2000	1/20 oz	5	14.6	100,000/ 29,325	Standard reverse	41	95

GOLD ISSUES : MULTIPLE DATES

SPECIMEN LUNAR SERIES ONE

FIRST ISSUE 1996 - LAST ISSUE 2007

2001 Specimen Snake | 2002 Specimen Horse | 2003 Specimen Goat | 2004 Colour Monkey

Date	Weight in oz's	Face Value	Size mm	Mintage Max/ Actual	Reverse Feature	Issue Price	Average Retail
2001 : YEAR OF THE SNAKE - GOLD SPECIMEN							
2001	1 kg	3,000	100.6	To order/ 156	Standard reverse	17,500	58,000
2001	10 oz	1,000	75.6	To order/ 153	Standard reverse	b/v	18,500
2001	2 oz	200	41.1	To order/ 1,295	Standard reverse	b/v	3,500
2001	1 oz	100	39.34	30,000/ All sold	Standard reverse	b/v	1,750
2001	1/4 oz	25	22.6	60,000/ 8,436	Standard reverse	259	455
2001	1/10 oz	15	18.6	80,000/ 19,281	Standard reverse	101	185
2001	1/20 oz	5	14.6	100,000/ 19,738	Standard reverse	41.5	45
2002 : YEAR OF THE HORSE - GOLD SPECIMEN							
2002	1 kg	3,000	100.6	To order/ 163	Standard reverse	19,000	58,000
2002	10 oz	1,000	75.6	To order/ 191	Standard reverse	b/v	18,500
2002	2 oz	200	41.1	To order/ 1,291	Standard reverse	b/v	3,500
2002	1 oz	100	39.34	30,000/ All sold	Standard reverse	b/v	1,750
2002	1/4 oz	25	22.6	60,000/ 10,187	Standard reverse	259	455
2002	1/10 oz	15	18.6	80,000/ 18,434	Standard reverse	118	185
2002	1/20 oz	5	14.6	100,000/ 27,338	Standard reverse	41.5	45
2003 : YEAR OF THE GOAT - GOLD SPECIMEN							
2003	1 kg	3,000	100.6	To order/ 109	Standard reverse	20,000	58,000
2003	10 oz	1,000	75.6	To order/ 153	Standard reverse	b/v	18,500
2003	2 oz	200	41.1	To order/ 1,355	Standard reverse	b/v	3,500
2003	1 oz	100	39.34	30,000/ 16,775	Standard reverse	b/v	1,750
2003	1/4 oz	25	22.6	60,000/ 8,479	Standard reverse	259	455
2003	1/10 oz	15	18.6	80,000/ 14,966	Standard reverse	25	185
2003	1/20 oz	5	14.6	100,000/ 17,892	Standard reverse	41.5	45
2004: YEAR OF THE MONKEY - GOLD SPECIMEN							
2004	1 kg	3,000	100.6	To order/ 195	Standard reverse	b/v	58,000
2004	10 oz	1,000	75.6	To order/ 265	Standard reverse	b/v	18,000
2004	2 oz	200	41.1	To order/ 1,470	Standard reverse	b/v	3,500
2004	1 oz	100	39.34	30,000/ 16,868	Standard reverse	b/v	1,750
2004	1 oz	100	39.34	6,000/ 1,605	Colour reverse	n/a	1,750
2004	1/2 oz	50	30.6	40,000/ 4,228	Standard reverse	b/v	895
2004	1/2 oz	50	30.6	8,000/ 1,732	Colour reverse	n/a	895
2004	1/4 oz	25	22.6	60,000/ 7,284	Standard reverse	b/v	455
2004	1/4 oz	25	22.6	8,000/ 2,896	Colour reverse	n/a	455
2004	1/10 oz	15	18.6	80,000/ 14,060	Standard reverse	b/v	185
2004	1/10 oz	15	18.6	28,000/ 14,365	Colour reverse	n/a	185
2004	1/20 oz	5	14.6	100,000,/ 15,898	Standard reverse	b/v	95
2004	1/20 oz	5	14.6	28,000,/ 15,073	Gilt reverse	b/v	95

GOLD ISSUES : MULTIPLE DATES

SPECIMEN LUNAR SERIES ONE

FIRST ISSUE 1996 - LAST ISSUE 2007

2005 Rooster Reverse

2005 coloured Rooster

2006 Coloured Dog

2007 Coloured Pig

Date	Weight in oz's	Face Value	Size mm	Mintage Max/ Actual	Reverse Feature	Issue Price	Average Retail
2005 : YEAR OF THE ROOSTER - GOLD SPECIMEN							
2005	1 kg	3,000	100.6	To order/ 230	Standard reverse	20,000	b/v
2005	10 oz	1,000	75.3	To order/ 240	Standard reverse	b/v	b/v
2005	2 oz	200	40.6	To order/ 2,129	Standard reverse	b/v	3,500
2005	1 oz	100	39.34	30,000/ 19,729	Standard reverse	b/v	1,750
2005	1 oz	100	39.34	6,000/ 1,770	Colour reverse	n/a	1,750
2005	1/2 oz	50	30.6	40,000/ 4,506	Standard reverse	b/v	895
2005	1/2 oz	50	30.6	8,000/ 1,848	Colour reverse	n/a	895
2005	1/4 oz	15	22.6	60,000/ 6,450	Standard reverse	259	455
2005	1/4 oz	15	22.6	8,000/ 2,889	Colour reverse	259	455
2005	1/10 oz	10	18.6	80,000/ 15,109	Standard reverse	152	185
2005	1/10 oz	10	18.6	28,000/ 16,700	Standard reverse	152	185
2005	1/10 oz	10	18.6	15,000/ 7,816	Standard reverse	149	185
2005	1/20 oz	5	14.6	100,000/ 18,200	Rose gold	b/v	95
2005	1/20 oz	5	14.6	28,000/ 22,564	Standard reverse	n/a	95
2005	1/20 oz	5	14.6	1,000/ n/a	Colour. ANDA	86	86
2006 : YEAR OF THE DOG - GOLD SPECIMEN							
2006	10 kg	30k	180.6	20/ 10	Standard reverse	525k	b/v
2006	1 kg	3,000	100.6	To order / 137	Standard reverse	b/v	58,000
2006	10 oz	1,000	75.6	To order/ 195	Standard reverse	18,500	18,500
2006	2 oz	200	41.1	To order/ 2,460	Standard reverse	b/v	3,500
2006	1 oz	100	39.34	30,000/ 26,334	Standard reverse	b/v	1,750
2006	1 oz	100	39.34	6,000/ 806	Colour reverse	n/a	1,750
2006	1/2 oz	50	30.6	40,000/ 5,767	Standard reverse	386	895
2006	1/2 oz	50	30.6	8,000/ 1,706	Colour reverse	n/a	895
2006	1/4 oz	25	22.6	60,000/ 6,009	Standard reverse	b/v	455
2006	1/4 oz	25	22.6	8,000/ 2,359	Colour reverse	n/a	455
2006	1/10 oz	15	18.6	80,000/ 12,017	Standard reverse	152	185
2006	1/10 oz	15	18.6	50,000/ 16,550	Colour reverse	n/a	185
2006	1/20 oz	5	14.6	100,000/ 15,737	Standard reverse	b/v	95
2006	1/20 oz	5	14.6	50,000 / 21,701	Colour reverse	57	95
2007 : YEAR OF THE PIG - GOLD SPECIMEN							
2007	10 kg	30k	180.6	20 / 6	Standard reverse	525k	b/v
2007	1 kg	3,000	100.6	To order/ 114	Standard reverse	b/v	58,000
2007	10 oz	1,000	75.6	To order/ 192	Standard reverse	b/v	18,500
2007	2 oz	200	41.1	To order/ 3,613	Standard reverse	b/v	3,500
2007	1 oz	100	39.34	30,000/ 18,149	Standard reverse	b/v	1,750
2007	1 oz	100	39.34	6,000/ 982	Colour reverse	b/v	1,750
2007	1/2 oz	50	30.6	40,000/ 7,694	Standard reverse	n/a	895
2007	1/2 oz	50	30.6	8,000/ 1,798	Colour reverse	n/a	895
2007	1/4 oz	25	22.6	60,000/ 6,486	Standard reverse	b/v	455
2007	1/4 oz	25	22.6	8,000/ 3 564	Colour reverse	n/a	455
2007	1/10 oz	15	18.6	80,000/ 11,216	Standard reverse	179	185
2007	1/10 oz	15	18.6	50,000/ 20,009	Colour reverse	n/a	185
2007	1/20 oz	5	14.6	100,000/ 10,308	Standard reverse	54	95
2007	1/20 oz	5	14.6	50,000/ 27,440	Colour reverse	n/a	95

GOLD ISSUES : MULTIPLE DATES

PROOF LUNAR SERIES TWO

SECOND SERIES COMMENCING 2008 -

Date	Weight in oz's	Face Value	Size mm	Mintage Max/ Actual	Reverse Feature	Issue Price	Average Retail
2008: YEAR OF THE MOUSE - GOLD PROOF							
2008	1 oz	100	39.34	3,000/ 141	Standard reverse	1,550	2,450
2008	1/4 oz	25	22.6	5,000/ 467	Standard reverse	464	695
2008	1/10 oz	15	18.6	5,000/ 989	Standard reverse	179	250
MOUSE : THREE COIN CASED PROOF GOLD SET							
2008	1 oz; 1/4 oz; 1/10 oz			3,000 / 1,036	Jarrah wood case	2,195	3,330
2009: YEAR OF THE OX - GOLD PROOF							
2009	1 oz	100	39.34	3,000/ 647	Standard reverse	2,230	2,450
2009	1/4 oz	25	22.6	5,000/ 1,308	Standard reverse	645	695
2009	1/10 oz	15	18.6	5,000/ 1,764	Standard reverse	243	250
OX : THREE COIN CASED PROOF GOLD SET							
2009	1 oz; 1/4 oz; 1/10 oz			3,000/ 967	Jarrah wood case	3,069	3,330
2010 : YEAR OF THE TIGER - GOLD PROOF							
2010	1 oz	100	39.34	3,000/ 826	Standard reverse	1,875	2,450
2010	1/4 oz	25	22.6	5,000/ 4,752	Standard reverse	555	695
2010	1/10 oz	15	18.6	5,000/ All sold	Standard reverse	215	250
TIGER : THREE COIN CASED PROOF GOLD SET							
2010	1 oz; 1/4 oz; 1/10 oz			3,000 / 1,071	Jarrah wood case	3,525	3,300
2011 : YEAR OF THE RABBIT - GOLD PROOF							
2011	1 oz	100	39.34	3000/ 595	Standard reverse	2,580	1,750
2011	1/4 oz	25	22.6	5,000/ 1,525	Standard reverse	687	455
2011	1/10 oz	15	18.6	5,000/ 2,523	Standard reverse	275	185
RABBIT : THREE COIN CASED PROOF GOLD SET							
2011	1 oz; 1/4 oz; 1/10 oz			3,000/ 2,056	Jarrah wood case	3,525	3,330
2012 : YEAR OF THE DRAGON - GOLD PROOF							
2012	1 oz	100	39.34	3,000/ 1,987	Standard reverse	2,580	3,000
2012	1 oz	100	27.3	388/ All sold	High Relief	2,580	3,000
2012	1 oz	100	39.34	5,000/ 1,068	Colour reverse	3,100	2,750
2012	1/4 oz	25	22.6	5,000/ 2,880	Standard reverse	687	700
2012	1/4 oz	25	22.6	5,000/ 1,731	Colour reverse	789	775
2012	1/10 oz	15	18.6	500/ 4,036	Standard reverse	275	300
2012	1/10 oz	15	18.6	5,000/ 3,445	Colour reverse	339	340
DRAGON : THREE COIN CASED PROOF GOLD SET							
2012	1 oz; 1/4 oz; 1/10 oz			3,000/ 2,056	Jarrah wood case	3,525	3,995
PROOF 1/20 oz FINE GOLD COLOURED COLLECTION							
2008 to 2012	Five x 1/20 oz coins			500/ n/a		595	595

GOLD ISSUES : MULTIPLE DATES

PROOF LUNAR SERIES TWO

SECOND SERIES COMMENCING 2008 -

2013 Snake Proof

2014 Horse Proof

2015 Goat Proof

2016 Monkey Proof

Date	Weight in oz's	Face Value	Size mm	Mintage Max/ Actual	Reverse Feature	Issue Price	Average Retail
2013 : YEAR OF THE SNAKE - GOLD PROOF							
2013	1 oz	100	39.34	3,000/ 807	Standard reverse	2,625	2,750
2013	1 oz	100	27.3	388/ All sold	High Relief	2,625	2,750
2013	1 oz	100	39.34	3,000/ n/a	Colour reverse	2,695	2,750
2013	1/4 oz	25	22.6	5,000/ 1,200	Standard reverse	695	725
2013	1/4 oz	25	22.6	5,000/ 1,159	Colour reverse	695	725
2013	1/10 oz	15	18.6	5,000/ 1,936	Standard reverse	299	299
2013	1/10 oz	15	18.6	5,000/ All sold	Colour reverse	299	299
SNAKE : THREE COIN CASED PROOF GOLD SET							
2013	1 oz; 1/4 oz; 1/10 oz				3,000/ 1,180	3,689	3,989
2014 : YEAR OF THE HORSE - GOLD PROOF							
2014	1 oz	100	27.3	388/ All sold	High Relief	2,695	2,750
2014	1 oz	100	39.34	6,000/ 679	Standard reverse	2,625	2,750
2014	1 oz	100	39.34	3,000/ 147	Colour reverse	2,695	2,625
2014	1/4 oz	25	22.6	5,000/ 1,048	Standard reverse	675	725
2014	1/4 oz	25	22.6	5,000/ 777	Colour reverse	695	725
2014	1/10 oz	15	18.6	8,000/ 2,557	Standard reverse	295	299
2014	1/10 oz	15	18.6	5,000/ 1,564	Colour reverse	299	299
HORSE : THREE COIN CASED PROOF GOLD SET							
2014	1 oz; 1/4 oz ; 1/10 oz			3,000/ 1,530		3,550	3,550
2015 : YEAR OF THE GOAT - GOLD PROOF							
2015	1 oz	100	39.34	6,000/ 405	Standard reverse	2,695	2,750
2015	1 oz	100	39.34	3,000/ 160	Colour reverse	2,695	2,750
2015	1 oz	100	27.3	388/ Sold out	High Relief	2,695	2,750
2015	1/4 oz	25	22.6	8,000/ 647	Standard reverse	695	725
2015	1/4 oz	25	22.6	5,000/ 592	Colour reverse	695	725
2015	1/10 oz	15	18.6	8,000/ 1,788	Standard reverse	299	299
2015	1/10 oz	15	18.6	5,000/ 1,152	Colour reverse	299	299
GOAT : THREE COIN CASED PROOF GOLD SET							
2015	1 oz; 1/4 oz ; 1/10 oz			3,000/ 1,291		3,550	3,550
2016 : YEAR OF THE MONKEY - GOLD PROOF							
2016	1 oz	100	39.34	6,000/ 511	Standard reverse	2,695	2,750
2016	1 oz	100	39.34	3,000/ 199	Colour reverse	2,695	2,750
2016	1 oz	100	27.3	388/ Sold out	High Relief	2,695	2,750
2016	1/4 oz	25	22.6	8,000/ 697	Standard reverse	695	725
2016	1/4 oz	25	22.6	5,000/ 407	Colour reverse	695	725
2016	1/10 oz	15	18.6	8,000/ 1,735	Standard reverse	299	299
2016	1/10 oz	15	18.6	5,000/ 937	Colour reverse	299	299
MONKEY : THREE COIN CASED PROOF GOLD SET							
2016	1 oz; 1/4 oz ; 1/10 oz			3,000/ 1,107		3,550	3,550

GOLD ISSUES : MULTIPLE DATES

PROOF LUNAR SERIES TWO

SECOND SERIES COMMENCING 2008 -

2017 Proof Rooster

Common Obverse

2017 Coloured Proof

Date	Weight in oz's	Face Value	Size mm	Mintage Max/ Actual	Reverse Feature	Issue Price	Average Retail
2017 : YEAR OF THE ROOSTER - GOLD PROOF							
2017	1 oz	100	39.34	6,000/ tba	Standard reverse	2,699	2,999
2017	1 oz	100	39.34	3,000/ tba	Colour reverse	2,999	2,999
2017	1 oz	100	27.3	388/ tba	High Relief	2,999	2999
2017	1/4 oz	25	22.6	8,000/ tba	Standard reverse	799	799
2017	1/4 oz	25	22.6	5,000/ 1,734	Colour reverse	695	695
2017	1/10 oz	15	18.6	8,000/ tba	Standard reverse	339	339
2017	1/10 oz	15	18.6	5,000/ tba	Colour reverse	299	299
ROOSTER : THREE COIN CASED PROOF GOLD SET							
2017	1 oz; 1/4 oz ; 1/10 oz			1,500/ n/a		3,599	3,599

SPECIMEN GOLD LUNAR ISSUES

SECOND SERIES COMMENCING 2008 -

2008 Rat. Coloured

2009 Ox. Coloured

2010 Tiger Specimen

Date	Weight in oz's	Face Value	Size mm	Mintage Max/ Actual	Reverse Feature	Issue Price	Average Retail
2008 : YEAR OF THE RAT - GOLD SPECIMEN							
2008	10 kg	30,000	180.6	100/ Nil	Standard reverse	—	—
2008	1 kg	3,000	100.1	To order/ 55	Standard reverse	32,000	58,000
2008	10 oz	1,000	75.6	To order/ 128	Standard reverse	b/v	18,500
2008	2 oz	200	41.1	To order/ 677	Standard reverse	b/v	3,500
2008	1 oz	100	39.34	30,000/ All sold	Standard reverse	b/v	1,700
2008	1 oz	100	39.34	6,000/ 542	Colour reverse	b/v	1,750
2008	1/2 oz	50	30.6	To order/ 3,474	Standard reverse	b/v	895
2008	1/2 oz	50	30.6	8,000/ 563	Colour reverse	b/v	895
2008	1/4 oz	25	22.6	To order/ 5,541	Standard reverse	b/v	455
2008	1/4 oz	25	22.6	8,000/ 2,555	Colour reverse	b/v	455
2008	1/10 oz	15	18.1	To order/ 5,821	Standard reverse	b/v	185
2008	1/10 oz	15	18.1	50,000/ 23,317	Colour reverse	b/v	185
2008	1/20 oz	5	14.6	To order/ 5,376	Standard reverse	b/v	95
2009 : YEAR OF THE OX - GOLD SPECIMEN							
2009	10 kg	30,000	180.6	100/ Nil	Standard reverse	—	—
2009	1 kg	3,000	100.1	To order/ 79	Standard reverse	43,500	b/v
2009	10 oz	1,000	75.6	To order/ 153	Standard reverse	b/v	18,500
2009	2 oz	200	41.1	To order/ 1,338	Standard reverse	b/v	3,500
2009	1 oz	100	39.34	30,000/ All sold	Standard reverse	b/v	1,750
2009	1 oz	100	39.34	6,000/ 537	Colour reverse	b/v	1,750
2009	1/2 oz	50	30.6	To order/ 5,054	Standard reverse	b/v	895
2009	1/2 oz	50	30.6	8,000/ 583	Colour reverse	b/v	895
2009	1/4 oz	25	22.6	To order/ 7,750	Standard reverse	b/v	455
2009	1/4 oz	25	22.6	8,000/ 3,069	Colour reverse	b/v	455
2009	1/10 oz	15	18.1	To order/ 10,836	Standard reverse	b/v	185
2009	1/10 oz	15	18.1	50,000/ 19,762	Colour reverse	b/v	185
2009	1/20 oz	5	14.6	To order/ 5,971	Plain reverse	b/v	95
2009	1/20 oz	5	14.6	50,000/ 23,604	Colour reverse	b/v	95
2010 : YEAR OF THE TIGER - GOLD SPECIMEN							
2010	10 kg	30,000	180.6	100/ 2	Standard reverse	435,000	b/v
2010	1 kg	3,000	101.0	To order/ 110	Standard reverse	43,500	b/v
2010	10 oz	1,000	75.6	To order/ 267	Standard reverse	b/v	18,500
2010	2 oz	200	41.1	To order/ 5,340	Standard reverse	b/v	3,500
2010	1 oz	100	39.34	30,000/ All sold	Standard reverse	b/v	1,750
2010	1 oz	100	39.34	6,000/ 316	Colour reverse	n/a	1,750
2010	1/2 oz	50	30.6	To order/ 9,781	Standard reverse	b/v	895
2010	1/2 oz	50	30.6	8,000/ 583	Colour reverse	n/a	895
2010	1/4 oz	25	22.6	To order/ 11,771	Standard reverse	b/v	455
2010	1/4 oz	25	22.6	8,000/ 1,783	Colour reverse	n/a	455
2010	1/10 oz	15	18.1	To order/ 22,699	Standard reverse	b/v	18
2010	1/10 oz	15	18.1	50,000/ 14,067	Colour reverse	n/a	185
2010	1/20 oz	5	14.6	To order/ 17,552	Standard reverse	b/v	95
2010	1/20 oz	5	14.6	50,000/ 20,302	Colour reverse	n/a	95

GOLD ISSUES : MULTIPLE DATES

SPECIMEN LUNAR SERIES TWO

SECOND SERIES COMMENCING 2008 -

2011 Rabbit Specimen

2012 Dragon Dragon

2013 Snake Specimen

Date	Weight in oz's	Face Value	Size mm	Mintage Max/ Actual	Reverse Feature	Issue Price	Average Retail
2011 : YEAR OF THE RABBIT - GOLD SPECIMEN							
2011	10 kg	30,000	180.6	100/ Nil	Standard reverse	—	—
2011	1 kg	3,000	100.6	To order/ 153	Standard reverse	45,000	57,000
2011	10 oz	1,000	75.6	To order/ 641	Standard reverse	b/v	18,500
2011	2 oz	200	41.1	To order/ 4,209	Standard reverse	b/v	3,500
2011	1 oz	100	39.34	30,000/ All sold	Standard reverse	2,580	1,750
2011	1 oz	100	39.34	6,000/ 289	Colour reverse	b/v	n/a
2011	1/2 oz	50	30.6	To order/ 8,885	Standard reverse	b/v	895
2011	1/2 oz	50	30.6	8,000/ 1,365	Colour reverse	b/v	n/a
2011	1/4 oz	25	22.6	To order/ 11,101	Standard reverse	b/v	455
2011	1/4 oz	25	22.6	8,000/ 1,265	Colour reverse	b/v	n/a
2011	1/10 oz	15	18.1	To order/ 21,901	Standard reverse	b/v	185
2011	1/10 oz	15	18.1	50,000/ 11,021	Colour reverse	b/v	n/a
2011	1/20 oz	5	14.6	To order/ 22,412	Standard reverse	b/v	95
2011	1/20 oz	5	14.6	50,000/ 17,142	Colour reverse	b/v	n/a
2012 : YEAR OF THE DRAGON - GOLD SPECIMEN							
2012	10 kg	30,000	180.6	100/ 3	Standard reverse	515,000	b/v
2012	1 kg	3,000	100.6	To order/ 241	Standard reverse	57,000	b/v
2012	10 oz	1,000	75.6	To order/ 1,087	Standard reverse	b/v	18,500
2012	2 oz	200	41.1	To order/ 5,986	Standard reverse	4,455	3,500
2012	1 oz	100	39.34	30,000/ Sold out	Standard reverse	b/v	1750
2012	1 oz	100	39.34	5,000/ 468	Colour reverse	n/a	n/a
2012	1/2 oz	50	30.6	To order/ 19,370	Standard reverse	n/a	n/a
2012	1/2 oz	50	30.6	8000/ 574	Gilt reverse	67.5	85
2012	1/4 oz	25	22.6	To order/ 18,620	Standard reverse	n/a	n/a
2012	1/4 oz	25	22.6	8000/ 6,099	Gilt reverse	n/a	n/a
2012	1/10 oz	15	18.1	To order/ 33,059	Standard reverse	203.5	185
2012	1/10 oz	15	18.1	50,000/ 19,939	Gilt reverse	n/a	n/a
2012	1/20 oz	5	14.6	To order/ 23,322	Standard reverse	b/v	95
2012	1/20 oz	5	14.6	50,000/ 20,450	Colour reverse	b/v	n/a
2013 : YEAR OF THE SNAKE - GOLD SPECIMEN							
2013	10 kg	30,000	180.6	100/ 11	Standard reverse	515,000	b/v
2013	1 kg	3,000	100.6	To order/ 256	Standard reverse	54,675	58,000
2013	10 oz	1,000	75.6	To order/ 981	Standard reverse	n/a	b/v
2013	2 oz	200	41.1	To order/ 6,693	Standard reverse	4,445b/v	
2013	1 oz	100	39.34	30,000/ all sold	Standard reverse	n/a	b/v
2013	1 oz	100	39.34	5,000/ 425	Orange snake	2,950	2,950
2013	1/2 oz	50	22.6	To order/ 14,681	Standard reverse	n/a	b/v
2013	1/2 oz	50	30.6	8,000/ 314	Orange snake	1,182.5	b/v
2013	1/4 oz	25	22.6	To order/ 16,159	Standard reverse	n/a	b/v
2013	1/4 oz	25	22.6	8,000/ 1,730	Orange snake	654.5	b/v
2013	1/10 oz	15	18.1	To order/ 23,700	Standard reverse	n/a	b/v
2013	1/10 oz	15	18.1	5,000/ 7,707	Orange snake	203.5	b/v
2013	1/20 oz	5	14.6	To order/ 15,598	Standard reverse	n/a	b/v
2013	1/20 oz	5	14.6	50,000/ 10,973	Orange snake	159	b/v

SPECIMEN LUNAR SERIES TWO

SECOND SERIES COMMENCING 2008 -

2014 Horse Specimen

2015 Goat Specimen

2016 Monkey Specimen

2017 Rooster Specimen

Date	Weight in oz's	Face Value	Size mm	Mintage Max/ Actual	Reverse Feature	Issue Price	Average Retail
2014 : YEAR OF THE HORSE - GOLD SPECIMEN							
2014	1 kg	3,000	100.6	To order/ 263	Standard reverse	b/v	58,000
2014	10 oz	1,000	75.6	To order/ 980	Standard reverse	b/v	18,500
2014	2 oz	200	41.1	To order/ 4,887	Standard reverse	4,455	b/v
2014	1 oz	100	39.34	30,000/ All sold	Standard reverse	b/v	b/v
2014	1/2 oz	50	30.6	To order/ 17,839	Standard reverse	1,182.5	b/v
2014	1/4 oz	25	22.6	To order/ 18,621	Standard reverse	654.5	b/v
2014	1/10 oz	15	18.1	To order/ 34,181	Standard reverse	203.5	b/v
2014	1/20 oz	5	14.6	To order/ 20,879	Standard reverse	b/v	95
2014	1/20 oz	5	14.6	To order/ n/a	Coloured reverse	159	b/v
2015 : YEAR OF THE GOAT - GOLD SPECIMEN							
2015	1 kg	3,000	100.6	To order/ 178	Standard reverse	b/v	58,000
2015	10 oz	1,000	75.6	To order/ 733	Standard reverse	b/v	18,500
2015	2 oz	200	41.1	To order/ 3,255	Standard reverse	4,455	b/v
2015	1 oz	100	39.34	30,000/ All sold	Standard reverse	2,695	b/v
2015	1 oz	100	39.34	6000/ 165	Coloured reverse	2,695	b/v
2015	1/2 oz	50	30.6	To order/ 11,961	Standard reverse	1,182.5	b/v
2015	1/2 oz	50	30.6	8,000/ 127	Coloured reverse	1,182.5	b/v
2015	1/4 oz	25	22.6	To order/ 13,650	Standard reverse	695	b/v
2015	1/4 oz	25	22.6	8,000/ 527	Coloured reverse	695	b/v
2015	1/10 oz	15	18.1	To order/ 43,036	Standard reverse	299	b/v
2015	1/10 oz	15	18.1	50,000/ 2,724	Coloured reverse	299	b/v
2015	1/20 oz	5	14.6	To order/ 66,693	Standard reverse	b/v	95
2015	1/20 oz	5	14.6	50,000/ 3,335	Coloured reverse	b/v	95
2015	1/20 oz	5	14.6	500/ 405	Coloured reverse	159	b/v
2016 : YEAR OF THE MONKEY - GOLD SPECIMEN							
2016	1 kg	3,000	100.6	To order/ 108	Standard reverse	b/v	58,000
2016	1 kg	3,000	100.6	500/ n/a	Cognac diamond eye	b/v	58,000
2016	10 oz	1,000	75.6	To order/ 597	Standard reverse	b/v	18,500
2016	2 oz	200	41.1	To order/ 4,472	Standard reverse	4,455	b/v
2016	1 oz	100	39.34	30,000/ All sold	Standard reverse	2,699	1,775
2016	1/2 oz	50	30.6	To order/ 11,947	Standard reverse	1,182.5	b/v
2016	1/4 oz	25	22.6	To order/ 12,833	Standard reverse	699	b/v
2016	1/10 oz	15	18.1	To order/ 27,920	Standard reverse	299	185
2016	1/20 oz	5	14.6	To order/ 20,147	Standard reverse	b/v	110
2016	1/20 oz	5	14.6	500/ n/a	Colour & certficate	159	b/v
2017 : YEAR OF THE ROOSTER - GOLD SPECIMEN							
2017	1 kg	3,000	100.6	To order/ 48	Standard reverse	b/v	58,950
2017	10 oz	1,000	75.6	To order/ 396	Standard reverse	b/v	16,750
2017	2 oz	200	41.1	To order/ 1,765	Standard reverse	3,338	3,350
2017	1 oz	100	39.34	30,000/ All sold	Standard reverse	1,674	1,700
2017	1/2 oz	50	30.6	To order/ 7,462	Standard reverse	n/a	875
2017	1/4 oz	25	22.6	To order/ 7,777	Standard reverse	449	460
2017	1/10 oz	15	18.1	To order/ 16,253	Standard reverse	185.4	210
2017	1/20 oz	5	14.6	To order/ 8,625	Standard reverse	109.7	120
2017	1/20 oz	5	14.6	500/ n/a	Colour	n/a	60

Mintage figures for 2017 issues not finalised.

GOLD ISSUES : MULTIPLE DATES

PROOF - DISCOVER AUSTRALIA - FAUNA

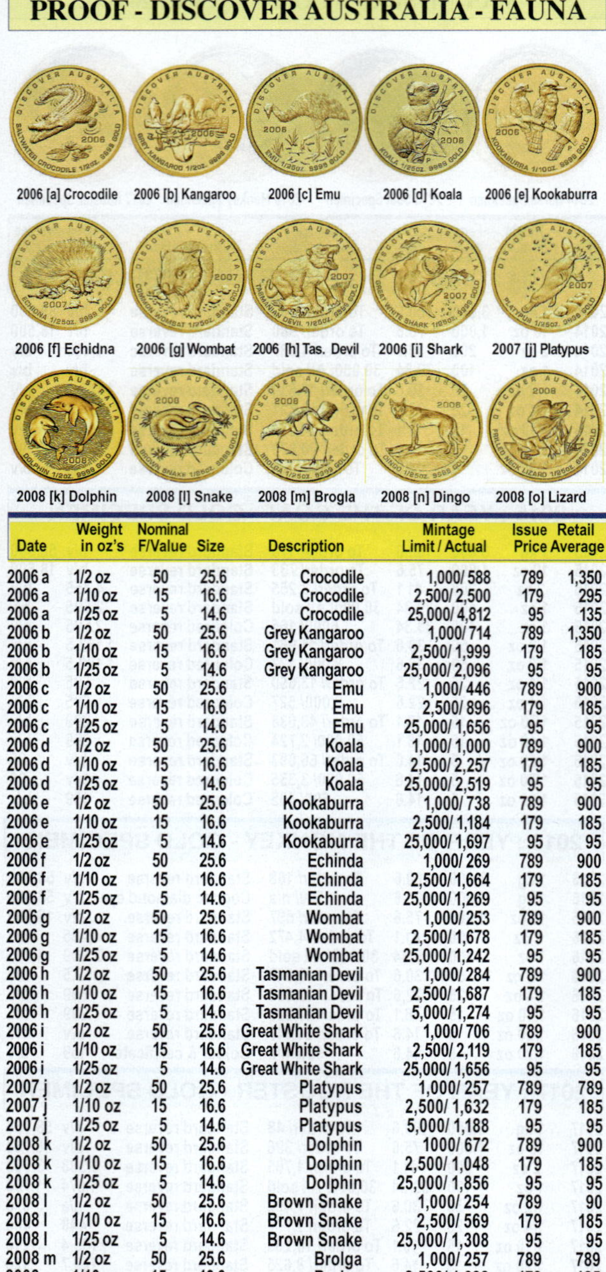

2006 [a] Crocodile — 2006 [b] Kangaroo — 2006 [c] Emu — 2006 [d] Koala — 2006 [e] Kookaburra

2006 [f] Echidna — 2006 [g] Wombat — 2006 [h] Tas. Devil — 2006 [i] Shark — 2007 [j] Platypus

2008 [k] Dolphin — 2008 [l] Snake — 2008 [m] Brogla — 2008 [n] Dingo — 2008 [o] Lizard

Date	Weight in oz's	Nominal F/Value	Size	Description	Mintage Limit / Actual	Issue Price	Retail Average
2006 a	1/2 oz	50	25.6	Crocodile	1,000/ 588	789	1,350
2006 a	1/10 oz	15	16.6	Crocodile	2,500/ 2,500	179	295
2006 a	1/25 oz	5	14.6	Crocodile	25,000/ 4,812	95	135
2006 b	1/2 oz	50	25.6	Grey Kangaroo	1,000/ 714	789	1,350
2006 b	1/10 oz	15	16.6	Grey Kangaroo	2,500/ 1,999	179	185
2006 b	1/25 oz	5	14.6	Grey Kangaroo	25,000/ 2,096	95	95
2006 c	1/2 oz	50	25.6	Emu	1,000/ 446	789	900
2006 c	1/10 oz	15	16.6	Emu	2,500/ 896	179	185
2006 c	1/25 oz	5	14.6	Emu	25,000/ 1,656	95	95
2006 d	1/2 oz	50	25.6	Koala	1,000/ 1,000	789	900
2006 d	1/10 oz	15	16.6	Koala	2,500/ 2,257	179	185
2006 d	1/25 oz	5	14.6	Koala	25,000/ 2,519	95	95
2006 e	1/2 oz	50	25.6	Kookaburra	1,000/ 738	789	900
2006 e	1/10 oz	15	16.6	Kookaburra	2,500/ 1,184	179	185
2006 e	1/25 oz	5	14.6	Kookaburra	25,000/ 1,697	95	95
2006 f	1/2 oz	50	25.6	Echinda	1,000/ 269	789	900
2006 f	1/10 oz	15	16.6	Echinda	2,500/ 1,664	179	185
2006 f	1/25 oz	5	14.6	Echinda	25,000/ 1,269	95	95
2006 g	1/2 oz	50	25.6	Wombat	1,000/ 253	789	900
2006 g	1/10 oz	15	16.6	Wombat	2,500/ 1,678	179	185
2006 g	1/25 oz	5	14.6	Wombat	25,000/ 1,242	95	95
2006 h	1/2 oz	50	25.6	Tasmanian Devil	1,000/ 284	789	900
2006 h	1/10 oz	15	16.6	Tasmanian Devil	2,500/ 1,687	179	185
2006 h	1/25 oz	5	14.6	Tasmanian Devil	5,000/ 1,274	95	95
2006 i	1/2 oz	50	25.6	Great White Shark	1,000/ 706	789	900
2006 i	1/10 oz	15	16.6	Great White Shark	2,500/ 2,119	179	185
2006 i	1/25 oz	5	14.6	Great White Shark	25,000/ 1,656	95	95
2007 j	1/2 oz	50	25.6	Platypus	1,000/ 257	789	789
2007 j	1/10 oz	15	16.6	Platypus	2,500/ 1,632	179	185
2007 j	1/25 oz	5	14.6	Platypus	5,000/ 1,188	95	95
2008 k	1/2 oz	50	25.6	Dolphin	1000/ 672	789	900
2008 k	1/10 oz	15	16.6	Dolphin	2,500/ 1,048	179	185
2008 k	1/25 oz	5	14.6	Dolphin	25,000/ 1,856	95	95
2008 l	1/2 oz	50	25.6	Brown Snake	1,000/ 254	789	90
2008 l	1/10 oz	15	16.6	Brown Snake	2,500/ 569	179	185
2008 l	1/25 oz	5	14.6	Brown Snake	25,000/ 1,308	95	95
2008 m	1/2 oz	50	25.6	Brolga	1,000/ 257	789	789
2008 m	1/10 oz	15	16.6	Brolga	2,500/ 1,632	179	185
2008 m	1/25 oz	5	14.6	Brolga	5,000/ 1,188	95	95

GOLD ISSUES : MULTIPLE DATES

PROOF - DISCOVER AUSTRALIA - FAUNA

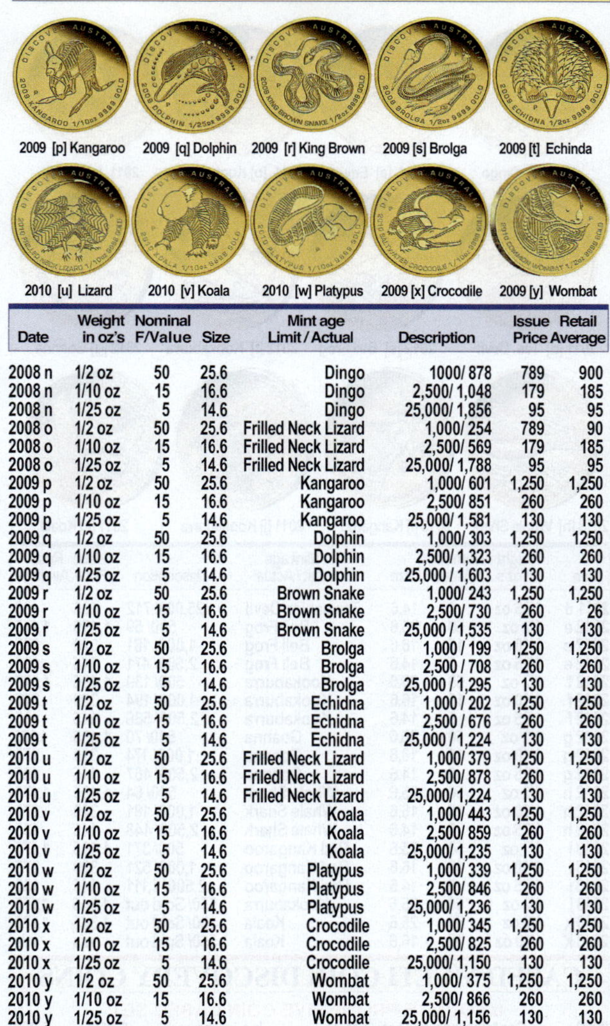

2009 [p] Kangaroo 2009 [q] Dolphin 2009 [r] King Brown 2009 [s] Brolga 2009 [t] Echinda

2010 [u] Lizard 2010 [v] Koala 2010 [w] Platypus 2009 [x] Crocodile 2009 [y] Wombat

Date	Weight in oz's	Nominal F/Value	Size	Mint age Limit / Actual	Description	Issue Price	Retail Average
2008 n	1/2 oz	50	25.6	Dingo	1000/ 878	789	900
2008 n	1/10 oz	15	16.6	Dingo	2,500/ 1,048	179	185
2008 n	1/25 oz	5	14.6	Dingo	25,000/ 1,856	95	95
2008 o	1/2 oz	50	25.6	Frilled Neck Lizard	1,000/ 254	789	90
2008 o	1/10 oz	15	16.6	Frilled Neck Lizard	2,500/ 569	179	185
2008 o	1/25 oz	5	14.6	Frilled Neck Lizard	25,000/ 1,788	95	95
2009 p	1/2 oz	50	25.6	Kangaroo	1,000/ 601	1,250	1,250
2009 p	1/10 oz	15	16.6	Kangaroo	2,500/ 851	260	260
2009 p	1/25 oz	5	14.6	Kangaroo	25,000/ 1,581	130	130
2009 q	1/2 oz	50	25.6	Dolphin	1,000/ 303	1,250	1250
2009 q	1/10 oz	15	16.6	Dolphin	2,500/ 1,323	260	260
2009 q	1/25 oz	5	14.6	Dolphin	25,000 / 1,603	130	130
2009 r	1/2 oz	50	25.6	Brown Snake	1,000/ 243	1,250	1,250
2009 r	1/10 oz	15	16.6	Brown Snake	2,500/ 730	260	26
2009 r	1/25 oz	5	14.6	Brown Snake	25,000 / 1,535	130	130
2009 s	1/2 oz	50	25.6	Brolga	1,000 / 199	1,250	1,250
2009 s	1/10 oz	15	16.6	Brolga	2,500 / 708	260	260
2009 s	1/25 oz	5	14.6	Brolga	25,000 / 1,295	130	130
2009 t	1/2 oz	50	25.6	Echidna	1,000 / 202	1,250	1250
2009 t	1/10 oz	15	16.6	Echidna	2,500 / 676	260	260
2009 t	1/25 oz	5	14.6	Echidna	25,000 / 1,224	130	130
2010 u	1/2 oz	50	25.6	Frilled Neck Lizard	1,000/ 379	1,250	1,250
2010 u	1/10 oz	15	16.6	Friledl Neck Lizard	2,500/ 878	260	260
2010 u	1/25 oz	5	14.6	Frilled Neck Lizard	25,000/ 1,224	130	130
2010 v	1/2 oz	50	25.6	Koala	1,000/ 443	1,250	1,250
2010 v	1/10 oz	15	16.6	Koala	2,500/ 859	260	260
2010 v	1/25 oz	5	14.6	Koala	25,000/ 1,235	130	130
2010 w	1/2 oz	50	25.6	Platypus	1,000/ 339	1,250	1,250
2010 w	1/10 oz	15	16.6	Platypus	2,500/ 846	260	260
2010 w	1/25 oz	5	14.6	Platypus	25,000/ 1,236	130	130
2010 x	1/2 oz	50	25.6	Crocodile	1,000/ 345	1,250	1,250
2010 x	1/10 oz	15	16.6	Crocodile	2,500/ 825	260	260
2010 x	1/25 oz	5	14.6	Crocodile	25,000/ 1,150	130	130
2010 y	1/2 oz	50	25.6	Wombat	1,000/ 375	1,250	1,250
2010 y	1/10 oz	15	16.6	Wombat	2,500/ 866	260	260
2010 y	1/25 oz	5	14.6	Wombat	25,000/ 1,156	130	130
2011 z	1/2 oz	50	25.6	Dingo	1,000/ 62	1,325	325
2011 z	1/10 oz	15	16.6	Dingo	2,500/ 263	275	275
2011 z	1/25 oz	5	14.6	Dingo	25,000/ 795	136	136
2011 a	1/2 oz	50	25.6	Emu	1,000/ 63	1,325	1,325
2011 a	1/10 oz	15	16.6	Emu	2,500/ 257	275	275
2011 a	1/25 oz	5	14.6	Emu	25,000/ 726	136	145
2011 b	1/2 oz	50	25.6	Kookaburra	1,000/ 70	1,325	1,325
2011 b	1/10 oz	15	16.6	Kookaburra	2,500/ 255	275	275
2011 b	1/25 oz	5	14.6	Kookaburra	25,000/ 779	136	145
2011 c	1/2 oz	50	25.6	White Shark	1,000 / 68	1,325	132
2011 c	1/10 oz	15	16.6	White Shark	2,500/ 272	275	275
2011 c	1/25 oz	5	14.6	White Shark	25,000/ 726	136	136
2011 d	1/2 oz	50	25.6	Tasmanian Devil	1,000/ 66	1,325	1,325
2011 d	1/10 oz	15	16.6	Tasmanian Devil	2,500/ 249	275	275

GOLD ISSUES : MULTIPLE DATES

PROOF - DISCOVER AUSTRALIA

2011 [z] Dingo | 2011 [a] Emu | 2011 [b] Kookaburra | 2011 [c] Shark

2011 [d] Tas. Devil | 2012 [e] Bell Frog | 2012 [f] Kookaburra | 2012 [g] Goanna

2013 [h] Whale Shark | 2013 [i] Kangaroo | 2011 [j] Kookaburra | 2011 [k] Koala

Date	Weight in oz's	Nominal F/Value	Size	Mint age Limit / Actual	Description	Issue Price	Retail Average
2011 d	1/25 oz	5	14.6	Tasmanian Devil	25,000/ 712	136	136
2012 e	1/2 oz	50	25.6	Bell Frog	500/ 59	1,495	1,175
2012 e	1/10 oz	15	16.6	Bell Frog	1,000/ 181	329	275
2012 e	1/25 oz	5	14.6	Bell Frog	2,500/ 471	145	135
2012 f	1/2 oz	50	25.6	Kookaburra	500/ 139	1,495	1,175
2012 f	1/10 oz	15	16.6	Kookaburra	1,000/ 194	329	275
2012 f	1/25 oz	5	14.6	Kookaburra	2,500/ 586	145	135
2012 g	1/2 oz	50	25.6	Goanna	500/ 70	1,495	1,175
2012 g	1/10 oz	15	16.6	Goanna	1,000/ 174	329	275
2012 g	1/25 oz	5	14.6	Goanna	2,500/ 467	145	135
2012 h	1/2 oz	50	25.6	Whale Shark	500/ 64	1,495	1,175
2012 h	1/10 oz	15	16.6	Whale Shark	1,000/ 181	329	275
2012 h	1/25 oz	5	14.6	Whale Shark	2,500/ 448	145	135
2013 i	1/2 oz	50	25.6	Red Kangaroo	500/ 371	1,495	1,175
2013 i	1/10 oz	15	16.6	Red Kangaroo	1,000/ 521	329	275
2013 i	1/25 oz	5	14.6	Red Kangaroo	2,500/ 1,111	145	135
2013 j	1/2 oz	50	25.6	Kookaburra	550/ Sold out	1,345	1,175
2013 k	1/2 oz	50	25.6	Koala	550/ Sold out	1,345	1,175
2013 k	1/10 oz	15	16.6	Koala	550/ Sold out	n/a	n/a

CASED MULTI COIN DISCOVERY COINS

1/2 OUNCE PROOF FIVE COIN CASED SET

2009	Contains one of each (a to e)	Inc in above	6,250	6,250
2010	Contains one of each (f to j)	Inc in above	6,250	6,250
2011	Contains one of each (k to o)	Inc in above	6,625	6,62
2012	Contains one of each (a to e)	Inc in above	7,475	n/a

1/10 OUNCE PROOF FIVE COIN CASED SET

2009	Contains one of each (a to e)	Inc in above	1,300	1,300
2010	Contains one of each (f to j)	Inc in above	1,300	1,300
2011	Contains one of each (k to o)	Inc in above	1,375	1,375
2012	Contains one of each (a to e)	Inc in above	1,645	n/a

1/25 OUNCE PROOF FIVE COIN CASED SET

2009	Contains one of each (a to e)	Inc in above	650	650
2010	Contains one of each (f to j)	Inc in above	650	650
2011	Contains one of each (k to o)	Inc in above	680	680
2012	Contains one of each (a to e)	Inc in above	725	650

GOLD ISSUES : MULTIPLE DATES

KANGAROO SPECIMEN & PROOF ISSUES

2007 : One Ounce

2008 : One Ounce

2009 : One Ounce

2013 : One Ounce

Date	Weight in oz's	Face Value	Reverse Design	Type	Size	Mintage Max/ Actual	Issue Price	Average Retail
2006	1 kg	3,000	Red Kangaroo	Spec	75.6	To order/ 155	n/a	b/v
2006	10 oz	1,000	Red Kangaroo	Spec	59.7	To order/ 499	n/a	b/v
2006	2 oz	200	Red Kangaroo	Spec	40.4	To order/ 2,760	n/a	b/v
2006	1 oz	100	Kangaroo	Spec	32.6	350k/ 49,991	n/a	b/v
2006	1/2 oz	50	Kangaroo	Spec	25.6	100k/ 15,350	n/a	b/v
2006	1/4 oz	25	Kangaroo	Spec	20.6	150k/ 17,009	n/a	b/v
2006	1/10 oz	15	Kangaroo	Spec	16.6	200k/ 28,453	n/a	b/v
2006	1/20 oz	5	Kangaroo	Spec	13.7	200k/ 12,299	n/a	b/v
2007	1 kg	3,000	Red Kangaroo	Spec	75.6	To order/ 131	740	b/v
2007	10 oz	1,000	Red Kangaroo	Spec	59.7	To order/ 504	251	b/v
2007	2 oz	200	Red Kangaroo	Spec	40.4	To order/ 2,398	56	b/v
2007	1 oz	100	Standing 'roo	Spec	32.6	350k/ 46,891	36	b/v
2007	1/2 oz	50	Standing 'roo	Spec	25.6	100k/ 13,780	n/a	b/v
2007	1/4 oz	25	Standing 'roo	Spec	20.6	150k/ 18,351	n/a	b/v
2007	1/10 oz	15	Standing 'roo	Spec	16.1	200k/ 22,583	n/a	b/v
2007	1/20 oz	5	Standing 'roo	Spec	13.7	200k/ 14,983	n/a	b/v
2008	1 kg	3,000	Red Kangaroo	Spec	75.6	To order/ 185	n/a	b/v
2008	10 oz	1,000	Red Kangaroo	Spec	59.7	To order/ 615	n/a	b/v
2008	2 oz	200	Red Kangaroo	Spec	40.4	To order/ 3,671	n/a	b/v
2008	1 oz	100	Kangaroo	Spec	32.6	350k/ 63,429	n/a	b/v
2008	1/2 oz	50	Kangaroo	Spec	25.6	100k/ 15,530	n/a	b/v
2008	1/4 oz	25	Kangaroo	Spec	20.6	150k/ 18,611	n/a	b/v
2008	1/10 oz	15	Kangaroo	Spec	16.1	200k/ 23,357	n/a	b/v
2008	1/20 oz	5	Kangaroo	Spec	13.7	200k/ 15,945	n/a	b/v
2009	1 kg	3,000	Red Kangaroo	Spec	75.6	To order/ 140	n/a	b/v
2009	10 oz	1,000	Red Kangaroo	Spec	59.7	To order/ 943	n/a	b/v
2009	2 oz	200	Red Kangaroo	Spec	40.4	To order/ 3,452	n/a	b/v
2009	1 oz	100	Kangaroo	Spec	32.6	350k/ 298,016	n/a	b/v
2009	1/2 oz	50	Kangaroo	Spec	25.6	100k/ 31,658	n/a	b/v
2009	1/4 oz	25	Kangaroo	Spec	20.6	150k/ 31,942	n/a	b/v
2009	1/10 oz	15	Kangaroo	Spec	16.1	200k/ 36,235	n/a	b/v
2009	1/20 oz	5	Kangaroo	Spec	13.7	200k/ 12,161	n/a	b/v
2010	1 kg	3,000	Red Kangaroo	Spec	75.6	To order/ 149	n/a	b/v
2010	1 oz	100	Kangaroo	Spec	32.6	350k/ 152,229	n/a	b/v
2010	1/2 oz	50	Kangaroo	Spec	25.6	100k/ 24,510	n/a	b/v
2010	1/4 oz	25	Kangaroo	Spec	20.6	150k/ 26,143	n/a	b/v
2010	1/10 oz	15	Kangaroo	Spec	16.1	200k/ 39,997	n/a	b/v
2010	1/20 oz	5	Kangaroo	Spec	13.7	200k/ 1,112	n/a	b/v
2011	1 kg	3,000	Red Kangaroo	Spec	75.6	To order/ 143	n/a	b/v
2011	1 oz	100	Kangaroo	Spec	32.6	350k/ 190,681	n/a	b/v
2011	1/2 oz	50	Kangaroo	Spec	25.6	100k/ 17,827	n/a	b/v
2011	1/4 oz	25	Kangaroo	Spec	20.6	150k/ 18,518	n/a	b/v
2011	1/10 oz	15	Kangaroo	Spec	16.1	200k/ 51,240	n/a	b/v
2011	1/20 oz	5	Kangaroo	Spec	13.7	200k/ 1,093	n/a	b/v
2012	1 kg	3,000	Red Kangaroo	Spec	75.6	To order/ 191	n/a	b/v
2012	1 oz	100	Kangaroo	Spec	32.6	350k/ 198,207	n/a	b/v
2012	1/2 oz	50	Kangaroo	Spec	25.6	100k/ 23,613	n/a	b/v
2012	1/4 oz	25	Kangaroo	Spec	20.6	150k/ 26,526	n/a	b/v
2012	1/10 oz	15	Kangaroo	Spec	16.1	200k/ 57,725	n/a	b/v
2013	1 kg	3,000	Red Kangaroo	Spec	75.6	To order/ 311	n/a	b/v
2013	1 oz	100	Kangaroo	Spec	32.6	350k/ 341,417	n/a	b/v
2013	1/2 oz	50	Kangaroo	Spec	25.6	100k/ 46,095	n/a	b/v
2013	1/4 oz	25	Kangaroo	Spec	20.6	150k/ 32,198	n/a	b/v
2013	1/10 oz	15	Chinese P'mark	Proof	16.1	30,000/ 6061	299	n/a
2013	1/10 oz	15	Kangaroo	Spec	16.1	200k/ 53,994	n/a	b/v

GOLD ISSUES : MULTIPLE DATES

KANGAROO SPECIMEN & PROOF ISSUES

2014 : 1/2 Ounce

2015 : One Ounce

2016 : 1/10 Ounce

2017 : One Ounce

Date	Weight in oz's	Face Value	Reverse Design	Type	Size	Mintage Max/ Actual	Issue Price	Average Retail
2014	1 kg	3,000	Red Kangaroo	Spec	75.6	To order/ 206	n/a	50,000
2014	1 oz	100	Kangaroo	Proof	32.6	2,000/ n/a	2,695	1,650
2014	1 oz	100	Kangaroo	Spec	32.6	350k/ 223,041	n/a	1,650
2014	1/2 oz	50	Kangaroo	Spec	25.6	100k/ 22,510	n/a	740
2014	1/4 oz	25	Kangaroo	Spec	20.6	150k/ 25,016	n/a	375
2014	1/4 oz	25	Kangaroo	Proof	20.6	1,000/ n/a	695	375
2014	1/10 oz	15	Kangaroo	Spec	16.6	200k/ 41,333	n/a	150
2015	1 kg	3,000	Red Kangaroo	Spec	75.6	To order/ 151	n/a	50,000
2015	5 oz	500	Red Kangaroo	Spec	N/A	To order/ 315	n/a	50,000
2015	2 oz	200	High relief	Proof	36.6	250/ All sold	5,099	5,100
2015	1 oz	100	Kangaroo	Spec	32.6	350k/ 206,743	n/a	1,65
2015	1 oz	100	High relief	Proof	32.6	500/ All sold	2,695	2,750
2015	1/2 oz	50	Kangaroo	Spec	25.6	100k/ 28,477	n/a	740
2015	1/4 oz	25	Kangaroo	Spec	20.6	150k/ 25,800	n/a	375
2015	1/4 oz	25	Kangaroo	Proof	20.6	1,000/ n/a	695	375
2015	1/10 oz	15	Kangaroo	Spec	16.6	200k/ 60,726	n/a	150
2016	1 kg	3,000	Red Kangaroo	Spec	75.6	To order/ 113	b/v	50,000
2016	2 oz	200	Kangaroo	Proof	36.6	250/ All sold	5,749	5,749
2016	1 oz	100	Kangaroo	Proof	32.6	2,000/ n/a	2,695	1,650
2015	1 oz	100	High relief	Proof	32.6	500/ All sold	2,695	3,000
2016	1 oz	100	Kangaroo	Spec	32.6	350k/ 221,817	b/v	1,650
2016	1/2 oz	50	Kangaroo	Spec	25.6	100k/ 23,140	b/v	740
2016	1/4 oz	25	Kangaroo	Spec	20.6	150k/ 26,613	475	375
2016	1/4 oz	25	Kangaroo	Proof	20.6	1,000/ n/a	695	375
2016	1/10 oz	15	Kangaroo	Spec	16.6	200k/ 52,669	b/v	15
2017	1 kg	3,000	Red Kangaroo	Spec	75.6	To order/ 21•	b/v	56,000
2017	1 oz	100	Kangaroo	Proof	32.6	2,000/ n/a	2,695	1,50
2017	1 oz	100	Kangaroo	Spec	32.6	350k/ 102,448•	b/v	1,750
2017	1/2 oz	50	Kangaroo	Spec	25.6	100k/ 12,666•	b/v	910
2017	1/4 oz	25	Kangaroo	Spec	20.6	150k/ 11,725•	465	475
2017	1/4 oz	25	Kangaroo	Proof	20.6	1,000/ n/a	695	375
2017	1/10 oz	15	Kangaroo	Spec	16.6	200k/ 31,029•	b/v	15

GOLD MINI ROO SPECIMEN

2010 [a] Issue

2011 [b] Issue

2012 [c] Issue

2013 [d] Issue

2014 [e] Issue

Date	Weight in oz's	Face Value	Reverse Design	Type	Size	Mintage Max/ Actual	Issue Price	Average Retail
2010	0.5g	2	Bounding Roo	Spec	11.6	To Order/ 15,713	69.95	95
2011	0.5g	2	Hunched Roo	Spec	11.6	To Order/ 12,185	69.95	95
2012	0.5g	2	Standing Roo	Spec	11.6	To Order/ 18,002	69.95	90
2013	0.5g	2	Classic stance	Spec	11.6	To Order/ 9,188	69.95	90
2014	0.5g	2	Looking back	Spec	11.6	To Order/ 15,713	69.95	85
2015	0.5g	2	Looking back	Spec	11.6	To Order/ 8,661	69.95	80
2016	0.5g	2	Bounding Roo	Spec	11.6	To Order/ 10,364	69.95	75
2017	0.5g	2	Bounding Roo	Spec	11.6	To Order/ n/a	69.95	70

GOLD ISSUES : MULTIPLE DATES

KOALA SPECIMEN & PROOF ISSUES

2009 : 1/10 oz

2012 : 1 oz

2015 : 5 ozs

2016 : 5 ozs

Date	Metal	Type	Face Value	Weight in oz's	Size	Mintage Max/ Actual	Issue Price	Average Retail
2008	Gold	Proof	200	2 oz	100.6	250/ 20	3,595	3,595
2008	Gold	Proof. High relief	100	1 oz	75.6	2,000/ 1,210	1,995	1,750
2008	Gold	Proof	15	1/10oz	40.6	15,000/ 8,577	207	210
2008	Gold	Proof	5	1/25oz	36.6	To order/ 26,664	107	110
2009	Gold	Proof	200	2 oz	100.6	250/ All sold	3,995	3,500
2009	Gold	Proof. High relief	100	1 oz	75.6	2,000/ 860	2,550	1,950
2009	Gold	Proof	15	1/10oz	40.6	5,000/ 1,545	260	210
2009	Gold	Proof	5	1/25oz	36.6	15,000/ 1,077	130	125
2010	Gold	Proof	200	2 oz	100.6	250/ All sold	3,995	3,500
2010	Gold	Proof. High relief	100	1 oz	75.6	2,000/ 1,567	2,550	1,950
2010	Gold	Proof	15	1/10oz	40.6	5,000/ 3,189	260	210
2010	Gold	Proof	5	1/25oz	36.6	15,000/ 1,007	130	135
2011	Gold	Proof	200	2 oz	100.6	250/ All sold	5,570	5,500
2011	Gold	Proof. High relief	100	1 oz	75.6	2,000/ 859	3,100	2,695
2011	Gold	Proof	15	1/10oz	40.6	5,000/ 1,628	329	b/v
2011	Gold	Proof	5	1/25oz	36.6	15,000/ 1,117	145	b/v
2012	Gold	Proof	200	2 oz	100.6	250/ All sold	5,570	b/v
2012	Gold	Proof. High relief	100	1 oz	75.6	2,000/ 659	3,100	b/v
2012	Gold	Proof	15	1/10oz	40.6	5,000/ 1,500	329	b/v
2012	Gold	Proof	5	1/25 oz	36.6	15,000/ 1,499	145	b/v
2013	Gold	Proof	200	2 oz	100.6	250/ All sold	3,595	3,595
2013	Gold	Proof. High relief	100	1 oz	75.6	2,000/ 659	n/a	b/v
2013	Gold	Proof	50	1/2 oz	25.6	550/ n/a	n/a	b/v
2013	Gold	Proof	15	1/10oz	40.6	5,000/ All sold	295	b/v
2013	Gold	Proof	5	1/25oz	36.6	15,000/ 1,499	n/a	299
2014	Gold	Proof. High relief	500	5 oz	50.5	19/ All sold	12,995	12,995
2014	Gold	Proof. High relief. Slabbed	500	5 oz	50.5	80/ All sold	12,995	b/v
2014	Gold	Proof. High relief	200	2 oz	36.6	250/ All sold	5,570	b/v
2014	Gold	Proof. High relief	100	1 oz	27.3	1,800/ 199	3,100	b/v
2014	Gold	Proof. High relief. Slabbed	100	1 oz	27.3	200/ All sold	3,100	b/v
2014	Gold	Proof	25	1/4 oz	20.6	1,000/ 628	799	b/v
2014	Gold	Proof	15	1/10oz	16.6	5,000/ 392	299	b/v
2015	Gold	Proof	500	5 oz	50.5	99/ 85	12,995	12,995
2015	Gold	Proof. High relief	200	2 oz	36.6	50/ All sold	5,050	5,050
2015	Gold	Proof. High relief. Slabbed	200	2 oz	36.6	100/ All sold	5,050	5,050
2015	Gold	Proof. High relief	100	1 oz	27.3	350/ All sold	2,695	2,695
2015	Gold	Proof. High relief. Slabbed	100	1 oz	27.3	150/ All sold	2,695	2,695
2015	Gold	Proof	25	1/4 oz	20.6	1,000/ 584	695	695
2015	Gold	Proof	15	1/10oz	16.6	1,500/ 592	299	299
2015	Gold	Proof	2	.5g	11.6	To order/ 3,027	59.5	60
2016	Gold	Proof	500	5 oz	50.5	99/ 77	14,449	12,999
2016	Gold	Proof. High relief	200	2 oz	36.6	150/ All sold	5,150	5,150
2016	Gold	Proof. High relief	100	1 oz	27.3	500/ 257	2,699	2,699
2016	Gold	Proof	25	1/4 oz	20.6	1,000/ 459	699	b/v
2016	Gold	Proof	15	1/10oz	16.6	1,500/ 672	229	b/v
2017	Gold	Proof	500	5 oz	50.5	99/ 77	14,449	14,449
2017	Gold	Proof. High relief	200	2 oz	36.6	150/ All sold	5,150	5,150
2017	Gold	Proof. relief	100	1 oz	27.3	500/ 257	2,699	2,699
2017	Gold	Proof	25	1/4 oz	20.6	1,000/ 459	699	799
2017	Gold	Proof	15	1/10oz	16.6	1,500/ 672	229	339

PLATINUM ISSUES : MULTIPLE DATES

KOALA : PROOF ISSUES

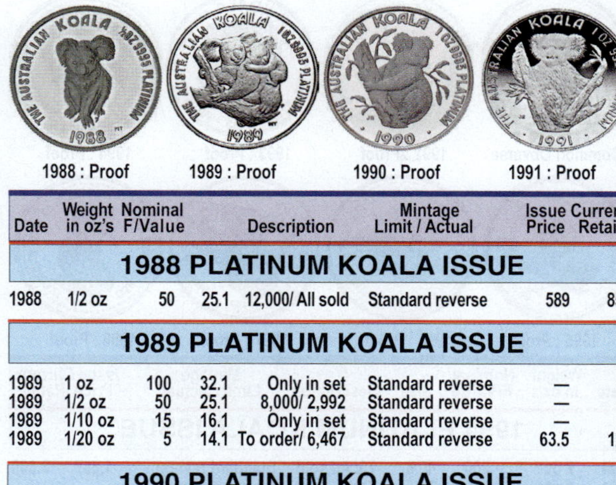

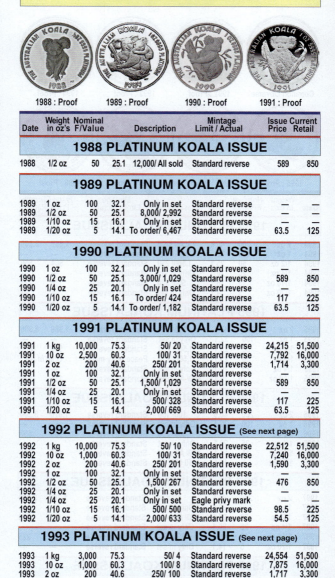

1988 : Proof | 1989 : Proof | 1990 : Proof | 1991 : Proof

Date	Weight in oz's	Nominal F/Value		Description	Mintage Limit / Actual	Issue Price	Current Retail
1988 PLATINUM KOALA ISSUE							
1988	1/2 oz	50	25.1	12,000/ All sold	Standard reverse	589	850
1989 PLATINUM KOALA ISSUE							
1989	1 oz	100	32.1	Only in set	Standard reverse	—	—
1989	1/2 oz	50	25.1	8,000/ 2,992	Standard reverse	—	—
1989	1/10 oz	15	16.1	Only in set	Standard reverse	—	—
1989	1/20 oz	5	14.1	To order/ 6,467	Standard reverse	63.5	125
1990 PLATINUM KOALA ISSUE							
1990	1 oz	100	32.1	Only in set	Standard reverse	—	—
1990	1/2 oz	50	25.1	3,000/ 1,029	Standard reverse	589	850
1990	1/4 oz	25	20.1	Only in set	Standard reverse	—	—
1990	1/10 oz	15	16.1	To order/ 424	Standard reverse	117	225
1990	1/20 oz	5	14.1	To order/ 1,182	Standard reverse	63.5	125
1991 PLATINUM KOALA ISSUE							
1991	1 kg	10,000	75.3	50/ 20	Standard reverse	24,215	51,500
1991	10 oz	2,500	60.3	100/ 31	Standard reverse	7,792	16,000
1991	2 oz	200	40.6	250/ 201	Standard reverse	1,714	3,300
1991	1 oz	100	32.1	Only in set	Standard reverse	—	—
1991	1/2 oz	50	25.1	1,500/ 1,029	Standard reverse	589	850
1991	1/4 oz	25	20.1	Only in set	Standard reverse	—	—
1991	1/10 oz	15	16.1	500/ 328	Standard reverse	117	225
1991	1/20 oz	5	14.1	2,000/ 669	Standard reverse	63.5	125
1992 PLATINUM KOALA ISSUE (See next page)							
1992	1 kg	10,000	75.3	50/ 10	Standard reverse	22,512	51,500
1992	10 oz	1,000	60.3	100/ 31	Standard reverse	7,240	16,000
1992	2 oz	200	40.6	250/ 201	Standard reverse	1,590	3,300
1992	1 oz	100	32.1	Only in set	Standard reverse	—	—
1992	1/2 oz	50	25.1	1,500/ 267	Standard reverse	476	850
1992	1/4 oz	25	20.1	Only in set	Standard reverse	—	—
1992	1/4 oz	25	20.1	Only in set	Eagle privy mark	—	—
1992	1/10 oz	15	16.1	500/ 500	Standard reverse	98.5	225
1992	1/20 oz	5	14.1	2,000/ 633	Standard reverse	54.5	125
1993 PLATINUM KOALA ISSUE (See next page)							
1993	1 kg	3,000	75.3	50/ 4	Standard reverse	24,554	51,500
1993	10 oz	1,000	60.3	100/ 8	Standard reverse	7,875	16,000
1993	2 oz	200	40.6	250/ 100	Standard reverse	1,717	3,300
1993	1 oz	100	32.1	Only in set	Standard reverse	—	—
1993	1/2 oz	50	25.1	1,500/ 250	Standard reverse	508	850
1993	1/4 oz	25	20.1	Only in set	Standard reverse	—	—
1993	1/10 oz	15	16.1	500/ 500	Standard reverse	104.6	225
1993	1/20 oz	5	14.1	2,000/ 2,000	Standard reverse	57.3	125

PLATINUM ISSUES : MULTIPLE DATES

KOALA : PROOF ISSUES

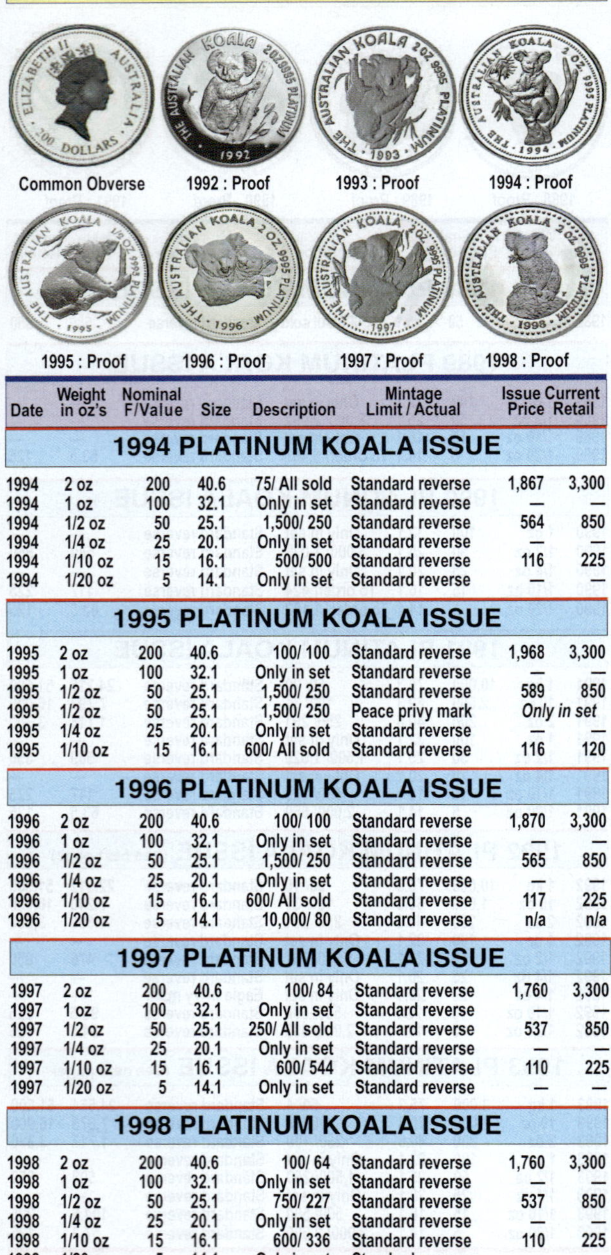

Common Obverse | 1992 : Proof | 1993 : Proof | 1994 : Proof

1995 : Proof | 1996 : Proof | 1997 : Proof | 1998 : Proof

Date	Weight in oz's	Nominal F/Value	Size	Description	Mintage Limit / Actual	Issue Price	Current Retail
1994 PLATINUM KOALA ISSUE							
1994	2 oz	200	40.6	75/ All sold	Standard reverse	1,867	3,300
1994	1 oz	100	32.1	Only in set	Standard reverse	—	—
1994	1/2 oz	50	25.1	1,500/ 250	Standard reverse	564	850
1994	1/4 oz	25	20.1	Only in set	Standard reverse	—	—
1994	1/10 oz	15	16.1	500/ 500	Standard reverse	116	225
1994	1/20 oz	5	14.1	Only in set	Standard reverse	—	—
1995 PLATINUM KOALA ISSUE							
1995	2 oz	200	40.6	100/ 100	Standard reverse	1,968	3,300
1995	1 oz	100	32.1	Only in set	Standard reverse	—	—
1995	1/2 oz	50	25.1	1,500/ 250	Standard reverse	589	850
1995	1/2 oz	50	25.1	1,500/ 250	Peace privy mark	*Only in set*	
1995	1/4 oz	25	20.1	Only in set	Standard reverse	—	—
1995	1/10 oz	15	16.1	600/ All sold	Standard reverse	116	120
1996 PLATINUM KOALA ISSUE							
1996	2 oz	200	40.6	100/ 100	Standard reverse	1,870	3,300
1996	1 oz	100	32.1	Only in set	Standard reverse	—	—
1996	1/2 oz	50	25.1	1,500/ 250	Standard reverse	565	850
1996	1/4 oz	25	20.1	Only in set	Standard reverse	—	—
1996	1/10 oz	15	16.1	600/ All sold	Standard reverse	117	225
1996	1/20 oz	5	14.1	10,000/ 80	Standard reverse	n/a	n/a
1997 PLATINUM KOALA ISSUE							
1997	2 oz	200	40.6	100/ 84	Standard reverse	1,760	3,300
1997	1 oz	100	32.1	Only in set	Standard reverse	—	—
1997	1/2 oz	50	25.1	250/ All sold	Standard reverse	537	850
1997	1/4 oz	25	20.1	Only in set	Standard reverse	—	—
1997	1/10 oz	15	16.1	600/ 544	Standard reverse	110	225
1997	1/20 oz	5	14.1	Only in set	Standard reverse	—	—
1998 PLATINUM KOALA ISSUE							
1998	2 oz	200	40.6	100/ 64	Standard reverse	1,760	3,300
1998	1 oz	100	32.1	Only in set	Standard reverse	—	—
1998	1/2 oz	50	25.1	750/ 227	Standard reverse	537	850
1998	1/4 oz	25	20.1	Only in set	Standard reverse	—	—
1998	1/10 oz	15	16.1	600/ 336	Standard reverse	110	225
1998	1/20 oz	5	14.1	Only in set	Standard reverse	—	—

PLATINUM ISSUES : MULTIPLE DATES

KOALA : PROOF & SPECIMEN FINISH

1999 : Proof

2000 : Proof

2001 : Proof

2001 : Federation

2002 : Proof

2002 : Multiculturalism

2003 : Proof

2003 : The Arts

Date	Weight in oz's	Face Value	Size	Mintage Max/ Actual	Reverse Design	Issue Price	Average Retail
1999 PLATINUM KOALA ISSUE							
1999	2 oz	200	40.6	100/ 100	Standard reverse	1,910	3,300
1999	1 oz	100	32.1	Only in set	Standard reverse	—	—
1999	1/2 oz	50	25.1	750/ 72	Standard reverse	595	850
1999	1/4 oz	25	20.1	Only in set	Standard reverse	—	—
1999	1/10 oz	15	16.1	600/ 221	Standard reverse	120	225
1999	1/20 oz	5	14.1	Only in set	Standard reverse	—	—
2000 PLATINUM KOALA ISSUE							
2000	2 oz	200	40.6	225/ 202	Standard reverse	2,732	3,300
2000	1 oz	100	32.1	Only in set	Standard reverse	—	—
2000	1/2 oz	50	25.1	350/ 101	Standard reverse	788	850
2000	1/4 oz	25	20.1	Only in set	Standard reverse	—	—
2000	1/10 oz	15	16.1	600/ 245	Standard reverse	161	225
2000	1/20 oz	5	14.1	Only in set	Standard reverse	—	—
2001 PLATINUM KOALA ISSUE							
2001	2 oz	200	40.6	250/ 134	Standard reverse	3,220	3,300
2001a	1 oz	100	32.1	1,000/ 57	Federation/ Parkes	1,950	1,650
2001	1/2 oz	50	25.1	350/ 67	Standard reverse	912	850
2001	1/4 oz	25	20.1	Only in set	Standard reverse	—	—
2001	1/10 oz	15	16.1	650/ 236	Standard reverse	186.5	225
2001	1/20 oz	5	14.1	5,000/ 219	Standard reverse	104	125
2002 PLATINUM KOALA ISSUE							
2002	2 oz	200	40.6	250/ 117	Standard reverse	3,220	3,300
2002 a	1 oz	100	32.1	1,000/ 22	Multiculturalism	1,950	1,650
2002	1/2 oz	50	25.1	350/ All sold	Standard reverse	912	850
2002	1/4 oz	25	20.1	Only in set	Standard reverse	—	—
2002	1/10 oz	15	16.1	650/ 527	Standard reverse	186.5	225
2003 PLATINUM KOALA ISSUE							
2003	2 oz	200	40.6	250/ 65	Standard reverse	3,584	3,300
2003 a	1 oz	100	32.1	1,000/ 55	The Arts	2,050	1,650
2003	1/2 oz	50	25.1	350/ 81	Standard reverse	1,008	850
2003	1/4 oz	25	20.1	Only in set	Standard reverse	—	—
2003	1/10 oz	15	16.1	650/ 332	Standard reverse	260	225

[a] From 2001 to 2005, the 1oz proof Koala coin features designs based on Australia's culture and heritage.

PLATINUM ISSUES : MULTIPLE DATES

KOALA : PROOF & SPECIMEN FINISH

2004 : Proof

2004 : Sport

2005 : Proof

2005 : Industry

Date	Weight in oz's	Nominal F/Value		Mintage Limit / Actual	Description	Issue Price	Current Retail
2004 PLATINUM KOALA ISSUE							
2004	2 oz	200	40.6	200/ 41	Standard reverse	4,250	3,300
2004a	1 oz	100	32.1	100/ 44	Sport	2,450	1,650
2004	1/2 oz	50	25.1	350/ 83	Standard reverse	1,250	850
2004	1/4 oz	25	20.1	Only in set	Standard reverse	—	—
2004	1/10 oz	15	16.1	500/ 237	Standard reverse	249	225
2005 PLATINUM KOALA ISSUE							
2005	2 oz	200	40.6	200/ 91	Standard reverse	3,220	3,300
2005a	1 oz	100	32.1	100/ 47	Industry	1,950	1,650
2005	1/2 oz	50	25.1	350/ 97	Standard reverse	912	850
2005	1/4 oz	25	20.1	Only in set	Standard reverse	—	—
2005	1/10 oz	15	16.1	500/ 500	Standard reverse	186.5	225

(a) From 2001 to 2005, the 1oz proof Koala coin features designs based on Australia's culture and heritage. The 2001 Federation coin features the original Parliament House in Canberra, Sir Henry Parkes and the Australian flag. The other themes to follow include *Multiculturalism, Industry, Sport and The Arts.*

SPECIAL PLATINUM KOALA SETS AND COMBINATIONS

ANNUAL PROOF PLATINUM KOALA FIVE COIN CASED SET

Date	Description	Mintage Limit / Actual	Issue Price	Current Retail
1989	1 oz to 1/20 oz plus medallion in jarrah case	2,500/ 2,500	2,090	3,350
1990	1 oz to 1/20 oz plus medallion in jarrah case	2,500/ 968	2,090	3,350
1991	1 oz to 1/20 oz plus medallion in jarrah case	1,000/ 328	2,090	3,350
1992	1 oz to 1/20 oz plus medallion in jarrah case	1000/ 227	1,677	3,350
1993	1 oz to 1/20 oz plus medallion in jarrah case	1000/ 165	1,797	3,350
1994	1 oz to 1/20 oz plus medallion in jarrah case	200/ 200	1,975	3,350
1995	1 oz to 1/20 oz plus medallion in jarrah case	200/ 200	2,072	3,350
1996	1 oz to 1/20 oz plus medallion in jarrah case	200/ 200	1,995	3,350
1997	1 oz to 1/20 oz plus medallion in jarrah case	200/ 153	1,875	3,350
1998	1 oz to 1/20 oz plus medallion in jarrah case	1000/ 155	1,875	3,350
1999	1 oz to 1/20 oz plus medallion in jarrah case	200/ 108	1,999	3,350
2000	1 oz to 1/20 oz plus medallion in jarrah case	250/ 135	2,812	3,350
2001	1 oz to 1/20 oz plus medallion in jarrah case	275/ 171	1,797	3,350
2002	1 oz to 1/20 oz plus medallion in jarrah case	275/ 138	1,797	3,350
2003	1 oz to 1/20 oz plus medallion in jarrah case	200/ 99	3,640	3,350
2004	1 oz to 1/20 oz plus medallion in jarrah case	200/ 65	4,300	3,350
2005	1 oz to 1/20 oz plus medallion in jarrah case	200/ 200	4,300	3,350

1999 : PROOF & SPECIMEN (TWO COIN) CASED SET

Date	Nominal F/Value	Weight	Description	Mintage Limit / Actual	Issue Price	Current Retail
1999	25.00	1/4 oz	Twin Set	200/ 187	520	625

PLATINUM PROOF : MULTIPLE DATES

DISCOVER AUSTRALIA : FLORA 2006 - 2008

[a] Cooktown Orchid

[b] Sturt's Desert Rose

[c] Royal Bluebell

[d] Kangaroo Paw

[e] Pink Heath

[f] Anemone Buttercup

[g] Sturt's Desert Pea

[h] Tas. Bluegum

[i] Waratah

[j] Golden Wattle

[k] Flax-Lily

([l] Native Frangipani

[m] Geraldton Wax

[n] Red Kurrajong

[o] Small Leaf

Date	Weight in oz's	Nominal F/Value	Description	Mintage Limit / Actual	Issue Price	Current Retail
2006 a	1/2 oz	50	Cooktown Orchid	1,000 / 169	1,460	1,460
2006 a	1/10 oz	15	Cooktown Orchid	2,500 / 1891	307	307
2006 b	1/2 oz	50	Sturt's Desert Rose	1,000 / 171	1,460	1,460
2006 b	1/10 oz	15	Sturt's Desert Rose	2,500 / 1713	307	307
2006 c	1/2 oz	50	Royal Bluebell	1,000 / 153	1,460	1,460
2006 c	1/10 oz	15	Royal Bluebell	2,500 / 615	307	307
2006 d	1/2 oz	50	Kangaroo Paw	1,000 / 155	1,460	1,460
2006 d	1/10 oz	15	Kangaroo Paw	2,500 / 1606	307	307
2006 e	1/2 oz	50	Common Pink Heath	1,000 / 138	1,460	1,460
2006 e	1/10 oz	15	Common Pink Heath	2,500 / 500	307	307
2007 f	1/2 oz	50	Anemone Buttercup	1,000 / 78	1,460	1,460
2007 f	1/10 oz	15	Anemone Buttercup	2,500 / 404	307	307
2007 g	1/2 oz	50	Sturt's Desert Pea	1,000 / 78	1,460	1,460
2007 g	1/10 oz	15	Sturt's Desert Pea	2,500 / 359	307	307
2007 h	1/2 oz	50	Tasmanian Bluegum	1,000 / 79	1,460	1,460
2007 h	1/10 oz	15	Tasmanian Bluegum	2,500 / 348	307	307
2007 i	1/2 oz	50	Waratah	1,000 / 83	1,460	1460
2007 i	1/10 oz	15	Waratah	2,500 / 364	307	307
2007 j	1/2 oz	50	Golden Wattle	1,000 / 80	1,460	1460
2007 j	1/10 oz	15	Golden Wattle	2,500 / 414	307	307
2008 k	1/2 oz	50	Black Flax-Lily	1,000 / 103	1,460	1460
2008 k	1/10 oz	15	Black Flax-Lily	2,500 / 352	307	307
2008 l	1/2 oz	50	Native Frangipani	1,000 /104	1,625	1460
2008 l	1/10 oz	15	Native Frangipani	2,500 / 356	345	307
2008 m	1/2 oz	50	Geraldton Wax	1,000 / 100	2,075	1,460
2008 m	1/10 oz	15	Geraldton Wax	2,500 / 373	345	307
2008 n	1/2 oz	50	Red Kurrajong	1,000 / 100	2,075	1,460
2008 n	1/10 oz	15	Red Kurrajong	2,500 / 338	345	307
2008 o	1/2 oz	50	Small Leaf Lillypilly	1,000 / 98	2,075	1,460
2008 o	1/10 oz	15	Small Leaf Lillypilly	2,500 / 380	345	307

PLATINUM PROOF : MULTIPLE DATES

DISCOVER AUSTRALIA : DREAMING 2009 - 2010

[a] Kangaroo

[b] Dolphin

[c] Brown Snake

[d] Brolga

[e] Echidna

[f] F/N Lizard

[g] Koala

[h] Platypus

[i] Crocodile

[j] Wombat

[k] Dingo

[l] Emu

[m] Kookaburra

[n] Great White

[o] Tassie Devil

Date	Weight in oz's	Nominal F/Value	Description	Mintage Limit / Actual	Issue Price	Current Retail
2009 a	1/2 oz	50	Kangaroo	1,000/ 420	1,250	1,250
2009 a	1/10 oz	15	Kangaroo	2,500/ 565	260	260
2009 b	1/2 oz	50	Dolphin	1,000/ 82	1,250	1,250
2009 b	1/10 oz	15	Dolphin	2,500/ 563	260	260
2009 c	1/2 oz	50	King Brown Snake	1,000/ 63	1,250	1,250
2009 c	1/10 oz	15	King Brown Snake	2,500/ 473	260	260
2009 d	1/2 oz	50	Brolga	1,000/ 75	1,250	1,250
2009 d	1/10 oz	15	Brolga	2,500/ 471	260	260
2009 e	1/2 oz	50	Echidna	1,000/ 74	1,250	1,250
2009 e	1/10 oz	15	Echidna	2,500/ 625	260	260
2010 f	1/2 oz	50	Frilled Neck Lizard	1,000/ 128	1,550	1,550
2010 f	1/10 oz	15	Frilled Neck Lizard	2,500/ 404	335	335
2010 g	1/2 oz	50	Koala	1,000/ 386	1,550	1,550
2010 g	1/10 oz	15	Koala	2,500/ 393	335	335
2010 h	1/2 oz	50	Platypus	1,000/ 394	1,550	1,550
2010 h	1/10 oz	15	Platypus	2,500/ 328	335	335
2010 i	1/2 oz	50	Saltwater Crocodile	1,000/ 134	1,550	1,550
2010 i	1/10 oz	15	Saltwater Crocodile	2,500/ 407	335	335
2010 j	1/2 oz	50	Common Wombat	1,000/ 128	1,550	1,550
2010 j	1/10 oz	15	Common Wombat	2,500/ 373	335	335
2011 k	1/2 oz	50	Dingo	1,000/ 21	1,550	1,550
2011 k	1/10 oz	15	Dingo	2,500/ 231	335	335
2011 l	1/2 oz	50	Emu	1,000/ 21	1,550	1,550
2011 l	1/10 oz	15	Emu	2,500/ 225	335	335
2011 m	1/2 oz	50	Kookaburra	1,000/ 24	1,550	1,550
2011 m	1/10 oz	15	Kookaburra	2,500/ 249	335	335
2011 n	1/2 oz	50	Great White Shark	1,000/ 29	1,550	1,550
2011 n	1/10 oz	15	Great White Shark	2,500/ 275	335	335
2011 o	1/2 oz	50	Tasmanian Devil	1,000/ 22	1,550	1,550
2011 o	1/10 oz	15	Tasmanian Devil	2,500/ 249	335	335

PROOF FIVE COIN CASED SETS (1/2oz & 1/10oz)

Date	Description	Mintage	Issue Price	Current Retail
2009	1/2 ounce. Contains one of each (a to e)	n/a / n/a	6,250	6,250
2010	1/2 ounce. Contains one of each (f to j)	n/a / n/a	7,750	7,750
2011	1/2 ounce. Contains one of each (k to o)	n/a / n/a	7,750	7,750

PLATINUM PROOF : MULTIPLE DATES

DISCOVER AUSTRALIA. SERIES TWO : 2012 -

[a] Bell Frog [b] Goanna [c] Kangaroo [d] Kookaburra [e] Whale Shark

Date	Weight in oz's	Nominal F/Value	Description	Mintage Limit / Actual	Issue Price	Current Retail
2012 a	1/0 oz	15	Bell Frog	1,000/ 210	345	295
2012 b	1/0 oz	15	Goanna	7,500/ 187	345	295
2012 c	1/0 oz	15	Red Kangaroo	7,500/ 231	345	295
2012 d	1/0 oz	15	Kookaburra	7,500/ 227	345	295
2012 e	1/0 oz	15	Whale Shark	7,500/ 196	345	295

ONE OUNCE PROOF FIVE COIN CASED SET

2012	Cased set contains one of each (a to e)	Inc in above	1,725	n/a

SILVER ISSUES : MULTIPLE DATES

1988 HOLEY DOLLAR & DUMP

Date	Weight in oz's	Nominal F/Value	Description	Mintage Limit /Actual	Issue Price	Current Retail
1988	1/.25¢	1oz & 1/4oz	Proof	100,000	45	55
1988			Sydney Fair issue (Nov. 12-13,1988)	500	45	65
1988			Singapore Fair issue (Feb. 1989)	300	n/a	7

1989 HOLEY DOLLAR & DUMP

1989	1.00 / .25¢	1 oz; 1/4 oz	45,000	45	55
1989	Sydney Fair issue (Nov 19 - 20)		500	45	65

1990 HOLEY DOLLAR & DUMP

1990	1.00 / .25¢	1 oz; 1/4 oz	30,000	45	70

Three year set (1988-1990) in history book style album. Current retail price = 225

KOOKABURRA PROOF & SPECIMEN

SERIES ONE : 1990 TO 2005 : FINE SILVER. 99.9%

Common obverse

1990 (a) Proof Reverse

1990 (b) Specimen

Date	Face Value	Description	Type	Weight in oz's	Size	Mintage Max/ Actual	Issue Price	Average Retail
1990 : PROOF FINISH STANDARD REVERSE ISSUES								
1990	5	Standard reverse	Proof	1 oz	40.6	35,000/ 21,671	45	35
1990 : PROOF FINISH. COIN FAIR SPECIAL CERTIFICATE								
1990 a	5	Sydney NAA Fair	Proof	1 oz	40.6	1,000/ All sold	45	40
1990 b	5	Albany NAA Fair	Proof	1 oz	40.6	200/ All sold	45	40
1990 : SPECIMEN FINISH STANDARD REVERSE ISSUES								
1990	5	Standard reverse	Spec	1 oz	40.6	300,000/ All sold	15	20
1990 : SPECIMEN FINISH. COIN FAIR SPECIAL CERTIFICATE								
1990 c	5	Sydney NAA Fair	Spec	1 oz	40.6	1,000/ All sold	18	20

(a) A proof version of this coin (dated 1990) was issued at the Sydney International Coin Fair on March 23 - 24, 1991. Numbered certificate.
(b) Similar to above and issued at the Albany Coin Fair on March 30 - 31.
(c) Issued at the Sydney Coin Fair on November 16 - 17, 1991. Coin issued without a privy mark but with a specially printed certificate.

1991 (d) Proof 2oz-1kg

1991 (e) Proof

1991 (f) Specimen

Date	Face Value	Description	Type	Weight in oz's	Size	Mintage Max/ Actual	Issue Price	Average Retail
1991 : PROOF FINISH STANDARD REVERSE ISSUES								
1991	150	Standard reverse	Proof	1 kg	100	1,000/ All sold	475	650
1991	50	Standard reverse	Proof	10oz	75	2,500/ All sold	245	250
1991	10	Standard reverse	Proof	2oz	50	5,000/ All sold	82	65
1991	5	Standard reverse	Proof	1oz	40.6	35,000/ 6,673	45	65
1991 : PROOF FINISH. COIN FAIR SPECIAL CERTIFICATE								
1991 **d**	10	Hobart NAA Fair	Proof	2oz	50	500/ All sold	82	70
1991 **e**	5	Sydney NAA Fair	Proof	1 oz	40.6	1,500/ All sold	45	40
1991 : SPECIMEN FINISH. COIN FAIR SPECIAL CERTIFICATE								
1991	5	Standard reverse	Spec	1 oz	40.6	300k/ All sold	15	20
1991 : SPECIMEN FINISH. COIN FAIR SPECIAL CERTIFICATE								
1991 **f**	5	Sydney NAA Fair	Spec	1 oz	40.6	1,000/ All sold	18	20

(d) Issued at the Hobart Coin Fair on May 11 - 12, 1991. Certificate only.
(e) Issued at the Sydney Coin Fair on November 16 - 17, 1991.
(f) Uncirculated (specimen finish) coin issued on November 17-18, 1990.

KOOKABURRA PROOF & SPECIMEN

SERIES ONE : 1990 TO 2005 : FINE SILVER. 99.9%

1992 : Proof reverse

1992 : 1 Kilo - 2 oz Specimen

1992 : Specimen

Date	Face Value	Description	Type	Weight in oz's	Size	Mintage Max/ Actual	Issue Price	Average Retail
From this year onwards the nominal values were significantly decreased								
1992 : PROOF FINISH STANDARD REVERSE ISSUES								
1992	30	Standard reverse	Proof	1 kg	100	1,000/ All sold	475	1,150
1992	10	Standard reverse	Proof	10 oz	75	2,500/ All sold	245	250
1992	2	Standard reverse	Proof	2 oz	50	5,000/ All sold	82	65
1992	1	Standard reverse	Proof	1 oz	40.6	350,000/ 6,766	45	40
1992 : PROOF FINISH MISCELLANEOUS PRIVY MARKED COIN								
1992 a	2	NAA Logo	Proof	2 oz	50	500/ All sold	82	125
1992 b	2	Adelaide Pound	Proof	2 oz	50	500/ All sold	82	125
1992 c	1	USA Eagle privy	Proof	1 oz	40.6	Exclusive to set	—	—
1992 : SPECIMEN FINISH STANDARD REVERSE ISSUES								
1992	30	Standard reverse	Spec	1 kg	100	To order/ 47,348	260	550
1992	10	Standard reverse	Spec	10 oz	75	To order/ 29,576	80	250
1992	2	Standard reverse	Spec	2 oz	50	To order/ 84,782	19	45
1992	1	Standard reverse	Spec	1 oz	40.6	300k/ 219,694	15	20
1992 : SPECIMEN FINISH MISCELLANEOUS PRIVY MARKED COIN								
1992 d	2	Holey Dollar privy	Spec	2 oz	50	1,000/ All sold	45	95

THE FIRST PERTH MINT PRIVY MARKS

1992 (a) NAA Logo

1992 (b) Adelaide Pound

1992 (c) Eagle Privy

1992 (d) Holey Dollar

[a] NAA Logo (First Perth Mint privy mark) Issued at the NAA Melbourne Coin Fair on July 11 - 12, 1992. The coin carried a privy mark in the form of the 'NAA' Logo (Numismatic Association of Australia). This created a world first for Australian Numismatics in that it was the first time that the mark of a private organisation was used on a legal tender coin. It was also the first coin fair privy mark. The certificate range for the 500 coins was from 4501 to 5000.
[b] Adelaide Pound privy mark : Issued at the NAA Adelaide Coin Fair on September 5 - 6, 1992. Has a privy mark resembling the obverse of the gold Adelaide Pound struck in 1852. The certificate range for the 500 coins was from 4001 to 4500.
[c] USA Eagle privy mark : Issued for the US market. Coins sold individually in a black wallet as well as a set comprised of 1992 Proof 1 oz Kookaburra, Proof 1/4 oz Nugget and Proof 1/4 oz Koala. 567 sets were sold at $1184.65.
([d]Holey Dollar privy mark : Issued at the NAA Sydney Coin Fair on Nov 21 - 22, 1992.

KOOKABURRA PROOF & SPECIMEN

SERIES ONE : 1990 TO 2005 : FINE SILVER. 99.9%

1993: Proof reverse

1993: 1 Kg - 2 oz Specimen

1993: 1 oz Specimen

Date	Face Value	Description	Type	Weight in oz's	Size	Mintage Max/ Actual	Issue Price	Average Retail
1993 : PROOF FINISH STANDARD REVERSE ISSUES								
1993	30	Standard reverse	Proof	1 kg	100	1,000/ All sold	494	1,150
1993	10	Standard reverse	Proof	10 oz	75	2,500/ 1,495	251	380
1993	2	Standard reverse	Proof	2 oz	50	5,000/ 3,290	82	150
1993	1	Standard reverse	Proof	1 oz	40.6	35,000/ 5,121	46	50
1993 PROOF MULTIPLE COIN CASED SETS								
Four Coin Proof Set :		1 Kg 10oz	2oz	1oz		1,000/ All sold	874	1,200
Three Coin Proof Set :		10oz	2oz	1oz		300/ 280	380	550
Two Coin Proof Set :			2oz	1oz		600/ All sold	129	180
1993 : PROOF FINISH MISCELLANEOUS PRIVY MARKED COIN								
1993 **a**	30	Royal Wedding	Proof	1 kg	100	210/ 200	425	550
1993 **b**	2	Sydney Mint Sov	Proof	2 oz	50	750/ All sold	85	95
1993	2	Ingot. Perth Fair	Proof	2 oz	50	500/ All sold	83	95
1993 **c**	1	Opera House privy	Proof	1 oz	40.6	15,000/ 5,121	46	50

1993 (a) Royal Wedding

1993 (b) Sydney Mint

1993 (d) Opera House

(a) Japanese Royal Wedding : Struck to commemorate the Japanese Royal Wedding of the Crown Prince Naruhito and Masako Owada on June 9, 1993. Although the official issue was supposed to be 1000 coins, only 210 were actually struck. It was the first privy mark on a One Kilogram Kookaburra coin and the first to commemorate a foreign event.
(b) Sydney Mint Sovereign : Issued at the NAA Sydney Coin Fair on November 20 - 21, 1993. Privy mark of the Sydney Mint Sovereign which was struck in a converted wing of the "Rum Hospital" from 1855 to 1870.
Perth Mint Coin Fair Series : Issued at the National Stamp and Coin Show in Perth on July 3 - 4, 1993. No privy mark but with an individually numbered silver medallion which included the wording : *"Australian Kookaburra 1993 Proof Issue. Issued at NS&CS, Perth Fair, 3 & 4 July. Maximum Mintage 500".*
(c) Opera House privy mark : The first of the non - fair Australian issued privy marked coins available to the general public. Opera House privy mark celebrates the 20th anniversary of this historic landmark. Coin Certificate Number One was donated to the Sydney Opera House for its memorabilia collection.

KOOKABURRA PROOF & SPECIMEN

SERIES ONE : 1990 TO 2005 : FINE SILVER. 99.9%

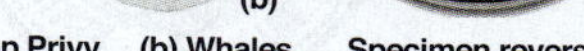

(a) Dump Privy (b) Whales Specimen reverse (c) Emu (d) Port Phillip

Date	Face Value	Description	Type	Weight in oz's	Size	Mintage Max/ Actual	Issue Price	Average Retail
1993 : USA EAGLE PRIVY SILVER PROOF CASED SETS								
Kookaburra trio :		One each	10oz	2oz	1oz	500/ All sold	n/a	n/a
1993 : USA EAGLE MIXED METAL PROOF PRIVY MARKED SETS								
Mixed trio :		Silver 1oz; Gold 1/4oz; Platinum 1/4oz				750/ All sold	n/a	n/a
1993 : SPECIMEN FINISH STANDARD REVERSE ISSUES								
1993	30	Standard reverse	Spec	1 kg	100	To order/ 13, 550	260	550
1993	10	Standard reverse	Spec	10 oz	75	To order/ 10,161	83	250
1993	2	Standard reverse	Spec	2 oz	50	To order/ 35,329	20	35
1993	1	Standard reverse	Spec	1 oz	40.6	300k/ 190,581	15	25
1993 : SPECIMEN FINISH MISCELLANEOUS PRIVY MARKED COINS								
1993 **a**	2	Dump privy	Spec	2 oz	50	1,000/ n/a	45	50
1993 **b**	2	Two Whales privy	Spec	2 oz	50	1,000/ n/a	45	50
1993 **c**	2	Emu privy	Spec	2 oz	50	1,000/ n/a	45	50
1993 **d**	2	Port Phillip privy	Spec	2 oz	50	1,000/ n/a	47	50
1993 **e**	1	Mint reopening	Spec	1 oz	40.6	200 presented	–	275

series. Included are a Kookaburra 1oz coin and a gold kangaroo/nugget and a platinum koala coin.

(a) Colonial Dump : Issued at the Sydney NAA Fair on March 20 - 21, 1993 to mark the 180th anniversary striking of the Colonial Dump of 1813.

(b) Whale privy mark : Issued at the Albany Fair on April 10 - 11, 1993. Privy mark of Whales in recognition of the area's historical role in this industry.

(c) Emu privy mark : Issued at the Brisbane NAA Fair on May 8 - 9, 1993. Emu privy mark similar to that used on a token issued by Stewart and Hemmant.

(d) Port Phillip privy mark : Issued at the NAA Melbourne Fair on July 17 - 18, 1993. Kangaroo drivy mark styled on the failed Kangaroo Office patterns of the 1800s.

(e) recommissioned Perth Mint coin & certificate : Issued in green presentation case with numbered certificate which states *"This is one of 200 One Ounce 1993 Australian Kookaburra silver bullion coins specially minted and presented to mark the official opening of the recommissioned Perth Mint and Perth Mint Exhibition on 8 December, 1993".* The coin was only presented to invited guests attending the reopening ceremony. Although not well known, it is the rarest of all the Kookaburra special interest issues to date.

There are two distinct obverse portraits related to the issues of George V which are commonly termed the "Large Head" and "Small Head" design. When the first coins were issued in 1911, the portrait of the King caused shadowing on the reverse of the coin. In 1929, the portrait was reduced slightly to improve the symmetry and prevent "ghosting" of the reverse design. The Smaller Head Type has two rows of beading around the rim. This amended portrait was used up until 1931 when the issuing of sovereigns in Australia was abandoned forever.

See details of Large Head & Small Head privy marks on next page.

LARGE HEAD

SMALL HEAD

KOOKABURRA PROOF & SPECIMEN

SERIES ONE : 1990 TO 2005 : FINE SILVER. 99.9%

1994 : Proof reverse

1994 : Specimen reverse

Date	Face Value	Description	Type	Weight in oz's	Size	Mintage Max/ Actual	Issue Price	Average Retail
1994 : PROOF FINISH STANDARD REVERSE ISSUES								
1994	30	Standard reverse	Proof	1 kg	100	Exclusive to sets	—	—
1994	10	Standard reverse	Spec	10 oz	75	Exclusive to sets	—	—
1994	2	Standard reverse	Proof	2 oz	50	500/ All sold	86	60
1994	1	Standard reverse	Proof	1 oz	40.6	2,500/ All sold	50	45
1994 PROOF MULTIPLE COIN CASED SET								
Four Coin Proof Set :		1 Kg	10oz	2oz	1oz	1,000/ All sold	935	1,200
Three Coin Proof Set :			10oz	2oz	1oz	250/ All sold	398	550
Two Coin Proof Set :				2oz	1oz	500/ All sold	135.5	180
1994 : PROOF & SPECIMEN PRIVY MARKED THEME - GOLD SOVEREIGNS								
1994 **a**	2	Veiled Head Sov.	Spec	2 oz	50	1,000/ All sold	55	95
1994 **b**	2	Edward VII Sov.	Proof	2 oz	50	1,500/ All sold	95	95
1994 **c**	2	Large Hd. G V Sov.	Spec	2 oz	50	1,500/ All sold	60	95
1994 **d**	2	Small Hd. G V Sov.	Proof	2 oz	50	1,500/ All sold	95	95
1994 : SPECIMEN FINISH STANDARD REVERSE ISSUES								
1994	30	Standard reverse	Spec	1 kg	100	To order/ 32,781	345	1,150
1994	10	Standard reverse	Spec	10 oz	75	All sold/ 11,231	112.5	380
1994	2	Standard reverse	Spec	2 oz	50	To order/ 39,603	30	95
1994	1	Standard reverse	Spec	1 oz	40.6	To order/ 174,561	22	30
1994 : SPECIMEN FINISH PRIVY MARKED MISCELLANEOUS ISSUES								
1994 **e**	1	C/wealth Games	Spec	1 oz	40.6	500/ All sold	29	35
1994 SPECIMEN FOUR COIN CASED SET								
Four Coin Specimen Set :		1 Kilo; 10 oz; 2 oz; 1 oz.				1,000/ All sold	495	1,700

(a) Veiled Head Sovereign mint mark : Issued at the Sydney NAA Fair on March 26 - 27, 1994. Queen Victoria *'Veiled Head Bust'* privy mark. This was the first of four special privy marks issued during 1994 to commemorate each of the four gold sovereign portraits struck by the Perth Mint from 1899 to 1931. The privy marks were gold layered over the top of the fine silver host coins.

(b) Edward VII Sovereign privy mark : Issued at the Melbourne NAA Fair on July 16 - 17, 1994. Privy mark of the obverse bust of King Edward VII who featured on Perth minted sovereigns from 1902 to 1910. Privy mark appears as a gold inlay.

(c) George V (Large Head Sovereign) : Issued at the Perth NAA Fair on August 20 - 21, 1994. Coin features the George V *'Large Head'* portrait privy mark which appeared on Perth minted sovereigns from 1911 to 1928.

(d) George V (Small Head Sovereign) : Issued at the Sydney NAA Fair on November 19 - 20, 1994. Issue depicts the George V *'Small Head'* portrait privy mark which appeared on Perth minted sovereigns from 1929 to 1931.

(e) Commonwealth Games : *'Team Australia'* privy mark on a One Ounce Specimen Kookaburra to mark Australia's participation in the XVth (15th) Commonwealth Games held in Victoria, British Columbia, Canada in August 1994. The Perth Mint (GoldCorp) donated $5 from the sale of each coin. The sellout raised $75,000 towards defraying the $7m cost of sending the Australian team to the Games.

KOOKABURRA PROOF & SPECIMEN

SERIES ONE : 1990 TO 2005 : FINE SILVER. 99.9%

Above. The four commemorative privy marks. Two were proof and two were specimen issues.

1995 : PROOF FINISH STANDARD REVERSE ISSUES

1995	30	Standard reverse	Proof	1 kg	100	In sets only	—	—
1995	10	Standard reverse	Spec	10 oz	75	In sets only	—	—
1995	2	Standard reverse	Proof	2 oz	50	600/ All sold	86	65
1995	1	Standard reverse	Proof	1 oz	40.6	3,000/ All sold	47.5	50

1995 PROOF MULTIPLE COIN CASED SET

Four Coin Proof Set :	1 Kg	10oz	2oz	1oz	1,000/ All sold	935	1,200
Three Coin Proof Set :		10oz	2oz	1oz	300/ 280	398	425
Two Coin Proof Set :			2oz	1oz	600/ All sold	133.5	180

1995 : PROOF FINISH MISCELLANEOUS PRIVY MARKED COIN

1995 a	30	Liberty Head privy	Proof	1 kg	100	500/ All sold	530	950
1995 b	10	Golden Eagle privy	Proof	10 oz	75	In sets only	—	—
1995 b	2	Golden Eagle privy	Proof	2 oz	50	In sets only	—	—
1995 c	2	WW2 Peace privy	Proof	2 oz	50	1,000/ All sold	86	75

1995 : PROOF TWO COIN CASE SET (EAGLE PRIVY MARK)

Proof 10 oz; 2 oz with natural gold nugget.	800/ 800	430	595

1995 : PROOF & SPECIMEN PRIVY MARKED THEME - PREDECIMAL COINS

1995 d	2	Canb. Florin privy	Proof	2 oz	50	1,500/ All sold	90	95
1995 e	2	Melb. Cent privy	Proof	2 oz	50	1,500/ All sold	90	95
1995 f	2	Federation Florin	Spec	2 oz	50	1,500/ All sold	55	65
1995 g	2	Royal Visit privy	Spec	2 oz	50	1,000/ All sold	55	65

(a) Liberty Head privy mark : Struck primarily for the USA market, only 100 of the 500 coins struck were held back for the Australian market. The privy mark features the obverse of the famed "Morgan" silver one dollar coin issued in the USA between 1878 and 1921.

(b) Golden Eagle privy mark : Actually issued in 1996, this two coin set featured a fine gold privy mark on each of the 10 oz and 2 oz proof coins. The set also contained a natural gold nugget. Only 150 of the 800 sets were allocated for Australia.

(c) WW2 Peace dual issue : Gold inlaid privy mark issued to mark the 50th Anniversary of the end of WWII. 1000 individual 2 oz coins as well as 300 sets were released. The sets also contained a 1/2 oz proof Koala and a 1 oz proof Nugget.

(d) Canberra Florin privy mark : Issued at the Sydney NAA Fair on April 1 - 2, 1995. Privy mark of commemorative florin to mark the opening of Parliament House, Canberra, 1927. This is the first of four special privy marks modelled on the designs of special commemorative pre-decimal silver florins issued between 1927 and 1954.

(e) Melbourne Centenary Florin privy mark : Issued at the Melbourne NAA Fair on July 15 - 16, 1995. Privy mark of the 1934 - 35 florin of George V issued to commemorate the centenary of the founding of Victoria in 1834 and the settling of Melbourne in 1835. This is the only one of the four original commemorative coins sold at a premium. 75,000 of the original coins were struck to be sold at three shillings each with the profits being used to off-set the cost of the celebrations. 21,000 unsold coins were returned to the Melbourne Mint for remelting.

(f) Federation Florin privy mark : Issued at the Hobart NAA Fair on May 13 - 14, 1995. Privy mark of the 1951 florin struck to commemorate the 50th anniversary of the establishment of the Australian Federation.

(g) Royal Visit Florin privy mark : Released at the Sydney NAA Fair on November 25 - 26, 1995. The privy mark featured the reverse of the 1954 florin struck to mark the first visit of Elizabeth II as Monarch.

KOOKABURRA PROOF & SPECIMEN

SERIES ONE : 1990 TO 2005 : FINE SILVER. 99.9%

Date	Face Value	Description	Type	Weight in oz's	Size	Mintage Max/ Actual	Issue Price	Average Retail
1995 : SPECIMEN FINISH STANDARD REVERSE ISSUES								
1995	30	Standard reverse	Spec	1 kg	100	To order/ 11,721	530	750
1995	10	Standard reverse	Spec	10 oz	75	To order/ 9,894	—	250
1995	2	Standard reverse	Spec	2 oz	50	To order/ 45,308	55	65
1995	1	Standard reverse	Spec	1 oz	40.6	300,000/ 154,247	15	30
1995	1	Gilt/ ANDA Fair	Spec	1 oz	40.6	3,000/ All sold	n/a	n/a
1995 : SPECIMEN FINISH PRIVY MARKED MISCELLANEOUS ISSUES								
1995 a	2	World Vision privy	Spec	2 oz	50	15,000/ n/a	50	65
1995 b	2	Ingot. Perth Mint	Spec	2 oz	50	500/ All sold	55	6
1995 c	1	Gilt Panda privy	Spec	1 oz	40.6	10,000/ All sold	35	25
1995 SPECIMEN FOUR COIN CASED SET								
Four Coin Specimen Set :		1 Kilo; 10 oz; 2 oz; 1 oz.				1000/ 1000	495	1,700

(a) World Vision/ 40 Hour Famine privy mark : 1995 marked the 20th anniversary of the World Vision 40 - Hour Famine Program. Profits from the sale of the 15,000 issue were donated to the international organisation. It has been claimed that the issue was not popular and that many coins were remelted after not selling. Unconfirmed speculation indicates that the issue could be as low as 2000 coins.
(b) NCSS issue with silver ingot : Issued at the National Coin and Stamp Show (NCSS) in Perth on July 1 - 2, 1995. No privy mark but the coin came cased with a silver ingot which was individually numbered.
(c) Beijing Coin Fair (Two coin set) : Issued at the inaugural Chinese Coin Fair held in Beijing during September 1995. It was a joint effort with the Chinese Central Bank with a one ounce Panda silver coin also being issued along with the Australian Kookaburra silver coin. Both coins featured the Panda privy mark which was the gold inlaid variety. Of the 10,000 issued only 500 were allocated to the Australian market.

YEAR	PROOF DESIGN	SPECIMEN DESIGN
1990	Kookaburra with beak down	Sitting on a stump
1991	Beak up	Beak down
1992	Feeding babies	Beak up
1993	Two on branch	Feeding babies
1994	Looking to left	Two on branch
1995	In flight	Looking to left
1996	With babies	In flight
1997	Sitting on a fence	With babies
1998	Big and small kookaburra	Sitting on a fence
1999	With clump of leaves	Big and small kookaburra
2000	Two birds on a branch	With clump of leaves
2001	With Australian map	Two birds on a branch
2002	Leaning to the right	With Australian map
2003	One in flight, other one at rest	Leaning to the right
2004	Resting on diagonal branch	One in flight, other one at rest
2005	Two birds, one with raised head	Resting on diagonal branch
2006	Branch half-submerged in water	Two birds, one with raised

KOOKABURRA PROOF & SPECIMEN

SERIES ONE : 1990 TO 2005 : FINE SILVER. 99.9%

Date	Face Value	Description	Type	Weight in oz's	Size	Mintage Max/ Actual	Issue Price	Average Retail
1996 : PROOF FINISH STANDARD REVERSE ISSUES								
1996	30	Standard reverse	Proof	1 kg	100	In sets only	—	—
1996	10	Standard reverse	Spec	10 oz	75	In sets only	—	—
1996	2	Standard reverse	Proof	2 oz	50	650/ All sold	86	65
1996	1	Standard reverse	Proof	1 oz	40.6	3,500/ All sold	47.5	50
1996 PROOF MULTIPLE COIN CASED SET								
Four Coin Proof Set :	1 Kg	10oz	2oz	1oz		1,000/ All sold	935	1,200
Three Coin Proof Set :		10oz	2oz	1oz		300/ All sold	398	425
Two Coin Proof Set :			2oz	1oz		650/ All sold	133.5	180
1996 : PROOF FINISH MISCELLANEOUS PRIVY MARKED COINS								
1996 a	10	Golden Eagle privy	Proof	10 oz	75	In sets only	—	—

1996 (b) Guinea

1996 (c) Johanna

1996 (d) Ducat

1996 (e) Pagoda

Date	Face Value	Description	Type	Weight in oz's	Size	Mintage Max/ Actual	Issue Price	Average Retail
1996 : PROCLAMATION COINS : PROOF & SPECIMEN PRIVY MARKED THEME								
1996 b	2	Spade Guinea privy	Proof	2 oz	50	1,500/ All sold	95	90
1996 c	2	Johanna privy	Proof	2 oz	50	1,500/ All sold	95	90
1996 d	2	Dutch Ducat privy	Spec	2 oz	50	1,500/ n/a	60	95
1996 e	2	Star Pagoda privy	Spec	2 oz	50	1,500/ n/a	60	95

(a) Golden Eagle privy mark : A two-coin set consisting of a 10 oz and 2 oz silver proof issue restricted to 800 sets with a *"Golden Eagle"* privy mark.

(b) Spade Guinea privy mark : Issued at the NAA Sydney Coin Fair on March 23 - 24, 1996. The gold inlaid privy mark represents a British gold coin issued around the time of the First Settlement in 1788. Called a *"Spade"* Guinea because of the shape of the shield on the reverse. With a face value of 21 Shillings it was named a *"Guinea"* after the area where the gold was mined in Africa. In his proclamation of 1800, Governor King gave the coin an increased value of 22 Shillings.

(c) The Johanna privy mark : Issued at the NAA Melbourne Coin Fair on July 6 - 7, 1996. The Portuguese Johanna is one of the most spectacular of all the coins covered by King's Proclamation of 1800. It is also interesting that King should include the coin when you consider that it was last struck in 1732. Governor King gave it a value of £4, making it the highest value of all the Proclamation coins.

(d) The Gold Ducat privy mark : Released at the NAA Adelaide Coin Fair on May 4 - 5, 1996. Struck in vast numbers the ducat was accepted internationally as a trade coin. In his Proclamation of 1800, Governor King gave the coin a value of 9/6.

(e) Star Pagoda : Issued at the NAA Sydney Coin Fair on November 16 - 17, 1996. A small lumpy gold coin which takes its name from the *"Star"* shaped design on one side of the coin. Governor King gave it a value of Eight Shillings.

KOOKABURRA PROOF & SPECIMEN

SERIES ONE : 1990 TO 2005 : FINE SILVER. 99.9%

1996 : SPECIMEN FINISH STANDARD REVERSE ISSUES

1996	30	Standard reverse	Spec	1 kg	100	To order/ 8,961	303	550
1996	10	Standard reverse	Spec	10 oz	75	To order/ 7,557	96	250
1996	2	Standard reverse	Spec	2 oz	50	To order/ 78,424	22.5	30
1996	1	Standard reverse	Spec	1 oz	40.6	To orde/ 170,105	15	30

1996 : SPECIMEN FINISH MISCELLANEOUS PRIVY MARKED COINS

1996 a	2	The Hague privy	Spec	2 oz	50	1,500/ n/a	60	95
1996 b	1	Tricentennial privy	Spec	1 oz	40.6	5,000/ n/a	36	60
1996 c	1	Basler Stab privy	Spec	1 oz	40.6	2,500/ n/a	43	75
1996 d	1	Goya privy	Spec	1 oz	40.6	2,500/ n/a	43	75
1996 e	1	Chinese Panda	Spec	1 oz	40.6	15,000/ n/a	43	75
1996 f	1	Foundation stone	Spec	1 oz	40.6	1,500/ n/a	39	65

1996 : EUROPEAN COUNTRIES SPECIMEN FINISH PRIVY MARKED COINS

1996 g	1	Germany privy	Spec	1 oz	40.6	5,000/ n/a	36	65
1996 h	1	France privy	Spec	1 oz	40.6	5,000/ n/a	36	65
1996 h	1	Great Britain privy	Spec	1 oz	40.6	5,000/ n/a	36	65
1996 h	1	Greece privy	Spec	1 oz	40.6	5,000/ n/a	36	65
1996 h	1	Belgium privy	Spec	1 oz	40.6	5,000/ n/a	36	65

1996 SPECIMEN FOUR COIN CASED SET

Four Coin Specimen Set : 1 Kilo; 10 oz; 2 oz; 1 oz.	1000/ 1000	490	1,650

1996 : SPECIMEN PERTH COIN FAIR COIN & MEDALLION SET

(i) NCSS Fair:	2 oz	1946 Perth Mint Shilling	500/ All sold	59	60

(a) The Hague privy mark : Struck to commemorate The Hague Coin Fair in Amsterdam in February 1996. The privy mark features the coat of arms of The Hague. Of the 1500 issued, 300 were reserved for Australian collectors.

(b) Tricentennial privy : Issued to mark the 300th anniversary of the European naming of the Swan River and Rottnest Island by Dutch explorer Willem de Vlamingh in 1696.

(c) The "Basler Stab" : is the emblem of Basel, Switzerland. This privy marked coin commemorated the Basel Coin Convention in January, 1996.

(d) Goya privy mark : The first of a series commemorating famous artists. This fine gold insert features the acclaimed *"La Maja Nude"* by Spanish painter, Goya.

(e) Panda privy mark : issued at the Beijing Coin Show from November 6 - 10.

(f) The Perth Mint foundation stone : was laid on September 23, 1896. To commemorate the centenary, the above specimen one ounce coin was issued along with a Nugget half ounce coin. Both were edge numbered with the date "23 - 9 - 96" along with an individually numbered certificate.

(g) The Brandenburg Gate privy mark : was the first of 15 such coins being struck over the next three years to mark the European Union.

(h) European Countries Theme (Part) : Further privy marks issued as part of the above series.

(i) NCSS Perth Fairs : The first of a four - year program to commemorate each of the Perth National Coin and Stamp Shows (NCSS) from 1997 to the year 2000. Each cased set contains a specimen 2 oz coin and a silver medallion which will feature privy marks of various pre-decimal coins struck at the Perth Mint. The first of the series was released on August 16 - 17, 1997. The medallion featured a 1943 penny and halfpenny privy mark in a copper coloured finish. The coins feature the Perth mint mark attributed to pence issued at that time. This is a dot after the letter "Y." of the word penny. The reverse of the medallion featured the Perth Mint's "Swan" logo.

KOOKABURRA PROOF & SPECIMEN

SERIES ONE : 1990 TO 2005 : FINE SILVER. 99.9%

Date	Face Value	Description	Type	Weight in oz's	Size	Mintage Max/ Actual	Issue Price	Average Retail
1997 : PROOF FINISH STANDARD REVERSE ISSUES								
1997	30	Standard reverse	Proof	1 kg	101	Exclusive to set	—	—
1997	10	Standard reverse	Proof	10 oz	75.5	Exclusive to set	—	—
1997	2	Standard reverse	Proof	2 oz	50.3	650/ All sold	84	75
1997	1	Standard reverse	Proof	1 oz	40.6	3,500/ 2,466	47	50
1997 : PROOF MULTIPLE COIN CASED SETS								
Four Coin Proof Set :	1 kg	10oz	2oz	1oz		1000 / 450	895	1125
Three Coin Proof Set :		10oz	2oz	1oz		300/ All sold	386	425
Two Coin Proof Set :			2oz	1oz		650/ All sold	131	170
PROOF & SPECIMEN PRIVY MARKED THEME - PREDECIMAL COINS								
1997 a	2	1937 Penny privy	Proof	2 oz	50.3	2,000/ n/a	90	80
1997 b	2	1937 Florin privy	Proof	2 oz	50.3	2,000/ n/a	90	80
1997 c	2	Threepence privy	Spec	2 oz	50.3	2,000/ n/a	55	60
1997 d	2	1937 Shilling privy	Spec	2 oz	50.3	2,000/ n/a	55	60
1997 e	2	1937 Crown privy	Spec	2 oz	50.3	4,000/ n/a	50	60
1997 : SPECIMEN FINISH STANDARD REVERSE ISSUES								
1997	30	Standard reverse	Spec	1 kg	101	To order/ 7,967	310	1,150
1997	10	Standard reverse	Spec	10 oz	75.5	To order/ 7,880	112	250
1997	2	Standard reverse	Spec	2 oz	50.3	To order/ 32,896	30	60
1997	1	Standard reverse	Spec	1 oz	40.6	300k/ 159,497	22	20
1997 : SPECIMEN FINISH PRIVY MARKED MISCELLANEOUS ISSUES								
1997 f	1	Finland privy	Spec	1 oz	40.6	5,000/ All sold	36	30
1997 f	1	Portugal privy	Spec	1 oz	40.6	5,000/ All sold	36	30
1997 f	1	Italy privy	Spec	1 oz	40.6	5,000/ All sold	36	30
1997 f	1	Netherlands privy	Spec	1 oz	40.6	5,000/ All sold	36	30
1997 f	1	Denmark privy	Spec	1 oz	40.6	5,000/ All sold	36	30

(a) 1937 Pattern Penny privy mark: Issued at the ANDA Fair in Sydney on March 21 - 23, 1997.

(b) 1937 Pattern Florin privy mark: Issued at the ANDA Coin, Note & Stamp Fair, Newcastle on August 23, 24, 2007.

(c) 1937 Pattern Threepence privy mark: Issued at the ANDA Coin, Note & Stamp Fair, Melbourne on July 18-20, 1997.

(d) 1937 Pattern Shilling privy mark : Issued at the ANDA Fair in Sydney on October 31 - November 2, 1997.

(e) 1937 Crown privy mark : Depicts the reverse design of the pre-decimal 1937 crown to commemorate the 60th anniversary of its issue - the only coin issued for circulation that year.The coin was distributed in a pink leatherette, hinged-lid presentation case. This coin was also included in an unofficial limited release of 500 60th Anniversary Collections, accompanied by a superior quality 1937 Crown. Issued by Australian Coin Dealer - Downies - the pair are housed in a green leatherette hinged-lid presentation case with a numbered certificate.

(f) European privy marks. Series two of privy marks to celecrate European land marks

KOOKABURRA PROOF & SPECIMEN

SERIES ONE : 1990 TO 2005 : FINE SILVER. 99.9%

Date	Face Value	Description	Type	Weight in oz's	Size	Mintage Max/ Actual	Issue Price	Average Retail
1997 : SPECIMEN FINISH PRIVY MARKED MISCELLANEOUS ISSUES								
1997 g	30	Walking Liberty	Spec	1 kg	100	1,000/ n/a	455	750
1997 h	1	Gilt Panda privy	Spec	1 oz	40.6	15,000/ All sold	43	50
1997 i	1	Zurich coat of arms	Spec	1 oz	40.6	2,500/ All sold	36	30
1997 j	1	Gaudi privy	Spec	1 oz	40.6	2,500/ All sold	43	50
1997 k	1	Japan. Gold Yen	Spec	1 oz	40.6	2,500/ All sold	43	50
1997 l	1	Chinese Dragon	Spec	1 oz	40.6	20,000/ n/a	43	30
1997 m	1	Chinese Phoenix	Spec	1 oz	40.6	20,000/ n/a	43	30
1997 n	1	Thomas Edison	Spec	1 oz	40.6	2,500/ All sold	43	30
1997 o	1	Oldsmobile privy	Spec	1 oz	40.6	2,500/ All sold	39	30
1997 p	1	Coin & Swan medal	Spec	1 oz	40.6	500/ n/a	36	30
(q) 1997 : SPECIMEN PERTH COIN FAIR COIN & MEDALLION SET								
NCSS Fair :		2 oz coin & 1943 Perth Penny & Halfpenny privy				500	86	90

(g) Walking Liberty privy mark : Struck for the USA market to mark the 50th anniversary since the last of the "Walking Liberty" fifty cent pieces were struck.
(h) Gilt Panda privy mark : Issued at the Shangai Coin Fair on November 19 - 23, 1997.
(i) Zurich privy mark : Issued at the Zurich Coin Fair on October 26, 1996. Privy struck on a 1997 dated coin.
(j) Gaudi privy mark : The second in the famous artist series and features a gold privy mark of Antoni Gaudi's "Sagrada Familia", a well - known landmark of Barcelona. He has been described as one of the most ingenious architects in modern history.
(k) Japanese Gold Yen privy mark : The Yen has become the recognised currency of Japan and although the design has been updated over the years, it is essentially the same. For this reason, the original 20 Yen coin is referred to as an 'Old Type' and it holds a significant place in Japanese numismatic history.
(l) Chinese Dragon privy mark : East and west have a different take on the personality of the dragon. Chinese culture sees the dragon as a benign animal that symbolises strength, adventure, prosperity and good luck.
(m) Phoneix privy mark : The phoenix is believed to control the 5 tones of Chinese music and to represent the Confucian virtues of loyalty, honesty, decorum and justice.
(n) Thomas Edison privy mark : To mark the 150th anniversary of the birth of Edison.
(o) Centenary of the Oldsmobile privy mark : Over a century ago Ranasom E. Olds built his first car, a three wheeled carriage with a one horsepower Olds steam engine. In his first year the Olds Gasoline Engine Works produced just four cars. In 1897 he incorporated the worlds first automobile company which was established in Michigan. This privy mark features the company's famous Curved Dash Oldsmobile.
(p) Black Swan Penny Stamp privy mark : Issued at the Fremantle Stamp and Coin Fair from October 23 - 26. The set consisted of a standard 1997 one ounce specimen Kookaburra & Chick $1 silver coin accompanied by a 1 ounce pure silver medallion, featuring the famous Western Australian 1854 Black Swan Penny Stamp. The pair are housed in a black leatherette, hinged-lid presentation case.
(q) NCSS Perth privy mark series : The first of a four year program to commemorate each of the NCSS Perth coin fairs from 1997 to the year 2000. Each set contains a specimen 2 oz coin and a silver medallion which features different pre-decimal coins on the reverse with the Perth Mint seal on the obverse. This year, the medallion set issued on August 16 -17, 1997 featured the 1943 penny and halfpenny which were originally struck at the Mint.

KOOKABURRA PROOF & SPECIMEN

SERIES ONE : 1990 TO 2005 : FINE SILVER. 99.9%

1998 : Proof Reverse 1998 : Specimen Reverse

1998 : PROOF FINISH STANDARD REVERSE ISSUES

1998 a	30	Standard reverse	Proof	1 kg	100	250/ 152	595	1,150
1998	10	Standard reverse	Proof	10 oz	75	Only in sets	—	—
1998	2	Standard reverse	Proof	2 oz	50	650/ 600	90	75
1998	1	Standard reverse	Proof	1 oz	40.6	2,500/ 2,114	49.5	55
1998 b	1	Coin & phonecard	Proof	1 oz	40.6	500/ 425	70	65

1998 : PROOF MULTIPLE COIN CASED SET

Four Coin Proof Set :	1 Kg	10oz	2oz	1oz	250/ All sold	1,015	1,250
Three Coin Proof Set :		10oz	2oz	1oz	300 / 272	420	525
Two Coin Proof Set :			2oz	1oz	650 / 633	139	180

1998 : PREDECIMAL COINS - PROOF & SPECIMEN PRIVY MARKED THEME

1998 c	2	Jubilee Sov. privy	Proof	2 oz	50	1,500/ n/a	98	75
1998 d	2	Syd Mint Sov. privy	Proof	2 oz	50	1,500/ n/a	98	75
1998 e	2	Shield rev privy	Spec	2 oz	50	1,500/ n/a	63	75
1998 f	2	St George rev privy	Spec	2 oz	50	1,500/ n/a	63	75

1998 : SPECIMEN FINISH STANDARD REVERSE ISSUES

1998	30	Standard reverse	Spec	1 kg	100	To order/ 4,688	305	600
1998	10	Standard reverse	Spec	10 oz	75	To order/ 5,424	105	350
1998	2	Standard reverse	Spec	2 oz	50	To order/ 21,184	30	50
1998	1	Standard reverse	Spec	1 oz	40.6	300,000/ 103,119	22	30

1998 : EUROPEAN COUNTRIES - SPECIMEN PRIVY MARKED THEME

1998 g	1	Ireland privy	Spec	1 oz	40.6	5,000/ n/a	39	50
1998 g	1	Luxembourg	Spec	1 oz	40.6	5,000/ n/a	39	50
1998 g	1	Spain privy	Spec	1 oz	40.6	5,000/ n/a	39	50
1998 g	1	Austria privy	Spec	1 oz	40.6	5,000/ n/a	39	50
1998 g	1	Sweden privy	Spec	1 oz	40.6	5,000/ n/a	39	50

1998 : SPECIMEN FOUR COIN CASED SET

Four Coin Proof Set :	1 Kg	10oz	2oz	1oz	250/ All sold	490	1,250

(h) 1998 : SPECIMEN PERTH COIN FAIR COIN & MEDALLION SET

NCSS Fair:	2 oz coin & 1946 Perth Shilling privy medallion	750	119	120

(a) Re-introduction of the One Kilo Coin : This was the first year since 1993 that the fine silver proof kilo coin was available as an individual coin.
(b) Coin & Phonecard set : Comprising of a 1oz Proof Kookaburra and the first ever Australian Kookaburra phonecard to be released by The Perth Mint.
(c) Jubilee Head sovereign privy mark : This gold coin was struck in Australia between 1887 to 1893. Issued at the ANDA Fair in Melbourne on March 20 - 22, 1998.
(d) Sydney Mint sovereign privy mark : Struck between 1855 and 1870. Issued at the ANDA Fair in Sydney on October 30 to November 1, 1998.
(e) Queen Victoria Shield reverse Sovereign Privy mark : Issued between 1871 and 1887. Privy mark issued at the ANDA Fair in Brisbane on June 12 -14, 1998.
(f) St George Reverse privy mark : Privy marked coin issued at the ANDA Fair in Adelaide from August 14 -16, 1998.
(g) European Series : Further privy marks issued as part of the European series.
(h) Perth Shilling NCSS issue : The second of a series to mark the NCSS Perth Fairs from 1997 to the year 2000. The medallion featured overlapping reverse and obverse designs of the 1946 shilling. This was the only pre-decimal silver coin struck at the Perth Mint.

KOOKABURRA PROOF & SPECIMEN

SERIES ONE : 1990 TO 2005 : FINE SILVER. 99.9%

1999 : Proof Reverse 1999 : Specimen Reverse 1999 : Perth Fair Pair

Date	Face Value	Description	Type	Weight in oz's	Size	Mintage Max/ Actual	Issue Price	Average Retail
1998 : PROOF FINISH STANDARD REVERSE ISSUES								
1999	30	Standard reverse	Proof	1 kg	100	250/ 72	595	1,150
1999	10	Standard reverse	Proof	10 oz	75	Exclusive to set	—	—
1999	2	Standard reverse	Proof	2 oz	50	650/ 459	90	75
1999	1	Standard reverse	Proof	1 oz	40.6	2,500/ 1,646	49.5	55
1999 : PROOF MULTIPLE COIN CASED SETS								
Four Coin Proof Set :		1 Kg	10oz	2oz	1oz	250/ 206	1,015	1,250
Three Coin Proof Set :			10oz	2oz	1oz	300/ 192	420	525
Two Coin Proof Set :				2oz	1oz	650/ 581	139	180
PREDECIMAL COINS : PROOF & SPECIMEN PRIVY MARKED THEME								
1999 a	2	1930 Penny privy	Proof	2 oz	50	1,500/ n/a	99	75
1999 b	2	1932 Florin privy	Proof	2 oz	50	1,500/ n/a	99	75
1999 c	2	1923 Halfpenny	Spec	2 oz	50	1,500/ n/a	63	40
1999 d	2	1933 Shilling	Spec	2 oz	50	1,500/ n/a	63	40
1999 TWIN SET : KOOKABURRA PROOF & SPECIMEN								
(e) Two coin cased set		Proof & Specimen 10oz pair				500/ 310	475	350

(a) 1930 Penny : This coin is Australia's most famous rare coin although not the most expensive. Even non - collectors know of the rarity of this glamour coin while ignorant of much rarer items such as the Adelaide Pound; the Holey Dollar; a number of rare gold sovereigns and half sovereigns as well as most pre-decimal proof and pattern coins. This is mainly due to the saturation coverage in the press Australia's pre-decimal coins received in the lead-up to the change-over to decimal currency in 1966. It was the only really rare coin the general public could still find in change. Only 1500 to 3000 are thought to exist.

(b) 1932 Florin : This coin owes its rarity as a result of the worst depression of modern times. In 1932, the industrial world was in the grip of the Great Depression. As a result, there was little call for new coinage to be released into the economy. Only 188,000 florins were struck in 1932. This is quite an insignificant amount when you compare it to the 3,129,000 struck in 1931 and the 5,054,000 issued in 1936.

(c) 1923 Halfpenny : This coin has many people scratching their heads. An indicated mintage figure of 1,113,000 hardly puts this date in the rarity basket. In actual fact the real number of halfpennies dated 1923 to come out of the Melbourne Mint was in the order of just 15,000. Research has shown that the 1923 dated dies started to fracture early into the minting process. To save time and money in preparing new dies, the bulk of the one million plus halfpennies struck in 1923 were actually dated 1922 when left over dies were pressed into service. Careful examination of the reverse of some 1923 halfpennies will clearly show die cracks as a result of the faulty dies.

(d) 1933 Shilling : Although this date has the lowest mintage in the series, advanced collectors will tell you it isn't the hardest coin to get in mint condition. While mint reports state that only 220,000 shillings were struck in 1933 they tend to be easier to obtain in mint condition (in relative terms) than the 1915 H issue which has a mintage figure of 500,000.

(e) Proof & Specimen cased pair : This set, limited to 500 sets, comprised a 1999 10 oz proof Kookaburra silver coin and a 1999 10 oz specimen Kookaburra. These coins feature a different reverse design and carry the "P100" mintmark.

KOOKABURRA PROOF & SPECIMEN

SERIES ONE : 1990 TO 2005 : FINE SILVER. 99.9%

Date	Face Value	Description	Type	Weight in oz's	Size	Mintage Max/ Actual	Issue Price	Average Retail
1999 : SPECIMEN FINISH STANDARD REVERSE ISSUES								
1999	30	Standard reverse	Spec	1 kg	100	To order/ 4,714	384	975
1999	10	Standard reverse	Spec	10oz	75	To order/ 4,012	129	225
1999	2	Standard reverse	Spec	2 oz	50	To order/ 20,602	36	40
1999	1	Standard reverse	Spec	1 oz	40.6	To order/ 109,364	26	30
1999 : FOUR COIN SPECIMEN FINISH STANDARD REVERSE SET								
1999 Specmen		1 Kilo; 10 oz; 2 oz; 1 oz.				1,000	490	1,680
AUSTRALIAN LANDMARKS : SPECIMEN FINISH PRIVY MARKED THEME								
1999 a	1	Perth Landmark	Spec	1oz	40.6	1,500/ n/a	42.95	45
1999 a	1	Gold Coast privy	Spec	1oz	40.6	1,500/ n/a	42.95	45
1999 a	1	Adelaide privy	Spec	1oz	40.6	1,500/ n/a	42.95	45
1999 a	1	MacDonnell Ranges	Spec	1oz	40.6	1,500/ n/a	42.95	45
1999 a	1	Sydney privy	Spec	1oz	40.6	1,500/ n/a	42.95	45
1999 : SPECIMEN FINISH PRIVY MARKED MISCELLANEOUS ISSUES								
1999 b	1	Centenary Sov	Spec	1oz	40.6	5,000/ n/a	45	40
1999 c	1	Tempo Koban	Spec	1oz	40.6	2,500/ n/a	47.95	45
1999 d	1	Nickel pattern Penny	Spec	1oz	40.6	4,000/ n/a	39	45
(e) 1999 : SPECIMEN PERTH COIN FAIR COIN & MEDALLION SET								
NCSS Fair		2 oz coin & 1899 Perth Mint Veiled Hd sovereign medal				750	119	130

(a) Australian Landmark privy marks : This privy mark series features ten different themes or landmarks of Australia. The first five coins were issued in 1999 with the remaining five privy marks being depicted on the 2000 dated specimen issue.

(b) Perth Mint Centenary Sovereign Privy Mark : This coin features the reverse design of the unique 1999 - dated proof Perth Mint centenary sovereign. The central area of the privy mark is in gold cameo.

(c) Koban Privy mark : In English, Koban means Small Stamp (or mould) and refers to the design of this Japanese issued gold coin. Small crests of the Kiri flower appear on the top, bottom and edges of these flat, oval shaped coins. Koban Kin means gold and the first of these issues, called Musashi Sumigaki or Sumiban Koban Kin appeared at the end of the 1600s. The privy mark is fine gold.

(d) Pattern Nickel Pence : Issued in October 1998 to commemorate the 80th anniversary of the first issue of experimental square nickel pennies and halfpennies by the Melbourne Mint.

(e) NCSS Perth Fair Series : The third of a four year program to commemorate each of the NCSS Perth coin and stamp fairs from 1997 to the year 2000. Each cased set contains a specimen 2 oz coin and a silver medallion. The medallion will feature different pre-decimal coins on the reverse with the Perth Mint seal on the obverse. This year, the medallion set issued on August 21 - 22, featured overlapping reverse and obverse designs of the Perth minted 1899 sovereign. From 1899 to 1931, the Perth Mint produced many millions of sovereigns and half sovereigns - many of which were exported to India.

KOOKABURRA PROOF & SPECIMEN

SERIES ONE : 1990 TO 2005 : FINE SILVER. 99.9%

Date	Face Value	Description	Type	Weight in oz's	Size	Mintage Max/ Actual	Issue Price	Average Retail
EUROPEAN MONETARY UNION - SPECIMEN FINISH								
1999 a	1	Germany/ Mark	Spec	1oz	40.6	5,000/ All sold	42.95	50
1999 b	1	Austria/ Schilling	Spec	1oz	40.6	5,000/ All sold	42.95	50
1999 c	1	Luxembourg/ Franc	Spec	1oz	40.6	5,000/ All sold	42.95	50
1999 d	1	Netherlands/ Guilder	Spec	1oz	40.6	5,000/ All sold	42.95	50
1999 e	1	Belgium/ Franc	Spec	1oz	40.6	5,000/ All sold	42.95	50
1999 f	1	Finland/ Markka	Spec	1oz	40.6	5,000/ All sold	42.95	50
1999 g	1	France. Franc	Spec	1oz	40.6	5,000/ All sold	42.95	50
1999 h	1	Italy. Lire	Spec	1oz	40.6	5,000/ All sold	42.95	50
1999 i	1	Spain/ Pesetas	Spec	1oz	40.6	5,000/ All sold	42.95	50
1999 j	1	Portugal/ Escudos	Spec	1oz	40.6	5,000/ All sold	42.95	50
1999 k	1	Ireland/ Punt	Spec	1oz	40.6	5,000/ All sold	42.95	50

The above series of 11 coins was released by the Perth Mint to commemorate the formation of the European Monetary Union on January 1, 1999.

(a) Deutsche Mark (Germany) : Originally a Mark was an ancient unit of account which was equal to two-thirds of the Roman pound. It became the major unit of currency of the German Empire from 1873.

(b) Schilling (Austria) : Introduced after WWI with 10,000 kronen to the schilling and later 100 groschen to the schilling. The silver coin was debased to cu/ni in 1934.

(c) Franc (Luxembourg) : The franc was used in Luxembourg during the Napoleonic Wars. Today the one franc is the smallest coin issued.

(d) Guilder (Netherlands) : Although struck by a number of neighbours the Netherlands Guilder or Gulden was first struck in 1601.

(e) Franc (Belgium) : The franc was established in 1830 by Catholic, Leopold of Saxe-Coburg who set himself up as the first King of the Belgians following a successful revolt against the Protestant Dutch.

(f) Markka (Finland) : The Finnish equivalent of the German mark, it was first struck as a silver coin in 1864 when under the domination of Russia.

(g) Franc (France) : The French franc was first struck as a medieval gold coin under John The Good (Jean II) in 1360. It was struck to either pay ransom money or celebrate his release from captivity in England after the Battle of Poitiers.

(h) Lira (Italy) : Derived from the Roman word Libra, meaning Pound. It was first struck in 1472 by the Doge, Nicolas Tron of Venice.

(i) Peseta (Spain) : A relatively new word, it traces its origins to the much older Spanish coin, the *Peso.* Peseta provincial coins of inferior silver content to the peso were struck for use only in Spain in the 18th century. The Peseta came into its own in 1868 when Spain joined the Latin Monetary Union and adopted a decimal currency.

(j) Escudos (Portugal) : Spanish word for Shield. First issued as a gold coin in 1536, it was valued at 16 silver reales. It remained the principal gold coin until 1833.

(k) Punt - Pound (Ireland) : One of many denominations since the time of Christ introduced by the conquering English. Often the Irish denominations were lightweight to ensure they did not circulate on the mainland.

KOOKABURRA PROOF & SPECIMEN

SERIES ONE : 1990 TO 2005 : FINE SILVER. 99.9%

Date	Face Value	Description	Type	Weight in oz's	Size	Mintage Max/ Actual	Issue Price	Average Retail
USA STATE QUARTERS SPECIMEN FINISH								
1999 a	1	Delaware	Spec	1oz	40.6	10,000/ n/a	40	45
1999 b	1	Pennsylvania	Spec	1oz	40.6	10,000/ n/a	40	45
1999 c	1	New Jersey	Spec	1oz	40.6	10,000/ n/a	40	45
1999 d	1	Georgia	Spec	1oz	40.6	10,000/ n/a	40	45
1999 e	1	Connecticut	Spec	1oz	40.6	10,000/ n/a	40	45
KILO COIN WITH FIVE FINE GOLD INSERT PRIVY MARKS								
1999	1 kg	30	Five gold privy marks			1,000	692.82	1,250
2 OZ COIN WITH FIVE SILVER INSERT PRIVY MARKS								
1999	2 oz	2	Five silver privy marks			9,999	67.81	120

Background information : In early 1999 the US Mint launched the first in a series of new circulating quarters, featuring historic designs honouring all of the US states in the order in which they joined the union. Each privy coin is packaged with an original US State quarter.

(a) Delaware : The US Delaware State, featuring Statesman Caesar Rodney on horseback, was the first coin in the series. He rode 80 miles to Philadelphia to break the tie among Delaware delegates at the Continental Congress and vote in favour of Delaware accepting the Declaration of Independence.

(b) Pennsylvania : Features the "Commonwealth" status which is atop the Pennsylvania capital dome, with an outline of the State, the State motto and a keystone.

(c) New Jersey : A design based on the 1851 painting by Emmanuel Leutze, it shows George Washington standing in his boat accompanied by members of the Colonial army on their way to victories against the British.

(d) Georgia : Shows a large peach within an outline of the State, bordered by oak sprigs and a banner with the State motto "Wisdom, Justice, Moderation."

(e) Connecticut : Features the *"Charter Oak"* which represents the hiding place of the Connecticut Charter which was kept from the British who challenged Connecticut's government structure.

KOOKABURRA PROOF & SPECIMEN

SERIES ONE : 1990 TO 2005 : FINE SILVER. 99.9%

Date	Face Value	Description	Type	Weight in oz's	Size	Mintage Max/ Actual	Issue Price	Average Retail
2000 : PROOF FINISH STANDARD REVERSE ISSUES								
2000	30	Standard reverse	Proof	1 kg	100	In sets only	—	—
2000	10	Standard reverse	Proof	10 oz	75	In sets only	—	—
2000	2	Standard reverse	Proof	2 oz	50	750/ 406	95	75
2000	1	Standard reverse	Proof	1 oz	40.6	3,000/ 2,583	53	50
2000 : PROOF FINISH STANDARD REVERSE ISSUES								
2000 a	2	Victoria Cross	Proof	2 oz	50	750/ 406	95	75
2000 : PROOF MULTIPLE COIN CASED SETS								
Four Coin Proof Set :		1 Kg	10oz	2oz	1oz	300/ 266	1,038	1,680
Three Coin Proof Set :			10oz	2oz	1oz	350/ 128	440	530
Two Coin Proof Set :				2oz	1oz	750/ 465	147	180

(a) Victoria Cross : On the 100th anniversary of the awarding of the first Victoria Cross to an Australian, The Perth Mint issued a limited number of commemorative, coloured privy mark coins, each presented in a serial-numbered frame with a replica of the Victoria Cross.

KOOKABURRA PROOF & SPECIMEN

SERIES ONE : 1990 TO 2005 : FINE SILVER. 99.9%

Date	Face Value	Description	Type	Weight in oz's	Size	Mintage Max/ Actual	Issue Price	Average Retail
2000 : SPECIMEN FINISH STANDARD REVERSE ISSUES								
2000	30	Standard reverse	Spec	1 kg	100	To order/ 4,556	384	1,150
2000	10	Standard reverse	Spec	10 oz	75	To order/ 4,790	129	350
2000	2	Standard reverse	Spec	2 oz	50	To order/ 23,872	36	30
2000	1	Standard reverse	Spec	1 oz	40.6	300k/ 104,169	21	25
2000 : FOUR COIN SPECIMEN FINISH STANDARD REVERSE SET								
2000		Bullion : 1 Kilo; 10 oz; 2 oz; 1 oz					629.75	1680
2000 : SPECIMEN FINISH PRIVY MARKED THEME - HISTORIC COINS								
2000 a	2	Antoninianus Silver	Spec	2 oz	50	2,000/ n/a	125	125
2000 b	2	Byzantine Bronze	Spec	2 oz	50	2,000/ n/a	125	125
2000 c	2	English Silver Penny	Spec	2 oz	50	2,000/ n/a	145	125
2000 d	2	Hungarian Denar	Spec	2 oz	50	2,000/ n/a	99	125
SPECIMEN FINISH PRIVY MARKED THEME - AUSTRALIAN LANDMARKS								
2000 e	1	Uluru (Ayers Rock)	Spec	1 oz	40.6	1,500/ n/a	42.95	50
2000 f	1	Great Barrier Reef	Spec	1 oz	40.6	1,500/ n/a	42.95	50
2000 g	1	Monkey Mia Privy	Spec	1 oz	40.6	1,500/ n/a	42.95	50
2000 h	1	Kalgoorlie Privy	Spec	1 oz	40.6	1,500/ n/a	42.95	50
2000 i	1	Australia 2000	Spec	1 oz	40.6	1,500/ n/a	42.95	50
2000 : SPECIMEN FINISH PRIVY MARKED MISCELLANEOUS ISSUES								
2000 j	1	Baby Pack Folder	Spec	1 oz	40.6	2,000/ n/a	35	50

(a) Roman Antoninianus : A coin from one of the worlds most famous and powerful Empires, the Roman silver Antoninianus is from the reign of Gordian III. This privy marked coin was issued at the Sydney ANDA fair held from February 18 - 20, 2000.
(b) Byzantine Empire : Founded by the Roman Emperor Constantine the Great, the Byzantine Empire endured for over a millennium, and was the axis of trade, culture and Christianity for centuries. Issued at the Melbourne ANDA fair from April 14 - 16.
(c) English Silver Penny : The silver Long Cross pennies of Edward I of England (1239 - 1307) was part of reforms that would revolutionise coinage across the world. Issued at the ANDA Brisbane Fair held from May 26 - 28, 2000.
(d) Hungarian Denar : Celebrating the silver denar of Ferdinand I of Hungary, this coin bears the famous Madonna design. It was renowned as a trading coin across Europe throughout the Renaissance. Kookaburra privy issued at the Melbourne ANDA fair held from October 22 - 22.
(e to i) Australian Landmarks : The second instalment in a ten coin series of famous Australian Landmarks that began in 1999.
(j) Baby Pack : Each Kookaburra Baby Pack contains a 2000-dated 1 oz Kookaburra specimen silver coin which is housed in a beautifully printed folder with blank areas to record the baby's personal details.

KOOKABURRA PROOF & SPECIMEN

SERIES ONE : 1990 TO 2005 : FINE SILVER. 99.9%

Date	Face Value	Description	Type	Weight in oz's	Size	Mintage Max/ Actual	Issue Price	Average Retail
USA STATE QUARTERS SPECIMEN FINISH								
2000 a	1	Massachusetts	Spec	1 oz	40.6	75,000/ n/a	45	50
2000 b	1	Maryland	Spec	1 oz	40.6	75,000/ n/a	45	50
2000 c	1	South Carolina	Spec	1 oz	40.6	75,000/ n/a	45	50
2000 d	1	New Hampshire	Spec	1 oz	40.6	75,000/ n/a	45	50
2000 e	1	Virginia	Spec	1 oz	40.6	75,000/ n/a	45	50
KILO COIN WITH FIVE PURE GOLD INSERT PRIVY MARKS								
2000	30	Kilo	Five gold privy marks			1,000	699	1,150
2 OZ COIN WITH FIVE SILVER INSERT PRIVY MARKS								
2000	2	2 oz	Five silver privy marks			10,000	74	120

Background information : In early 1999 the US Mint launched the first in a series of new circulating quarters, featuring historic designs honouring all of the US states in the order in which they joined the union. Each privy coin is packaged with an original US State quarter. This is the second issue.

(a) Massachusetts : Against an outline of the *"Bay State"*, the famous statue of *"The Minuteman"* is depicted. The Minuteman rallied together to help defeat the British during the Revolutionary War. Consisting of regular farmers and colonists, these small forces were trained to assemble and fight at just a minute's notice -hence the term *"minutemen."*

(b) Maryland : The central design shows the dome of the Maryland State-house, which dates back to 1772. It is the country's largest wooden dome built without nails and is the country's oldest state capital building still in legislative use. Leaf clusters from the official State tree, the White Oak, decorate the border. Maryland is nicknamed the Old Line State in honour of its *"troops of the Line."*

(c) South Carolina: Key State symbols are depicted against the State outline. A Palmetto Tree relates to when colonists, assembled in a small fort built of Palmetto logs, successfully defeated a British fleet trying to capture Charleston Harbour. The Carolina Wren and Yellow Jessamine are native to the state.

(d) New Hampshire : Honouring one of the state's most unique natural attractions - *"The Old Man of the Mountain"*. Measuring over 40 feet high with a lateral distance of 25 feet, this impressive rock formation depicts the distinct profile of an elderly man gazing eastward. The state motto *"Live free or die"* and nine stars signifying that New Hamshire was the ninth state to ratify the Constitution.

(e) Virginia : Three ships, *Susan Constant, Godspeed* and *Discovery* brought the first English settlers to Jamestown, the nation's first permanent English settlement. Departing from London on December 20, 1606, 104 men and boys arrived on a small island along the James River on May 12, 1607 and established Jamestown in honour of King James 1.

KOOKABURRA PROOF & SPECIMEN

SERIES ONE : 1990 TO 2005 : FINE SILVER. 99.9%

Date	Face Value	Description	Type	Weight in oz's	Size	Mintage Max/ Actual	Issue Price	Average Retail
THE CALENDAR : SPECIMEN FINISH PRIVYMARKED THEME								
2000	1	Valentines Day	Spec	1 oz	40.6	2,000/ n/a	46	50
SPECIMEN FINISH PRIVY MARKED THEME - THE CALENDAR								
2000		Only available as a full set				5,000	552	600

In setting out the descriptions below we first give the name of the month we are all familiar with; eg : *January.* This is followed by the Latin name; eg : *Januarius* and then the Roman / Latin association; eg : *Janus.*

(a) January / Januarius (Janus). Janus - the god of beginnings and endings is represented with two heads, one as a youth signifying beginning, the other of an aged man, indicating the end. The key symbolizes that he opened all things in the beginning.
(b) February / Februarius (Februa). Februa - the feast of purification held on the 15th. A month devoted to expiation *(to atone or make amends for)* and heralding the rebirth of Spring and its associated fertility.
(c) March / Martius (Mars). Mars - the Roman god of war, the storm and hurricane, regarded as the father of the Roman people.
(d) April / Aprilis (Venus). Venus - the goddess of love epitomizes all that is beautiful and pure and is associated with beautiful plants such as the rose.
(e) May / Maius (Maia). Maia - the wife of Mars who was the goddess of spring and growth.
(f) June / Junius (Juno). Juno - the wife of Jupiter and the queen of the gods. She was also regarded as the goddess of wisdom, marriage, childbirth and protector of married women.
(g) July / Julius (Julius Caesar). One of the most influential political and military leaders in history, Julius Caesar helped establish the vast Roman Empire, but political jealousies among his opponents led to his assassination.
(h) August / Augustus (Augustus Caesar). Originally called Sextilis, or the sixth month after March, it was renamed in honour of Augustus Caesar, the most revered of the Roman emperors.
(i) September / Septem (Seven). An ostentatious, seven - eyed plumage display of the peacock symbolizes Rome's far flung empire.
(j) October / Octo (Eight). A design in the shape of an octogon, depicting Roman art and ceramics.
(k) November / Nove (Nine). Depiction of a lyre which is symbolic of Roman culture.
(l) December / Decem (Ten). Design of an eagle which appears on the standards of Roman legions.
(m) Valentine's Day : Highlights the origins of the month of February and its link with Valentine's Day, and forms part of the Millennium Calendar Privy Mark Series which highlights the gods, emperors and symbols that have become associated with each of the 12 months in the Gregorian calendar.

KOOKABURRA PROOF & SPECIMEN

SERIES ONE : 1990 TO 2005 : FINE SILVER. 99.9%

2001 : Proof Reverse

2001 : 10 oz Calendar

2001 : Specimen Reverse

Date	Face Value	Description	Type	Weight in oz's	Size	Mintage Max/ Actual	Issue Price	Average Retail
2001 : PROOF SILVER KOOKABURRA ISSUES								
2001	30	Standard reverse	Proof	1 kg	100	Exclusive to sets	—	—
2001a	10	Calendar/ Evolution	Proof	10 oz	75	Exclusive to sets	—	—
2001	2	Standard reverse	Proof	1 oz	50	800/ 405	99	60
2001	1	Standard reverse	Proof	1 oz	40.6	5,000/ 3,241	53	30
2001 : PROOF MULTIPLE COIN CASED SETS								
Four Coin Proof Set :	1 Kg	10oz	2oz	1oz		350/ 212	1,050	1,680
Three Coin Proof Set :		10oz	2oz	1oz		400/ 321	450	530
Two Coin Proof Set :			2oz	1oz		800/ 323	149	180
2001 : CALENDAR : PART OF EVOLUTION THEME - TEN OUNCE PROOF								
2001	Individual 10 oz : Cased in Free standing display					1,500/ 1,269	325	325
2001 : SPECIMEN FINISH STANDARD REVERSE ISSUES								
2001	30	Standard reverse	Spec	1 kg	100	To order/ 3,108	384	1,150
2001	10	Standard reverse	Spec	10 oz	75	To order/ 2,766	129	350
2001	2	Standard reverse	Spec	2 oz	50	To order/ 17,050	36	30
2001	1	Standard reverse	Spec	1 oz	40.6	300k/ 169,265	21	25
2001 : SPECIMEN FINISH PRIVY MARKED MISCELLANEOUS ISSUES								
2001b	30	Royal baby. Japan	Spec	1 kg	n/a	300/ n/a	850	975
2001c	1	Federation star	Spec	1 oz	40.6	To order/ n/a	45	60
2001d	1	Love token set	Spec	1 oz	40.6	1,000/ 201	45	60
2001e	1	Santa Claus privy	Spec	1 oz	40.6	50,000/ n/a	45	60
2001	1	Baby Pack Folder	Spec	1 oz	40.6	2,000/ n/a	35	50

(a) Calendar 10 oz set : This was the first of the 10 ounce proof Kookaburra coins featuring a series of designs based on the evolution of the tools or instruments that have influenced the universe through the ages. The 2001 issue featured "Evolution" of the Calendar. This was followed by Time (2002); Alphabet (2003), Numbers (2004) and Knowledge (2005).
(b) Japan's Royal Baby : Just 300 one kilo fine silver proof coins were struck to commemorate the birth of the first child of Japanese Crown Prince Naruhito and Princess Masako on December 1, 2001. The coin featured a pure gold privy mark.
(c) Federation star privy mark : The seven pointed star privy that represents Australia's Federation in January 1901 is a fine gold insert. The Mint issued 9,000 individual coins and offered a further 1,000 coins as part of a three coin set which also featured the 1951 Federation Florin and the Holey Dollar and Dump.
(d) Love token/ Crown set : This Love Token gift set contained a 2001 Australian Kookaburra 1 oz silver specimen coin and an original Queen Victoria Veiled Head silver crown issued from 1893 to 1900. Part of the purchase price included a personal message on the obverse of the crown for each customer, thereby creating a unique gift. The use of coins as love tokens is thought to have begun in the early 17th century, especially by sailors and soldiers who were leaving their homes for destinations from which they might not return.
(e) Santa Claus : The coloured hanging decoration of Santa Claus holds the Christmas privy mark coin. Space on the back of the decoration allows for space for it to be personalised.

KOOKABURRA PROOF & SPECIMEN

SERIES ONE : 1990 TO 2005 : FINE SILVER. 99.9%

Date	Face Value	Description	Type	Weight in oz's	Size	Mintage Max/ Actual	Issue Price	Average Retail
2001 : SPECIMEN FINISH STANDARD REVERSE ISSUES								
2001	30	Standard reverse	Spec	1 kg	100	To order/ 2,856	384	1,150
2001	10	Standard reverse	Spec	10 oz	75	To order/ 2,438	129	350
2001	2	Standard reverse	Spec	2 oz	50	To order/ 15,696	36	30
2001	1	Standard reverse	Spec	1 oz	40.6	300,000/ 291,604	21	25
2001 : PROOF SILVER KOOKABURRA ISSUES								
2001a	1	New York privy	Spec	1 oz	40.6	75k/ n/a	45	50
2001b	1	North Carolina	Spec	1 oz	40.6	75k/ n/a	45	50
2001c	1	Rhode Island	Spec	1 oz	40.6	75k/ n/a	45	50
2001d	1	Vermont privy	Spec	1 oz	40.6	75k/ n/a	45	50
2001e	1	Kentucky privy	Spec	1 oz	40.6	75k/ n/a	45	50
KILO COIN WITH FIVE FINE GOLD INSERT PRIVY MARKS								
2001	30	Kilo	Five gold privy marks			1000	710	1,150
2 oz COIN WITH FIVE FINE SILVER INSERT PRIVY MARKS								
2001	2	2 oz	Five silver privy marks			10,000	78	120

(a) New York : Features the Statue of Liberty and 11 stars representing the number of States in the Union when New York joined.
(b) North Carolina : Depicts the famous 1903 photograph of the "First Flight". This historic feat took place on December 17, 1903, at Kitty Hawk, North Carolina.
(c) Rhode Island : Shows a vintage sailboat in Rhode Island's famous Narragansett Bay. It was here in 1983 that Australia II won the feted America's Cup.
(d) Vermont : Camel's Hump Mountain with an image of maple trees and sap buckets.
(e) Kentucky : Shows a thoroughbred racehorse, standing behind a fence.

2001 ERROR / MULE PROOF

Platinum or gold $200 obverse accidently muled with a 2001 Proof silver reverse

Date	Face Value	Weight in oz's	Description	Mintage Max/ Actual	Issue Price	Average Retail
2001	1.00	1 oz	Mule. Wrong obverse	20?	53	7,750

This unusual error occurred in 2001 when the normal reverse of the one ounce silver proof Kookaburra coin was accidentally muled, or mixed up, with the two ounce proof gold or platinum obverse. Originally around 100 were struck and shipped to clients before the error was detected. The Perth Mint sent a letter to collectors and some 80 coins were returned for replacement. The resulting mintage could be as low as 20 coins. An example sold for $2,330 *(including commission)* against a $1,500 estimate in Downies Sale 277, in October, 2001. In February 2005, another example sold by Downies (Sale 287, lot 692) for $5,500, plus commission. In July 2010, Peter Tickenoff, the manager of the WA based company, Mint Coins, reported that they sold an example for $7,000.

KOOKABURRA PROOF & SPECIMEN

SERIES ONE : 1990 TO 2005 : FINE SILVER. 99.9%

2002 : Proof Reverse

2002 : 10 oz Time

2002 : Specimen

Date	Face Value	Description	Type	Weight in oz's	Size	Mintage Max/ Actual	Issue Price	Average Retail
2002 : PROOF FINISH STANDARD REVERSE ISSUES								
2002	30	No privy mark	Proof	1 kg	100	Exclusive to sets	—	—
2002	10	Evolution Time	Proof	10 oz	100	See entries below	—	—
2002	2	No privy mark	Proof	2 oz	50	800/ 497	103	65
2002	1	No privy mark	Proof	1 oz	40.6	5,000/ 1,733	56.5	60
TIME : PART OF EVOLUTION THEME - TEN OUNCE PROOF								
2002		Individual 10 oz : Cased in Free standing display				1,500/ 1,269	325	375
2002 : PROOF FINISH MISCELLANEOUS PRIVY MARKED COIN								
2002 a	1	Tribute to Freedom	Spec	1 oz	40.6	18,500/ n/a	55	50
2002 : PROOF MULTIPLE COIN CASED SETS								
Five coins. Kilo set :		1 kg 10 oz 2 oz	1 oz	1/2oz•		350/ 198	1,184	1,700
Four coins. Ten oz set :		10 oz 2 oz	1 oz	n/a		400/ 225	481	480
Two Coins. Two oz set :		2 oz	1 oz	n/a		800/ 342	160	1,800
* The 1/2 oz in the the five coin kilo set was the .50¢ square kookaburra pattern design								
2002 : SPECIMEN FINISH STANDARD REVERSE ISSUES								
2002	30	Standard reverse	Spec	1 kg	100	To order/ 2,856	384	1,150
2002	10	Standard reverse	Spec	10 oz	75	To order/ 2,438	129	350
2002	2	Standard reverse	Spec	2 oz	50	To order/ 15,696	36	30
2002	1	Standard reverse	Spec	1 oz	40.6	300,000/ 91,604	21	25
2002 : PALINDROME PRIVY MARKED SPECIMEN FINISH								
2002 b	2	1661 Spanish Cob	Spec	2 oz	50	1,500/ n/a	77.5	80
2002 c	2	1771 Spanish Dollar	Spec	2 oz	50	1,500/ n/a	77.5	80
2002 d	2	1881 Gold Sov. privy	Spec	2 oz	50	1,500/ n/a	77.5	80
2002 e	2	1991 Aust. Nugget	Spec	2 oz	50	1,500/ n/a	77.5	80
2002 f	2	Cased box of four	Spec	2 oz	50	1,000/ n/a	n/a	n/a

(a) Tribute to Freedom : A coloured representation of the "Stars and Stripes" issued as a commemoration of the 225th anniversary of its design. This coin was also issued in a three-piece set that featured a half-ounce and a one-ounce gold nugget which carried a .999 fine silver Liberty Bell privy.
(b) Spanish Cob : Featuring a 1661 copper Spanish Cob that shows a Spanish crown and shield. Released at the Sydney ANDA Fair from April 19-21, 2002. Ironically the copper cob privy on the coin is actually coloured blue.
(c) Pillar Dollar : Issued at the Brisbane ANDA Fair on May 24-26, this privy mark features a 1771 silver Spanish Pillar Dollar depicting the Pillars of Hercules.
(d) St George & the Dragon : Released at the Sydney ANDA Fair from August 9-11, and features Italian engraver Benedetto Pistrucci's masterpiece of St. George and the Dragon.
(e) Australian Proof Nugget privy mark : Released at the Melbourne ANDA Fair held from October 18-22. The first Nugget coin was released in 1986 when the one-ounce piece was the biggest of four issues.
(f) Palindrome privy mark : The figures in the year 2002 represent a palindrome - and word or phrase which reads the same backwards or forwards. The Perth Mint released this 4-coin set to celebrate this once in a century occurrence. The coins were released at ANDA Coin Fairs held throughout 2002. A separate ballot was held for Perth Mint customers for a small allocation of full four coin sets.

KOOKABURRA PROOF & SPECIMEN

SERIES ONE : 1990 TO 2005 : FINE SILVER. 99.9%

2003 : Proof Reverse

2003 : 10 oz Alphabet

2003 : Specimen Reverse

Date	Face Value	Description	Type	Weight in oz's	Size	Mintage Max/ Actual	Issue Price	Average Retail
2003 : PROOF FINISH STANDARD REVERSE ISSUES								
2003	30	No privy mark	Proof	1 kg	100	Exclusive to sets	—	—
2003	10	Alphabet Evolution	Proof	10 oz	100	Exclusive to sets	—	—
2003	2	No privy mark	Proof	2 oz	50	800/ 497	103	65
2003 b	1	No privy mark	Proof	1 oz	40.6	5.000/ 1,733	56.5	60
ALPHABET : PART OF EVOLUTION THEME - TEN OUNCE PROOF								
2003		Individual 10 oz : Cased in Free standing display				1,500/ 799	325	375
2003 : PROOF MULTIPLE COIN CASED SETS								
Five coins. Kilo set :	1 kg	10 oz	2 oz	1 oz	*1/2oz	350/ 135	1,184	1,700
Four coins. Ten oz set :		10 oz	2 oz	1 oz	n/a	400/ 127	481	480
Two Coins. Two oz set :			2 oz	1 oz	n/a	800/ 232	160	1,800
*** The 1/2oz in the the above set was the .50¢ square kookaburra pattern design**								
2003 : SPECIMEN FINISH STANDARD REVERSE ISSUES								
2003	30	Standard reverse	Spec	1 kg	100	To order/ 3,016	384	1,150
2003	10	Standard reverse	Spec	10 oz	75	To order/ 3,558	129	350
2003	2	Standard reverse	Spec	2 oz	50	To order/ 16,663	36	50
2003	1	Standard reverse	Spec	1 oz	40.6	300,000/ 109,439	21	25
2003 : FOUR COIN SPECIMEN STANDARD REVERSE SET								
2003 :		Bullion : 1 Kilo; 10 oz; 2 oz; 1 oz.				2,500/ n/a	629.75	1,680
2003 : AUSTRALIANS AT WAR SPECIMEN COINS								
2003	2	Boer War Set	Spec	2 oz	50	1,000/ n/a	125	80
2003	2	World War I Set	Spec	2 oz	50	1,000/ n/a	125	80
2003	2	World War II Set	Spec	2 oz	50	1,000/ All sold	125	80
2003	2	Korean War Set	Spec	2 oz	50	1,000/ n/a	125	80
2003	2	Vietnam War Set	Spec	2 oz	50	1,000/ All sold	125	80
2003		One of each of the above cased				2,500/ n/a	695	750

Australians at War is a tribute series of silver privy mark coins, miniature service medals and specially designed and coloured medallions that pay tribute to the five major international conflicts of the twentieth century. Produced with the support and cooperation of the Australian War Memorial, the Commonwealth Departments of Veterans' Affairs and Defence and the Returned & Services League of Australia, it includes five 2003-dated specimen quality Australian Kookaburra two-ounce coins. The reverse features a colour privy mark representation of a service medal and ribbon awarded to personnel who served in either the Boer War, World War I, World War II, the Korean War or the Vietnam War. The medals featured include the Queen's South Africa Medal; the Victory Medal 1914-1919; the Australia Service Medal 1939-1945; the Korea Medal and the Vietnam Medal. The five coloured medallions portray images associated with one of the five conflicts, each medallion is a unique reminder of the personnel and fighting equipment of that era. As well as the individual sets, the mint also produced 2,500 Complete Collections, compromising all five coins, five miniature medals and five medallions. The set is housed in a magnificent handmade blue presentation box featuring the official Australians at War emblem and a replica of the Australian Army's Rising Sun badge on the lid and comes complete with a 12 page booklet.

KOOKABURRA PROOF & SPECIMEN

SERIES ONE : 1990 TO 2005 : FINE SILVER. 99.9%

2004 [a] Proof Reverse

2004 [b] 10 oz Numbers

2004 [c] Gilded Specimen

Date	Face Value	Description	Type	Weight in oz's	Size	Mintage Max/ Actual	Issue Price	Average Retail
2004 : PROOF FINISH STANDARD REVERSE ISSUES								
2004	30	Standard reverse	Proof	1 kg	100	Exclusive to sets	—	—
2004	10	Numbers/ Evolution	Proof	10 oz	70	See entry below	—	—
2004	2	Standard reverse	Proof	2 oz	50	800/ 497	62	60
2004	1	Standard reverse	Proof	1 oz	40.6	5,000/ 1,446	62	60
NUMBERS : PART OF EVOLUTION THEME - TEN OUNCE PROOF								
2004 b	10	Numbers/ Evolution	Proof	10 oz	75	1,500/ 886	357	375

2004 : PROOF MULTIPLE COIN CASED SETS

Set						Mintage Max/ Actual	Issue Price	Average Retail
Five coins. Kilo set :	1 kg	10 oz	2 oz	1 oz	*1/2oz	350/ 165	1,295	1,650
Two Coins. Two oz set :			2 oz	1 oz		800/ 545	174.5	180

(*) The 1/2 oz in the the five coin kilo set was the .50¢ square kookaburra pattern design

Date	Face Value	Description	Type	Weight in oz's	Size	Mintage Max/ Actual	Issue Price	Average Retail
2004 : SPECIMEN FINISH STANDARD REVERSE ISSUES								
2004	30	Standard reverse	Spec	1 kg	100	To order/ 2,712	n/a	1,150
2004	10	Standard reverse	Spec	10 oz	75	To order/ 2,270	n/a	350
2004	2	Standard reverse	Spec	2 oz	50	To order/ 13,969	n/a	50.5
2004	1	Standard reverse	Spec	1 oz	40.6	300,000/ 84,455	n/a	25
2004 : SPECIMEN GILDED ONE OUNCE SILVER COIN								
2004 c	1	Gilded kookaburra	Spec	1 oz	40.6	10,000/ Sold out	55	70

[c] This coin was sold individually in a free-standing perspex display case. This is the first gold gilded specimen quality coin issued by the Perth Mint.

b

c

d

e

f

Date	Face Value	Description	Type	Weight in oz's	Size	Mintage Max/ Actual	Issue Price	Average Retail
ASTROLOGY : SPECIMEN FINISH PRIVY MARKED THEME								
2005 b	1	Aquarius privy	Spec	1 oz	40.6	5,000/ n/a	49.5	45
2005	1	Pisces privy	Spec	1 oz	40.6	5,000/ n/a	49.5	45
2005	1	Aries privy	Spec	1 oz	40.6	5,000/ n/a	49.5	45
2005	1	Tauris privy	Spec	1 oz	40.6	5,000/ n/a	49.5	45
2005 c	1	Gemini privy	Spec	1 oz	40.6	5,000/ n/a	49.5	45
2005	1	Cancer privy	Spec	1 oz	40.6	5,000/ n/a	49.5	45
2005 d	1	Leo privy	Spec	1 oz	40.6	5,000/ n/a	49.5	45
2005	1	Virgo privy	Spec	1 oz	40.6	5,000/ n/a	49.5	45
2005	1	Libra privy	Spec	1 oz	40.6	5,000/ n/a	49.5	45
2005 e	1	Scorpio privy	Spec	1 oz	40.6	5,000/ n/a	49.5	45
2005	1	Sagittarius privy	Spec	1 oz	40.6	5,000/ n/a	49.5	45
2005 f	1	Capricorn privy	Spec	1 oz	40.6	5,000/ n/a	49.5	45
2005		Boxed set of each of the above coins				5,000/ n/a	594	575

KOOKABURRA PROOF & SPECIMEN

SERIES ONE : 1990 TO 2005 : FINE SILVER. 99.9%

2005 : Proof Reverse

2005 : 10 oz Knowledge

2005 : Gilded Specimen

Date	Face Value	Description	Type	Weight in oz's	Size mm	Mintage Max/ Actual	Issue Price	Average Retail
2005 : PROOF FINISH STANDARD REVERSE ISSUES								
2005	30	Standard reverse	Spec	1 kg	100	To order/ 2,100	n/a	n/a
2005	30	Standard reverse	Proof	1 kg	100	Exclusive to set	–	–
2005	10	Knowledge	Proof	10 oz	70	Exclusive to set	–	–
2005	2	No privy mark	Proof	2 oz	50	Exclusive to set	–	–
2005	1	No privy mark	Proof	1 oz	40.6	5,000/ 2,346	65	70
KNOWLEDGE : TEN OUNCE PROOF - EVOLUTION THEME								
2005	10	Knowledge	Proof	10 oz	75	1,500/ 998	357	375
2005 : PROOF MULTIPLE COIN CASED SETS								
Five Coin Proof Set :		1 Kg 10oz 2oz 1oz 1/2oz				350/ 316	1,355	1,355
Two Coin Proof Set :		2oz 1oz				800/ 795	178	180
The 50¢ ,1/2 oz square kookaburra pattern was part of the five coin kilo set.								
2005 : SPECIMEN FINISH STANDARD REVERSE ISSUES								
2005	30	Standard reverse	Spec	1 kg	100	To order/ 2,100	n/a	n/a
2005	10	Standard reverse	Spec	10 oz	75	To order/ 2,112	n/a	n/a
2005	2	Standard reverse	Spec	2 oz	50	To order/ 14,082	n/a	n/a
2005	1	Standard reverse	Spec	1 oz	40.6	300,000/ 95,145	n/a	n/a
2005 : SPECIMEN GILDED ONE OUNCE SILVER COIN								
2005	1	Gilded kookaburra	Spec	1 oz	40.6	10,000/ 9,175	55	70

KOOKABURRA SQUARE PROOF ISSUE

(a) 2002 Rev

(b) 2003 Rev

(c) 2004 Rev

(d) 2005 Rev

Date	Face Value	Weight in oz's	Finish	Mintage Max/ Actual	Issue Feature	Retail Price
2002 a	.50¢	1/2 oz	Proof	75,000/ 35,365	39.5	60
2002 a	.50¢	1/2 oz	Proof	350/ 198	*Only sold in sets*	
2003 b	.50¢	1/2 oz	Proof	30,000/ 11,450	39.5	65
2003 b	.50¢	1/2 oz	Proof	350/ 135	*Only sold in sets*	
2004 c	.50¢	1/2 oz	Proof	30,000/ 9674	43	65
2004 c	.50¢	1/2 oz	Proof	350/ 165	*Only sold in sets*	
2005 d	.50¢	1/2 oz	Proof	30,000/ 8,117	44	70
2005 d	.50¢	1/2 oz	Proof	350/ 316	*Only sold in sets*	

The design of this issue draws heavily on a series of cupro-nickel one penny and halfpenny patterns devised during 1919 and 1921 to replace the larger and heavier bronze issues. In total, 13 of the very rare patterns were produced before the concept was finally abandoned. The above fine silver proof issue closely follows the reverse theme of a kookaburra sitting on a tree branch but the new design does not specifically match any of the 13 known patterns.

SILVER ISSUES : MULTIPLE DATES

SERIES TWO : 2006 TO PRESENT : FINE SILVER. 99.9%

c2006 (a) Specimen

2007 (b) Specimen

2008 (c) Specimen

2009 (d) Specimen

2011 (e) Specimen

Date	Weight in oz's	Face Value	Description	Type	Size mm	Mintage Max/ Actual	Issue Price	Average Retail
2006	1 kg	30	Two Kookaburra's	Sp'men	101.1	To order/ 4,467	b/v	b/v
2006	10 oz	10	Two Kookaburra's	Sp'men	75.6	To order/ 2,999	b/v	b/v
2006	2 oz	2	Two Kookaburra's	Sp'men	53.3	To order/ 12,802	b/v	b/v
2006	1 oz	1	Two Kookaburra's	Sp'men	40.6	300k/ 87,044	b/v	b/v
2007	1 kg	30	Kooka facing left	Sp'men	101.1	To order/ 17,314	b/v	b/v
2007	10 oz	10	Kooka facing left	Sp'men	75.6	To order/ 5,993	b/v	b/v
2007	2 oz	2	Kooka facing left	Sp'men	53.3	To order/ 13,938	b/v	b/v
2007	1 oz	1	Kooka facing left	Sp'men	40.6	300k/ 213,436	b/v	b/v
2007	1 oz	1	Gilt reverse. ANDA	Sp'men	40.6	10,000/ 5,323	70	90
2008	1 kg	30	Kooka with web	Sp'men	101.1	To order/ 32,973	b/v	b/v
2008	10 oz	10	Kooka with web	Sp'men	75.6	To order/ 17,213	b/v	b/v
2008	2 oz	2	Kooka with web	Sp'men	53.3	To order/ 20,083	b/v	b/v
2008	1 oz	1	Kooka with web	Sp'men	40.6	300,000/ All sold	n/a	n/a
2008	1 oz	1	Gilt reverse	Sp'men	40.6	10,000/ 5,323	65	b/v
2009	1 kg	30	Kooka & sun rays	Sp'men	101.1	To order/ 74,757	b/v	b/v
2009	10 oz	10	Kooka & sun rays	Sp'men	75.6	To order/ 13,360	b/v	b/v
2009	2 oz	2	Kooka & sun rays	Sp'men	53.3	To order/ 20,991	b/v	b/v
2009	1 oz	1	Kooka & sun rays	Sp'men	40.6	300,000/ All sold	b/v	b/v
2010	1 kg	30	Kooka sleeping	Sp'men	101.1	To order/ 58,968	b/v	b/v
2010	10 oz	10	Kooka sleeping	Sp'men	75.6	To order/ 18,782	b/v	b/v
2010	2 oz	2	Gilt reverse	Sp'men	53.3	To order/ 13,938	b/v	b/v
2010	1 oz	1	Kooka sleeping	Sp'men	40.6	300,000/ All sold	b/v	b/v
2011	1 kg	30	Stretching wings	Sp'men	101.1	To order/ 78,145	b/v	b/v
2011	10 oz	10	Stretching wings	Sp'men	75.6	To order/ 45,901	b/v	b/v
2011	2 oz	2	Gilt reverse	Sp'men	53.3	To order/ 13,938	b/v	b/v
2011	1 oz	1	Stretching wings	Sp'men	40.6	500,000/ All sold	b/v	b/v
2011	1 oz	1	Piedfort. High relief	Proof	32.6	10,000/ 7,548	102	112
2012	1 kg	30	Kooka facing left	Sp'men	101.1	To order/ 51,596	b/v	b/v
2012	10 oz	10	Kooka facing left	Sp'men	75.6	To order/ 25,608	b/v	b/v
2012	1 oz	1	Kooka sleeping	Sp'men	40.6	To order/ 13,938	b/v	b/v
2012	1 oz	1	Piedfort. High relief	Proof	32.6	10,000/ All sold	102	110
2012	1 oz	1	Beijing Show Colour	Sp'men	40.6	5,000/ 4,951	99	b/v
2012	1 oz	1	Specimen	Sp'men	40.6	500,000/ All sold	b/v	50
2012	1 oz	1	Dragon Privymark	Sp'men	40.6	80,000/ 64,989	b/v	b/v
2013	1 kg	30	Two Kooka's	Sp'men	101.1	To order/ 41,911	b/v	b/v
2013	10 oz	10	Two Kooka's	Sp'men	75.6	To order/ 24,481	b/v	b/v
2013	1 oz	1	Specimen	Sp'men	40.6	500,000/ All sold	40	b/v
2013	1 oz	1	Spec/ Snake privy	Sp'men	40.6	50,000/ All sold	b/v	b/v
2013	1 oz	1	Piedfort. High relief	Sp'men	40.6	500,000/ n/a	40	b/v
2013	1 oz	1	Piedfort. High relief	Proof	32.6	10,000/ 7,548	102	102
2013 a	1 oz	1	F15 Privymark	Sp'men	40.6	15,000/ 7,600	b/v	b/v
2014	1 kg	30	Kooka facing right	Sp'men	101.1	To order/ 34,534	b/v	b/v
2014	10 oz	10	Kooka facing right	Sp'men	75.6	To order/ 28,547	b/v	b/v
2014	5 oz	8	Piedfort. High relief	Proof	50.6	1,000/ All sold	485	550
2014	1 oz	1	Kooka facing right	Sp'men	40.6	500,000/ All sold	40	b/v
2014	1 oz	1	Piedfort. High relief	Proof	32.6	10,000/ 2,757	104	110
2014	1 oz	1	Horse Privymark	Sp'men	40.6	50,000/ All sold	b/v	95
2014	1 oz	1	F15 Privymark	Sp'men	40.6	15,000/ 7,000	b/v	b/v
2015	1 kg	30	P25 privymark	Proof	100.6	500/ 382	n/a	n/a
2015	1 kg	30	Original design	Sp'men	100.6	To order/ 27,094	1,009	750
2015	10 oz	10	Original design	Sp'men	75.6	To order/ 26,272	b/v	b/v
2015	5 oz	8	Piedfort. High relief	Proof	50.6	1,000/ All sold	485	485
2015	2 oz	2	Gilt reverse	Sp'men	53.3	To order/ 13,938	b/v	57
2015	1 oz	1	Original design	Sp'men	40.6	500,000/ All sold	45	32
2015	1 oz	1	Goat privymark	Sp'men	40.6	50,000/ All sold	45	32
2015	1 oz	1	F15 Privymark	Sp'men	40.6	15,000/ 7,350	45	32
2015	1 oz	1	Piedfort. High relief	Proof	32.6	10,000/ 3,182	109	109
2015	1/2 oz	.50¢	Original design	Sp'men	32.6	2,000/ All sold	65	65

SILVER ISSUES : MULTIPLE DATES

2012 (f) Specimen

2013 (g) Specimen

2014 (h) Specimen

2015 (i) Specimen

2016 (j) Specimen

.999% SILVER AUSTRALIAN KOOKABURRA

Date	Weight in oz's	Face Value	Description	Type	Size mm	Mintage Max/ Actual	Issue Price	Average Retail
2016	1 kg	30	Pr P25 privymark	Proof	100.6	500/ 163	1,750	1,750
2016	1 kg	30	Original design	Sp'men	100.6	To order/ 13,355	1,009	1,000
2016	10 oz	10	Original design	Sp'men	75.6	To order/ 22,266	345	250
2016	5 oz	8	Piedfort. High relief	Proof	50.6	1,000/ 393	n/a	485
2016	2 oz	2	Gilt reverse	Sp'men	53.3	To order/ 13,938•	b/v	57
2016	1 oz	1	Piedfort. High relief	Proof	32.6	10,000/ 2,102	109	109
2016	1 oz	1	Berlin Show Colour	Sp'men	40.6	2,000/ All sold	45	32
2016	1 oz	1	Kooka on Post	Sp'men	40.6	500,000/ 292,096	45	32
2016	1 oz	1	Monkey Privy	Sp'men	40.6	50,000/ all sold	45	32
2016	1 oz	1	F15 Privymark	Sp'men	40.6	15,000/ 5,252	45	32
2017	1 kg	30	Facing kookaburra	Proof	100.6	300/ tba	1,750	na
2017	1 kg	30	Facing kookaburra	Sp'men	100.6	To order/ 3,628	na	1,750
2017	10 oz	10	Original design	Sp'men	75.6	To order/ 7,962	na	na
2017	2 oz	2	Gilt reverse	Sp'men	53.3	To order/ tba	b/v	57
2017	1 oz	1	Original design	Sp'men	40.6	500k/ 186,184	b/v	b/v
2017	1 oz	1	Monkey Privy	Sp'men	40.6	50,000/ 29,195	45	32

2010 (f) Proof

2011 (g) Proof

2016 (h) Gilt Specimen

2016 (i) Gilt Specimen

.9999% SILVER AUSTRALIAN KANGAROO

Date	Weight in oz's	Face Value	Description	Metal	Type	Size mm	Mintage Max/ Actual	Issue Price	Averag Retail
2010	1 oz	1	High Relief	Silver	Proof	32.6	20,000/ tba	109	109
2011	1 oz	1	High Relief	Silver	Proof	32.6	20,000/ tba	96	109
2012	1 oz	1	High Relief	Silver	Proof	32.6	20,000/ tba	109	109
2013	1 oz	1	High Relief	Silver	Proof	32.6	20,000/ tba	109	109
2014	1 oz	1	High Relief	Silver	Proof	32.6	20,000/ tba	109	109
2015	5 oz	8	High Relief	Silver	Proof	50.6	1,750/ 1,666	499	499
2015	1 oz	1	High Relief	Silver	Proof	40.6	20,000/ 6,446	99	99
2016	1 oz	1	Standard	Silver	Spec	40.6	300,000	b/v	b/v
2016	1 kg	30	Standard	Silver	Proof	50.6	500/ 163	499	499
2016	5 oz	8	High Relief	Silver	Proof	50.6	1,000/ 623	499	499
2016	1 oz	1	High Relief	Silver	Proof	32.6	20,000/ 4,771	109	109
2016	1 oz	1	Gilt Rev	Silver	Spec	40.6	5,000/ n/a	95	95
2016	1 oz	1	Standard	Silver	Proof	32.6	20,000/ n/a	109	109
2016	1 oz	1	Standard	Silver	Spec	40.6	11,245,615	b/v	b/v
2016a	1/4oz	.50¢	Standard	Silver	Proof	25.5	1,500/ 1,073	29	29
2016	1/10 oz	.10¢	Standard	Silver	Proof	20.6	13,000/ 2,753	29	29
2017	1 kg	30	Standard	Silver	Proof	100.6	300/ b/v	1,750	499
2017	5 oz	8	High Relief	Silver	Proof	50.6	1,000/ 623	499	499
2017	1 oz	1	Spec. Gilt	Silver	Proof	32.6	5,000/ n/a	95	100
2017	1 oz	1	High Relief	Silver	Proof	32.6	20,000/ n/a	109	109

[a] Melbourne Coin Fair coloured silver spec

FOUR COIN CASED PROOF SILVER SET

Date	Description	Mintage	Issue Price	Retail
2016	1 oz, 1/2 oz, 1/4oz, 1/10oz	300 / 289	219	219

SILVER ISSUES : MULTIPLE DATES

KOALA PROOF SERIES TWO - 2008

2008 Silver Gilt

2009 Silver Gilt

2011 Silver Gilt

2014 Silver Gilt

2016 Silver Gilt

Date	Metal	Description	Face Value	Weight in oz's	Size	Mintage Limit / Actual	Issue Price	Current Retail
2011	Silver	Proof	30	1 kg	100.6	500/ 471	69	b/v
2011	Silver	Proof	8	5 oz	60.6	5,000/ Sold out	495	500
2011	Silver	Proof. High Relief	1	1 oz	32.6	10,000/ 9,302	n/a	b/v
2011	Silver	Proof	10¢	1/10oz	20.6	To order/ 26,509	69	b/v
2012	Silver	Proof	30	1 kg	100.6	500/ 471	1,750	b/v
2012	Silver	Proof	8	5 oz	60.6	5,000/ 4,178	495	b/v
2012	Silver	Proof. High relief	1	1 oz	32.6	10,000/ 9,302	104	b/v
2012	Silver	Proof	10¢	1/10oz	20.6	To order/ 13,567	69	b/v
2013	Silver	Proof	30	1 kg	100.6	500/ 471	1,750	b/v
2013	Silver	Proof	8	5 oz	60.6	5,000/ 4,178	495	b/v
2013	Silver	Proof. High relief	1	1 oz	32.6	10,000/ 9,302	102	b/v
2013	Silver	Proof. Gilt Reverse	1	1 oz	36.6	5,000/ n/a	94	b/v
2013	Silver	Proof	10¢	1/10 oz	20.6	To order/ 13,561	69	b/v
2014	Silver	Proof. High relief	8	5 oz	50.6	5,000/ n/a	485	485
2014	Silver	Proof. Gilt	1	1 oz	36.6	5,000/ n/a	94	b/v
2014	Silver	Proof. High relief	1	1 oz	32.6	10,000/ n/a	104	b/v
2015	Silver	Proof	30	1 kg	100.6	500/ 227	1,750	1,750
2015	Silver	Proof. High relief	8	5 oz	50.6	1,000/ n/a	485	525
2015	Silver	Proof. High relief	8	5 oz	50.6	5,000/ 999	485	485
2015	Silver	Proof. High relief	1	1 oz	32.6	10,000/ 3,625	104	104
2015	Silver	Proof	.10¢	1/10 oz	36.6	To order/ 3,530	14.95	14.95
2016	Silver	Proof	30	1 kg	100.6	500/ 93	1,750	1,750
2016	Silver	Proof. High relief	8	5 oz	50.6	5,000/ 879	485	499
2016	Silver	Proof. High relief	1	1 oz	40.6	10,000/ 2,231	109	109
2017	Silver	Proof	30	1 kg	100.6	500/ 93	1,750	1,750
2017a	Silver	Proof. 10th Anniv	10	10 oz	75.6	750/ tba	799	799
2017	Silver	Proof. High relief	8	5 oz	50.6	5,000/ n/a	499	499
2017	Silver	Proof. High relief	1	1 oz	40.6	10,000/ 2,231	109	109

SILVER ISSUES : MULTIPLE DATES

KOALA SPECIMEN SERIES. 2007 -

2008 Silver Gilt

2009 Silver Gilt

2011 Silver Gilt

2014 Silver Gilt

2015 Silver Gilt

Gold Issues 99.99% fine. Silver Issues 99.9% fine

Date	Metal	Description	face Value	Weight in oz's	Size	Mintage Limit / Actual	Issue Price	Current Retail
2007	Silver	Specimen	1	1 oz	40.6	To order/ 137,768	n/a	n/a
2008	Silver	Specimen	30	1 kg	100.6	To order/ 13,188	n/a	n/a
2008	Silver	Specimen	10	10oz	75.6	To order/ 4,367	n/a	n/a
2008	Silver	Specimen	1	1 oz	40.6	To order/ 84,057	n/a	n/a
2008	Silver	Specimen	.50¢	1/2oz	36.6	To order/ 13,944	n/a	n/a
2009	Silver	Specimen	30	1 kg	100.6	To order/ 34,947	n/a	n/a
2009	Silver	Specimen	10	10 oz	75.6	To order/ 6,556	n/a	n/a
2009	Silver	Specimen	1	1 oz	40.6	To order/ 336,757	n/a	n/a
2009	Silver	Specimen	.50¢	1/2oz	36.6	To order/ 15,334	n/a	n/a
2010	Silver	Specimen	30	1 kg	100.6	To order/ 30,692	n/a	n/a
2010	Silver	Specimen	10	10oz	75.6	To order/ 12,928	n/a	n/a
2010	Silver	Specimen	1	1 oz	40.6	To order/ 233,531	n/a	n/a
2010	Silver	Specimen	.50¢	1/2oz	36.6	To order/ 13,315	n/a	n/a
2011	Silver	Specimen	30	1 kg	100.6	To order/ 75,712	n/a	b/v
2011	Silver	Specimen	10	10 oz	75.6	To order/ 10,051	n/a	n/a
2011	Silver	Specimen	1	1 oz	40.6	To order/ 910,480	n/a	n/a
2011	Silver	Spec. Bear Privy	1	1 oz	40.6	50,000/ 48,922	n/a	n/a
2011	Silver	Specimen	.50¢	1/2oz	36.6	To order/ 76,755	n/a	n/a
2012	Silver	Specimen	30	1 kg	100.6	To order/ 19,551	b/v	b/v
2012 a	Silver	Specimen	10	10 oz	75.6	To order/ 17,132	n/a	b/v
2012	Silver	Specimen	1	1 oz	40.6	To order/ 388,046	n/a	b/v
2012	Silver	Spec. Coloured	1	1 oz	40.6	500/ n/a	99	b/v
2012	Silver	Spec. Gilt Reverse	1	1 oz	40.6	10,000/ 4,466	69	b/v
2012	Silver	Spec .Bear Privy	1	1 oz	40.6	50,000/ 32,361	n/a	n/a
2012	Silver	Specimen	.50¢	1/2 oz	36.6	To order/ 118,577	n/a	b/v
2013	Silver	Specimen	30	1 kg	100.6	To order/ 51,296	b/v	b/v
2013	Silver	Specimen	10	10 oz	75.6	To order/ 15,642	b/v	b/v
2013	Silver	Specimen	1	1 oz	40.6	To order/ 477,209	b/v	b/v
2015	Silver	Spec. Gilt Reverse	1	1 oz	40.6	10,000/ n/a	94	94
2013	Silver	Spec. Colour rev	1	1 oz	40.6	To order/ n/a	75	b/v
2013	Silver	Chinese Privy	1	1 oz	40.6	100,000/ 10,392	69	b/v
2013	Silver	Specimen	.50¢	1/2 oz	36.6	To order/ 84,184	b/v	b/v
2013	Silver	Specimen	.10¢	1/10 oz	20.6	To order/ n/a	14.95	18
2014	Silver	Specimen	30	1 kg	100.6	To order/ 25,194	n/a	b/v
2014	Silver	Specimen	10	10 oz	75.6	To order/ 17,985	n/a	b/v
2014	Silver	Specimen	1	1 oz	40.6	To order/ 334,884	n/a	b/v
2014	Silver	Chinese Privy	1	1 oz	40.6	100,000/ 8,397	69	b/v
2014	Silver	Specimen	.50¢	1/2 oz	36.6	To order/ 81,752	n/a	b/v
2015	Silver	Specimen	30	1 kg	100.6	To order/ 37,669	n/a	750
2015	Silver	Specimen	10	10 oz	75.6	To order/ 20,120	n/a	250
2015	Silver	Specimen	1	1 oz	36.6	To order/ 450,899	n/a	b/v
2015	Silver	Spec. Gilt Reverse	1	1 oz	40.6	10,000/ 1,776	94	94
2015	Silver	Specimen	.50¢	1/2 oz	36.6	To order/ 97,157	n/a	17
2015	Silver	Specimen	.10¢	1/10 oz	20.6	To order/ 3,530	14.95	17
2016	Silver	Specimen	30	1 kg	100.6	To order/ 27,513	n/a	b/v
2016	Silver	Specimen	10	10 oz	75.6	To order/ n/a	n/a	250
2016	Silver	Specimen	1	1 oz	40.6	300,000/ All sold	n/a	n/a
2016	Silver	Specimen	.50¢	1/2 oz	36.6	To order/ n/a	n/a	17
2017	Silver	Specimen	30	1 kg	100.6	To order/ n/a	1,750	1,750
2017	Silver	Specimen	10	10 oz	75.6	To order/ n/a	830	830
2017	Silver	Specimen	1	1 oz	36.6	300,000/ n/a	n/a	b/v
2017	Silver	Specimen	1	1 oz	36.6	25,000/ n/a	n/a	b/v
2017	Silver	Specimen	.50¢	1/2 oz	36.6	To order/ n/a	32	32

On this page, and others, you will see notations giving a 'B/V' [Bullion Value] rather than a regular price. This generally concerns high volume issues that trade at prices reflecting the intrinsic 'melt value' of the coin. Even offering an issue price can be tricky as even this can change from week to week as the 'spot' price of the metal. The Perth Mint, and most other dealers, have constantly updated buying and selling prices on their websites.

SILVER ISSUES : MULTIPLE DATES

LUNAR PROOF FINISH

SERIES ONE - 1999 TO 2010

1999 Proof Rabbit

2000 Proof Dragon

2001 Proof Snake

Date	Face Value	Weight in oz's	Size mm	Mintage Max/ Actual	Reverse Feature	Issue Price	Average Retail
1999 : YEAR OF THE RABBIT - SILVER PROOF							
1999	30	1 kg	101	250/ 111	Standard reverse	599	1,250
1999	10	10oz	75.5	Sets only	Standard reverse	–	475
1999	2	2oz	50.3	1,000/ 424	Standard reverse	100	110
1999	1	1 oz	40.6	2.500/ 1,490	With gilt pin	53	90
1999	.50¢	1/2oz	32.1	5,000/ 1081	Standard reverse	39	30
RABBIT : THREE COIN CASED PROOF SILVER SET							
1999		2 oz, 1 oz, 1/2 oz			1,000/ 487	195	1,250
FIVE COIN CASED PROOF SILVER SET							
1999	1kg 10 oz, 2 oz , 1 oz & 1/2 oz				500/ 129	1,085	1,950
2000 : YEAR OF THE DRAGON - SILVER PROOF							
2000	30	1 kg	101	250/ 220	Standard reverse	618	1,250
2000	10	10 oz	75.5	Sets only	Standard reverse	—	—
2000	2	2 oz	50.3	1,000 / 838	Standard reverse	101	110
2000	1	1 oz	40.6	2,500/ All sold	Standard reverse	53	90
2000	.50¢	1/2oz	32.1	5,000 / 1,750	Standard reverse	39	30
DRAGON : THREE COIN CASED PROOF SILVER SET							
2000		2 oz, 1 oz, 1/2 oz			1000 / 982	197	200
FIVE COIN CASED PROOF SILVER SET							
2000	1 Kilo, 10 oz, 2 oz, 1 oz, 1/2 oz				500 / 266	1,112	1,950
2001 : YEAR OF THE SNAKE - SILVER PROOF							
2001	30	1 kg	101.0	250 / 201	Standard reverse	678	1250
2001	10	10oz	75.5	Sets only	Standard reverse	—	—
2001	2	2 oz	50.3	1000 / 939	Standard reverse	1,12.5	110
2001	1	1 oz	40.6	2,500 / 2,466	Standard reverse	59.5	90
2001	.50¢	1/2oz	32.1	5,000 / 1,135	Standard reverse	44	30
SNAKE : THREE COIN CASED PROOF SILVER SET							
2001		2 oz, 1 oz, 1/2 oz			1000 / 599	215.6	200
FIVE COIN CASED PROOF SILVER SET							
2001	1 Kilo, 10 oz, 2 oz, 1 oz, 1/2 oz500 / 289				1,215		1,950

Due to the volatile bullion market in recent years, it cannot be stressed enough that the prices listed here are a guide at best and based on world bullion prices as listed on June 12th, 2017. It is strongly suggested that you check the latest bullion prices before buying or selling.

LUNAR PROOF FINISH

SERIES ONE- 1999 TO 2010

2002 Proof Horse

2003 Proof Goat

2004 Proof Monkey

2005 Proof Rooster

Date	Face Value	Weight in oz's	Size mm	Mintage Max/ Actual	Reverse Feature	Issue Price	Average Retail
2002 : YEAR OF THE HORSE - SILVER PROOF							
2002	30	1 kg	101.1	250/ 71	Standard reverse	678	1,250
2002	10	10 oz	75.5	*Sets only*	Standard reverse	—	—
2002	2	2 oz	50.3	1,000/ 772	Standard reverse	112.5	110
2002	1	1 oz	40.6	2,500/ 1,665	Standard reverse	59.5	90
2002	.50¢	1/2 oz	32.1	5,000/ 1,464	Standard reverse	39	30
HORSE : THREE COIN CASED PROOF SILVER SET							
2002	2 oz, 1 oz, 1/2 oz				1000 / 278	n/a	200
FIVE COIN CASED PROOF SILVER SET							
2002	1 kilo, 10 oz, 2 oz, 1 oz, 1/2 oz				500 / 68	1,950	n/a
2003 : YEAR OF THE GOAT - SILVER PROOF							
2003	30	1 kg	101.1	250/ 57	Standard reverse	699	1,250
2003	10	10 oz	75.5	Sets only	Standard reverse	—	—
2003	2	2 oz	50.3	1,000/ 417	Standard reverse	120	100
2003	1	1 oz	40.6	2,500/ 1,237	Standard reverse	63.5	90
2003	.50¢	1/2 oz	32.1	5,000/ 776	Standard reverse	47	50
2003 GOAT : CASED SILVER PROOF COIN SETS							
Five coin set :	1 Kg 10oz 2oz 1oz 1/2oz			500 / 48		1,290	1,925
Three coin set :	2oz 1oz 1/2oz			1,000/ 172		251	200
2004 : THE LUNAR MONKEY - SILVER PROOF							
2004	30	1 kg	101.1	250/ 39	Standard reverse	767.5	125
2004	10	10 oz	75.5	Sets only	Standard reverse	—	—
2004	2	2 oz	50.3	1,000/ 264	Standard reverse	131	110
2004	1	1 oz	40.6	2,500 / 931	Standard reverse	69	90
2004	.50¢	1/2 oz	32.1	5,000 / 674	Standard reverse	51	30
MONKEY : CASED SILVER PROOF COIN SETS							
Five coin set :	1 Kg 10oz 2oz 1oz 1/2oz			1,000/ 172		251	200
Three coin set :	2oz 1oz 1/2oz			500/ 84		1,417	192
2005 : THE LUNAR ROOSTER - SILVER PROOF							
2005	2	2 oz	50.3	1,000/ 262	Standard reverse	134.5	110
2005	1	1 oz	40.6	2,500/ 1,441	Coin with pin	71	80
2005	.50¢	1/2 oz	32.1	5,000/ 607	Standard reverse	52	30
ROOSTER : THREE COIN CASED PROOF SILVER SET							
2005	2 oz 1 oz 1/2oz				1,000/ 293	257	200

SILVER ISSUES : MULTIPLE DATES

LUNAR PROOF FINISH

SERIES ONE - 1999 TO 2010

Date	Face Value	Weight in oz's	Size mm	Mintage Max/ Actual	Reverse Feature	Issue Price	Average Retail
2006 : YEAR OF THE DOG - SILVER PROOF							
2006	30	1 kg	101.1	100/ All sold	Standard reverse	n/a	n/a
2006	2	2 oz	50.3	1,000/ 688	Standard reverse	134.5	110
2006	1	1 oz	40.6	2,500/ All sold	Standard reverse	71	80
2006	.50¢	1/2 oz	32.1	5,000/ 1,281	Standard reverse	52	30
DOG : THREE COIN CASED PROOF SILVER SET							
2006	2 oz, 1 oz, 1/2 oz			1000/ 387		257	200
2007 : YEAR OF THE PIG - SILVER PROOF							
2007	30	1 kg	101.1	100/ 100	Standard reverse	n/a	n/a
2007	2	2 oz	50.3	1,000/ 369	Standard reverse	148	110
2007	1	1 oz	40.6	2,500/ All sold	Standard reverse	75	80
2007	.50¢	1/2 oz	32.1	5,000/ 1,006	Standard reverse	55	30
PIG : THREE COIN CASED PROOF SILVER SET							
2007	2 oz, 1 oz, 1/2 oz			1,000 / 333		278	200
2008 : YEAR OF THE MOUSE - SILVER PROOF							
2008	2	2 oz	50.3	1,000/ 136	Standard reverse	165	110
2008	1	1 oz	40.6	2,500/ 324	Standard reverse	82.5	90
2008	.50¢	1/2 oz	32.1	5,000/ 202	Standard reverse	69.5	30
MOUSE : THREE COIN CASED PROOF SILVER SET							
2008	2 oz, 1 oz, 1/2 oz			1,000/ 75		329.5	200
2009 : YEAR OF THE OX - SILVER PROOF							
2009	2	2 oz	50.3	1,000 / 171	Standard reverse	165	110
2009	1	1 oz	40.6	2,500 / 534	Standard reverse	82.5	90
2009	.50¢	1/2 oz	32.1	5,000 / 474	Standard reverse	69.5	30
OX : THREE COIN CASED PROOF SILVER SET							
2009	2 oz, 1 oz, 1/2 oz			1,000/ 87		329.5	200
2010 : YEAR OF THE TIGER - SILVER PROOF							
2010	2	2 oz	50.3	1,000/ 287	Standard reverse	165	170
2010	1	1 oz	40.6	2,500/ 541	Standard reverse	82.5	90
2010	.50¢	1/2 oz	32.1	5000/ 396	Standard reverse	69.5	30
TIGER : THREE COIN CASED PROOF SILVER SET							
2010	2 oz, 1 oz, 1/2 oz			1,000/ 83		329.5	200

SILVER ISSUES : MULTIPLE DATES

LUNAR SPECIMEN FINISH

SERIES ONE - 1999 TO 2010

1999 Year of the Rabbit

2000 Year of the Dragon

2001 Year of the Snake

1999 : YEAR OF THE RABBIT - SPECIMEN SILVER

1999	30	1 kg	101.1	To order/ 1,983	Standard reverse	599	1,250
1999 a	30	1 kg	101.1	5,000 / 318	Diamond eyes	785	1,500
1999 b	30	1 kg	101.1	n/a	Chinese privy	475	1,250
1999	10	10 oz	75.5	To order/ 2,486	Standard reverse	b/v	475
1999	2	2 oz	50.3	To order/ 12,869	Standard reverse	b/v	100
1999	1	1 oz	40.6	300,000/ 63,644	Standard reverse	23	60
1999 c	1	1 oz	40.6	50,000/ 15,482	Gilt reverse	75	60
1999	50¢	1/2 oz	40.6	500,000/ 16,913	Plain reverse	b/v	30

CHINESE PRIVY MARKED COINS

(b) This is the first privy mark to appear on a lunar issue. This 1999 - dated issue celebrated the 50th anniversary of the People's Republic of China on October 1, 1949 and the December 20, 1999 return of Macau to China. The double privy depicts the symbol for Macau and the flag of the People's Republic of China, both in colour on a gold insert.

2000 : YEAR OF THE DRAGON - SPECIMEN SILVER

2000	30	1 kg	101.1	To order/ 7,805	Standard reverse	460	750
2000 a	30	1 kg	101.1	5,000/ 3,404	Diamond eyes	695	1,500
2000	10	10 oz	75.5	To order/ 7,926	Standard reverse	153	475
2000	2	2 oz	50.3	To order/ 29,110	Standard reverse	32.95	110
2000	1	1 oz	40.6	300,000/ 118,697	Standard reverse	25.5	60
2000 c	1	1 oz	40.6	50,000/ 22,407	Gilt reverse	75	60
2000	50¢	1/2 oz	31.9	500,000/ 52,956	Plain reverse	19.95	36

2001 : YEAR OF THE SNAKE - SPECIMEN SILVER

2001	30	1 kg	101.1	To order/ 3013	Standard reverse	795	1,250
2001 a	30	1 kg	101.1	5000/ 349	Diamond eyes	b/v	1,500
2001	10	10 oz	75.5	To order/ 3962	Standard reverse	b/v	475
2001	2	2 oz	50.3	To order/ 14,062	Standard reverse	b/v	110
2001	1	1 oz	40.6	300,000/ 71,301	Standard reverse	b/v	60
2001 c	1	1 oz	40.6	50,000/ 66,335	Gilt reverse	75	60
2001	50¢	1/2 oz	32.1	500,000/ 30,904	Standard reverse	b/v	30

2001 : AUSTRALIA'S 21st CENTURY SILVER COIN SET

2001	Four silver 1oz proof coins	5000/ n/a	225	200

[a] The diamond eyed and coloured 1 kilo coins dated 1999 to 2004 are restrikes, having been produced in 2005 to be part of a continuing boxed series. .

[c] Quoted mintage figures for this gilt issue can be confusing with both 50,000 and 10,000 pieces being given as the official mintages. A total of 50,000 were struck for world-wide distribution including 10,000 put aside for the Australian market.

SILVER ISSUES : MULTIPLE DATES

LUNAR SPECIMEN FINISH

SERIES ONE - 1999 TO 2010

2002 Gilt Horse

2003 Gilt Reverse

2004 Coloured Monkey

Date	Face Value	Weight in oz's	Size mm	Mintage Max/ Actual	Reverse Feature	Issue Price	Average Retail
2002 : YEAR OF THE HORSE - SPECIMEN SILVER							
2002	30	1 kg	101.1	To order/ 4,338	Standard reverse	460	1,250
2002	30	1 kg	101.1	5,000/ 883	Diamond eyes	785	1,500
2002	10	10 oz	75.5	To order/ ,537	Standard reverse	b/v	475
2002	2	2 oz	50.3	To order/ 19,359	Standard reverse	b/v	110
2002	1	1 oz	40.6	300,000/ 99,632	Standard reverse	b/v	1,250
2002	1	1 oz	40.6	150,000/ 16,859	Gilt reverse	75	60
2003 : YEAR OF THE GOAT - SPECIMEN SILVER							
2003	30	1 kg	101.1	To order/ 6,931	Standard reverse	785	1,250
2003	30	1 kg	101.1	5000/ 492	Diamond eyes	785	1,250
2003	10	10 oz	75.5	To order/ 6,974	Standard reverse	b/v	475
2003	2	2 oz	50.3	To order/ 20,466	Standard reverse	b/v	110
2003	1	1 oz	40.6	300,000/ 102,164	Standard reverse	b/v	60
2004 : YEAR OF THE MONKEY - SPECIMEN SILVER							
2004	30	1 kg	101.1	No limit/ 5,095	Standard reverse	599	1,250
2004	30	1 kg	101.1	5,000/ 466	Diamond eyes	855	1,250
2004	30	1 kg	101.1	6,800/ 1,927	Colour reverse	855	1,250
2004	30	1 kg	101.1	1,000/ n/a	Gilt reverse	855	1,250
2004	15	1/2 kg	101.1	No limit/ 1287	Standard reverse	b/v	625
2004	15	1/2 kg	101.1	3,800/ n/a	Colour reverse	399	625
2004	10	10 oz	75.5	To order/ 3,735	Standard reverse	b/v	475
2004	10	10 oz	75.5	5,000/ 2,329	Colour reverse	n/a	475
2004	8	5 oz	60.3	No limit/ 3,592	Standard reverse	b/v	225
2004	8	5 oz	60.3	8,800/ 4,670	Colour reverse	n/a	225
2004	8	5 oz	60.3	6,000/ n/a	Gilt reverse	199	225
2004	2	2 oz	50.3	No limit/ 18,124	Standard reverse	b/v	110
2004	2	2 oz	50.3	28,000/ 6,399	Colour reverse	n/a	110
2004	1	1 oz	40.6	300,000/ 105,680	Standard reverse	b/v	60
2004	1	1 oz	40.6	38,000/31,406	Colour reverse	n/a	60
2004 a	1	1 oz	40.6	1,500/ n/a	Colour ANDA Melb	65	60
2004 a	1	1 oz	40.6	1,500/ n/a	Colour ANDA Syd	65	60
2004	1	1 oz	40.6	50,000/ 25,599	Gilt reverse	75	60
2004	.50¢	1/2 oz	31.9	500,000/ 52,792	Colour reverse	b/v	30
2004	.50¢	1/2 oz	31.9	38,000/ 26,192	Gilt reverse	n/a	30
2004 : MONKEY 1 oz FOUR COIN LUNAR SILVER TYPESET							
2004	Proof; Specimen; Gilded; Coloured				800 / 509	199	225

[a] This was the first ever coloured lunar coin released by the Perth Mint.

LUNAR SPECIMEN FINISH

SERIES ONE - 1999 TO 2010

2005 Coloured Rooster

2005 Silver Gilt Dog

2016 Silver Gilt Dog

2016 Silver Colour Dog

Date	Face Value	Weight in oz's	Size mm	Mintage Max/ Actual	Reverse Feature	Issue Price	Average Retail
2005 : YEAR OF THE ROOSTER - SPECIMEN SILVER							
2005	30	1 kg	101.1	To order/ 4,338	Standard reverse	460	1,250
2005	30	1 kg	101.1	To order/ 3,818	Standard reverse	460	1250
2005	30	1 kg	101.1	5,000 / 588	Diamond eyes	785	b/v
2005	30	1 kg	101.1	6,800/ 2124	Colour reverse	n/a	b/v
2005	15	1/2 kg	101.1	To order / 1307	Standard reverse	b/v	625
2005	15	1/2 kg	101.1	3,800/ All sold	Standard reversee	n/a	625
2005	10	10 oz	75.5	To order/ 2775	Standard reverse	b/v	295
2005	10	10 oz	75.5	5,000/ 1,280	Colour reverse	n/a	475
2005	8	5 oz	60.3	To order/ 5,585	Standard reverse	b/v	225
2005	8	5 oz	60.3	8,800/ All sold	Standard reverse	n/a	165
2005	8	5 oz	60.3	10,000/ 4665	Gilt reverse	n/a	165
2005	8	5 oz	60.3	To order/ 16,292	Standard reverse	n/a	165
2005	2	2 oz	50.3	28,000/ 6868	Colour reverse	n/a	110
2005	2	2 oz	50.3	1,000/ Sold out	Colour. ANDA Syd	125	125
2005	2	2 oz	50.3	1,000/ Sold out	Colour. ANDA Bris	125	125
2005	1	1 oz	40.6	300,000/ 92,691	Standard reverse	b/v	60
2005	1	1 oz	40.6	38,000/ All sold	Colour reverse	49.5	60
2005	1	1 oz	40.6	15,000/ 8832	Gilt & Colour	n/a	60
2005	1	1 oz	40.6	50,000/ 28,960	Gilt reverse in case	57	60
2005	1	1 oz	40.6	Inc in above	Gilt rev. in Shipper	52	56
2005	.50¢	1/2 oz	31.9	500,000/ 37,994	Standard reverse	b/v	30
2005	.50¢	1/2 oz	31.9	38,000/ All sold	Colour reverse	n/a	30
2005	.50¢	1/2 oz	31.9	1,000/ All sold	Colour. ANDA. Syd	n/a	30
2005	.50¢	1/2 oz	31.9	1,000/ All sold	Colour. ANDA. Melb	n/a	30
2005	.50¢	1/2 oz	31.9	100,000/ 35,537	Al/Br money packet	n/a	30
2006 : YEAR OF THE DOG - SILVER SPECIMEN							
2006	300	10 kg	221.1	1,000/ 78	Standard reverse	7,500	b/v
2006	30	1 kg	101.1	To order/ 4,145	Standard reverse	460	1,250
2006	30	1 kg	101.1	7,000 / 2,004	Colour reverse	785	1,250
2006	30	1 kg	101.1	5,000/ 504	Diamond eyes	899	1,250
2006	15	1/2 kg	101.1	To order/ 785	Standard reverse	b/v	625
2006	15	1/2 kg	101.1	7,000/ 3,406	Colour reverse	n/a	625
2006	10	10 oz	75.5	To order/ 2,813	Standard reverse	b/v	475
2006	10	10 oz	75.5	5,000/ 1,014	Colour reverse	n/a	475
2006	8	5 oz	60.3	To order/ 5,080	Standard reverse	b/v	225
2006	8	5 oz	60.3	20,000/ All sold	Colour reverse	b/v	225
2006	2	2 oz	50.3	To order/ 17,106	Standard reverse	b/v	110
2006	2	2 oz	50.3	40,000/ 3,240	Colour reverse	n/a	110
2006 a	2	2 oz	50.3	750/ All sold	ANDA Colour	75	95
2006	1	1 oz	40.6	300,000/ 98,825	Standard reverse	b/v	60
2006	1	1 oz	40.6	70,000/ 58,373	Colour reverse	55	60
2006	1	1 oz	40.6	50,000/ 30,156	Gilt reverse	n/a	60
2006	.50¢	1/2 oz	31.9	500,000/ 39,361	Standard reverse	b/v	30
2006	.50¢	1/2 oz	31.9	70,000/ 29,158	Colour reverse	n/a	30

[a] Released at the Canberra ANDA Coin, Note & Stamp Show

SILVER ISSUES : MULTIPLE DATES

LUNAR SPECIMEN FINISH

SERIES ONE - 1999 TO 2010

2007 Pig Colour

2008 Mouse Colour

2009 Gilt Ox

2010 Tiger Colour

Date	Face Value	Weight in oz's	Size mm	Mintage Max/ Actual	Reverse Feature	Issue Price	Average Retail
2007 : YEAR OF THE PIG - SILVER SPECIMEN							
2007	300	10 kg	221.1	1,000/ 105	Standard reverse	9,000	n/a
2007	30	1 kg	101.1	To order/ 4838	Standard reverse	460	1,250
2007	30	1 kg	101.1	7000/ 1695	Colour reverse	785	1,250
2007	30	1 kg	101.1	5000/ 525	Diamond eye	1,050	n/a
2007	15	1/2 kg	101.1	To order/ 962	Standard reverse	b/v	625
2007	15	1/2 kg	101.1	7000/ 2524	Colour reverse	n/a	625
2007	15	1/2 kg	101.1	To order/ 3061	Standard reverse	b/v	625
2007	10	10 oz	75.5	5000/ 1064	Colour reverse	n/a	475
2007	8	5 oz	60.3	To order/ 3,229	Standard reverse	b/v	225
2007	8	5 oz	60.3	20,000/ 13,201	Colour reverse	274	225
2007	8	5 oz	60.3	To order/ 14,180	Standard reverse	b/v	225
2007	2	2 oz	50.3	40,000/ 2,144	Colour reverse	n/a	110
2007	1	1 oz	40.6	300,000/ 87,009	Standard reverse	b/v	60
2007	1	1 oz	40.6	70,000/ All sold	Colour reverse	62	60
2007	1	1 oz	40.6	50,000/ 29,251	Gilt reverse	62	62
2007	.50¢	1/2 oz	31.9	500,000/ 32,495	Standard reverse	b/v	30
2007	.50¢	1/2 oz	31.9	70,000/ 63,224	Colour reverse	n/a	30
2008 : YEAR OF THE MOUSE - SILVER SPECIMEN							
2008	300	10 kg	221.1	1,000/ 78	Standard reverse	7,500	b/v
2008	30	1 kg	101.1	5,000/ 525	Diamond eye	1,150	1,250
2008	30	1 kg	101.1	To order/ 3,344	Standard reverse	460	1,250
2008	2	2 oz	50.3	To order/ 7,221	Standard reverse	b/v	110
2008	1	1 oz	45.6	To order/ 59,623	Standard reverse	b/v	60
2008	1	1 oz	45.6	50,000/ 13,538	Gilt reverse	n/a	60
2009 : YEAR OF THE OX - SILVER SPECIMEN							
2009	30	1 kg	101.1	5,000/ 288	Diamond eye	1,495	1,250
2009	2	2 oz	50.3	To order/ 6465	Standard reverse	b/v	110
2009	1	1 oz	40.6	To order/ 52,267	Standard reverse	b/v	60
2009	1	1 oz	40.6	50,000/ 18,470	Gilt reverse	n/a	60
2010 : YEAR OF THE TIGER - SILVER SPECIMEN							
2010	30	1 kg	101.1	To order/1,877	Standard reverse	460	1,250
2010	30	1 kg	101.1	5,000/ 1888	Diamond eyes	1,595	1,250
2010	30	1 kg	101.1	5,000/ 3785	Standard reverse	1,250	1,250
2010	2	2 oz	50.3	To order/ 6520	Standard reverse	b/v	110
2010	1	1 oz	40.6	To order/ 56,077	Standard reverse	b/v	60
2010	1	1 oz	40.6	50,000/ 17,218	Gilt reverse	n/a	60

SILVER ISSUES : MULTIPLE DATES

LUNAR PROOF FINISH

SERIES TWO - 2008 TO PRESENT

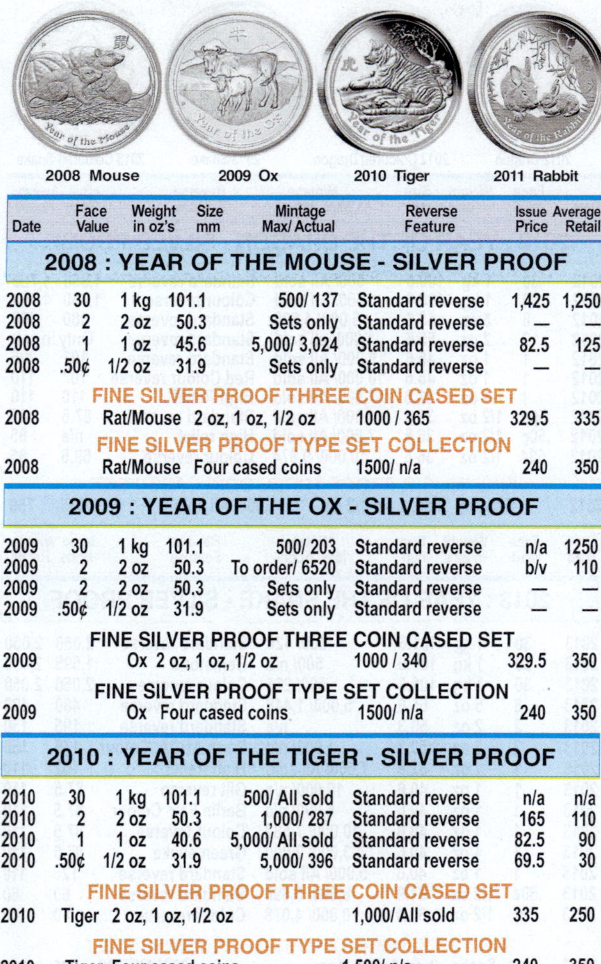

2008 Mouse 2009 Ox 2010 Tiger 2011 Rabbit

Date	Face Value	Weight in oz's	Size mm	Mintage Max/ Actual	Reverse Feature	Issue Price	Average Retail
2008 : YEAR OF THE MOUSE - SILVER PROOF							
2008	30	1 kg	101.1	500/ 137	Standard reverse	1,425	1,250
2008	2	2 oz	50.3	Sets only	Standard reverse	—	—
2008	1	1 oz	45.6	5,000/ 3,024	Standard reverse	82.5	125
2008	.50¢	1/2 oz	31.9	Sets only	Standard reverse	—	—
FINE SILVER PROOF THREE COIN CASED SET							
2008		Rat/Mouse	2 oz, 1 oz, 1/2 oz	1000 / 365		329.5	335
FINE SILVER PROOF TYPE SET COLLECTION							
2008		Rat/Mouse	Four cased coins	1500/ n/a		240	350
2009 : YEAR OF THE OX - SILVER PROOF							
2009	30	1 kg	101.1	500/ 203	Standard reverse	n/a	1250
2009	2	2 oz	50.3	To order/ 6520	Standard reverse	b/v	110
2009	2	2 oz	50.3	Sets only	Standard reverse	—	—
2009	.50¢	1/2 oz	31.9	Sets only	Standard reverse	—	—
FINE SILVER PROOF THREE COIN CASED SET							
2009		Ox	2 oz, 1 oz, 1/2 oz	1000 / 340		329.5	350
FINE SILVER PROOF TYPE SET COLLECTION							
2009		Ox	Four cased coins	1500/ n/a		240	350
2010 : YEAR OF THE TIGER - SILVER PROOF							
2010	30	1 kg	101.1	500/ All sold	Standard reverse	n/a	n/a
2010	2	2 oz	50.3	1,000/ 287	Standard reverse	165	110
2010	1	1 oz	40.6	5,000/ All sold	Standard reverse	82.5	90
2010	.50¢	1/2 oz	31.9	5,000/ 396	Standard reverse	69.5	30
FINE SILVER PROOF THREE COIN CASED SET							
2010		Tiger	2 oz, 1 oz, 1/2 oz	1,000/ All sold		335	250
FINE SILVER PROOF TYPE SET COLLECTION							
2010		Tiger	Four cased coins	1,500/ n/a		240	350
2011 : YEAR OF THE RABBIT - SILVER PROOF							
2011	30	1 kg	101.1	500/ All sold	Standard reverse	1,890	1,250
2011	2	2 oz	50.3	Sets Only	Standard reverse	—	—
2011	1	1 oz	45.6	5,000/ All sold	Standard reverse	105	150
2011	.50¢	1/2 oz	31.9	3,000/ All sold	Standard reverse	n/a	n/a
FINE SILVER PROOF THREE COIN CASED SET							
2011		Set consists of :	2 oz, 1 oz, 1/2 oz	1,000/ All sold		380	420
FINE SILVER PROOF TYPE SET COLLECTION							
2011		Rabbit	Four cased coins	1,500/ 1,500		240	350

SILVER ISSUES : MULTIPLE DATES

LUNAR PROOF FINISH

SERIES TWO - 2008 TO PRESENT

2012 Dragon

2012 Coloured Dragon

2013 Snake

2013 Coloured Snake

2012 : YEAR OF THE DRAGON - SILVER PROOF

Date	Face Value	Weight in oz's	Size mm	Mintage Max/ Actual	Reverse Feature	Issue Price	Average Retail
2012	30	1 kg	100.6	500/ All sold	Standard reverse	1,950	1,750
2012	30	1 kg	100.6	500/ All sold	Colour reverse	1,750	1,750
2012	8	5 oz	65.6	5,000/ 4,526	Standard reverse	480	480
2012	2	2 oz	55.6	1,000/ all sold	Standard reverse	Only in sets	
2012	1	1 oz	45.6	5,000/ All sold	Standard reverse	107	295
2012	1	1 oz	45.6	10,000/ All sold	Red Colour reverse	107	110
2012	1	1 oz	32.6	7,500/ All sold	High Relief	110	110
2012	.50¢	1/2 oz	36.6	4,000/ All sold	Standard reverse	67.5	85
2012	.50¢	1/2 oz	36.6	7,500/ All sold	High relief	n/a	85
2012	.50¢	1/2 oz	36.6	10,000/ 9,874	Colour reverse	69.5	85

FINE SILVER PROOF THREE COIN CASED SET

Date	Description	Mintage	Issue Price	Average Retail
2012	Dragon 2 oz, 1 oz, 1/2 oz	1,000/ All sold	335	750

2013 : YEAR OF THE SNAKE - SILVER PROOF

Date	Face Value	Weight in oz's	Size mm	Mintage Max/ Actual	Reverse Feature	Issue Price	Average Retail
2013	30	1 kg	101.6	500/ 426	Standard reverse	2,050	2,050
2013	30	1 kg	101.6	500/ n/a	Gemstone	1,595	2,050
2013	30	1 kg	101.6	500/ 265	Colour reverse	2,050	2,050
2013	8	5 oz	65.6	5,000/ 1,448	Standard reverse	480	480
2013	2	2 oz	50.3	n/a	Standard reverse	195	150
2013	2	2 oz	50.3	1,000/ n/a	Perth ANDA. Colour	175	150
2013	1	1 oz	32.6	7,500/ All sold	High Relief	102	110
2013	1	1 oz	40.6	10,000/ n/a	Gilt reverse	87.5	110
2013	1	1 oz	40.6	5,000/ n/a	Berlin Fair. Colour	87.5	110
2013	1	1 oz	40.6	10,000/ 7,582	Colour reverse	87.5	110
2013	1	1 oz	40.6	3,000/ 2,000	Green snake	87.5	110
2013	1	1 oz	40.6	5,000/ All sold	Standard reverse	125	110
2013	.50¢	1/2 oz	31.9	8,000/ 5,890	Standard reverse	60	60
2013	.50¢	1/2 oz	31.9	10,000/ 4,078	Colour reverse	60	60

FINE SILVER PROOF THREE COIN CASED SET

Date	Description	Mintage	Issue Price	Average Retail
2013	Snake 2 oz, 1 oz, 1/2 oz	1000/ All sold	335	250

TWELVE COIN CASED SILVER PROOF SET

Date	Description	Mintage	Issue Price	Average Retail
2013	One of each 2 oz coins. 2008 to 2013 inclusive	1000/ All sold	n/a	n/a

FINE SILVER PROOF THREE COIN CASED SET

Date	Design	Coins	Mintage	Issue Price	Average Retail
2012	Dragon	2 oz, 1 oz, 1/2 oz	1,000/ All sold	379	895
2013	Snake	2 oz, 1 oz, 1/2 oz	1,000/ tba	385	380
2014	Horse	2 oz, 1 oz, 1/2 oz	1,000/ tba	340	340

FINE SILVER ONE OUNCE TYPE SET

Date	Design	Coins	Mintage	Issue Price	Average Retail
2012	Dragon	Proof, colour, gilt, specimen	1,500/ tba	395	695
2013	Snake	Proof, colour, gilt, specimen	1,500/ tba	365	360
2014	Horse	Proof, colour, gilt, specimen	1,500/ tba	350	350

SILVER ISSUES : MULTIPLE DATES

LUNAR PROOF FINISH

SERIES TWO - 2008 TO PRESENT

2014 Coloured Horse

2014 Horse. Specimen

2015 Coloured Goat

2015 High Relief Goat

Date	Face Value	Weight in oz's	Size mm	Mintage Max/ Actual	Reverse Feature	Issue Price	Average Retail
2014 : YEAR OF THE HORSE - SILVER PROOF							
2014	30	1 kg	100.6	500/ All sold	Standard reverse	1,750	1,750
2014	30	1 kg	100.6	500/ All sold	Coloured reverse	1750	1750
2014	8	5 oz	65.6	5,000/ 869	Standard reverse	480	480
2014 a	2	2 oz	56.6	1,000/ n/a	Perth ANDA Fair	179	150
2014	2	2 oz	56.6	2,000/ 963	Standard reverse	179	150
2014	1	1 oz	45.6	5,000/ All sold	Standard reverse	99	99
2014	1	1 oz	32.6	7,500/ 7,461	High Relief reverse	102	105
2014	1	1 oz	45.6	10,000/ 7,582	Colour reverse	99	99
2014	.50¢	1/2 oz	36.6	8,000/ 4,790	Standard reverse	63.5	60
2014	.50¢	1/2 oz	36.6	10,000/ 4,078	Colour reverse	63.5	60
FINE SILVER ONE OUNCE THREE COIN CASED SET							
2014	2oz, 1oz, 1/2 oz			1,000/ All sold		340	340
FINE SILVER ONE OUNCE FOUR COIN CASED SET							
2014	Proof, Specimen, Colour & Gilt 1oz			1,500/ All sold		n/a	n/a

[a] This two ounce coloured coin was issued at the Perth ANDA coin fair held at the Belmont Racecourse complex on March 1 & 2, 2014.

Date	Face Value	Weight in oz's	Size mm	Mintage Max/ Actual	Reverse Feature	Issue Price	Average Retail
2015 : YEAR OF THE GOAT - SILVER PROOF							
2015	30	1 kg	100.6	500/ 410	Standard reverse	1,750	1,750
2015	30	1 kg	100.6	500/ 300	Colour reverse	1,750	1,750
2015	8	5 oz	65.6	5,000/ 637	Standard reverse	450	480
2015	2	2 oz	55.6	2,000/ 1,508	Standard reverse	179	150
2015 a	2	2 oz	55.6	1,000/ 833	Colour. Perth ANDA	179	150
2015	1	1 oz	45.6	8,500/ 7,891	Standard reverse	99	99
2015	1	1 oz	32.6	7,500/ 5,602	High Relief	102	102
2015	1	1 oz	45.6	10,000/ 6,838	Colour reverse	99	100
2015	.50¢	1/2 oz	36.6	9,000/ 6,950	Standard reverse	63.5	60
2015	.50¢	1/2 oz	36.6	10,000/ 4,410	Colour reverse	63.5	60
FINE SILVER ONE OUNCE THREE COIN CASED SET							
2015	Goat	2oz, 1oz, 1/2 oz		tba/ 1,984		340	350
FINE SILVER HALF OUNCE TWO BEIJING COIN FAIR SET							
2015	Goat			1,500/ 1,196		340	340
FINE SILVER ONE OUNCE FOUR COIN CASED SET							
2015	Proof, Specimen, Colour & Gilt 1oz			1,500/ 1,196		tba	tba
2015	Silmilar to above but for Japanese market			1,000/ 475		tba	tba

[a] This two ounce specimen coloured coin was released at the ANDA Perth coin fair held on March 7 - 8, 2015. Both goats on the reverse design were coloured.

SILVER ISSUES : MULTIPLE DATES

LUNAR PROOF FINISH

SERIES TWO - 2008 TO PRESENT

2016 Coloured Monkey

2016 Monkey. Proof Rev

2017 Coloured Rooster

2017 High Relief Rooster

Date	Face Value	Weight in oz's	Size mm	Mintage Max/ Actual	Reverse Feature	Issue Price	Average Retail
2016 : YEAR OF THE MONKEY - SILVER PROOF							
2016	30	1 kg	100.6	500/ 249	Standard reverse	1,750	1,795
2016	30	1 kg	100.6	500/ 150	Coloured reverse	1,795	1,750
2016	8	5 oz	65.6	5,000/ n/a	Standard reverse	450	480
2016	2	2 oz	55.6	2,000/ 843	Standard reverse	179	150
2016 a	2	2 oz	55.6	1,000/ n/a	Colour. Perth ANDA	175	175
2016	1	1 oz	45.6	8,500/ 4,154	Standard reverse	99	99
2016	1	1 oz	32.6	7,500/ 3,025	High Relief	102	102
2016	1	1 oz	45.6	10,000/ 4,738	Colour reverse	99	100
2016	.50¢	1/2 oz	36.6	9,000/ 1,765	Standard reverse	63.5	60
2016	.50¢	1/2 oz	36.6	10,000/ 2,600	Colour reverse	63.5	60
FINE SILVER ONE OUNCE THREE COIN CASED SET							
2016	2oz, 1oz, 1/2 oz			1,000/ All sold		350	350
FINE SILVER HALF OUNCE TWO BEIJING COIN FAIR SET							
2016	Monkey	Two silver cased set		1,500/ tba		340	340
FINE SILVER ONE OUNCE FOUR COIN CASED TYPE SET							
2016	Proof, Specimen, Colour & Gilt 1oz			1,500/ tba		tba	tba

Date	Face Value	Weight in oz's	Size mm	Mintage Max/ Actual	Reverse Feature	Issue Price	Average Retail
2017 : YEAR OF THE ROOSTER - SILVER PROOF							
2017	30	1 kg	100.6	500/ n/a	Standard reverse	1,750	1,750
2017	30	1 kg	100.6	500/ n/a	Colour reverse	1,795	1,750
2017	8	5 oz	65.6	5,000/ n/a	Standard reverse	450	480
2017	2	2 oz	55.6	2,000/ n/a	Standard reverse	179	150
2017 b	2	2 oz	55.6	1,000/ n/a	Colour. Perth ANDA	179	150
2017	1	1 oz	45.6	8,500/ n/a	Standard reverse	99	99
2017	1	1 oz	32.6	7,500/ n/a	High Relief	109	109
2017	1	1 oz	45.6	10,000/ n/a	Colour reverse	99	100
2017	.50¢	1/2 oz	36.6	9,000/ n/a	Standard reverse	63.5	60
2017	.50¢	1/2 oz	36.6	10,000/ n/a	Colour reverse	63.5	60
2017 c	.25¢	1/4 oz	25.5	To order/ 2,500	Colour. Melb. ANDA	29	30
FINE SILVER ONE OUNCE THREE COIN CASED SET							
2017	Rooster 2oz, 1oz, 1/oz			1,500/ All sold		350	350
FINE SILVER HALF OUNCE TWO BEIJING COIN FAIR SET							
2017	Rooster	Two silver cased set		1,500/ tba		340	340
FINE SILVER ONE OUNCE FOUR COIN CASED SET							
2017	Rooster	Proof, Specimen, Colour & Gilt 1oz		1500/ tba		359	tba

[a] This coloured 2oz silver proof coin was released at the ANDA/ APTA fair held at the Domain Stadium, Subiaco, Perth from March 12-13th, 2016
[b] This two ounce proof coloured coin was released at the ANDA Money Expo held at the Domain Stadium, Subiaco, on February 11-12th, 2017.
[c] This coloured 1/4oz proof coin was offered at the Melbourne Stamp & Coin fair held from March 30 to April 2, 2017.

SILVER ISSUES : MULTIPLE DATES

LUNAR SPECIMEN FINISH

SERIES TWO - 2008 TO PRESENT

2008 Coloured Mouse   2008 Gilt Mouse   2009 Coloured Ox   2009 Gilt Ox

Date	Face Value	Weight in oz's	Size mm	Mintage Max/ Actual	Reverse Feature	Issue Price	Average Retail
2008 : YEAR OF THE MOUSE - SPECIMEN SILVER							
2008	300	10 kg	221.1	1,000/ 35	Standard reverse	b/v	15,000
2008	30	1 kg	101.6	To order/ 9,129	Standard reverse	b/v	1,250
2008	30	1 kg	101.6	5,000/	Sapphire eyes	1,250	1,500
2008	30	1 kg	101.6	7,000/ 1,169	Colour reverse	b/v	1,250
2008	15	1/2 kg	101.1	To order/ 739	Standard reverse	625.5	700
2008	15	1/2 kg	101.1	7,000/ 1,259	Colour reverse	625.5	700
2008	10	10 oz	75.5	To order/ 3,718	Standard reverse	b/v	475
2008	10	10 oz	75.5	5,000/ 2,927	Colour reverse	n/a	475
2008	8	5 oz	60.3	To order/ 3,005	Standard reverse	225.5	250
2008	8	5 oz	60.3	20,000/ 7,858	Colour reverse	225.5	250
2008	2	2 oz	50.3	To order/ 9,126	Standard reverse	b/v	110
2008	2	2 oz	50.3	40,000/ 3,913	Colour reverse	n/a	110
2008	1	1 oz	40.6	300,000/ All sold	Standard reverse	b/v	60
2008	1	1 oz	40.6	170,000/ 69,450	Colour reverse	62	60
2008	1	1 oz	40.6	50,000/ 5,394	Gilt / Case	76.5	50
2008	1	1 oz	40.6	Inc above	Gilt / Shipper	72.5	60
2008	.50¢	1/2 oz	31.9	To order/ 17,114	Standard reverse	b/v	30
2008	.50¢	1/2 oz	31.9	170,000/ 57,073	Colour reverse	30	30
FINE SILVER ONE OUNCE FOUR COIN CASED SET							
2008	Proof, Specimen, Colour & Gilt 1oz			1,500/ 857		239.5	350
2009 : YEAR OF THE OX - SPECIMEN SILVER							
2009	300	10 kg	221.1	1000/ 46	Standard reverse	9,000	15,000
2009	30	1 kg	101.6	No limit/ 16,163	Standard reverse	b/v	1,250
2009	30	1 kg	101.6	5,000/ 346	Citrine eyes	1,495	1,500
2009	30	1 kg	101.6	7,000/ 1112	Colour reverse	n/a	1250
2009	15	1/2 oz	101.1	No limit/ 1535	Standard reverse	b/v	625
2009	10	10 oz	75.5	No limit/ 9,020	Standard reverse	b/v	475
2009	10	10 oz	75.5	5,000/ 1,051	Colour reverse	n/a	475
2009	8	5 oz	60.3	No limit/ 4,720	Standard reverse	b/v	225
2009	8	5 oz	60.3	20,000/ 5,973	Colour reverse	n/a	225
2009	2	2 oz	50.3	No limit/ 18,570	Standard reverse	b/v	110
2009	2	2 oz	50.3	40,000/ 3,997	Colour reverse	n/a	110
2009	1	1 oz	40.6	300,000/ All sold	Standard reverse	b/v	60
2009	1	1 oz	40.6	170,000/ 55,189	Colour reverse	69.5	60
2009	1	1 oz	40.6	50,000/ 18,167	Gilt/ Case	76.5	60
2009	1	1 oz	40.6	Inc above	Gilt/ Shipper	72.5	60
2009	.50¢	1/2 oz	31.9	No limit/ 17,674	Standard reverse	b/v	30
2009	.50¢	1/2 oz	31.9	170,000/ 47,018	Colour reverse	n/a	30
FINE SILVER ONE OUNCE FOUR COIN CASED SET							
2009	Proof, Specimen, Colour & Gilt 1oz			1,500/ 1,137		265	330

LUNAR SPECIMEN FINISH

SERIES TWO - 2008 TO PRESENT

2010 Coloured Tiger

2010 Silver specimen

2010 Silver gilt

Date	Face Value	Weight in oz's	Size mm	Mintage Max/ Actual	Reverse Feature	Issue Price	Average Retail
2010 : YEAR OF TIGER - SPECIMEN SILVER							
2010	300	10 kg	221.1	500/ 173	Standard reverse	10,000	b/v
2010	30	1 kg	101.6	To order/ 34,104	Standard reverse	n/a	1,250
2010	30	1 kg	101.6	5,000/ 856	Topaz eyes	1,595	1,450
2010	30	1 kg	101.6	7,000/ 1,112	Colour reverse	1,750	1,250
2010	15	1/2 oz	101.1	To order/ 5,058	Standard reverse	b/v	650
2010	10	10 oz	75.5	To order/ 16,727	Standard reverse	480	475
2010	10	10 oz	75.5	5,000/ 1,029	Colour reverse	n/a	475
2010	8	5 oz	60.3	To order/ 14,553	Standard reverse	225	225
2010	8	5 oz	60.3	20,000/ 6,287	Colour reverse	n/a	225
2010	2	2 oz	50.3	To order/ 63,005	Standard reverse	107	110
2010	2	2 oz	50.3	40,000/ 5,033	Colour reverse	n/a	110
2010	2	2 oz	50.3	1,000/ All sold	Perth ANDA Fair	375	110
2010	1	1 oz	40.6	300,000/ All sold	Bullion issue	60	75
2010	1	1 oz	40.6	7,500/ tba	High Relief Piedfort	160	175
2010	1	1 oz	40.6	170,000/ 57,920	Colour reverse	69	75
2010 a	1	1 oz	40.6	5,000/ tba	Colour. Berlin Fair	89	80
2010	1	1 oz	40.6	2,500/ All sold	Colour. Bris. ANDA	99	99
2010 c	1	1 oz	40.6	5,000/ tba	Colour. Melb. ANDA	99	99
2010 d	1	1 oz	40.6	5,000/ tba	Philadelphia Fair	99	99
2010 e	1	1 oz	40.6	5,000/ tba	Sydney ANDA	99	99
2010	1	1 oz	40.6	200,000/ tba	Bavarian Lion Privy	4.5	50
2010	1	1 oz	40.6	50,000/ 17,218	Gilt reverse in case	104	107
2010	1	1 oz	40.6	Inc in above	Gilt rev. in Shipper	99.5	100
2010	.50¢	1/2 oz	31.9	To order/ 50,035	Standard reverse	32	32
2010	.50¢	1/2 oz	31.9	170,000/ 62,697	Colour reverse	32	32

CASED FOUR COIN SILVER TYPE SET

Date	Description	Mintage Max/ Actual	Issue Price	Average Retail
FINE SILVER ONE OUNCE FOUR COIN CASED SET				
2010	Proof, Specimen, Colour & Gilt 1oz	1,500/ All sold	280	350

SILVER ISSUES : MULTIPLE DATES

LUNAR SPECIMEN FINISH

SERIES TWO - 2008 TO PRESENT

c2011 Coloured Rabbit

2011 Gilt Rabbit

2011 Specimen Rabbit

2011 Gem stone Rabbit

Date	Face Value	Weight in oz's	Size mm	Mintage Max/ Actual	Reverse Feature	Issue Price	Average Retail
2011 : YEAR OF RABBIT - SPECIMEN SILVER							
2011	300	10 kg	221.1	500/ 173	Standard reverse	10,000	15,000
2011	30	1 kg	101.6	To order/ 46,337	Standard reverse	1,432	1,250
2011	30	1 kg	101.6	5,000/ 428	Emerald eyes	1,595	1,450
2011	30	1 kg	101.6	7,000/ 2,118	Colour reverse	1,750	1,250
2011	15	1/2 kg	101.1	To order/ 5,058	Standard reverse	b/v	650
2011	10	10 oz	75.5	To order/ 12,563	Standard reverse	480	475
2011	10	10 oz	75.5	5,000/ 888	Colour reverse	n/a	475
2011	8	5 oz	60.3	To order/ 8,030	Standard reverse	225	225
2011	8	5 oz	60.3	20,000/ 5,028	Colour reverse	n/a	225
2011	2	2 oz	50.3	To order/ 118,738	Standard reverse	107	110
2011	2	2 oz	50.3	40,000/ 4,676	Colour reverse	n/a	110
2011	2	2 oz	50.3	1000/ All sold	Perth ANDA Fair	n/a	110
2011	1	1 oz	40.6	300,000/ All sold	Bullion issue	60	75
2011	1	1 oz	40.6	7,500/ TBA	High Relief Piedfort	160	175
2011	1	1 oz	40.6	170,000/ 44,093	Colour reverse	69	175
2011 a	1	1 oz	40.6	5,000/ TBA	Colour. Berlin Fair	89	175
2011 b	1	1 oz	40.6	5,000/ All sold	Colour. Bris.ANDA	99	99
2011 c	1	1 oz	40.6	5,000/ TBA	Colour. Melb. ANDA	99	99
2011 d	1	1 oz	40.6	5,000/ TBA	Philadelphia Fair	99	99
2011 e	1	1 oz	40.6	5,000/ TBA	Sydney ANDA	99	99
2011	1	1 oz	40.6	200,000/ TBA	Bavarian Lion Privy	n/a	n/a
2011	1	1 oz	40.6	50,000/ 8,413	Gilt reverse in case	104	107
2011	1	1 oz	40.6	Inc in above	Gilt rev. in Shipper	99.5	100
2011	.50¢	1/2 oz	31.9	To order/ 389,161	Standard reverse	32	32
2011	.50¢	1/2 oz	31.9	170,000/ 53,372	Colour reverse	32	32
FINE SILVER ONE OUNCE FOUR COIN CASED SET							
2014	Proof, Specimen, Colour & Gilt 1oz			1,500/ All sold		350	350

(a) Issued at the *World Money Fair* held in Berlin, Germany on February 8, 2012. The coin featured red and charcoal highlights on the reverse of the dragon.
(b) Issued at the ANDA Brisbane fair held from May 26 - 27, 2012. The coin featured purple highlights on the reverse of the dragon.
(c) Issued at the ANDA Melbourne fair held from July 7-8, 2012. The coin featured gold highlights on the reverse of the dragon.
(d) Released at the *American Numismatic Association* fair held in Philadelphia, USA from August 7 - 11, 2012. The coin featured light blue colouring to the reverse of the coin.
(e) Issued at the ANDA Sydney fair held at the Canterbury Racecourse from August 18-19, 2012. The coin featured royal blue highlights on the reverse.

See their advertisement on page 157

SILVER ISSUES : MULTIPLE DATES

LUNAR SPECIMEN FINISH

SERIES TWO - 2008 TO PRESENT

[a] ANDA Brisbane

[b] ANDA Melbourne

[c] ANA Philadelphia

[d] ANDA Sydney

2012 : YEAR OF DRAGON - SPECIMEN SILVER

2012	300	10 kg	221.1	500/ 234	Standard reverse	13,000	15,000
2012	30	1 kg	101.6	To order/ 54,083	Standard reverse	1,432	1,250
2012	30	1 kg	101.6	5,000/ 1,895	Ruby eyes inset	1,950	1,920
2012	30	1 kg	101.6	7,000/ 3,251	Red. Colour reverse	2,100	1,950
2012	10	10 oz	75.5	To order/ 47,390	Standard reverse	480	475
2012	10	10 oz	75.5	5,000/ 2,468	Red. Colour reverse	n/a	475
2012	8	5 oz	60.3	To order/ 31,664	Standard reverse	225	225
2012	8	5 oz	60.3	20,000/ 10,762	Red. Colour reverse	n/a	225
2012	2	2 oz	55.6	To order/ 118,738	Standard reverse	107	110
2012	2	2 oz	55.6	39,000/ 8,391	Red. Colour reverse	n/a	110
2012 a	2	2 oz	55.6	1000/ All sold	Red. Perth ANDA	175	290
2012	1	1 oz	45.6	300,000/ All sold	Standard reverse	42	60
2012	1	1 oz	45.6	200,000/ All sold	Bavarian Lion Privy	n/a	60
2012	1	1 oz	45.6	170,000/ 7,375	Brown Snake reverse	99	99
2012	1	1 oz	45.6	170,000/ 7,365	Gold Snake reverse	99	99
2012	1	1 oz	45.6	170,000/ 7,405	Black Snake reverse	99	99
2012	1	1 oz	45.6	170,000/ 8,162	Blue Snake reverse	99	99
2012	1	1 oz	45.6	170,000/ 7,402	Purple Snake reverse	99	99
2012	1	1 oz	45.6	170,000/ 60,442	Red Snake reverse	99	99
2012	1	1 oz	45.6	170,000/ 7,377	Silver Snake reverse	99	99
2012	1	1 oz	45.6	170,000/ 9,251	White Snake reverse	99	99
2012	1	1 oz	45.6	170,000/ 8,533	Yellow Snake reverse	99	99
2012 b	1	1 oz	45.6	5,000/ 2,881	Black. Berlin Fair	99	170
2012 c	1	1 oz	45.6	5,000/ All sold	Purple. Bris. ANDA.	99	90
2012 d	1	1 oz	45.6	5,000/ 3,948	Gold. Melb. ANDA.	99	90
2012 e	1	1 oz	45.6	5,000/ All sold	Blue & White. ANA.USA	99	99
2012 f	1	1 oz	45.6	5,000/ 2,455	Yellow. Sydney ANDA	99	99
2012	1	1 oz	45.6	50,000/ All sold	Gilt reverse. In case	104	107
2012	1	1 oz	45.6	Inc in above	Gilt reverse. In Shipper	99	100
2012	.50¢	1/2 oz	31.9	To order/ 389,161	Standard reverse	32	32
2012	.50¢	1/2 oz	31.9	170,000/ 51,196	Red. Colour reverse	32	32

(a) Perth ANDA Show (Red reverse) : This was the only 2oz silver Dragon coin issued at coin fairs during the year. It was issued at the two day fair held in Perth from March, 3 & 4, 2012. The red reverse is the main colour used on other non-fair or commemorative issues.
(b) Berlin Coin Show (Black reverse): The coin depicts a black dragon with red detailing and a representation of a 'pearl of wisdom'. The colour black is regarded as highly spiritual and most fundamental of all colours. The coin is housed in a display case and shipper identifying it as The Perth Mint's official 2012 World's Money Fair Berlin Coin Show Special at the fair issued from February 3-5, 2012.
(c) Brisbane ANDA Show (Purple reverse): The coin's reverse depicts a purple dragon with a representation of a pearl. The colour purple symbolises wealth and well-being. The issue was released at the Brisbane Table Tennis Centre, Windsor, on May 26 & 27.
(d) Melbourne ANDA Show (Yellow reverse): Depicts a yellow dragon with purple highlights and a representation of a 'pearl of wisdom'. The fair took place at the Caulfield Racecourse, on July 7 & 8.
(e) Philadelphia ANA Coin Show (Silver & Blue): This was the Perth Mint's official product issued at the 2012 Philadelphia ANA World's Fair of Money Show The American Numismatic Association World's Fair of Money in Philadelphia, Pennsylvania, was held from August 7, 12, 2012.
(f) Sydney ANDA Show (Blue & Yellow): This predominately blue ANDA Coin Show Special was released at the Canterbury Racecourse, on August 18th & 19th, 2012.

SILVER ISSUES : MULTIPLE DATES

LUNAR SPECIMEN FINISH

SERIES TWO - 2008 TO PRESENT

2013 Snake colour

2013 Snake. Gilt

2014 Horse Plain

2014 Horse colour

Date	Face Value	Weight in oz's	Size mm	Mintage Max/ Actual	Reverse Feature	Issue Price	Average Retail
2013 : YEAR OF SNAKE - SPECIMEN SILVER							
2013	300	10 kg	221.1	200/ All sold	Standard reverse	14,320	15,000
2013	30	1 kg	101.1	No limit/ 30,966	Standard reverse	2,095	2,095
2013	30	1 kg	101.1	5,000/ 1,003	Black Diamond	1,595	1,595
2013	30	1 kg	101.1	7,000/ 1,082	Green Snake	1,595	1,595
2013	10	10 oz	75.5	No limit/28,213	Standard reverse	480	480
2013	10	10 oz	75.5	5,000/ 914	Green Snake	480	480
2013	8	5 oz	60.3	No limit/ 20,552	Plain reverse	255	255
2013	8	5 oz	60.3	20,000/ 3,250	Green Snake	255	255
2013	2	2 oz	50.3	To order/ 56,133	Standard reverse	107	110
2013	2	2 oz	50.3	10,000/ 3,478	Green Snake	110	175
2013	2	2 oz	50.3	No limit/ tba	Colour/ ANDA	110	175
2013	1	1 oz	40.6	300,000/ All sold	Standard reverse	50	99
2013	1	1 oz	40.6	170,000/ 36,520	Green Snake	69	175
2013	1	1 oz	40.6	5,000/ 2,340	Colour	99	99
2013 a	1	1 oz	40.6	100,000/ 56,241	Bavarian Lion Privy	n/a	89
2013 b	1	1 oz	40.6	5,000/ 2,854	Green/ Berlin	89	89
2013	1	1 oz	40.6	50,000/ 9,253	Gilt /Case	87.5	99
2013	1	1 oz	40.6	*Inc in above*	Gilt /Shipper	95	95
2013	.50¢	1/2 oz	31.9	To order/ 88,073	Standard reverse	95	95
2013	.50¢	1/2 oz	31.9	200,000/ 32,054	Green Snake	95	95
2013	.50¢	1/2 oz	31.9	10,000/ 4,078	Green Snake	95	95
2013	.50¢	1/2 oz	31.9	No limit/ 160,616	Standard reverse	67.5	32
FINE SILVER ONE OUNCE FOUR COIN CASED SET							
2013	Proof, Specimen, Colour & Gilt 1oz			1500/ TBA		395	395
2014 : YEAR OF THE HORSE - SILVER SPECIMEN							
2014	300	10 kg	221.1	200/ 194	Standard reverse	n/a	n/a
2014	30	1 kg	101.1	To order 19,678	Standard reverse	n/a	1,750
2014	30	1 kg	100.6	5000/n/a	White Diamond	1,750	1,750
2014	30	1 kg	101.1	6,500/ 448	Coloured	1,750	1,750
2014	10	10 oz	75.5	To order/ 29,983	Standard reverse	n/a	480
2014	8	5 oz	65.6	To order/ 31,232	Standard reverse	n/a	225
2014	2	2 oz	55.6	To order/ 112,801	Standard reverse	n/a	170
2014 c	2	2 oz	55.6	1,000/ n/a	Colour. ANDA	169	170
2014	1	1 oz	40.6	300,000/ All sold	Standard reverse	99	99
2014 a	1	1 oz	40.6	100,000/ 56,241	Bavarian Lion Privy	n/a	89
2014	1	1 oz	45.6	47,500/ 11,778	Gilt/ Cased	94	94
2014	1	1 oz	45.6	Inc in above	Gilt/ Certificate	89	89
2014	.50¢	1/2 oz	31.9	To order/ 249,155	Standard reverse	63.5	n/a
FINE SILVER ONE OUNCE FOUR COIN CASED SET							
2014	Proof, Specimen, Colour & Gilt 1oz			1,500/ All sold		350	350

[a] Issued with a Bavarian Lion privymark, this entire issue was struck for a German - based Perth Mint wholesaler.
[b] Released at the annual Berlin Money Show.
[c] This coloured 2 ounce coin was released at the Perth ANDA Coin and Banknote Show

SILVER ISSUES : MULTIPLE DATES

LUNAR SPECIMEN FINISH

SERIES TWO - 2008 TO PRESENT

2015 [a] Goat. High Relief

2015 [b] Goat. Colour

2016 [c] Monkey Gilt

2016 [d] Monkey Coloured

Date	Face Value	Weight in oz's	Size mm	Mintage Max/ Actual	Reverse Feature	Issue Price	Average Retail
2015 : YEAR OF THE GOAT - SILVER SPECIMEN							
2015	300	10 kg	221	150/ All sold	Standard reverse	15,000	b/v
2015	30	1 kg	100.6	5,000/ n/a	Standard reverse	1,750	1,750
2015	30	1 kg	100.6	5,000/ 820	Emerald eyes	1,799	1,750
2015	30	1 kg	100.6	7,000/ 2,916	Coloured reverse	1,799	1,750
2015	10	10 oz	85.6	To order/ 26,932	Standard reverse	n/a	n/a
2015	10	10 oz	85.6	5,000/ 1,816	Coloured reverse	n/a	n/a
2015	8	5 oz	65.6	5,000/ 16,920	Standard reverse	450	450
2015	8	5 oz	65.6	20,000/ 3,588	Coloured reverse	450	450
2015	2	2 oz	55.6	To order/ 61,843	Standard reverse	179	150
2015	2	2 oz	55.6	40,000/ 6,878	Coloured reverse	179	150
2015 a	2	2 oz	55.6	1,000/ n/a	ANDA Perth fair	179	185
2015 b	2	2 oz	55.6	1,500/ n/a	ANDA Sydney fair	179	185
2015	1	1 oz	45.6	300 k/ All sold	Standard reverse	94	94
2015	1	1 oz	45.6	170,000/ 48,563	Coloured reverse	94	94
2015	1	1 oz	32.6	7,500/ n/a	High relief plain rev	102	102
2015	1	1 oz	45.6	50,000/ 11,011	Gilt/ Cased	94	94
2015	1	1 oz	45.6	Inc in above	Gilt/ Capsule	89	89
2015	.50¢	1/2 oz	36.6	To order/ 188,442	Standard reverse	63.5	30
2015	.50¢	1/2 oz	36.6	200,000/ 14,990	Coloured reverse	63.5	30

[a] This coloured 2 ounce coin was issued at the 2015 Perth ANDA fair held at the Paterson's Stadium on March 7 & 8th. Only 1,000 coins were struck.
[b] This two ounce silver coloured coin was limited to 1500 and distributed at the ANDA Sydney Show held in the Sydney Lower Town Hall, on October 24,25 2014.

Date	Face Value	Weight in oz's	Size mm	Mintage Max/ Actual	Reverse Feature	Issue Price	Average Retail
2016 : YEAR OF THE MONKEY - SILVER SPECIMEN							
2016	300	10 kg	221	150/ Nil	Standard reverse	15,000	b/v
2016	30	1 kg	100.6	To order/ 9,755	Standard reverse	1,750	1,750
2016	30	1 kg	100.6	7,000/ 30	Standard reverse	1,750	1,750
2016 a	30	1 kg	100.6	500/ 372	Cognac diamond	1,799	1,799
2016	10	10 oz	85.6	To order/ 4,226	Standard reverse	1,750	1,750
2016	8	5 oz	65.6	20,000/ 812	Standard reverse	450	450
2016	2	2 oz	55.6	To order/ 10,414	Standard reverse	179	150
2016	2	2 oz	55.6	40,000/ 3,050	Colour reverse	179	185
2016	2	2 oz	55.6	1,000/ n/a	ANDA Perth fair	179	185
2016 b	2	2 oz	55.6	1,500/ n/a	ANDA Sydney fair	179	185
2016	1	1 oz	45.6	300,000k/ All sold	Standard reverse	94	94
2016	1	1 oz	32.6	7,500/ n/a	High relief plain rev	102	102
2016	1	1 oz	36.6	170,000/ 19,500	Colour reverse	63.5	20
2016	1	1 oz	45.6	50,000/ 6,341	Gilt highlights. Cased	94	94
2016	1	1 oz	45.6	Inc in above	Gilt/ Capsule	89	89
2016	.50¢	1/2 oz	36.6	To order/ 127,688	Standard reverse	63.5	20
2016	.50¢	1/2 oz	36.6	200,000/ 10,070	Colour reverse	63.5	20

[a] The mintage figure for this issue was reduced from 5,000 to 500 coins.
[b] This coloured 2 ounce coin was issued at the 2015 Perth ANDA fair held at the Paterson's Stadium on March 7 & 8th. Only 1,000 coins were struck.
[c] This two ounce silver coloured coin was limited to 1500 and distributed at the ANDA Sydney Show held in the Sydney Lower Town Hall, on October 24,25 2014.

SILVER ISSUES : MULTIPLE DATES

LUNAR SPECIMEN FINISH

SERIES TWO - 2008 TO PRESENT

2017 High Relief | 2017 Gilt specimen | 2017 Coloured Rooster

Date	Face Value	Weight in oz's	Size mm	Mintage Max/ Actual	Reverse Feature		Issue Price	Average Retail
2017 : YEAR OF THE ROOSTER - SILVER SPECIMEN								
2017	300	10 kg	221	100/ n/a	Standard reverse		15,000	b/v
2017	30	1 kg	100.6	To order/ n/a	Standard reverse		1,750	1,750
2017	30	1 kg	100.6	500/ n/a	Citrine diamond		1,799	1,799
2017	10	10 oz	85.6	To order/ n/a	Standard reverse		1,750	1,750
2017	8	5 oz	65.6	To order/ n/a	Standard reverse		175	450
2017	2	2 oz	55.6	To order/ n/a	Standard reverse		179	150
2017 a	2	2 oz	55.6	1,000/ n/a	Colour, ANDA Perth		179	185
2017	1	1 oz	45.6	300 k/ All sold	Standard reverse		94	94
2017	1	1 oz	45.6	170,000/ n/a	Colour reverse		40	60
2017	1	1 oz	32.6	7,500/ n/a	High relief plain rev		102	102
2017	1	1 oz	45.6	50,000/ n/a	Gilt/ Cased		95	95
2017	1	1 oz	45.6	Inc in above	Gilt/ Capsule		89	89
2017	.50¢	1/2 oz	36.6	To order/ n/a	Standard reverse		63.5	30
2017	.50¢	1/2 oz	36.6	To order/ n/a	Colour reverse		28	30

[a] This proof quality 99.99% pure silver coloured coin was issued at the Perth ANDA Money Expo held on February 11 & 12, 2017. Limited to just 1,000 coins, the ANDA logo featured on the packaging. Collectors attending the fair were offered the coins and a discount price.

Date	Face Value	Weight in oz's	Size mm	Mintage Max/ Actual	Reverse Feature		Issue Price	Average Retail
2014 : YEAR OF THE HORSE LUNAR ISSUES								
2014	15	1/10oz	Gold	7,500/ 1011	Brown Horse	15,000	b/v	b/v
2014	15	1/10oz	Gold	7,500/ 1011	Buckskin	15,000	b/v	b/v
2014	15	1/10oz	Gold	7,500/ 1011	Chestnut Pinto	15,000	b/v	b/v
2014	15	1/10oz	Gold	7,500/ 1011	Dapple Grey	15,000	b/v	b/v
2014	15	1/10oz	Gold	7,500/ 1011	Palamino	15,000	b/v	b/v
2014	15	1/10oz	Gold	7,500/ 1511	Pinto 2	15,000	b/v	b/v
2014	15	1/10oz	Gold	7,500/ 1511	Pinto 3	15,000	b/v	b/v
2014	15	1/10oz	Gold	7,500/ 1011	White Horse 1	15,000	b/v	b/v
2014	15	1/10oz	Gold	7,500/ 1011	White Horse 2	15,000	b/v	b/v
2014	15	1/10oz	Gold	7,500/ 1011	White Horse 3	15,000	b/v	b/v

THEMED ISSUES : MULTIPLE DATES

ALL GOLD, SILVER OR ALUM/BRONZE ISSUES

2004 (a) Mawson Station

2005 (b) Leopard Seal

2006 (c) Edgeworth Base

2007 (d) Davis Station

2008 (e) Whale

2009 (f) South Pole

2010 (g) Husky

2011 (h) Killer Whale

2012 (i) Penguin

2013 (j) Aurora Australis

2014 (k) Albatross

2015 (l) Elephant Seal

Date	Face Value	Description	Weight in oz's	Metal	Finish	Size mm	Mintage Max/ Actual	Issue Price	Average Retail

2004 - ANTARCTIC TERRITORIES. PROOF ISSUES

Date	Face Value	Description	Weight in oz's	Metal	Finish	Size mm	Mintage Max/ Actual	Issue Price	Average Retail
2004 a	1	Mawson Station	1oz	Silver	Proof	40.6	7,500/ All sold	75	250
2005 b	1	Leopard Seal	1oz	Silver	Proof	40.6	7,500/ All sold	75	200
2006 c	1	Edgeworth Base	1oz	Silver	Proof	40.6	7,500/ All sold	75	125
2007 d	1	Davis Station	1oz	Silver	Proof	40.6	7,500/ All sold	75	95
2008 e	1	H'back Whale	1oz	Silver	Proof	40.6	7,500/ All sold	82	125
2009 f	1	South Pole	1oz	Silver	Proof	40.6	7,500/ All sold	82	125
2010 g	1	Husky	1oz	Silver	Proof	40.6	7,500/ All sold	82	125
2011 h	1	Killer Whale	1oz	Silver	Proof	40.6	7,500/ All sold	107	125
2012 i	1	Penguin	1oz	Silver	Proof	40.6	7,500/ All sold	107	125
2013 j	1	Aurora Australis	1oz	Silver	Proof	40.6	7,500/ All sold	92.5	125
2014 k	1	Albatross	1oz	Silver	Proof	40.6	7,500/ 3,670	99	105
2015 l	1	Elephant Seal	1oz	Silver	Proof	40.6	7,500/ tba	99	105

2007 (a) Sapphires

2008 (b) Opals

2009 (c) Diamonds

2010 (d) Nuggets

2007 - 2011 AUSTRALIA LOCKET SERIES

Date	Face Value	Description	Weight in oz's	Metal	Finish	Size mm	Mintage Max/ Actual	Issue Price	Average Retail
2007 a	1	Sapphires	1oz	Silver	Proof	36.6	7,500/ All sold	105	50
2007	100	Sapphires	1oz	Gold	Proof	31.1	1,000/ All sold	1,895	3,250
2008	1	Opals	1oz	Silver	Proof	36.6	7,500/ All sold	105	150
2008 b	100	Opals	1oz	Gold	Proof	31.1	1,000/ 550	1,895	3,250
2009 c	1	Diamonds	1oz	Silver	Proof	36.6	7,500/ All sold	105	150
2009	100	Diamonds	1oz	Gold	Proof	31.1	1,000/ 715	1,895	3,250
2010	1	Nuggets	1oz	Silver	Proof	36.6	7,500/ All sold	105	150
2010 d	100	Nuggets	1oz	Gold	Proof	31.1	1,000/ 679	1,895	3,250
2011	1	Pearls	1oz	Silver	Proof	36.6	7,500/ All sold	105	150
2011	100	Pearls	1oz	Gold	Proof	31.1	1,000/ 748	2,650	3,250

THEMED ISSUES : MULTIPLE DATES

ALL GOLD, SILVER OR ALUM/BRONZE ISSUES

2006 (a) Melbourne · 2006 (b) Uluru · 2006 (c) Canberra · 2006 : (d) Perth

2006 (e) Barrier Reef · 2007 (f) Gold Coast · 2007 (g) Phillip Island · 2007 (h) Port Arthur

2007 (i) Adelaide · 2007 (j) Sydney · 2008 (k) Broome · 2008 (l) Darwin

2008 (m) Brisbane · 2008 (n) Hobart · 2008 (o) Kakadu · Common obverse

Date	Face Value	Description	Weight in oz's	Metal	Finish	Size mm	Mintage Max/ Actual	Issue Price	Average Retail
2006 - 2008 AUSTRALIAN LANDMARK									
2006 a	1	Melbourne	1oz	Silver	Proof	40.6	7,500/ 5,923	75	75
2006 b	1	Uluru	1oz	Silver	Proof	40.6	7,500/ 5,938	75	75
2006 c	1	Canberra	1oz	Silver	Proof	40.6	7,500/ 4,926	75	75
2006 d	1	Perth	1oz	Silver	Proof	40.6	7,500/ All sold	75	9
2006 e	1	Barrier Reef	1oz	Silver	Proof	40.6	7,500/ 5,751	75	75
2007 f	1	Gold Coast	1oz	Silver	Proof	40.6	7,500/ 4,558	75	75
2007 g	1	Phillip Island	1oz	Silver	Proof	40.6	7,500/ 4,668	75	75
2007 h	1	Port Arthur	1oz	Silver	Proof	40.6	7,500/ 6,105	75	75
2007 i	1	Adelaide	1oz	Silver	Proof	40.6	7,500/ 6,376	75	75
2007 j	1	Sydney	1oz	Silver	Proof	40.6	7,500/ 5,945	75	75
2008 k	1	Broome	1oz	Silver	Proof	40.6	7,500/ 7,251	82.5	90
2008 l	1	Darwin	1oz	Silver	Proof	40.6	7,500/ 7,319	82.5	85
2008 m	1	Brisbane	1oz	Silver	Proof	40.6	7,500/ 7,500	82.5	85
2008 n	1	Hobart	1oz	Silver	Proof	40.6	7,500/ 7,276	82.5	85
2008 o	1	Kakadu	1oz	Silver	Proof	40.6	7,500/ 7,252	82.5	85

THEMED ISSUES : MULTIPLE DATES

EITHER GOLD, SILVER OR ALUM/BRONZE ISSUES

2008 - 2011 SPECIMEN RECTANGULAR THEMES

Gold Issues 99.99% fine. Silver Issues 99.9% fine

2008 : INDIGENOUS DREAMING SERIES

2008	1	Kangaroo	1 oz	Silver	Sp'men	To order/ 5,797	59.95	60
2008	15	Kangaroo	2.5g	Gold	Sp'men	To order/ 1,078	175	175
2008	20	Kangaroo	5 g	Gold	Sp'men	To order/ 1,053	350	350
2008	25	Kangaroo	10 g	Gold	Sp'men	To order/ 1,062	650	650
2008	1	Turtle	1 oz	Silver	Sp'men	To order/ 3,177	59.95	60
2008	15	Turtle	2.5g	Gold	Sp'men	To order/ 1,084	175	175
2008	20	Turtle	5 g	Gold	Sp'men	To order/ 1,053	350	350
2008	25	Turtle	10 g	Silver	Sp'men	To order/ 1,021	650	650

2008 : CHINESE MYTHOLOGY SERIES

2008	8	Fortune	5 g	Gold	Sp'men	20,000 / 1,181	n/a	350
2008	25	Fortune	10 g	Gold	Sp'men	10,000 / 373	650	650
2008	8	Success	5 g	Gold	Sp'men	20,000 / 1,181	n/a	350
2008	25	Success	10 g	Gold	Sp'men	10,000 / 375	650	650
2008	8	Longevity	5 g	Gold	Sp'men	20,000 / 1,187	n/a	350
2008	25	Longevity	10 g	Gold	Sp'men	10,000 / 382	650	650
2008	8	Wealth	5 g	Gold	Sp'men	20,000 / 1,168	n/a	350
2008	25	Wealth	10 g	Gold	Sp'men	10,000 / 375	650	650

2009 : CHINESE MYTHOLOGY SERIES

2009	1	Fortune	1 oz	Silver	Sp'men	To order/ 2,153	n/a	60
2009	8	Fortune	5 g	Gold	Sp'men	To order/, 256	n/a	180
2009	25	Fortune	10 g	Gold	Sp'men	To order/ 68	850	650
2009	1	Success	1 oz	Silver	Sp'men	To order/ 2,142	n/a	60
2009	8	Success	5 g	Gold	Sp'men	To order,/ 251	n/a	180
2009	25	Success	10 g	Gold	Sp'men	To order / 71	850	650
2009	1	Longevity	1 oz	Silver	Sp'men	To order/ 2,159	n/a	60
2009	8	Longevity	5 g	Gold	Sp'men	To order,/ 258	n/a	180
2009	25	Longevity	10 g	Gold	Sp'men	To order / 72	850	650
2009	1	Wealth	1 oz	Silver	Sp'men	To order, 2,155	n/a	60
2009	8	Wealth	5 g	Gold	Sp'men	To order/, 266	n/a	180
2009	25	Wealth	10 g	Gold	Sp'men	To order / 68	850	650

2010 & 2011 : INDIGENOUS DREAMING SERIES

2010	1	Dolphin	1 oz	Silver	Sp'men	To order / 2984	69.5	60
2010	15	Dolphin	2.5 g	Gold	Sp'men	To order / 504	229	180
2010	25	Dolphin	10 g	Gold	Sp'men	To order / 390	850	650
2011	1	Playpus	1 oz	Silver	Sp'men	To order / 1737	85	60
2011	15	Playpus	2.5 g	Gold	Sp'men	To order / 213	260	180
2011	25	Playpus	10 g	Gold	Sp'men	To order / 77	995	650

THEMED ISSUES : MULTIPLE DATES

ALL GOLD, SILVER & BRONZE ISSUES

2009 : (a) Kangaroo 2009 : (b) Dolphin 2009 : (c) Brown Snake 2009 : (d) Brolga

2009 : (e) Echidna 2010 : (f) Lizard 2010 : (g) Koala 2010 : (h) Platypus

2010 : (i) Crocodile 2010 : (j) Wombat 2011 : (k) Dingo 2011 : (l) Emu

2011 : (m) Kookaburra 2011 : (n) White Shark 12011 : (o) Tasmanian Devil

Date	Face Value	Description	Weight in oz's	Metal	Finish	Size mm	Mintage Max/ Actual	Issue Price	Average Retail
2009 - 2011 AUSTRALIAN DREAMING									
2009 a	1	Kangaroo	1 oz	Silver	Proof	36.6	10,000/ 7,390	89.5	89
2009 b	1	Dolphin	1 oz	Silver	Proof	36.6	10,000/ 6,651	89.5	89
2009 c	1	Brown Snake	1 oz	Silver	Proof	36.6	10,000/ 5,972	89.5	89
2009 d	1	Brolga	1 oz	Silver	Proof	36.6	10,000/ 6,213	89.5	89
2009 e	1	Echidna	1 oz	Silver	Proof	36.6	10,000/ 5,859	89.5	89
2010 f	1	Frilled Neck	1 oz	Silver	Proof	36.6	10,000/ 4,995	89.5	89
2010 g	1	Koala	1 oz	Silver	Proof	36.6	10,000/ 5,143	89.5	89
2010 h	1	Platypus	1 oz	Silver	Proof	36.6	10,000/ 4,934	89.5	89
2010 i	1	Crocodile	1 oz	Silver	Proof	36.6	10,000/ 4,768	89.5	89
2010 j	1	Wombat	1 oz	Silver	Proof	36.6	10,000/ 5,065	89.5	89
2011 k	1	Dingo	1 oz	Silver	Proof	36.6	10,000/ 3,325	105	105
2011 l	1	Emu	1 oz	Silver	Proof	36.6	10,000/ 3,288	105	105
2011 m	1	Kookaburra	1 oz	Silver	Proof	36.6	10,000/ 3,296	105	105
2011 n	1	White Shark	1 oz	Silver	Proof	36.6	10,000/ 3,404	105	105
2011 o	1	Tas. Devil	1 oz	Silver	Proof	36.6	10,000/ 3,254	105	105
ONE OUNCE PROOF FIVE COIN CASED SET									
2009		Contains one of each [a to e]					n/a	447.50	450
2010		Contains one of each [f to j]					n/a	447.50	450
2011		Contains one of each [k to o]					n/a	525.00	450

THEMED ISSUES : MULTIPLE DATES

ALL GOLD, SILVER OR ALUM/BRONZE ISSUES

Common obverse

(a) Lion Fish

(b) Sea Dragon

(c) Clown Fish

(d) Seahorse

(e) Turtle

(f) Starfish

(g) Surgeonfish

(h) Octopus

(i) Mantra Ray

Date	Face Value	Description	Weight in oz's	Metal	Finish	Size mm	Mintage Max/ Actual	Issue Price	Average Retail
2009 - 2012 : SEA LIFE SERIES									
2009 a	.50¢	Lion Fish	1/2oz	Silver	Proof	36.6	10,000/ All sold	55	60
2009 b	.50¢	Sea Dragon	1/2oz	Silver	Proof	36.6	10,000/ All sold	55	60
2010 c	.50¢	Clown Fish	1/2oz	Silver	Proof	36.6	10,000/ All sold	55	60
2010 d	.50¢	Seahorse	1/2oz	Silver	Proof	36.6	10,000/ All sold	55	60
2011 e	.50¢	Turtle	1/2oz	Silver	Proof	36.6	10,000/ 7,283	55	60
2011 f	.50¢	Starfish	1/2oz	Silver	Proof	36.6	10,000/ 9,525	55	60
2012 g	.50¢	Surgeonfish	1/2oz	Silver	Proof	36.6	10,000/ 7,283	55	60
2012 h	.50¢	Octopus	1/2oz	Silver	Proof	36.6	10,000/ 6,983	55	60
2012 i	.50¢	Manta Ray	1/2oz	Silver	Proof	36.6	10,000/ 6,408	55	60

2010 (a) Kangaroo

2010 (b) Glider

2011 (c) Dingo

2011 (d) Bilby

2011 (e) Koala

2012 (f) Kookaburra

2013 (g) Possum

2013 (h) Echinda

2013 (i) Platypus

2013 (j) Wombat

2010 - BUSH BABIES. DISCOVER AUSTRALIA

Date	Face Value	Description	Weight in oz's	Metal	Finish	Size mm	Mintage Max/ Actual	Issue Price	Average Retail
2010 a	.50¢	Kangaroo	1/2 oz	Silver	Proof	36.6	10,000/ All sold	55	110
2010 b	.50¢	Sugar Glider	1/2 oz	Silver	Proof	36.6	10,000/ All sold	55	80
2011 c	.50¢	Dingo	1/2 oz	Silver	Proof	36.6	10,000/ n/a	56	80
2011 d	.50¢	Bilby	1/2 oz	Silver	Proof	36.6	10,000/ n/a	65	85
2011 e	.50¢	Koala	1/2 oz	Silver	Proof	36.6	10,000/ n/a	65	85
2012 f	.50¢	Kookaburra	1/2 oz	Silver	Proof	36.6	10,000/ n/a	67	65
2013 g	.50¢	Possum	1/2 oz	Silver	Proof	36.6	10,000/ n/a	67	65
2013 h	.50¢	Echidna	1/2 oz	Silver	Proof	36.6	10,000/ n/a	65	65
2013 i	.50¢	Platypus	1/2 oz	Silver	Proof	36.6	10,000/ n/a	65	65
2013 j	.50¢	Wombat	1/2 oz	Silver	Proof	36.6	10,000/ n/a	65	65

THEMED ISSUES : MULTIPLE DATES

ALL GOLD, SILVER OR ALUM/BRONZE ISSUES

2010 (a) Brisbane 2010 (b) Melbourne 2010 (c) Adelaide 2010 (d) Boston/Darwin 2010 (e) Sydney

2010 (f) Canberra 2010 (g) Tasmania 2011 (h) Perth 2011 (i) Brisbane 2011 (j) Melbourne

2011 (k) Sydney 2011 (l) Adelaide 2012 (m) Perth 1oz Common Obverse

Date	Description	Mintage Limit / Actual	Issue Price	Current Retai
2010 - 2012 CELEBRATE AUSTRALIA. ANDA				
2010 a	Brisbane ANDA Fair held May 2010	2,500/ All sold	95	95
2010 b	Melbourne ANDA Fair held July 2010	2,500/ All sold	95	110
2010 c	Adelaide No show association	2,500/ n/a	107	110
2010 d	Darwin/ Boston ANA. August 2010	1,500/ All sold	95	95
2010 e	Sydney ANDA August 2010	2,500/ 2,400	107	95
2010 f	Canberra ANDA November 2010	2,500/ 2,170	107	110
2010 g	Tasmnian Proof. No show association	2,500/ n/a	107	110
2011 h	Perth ANDA February 2011	2,500/ 2,187	107	110
2011 i	Brisbane ANDA held May 2011	2,500/ 2,499	107	110
2011 j	Heard Island. Melb. ANDA July 2011	2,500/ 1,644	107	110
2011 k	Blue Mths. Sydney ANDA Aug 2011	2,500/ 1,857	107	110
2011 l	Tas Wilderness. Adel ANDA. Oct 2011	2,500/ 1,231	107	110
2012 m	Shark Bay. Perth ANDA . March 2012	2,500/ 1,540	107	110

2011 (a) Gallipoli 2011 (b) Tobruk 2012 (c) Kokoda 2012 (d) Kapyong 2012 (e) Long Tan

Date	Face Value	Description	Weight in oz's	Metal	Finish	Size mm	Mintage Max/ Actual	Issue Price	Average Retail
FAMOUS BATTLES IN AUSTRALIAN HISTORY									
2011 a	1	Gallipoli	1oz	Silver	Proof	40.6	5,000/ All sold	107	125
2011 b	1	Tobruk	1oz	Silver	Proof	40.6	5,000/ 4,561	104	135
2012 c	1	Kokoda	1oz	Silver	Proof	40.6	5,000/ All sold	104	135
2012 d	1	Kapyong	1oz	Silver	Proof	40.6	5,000/ 3,328	104	125
2012 e	1	Long Tan	1oz	Silver	Proof	40.6	5,000/ 3,631	104	125

THEMED ISSUES : MULTIPLE DATES

ALL GOLD, SILVER OR ALUM/BRONZE ISSUES

2012 (a) Kookaburra 2012 (b) Emu 2013 (c) Kangaroo 2013 (d) Platypus 2014 (e) Koala

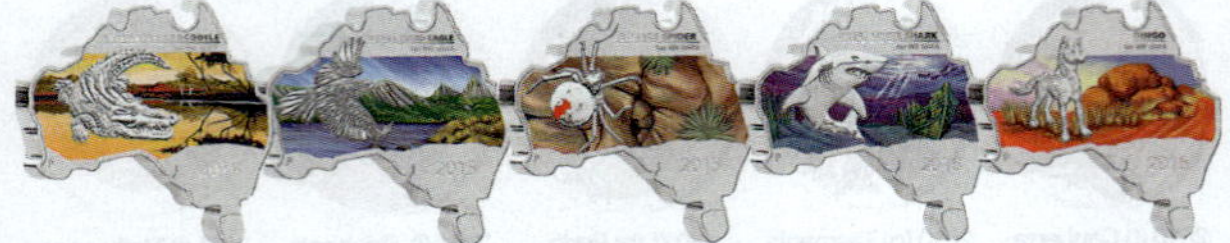

2014 (f) Crocodile 2015 (g) Eagle 2015 (h) Spider 2016 (i) Shark 2016 (j) Dingo

2012 - AUSTRALIAN MAP SHAPED COINS

2012 a	1	Kookaburra	1 oz	Silver	Proof	40.6	6,000/ All sold	112.5	250
2012 b	1	Emu	1 oz	Silver	Proof	40.6	6,000/ All sold	109.5	200
2013 c	1	Kangaroo	1 oz	Silver	Proof	40.6	6,000/ All sold	104.5	175
2013 d	1	Platypus	1 oz	Silver	Proof	40.6	6,000/ 5,256	104	150
2014 e	1	Koala	1 oz	Silver	Proof	40.6	6,000/ 5,529	104	125
2014 f	1	Crocodile	1 oz	Silver	Proof	40.6	6,000/ 3,866	104	125
2015 g	1	Wedge Tail	1 oz	Silver	Proof	40.6	6,000/ 5,256	104	150
2015 h	1	Red Back	1 oz	Silver	Proof	40.6	6,000/ 3,436	104	125
2016 i	1	Great White	1 oz	Silver	Proof	40.6	6,000/ 2,937	104	125
2016 i	1	Dingo	1 oz	Silver	Proof	40.6	6,000/ 2,314	104	125

2012 (a) Bell Frog 2012 (b) Red Kangaroo 2012 (c) Kookaburra 2012 (d) Goanna 2012 (e) Whale Shark

2013 (f) Emu 2013 (g) Kangaroo 2013 (h) Koala 2013 (i) Kookaburra 2013 (j) Platypus

2012 - DISCOVER AUSTRALIA SERIES TWO

2012 a	1	Bell Frog	1 oz	Silver	Proof	40.6	7,500/ 5,237	104	110
2012 b	1	Red Kangaroo	1 oz	Silver	Proof	40.6	7,500/ 5,872	104	110
2012 c	1	Kookaburra	1 oz	Silver	Proof	40.6	7,500/ 5,672	104	110
2012 d	1	Goanna	1 oz	Silver	Proof	40.6	7,500/ 5,217	104	110
2012 e	1	Whale Shark	1 oz	Silver	Proof	40.6	7,500/ 5,414	104	110
2013 f	1	Emu	1 oz	Silver	Proof	40.6	5,000/ 366	92.5	95
2013 g	1	Kangaroo	1 oz	Silver	Proof	40.6	5,000/ 514	92.5	95
2013 h	1	Koala	1 oz	Silver	Proof	40.6	5,000/ 462	92.5	95
2013 i	1	Kookaburra	1 oz	Silver	Proof	40.6	5,000/ 374	92.5	95
2013 j	1	Platypus	1 oz	Silver	Proof	40.6	5,000/ 369	92.5	95

ONE OUNCE PROOF FIVE COIN CASED SET

2012	Cased set contains one of each (a to e)	Inc in above	520	550
2013	Cased set contains one of each (f to j)	1,500/ 1,237	462.5	550

THEMED ISSUES : MULTIPLE DATES

2012 : OUTBACK AUSTRALIA

2012 [a] Kookaburra

2012 [b] Kangaroo

2012 [c] Koala

2013 [d] Kookaburra

2013 [e] Koala

2014 [f] Kookaburra

2014 [g] Kangaroo

2014 [h] Koala

Date	Face Value	Description	Weight in oz's	Metal	Finish	Size mm	Mintage Max/ Actual	Issue Price	Average Retail
2012 a	.50¢	Kookaburra	1/2 oz	Silver	Proof	36.6	5,000/ tba	Part of Set	
2012 b	.50¢	Kangaroo	1/2 oz	Silver	Proof	36.6	Inc in above	Part of Set	
2012 c	.50¢	Koala	1/2 oz	Silver	Proof	36.6	3 coin set	159	175
2012	1	Kookaburra	1 oz	Silver	Proof	40.6	5,000/ n/a	99	99
2012	1	Koala	1 oz	Silver	Proof	40.6	5,000/ n/a	99	99
2013 d	.50¢	Kookaburra	1/2 oz	Silver	Proof	36.6	5,000/ tba	Part of Set	
2013	.50¢	Kangaroo	1/2 oz	Silver	Proof	36.6	Inc in above	Part of Set	
2013 e	.50¢	Koala	1/2 oz	Silver	Proof	36.6	3 coin set	159	175
2013	1	Koala	1 oz	Silver	Proof	40.6	5,000/ 4,958	99	99
2014 f	.50¢	Kookaburra	1/2 oz	Silver	Proof	36.6	5,000/ tba	Part of Set	
2014 g	.50¢	Kangaroo	1/2 oz	Silver	Proof	36.6	Inc in above	Part of Set	
2014 h	50¢	Koala	1/2 oz	Silver	Proof	36.6	3 coin set	159	175
2014	1	Koala	1 oz	Silver	Proof	40.6	5,000/ 4,958	99	99

I oz SPECIAL INTERNATIONAL COIN FAIR RELEASES

2012	Beijing International Coin Exposition.	**a** & **c** as a set	2,000/ n/a	99	99
2014	Berlin World Money Fair	**g** as a single coin	2,000/ n/a	74	75

a & c. Special 1oz version released at the 2012 Beijing International Coin Exposition. The coin was presented in a vibrantly coloured, slide-out display card and outer shipper.
b. Issued at the 2012 ANA World's Fair of Money in Philadelphia.
e. This larger (1oz) Koala coin was offered as a stand alone issue on a mint-to-order basis.

1/2 oz SPECIAL INTERNATIONAL COIN FAIR RELEASES

[a] Collectors buying this coin at the Melbourne ANDA Money Expo were treated to a discount. Normally the coin had a RRP of $65, but fair attendees paid $59 for the coin with a bonus bespoke box featuring the ANDA logo.

[a] Wombat [b] Koala [c] Kangaroo [d] Possum [e] Devil [f] Owl [g] Python [h] Bat [i] Rooster

2012 - AUSTRALIAN OPAL SERIES

Date	Face Value	Description	Weight	Metal	Finish	Size	Mintage	Issue	Retail
2012 a	1	Wombat	1 oz	Silver	Proof	36.6	8,000/ All sold	110	130
2012 b	1	Koala	1 oz	Silver	Proof	36.6	8,000/ All sold	115	130
2013 c	1	Kangaroo	1 oz	Silver	Proof	36.6	8,000/ All sold	115	130
2013 d	1	Pygmy Possum	1 oz	Silver	Proof	36.6	8,000/ 6,485	115	120
2014 e	1	Tas. Devil	1 oz	Silver	Proof	36.6	8,000/ 6,159	115	130
2014 f	1	Masked Owl	1 oz	Silver	Proof	36.6	8,000/ 5,363	115	130
2015 g	1	Python	1 oz	Silver	Proof	36.6	8,000/ 4,337	115	115
2015 h	1	Ghost Bat	1 oz	Silver	Proof	36.6	8,000/ 3,717	115	115
1152016 i1		Rooster	1 oz	Silver	Proof	36.6	5,000/ n/a	115	115

THEMED ISSUES : MULTIPLE DATES

EITHER GOLD, SILVER OR ALUM/BRONZE ISSUES

2013 [a] 1oz Silver

2014 [b] 1oz Silver

2014 [c] 5oz Gold

2015 [d] 1oz Silver

2015 [e] 5oz Gold

2016 [f] 1oz Silver

2016 [g] 5oz Gold

2017 [h] 1oz Silver

2013 - AUSTRALIAN STOCK HORSE

Date	Face Value	Description	in oz's	Metal	Type	Size	Mintage Max/ Actual	Issue Price	Retail Average
2013	1	Rearing Horse	1 oz	Silver	Spec	40.6	10k/ All sold	59	59
2013 a	1	Rearing Horse	1 oz	Silver	Proof	40.6	1,000/ All sold	59	59
2014	1	Galloping Horse	1 oz	Silver	Spec	40.6	10,000/ tba	59	59
2014 b	1	Galloping Horse	1 oz	Silver	Proof	40.6	1,000/ tba	59	59
2014 c	500	Rearing Horse	5 oz	Gold	Spec	50.5	99/ All sold	12,995	13,000
2015 d	1	Horse & Fence	1 oz	Silver	Spec	40.6	10,000/ All sold	59	59
2015 e	500	Galloping Horse	5 oz	Gold	Spec	50.5	99/ All sold	12,999	13,000
2016 f	1	Grazing Horse	1 oz	Silver	Spec	40.6	10,000/ All sold	59	59
2016 g	500	Horse & Fence	5 oz	Gold	Spec	50.5	99/ All sold	14,449	15,000
2017 h	1	Rearing Horse	1 oz	Silver	Spec	40.6	10,000/ tba	59	59
2017	500	Rearing Horse	5 oz	Gold	Spec	50.5	99/ All sold	12,999	13,000

Packaging details, 1,000 in coloured card and 9,000 in capsules.

2013 [i] European Garnets

2014 [j] Australian Nuggets

[k] Nth America Turquoise

[l] New Born Baby

2013 - TREASURES OF THE WORLD SERIES

Date	Face Value	Description	Metal	Type	in oz's	Size	Mintage Max/ Actual	Issue Price	Retail Average
2013 i	1	Europe Garnets	Silver	Proof	1 oz	40.6	7,500/ 4,099	125	125
2013	100	Europe Garnets	Gold	Proof	1 oz	32.6	750/ 98	2,765	2,765
2014 j	1	Australian Gold	Silver	Proof	1 oz	40.6	7,500/ 4,061	125	125
2014	100	Australian Gold	Gold	Proof	1 oz	32.6	750/ 163	2,765	2,765
2015	1	Nth Amer Turquoise	Silver	Proof	1 oz	40.6	7,500/ 2,340	118.5	125
2015 k	100	Nth Amer Turquoise	Gold	Proof	1 oz	32.6	750/ 128	2,765	2,765

2013 - NEW BORN BABY COMMEMORATIVE

Date	Face Value	Description	Type	Metal	in oz's	Mintage Max/ Actual	Issue Price	Retail Average
2013 l	.50¢	Newborn Baby	Proof	Silver	1/2oz	To order/ 3,632	63.5	64
2014 l	.50¢	Newborn Baby	Proof	Silver	1/2oz	To order/ n/a	63.5	64
2015 l	.50¢	Newborn Baby	Proof	Silver	1/2oz	To order/ 2.266	63.5	64
2015 l	.50¢	Newborn Baby	Proof	Silver	1/2oz	To order/ n/a	63.5	64
2016 l	.50¢	Newborn Baby	Proof	Silver	1/2oz	To order/ n/a	63.5	64

THEMED ISSUES : MULTIPLE DATES

EITHER GOLD, SILVER OR ALUM/BRONZE ISSUES

2013 (a) Opera House 2013 (b) Opera House 2013 (c) Didgeridoo 2013 (d) Didgeridoo

2013 (e) Capt Cook 2013 (f) Capt Cook 2013 (g) Surfing 2013 (h) Surfing

2014 (i) Gold Rush 2014 (j) Gold Rush 2014 (k) Reef 2014 (l) Reef

2014 (m) Stockman 2014 (n) Stockman 2014 (o) Fishing 2014 (p) Fishing

Date	Face Value	Description	Weight in oz's	Metal	Finish	Size mm	Mintage Max/ Actual	Issue Price	Average Retail
2013 - THE LAND DOWN UNDER									
2013 a	1	Opera House	1 oz	Silver	Proof	40.6	5,000/ 3,753	99	99
2013	2	Opera House	10 oz	Silver	Proof	75.6	750/ 331	950	950
2013 b	25	Opera House	1/4 oz	Gold	Proof	20.6	1,000/ 646	795	795
2013	200	Opera House	2 oz	Gold	Proof	20.6	200/129	5,495	5,600
2013 c	1	Didgeridoo	1 oz	Silver	Proof	40.6	5,000/ 2,228	99	99
2013 d	25	Didgeridoo	1/4 oz	Gold	Proof	20.6	1,000/ 142	675	675
2013 e	1	Capt. Cook	1 oz	Silver	Proof	40.6	5,000/ 1,873	99	99
2013 f	25	Capt. Cook	1/4 oz	Gold	Proof	20.6	1,000/ 142	675	675
2013 g	1	Surfing	1 oz	Silver	Proof	40.6	5,000/ 1,614	99	99
2013 h	25	Surfing	1/4 oz	Gold	Proof	20.6	1,000/ 74	675	675
2014 i	1	Gold Rush	1 oz	Silver	Proof	40.6	5,000/ 2,361	99	99
2014 j	25	Gold Rush	1/4 oz	Gold	Proof	20.6	1,000/ 343	675	675
2014 k	1	Barrier Reef	1 oz	Silver	Proof	40.6	5,000/ 1,946	99	99
2014	8	Barrier Reef	5 oz	Silver	Proof	65.6	400/ All sold	485	485
2014	25	Barrier Reef	1/4 oz	Gold	Proof	20.6	1,000/ 343	675	675
2014 l	200	Reef - Turtle	2 oz	Gold	Proof	41.1	200/ Sold out	5,050	675
2014 m	1	Stockman	1 oz	Silver	Proof	40.6	5,000/ 1,763	99	99
2014 n	25	Stockman	1/4 oz	Gold	Proof	20.6	1,000/ 189	675	675
2014 o	1	Rock Fishing	1 oz	Silver	Proof	40.6	5,000/ 1,389	99	99
2014 p	25	Rock Fishing	1/4 oz	Gold	Proof	20.6	1,000/ 142	675	675

THEMED ISSUES : MULTIPLE DATES

EITHER GOLD, SILVER OR ALUM/BRONZE ISSUES

2014 [a] Declaration of War

2014 [b] Our Last Man

2015 [c] Making a Nation

1915 [d] Lest We Forget

2015 [e] Goodbye Cobber

2015 [f] Baptism of Fire

2015 [g] The Somme

2015 [h] ANZAC Day

Date	Face Value	Description	Weight in oz's	Metal	Finish	Size mm	Mintage Max/ Actual	Issue Price	Average Retail
2014 - ANZAC SPIRIT : 100 YEARS									
2014 a	1	Declaration of war	1 oz	Silver	Proof	40.6	7,500/ 3,438	99	99
2014 b	25	To Our Last Man	1/4 oz	Gold	Proof	20.6	1,000/ 636	695	695
2015 c	1	Making a Nation	1 oz	Silver	Proof	40.6	7500/ 3,312	99	99
2015 d	30	Lest We Forget	1 kg	Silver	Proof	100.6	500/ 176	1,750	1,750
2015 e	25	Goodbye Cobber	1/4 oz	Gold	Proof	20.6	1,000/ 338	695	695
2015 f	200	Baptism of Fire	2 oz	Gold	Proof	36.6	100/ All sold	5,050	5,050
2016 g	1	The Somme	1 oz	Silver	Proof	40.6	7,500/ n/a	99	99
2016 h	25	ANZAC Day 100th	1/4 oz	Gold	Proof	20.6	1,000/ na	799	799

2014 [i] Travel

2014 [j] Enlist

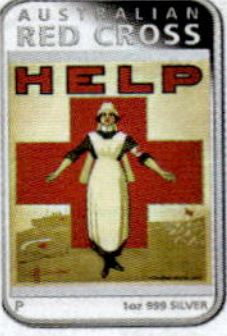
2015 [k] Red Cross

2016 [l] War Bonds

2016 [m] Home Front

Date	Value	Description	Finish	Metal	Weight in oz's	Mintage Max/ Actual	Issue Price	Average Retail
2014 - TRAVEL POSTERS								
2014 i	1.00	Kangaroo Travel	Proof	Silver	1oz	5,000/ tba	99	99
2014 - WORLD WAR ONE POSTERS								
2014 j		Coo-ee. Enlistment	Proof	Silver	1oz	5,000/ 2,400	99	99
2015 k		Red Cross	Proof	Silver	1oz	5,000 / 1,406	99	99
2016 l		War Bonds	Proof	Silver	1oz	5,000 / tba	99	99
2017 m		Home Front	Proof	Silver	1oz	5,000 / tba	99	99

THEMED ISSUES : MULTIPLE DATES

EITHER GOLD, SILVER OR ALUM/BRONZE ISSUES

2014 [a] Silver Proof

2014 [b] Gold Proof

2015 [c] Silver Proof

2015 [d] Gold Proof

2016 [e] Silver Proof

2015 [f] Bimetal Obv

2016 [g] Bimetal Rev

2017 [h] Gold Proof

2014 - WEDGE TAILED EAGLE

Date	Face Value	Description	Weight in oz's	Metal	Finish	Size mm	Mintage Max/ Actual	Issue Price	Average Retail
2014	1	Standard	1 oz	Silver	Spec	40.6	50k/ All sold	99	99
2014	1	Standard	1 oz	Silver	Proof	40.6	5,000/ All sold	99	195
2014 a	1	High relief	1 oz	Silver	Proof	32.6	10,000/ All sold	102	275
2014	8	High relief	5 oz	Silver	Proof	50.6	5,000/ All sold	485	550
2014 b	100	High relief	1 oz	Gold	Proof	27.3	1,000/ All sold	2,695	2,695
2014	200	High relief	2 oz	Gold	Proof	36.6	1,000/ All sold	5,050	5,050
2015	.50¢	Standard	1/2oz	Silver	Spec	36.6	118,577	n/a	b/v
2015	1	Standard	1 oz	Silver	Spec	40.6	81,381	n/a	b/v
2015	1	Part Gilt	1 oz	Silver	Spec	40.6	10,000/ 4,466	69	b/v
2015 c	1	Standard	1 oz	Silver	Proof	40.6	5,000/ 3,882	99	100
2015	1	High relief	1 oz	Silver	Proof	32.6	10,000/ All sold	104	110
2015	8	High relief	5 oz	Silver	Proof	50.6	2,500/ All sold	485	599
2015	10	Standard	10 oz	Silver	Proof	75.6	17,132	n/a	b/v
2015 d	2	Standard	0.5g	Gold	Proof	11.6	To order/ 4,375	59.5	60
2015	100	High relief	1 oz	Gold	Proof	27.3	1,000/ 732	2,695	2,695
2015	200	High relief	2 oz	Gold	Proof	36.6	500/ 254	5,050	5,050
2015	500	Standard	5 oz	Gold	Proof	50.5	99/ All sold	12,995	12,995
2015	100	Standard	1 oz	Platinum	Proof	32.6	500/ All sold	2,699	2,750
2016	1	Standard	1oz	Silver	Spec	40.6	109,366	n/a	n/a
2016	1	Standard	1oz	Silver	Proof	40.6	5,000/ 1,385	99	100
2016	1	High Relief	1 oz	Silver	Proof	32.6	20,000/ 14,459	109	110
2016 e	8	High Relief	5 oz	Silver	Proof	50.6	5,000/ 3,798	499	b/v
2016 f/g	50	Bi-metal	15.6g	–	Proof	32.6	750/ 698	1,599	1,599
2016	15	Standard	1/10oz	Gold	Proof	16.1	10,000/ 9,839	b/v	b/v
2016	100	High Relief	1 oz	Gold	Proof	27.3	1,000/ 866	2,699	2,750
2016	200	High Relief	2 oz	Gold	Proof	36.6	500/ 224	5,150	5,250
2016	500	High Relief	5 oz	Gold	Proof	40.5	199/ All sold	12,995	b/v
2016 g	100	Standard	1 oz	Platinum	Proof	32.6	350/ 344	2,799	2,799
2017	1	Standard	1 oz	Silver	Spec	40.6	To order/ tba	b/v	b/v
2017	1	High Relief	1 oz	Silver	Spec	32.6	10,000/ tba	99	99
2017	30	Standard	1 kg	Silver	Spec	100.6	To order/ n/a	n/a	n/a
2017	2	Standard	0.5g	Gold	Spec	11.6	To order/ n/a	59.5	60
2017	100	High Relief	1 oz	Gold	Proof	27.3	500/ n/a	2,899	b/v
2017 h	200	High Relief	2 oz	Gold	Proof	36.6	150/ n/a	5,749	b/v

In 2017 the Perth Mint commissioned American sculptor and engraver, John M. Mercanti, the 12th chief engraver of the U.S. Mint. He created the reverse design of the American Silver Eagle bullion coin and has produced more coin and medal designs than any other employee in the history of the U.S. Mint.

This listing in incomplete and will updated in the next edition.

THEMED ISSUES : MULTIPLE DATES

ALL GOLD, SILVER OR ALUM/BRONZE ISSUES

1914 [a] Answering the call

1914 [b] Family Farewell

1914 [c] First Action

1915 [d] The Bravest

1915 [e] Billies for Troops

1915 [f] Fallen Spirit

1916 [g] Not Forgotten

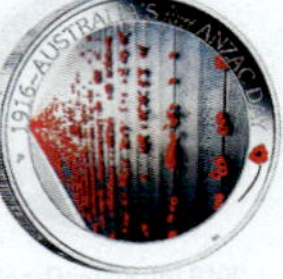
1916 [h] First Anzac Day

1916 [i] Brothers in Arms

1917 [j] Grim Path Back

2017 [k] Speed & Surprise

2017 [l] Front Line

2014 - THE ANZAC SPIRIT : 1/2oz SILVER SET

2014 a	50¢	Answer the Call	Proof	Silver	1/2 oz	32.6	5,000/ 1,633	Part set	
2014 b	50¢	Family Farewell	Proof	Silver	1/2 oz	32.6	Inc above	99	99
2014 c	50¢	First Action	Proof	Silver	1/2 oz	32.6	Cased trio	189	189
2015 d	50¢	Bravest the Brave	Proof	Silver	1/2 oz	32.6	5,00/1,633	189	189
2015 e	50¢	Billies for Troops	Proof	Silver	1/2 oz	32.6	Inc above	Part set	
2015 f	50¢	Spirit of the fallen	Proof	Silver	1/2 oz	32.6	Cased trio	189	189
2016 g	50¢	Not Forgotten	Proof	Silver	1/2 oz	32.6	5,000/tba	Part set	
2016 h	50¢	First Anzac Day	Proof	Silver	1/2 oz	32.6	Inc above	Part set	
2016 i	50¢	Brothers in Arms	Proof	Silver	1/2 oz	32.6	Cased trio	189	189
2017 j	50¢	Grim Path Back	Proof	Silver	1 oz	32.6	5,000/tba	Part set	
2017 k	50¢	Speed & Surprise	Proof	Silver	1 oz	32.6	Inc above	Part set	
2017 l	50¢	Front Line Angels	Proof	Silver	1 oz	32.6	Cased trio	189	189

1914 [l] Abalone

1915 [m] Mother of Pearl

1915 [n] Snugglepot

1916 [o] Gumnuts

2014 - AUSTRALIAN SHELLS

2014 l	1	Abalone	Proof	Silver	1 oz	36.6	5,000/ 4,963	109	109
2015 m	1	Mother/Pearl	Proof	Silver	1 oz	36.6	5,000/ 2,110	109	109

2015 - SNUGGLE POT & CUDDLE PIE

2015 n	1	Snugglepot	Proof	Silver	1/2 oz	32.6	5,000/ 1,567	58	58
2016 o	1	Snugglepot	Proof	Silver	1/2 oz	32.6	5,000/ 889	59	60

THEMED ISSUES : MULTIPLE DATES

1915 [a] Battle of Britain 1916 [b] Rats of Tobruk 1915 [c] Xmas Tree 1916 [d] Xmas Candle

2015 - THEME : 75TH ANNIVERSARY OF WWII

2015 a	1	Battle of Britain	Proof	Silver	1 oz	40.6	5,000/ 1,885	99	99
2016 b	1	Rats of Tobruk	Proof	Silver	1 oz	40.6	5,000/ n/a	99	99

2015 - THEME : CHRISTMAS SILVER PROOF

2015 c	1	Tree show scene	Proof	Silver	1 oz	40.6	3,000/ All sold	109	109
2016 d	1	Scene with candle	Proof	Silver	1 oz	40.6	3,000/ 2,255	109	109

2015 [e] Weddings 1915 [f] Obv & Rev Pink Gold Argyle Diamond 1916 [g] White Diamond

2015 - THEME : WEDDING CELEBRATION

2015 e	1	Wedding	Proof	Silver	1 oz	40.6	To order/ 2,582	104	104
2016 e	1	Wedding	Proof	Silver	1 oz	40.6	To order/ 3,078	109	109
2017 e	1	Wedding	Proof	Silver	1 oz	40.6	To order n/a	109	109

2015 KIMBERLEY GOLDEN GEMS

2015 f	100	Pink Argyle Di'md [.04 ct]	Proof	91.67	2 oz	40.6	400/ n/a	8,888	b/v
2016 g	100	White Diamond [.03 ct]	Proof	99.99	2 oz	40.6	500/ 393	8,499	b/v

Common Obverse

1915 [f] Kangaroo

1916 [g] Koala

2016 - THEME : 2oz SILVER ANTIQUE FINISH

2016 h	2	Kangaroo antique Silver Proof	2 oz	40.6	3,000/ All sold	199	199
2017 i	2	Koala antique Silver Proof	2 oz	40.6	3,000/ n/a	109	109

To capture the depth and detail of the design, the coin is struck in high relief to a rimless format and features an antique finish.

See their advertisement on page 19 & 430

ONE YEAR : MULTIPLE COIN DESIGNS

ALL GOLD, SILVER OR ALUM/BRONZE ISSUES

1999 (a) Perth Mint Bi-metal Centenary

2000 (b) Earth, Moon, Stars

2000 (c) View of the Earth

2001 (d) Cleopatra's Needle

2001 (e) Gregorian Calendar

Date	Face Value	Description	Weight in oz's	Metal	Finish	Size mm	Mintage Max/ Actual	Issue Price	Average Retail
1999 : CENTENARY OF THE PERTH MINT									
Bimetal issue : 0.2354 oz fine gold & 0.161oz fine silver									
1999 a	100	1899 sov rev.	1 oz	Bimetal	Proof	n/a	7,500/ 5,625	285	475
1999 a	100	1899 sov rev.	1 oz	Bimetal	Unc	n/a	50,000/ 9752	210	395

[a] To commemorate the 100th anniversary of the opening of The Perth Mint, a bi-metal coin dated 1999 was struck in both proof and uncirculated condition with a mintmark P100. The centrepiece of the bi-metal coin is a 22-carat core with the same specifications as the original 22 - carat Perth Mint sovereign. The proof coin was issued in a timber case while the uncirculated version in a green crocodile skin patterned black and green case.

2000 : VARIOUS MILLENNIUM ISSUES

Date	Face Value	Description	Weight in oz's	Metal	Finish	Size mm	Mintage Max/ Actual	Issue Price	Average Retail
2000 b	1	Earth,moon,stars	1 oz	Colour	Proof	40.6	30,000 / n/a	59	65
2000 c	20	View of the Earth	1 oz	Bimetal	Proof	n/a	7,500/ n/a	310	450

2001 : VARIOUS MILLENNIUM ISSUES

Date	Face Value	Description	Weight in oz's	Metal	Finish	Size mm	Mintage Max/ Actual	Issue Price	Average Retail
2001 d	1	Cleopatras Needle	1 oz	Colour	Proof	40.6	30,000/ n/a	65	65
2001 e	20	Gregorian calendar	1 oz	Bimetal	Proof	n/a	7,500/ n/a	332	450

New South Wales

South Australia

Victoria

Western Australia

Tasmania

Queensland

Date	Face Value	Description	Weight in oz's	Metal	Finish	Size mm	Mintage Max/ Actual	Issue Price	Average Retail
2001 - ANDA FAIR FEDERATION STATE TRIBUTE									
2001	1& 25¢	Perth ANDA	1oz	Silver	Proof	40.6	1,500/ n/a	99	80
2001	1& 25¢	Hobart ANDA	1oz	Silver	Proof	40.6	1,500/ n/a	99	80
2001	1& 25¢	Brisbane ANDA	1oz	Silver	Proof	40.6	1,500/ n/a	99	80
2001	1& 25¢	Sydney ANDA	1oz	Silver	Proof	40.6	1,500/ n/a	99	80
2001	1& 25¢	Adelaide ANDA	1oz	Silver	Proof	40.6	1,500/ n/a	99	80
2001	1& 25¢	Melb. ANDA	1oz	Silver	Proof	40.6	1,500/ n/a	99	80
2001	Case containing one of the each of the above						Inc above	594	750

ONE YEAR : MULTIPLE COIN DESIGNS

ALL GOLD, SILVER OR ALUM/BRONZE ISSUES

2001 (a) Federation silver two piece issue   2001 (b) Federation bi-metal two piece issue

Date	Face Value	Description	Weight in oz's	Metal	Finish	Size mm	Mintage Max/ Actual	Issue Price	Average Retail
2001 - FEDERATION. FINE SILVER PAIR									
2001	1&25¢	Federation	n/a	Silver	Proof	50	30,000/21,668	99	80

The reverse portrays the official badges of the six states and the NT. The central motif features a detailed illustration of Parliament House. 27,500 of the above mintage were issued individually. 2000 coins were reserved for other sets.

Date	Face Value	Description	Weight in oz's	Metal	Finish	Size mm	Mintage Max/ Actual	Issue Price	Average Retail
2001 - FEDERATION. BI - METAL ISSUE									
2001	1&25¢	Federation	n/a	Silver	Proof	50	7,500/7,350	325	300

The reverse depicts the Australian coat of arms, laid on a bed of golden wattle, the national floral emblem of Australia. This central gold insert is surrounded with the floral emblems of the individual states and territories. 7500 of the above mintage were issued individually. 2500 coins were reserved for other sets.

2002 (f) Jubilee Silver   2002 (g) Accession Bimetal   2003 (h) Coronation Silver   2003 (i) Coronation Bimetal

2002 GOLDEN JUBILEE COIN THEMES

Gold Issues 99.99% fine. Silver Issues 99.9% fine

Date	Face Value	Description	Weight	Metal	Finish	Size	Mintage Max/ Actual	Issue Price	Average Retai
2002 f	1	Accession	1 oz	Silver	Proof	n/a	40,000/ n/a	60	90
2002 g	20	Jubilee	1 oz	Bimetal	Proof	36.6	7,500/ n/a	575	600
2003 h	1	Coronation	1 oz	Silver	Proof	n/a	40,000/ 23,733	60	90
2003 i	20	Coronation	1 oz	Bimetal	Proof	36.6	7,500/ 621	395	425

(f) The central design depicts the Queen on horseback during the Trooping the Colour ceremony, held each year to commemorate her official birthday.
(g) Modelled on the Order of the Thistle breast star, this award is the most exclusive British order of chivalry and was founded by Edward III in 1348.
(h) The central design features a coloured image of St Edward's Crown surrounded by a decorative border and a representation of the breast star of the Order of the Thistle.
(i) The reverse of the fine gold centrepiece depicts the four different effigies used to date to portray the image of Queen Elizabeth II on Australian currency.

See their advertisement on page 22

ONE YEAR : MULTIPLE COIN DESIGNS

ALL GOLD, SILVER OR ALUM/BRONZE ISSUES

NEW ZEALAND REVERSE AUSTRALIAN REVERSE

NZ Uncirc al/br Proof Silver Proof gold AUST Al/br Silver Gold

Date	Face Value	Description	Weight	Metal	Finish	Size	Mintage Max/ Actual	Issue Price	Average Retail
2005 : ANZAC 90TH ANNIVERSARY									
2005	1	Aust or NZ	20g	Al/Br	Unc	n/a	15,000/ 14,183	32.95	40
2005	1	Aust or NZ	1 oz	Silver	Proof	n/a	15,000/ All sold	152.9	140
2005	10	Aust or NZ	1/4 oz	Gold	Proof	n/a	1,000/ All sold	875	550

2005. Gold & Silver 'Dancing man' pair 2005. Icons of Australia & New Zealand

Date	Face Value	Description	Weight in oz's	Metal	Finish	Size mm	Mintage Max/ Actual	Issue Price	Average Retail
2005 - DANCING MAN. END OF WWII. 60 YEARS									
2005	1	WWII 60th	1 oz	Silver	Proof	36.6	25,000/ 20,558	79.50	60
2005	100	WWII 60th	1 oz	Gold	Proof	n/a	750/ n/a	1,349	1,400
2005	1 & 10	1 oz pair		Gold & Silver	Proof	--	750/ n/a	1,890	1,890
2005 - ICONS OF AUSTRALIA & NEW ZEALAND									
2005		Two coin set		Alum/ Bronze			20,000/ 16,547	29.95	30

2005 (a) Australia's Peacekeepers

2006 (c) TV. Set of 5 Silver Proofs

Date	Face Value	Description	Metal	Finish	Weight	Mintage Max/ Actual	Issue Price	Retail Average
2005 : AUSTRALIA'S PEACEKEEPERS								
2006 a	2	Five coin cased set	Silver	Proof	1 oz	2,500/ 1,259	499	599
2006 : 50 YEARS OF TELEVISION								
2006 c	1	Proof Five coin set	Silver 99.9 fine		1 oz	12,500/ 9,470	85	110

ONE YEAR : MULTIPLE COIN DESIGNS

ALL GOLD, SILVER OR ALUM/BRONZE ISSUES

2006 [a] Dame Edna Silver & Alum/bronze

2006 [c] Banknote portraits

Date	Face Value	Description	Metal	Finish	Weight in oz's	Mintage Max/ Actual	Issue Price	Retail Average
[a/b]		**2006 : DAME EDNA EVERAGE**						
2006 a	1	Dame Edna Everage	Silver	Proof	1 oz	8,500/ 4,612	69	70
2006 b	1	Dame Edna Everage	Al/br	Uncirc	1 oz	*Only available as a PNC*		
[c]		**2006 : PORTRAITS ON BANKNOTES**						
2006	1	Elizabeth II/ Artwork	Silver	Proof	1 oz	1,000/ 789	80	80
2006	1	Macarther/ Farrer	Silver	Proof	1 oz	1,000/ All sold	80	80
2006	1	Banks/ Chisholm	Silver	Proof	1 oz	1,000/ 862	80	80
2006	1	Greenway/ Lawson	Silver	Proof	1 oz	1,000/ 800	80	80
2006	1	K'Smith/ Hargraves	Silver	Proof	1 oz	1,000/ 879	80	80
2006 c		Cased set. One of each	Silver	Proof	1 oz	2,500/ 1,259	375	300

2006 (d) 1oz Silver

2006 (e) 1/25oz Gold

2006 (f) 1/4 oz Gold

d/e/f] 2006 FIFA WORLD CUP - GERMANY

Date	Face Value	Description	Weight	Metal	Finish		Mintage Max/ Actual	Issue Price	Retail Average
2006 d	1&25¢	Holey $1 & Dump	1oz	Silver	Proof	40.6	50,000/ 21,630	99	75
2006 e	4	World Cup Trophy	1/25oz	Gold	Proof	40.6	50,000/ 23,474	79	165
2006 f	25	Players with ball	1/4oz	Gold	Proof	20.1	25,000/ 3,190	385	350

AUSTRALIAN GOLD ICONS

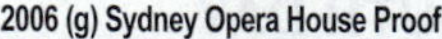

2006 (g) Sydney Opera House Proof

2007 : (h) Harbour Bridge Proof

Date	Weight in oz's	Face Value	Description	Max/ Actual	Issue Price	Retail Average
2006 g	1/25oz	5	Sydney Opera House	12,727	95	105
2007 h	1/25 oz	5	Sydney Harbour Bridge	9,420	95	105

ONE YEAR : MULTIPLE COIN DESIGNS

ALL GOLD, SILVER OR ALUM/BRONZE ISSUES

(a) 1oz Silver

(b) 1 oz Gold

(c) 1oz Silver

(d) 1/25 oz Gold

Date	Face Value	Description	Weight in oz's	Metal	Finish	Size mm	Mintage Max/ Actual	Issue Price	Average Retail
2007 : DIAMOND WEDDING JUBILEE									
2007 a	1	Diamond Jubilee	1 oz	Silver	Proof	36.6	12,000/ 5,069	80	45
2007 b	100	Diamond Jubilee	1 oz	Gold	Proof	36.6	1,000/ 411	1,595	1,600
2007 - SYDNEY HARBOUR BRIDGE									
2007 c	1	Fireworks / Br	1 oz	Silver	Proof	36.6	12,000/ 5,069	80	45
2007 d	25	Plain bridge rev	1/25 oz	Gold	Proof	36.6	100,000/ n/a	195	210

(e) 1/4 oz Gold Proof

(f) 1 oz Silver Proof

(g) Al/br Unc & PNC

Date	Face Value	Description	Weight in oz's	Metal	Finish	Size mm	Mintage Max/ Actual	Issue Price	Average Retail
2008 e	25	Cross	1/4 oz	Gold	Proof	20.1	1918/ 698	555	555
2008 f	1	Bugler	1 oz	Silver	Proof	36.6	12,500/ 7,354	82.5	100
2008 g	1	Rising Sun	1 oz	Al/br	Unc	*Coin & Stamp cover. Priced in PNC section*			

(h) Silver Proof

(i) Al/br Unc

(j) Gold Proof

(k) Al/br Unc

Date	Face Value	Description	Weight in oz's	Metal	Finish	Size mm	Mintage Max/ Actual	Issue Price	Average Retail
2008 : AFL CENTENARY									
2008 h	1	The 'Mark'	1 oz	Silver	Proof	n/a	12,500/ 4,573	95	95
2008 i	1	The 'Mark'	1 oz	Al/br	Unc	n/a	To order/ 31,015	13.5	13.5
2008 i	1	PNC	1 oz	Al/br	Unc	*Coin & Stamp cover. Priced in PNC section*			
2008 : WORLD YOUTH DAY									
2008	1	No colour	1 oz	Silver	Proof	n/a	25,000/ 3,638	89	80
2008 j	100	No colour	1/4 oz	Gold	Proof	n/a	1,000/ 273	1,750	1,750
2008 k	1	Coloured	1 oz	Al/br	Unc	n/a	500,000/ 40,953	13.5	16
2008 k	1	PNC	1 oz	Al/br	Unc	*Coin & Stamp cover. Priced in PNC*			

ONE YEAR : MULTIPLE COIN DESIGNS

ALL GOLD, SILVER OR ALUM/BRONZE ISSUES

2009 : REJECTED DESIGNS FOR 1966 DECIMALS

2009	Five 1966 silver proof coins in case	7,500/ 3,344	169	185
2009	Single 20¢. Gold Coast ANDA Fair	2,500/ 2,115	n/a	n/a

INDIVIDUAL TECHNICAL DETAILS

Monetary Denomination (AUD)	20¢	10¢	5¢	2¢	1¢
Silver Content (Troy oz)	0.4456	0.2273	0.1202	0.2099	0.1102
Fineness (% purity)	99.9	99.9	99.9	99.9	99.9
Minimum Gross Weight (gms)	12.86	6.07	2.74	5.53	2.43
Maximum Diameter (mm)	28.60	23.60	19.60	21.60	17.60
Maximum Thickness (mm)	3.00	3.00	3.00	3.00	3.00

2009 (a) Silver Proof

2009 (b) Al/br Unc

2009 (c) Al/br Unc

2009 (d) Silver Proof

Date	Face Value	Description	Weight in oz's	Metal	Finish	Size	Mintage Max/ Actual	Issue Price	Retail Average
2009 : SYDNEY WORLD MASTERS GAMES									
2009 a	1	Colour reverse	1 oz	Silver	Proof	40.6	5,000/ 1,993	95.5	75
2009 b	1	Plain reverse	13.8	Al/br	Unc	30.2	To order/ 8,467	13.95	15
2009 : CENTENARY OF AUST. SWIMMING									
2009 c	1	Plain reverse	13.8	Al/br	Unc	30.2	To order/ 8,467	13.95	15
2009 d	1	Colour reverse	1 oz	Silver	Proof	40.6	7,500/ 1,993	97.5	75

2010 (a) Panda/ Koala 2010 (b) Pavillion 2010 (c) Map 2010 (d) Kookaburra 2010 (e) Citiscape

2010 : SHANGHAI WORLD EXPO

2010 a	1	Panda & Koala	1oz	Silver	Proof	40.6	30,000/ 10,244	97.5	97.5
2010 b	1	Aust. Pavillion	1oz	Silver	Proof	40.6	30,000/ 4,299	97.5	97.5
2010 c	1	Aust. Map	1oz	Silver	Proof	40.6	30,000/ 10,286	107.5	200
2010 d	1	Kookaburra	1oz	Silver	Proof	40.6	30,000/ 10,481	97.5	97.5

ONE YEAR : MULTIPLE COIN DESIGNS

ALL GOLD, SILVER OR ALUM/BRONZE ISSUES

2010 (a) 1 oz Silver Rev

2010 (b) 5 gms Gold Rev

2010 (c) 1/4 oz Gold Rev

Date	Nominal F/Value	Description	Weight	Metal	Type	Size	Mintage Max/ Actual	Issue Price	Current Retail
2010 - FIFA WORLD CUP. SOUTH AFRICA									
2010 a	1	Runner	1 oz	Silver	Proof	36.6	15,000/ 7138	97.5	97.5
2010 b	2	Kangaroo	5gm	Gold	Proof	11.6	40,000/ n/a	60	75

(a) Silver Reverse

(b) Gold Reverse

(c) Silver Reverse

(d) Gold Reverse

Date	Nominal F/Value	Description	Weight	Metal	Type	Size	Mintage Max/ Actual	Issue Price	Current Retail
2010 - OUR FIRST SAINT SISTER MARY McKILLOP									
2010 a	1	Coloured	1 oz	Silver	Proof	40	7,500/ All sold	89.5	90
2010 b	15	Coloured	1/10oz	Gold	Proof	18.6	2,010/ All sold	275	450

2012 : QEII DIAMOND JUBILEE ISSUES

Date	Nominal F/Value	Description	Weight	Metal	Type	Size	Mintage Max/ Actual	Issue Price	Current Retail
2012 c	1	Portrait	1 oz	Silver	Proof	40.6	7,500/ n/a	104	104
2012	25	Young head	1/4oz	Silver	Proof	20.6	1,000/ All sold	717	760
2012 d	200	YH diamond	2 oz	Gold	Proof	41.1	60/ All sold	5,995	5,995

(a) Two coin Proof Silver cased set

(b) Silver Kilo

(c) Gold Kilo

Date	Face Value	Description	Weight in oz's	Metal	Finish	Size	Mintage Max/ Actual	Issue Price	Retail Average
2012 : QEII DIAMOND JUBILEE ISSUES									
2012 a	1 x 2	Cased pair	2 oz	Silver	Proof	40.6	1,000/ All sold	210	250
2012 b	100	Crown	1 kg	Silver	Proof	100.6	600/ All sold	1,990	2,200
2012 c	3,000	Crown	1 kg	Gold	Proof	75.6	60/ All sold	62,950	60,000

ONE YEAR : MULTIPLE COIN DESIGNS

ALL GOLD, SILVER OR ALUM/BRONZE ISSUES

(a) FIFA 1/2 oz Silver

(b) FIFA .5g Gold

(c) Royal Birth Silver

(d) Royal Birth Gold

Date	Face Value	Description	Weight in oz's	Metal	Finish	Size mm	Mintage Max/ Actual	Issue Price	Average Retail
2012 for 2014 : FIFA WORLD CUP BRAZIL									
2012 a	.50¢	Plain rev	1/2 oz	Silver	Proof	n/a	10,000/ 3,749	67	67
2012 b	1	Colour rev	.5 gm	Gold	Proof	11.6	7,500/ 2,432	74.5	80
2013 : BIRTH OF HRH PRINCE GEORGE									
2013 c	1	HRH George	1 oz	Silver	Proof	40.6	10,000 / 5,885	99	99
2013 d	25	HRH George	1/4 oz	Gold	Proof	20.6	1,000 / All sold	675	675

(e) Victoria Silver

(f) Victoria gold

(g) Elizabeth II Silver

(h) Elizabeth II Gold

Date	Face Value	Description	Weight in oz's	Metal	Finish	Size mm	Mintage Max/ Actual	Issue Price	Average Retail
2013 - VICTORIA'S 175TH CORONATION									
2013 e	1	Victoria	1 oz	Silver	Proof	40.6	5,000/ 1,803	99	99
2013 f	200	Victoria	1/4 oz	Gold	Proof	21.1	150/ All sold	675	675
2013 - ELIZABETH II 60TH CORONATION									
2013 g	1	Elizabeth II	1 oz	Silver	Proof	40.6	5,000/ 1,803	99	99
2013 h	1	Elizabeth II	1/4 oz	Gold	Proof	20.6	150/ All sold	675	675

(i) Cockatoo

(j) Budgerigar

(k) Bowerbird

(l) Lorikeet

(m) Fairy Wren

Date	Face Value	Description	Weight in oz's	Metal	Finish	Size	Mintage Max/ Actual	Issue Price	Retail Average
2013 - BIRDS OF AUSTRALIA									
2013 i	.50¢	Cockatoo	1/2 oz	Silver	Proof	36.6	10,000/ 8,651	67	67
2013 j	.50¢	Budgerigar	1/2 oz	Silver	Proof	36.6	10,000/ 4,767	67	67
2013 k	.50¢	Bowerbird	1/2 oz	Silver	Proof	36.6	10,000/ 3,559	67	67
2013 l	.50¢	Lorikeet	1/2 oz	Silver	Proof	36.6	10,000/ 3,951	67	67
2013 m	50¢	Fairy Wren	1/2 oz	Silver	Proof	36.6	10,000/ 3,396	67	67

ONE YEAR : MULTIPLE COIN DESIGNS

EITHER GOLD, SILVER OR ALUM/BRONZE ISSUES

2013 (a) Dump

2013 (b) Holey Dollar

2013 (c) Melbourne

2013 (d) St Peterburg

Date	Face Value	Description	Weight in oz's	Metal	Finish	Size	Mintage Max/ Actual	Issue Price	Retail Average
2013 HOLEY DOLLAR & DUMP BICENTENARY									
2013 a	25¢	Dump	6g	Silver	Proof	17.6	4,000/ All sold	115	125
2013 b	1.00	Holey Dollar	25.2g	Silver	Proof	40.6	Inc above		2 x coins
2013 SISTER CITIES. ANDA MELBOURNE FAIR									
2013 c/d	1	Melb/ St Petersburg	1 oz	Silver	Proof	40.6	5,000/ 2,000	104	110

The pairing of Melbourne and St Petersburg, Russia, as Sister Cities was celebrated in a special ANDA issue for it's 2013 Melbourne Coin Fair. The reverse of the coin features iconic landmarks of both cities due to the use of lenticular technology. The front façade of Flinders Street Station in Melbourne is depicted with a passing tram. The Admiralty building of St Petersburg, which faces the Neva River, is also shown with Isaac Cathedral in the background.

2014 (a) Summer

2014 (b) Autumn

2014 (c) Winter

2014 (d) Spring

2014 - AUSTRALIAN SEASONS

Date	Face Value	Description	Weight in oz's	Metal	Finish	Size	Mintage Max/ Actual	Issue Price	Retail Average
2014 a	1	Summer	1 oz	Silver	Proof	33.2	5,000/ Sold out	99	99
2014 b	1	Autumn	1 oz	Silver	Proof	33.2	5,000/ 3,509	99	99
2014 c	1	Winter	1 oz	Silver	Proof	33.2	5,000/ 2,502	99	99
2014 d	1	Spring	1 oz	Silver	Proof	33.2	5,000/ 2,896	99	99

(a) Genyornis

(b) Thylacolen

(c) Megalania

(d) Procoptodon

(e) Diprotodon

Date	Face Value	Description	Weight in oz's	Metal	Finish	Size	Mintage Max/ Actual	Issue Price	Retail Average
2014 - AUSTRALIAN MEGAFAUNA									
2014 a	1	Genyornis	1 oz	Silver	Proof	40.6	6,500 / 1,336	99	99
2014 b	1	Thylacolen	1 oz	Silver	Proof	40.6	6,500 / 1,287	99	99
2014 c	1	Megalania	1 oz	Silver	Proof	40.6	6,500 / 1,156	99	99
2014 d	1	Procoptodon	1 oz	Silver	Proof	40.6	6,500 / tba	99	99
2014 e	1	Diprotodon	1 oz	Silver	Proof	40.6	6,500 / 1,479	99	99

ONE YEAR : MULTIPLE COIN DESIGNS

EITHER GOLD, SILVER OR ALUM/BRONZE ISSUES

2014 (a) Australovenator 2015 (b) Diamantinasaurus 2015 (c) Leaellynasaura 2016 (d) Minmi

2014 - AUSTRALIAN AGE OF DINOSAURS

Date	Face Value	Description	Weight in oz's	Metal	Finish	Size	Mintage Max/ Actual	Issue Price	Retail Average
2014 a	1	Australovenator	1 oz	Silver	Proof	40.6	5,000 / 2,412	99	99
2015 b	1	Diamantinasaurus	1 oz	Silver	Proof	40.6	5,000 / 2,014	99	99
2015 c	1	Leaellynasaura	1 oz	Silver	Proof	40.6	5,000 / 1,898	99	99
2015 d	1	Minmi Paravertebra	1 oz	Silver	Proof	40.6	5,000 / 1,640	99	99
2015	1	Muttaburrasaurus	1 oz	Silver	Proof	40.6	5,000 / 1,888	99	99

(e&f) Banjo Silver (g) Banjo gold (h) Shark Silver (i) Shark Gold

2014 - BANJO PATERSON 150TH BIRTHDAY

Date	Face Value	Description	Weight in oz's	Metal	Finish	Size	Mintage Max/ Actual	Issue Price	Retail Average
2014 e	1	Coloured coin	1 oz	Silver	Proof	40.6	4,000/ 1,315	99	99
2014	1	Coin & gilt $10	5 oz	Silver	Proof	60.6	250/ 249	695	695
2014 g	1	A.B. Paterson	1/4 oz	Gold	Proof	20.6	500/ 148	695	695

2015 - GREAT WHITE SHARK - HIGH RELIEF

Date	Face Value	Description	Weight in oz's	Metal	Finish	Size	Mintage Max/ Actual	Issue Price	Retail Average
2015 h	1	Great White Shark	1 oz	Silver	Proof	32.6	10,000 5,179	104	104
2015 i	100	Great White Shark	1 oz	Silver	Proof	27.3	500 / tha	2,695	104

2015 [j] Silver High relief 2015 [k] 1/4 oz Gold 2015 [l] Charlotte. Silver 2015 [m] Charlotte. Gold

2015 - THE LONGEST REIGNING MONARCH

Date	Face Value	Description	Weight in oz's	Metal	Finish	Size	Mintage Max/ Actual	Issue Price	Retail Average
2015 j	1	QE2 Longest reign	1 oz	Silver	Proof	40.6	5,000/ 2,937	99	99
2015	25	QE2 Longest reign	1/4oz	Gold	Proof	20.6	1,000/ 862	695	695
2015 k	200	QE2 Longest reign	2 oz	Gold	Proof	41.1	350/ All sold	5,150	5,150

2015 - BIRTH OF PRINCESS CHARLOTTE

Date	Face Value	Description	Weight in oz's	Metal	Finish	Size	Mintage Max/ Actual	Issue Price	Retail Average
2015 l	1	Babe in arms	1 oz	Silver	Proof	40.6	5,000 / 3,604	99	99
2015 m	25	Babe in arms	1/4oz	Gold	Proof	20.6	1,000 / 736	695	695

ONE YEAR : MULTIPLE COIN DESIGNS

EITHER GOLD, SILVER OR ALUM/ BRONZE ISSUES

2015 - AUSTRALIAN SUNBURNT COUNTRY

2015 a	1	Sweeping Plains	1 oz	Silver	Proof	4,250 / 630	104	99
2015 b	1	Mountain Ranges	1 oz	Silver	Proof	4,250 / 565	104	99
2015 c	1	Drought & Flood	1 oz	Silver	Proof	4,250 / 476	104	99
2015 d	1	Jewel Sea	1 oz	Silver	Proof	4,250 / 567	104	99
2015		Four coin set	1x4	Silver	Proof	750 / tba	416	99

2016 [e] RSL Proof Silver

2016 [f] RSL Proof Gold

2016 [g] One Cent

2016 [h] Two Cents

Date	Face Value	Description	Weight in oz's	Metal	Finish	Size	Mintage Max/ Actual	Issue Price	Retail Average
2016 - CENTENARY OF THE RSL									
2016 e	1	Coloured Badge	1 oz	Silver	Proof	40.6	1,000 / 991	99	99
2016 f	25	RSL Badge	1/4oz	Gold	Proof	40.6	5,000 / 1,946	799	799
2016 - 50TH ANNIVERSARY DECIMAL CURRENCY									
2016 g/h		One & Two coins, Cased		Silver	Proof	—	2,000 / tha	149	149

2016 [i] Proof 1oz Silver

2016 [j] 1/4 oz Gold

2016 Gold Obverse

2016 [k] Gold High relief

2016 - QE2 90th BIRTHDAY

2016 i	1	Cased high relief	1 oz	Silver	Proof	32.6	5,000 / tha	109	109
2016 j	25	St Edwards	1/4oz	Gold	Proof	20.6	5,000 / tha	799	799
2016 k	200	Cased high relief	2 oz	Gold	Proof	40.6	300 / tha	5,150	5,500

STANDARD DESIGN - ANNUAL

THE DESIGN REMAINS CONSTANT FROM YEAR TO YEAR

Coat of Arms Sovereign

Half Sovereign Replica

Full Sovereign Replica

Citizen Reverse Al/br

Date	Face Value	Metal	Type	Purity	Weight in gms	Mintage Max/ Actual	Issue Price	Average Retail
COAT OF ARMS & SYDNEY MINT REPLICAS								
2009 - 2012 AUSTRALIAN COAT OF ARMS								
2009	25	Gold	Proof	22 ct. 91.67%	22.6	2,500/ All sold	649	750
2010	25	Gold	Proof	22 ct. 91.67%	22.6	2,500/ 1,482	649	750
2011	25	Gold	Proof	22 ct. 91.67%	22.6	2,500/ 1,094	675	750
2012	25	Gold	Proof	22 ct. 91.67%	22.6	2,500/ 1,033	750	750
SYDNEY MINT REPLICA HALF SOVEREIGN								
2015	15	Gold	Proof	22 ct. 91.67%	11.3	1,500/ tba	375	395
2016	15	Gold	Proof	22 ct. 91.67%	11.3	1,500/ 794	399	399
SYDNEY MINT REPLICA FULL SOVEREIGN								
2013	25	Gold	Proof	22 ct. 91.67%	22.6	1,750/ 1,096	650	750
2014	25	Gold	Proof	22 ct. 91.67%	22.6	1,500/ All sold	675	750
2015	25	Gold	Proof	22 ct. 91.67%	22.6	1,500/ n/a	675	750
2016	25	Gold	Proof	22 ct. 91.67%	22.6	1,500/ 1,287	675	750
2017	25	Gold	Proof	22 ct. 91.67%	22.6	1,000/ n/a	749	775

2014 - AUSTRALIAN CITIZENSHIP

Date	Face Value	Description	Finish	Metal	Weight in gm's	Size	Mintage Max/Actual	Issue Price	Retail Average
2009	1	Coat of Arms	Spec	Al/br	13	30.6	12,883	12.95	14
2010	1	Coat of Arms	Spec	Al/br	13	30.6	n/a	12.95	14
2011	1	Coat of Arms	Spec	Al/br	13	30.6	22,598	12.95	14
2012	1	Coat of Arms	Spec	Al/br	13	30.6	n/a	12.95	14
2013	1	Coat of Arms	Spec	Al/br	13	30.6	n/a	12.95	14
2014	1	Coat of Arms	Spec	Al/br	13	30.6	35,755	12.95	14
2015	1	Coat of Arms	Spec	Al/br	13	30.6	36,031	12.95	14
2016	1	Coat of Arms	Spec	Al/br	13	30.6	37,472	12.95	14
2017	1	Coat of Arms	Spec	Al/br	13	30.6	tba	13.90	14

For most of the first 50 years of the 20th century, "home grown" or immigrants to Australia were regarded as British citizens. The first "Australian" citizenship ceremony took place on February 3, 1949 at Albert Hall in Canberra. Since then more than four million migrants have made the pledge of commitment to Australia. A record 169,123 people became Australian citizens during 2006/ 2007. The commemorative will also allow new citizens to mark the year in which they were naturalised, as each annual release will display a new year-date. The base metal coin is mint to order and enclosed in a colourful folder.

BULLION SILVER COINS

2013 [a] Silver Alliance

2013 [b&c] Gold Alliance

2014 [d] Silver Coral Sea

2014 [e] Silver Coral Sea

2014 [f] Great White 2015 [g] Hammerhead 2016 [h] Tiger Shark 2014 [i] Crocodile 2015 [j] Funnel Web

Date	Face Value	Weight in oz's	Metal	Size	Type	Size	Mintage Max/ Actual	Issue Price	Retail Average
2013 - AUSTRALIA USA ALLIANCE									
2013 a	.50¢	1/2 oz	Silver	99.9	Specimen	32.6	1,069,980	39	b/v
2013 b	15	1/10 oz	Gold	99.99	Specimen	16.6	262,142	b/v	b/v
2013 c	25	1/4 oz	Gold	99.99	Specimen	20.6	22,589	b/v	b/v
2013 - BATTLE OF THE CORAL SEA									
2014 d	.50¢	1/2 oz	Silver	99.99	Specimen	32.6	615,017	39	b/v
2014	15	1/10 oz	Gold	99.99	Specimen	16.6	148,937	b/v	b/v
2014 e	25	1/4 oz	Gold	99.99	Specimen	20.6	15,093	b/v	b/v
2015	.50¢	1/2 oz	Silver	99.99	Specimen	32.6	1,185,003	39	b/v
2015	15	1/10 oz	Gold	99.99	Specimen	16.6	184,993	b/v	b/v
2015	25	1/4 oz	Gold	99.99	Specimen	20.6	16,995	b/v	b/v
2014 - AUSTRALIAN SHARKS									
2014 f	.50¢	1/2 oz	Silver	99.99	Specimen	32	298,852	39	b/v
2015 g	.50¢	1/2 oz	Silver	99.99	Specimen	32	115,005	39	b/v
2016 h	.50¢	1/2 oz	Silver	99.99	Specimen	32	tba	39	b/v

The shark issue was only released in Australia. The mininium order from the Perth Mint was 25 coins or more. The complete issue was limited to 300,000 coins.

Date	Face Value	Weight in oz's	Metal	Size	Type	Size	Mintage Max/ Actual	Issue Price	Retail Average
1914 : SALTWATER CROCODILE									
2014 i	1	1 oz	Silver	99.99	Specimen	40.6	1,000,000	b/v	b/v
2015 j	1	1 oz	Silver	99.99	Proof	40.6	5,000	b/v	b/v
2015 : FUNNEL WEB SPIDER									
2015 k	.50¢	1/2 oz	Silver	99.99	Specimen	32	115,005	b/v	b/v
2015	1	1 oz	Silver	99.9	Specimen	40.6	1,000,000	b/v	b/v

ONE YEAR : SINGLE COIN DESIGNS

ALL GOLD, SILVER OR ALUM/BRONZE ISSUES

2003 (a) Golden Pipeline
Silver 1 oz Proof

2003 (b) William's 21st
Silver 1 oz Proof

2004 (c) Royal Visit
Gilt 1 oz Specimen

2004 (d) Eureka Stockade
Silver 1 oz Proof

2004 (e) Man on Moon
Silver 1 oz Proof

2005 (f) Tennis Open
Silver 1 oz Proof

2005 (g) PGA Golf Open
Silver 1 oz Proof

(h) Rotary Centenary
Silver 1 oz Proof

2005 (i) Cocos (Keeling) Is.
Silver 1 oz Proof

2005 (j) Prince Harry
Silver 1 oz Proof

(k) 2006 Aust/Japan
Silver 1 oz Proof

(l) 2006 Duyfken
Silver 1 oz Proof

(m) 2006 QEII Birthday
Silver 1 oz Proof

(n) 2007 Lunar Pig
Silver 1 oz Proof

(o) 2007 SAS
Silver 1 oz Proof

2007 (p) Lunar Dollar
Silver & Gold Bimetal

Date	Face Value	Description	Type	Metal	Weight in oz's	Size mm	Mintage Max/ Actual	Issue Price	Retail Average
2003 a	1	Golden Pipeline	Proof	Silver	1 oz	40.6	5,000/ All sold	60	80
2003 b	1	Prince William	Proof	Silver	1 oz	40.6	12,500/ All sold	75	90
2004 c	1	Royal Visit	Proof	Gilt	1 oz	40.6	12,500/ All sold	65	65
2004 d	1	Eureka Stockade	Proof	Silver	1 oz	40.6	12,500/ 11,138	99	110
2004 e	1	First Moon Walk	Proof	Silver	1 oz	40.6	40,000/ 18,415	79.5	80
2005 f	1	Tennis Open	Proof	Silver	1 oz	40.6	10,000/ All sold	69.5	80
2005 g	1	PGA Golf Open	Proof	Silver	1 oz	40.6	10,000/ 4,571	69.5	80
2005 h	1	Rotary coin cent.	Proof	Silver	1 oz	40.6	100,000/ 6,989	79.5	80
2005 h	1	Rotary coin/stamp	Proof	Silver	1 oz	40.6	7,500/ 3,881	79.5	90
2005 i	1	Cocos (Keeling)	Proof	Silver	1 oz	40.6	7,500/ 6,436	69	90
2005 j	1	Prince Harry's 21	Proof	Silver	1 oz	40.6	12,500/ 6,008	69	90
2006 k	1	Aust/ Japan Exch	Proof	Silver	1 oz	40.6	80,000/ 48,279	75	90
2006 l	1	Duyfken (1606)	Proof	Silver	1 oz	40.6	10,000/ 9,941	75	90
2006 m	1	Queen's 80th	Proof	Silver	1 oz	40.6	12,500/ 5,823	69	80
2007 n	1	Lunar Pig Year	Proof	Silver	1 oz	40.6	7,500/ n/a	88	90
2007 o	1	Special Air Service	Proof	Silver	1 oz	40.6	7,500/ All sold	69	225
2007 p	1	Holey Dollar & Dump	Proof	Bimetal	1 oz	40.6	8888/ 5,994	99	110

ONE YEAR : SINGLE COIN DESIGNS

2007 (a) Phar Lap
Silver 1 oz Proof

2008 (b) Rum Rebellion
Silver 1 oz Proof

2008 (c) First Fleet
Silver 1 oz Proof

2008 (d) Coat of Arms
Silver 1 oz Proof

2008 (f) America's Cup
Silver 1 oz Proof

2008 (g) Proclamation
Silver 1 oz Proof

2008 (h) Christmas Island
Silver 1 oz Proof

2008 (i) HMAS Sydney
Silver 1 oz Proof

2008 (j) Prince Charles
1 oz Silver Proof

2009 (k) Postal Service
1 oz Silver Proof

2009 (l) Astronomy
1 oz Silver Proof

2010 (m) Aust 1st Flight
1 oz Silver Proof

2010 (n) 1st Silver Coins
1 oz Silver Proof

2010 (o) Macquarie
1 oz Silver Proof

2010 (p) Winter Olympics
1 oz Silver Proof

2010 (q) Burke & Wills
1 oz Silver Proof

Date	Face Value	Description	Type	Metal	Weight in oz's	Size mm	Mintage Max/ Actual	Issue Price	Retail Average
2007 a	1	Phar Lap 75th	Proof	Silver	1 oz	40.6	7,500/ 5,055	78	95
2008 b	1	Rum Rebellion	Proof	Silver	1 oz	40.6	3,000/ 2,812	115	125
2008 c	1	First Fleet jigsaw	Proof	Silver	1 oz	40.6	1,500/ All sold	525	1,200
2008 c	1	Fleet coin & medal	Proof	Silver	1 oz	40.6	5,000/ All sold	82.5	80
2008 e	1	Coat of Arms	Proof	Silver	1 oz	40.6	7,500/ 6,611	82.5	80
2008 f	1	Australia II 25th	Proof	Silver	1 oz	40.6	5,000/ 4,864	95	80
2008 g	50¢	GB (Proc.) Shilling	Proof	Silver	1 oz	40.6	3,000/ n/a	39.5	90
2008 h	1	Christmas Island	Proof	Silver	1 oz	40.6	5,000/ All sold	82.5	95
2008 i	1	Discovery Sydney II	Proof	Silver	1 oz	40.6	5,000/ 3,762	82.5	90
2008	1	Sydney & Kormoran	Proof	Silver	1 oz	40.6	2,500/ All sold	179	225
2008 j	1	Prince Charles 60th	Proof	Silver	1 oz	40.6	12,500/ 1,968	82.5	85
2009 k	1	Postal Service 200th	Proof	Silver	1 oz	40.6	7,500/ 4,894	89.95	90
2009 l	1	Astronomy	Proof	Silver	1 oz	40.6	7,500/ 6,814	89.95	95
2010 m	1	First Aust. flight	Proof	Silver	1 oz	40.6	7,500/ 5,442	89.95	90
2010 n	1	First silver coinage	Proof	Silver	1 oz	40.6	7,500/ 3,814	89.95	90
2010 o	1	Lachlan Macquarie	Proof	Silver	1 oz	40.6	7,500/ 4,613	89.95	90
2010 p	1	Winter Olympics	Proof	Silver	1 oz	40.6	5,000/ 3,582	89.95	90
2010 q	1	Burke & Wills	Proof	Silver	1 oz	40.6	7,500/ 5,488	89.95	90

[g] 1,000 coins were released at each of the ANDA fairs in Sydney and Melbourne. The remaining 1,000 were offered direct to Perth Mint clients in a ballot that closed on October 31, 2008.

ONE YEAR : SINGLE COIN DESIGNS

ALL GOLD, SILVER OR ALUM/BRONZE ISSUES

2011 (a) First Bronze
Silver 1 oz Proof

2011 (b) Sydney Cove
Silver 1 oz Piefort

2011 (c) Nugget 25th
Gold 1 oz Proof

2011 (d) Duntroon
Silver 1 oz Proof

2011 (e) RAN Centenary
Silver 1 oz Proof

2011 (f) Royal Wedding
Silver 1 oz Proof

2011 (g) Nellie Melba
Silver 1 oz Proof

2011 (h) Rugby Union
Silver 1 oz Proof

2012 (i) Ginger Meggs
Silver 1 oz Proof

2012 (j) China & Australia
Silver 1 oz Proof

2012 (k) Christmas
Silver 1/2 oz Proof

2013 (l) Leichhardt
Silver 2 oz Proof

2013 (m) Kangaroo
Silver 1 oz Proof

2013 (n) First Banknote Centenary
Silver 1 oz Proof

2014 (o) George V
Silver 1 oz Proof

Date	Face Value	Description	Type	Metal	Weight in oz's	Weight mm	Mintage Max/ Actual	Issue Price	Retail Average
2011 a	1	First bronze coins	Proof	Silver	1 oz	40.6	7,500/ 1,938	89.5	95
2011 b	1	Sydney Cove	Piedfort	Silver	1 oz	n/a	2,500/ 2,201	199	200
2011 c	100	Nugget 25th anniv	Proof	Gold	1 oz	32.6	1,500/ 1,153	2,580	2,700
2011 d	1	Duntroon 100 yrs	Proof	Silver	1 oz	40.6	7,500/ 3,457	115	120
2011 e	1	Centenary of RAN	Proof	Silver	1 oz	40.6	7,500/ 5,209	99	110
2011 f	1	Royal Wedding	Proof	Silver	1 oz	40.6	12,500/ All sold	78	85
2011 g	1	Nellie Melba	Proof	Silver	1 oz	40.6	5,000/ 3,102	105	105
2011 h	1	Rugby Men of Gold	Proof	Silver	1 oz	40.6	5,000/ 2,138	82.5	80
2012 i	1	Ginger Meggs	Proof	Silver	1 oz	40.6	3,000/ All sold	69	80
2012 j	1	China Friendship	Proof	Silver	1 oz	40.6	5,000/ 4,864	95	80
2012 k	50¢	Christmas locket	Proof	Silver	1/2oz	40.6	5,000/ 2,911	125	125
2013 l	2	Ludwig Leichhardt	Proof	Silver	2 oz	55.6	2013/ 917	175	175
2013 m	50¢	Roo Stamp	Proof	Silver	1/2oz	—	4,000/ All sold	89.95	90
2013 n	1	First Banknote	Proof	Silver	1oz	—	3,000/ All sold	110	110
2014 o	50¢	George V Stamp	Proof	Silver	1/2oz	—	2,500/ All sold	99.95	100

ONE YEAR : SINGLE COIN DESIGNS

ALL GOLD, SILVER OR ALUM/BRONZE ISSUES

2013 (a) Snake Success

2013 (b) Christmas

2013 (c) Koala 25th

2014 (d) Christmas

2014 (e) Military Aviation

2014 (f) Submarine 100th

2015 (g) Red Cross

2015 (h) Berlin Expo

2015 (i) Lion Dance

2015 (j) ANZAC Stamp

2016 (j) Dragon & Phonenix

2016 (k) Dirk Hartog

2016 (l) Monkey King

2016 (m) Gumnuts 100th

2016 (n) Five Blessings

2017 (o) Happy Birthday

Date	Face Value	Description	Type	Metal	Weight in oz's	Weight mm	Mintage Max/ Actual	Issue Price	Retail Average
2013 a	1	Snake Success	Proof	Silver	1 oz	40.6	5,513/ n/a	104	104
2013 b	50¢	Christmas Tree	Proof	Silver	1/2oz	36.6	To order/ 5,000	63.5	63.5
2013 c	50¢	Koala 25th	Proof	Plat'um	1/2oz	25.1	1,200/ All sold	1,595	1,595
2014 d	50¢	Christmas	Proof	Silver	1/2oz	36.6	To order/ 1,519	63.5	63.5
2014 e	1	Military Aviation	Proof	Silver	1 oz	40.6	5,000/ 2,180	99	99
2014 f	1	Submarine Cent.	Proof	Silver	1 oz	40.6	3,000/ 2,476	105	105
2014 g	50¢	Red Cross	Proof	Silver	1/2 oz	36.6	5,000/ 1,151	99	99
2015 h	1	Berlin Money Expo	Proof	Silver	1 oz	40.6	5,000/ n/a	99	99
2015 i	1	Chinese Lion Dance	Proof	Silver	1 oz	40.6	5,000/ n/a	99	99
2016 j	1	Dragon & Phoenix	Spec	Silver	1 oz	40.6	50,000/ n/a	84	84
2016 k	1	Dirk Hartog	Proof	Slver	1 oz	32.6	3,000/ n/a	109	109
2016 l	1	Monkey King	Spec	Silver	1 oz	45.6	61,457	75	75
2016 m	1	Gumnuts 100th	Proof	Silver	1 oz	45.6	10,000/ 5,000	69	69
2016 n	1	Five Blessings	Proof	Silver	1 oz	45.6	10,000/ All sold	69	69
2017 o	1	Happy Birthday	Spec	Silver	1 oz	45.6	To order/ n/a	99	109

[a] Officially issued under the auspices of the Kingdom of Tuvalu, this issue would not normally included in this book. However it was adopted by ANDA as a special release at its Perth Coin Fair. The maximum mintage figure was capped at 5,513 coins, of which 1,000 were made available at the fair. The coin shows the staff or 'caduceus' of the god Mercury, featuring two snakes and wings, adjacent to the Roman gods Mercury and Fortuna, both symbolising success and abundance.
[h] In association with the *Australian Philatelic Traders Association*, ANDA promoted this coin at its Sydney fair held in the Lower Town Hall from October 24 & 25th. As with the Perth Issue, ANDA featured a Tuvalu coin as the host coin. Each of housed in special ANDA Coin Show packaging. The reverse depicts a coloured representation of a young mountain goat leaping between two cliff tops. The sun is rising in the background, signifying the dawn of a new day and good health.
[l] The above coin was one of a series of gold and silver coins produced by the Perth Mint on behalf of a Chinese bullion agency. At least 11 denominations were struck with only a small allocation of the specimen 1oz coins being sold in Australia at this stage. As usual, the other denominations will filter back to Australia on the secondary market and we will include these in future editions.

2011 - PLATINUM BULLION PLATYPUS SERIES

Date	Weight in oz's	Nominal F/Value	Description	Type	Size	Mintage Limit / Actual	Issue Price	Retail Average
2011	1 oz	100	Platypus	Specimen	32.6	30,000/ All sold	1,665	1,550
2012	1 oz	100	Platypus	Specimen	32.6	30,000/ 26,580	2,155	1,550
2013	1 oz	100	Platypus	Specimen	32.6	To order/ 2,000•	1,665	1,550
2014	1 oz	100	Platypus	Specimen	32.6	To order/ 1,616	1,616	1,550
2015	1 oz	100	Platypus	Specimen	32.6	To order/ 12,420	1,616	1,550
2016	1 oz	100	Platypus	Specimen	32.6	To order/ 6,218	1,616	1,550
2017	1 oz	100	Platypus	Specimen	32.6	To order/ tba	1,616	1,550

In a press released dated January 31, 2011, The Perth Mint announced it intended to introduce an Australian Platypus platinum investment coin. The new coin complements the popular range of gold and silver offerings which make up Australia's official bullion coin program. Struck from 1 ounce of 99.95% pure platinum, the Australian Platypus portrays the aquatic mammal diving beneath the water among the reeds and incorporates The Perth Mint's traditional 'P' mintmark. Illustrating identical artistry each year, the feature design is bordered by the inscriptions AUSTRALIAN PLATYPUS, the year-date, and the weight and purity of the coin. The new coin fills a gap in The Perth Mint's line up of investment coins, which has existed since the withdrawal of the platinum Australian Koala series in 2005.

NB : A dot [•] after the mintage figure indicates that the final mintage has yet to be determined or the last price published.

PRICING : The price of the above coin will change with the prevailing bullion price of platinum. The above figure was the Perth Mint selling price on May 10, 2015.

2009 - LEST WE FORGET

2009 (a) ANZAC 2010 (b) RAN Tribute 2011 (c) RAAF Tribute 2012 (d) Nursing

2013 (e) Engineers 2014 (f) Submarines 2015 (g) Gallipoli 2016 (g) ANZAC 1917 [h] Intelligence

Date	Face Value	Description	Finish	Metal	Weight in gm's	Size	Mintage Max/ Actual	Issue Price	Retail Average
2009 a	1	ANZAC Tribute	Unc	Al/br	13.5gm	30.6	18,561	12.5	14
2010 b	1	RAN Tribute	Unc	Al/br	13.5gm	30.6	17,675	12.5	14
2011 c	1	RAAF Tribute	Unc	Al/br	13.5gm	30.6	12,696	12.5	14
2012 d	1	Nurses Tribute	Unc	Al/br	13.5gm	30.6	30,557	12.5	14
2013 e	1	Engineers Tribute	Unc	Al/br	13.5gm	30.6	17,675	13.5	14
2014 f	1	Submariners Tribute	Unc	Al/br	13.5gm	30.6	9,857	13.5	14
2015 f	1	Gallipoli Tribute	Unc	Al/br	13.5gm	30.6	9,857	13.5	14
2016 g	1	ANZAC Day Tribute	Unc	Al/br	13.5gm	30.6	19,640	13.5	14
2017 h	1	Intelligence Tribute	Unc	Al/br	13.5gm	30.6	To order	14.5	14

ALUMINIUM BRONZE ISSUES

2009 - 2012 CELEBRATE AUSTRALIA

2009 (a) TAS

2009 (b) NT

2009 (c) QLD

2009 (d) ACT

2009 (e) WA

2009 (f) NSW

2009 (g) SA

2009 (h) VIC

2010 (i) Blue Mts

2010 (j) Reef

2010 (k) Heard Is.

2010 (l) Shark Bay

2010 (m) Tas W'ness

2011 (n) Wet Tropics

2011 (o) Macquarie

2011 (p) Gondwana

2011 (q) Fossils

2011 (r) Purnulula Park

2012 (s) Fraser Is

2012 (t) Willandra

2012 (u) Kakadu

2012 (v) Lord Howe

2012 (w) Ulura-Kata

2013 [x] Sydney ANDA Show

Date	Nominal F/Value	Description	Mintage Figures	Issue Price	Current Retail
2009 a	1.00	Tasmania	9,689	14.95	14.95
2009 b	1.00	Northern Territory	9,813	14.95	14.95
2009 c	1.00	Queensland	9,666	14.95	14.95
2009 d	1.00	Aust Capital Territory	9,735	14.95	14.95
2009 e	1.00	Western Australia	13,067	14.95	14.95
2009 f	1.00	New South Wales	13,657	14.95	14.95
2009 g	1.00	South Australia	8,591	14.95	14.95
2009 h	1.00	Victoria	9,499	14.95	14.95
2010 i	1.00	Greater Blue Mountains	11,129	14.95	14.95
2010 j	1.00	Great Barrier Reef	14,899	14.95	14.95
2010 k	1.00	Heard & McDonald Islands	11,215	14.95	14.95
2010 l	1.00	Shark Bay	11,183	14.95	14.95
2010 m	1.00	The Tasmanian Wilderness	10,784	14.95	14.95
2011 n	1.00	Wet Tropics of Queensland	2,898	14.95	14.95
2011 o	1.00	Macquarie IHeritage Site	3,425	14.95	14.95
2011 p	1.00	Gondwana Rainforests	1,970	14.95	14.95
2011 q	1.00	Aust. Fossil Mammal Sites	1,825	14.95	14.95
2011 r	1.00	Purnululu National Park	5,270	14.95	14.95
2012 s	1.00	Fraser Island	1,676	14.95	14.95
2012 t	1.00	Willandra Lakes Region	1,592	14.95	14.95
2012 u	1.00	Kakadu National Park	1,587	14.95	14.95
2012 v	1.00	Lord Howe Island	1,429	14.95	14.95
2012 w	1.00	Uluru-Kata Tjuta Nat. Park	1,679	14.95	14.95
2013 x	1.00	Willandra Lakes Region	2,500	92.50	92.50

[x] This ANDA special pure silver proof coin was based on the 2012 Willandra Lakes Region aluminium bronze coin [See entry T]. This one -off issue was dated 2013 and was issued by the Perth Mint for the ANDA Sydney Fair held from September 7-8, 2013. Mention of the World Heritage Site was included on the certificate.

ALUMINIUM BRONZE ISSUES

2008 NATIVE ANIMALS - YOUNG COLLECTORS

Date	Nominal Value	Description	Mintage	Issue Price	Average Retail
2008	1.00	Australian Sea Lion	13,884	9.95	9.95
2008	1.00	Common Wombat	11,908	9.95	9.95
2008	1.00	Echidna	11,850	9.95	9.95
2008	1.00	Frilled Neck Lizard	11,864	9.95	9.95
2008	1.00	Ghost Bat	11,914	9.95	9.95
2008	1.00	Green Turtle	11,881	9.95	9.95
2008	1.00	Grey Kangaroo	14,385	9.95	9.95
2008	1.00	Palm Cockatoo	11,759	9.95	9.95
2008	1.00	Platypus	11,960	9.95	9.95
2008	1.00	Splendid Wren	11,796	9.95	9.95
2008	1.00	Wedge Tailed Eagle	14,034	9.95	9.95
2008	1.00	Whale Shark	11,943	9.95	9.95
2008	Complete set. 12 coins + medallion		n/a	79.95	79.95

2009 SPACE ISSUES - YOUNG COLLECTORS

Date	Nominal Value	Description	Mintage	Issue Price	Average Retail
2009	1.00	Nine aluminium bronze coins	5,217	79.95	79.95

2010 BACKYARD BUGS - YOUNG COLLECTORS

Date	Nominal Value	Description	Mintage	Issue Price	Average Retail
2010	1.00	Nine aluminium bronze coins	5,234	79.95	79.95

ALUMINIUM BRONZE ISSUES

2011 THE WIGGLES - YOUNG COLLECTORS

(a) Wiggles Characters

(b) Band members

(c) Wiggles Band

(d) Big Red Car

Date	Nominal Value	Description	Mintage	Issue Price	Current Retail
2011 a	1	Wiggles Characters	Unlimited/ 1,126	15.95	15.95
2011 b	1	Band members	Unlimited/ 1,169	15.95	15.95
2011 c	1	Wiggles band	Unlimited/ 1,175	15.95	15.95
2011 d	1	Big Red Car	Unlimited/ 1,331	15.95	15.95
2011	Set	Four coin boxed set	Unlimited/ 3,111	59.50	59.50

2012 ANIMAL ATHLETES - YOUNG COLLECTORS

[a] Rocket Frog [b] Rhino Beetle [c] Sailfish [d] Cheetah [e] Butterfly

Date	Nominal Value	Description	Type	Metal	Weight	Size	Mintage	Issue Price	Current Retail
2012 a	1	Rocket Frog	Spec	Al/ br	13.8	30.2	7,500/ n/a	14.95	15
2012 b	1	Rhino Beetle	Spec	Al/ br	13.8	30.2	7,500/ 2,943	14.95	15
2012 c	1	Sailfish	Spec	Al/ br	13.8	30.2	7,500/ 2,932	14.95	15
2012 d	1	Cheetah	Spec	Al/ br	13.8	30.2	7,500/ 3,175	14.95	15
2012	1	Butterfly	Spec	Al/ br	13.8	30.2	7,500/ 3,824	14.95	15
2012	1	Kangaroo	Spec	Al/ br	13.8	30.2	7,500/ 5,890	14.95	15

2013 "EXPERIENCE IT" - YOUNG COLLECTORS

Date	Nominal Value	Description	Type	Metal	Weight	Size	Mintage	Issue Price	Current Retail
2013	1	Surfing	Spec	Al/ br	13.8	30.2	1,500/ 1,400	14.95	15
2013		Coin + album	—	—	–	–	To Order/ 981	19.95	--
2013	1	Snorkling	Spec	Al/ br	13.8	30.2	1,500/ 1,412	14.95	15
2013	1	Snow Skiing	Spec	Al/ br	13.8	30.2	1,500/ 1,358	14.95	15
2013	1	BMX Riding	Spec	Al/ br	13.8	30.2	1,500/ 959	14.95	15
2013	1	Horse Riding	Spec	Al/ br	13.8	30.2	1,500/ 1,461	14.95	15
2013	1	Skateboarding	Spec	Al/ br	13.8	30.2	1,500/ 1,431	14.95	15

2014 "SUPER POWERS" - YOUNG COLLECTORS

Date	Nominal Value	Description	Type	Metal	Weight	Size	Mintage	Issue Price	Current Retail
2014	1	Super Senses	Spec	Al/ br	13.8	30.2	1,500/ 2,308	14.95	15
2014		Above + album	-	-	-	-	–	19.95	19.95
2014	1	Invisibility	Spec	Al/ br	13.8	30.2	1,500/ 1,763	14.95	15
2014	1	Cybernetics	Spec	Al/ br	13.8	30.2	1,500/ 1,591	14.95	15
2014	1	Skateboarding	Spec	Al/ br	13.8	30.2	1,500/ n/a	14.95	15
2014	1	Flight	Spec	Al/ br	13.8	30.2	1,500/ 1,562	14.95	15
2014	1	Weather Control	Spec	Al/ br	13.8	30.2	1,500/ 1,484	14.95	15
2014	1	Strength	Spec	Al/ br	13.8	30.2	1,500/ 1,185	14.95	15

SUPERSCRIBED BANKNOTES

In 1910, the Commonwealth passed the *Australian Notes Act of 1910* to reform the banking and currency sector which had become fragmented and unruly over the years. The Act stipulated that six months after the date of passage, set as September 16, 1910, private banks could no longer issue any form of currency, and any subsequent issue by a State Bank would no longer be considered legal tender. The Act further established the powers of the Commonwealth to issue, re-issue, and cancel Australian notes. The Act also established denominations, legal tender status, and the amount of gold coin held in reserve to secure the issues. On October 10, 1910 a Bank Notes Tax Act 1910 imposed a 10% tax on all issued or re-issued bank notes. A third currency reform act was passed on December 22, 1911 establishing the Commonwealth Bank Act. This specifically stated that the Bank was not to issue bills or notes for circulation. The Australian Treasury issued banknotes until a 1920 amendment to the Commonwealth Bank Act of 1911. The amendment established a note-issuing department within the bank which assumed those responsibilities previously held by the Treasury.

AUSTRALIAN BANK OF COMMERCE LIMITED

Reference # McDonald	Face Value	Branch Location	VG	Fine	Very Fine	Extra Fine
McSB 01/01	£ 1	Sydney	11,000	17,500	24,500	34,500
McSB 01/02	£ 1	Brisbane	11,000	17,500	24,500	34,500
McSB 01/03	£ 5	Sydney	22,000	45,000	55,000	75,000
McSB 01/04	£ 5	Brisbane	22,000	45,000	55,000	75,000
McSB 01/05	£ 10	Sydney	33,000	52,000	75,000	95,000
McSB 01/06	£ 10	Brisbane	33,000	52,000	75,000	95,000
McSB 01/07	£ 50	Adelaide	75,000	110,000	140,000	175,000

BANK OF ADELAIDE

Reference # McDonald	Face Value	Branch Location	VG	Fine	Very Fine	Extra Fine
McSB 02/01	£ 1	Adelaide	9,000	13,650	22,000	36,000
McSB 02/02	£ 5	Adelaide	26,500	37,500	50,000	62,000
McSB 02/03	£ 10	Adelaide	50,000	60,000	75,000	95,000
McSB 02/04	£ 20	Adelaide	80,000	95,000	110,000	145,000
McSB 02/05	£ 50	Adelaide	85,000	110,000	135,000	170,000

BANK OF AUSTRALASIA

Reference # McDonald	Face Value	Branch Location	VG	Fine	Very Fine	Extra Fine
McSB 03/01	£ 1	Perth	5,500	11,650	22,000	36,000
McSB 03/02	£ 1	Hobart	5,500	11,650	22,000	36,000
McSB 03/03	£ 1	Sydney	5,500	11,650	22,000	36,000
McSB 03/04	£ 5	Perth	34,500	45,000	60,000	75,000
McSB 03/05	£ 5	Sydney	34,500	45,000	60,000	75,000
McSB 03/06	£10	Perth	40,000	50,500	65,000	82,500
McSB 03/07	£10	Hobart	40,000	50,500	65,000	82,500
McSB 03/08	£10	Sydney	40,000	50,500	65,000	82,500
McSB 03/09	£10	Brisbane	40,000	50,500	65,000	82,500
McSB 03/10	£10	Melbourne	40,000	50,500	65,000	82,500
McSB 03/11	£20	No domicle	40,000	50,500	65,000	82,500
McSB 03/12	£50	No domicle	65,000	80,000	110,000	155,000
McSB 03/13	£100	No domicle	85,000	95,000	125,000	165,000

SUPERSCRIBED BANKNOTES

BANK OF NEW SOUTH WALES

Reference # McDonald	Face Value	Branch Location	VG	Fine	Very Fine	Extra Fine
McSB 04/01	£ 1	Sydney	10,750	18,750	28,500	45,000
McSB 04/02	£ 5	Sydney	42,500	54,500	72,000	90,000
McSB 04/03	£ 10	Perth	52,500	67,500	86,250	110,000
McSB 04/04	£ 10	Sydney	52,500	67,500	86,250	110,000
McSB 04/05	£ 10	Adelaide	52,500	67,500	86,250	110,000
McSB 04/06	£ 10	Melbourne	52,500	67,500	86,250	110,000
McSB 04/07	£ 10	No domicile	52,500	67,500	86,250	110,000
McSB 04/08	£ 20	Perth	65,000	80,000	110,000	155,000
McSB 04/09	£ 20	Sydney	65,000	80,000	110,000	155,000
McSB 04/10	£ 20	Adelaide	65,000	80,000	110,000	155,000
McSB 04/11	£ 20	Melbourne	65,000	80,000	110,000	155,000
McSB 04/13	£ 50	Perth	90,000	120,000	160,000	195,000
McSB 04/14	£ 50	Sydney	90,000	120,000	160,000	195,000
McSB 04/15	£ 50	Adelaide	90,000	120,000	160,000	195,000
McSB 04/16	£ 50	Melbourne	90,000	120,000	160,000	195,000
McSB 04/17	£ 100	Perth	95,000	135,000	172,000	200,000
McSB 04/18	£ 100	Sydney	95,000	135,000	172,000	200,000
McSB 04/19	£ 100	Adelaide	95,000	135,000	172,000	200,000
McSB 04/20	£ 100	Melbourne	95,000	135,000	172,000	200,000

BANK OF VICTORIA LIMITED

Reference # McDonald	Face Value	Branch Location	VG	Fine	Very Fine	Extra Fine
McSB 05/01	£ 1	Melbourne	10,500	16,500	26,500	42,500
McSB 05/02	£ 5	Melbourne	42,000	55,000	70,000	90,000
McSB 05/03	£ 10	Melbourne	52,500	67,500	86,250	110,000
McSB 05/04	£ 20	Melbourne	55,000	75,000	95,000	145,000
McSB 05/05	£ 50	Melbourne	65,000	80,000	110,000	155,000

CITY BANK OF SYDNEY

Reference # McDonald	Face Value	Branch Location	VG	Fine	Very Fine	Extra Fine
McSB 06/01	£ 1	Sydney	29,500	38,000	49,000	65,000
McSB 06/02	£ 5	Sydney	35,000	45,000	58,000	78,000
McSB 06/03	£10	Sydney	45,000	59,000	75,000	95,000
McSB 06/04	£20	Sydney	70,000	85,000	115,000	165,000
McSB 06/05	£50	Sydney	65,000	80,000	110,000	155,000

SUPERSCRIBED BANKNOTES

COMMERCIAL BANK OF AUSTRALIA LIMITED

Reference # McDonald	Face Value	Branch Location	VG	Fine	Very Fine	Extra Fine
McSB 07/01	£ 1	Perth	29,500	39,000	49,000	65,000
McSB 07/02	£ 5	Hobart	36,000	45,500	58,000	78,000

COMMERCIAL BANK OF TASMANIA LIMITED

Reference # McDonald	Face Value	Branch Location	VG	Fine	Very Fine	Extra Fine
McSB 08/01	£ 1	Hobart	10,500	16,650	26,000	39,000
McSB 08/02	£ 1	Launceston	29,500	39,000	48,500	65,000
McSB 08/03	£ 5	Launceston	32,000	42,000	50,000	70,000
McSB 08/04	£ 10	Launceston	45,500	58,000	75,000	95,000
McSB 08/05	£ 20	Launceston	78,000	95,000	125,000	150,000

COMMERCIAL BANKING COMPANY OF SYDNEY

Reference # McDonald	Face Value	Branch Location	VG	Fine	Very Fine	Extra Fine
McSB 09/01	£ 1	Sydney	7,250	11,250	16,500	30,000
McSB 09/02	£ 5	Sydney	41,250	52,500	63,750	87,500
McSB 09/03	£ 10	Sydney	52,500	67,500	86,250	110,000

ENGLISH SCOTTISH & AUSTRALIAN BANK LTD

Reference # McDonald	Face Value	Branch Location	VG	Fine	Very Fine	Extra Fine
McSB 10/01	£ 1	Sydney	11,500	16,250	22.500	38,500
McSB 10/02	£ 1	Adelaide	11,500	16,250	22.500	38,500
McSB 10/03	£ 1	Melbourne	11,500	16,250	22.500	38,500
McSB 10/04	£ 5	Sydney	34,250	42,500	55,250	71,500
McSB 10/05	£ 5	Adelaide	34,250	42,500	55,250	71,500
McSB 10/06	£ 5	Melbourne	34,250	42,500	55,250	71,500
McSB 10/07	£10	Adelaide	46,500	58,500	71,500	84,500
McSB 10/08	£20	Adelaide	85,000	110,000	125,000	147,500
McSB 10/09	£20	Melbourne	85,000	110,000	125,000	147,500
McSB 10/10	£50	Sydney	90,000	115,000	137,500	160,000
McSB 10/11	£50	Adelaide	90,000	115,000	137,500	160,000
McSB 10/12	£50	Melbourne	90,000	115,000	137,500	160,000

SUPERSCRIBED BANKNOTES

Reference # McDonald	Face Value	Branch Location	VG	Fine	Very Fine	Extra Fine
LONDON BANK OF AUSTRALIA LIMITED						
McSB 11/01	£ 1	Adelaide	2,750	4,500	8,750	17,500
McSB 11/02	£ 1	Melbourne	2,750	4,500	8,750	17,500
McSB 11/03	£ 5	Melbourne	42,500	52,000	72,000	90,000
McSB 11/04	£10	Sydney	42,500	52,000	72,000	90,000
McSB 11/05	£10	Adelaide	42,500	52,000	72,000	90,000
McSB 11/06	£10	Melbourne	42,500	52,000	72,000	90,000
McSB 11/07	£50	Sydney	90,000	125,000	165,000	190,000
McSB 11/08	£50	Adelaide	90,000	125,000	165,000	190,000
McSB 11/09	£50	Melbourne	90,000	125,000	165,000	190,000
McSB 11/10	£100	Sydney	95,000	135,000	172,000	200,000
McSB 11/11	£100	Adelaide	95,000	135,000	172,000	200,000
McSB 11/12	£100	Melbourne	95,000	135,000	172,000	200,000
NATIONAL BANK OF AUSTRALASIA LIMITED						
McSB 12/01	£ 1	Perth	3,250	5,500	9,750	19,500
McSB 12/02	£ 1	Adelaide	3,250	5,500	9,750	19,500
McSB 12/03	£ 1	Melbourne	3,250	5,500	9,750	19,500
McSB 12/04	£ 5	Adelaide	15,500	24,000	36,000	52,000
McSB 12/05	£ 5	Melbourne	15,500	24,000	36,000	52,000
McSB 12/06	£10	Perth	32,000	42,500	56,000	76,000
McSB 12/07	£10	Adelaide	32,000	42,500	56,000	76,000
McSB 12/08	£10	Melbourne	32,000	42,500	56,000	76,000
McSB 12/09	£20	Perth	90,000	120,000	160,000	195,000
McSB 12/10	£20	Adelaide	90,000	120,000	160,000	195,000
McSB 12/11	£20	Melbourne	90,000	120,000	160,000	195,000
McSB 12/12	£50	Sydney	100,000	128,000	165,000	210,000
McSB 12/13	£50	Adelaide	100,000	128,000	165,000	210,000
McSB 12/14	£50	Melbourne	100,000	128,000	165,000	210,000
McSB 12/15	£100	Melbourne	110,000	140,000	175,000	215,000

Reference # McDonald	Face Value	Branch Location	VG	Fine	Very Fine	Extra Fine
QUEENSLAND GOVERNMENT						
McSB 13/01	£ 1	Brisbane	47,500	60,000	75,000	100,000
McSB 13/02	£ 5	Brisbane	55,000	70,000	90,000	120,000

SUPERSCRIBED BANKNOTES

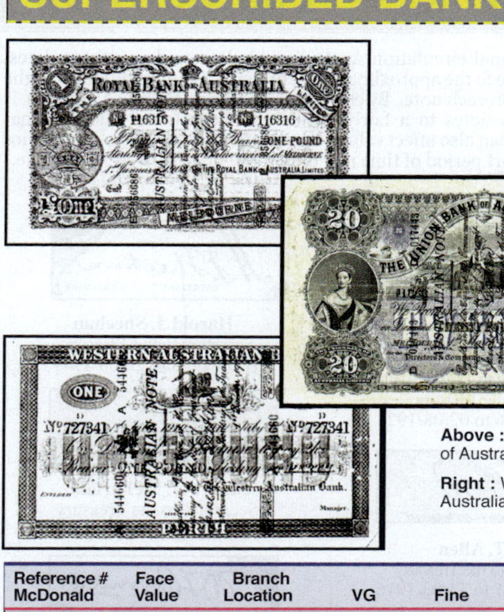

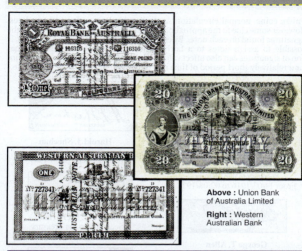

Above : Union Bank of Australia Limited

Right : Western Australian Bank

Reference # McDonald	Face Value	Branch Location	VG	Fine	Very Fine	Extra Fine
ROYAL BANK OF AUSTRALIA LIMITED						
McSB 14/01	£ 1	Sydney	35,000	45,000	70,000	100,000
UNION BANK OF AUSTRALIA LIMITED						
McSB 15/01	£ 1	Perth	7,200	12,000	20,000	36,000
McSB 15/02	£ 1	Hobart	7,200	12,000	20,000	36,000
McSB 15/03	£ 1	Sydney	7,200	12,000	20,000	36,000
McSB 15/04	£ 1	Adelaide	7,200	12,000	20,000	36,000
McSB 15/05	£ 1	Melbourne	7,200	12,000	20,000	36,000
McSB 15/06	£ 5	Perth	40,000	52,000	72,000	92,000
McSB 15/07	£ 5	Hobart	40,000	52,000	72,000	92,000
McSB 15/08	£ 5	Sydney	40,000	52,000	72,000	92,000
McSB 15/09	£ 5	Adelaide	40,000	52,000	72,000	92,000
McSB 15/10	£ 5	Melbourne	40,000	52,000	72,000	92,000
McSB 15/11	£10	Perth	56,000	72,000	92,000	110,000
McSB 15/12	£10	Hobart	56,000	72,000	92,000	110,000
McSB 15/13	£10	Sydney	56,000	72,000	92,000	110,000
McSB 15/14	£10	Adelaide	56,000	72,000	92,000	110,000
McSB 15/15	£10	Melbourne	56,000	72,000	92,000	110,000
McSB 15/16	£20	Perth	96,000	125,000	155,000	195,000
McSB 15/17	£20	Hobart	96,000	125,000	155,000	195,000
McSB 15/18	£20	Sydney	96,000	125,000	155,000	195,000
McSB 15/19	£20	Adelaide	96,000	125,000	155,000	195,000
McSB 15/20	£20	Melbourne	96,000	125,000	155,000	195,000
McSB 15/21	£50	Perth	110,000	135,000	165,000	210,000
McSB 15/22	£50	Hobart	110,000	135,000	165,000	210,000
McSB 15/23	£50	Sydney	110,000	135,000	165,000	210,000
McSB 15/24	£50	Adelaide	110,000	135,000	165,000	210,000
McSB 15/25	£50	Melbourne	110,000	135,000	165,000	210,000
WESTERN AUSTRALIAN BANK						
McSB 16/01	£ 1	Perth	47,500	60,000	95,500	130,000
McSB 16/02	£ 5	Perth	55,000	70,000	90,000	120,000
McSB 16/03	£ 10	Perth	75,000	95,000	150,000	175,000

SIGNATURES ON BANKNOTES

Unlike coins, normal circulation Australian banknotes do not bear dates. However some clue to the approximate date of issue does exist by studying the signatures found on each note. By checking signatories' terms of office, it is possible to assign notes to a fairly accurate period of issue. The combination of signatures can also affect values, as some individuals shared portfolios for a relatively short period of time and only small print runs were possible.

James R. Collins
First Assistant Secretary to the Treasury
From 01/07/1910 to 14/03/1916
Secretary to the Treasury
From 14/03/1916 to 02/08/1926

George T. Allen
First Secretary to the Treasury
From 01/01/1901 to 13/03/1916

Charles J. Cerutty
Director of the Note Issue Department
and Chairman of Directors
From 1918 to 1923

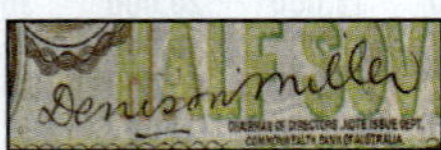

Denison S. Miller
First Governor of the Commonwealth Bank
01/06/1923. 06/06/1923 (Died in office).

James Kell
Governor of the Commonwealth Bank
10/10/1924 to 31/05/1927

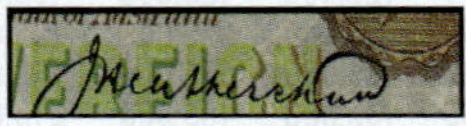

James T. Heathershaw
Secretary to the Treasury
03/08/1926 to 28/04/1932

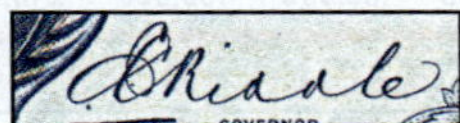

Ernest C. Riddle
Governor of the Commonwealth Bank
01/06/1927 to 28/02/1938

Harold J. Sheehan
Secretary to the Treasury
01/03/1938 to 26/03/1941

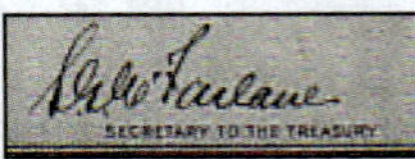

Stuart G. McFarlane
Secretary to the Treasury
24/03/1938 to 29/01/1948

Hugh T. Armitage
Governor of the Commonwealth Bank
01/07/1941 to 31/12/1948

George P. Watt
Secretary to the Treasury
23/11/1948 to 31/03/1951

Herbert C. Coombs
Governor of the Commonwealth Bank
01/01/1949 to 13/01/1960
Governor of the Reserve Bank
14/01/1960 to 22/07/1968

Roland Wilson
Secretary to the Treasury
01/04/1951 to 27/10/1966

Richard J. Randall
Secretary to the Treasury
From 28/10/1966 to 31/10/1971

SIGNATURES ON BANKNOTES

John G. Phillips
Governor of the Reserve Bank
23/07/1968 to 22/07/1975

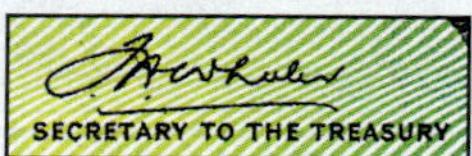

Frederick H. Wheeler
Secretary to the Treasury
01/11/1971 to 08/01/1979

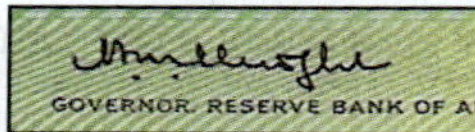

Harold M. Knight
Governor of the Reserve Bank
23/07/1975 to 13/08/1982

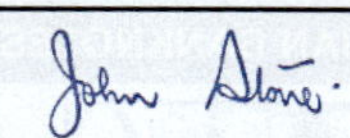

John O. Stone
Secretary to the Treasury
08/01/1979 to 14/09/1984

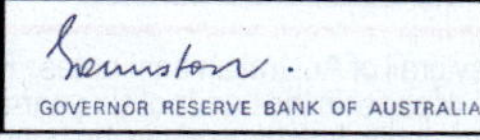

Robert A. Johnston
Governor of the Reserve Bank
14/08/1982 to 18/07/1989

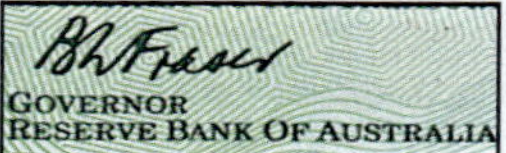

Bernie W. Fraser
Secretary to the Treasury
17/09/1984 to 17/09/1989
Governor of the Reserve Bank
18/09/1989 to 17/09/1996

Mervyn John Phillips
Was the first Deputy Governor of the Reserve Bank to appear on our banknotes ($20 & $50 only). He filled in for a two month period in 1989 between Robert Johnston retiring and the former Secretary to the Treasurer, Bernie Fraser taking up the position.

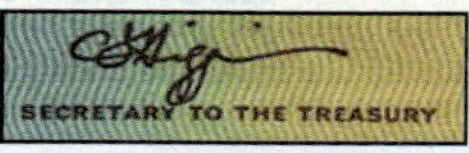

Christopher Higgins
Secretary to the Treasury
09/09/1989 to 06/12/1990 (Died in office)

Tony Cole
Secretary to the Treasury
14/02/1991 to 23/03/1993

Ted Evans
Secretary to the Treasury
10/05/1993 to 16/04/2001

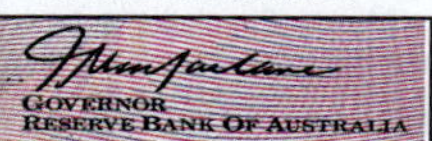

Ian Macfarlane
Governor of the Reserve Bank
18/09/1996 to 17/09/2006

Glenn Stevens
Governor of the Reserve Bank
18/09/2006 to present

Dr. Ken Henry
Secretary to the Treasury
2001 to 2011

Dr. Martin Parkinson
Secretary to the Treasury
2011 to 2014

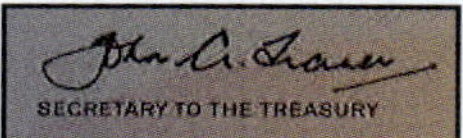

John Fraser
Secretary to the Treasury
2015 to present

PLEASE NOTE : For this edition we have not included several banknote series such as Pre Federation, Superscribed and Pre Decimal specimen issues. Throughout this book we have endeavoured to bring all prices back in line with the market. Prices in the above areas are still too volatile to pick a mean average. Hopefully, by the time the next issue comes out mid 2016, the market will have settled.

HALF SOVEREIGN

GEORGE V : 1913 - 1914 ISSUE

Red Serials. No border imprint. Predominately Blue. 197mm x 88mm

Reference # McD - Rks		Description	VG	Fine	VF	EF	aUnc	Unc
		COLLINS / ALLEN						
		First year of issue - 1913						
1	01a	a. Presentation note	22,500	36,000	80,000	175,000	225,000	320,000
1a		First Note. M 000001						
1b		Last Note. M 000526	One of six consecutive notes 'balloted' to D. Miller					
2	01b	b. With letter from G.T. Allen	31,000	48,000	70,000	120,000	175,000	300,000
3	01c	c. Circulation note	3,600	4,900	10,000	30,000	65,000	180,000

#1. THE HOLEY GRAIL OF AUSTRALIAN BANKNOTES

PRESENTATION NOTE # M 000001. The holey grail of Australian banknotes. For many years it was only known as a grainy wedge of paper in the hands of six-year-old daughter of the Governor General, Lord Denham. Judith had been given the honour of impressing, and keeping, the number one serial number on the note at a ceremony in the Kings Warehouse, Melbourne in May 1913. The note went back to London with the family and largely forgotten until being tracked down and purchased by then Monetarium director Barrie Winsor some 20 years ago. The note, now worth seven figures is currently in the hands of Coinworks, director Belinda Downie. Now housed a beautiful bespoke timber case, Belinda has been exhibiting the historic note at selected ANDA Expos throughout 2016. Although available for sale, it is hoped, in the meantime,that Coinworks will continue to feature the note at future ANDA fairs.

[McD 1]. Banknote Mc 1 - R 1a is normally found with several pin holes as the presentation note was pinned to the Treasury letter signed by the Secretary to the Treasury, George T. Allen.

[McD 1a & 1b]. It has been generally thought that presentation note M 000501 was the first "circulation issue" banknote. Research I have been conducting for around ten years indicates this is not correct. In short there was an "A" and a "B" list of VIP's offered the notes. The first 500 were set aside for the "A" list (mainly Labor MP's and their families). A certain Mr C.W. Darley accepted the last of the "A" list notes when offered M000102. Notes M000103 to M000500 were either destroyed or (hopefully) put into circulation. The "B" list was basically made up of *Captains of Industry* or senior public servants. A familiar name to banknote collectors will be that of Denison Miller, the Governor of the Commonwealth Bank who accepted note 000517 as well as a run of notes from 000520 to 000526. This last note was the final offering in what has often been mistakenly referred to as notes being drawn from a ballot. Miller was not the only person to "fluke" seven running numbers in a "ballot." The future Prime Minister Billy Hughes received a consecutive run of ten notes (M000033 to M000042). Other MP's received runs of four to seven notes in running numbers which would indicate that anyone with "Ten Bob" in their pocket could get as many notes as they wanted. However not everyone got what they wanted. The colourful MP, King O'Malley *(in charge of the construction of Canberra)* rejected note 000027 after making a written request for number 13! This is just a potted history of this fascinating issue. For the full story please refer to our Insiders Club newsletter Volume 1, Number 1, March 1999. Information only available to current or new subscribers.

HALF SOVEREIGN

GEORGE V : 1915 - 1923 ISSUE

' Half Sovereign' border imprint. Predominately Blue. 197mm x 88mm

Reference # McD	Rks	Description	VG	Fine	VF	EF	aUnc	Unc
		COLLINS / ALLEN - 1915						
		• Small seriffed prefix letter						
4	02a	No General prefixes	—	—	—	—	—	—
4a	02aF	M First prefix	3,000	5,000	15,000	25,000	35,000	120,000
4b	02aL	N Last prefix	3,000	5,000	11,000	30,000	40,000	110,000
		• Bold suffix letter						
5	02b	No general prefixes	—	—	—	—	—	—
5a	02bF	M First suffix	2,500	5,000	15,000	22,500	40,000	105,000
5b	02bL	N Last suffix	2,500	6,000	15,000	25,000	40,000	98,000
		• Bold prefix/suffix letters						
6	02c	No general issues	—	—	—	—	—	—
6a	02cF	M/M First prefix/suffix	2,000	4,000	8,000	22,500	41,000	82,000
6b	02cL	N/N Last prefix/suffix	2,250	3,000	7,000	24,000	40,000	80,000
		• Bold prefix/suffix letters						
7	02d	General issues	2,200	3,200	6,000	18,000	40,000	72,000
7a	02dF	M/A First prefix/suffix	2,200	3,200	6,000	18,000	40,000	72,000
7b	02dL	M/L Last prefix/suffix	2,300	3,400	6,350	19,750	42,500	75,000
		• Medium seriffed prefix/suffix letters						
8	02e	General issues	2,200	3,200	6,000	18,000	41,000	72,000
8a	02eF	M/B First prefix/suffix	2,200	3,200	6,000	18,000	41,000	72,000
8b	02eL	M/F Last prefix/suffix	2,300	3,400	6,200	19,550	42,000	75,000
		CERUTTY / COLLINS - 1918						
		• Medium seriffed prefix/suffix letters						
9	03a	General issues	1,200	1,800	8,000	35,000	70,000	110,000
9a	03aF	M/C First prefix/suffix	1,950	3,250	10,000	35,750	71,000	112,500
9b	03aL	M/F Last prefix/suffix	1,800	3,250	10,000	35,750	71,000	112,500
		• Bold prefix/suffix letters						
10	03b	General issues	1,200	1,800	3,000	8,000	20,000	36,000
10a	03bF	M/D First prefix/suffix	1,600	2,500	3,600	9,500	25,000	42,500
10b	03bL	N/Z Last prefix/suffix	1,500	2,200	3,250	9,500	24,000	40,000

STYLE VARIATIONS OF THE NUMBERS AND LETTERING

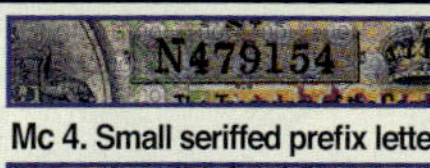

Mc 4. Small seriffed prefix letter

Mc 6&7. Bold prefix/suffix letters

Mc 8&9.• Medium seriffed prefix/suffix letters prefix

Mc10. Bold prefix/suffix letters

NOTE REGARDING PRICING

All the banknote prices published in this guide are for "natural" notes that have not been cleaned, pressed or artificially enhanced. Banknotes that have been treated in some way will be worth substantially less. For more information on how we arrive at our pricing, please read the information on page 8 of this guide.

HALF SOVEREIGN

GEORGE V : 1923 - 1932 ISSUE

'Half Sovereign' border imprint. Predominately Brown. 197mm x 88mm

Reference # McD	Rks	Description	VG	Fine	VF	EF	aUnc	Unc
		MILLER / COLLINS First year of issue - 1923						
11	04	General prefix	400	1,100	3,200	8,000	16,000	35,000
11a	04F	A/0 First prefix	500	1,400	3,600	10,000	18,750	38,000
11b	04L	A/23 Last prefix	650	1,750	4,400	13,000	21,000	41,000
		KELL / COLLINS First year of issue - 1926						
12	05	General prefix	600	1,200	2,200	6,500	16,000	34,000
12a	05F	A/24 First prefix	600	1,400	3,400	7,500	17,000	36,000
12b	05L	A/41 Last prefix	700	1,600	3,950	8,000	18,500	38,000
		KELL / HEATHERSHAW First year of issue - 1927						
13	06	General prefix	900	1,800	4,000	13,000	30,500	55,000
13a	06F	A/41 First prefix	1,000	2,200	5,000	18,000	35,000	56,000
13b	06L	A/51 Last prefix	950	2,000	4,400	13,500	32,000	54,500
		RIDDLE / HEATHERSHAW First year of issue - 1928						
14	07	General prefix	200	395	1,100	3,500	6,000	12,000
14a	07F	A/51 First prefix	350	575	1,250	4,500	13,500	16,000
14b	07L	B/36 Last prefix	325	550	1,100	4,200	7,000	16,000
		RIDDLE / SHEEHAN - 1933 • Thick Sheehan signature						
15	08a	General prefix	1,400	2,500	5,000	12,000	24,000	45,000
15a	08aF	A/36 First prefix	1,450	2,600	5,000	16,000	28,000	47,500
15b	08aL	A/38 Last prefix	1,500	2,500	5,000	15,000	22,500	45,000
		RIDDLE / SHEEHAN - 1933 • Thin Sheehan signature						
16	08b	General prefix	500	600	2,000	5,250	12,000	24,000
16a	08bF	B/38 First prefix	650	1,000	3,000	6,500	14,000	28,000
16b	08bL	B/43 Last prefix	600	900	2,500	6,250	13.500	27,500

THICK AND THIN SHEEHAN SIGNATURE

The Riddle/Sheehan thick signature ten shillings notes were limited to the early issues of the series. The thick signature prefix features a large B over numerals B/36 822001 to approximately B/38 and are encountered less frequently than the thin signature variety.

TEN SHILLINGS

GEORGE V : 1933 ISSUE

First Legal tender issue. Predominantly brown. 155 x 81 to 157 x 82 mm

Reference # McD	Rks	Description	VG	Fine	VF	EF	aUnc	Unc
		RIDDLE / SHEEHAN / *First year of issue - 1933*						
17	09	General issues	700	1,250	2,850	6,500	18,000	29,000
17a	09F	C/0 First prefix	800	1,750	3,000	7,500	18,500	30,000
17b	09L	C/20 Last prefix	850	1,950	3,200	8,200	19,000	30,500

TEN SHILLINGS

GEORGE V : 1934 ISSUE

Overprinted TEN SHILLINGS around borders. 155 x 81 to 157 x 82 mm

Reference # McD	Rks	Description	VG	Fine	VF	EF	aUnc	Unc
		RIDDLE / SHEEHAN / *First year of issue - 1934*						
18	10	General issues	450	800	1,600	5,000	11,000	16,000
18 a	10F	C/21 First prefix	550	900	2,450	6,000	11,500	19,500
18 b	10L	C/69 Last prefix	625	950	2,700	6,500	13,000	21,000

TEN SHILLINGS

GEORGE V : 1936 ISSUE

Redesigned smaller issue. Predominantly orange. 137 x 76 to 137 x 78 mm

Reference # McD	Rks	Description	VG	Fine	VF	EF	aUnc	Unc
		RIDDLE / SHEEHAN *First year of issue - 1936*						
19	11	General prefix	175	250	550	2,250	4,800	8,000
19a	11F	D/0 First prefix	200	325	750	3,500	5,500	10,000
19b	11L	D/98 Last prefix	325	500	1,150	3,975	6,500	10,500

TEN SHILLINGS

GEORGE VI : 1938 - 1952 ISSUE

Portrait of George VI. Predominantly orange. 137 x 76 to 137 x 78 mm

Reference # McD	Rks	Description	VG	Fine	VF	EF	aUnc	Unc
		SHEEHAN / MCFARLANE						
		First year of issue - 1939						
20	12	General prefix	60	125	350	850	1,500	2,500
20a	12F	D/98 First prefix	150	250	950	1,500	3,000	6,500
20b	12L	F/24 Last prefix	120	225	550	2,500	4,000	6,500
		ARMITAGE / MCFARLANE						
		First year of issue - 1942						
21	13	General prefix	30	70	150	275	475	1,000
21a	13F	F/24 First prefix	80	180	450	1,000	1,750	4,250
21b	13L	G/84 Last prefix	70	175	400	900	1,900	3,500
21s	13s	*Star.* General issue	2,750	7,000	15,000	30,000	45,000	70,000
21as	13sF	*Star.* G/50 First prefix	4,500	9,250	19,000	42,600	70,000	105,000
21bs	13sL	*Star.* G/95 Last prefix	4,500	8,750	18,500	37,500	70,000	95,000
		COOMBS / WATT						
		First year of issue - 1949						
22	14	General prefix	25	50	125	275	475	1,250
22a	14F	G/ 85 First prefix	75	160	400	1,000	1,800	3,200
22b	14L	A/ 74 Last prefix	75	160	400	1,000	1,800	3,200
22s	14s	*Star.* General issue	800	1,950	4,750	12,500	28,000	40,000
22as	14sF	*Star.* G/ 96 First prefix	1,100	2,750	5,750	15,000	35,000	47,000
22bs	14sL	*Star.* A/ 2 Last prefix	950	2,250	7,000	18,000	25,000	38,000
		COOMBS / WILSON						
		First year of issue - 1952						
23	15	General prefix	25	50	125	275	450	1,200
23a	15F	A/ 7 First prefix	70	170	400	1,000	1,750	3,000
23b	15L	B/ 49 Last prefix	75	170	450	1,200	1,950	3,500
23s	15s	*Star.* General issue	1,100	2,250	4,750	11,500	26,000	45,000
23as	15sF	*Star.* A/ 3 First prefix	950	2,250	5,250	12,500	25,000	42,000
23bs	15sL	*Star.* A/ 9 Last prefix	1,100	2,375	5,500	13,750	26,500	43,500

IDENTIFYING A STAR NOTE?

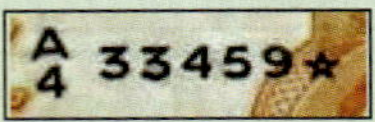

Pre-Decimal Type Style

ZFR 76161 *

Decimal Type Style

Star notes are a rare and interesting series of notes especially produced to replace a note spoilt during the printing cycle. The process of replacing damaged notes with 'star' issues was first adopted in the USA around 1910. Australia was slow to adopt the idea and up to 1948 each spoilt note was replaced with another bearing the same serial number which had to be hand set. The star note was introduced to do away with this time consuming and laborious practice. Any time an error note was discovered, it was plucked out of the system and replaced with a "star" note. These were printed as a special run and were almost identical to the normal note with the exception of the serial number. Instead of the normal six digits, the replacement note had five digits and a star in place of the last digit. The predecimal printers preferred a hollow five-pointed star while the decimal designers favoured an asterisk and went one step further by using the letter "Z" as a prefix. The idea of the system was to keep each bundle of 100 notes in serial number sequence to make counting bundles easier for tellers. Automatic counting machines made the process redundant. The system was discontinued in 1971. There are no stars above £5 and no $50 or $100 star notes.

TEN SHILLINGS

ELIZABETH II : 1954 - 1962 ISSUE

Navigator Matthew Flinders. Predominantly brown. 137 x 76 mm

Reference # McD	- Rks	Description	VG	Fine	VF	EF	aUnc	Unc
		COOMBS / WILSON - 1954. *Commonwealth Bank*						
24	16	General prefixes	15	20	35	65	150	275
24a	16F	AC/00 First prefix	150	250	600	1,200	2,650	3,650
24b	16L	AF/19 Last prefix	190	250	600	1,200	2,250	3,250
24s	16s	*Star.* General issue	550	1,450	3,250	9,750	23,500	40,000
24as	16sF	*Star.* C/90 First prefix	650	1,250	3,250	7,750	25,500	42,500
24bs	16sL	*Star.* AE/92 Last prefix	650	1,250	3,250	7,750	25,500	42,500
		COOMBS / WILSON - 1961. *Reserve Bank*						
25	17	General prefixes	10	20	40	80	150	250
25a	17F	AF/20 First prefix	150	250	550	950	1,450	2,250
		• Circulation issue						
25b	17L	AH/65 Last prefix	100	250	495	950	1,500	2,300
		• Note Printing Australia issue						
25c	17X	AH/69 Last prefix	*Banknotes usually flicked*				950	1,250
25s	17s	*Star.* General issue	445	950	2,000	5,000	11,000	19,000
25as	17sF	*Star.* AE/93 First prefix	500	1,000	2,950	8,250	16,500	25,000
25bs	17sL	*Star.* AG/51 Last prefix	550	1,100	2,950	8,750	14,000	22,500

Towards the end of this book you will find details of the special 25th Anniversary of Decimal Currency Portfolio issued in 1991. The notes came from the archives of Note Printing Australia (NPA) and consisted of the last 800 ten shillings, one pounds, five pounds and ten pounds issues coupled with the first issue of the one, two, ten and twenty dollar notes. In recent years, collectors and dealers have been breaking up these sets and buying or selling the notes individually. These notes are causing a confusing situation when compared with the normal circulation "Last Prefix" issues. We have decided to give both issues a separate Reference Number.

COMMONWEALTH OR RESERVE BANK ISSUE

Ten shillings. 1953 Commonwealth Bank — Ten shillings. 1961 Reserve Bank

One Pound. 1953 Commonwealth Bank — One Pound. 1961 Reserve Bank

Five Pounds. 1953 Commonwealth Bank — Five Pounds. 1961 Reserve Bank

Ten Pounds. 1953 Commonwealth Bank — Ten Pounds. 1961 Reserve Bank

By the end of the 1950s, controversy over the Commonwealth Bank's dual functions as a central bank as well as a trading/savings bank came to a head. Legislative changes in the form of the Commonwealth Banks Act 1959 and the Reserve Bank Act 1959 formally divided the two operations. The Reserve Bank of Australia was established on 14 January 1960 as the successor in law of the Commonwealth Bank, assuming control of all central banking activities. The remaining functions (trading/savings bank activities), together with the newly constituted Commonwealth Development Bank, became the Commonwealth Banking Corporation. In the months that followed, there was a subtle change to each denomination to reflect the change.

ONE POUND

GEORGE V : 1913 - 1918 ISSUE

First Gold Standard issue. Predominantly blue. 183 x 94 mm

Reference # McD	Rks	Description	VG	Fine	VF	EF	aUnc	Unc
		COLLINS / ALLEN. First year of issue - 1913						
		• Red small seriffed numbers						
26	18a	P Prefix letter	8,500	20,000	45,000	78,000	125,000	175,000
		• Dark blue serial numbers						
27	18b	General prefix	1,600	3,200	8,000	21,000	46,000	95,000
27a	18bF	Q First prefix	1,600	3,200	8,000	21,000	46,000	95,000
27b	18bL	T Last prefix	2,000	4,000	10,500	24,000	47,000	110,000
		• Large black serial numbers						
28	18c	T Prefix letter	4,000	6,500	12,500	20,000	60,000	110,000
29	18d	General suffixes	750	2,200	10,500	16,500	24,500	42,000
29a	18dF	A First suffix	950	2,500	11,500	19,000	26,000	45,000
29b	18dL	T Last suffix	900	2,200	10,500	16,500	24,000	42,500
		• Prefix and suffix letters						
30	18e	General prefix	1,200	2,100	5,500	13,500	22,500	45,000
30a	18eF	A/B First prefix and suffix	1,350	2,200	6,200	16,600	28,000	46,000
30b	18eL	A/P Last prefix and suffix	1,400	2,500	6,500	18,000	30,000	49,500
		CERUTTY / COLLINS. First year of issue - 1918 • Prefix & suffix letters						
31	21	General prefix & suffix	650	950	3,100	7,500	21,000	35,000
31a	21F	A/D First prefix and suffix letter	750	1,200	3,500	15,000	25,000	45,000
31b	21L	E/C Last prefix and suffix letter	800	1,250	3,400	14,000	24,500	40,000

NEW DISCOVERY. MIXED SERIAL NUMBERS

I'm not sure if serial number shown above is an important new find, deserving of its own reference number or simply a note in passing. An eagle eyed collector sent me a scan of this interesting banknote of 1918 that shows a slight difference with the fonts used to make up the serial number. The enlarged sections of the note shows the "1" on both sides of the note showing different fonts. Whether this is rare or not still has to be determined. Please let me know if you have any mixed font notes.

ONE POUND

GEORGE V : 1914 - 1915 ISSUE

EMERGENCY ISSUE : Predominantly blue and pink. 182 x 118 mm

Reference # McD - Rks		Description	VG	Fine	VF	EF	aUnc	Unc
		COLLINS / ALLEN *First year of issue - 1914*						
		No general prefix						
32a	19F	No prefix and A/A suffix letters	20,000	35,000	56,500	97,500	167,500	237,500
32b	19L	No prefix and B/B suffix letters	21,250	40,000	62,500	112,500	177,500	247,500

The previous one pound note (Mc31 - R21) was designed to replace all superscribed notes that had circulated from 1910 to 1913. However the outbreak of WW1 resulted in a much larger demand for banknotes that far outstripped the capabilities of the Australian Note Printer. Banknotes from the E.S. & A. Bank, originally dated September 1, 1894 were pressed into service after being suitably superscribed (overprinted). This type of note is regarded as the "Type Two" Superscribed note and differs from the 1910 - 1913 superscribed issues of the 1890s in that only two serial numbers were used instead of three.

ONE POUND. GEORGE V : 1914 - 1915 ISSUE

EMERGENCY ISSUE : 137 x 76 to 137 x 78 mm

Reference # McD - Rks		Description	VG	Fine	VF	EF	aUnc	Unc
		COLLINS / ALLEN - 1914						
		• Letters "No." between prefix and serial number						
33	20a	No General issues	—	—	—	—	—	—
33a	20aF	First prefix and suffix letters C/C	18,000	29,000	58,000	90,000	135,000	200,000
33b	20aL	Last prefix and suffix letters D/D	17,000	29,000	55,000	85,000	125,000	230,000
		• Letters "No." missing between prefix and serial number						
34	20b	No General issues	—	—	—	—	—	—
34a	20bF	First prefix and suffix letters E/E	25,000	38,000	65,000	135,000	235,000	295,000
34b	20bL	Last prefix and suffix letters F/F	24,000	36,000	62,000	120,000	200,000	275,000

ONE POUND

GEORGE V : 1923 - 1933 ISSUE

Portrait of George V. Predominantly dark green.
Size varies from 180 x 79 to 181 x 81 mm

Reference # McD	Rks	Description	VG	Fine	VF	EF	aUnc	Unc
		MILLER / COLLINS - 1923						
		• Includes imprint "T.S. Harrison Australian Note Printer." Large prefix letter						
35	22a	General prefix	4,850	8,500	15,000	36,000	60,000	110,000
35a	22a	FH First prefix letter	5,000	9,000	16,000	37,500	62,500	115,000
35b	22a	LK Last prefix letter	5,000	9,000	16,000	37,500	62,500	115,000
		• Includes imprint "T.S. Harrison Australian Note Printer." Small H prefix letter over numerals.						
36	23a	General prefix	600	950	2,500	6,250	16,000	30,000
36a	23a	FH/0 First prefix letter	750	1,150	3,000	8,500	17,250	32,500
36b	23a	LH/56 Last prefix letter	975	1,250	3,100	9,000	20,000	34,000
		MILLER / COLLINS. First year of issue - 1923						
		• Large prefix. Missing imprint "T.S. Harrison."						
37	22b	No general prefixes	—	—	—	—	—	—
37a	22b	FJ First prefix letter	20,000	35,000	55,000	80,000	150,000	200,000
37b	22b	LK Last prefix letter	21,000	30,000	60,000	85,000	152,000	205,000
		• Small H prefix. Missing imprint "T.S. Harrison."						
38	23b	General prefix	400	750	1,500	5,000	12,000	26,000
38a	23b	FH/0 First prefix	550	850	2,000	7,000	17,500	30,000
38b	23b	LH/61 Last prefix	600	900	2,200	8,500	18,500	31,000
		KELL / COLLINS - 1926						
39	24	General prefix	425	650	1,200	5,000	10,500	20,000
39a	24F	H/49 First prefix	550	800	1,750	6,000	11,500	21,500
39b	24L	H/80 Last prefix	575	750	1,500	5,500	12,000	23,000
		KELL / HEATHERSHAW - 1926						
40	25	General prefix	600	800	1,900	4,750	11,250	25,000
40a	25F	H/69 First prefix	700	1,000	2,500	7,500	15,000	30,500
40b	25L	J/2 Last prefix	750	1,000	2,600	8,250	17,000	32,500
		RIDDLE / HEATHERSHAW - 1927						
41	26	J/3 - K/71 General prefix	175	295	600	1,500	3,500	6,500
41a	26F	J/2 First prefix	200	300	800	2,500	4,250	8,000
41b	26L	K/72 Last prefix	200	300	800	2,500	4,250	8,000
		RIDDLE / SHEEHAN - 1932						
		• Thick Sheehan signature						
42	27a	K/73 - K97 General prefix	550	950	1,750	5,250	14,000	25,000
42a	27a	FK/72 First prefix	700	1,200	2,250	6,500	15,000	30,000
42b	27aL	K/98 Last prefix	750	1,250	2,100	7,500	15,500	31,000

The bottom centre of the notes carried the imprint 'T.S. Harrison Australian Note Printer.' from 1913 to around 1924. Harrison came over to Australia from London in September 1912, having previously worked for Waterlow's. At a meeting in 1919 of the Parliamentary Standing Committee on Public Works, Harrison stated that: "I was told in London that a first-class building awaited me. Instead of that I found a rat-hole of a place, with broken windows and dust some inches deep on them."

ONE POUND

FIRST LEGAL TENDER ISSUE : 1933 - 1938 ISSUE

Portrait of George V. Predominantly dark green. 180 x 79 to 181 x 81 mm

Reference # McD	Rks	Description	VG	Fine	VF	EF	aUnc	Unc
		RIDDLE / SHEEHAN : *First year of issue - 1933*						
44	28	L/T-N/70 General prefix	100	150	300	1,100	2,500	4,500
44a	28F	L/0 First prefix	125	225	750	1,500	3,000	7,000
44b	28L	N/71 Last prefix	150	300	895	2,000	3,500	8,000

ONE POUND GEORGE VI : 1938 - 1953 ISSUE

Portrait of George VI. Predominantly dark green. 180 x 79 to 181 x 81 mm

Reference # McD	Rks	Description	VG	Fine	VF	EF	aUnc	Unc
		SHEEHAN / MCFARLANE : *First year of issue - 1938*						
45	29	General prefix	30	70	150	350	750	2,000
45a	29F	N/71 First prefix	150	250	750	1,800	3,500	6,000
45b	29L	P/76 Last prefix	150	260	850	1,900	3,750	6,500
		ARMITAGE / MCFARLANE : *First year of issue - 1942*						
		• Dark green main print						
46	30a	General prefix	20	30	75	150	300	850
46a	30aF	P/76 First prefix	95	195	375	850	1,600	2,000
46b	30aL	K/96 Last prefix	70	150	275	700	1,250	2,300
		• Light green main print						
47	30b	General prefix	20	30	70	110	350	850
47a	30bF	First prefix To be advised	—	—	—	—	—	—
47b	30bL	Last prefix To be advised	—	—	—	—	—	—
47s	30s	STAR General prefix	4,750	6,250	13,500	32,500	55,000	80,000
47sa	30sF	*Star* K/46 First prefix	4,000	9,000	17,000	35,000	65,000	95,000
47sb	30sL	*Star* I/0 Last prefix	3,500	6,750	13,000	30,000	50,000	75,000
		COOMBS / WATT : *First year of issue - 1949*						
48	31	General prefix	20	35	100	250	375	850
48a	31F	K/97 First prefix	95	250	500	1,000	1,500	3,200
48b	31L	W/79 Last prefix	95	250	500	1,000	1,500	3,200
48s	31s	*Star.* General prefix	850	2,000	5,250	12,500	25,000	42,500
48sa	31sF	*Star.* I/1 First prefix	900	2,250	6,000	10,500	27,500	60,000
48sb	31sL	*Star.* W/1 Last prefix	950	2,500	6,500	11,500	32,000	62,500
		COOMBS / WILSON : *First year of issue - 1952*						
49	32	General prefix	20	35	95	240	330	850
49a	32F	W/72 First prefix	100	225	350	850	1,600	2,000
49b	32L	X/55 Last prefix	150	275	450	1,100	1,700	3,400
49s	32s	*Star.* General prefix	800	1,500	5,000	14,500	25,000	42,500
49sa	32sF	*Star.* W/2 First prefix	750	1,700	6,000	16,500	27,500	50,000
49sb	32sL	*Star.* W/6 Last prefix	650	1,500	5,500	15,500	26,500	47,500

ONE POUND

ELIZABETH II : 1953 - 1966 ISSUE

Portrait of. Elizabeth II. Predominantly green. 180 x 79 to 181 x 81 mm

Reference # McD	- Rks	Description	VG	Fine	VF	EF	aUnc	Unc
		COOMBS / WILSON *Commonwealth : Bank - First year of issue - 1953*						
50	33	General prefix	15	20	30	60	180	225
50a	33F	HA/00 First prefix	160	325	675	1,450	2,150	3,250
50b	33L	HF/65 Last prefix	175	375	750	1,750	2,500	3,750
50s	33s	*Star.* General prefix	225	600	1,650	3,000	7,500	9,500
50sa	33sF	*Star.* HA/50 First prefix	350	850	2,000	5,500	13,500	22,500
50sb	33sL	*Star.* HE/92 Last prefix	450	995	2,500	6,750	16,500	27,500
		COOMBS / WILSON : *Reserve Bank - First year of issue - 1961*						
		• Dark green reverse						
51	34a	HF/ 66? General prefix	15	20	30	55	160	225
51a	34aF	HF/ 65 First prefix	175	300	750	1,550	2,600	3,650
51b	34aL	Last prefix. To be advised	—	—	—	—	—	—
		• Star Dark green reverse						
51s	34sa	*Star.* General prefix	375	800	2,000	5,000	9,000	25,000
51sa	34saF	*Star.* HE/ 95 First prefix	410	925	2,300	5,750	15,000	30,000
51sb	34saL	*Star.* HE/ 99 Last prefix	500	1,500	3.250	8.000	19,000	27,500
		• Emerald green reverse						
52	34b	Unknown general prefix	8	15	30	65	100	165
52a	34bF	First prefix. To be advised	—	—	—	—	—	—
52b	34bL	HK/ 65 Last prefix for Circulation Issue	110	225	400	800	1,400	2,200
52c	34bX	HK/ 68 Last prefix for Reserve Bank Archives	Notes *usually flicked*			—	—	1,500
		• Star Emerald green reverse						
52	34b	Unknown general prefix	8	15	30	65	100	165
52s	34sb	*Star.* General prefix	275	600	1,500	3,750	12,500	22,500
52sa	34sbF	*Star.* HE/ 80 First prefix	395	825	2,000	5,500	14,500	23,500
52sb	34sbL	*Star.* HE/ 94 Last prefix	375	650	1,575	4,250	11,500	21,000

Towards the end of this book you will find details of the special 25th Anniversary of Decimal Currency Portfolio issued in 1991. The notes came from the archives of Note Printing Australia (NPA) and consisted of the last 800 ten shillings, one pounds, five pounds and ten pounds issues coupled with the first issue of the one, two, ten and twenty dollar notes. In recent years, collectors and dealers have been breaking up these sets and buying or selling the notes individually. These notes are causing a confusing situation when compared with the normal circulation "Last Prefix" issues. We have decided to give both issues a separate Reference Number.

PRICING OF BANKNOTES AND COINS

Prices in this book are based on comparative rarity, auction results and dealer buying and selling prices. With most of the early banknotes, Uncirculated condition is extremely rare and prices for such items can only be an estimate. Although not priced due to space restrictions, George V notes in even "Fair" or "Good" condition in some instances are still very collectable. Consecutive pairs, trios etc will usually carry a premium over a single note. The amount will depend on the rarity of the single banknote.

For an explanation of how we determine our pricing, please read the information found on page 8 of this book.

FIVE POUNDS

GEORGE V : NO MOSAIC ISSUE. 1914 - 1915

First Gold Standard issue : Predominantly blue. 167 x 105 mm

Reference # McD - Rks		Description	VG	Fine	VF	EF	aUnc	Unc
		COLLINS / ALLEN : First year of issue - 1913						
53	35	No mosaic on reverse. Preffix U only. No first & last prefix	30,000	60,000	20,000	170,000	240,000	350,000

FIVE POUNDS GEORGE V : MOSAIC ISSUE. 1914 - 1915

SECOND TYPE REVERSE : Predominantly blue. 167 x 105 mm

Reference # McD	Rks	Description	VG	Fine	VF	EF	aUnc	Unc
		COLLINS / ALLEN. *First year of issue - 1914*						
		• *Mosaic of '5's on reverse. Small letter prefix*						
		• *Dark blue serials*						
48	31	General prefix	20	35	100	250	375	850
54	36	No general prefixes	—	—	—	—	—	—
54a	36a	Letter prefix U	25,000	37,000	70,000	145,000	225,000	325,000
		• *Black serials*						
54b	36b	No general prefixes	—	—	—	—	—	—
54b/1	36bF	First prefix letter U	3,500	7,000	21,000	40,000	85,000	135,000
54b/2	36bL	Last prefix letter V	3,000	7,000	21,000	42,000	75,000	130,00
55	36c	No general suffixes	—	—	—	—	—	—
55b/1	36cF	First suffix letter U	3,500	6,900	17,500	37,000	70,000	110,000
55b/2	36cL	Last suffix letter V	3,300	8,000	19,500	45,000	75,000	125,000
		CERUTTY / COLLINS. First year of issue - 1918						
56	37a	Suffix letter V	5,200	12,250	24,000	49,500	95,000	145,000
57	37b	Prefix & suffix U- B to U- H	1,975	3,950	9,500	20,000	45,000	80,000
57a	37bF	First prefix and suffix U- A	2,750	4,250	9,750	22,500	46,000	80,000
57b	37bL	Last prefix and suffix U- J	2,800	4,250	11,750	27,500	55,000	77,500

There has been a rearrangement of reference numbers with the above Collins/Allen issue following the recent discovery of an issue with blue serial numbers rather than black. This blue issue is now McD54a. The original 54/36a is now 54b/36b.

FIVE POUNDS

GEORGE V : 1924 - 1933 ISSUE

Portrait of George V. Predominantly Blue. 180 x 78 mm

Reference # McD	Rks	Description	VG	Fine	VF	EF	aUnc	Unc
		KELL / COLLINS - 1924 • *Black signatures*						
58	38a	General prefixes	1,250	2,800	7,000	15,000	62,500	110,000
58a	38aF	Q/0 First prefix	1,575	3,650	9,000	17,500	67,500	117,000
58b	38aL	Q/5 Last prefix	1,750	4,000	10,500	19,500	70,000	125,000
		KELL / COLLINS - 1924 • *Dark blue signatures*						
59	38b	General prefixes	2,200	5,000	10,000	20,000	90,000	135,000
59a	38bF	Q/5 First prefix	2,500	6,000	12,000	27,500	110,000	155,000
59b	38bL	Q/7 Last prefix	2,750	6,500	13,500	32,500	115,000	165,000
		KELL / HEATHERSHAW - 1927 • *Note Issue Department*						
60	39	General prefixes	1,750	3,500	9,000	20,000	72,000	120,000
60a	39F	Q/7 First prefix	2,200	3,750	12,500	27,500	77,000	130,000
60b	39L	Q/11 Last prefix	2,500	4,000	13,000	30,000	82,000	135,000
		KELL / HEATHERSHAW - 1927 • *Commonwealth Bank issue*						
61	40	General prefixes	1,575	3,250	7,000	18,000	70,000	115,000
61a	40F	Q/7 First prefix	1,850	4,750	9,000	25,000	92,000	140,000
61b	40L	Q/11 Last prefix	1,750	4,500	8,250	22,500	90,000	147,500
		RIDDLE / HEATHERSHAW - 1927 • *Note Issue Department*						
62	41	No general prefixes	—	—	—	—	—	—
62a	41F	Q/11 First prefix	12,500	23,000	52,500	125,000	200,000	315,000
62b	41L	Q/12 Last prefix	21,000	40,000	75,000	157,500	236,000	357,000
		RIDDLE / HEATHERSHAW - 1927 • Commonwealth Bank						
63	42	General prefixes	550	1,350	4,250	11,500	22,000	37,500
63a	42F	Q/11 First prefix	700	1,750	3,500	12,750	24,000	41,500
63b	42L	Q/26 Last prefix	625	1,500	3,000	9,500	22,000	38,500
		RIDDLE / SHEEHAN - 1932 • Commonwealth Bank						
64	43	General prefixes	1,000	2,000	10,000	33,000	62,500	111,500
64a	43F	Q/26 First prefix	1,250	2,500	12,750	35,500	65,000	115,000
64b	43L	Q/29 Last prefix	1,250	2,500	12,750	37,500	67,000	117,000

GEORGE V : 1933 - 1936 ISSUE

Portrait of George V. Predominantly Blue. 180 x 78 mm

Reference # McD	Rks	Description	VG	Fine	VF	EF	aUnc	Unc
		RIDDLE / SHEEHAN - *First year of issue - 1933*						
65	44a	a. Pink face of King (*Cross hatching*) General issue	475	1,000	4,500	12,500	25,000	48,000
65a	44aF	R/0 First prefix	575	1,500	3,250	9,750	27,500	52,500
65b	44aL	R/10 Last prefix	650	1,650	3,650	11,250	29,000	57,500
66	44b	b. White face of King (*No cross hatching*) General issue	475	1,000	4,750	11,750	27,000	51,000
66a	44bF	R/10 First prefix	575	1,500	3,250	9,750	29,000	55,000
66b	44bL	R/29 Last prefix	600	1,175	4,000	11,500	31,500	59,000

FIVE POUNDS

GEORGE VI : 1939 - 1952 ISSUE

Portrait of George VI. Predominantly Blue. 181 x 79 mm

Reference # McD	Rks	Description	VG	Fine	VF	EF	aUnc	Unc
		SHEEHAN / MCFARLANE *- First year of issue - 1939*						
67	45	General prefixes	145	225	575	2,250	6,500	14,000
67a	45F	R/20 First prefix	170	350	675	2,950	9,000	16,000
67b	45L	R/34 Last prefix	180	350	700	3,200	8,000	18,000
		ARMITAGE / MCFARLANE *- First year of issue - 1941*						
68	46	General prefixes	40	90	200	450	1,500	4,000
68a	46F	R/34 First prefix	80	120	400	850	2,500	5,500
68b	46L	R/84 Last prefix	80	120	400	850	2,500	5,500
		COOMBS / WATT *- First year of issue - 1949*						
69	47	General prefixes	40	90	210	600	1,950	4,200
69a	47F	R/85 First prefix	80	150	400	900	3,400	6,000
69b	47L	S/26 Last prefix	80	150	400	900	3,400	6,000
		COOMBS / WILSON *- First year of issue - 1952*						
70	48	General prefixes	40	90	230	650	2,000	4,200
70a	48F	S/27 First prefix	70	225	400	850	3,000	6,100
70b	48L	S/57 Last prefix	80	250	425	950	3,250	6,500

FIVE POUNDS

ELIZABETH II : 1954 - 1966 ISSUE

Portrait of Sir John Franklin. Predominantly Blue. 181 x 79 mm

Reference # McD	Rks	Description	VG	Fine	VF	EF	aUnc	Unc
		COOMBS / WILSON						
		Commonwealth Bank - First year of issue - 1954						
71	49	General prefix	25	35	90	190	450	800
71a	49F	TA/00 First prefix	100	300	700	1,300	2,500	4,000
71b	49L	TB/41 Last prefix	225	400	850	1,750	3,200	5,500
		COOMBS / WILSON						
		Reserve Bank - First year of issue - 1961						
72	50	General prefix	25	35	95	190	400	750
72a	50F	TB/41 First prefix	110	250	750	1,450	2,500	4,550
72b	50L	TD/10 Last prefix •Circulation Issue	90	250	600	1,250	1,750	3,750
		TD/10 Last prefix • NPA Archives						
72c	50X	Serials unknown	*Banknotes usually flicked*			950	1,650	
72s	50s	*Star.* General prefix	650	1,750	2,500	20,000	50,000	80,000
72sa	50sF	*Star.* TC/10 First prefix	1,000	2,600	3,750	23,500	52,000	70,000
72sb	50sL	*Star.* TC/13 Last prefix	1,100	3,000	4,500	25,500	55,000	85,000

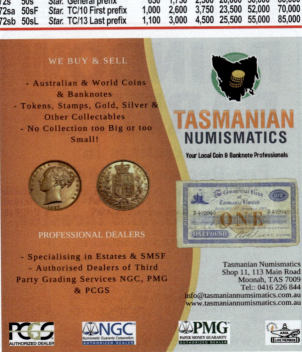

TEN POUNDS

GEORGE V : 1913 - 1925 ISSUE

Portrait of George V. Predominantly Red. 181 x 79 mm

Reference # McD	Rks	Description	VG	Fine	VF	EF	aUnc	Unc
		COLLINS / ALLEN : *First year of issue - 1913*						
73	51	Only W prefix used	19,500	30,000	65,000	100,000	150,000	255,000
		CERUTTY / COLLINS : *First year of issue - 1918*						
74	52a	• *Small black seriffed serials* Reverse colours mauve, green, mauve shading Only W prefix used	35,000	60,000	100,000	150,000	250,000	350,000
75	52b	• *Small black seriffed serials* Reverse colours green mauve, green shading Only W prefix used	13,500	26,000	60,000	90,000	175,000	240,000
76	52c	• *Bold serials* Only W suffix used	12,000	23,000	58,000	90,000	175,000	225,000
76a	52d	• *Bold serials* U over O prefix	12,000	23,000	58,000	90,000	175,000	225,000

TEN POUNDS

GEORGE V : 1925 - 1934 ISSUE

Portrait of George V in profile. Predominantly red & yellow 180 x 78 mm

Reference # McD	Rks	Description	VG	Fine	VF	EF	aUnc	Unc
		KELL / COLLINS *First year of issue - 1925*						
77a	53	Note Issue Dept. Specimen	—	—	—	300,000	—	—
77b	54	Commonwealth issue. U/1 only prefix	4,000	9,000	17,500	28,500	56,000	72,000
		RIDDLE / HEATHERSHAW *First year of issue - 1927*						
78	55	General issue	1,250	3,000	4,200	15,500	29,000	65,000
78a	55F	U/1 First prefix	1,750	3,500	7,000	20,000	32,500	68,000
78b	55L	U/4 Last prefix	1,600	3,000	6,500	17,500	29,000	65,000
		RIDDLE / SHEEHAN *First year of issue - 1932*						
79	56	U/4 Only prefix	11,000	24,500	55,000	110,000	160,000	200,000

TEN POUNDS

GEORGE V : 1934 - 1940 ISSUE

Portrait of George V. Predominantly Red. 181 x 79 mm

Reference # McD	Rks	Description	VG	Fine	VF	EF	aUnc	Unc
		RIDDLE / SHEEHAN First year of issue - 1934						
80	57	General prefix	800	1,500	2,650	9,250	15,000	20,000
80a	57F	V/0 First prefix	600	1,000	3,000	10,500	17,500	29,500
80b	57L	V/3 Last prefix	600	1,000	3,000	10,500	17,500	29,500

TEN POUNDS

GEORGE VI : 1940 - 1954 ISSUE

Portrait of George VI. Predominantly Red. 181 x 79 mm

Reference # McD	Rks	Description	VG	Fine	VF	EF	aUnc	Unc
		SHEEHAN / MCFARLANE 1940 : First year of issue						
81	58	General prefix	200	400	950	3,250	8,500	22,000
81a	58F	V/3 First prefix	250	650	1,750	4,750	9,000	24,000
81b	58L	V/5 Last prefix	300	700	2,500	5,500	10,000	26,000
		ARMITAGE / MCFARLANE 1943 : First year of issue						
82	59	General prefix	125	200	400	1,600	3,000	6,500
82a	59F	V/5 First prefix	180	250	700	2,500	3,500	7,500
82b	59L	V/14 Last prefix	180	250	600	2,000	3,500	7,000
		COOMBS / WATT 1949 : First year of issue						
83	60	General prefix	125	200	450	1,600	3,000	6,500
83a	60F	V/15 First prefix	150	300	600	2,000	3,500	7,250
83b	60L	V/22 Last prefix	180	250	700	2,500	3,750	7,500
		COOMBS / WILSON 1952 : First year of issue						
84	61	General prefix	225	400	1,000	4,500	9,000	20,000
84a	61F	V/22 First prefix	350	800	1,500	3,000	9,500	21,500
84b	61L	V/24 Last prefix	300	700	2,500	5,500	10,000	22,500

TEN POUNDS

ELIZABETH II : 1954 - 1966 ISSUE

Governor Arthur Phillip. Predominantly Red. 181 x 79 mm

Reference # McD	Rks	Description	VG	Fine	VF	EF	aUnc	Unc
		COOMBS / WILSON Commonwealth Bank. First year of issue - 1954						
85	62	General prefix	115	195	325	400	950	1,650
85a	62F	WA/00 First prefix	200	300	800	1,500	2,600	4,500
85b	62L	WA/28 Last prefix	250	600	1,200	2,000	4,100	6,500
		COOMBS / WILSON Reserve Bank. First year of issue - 1960						
86	63	General prefix	70	120	175	425	950	1,650
86a	63F	WA/28 First prefix	220	350	800	1,500	2,600	4,500
86b	63L	WA/62 Last prefix for circulation issue Serials to 061000	150	250	600	1,200	2,600	3,750
86c	63X	WA/62 Last prefix for NPA archives Serials from 089001	*Banknotes usually flicked*				1,850	—

86a Serial numbers for circulation issues to WA/62. Only 61,000 notes were issued and few would have survived - especially in better grade.

86c Serial numbers for the NPA Archive sets range from 089001 and above.

TWENTY POUNDS

KING GEORGE V : 1914 - 1938

GOLD STANDARD. Predominantly dark blue 165 x 98 to 168 x 102 mm

Reference # McD	Rks	Description	VG	Fine	VF	EF	aUnc	Unc
		COLLINS / ALLEN : First year of issue - 1913						
87	64	Prefix X	30,000	50,000	90,000	140,000	200,000	270,000
		CERUTTY / COLLINS : First year of issue - 1918						
88	65a	a. Small serials Prefix X	35,000	56,000	100,000	160,000	260,000	325,000
89	65b	b. Bold serials Suffix X	30,000	52,000	90,000	100,000	195,000	220,000

FIFTY POUNDS

GEORGE V : 1914 - 1945 ISSUE

Predominantly blue & pink . 166 x 102 mm to 168 to 102 mm

Reference # McD	Rks	Description	VG	Fine	VF	EF	aUnc	Unc
		COLLINS / ALLEN : First year of issue - 1914						
90	66	Prefix Y	90,000	120,000	175,000	220,000	325,000	425,000
		CERUTTY / COLLINS : First year of issue - 1918						
		Suffix Z	35,000	65,000	120,000	185,000	265,000	330,000
91	67a	a. Prefix Y Small type	45,000	70,000	110,000	145,000	275,000	325,000
92	67b	b. Suffix Y Bold type	43,500	70,000	95,000	125,000	225,000	290,000
93	67c	c. Prefix Medium type	30,000	45,000	55,000	93,500	180,000	260,000

ONE HUNDRED POUNDS

KING GEORGE V : 1914 - 1938

GOLD STANDARD. Predominantly dark blue 165 x 98 to 168 x 102 mm

Reference # McD	Rks	Description	VG	Fine	VF	EF	aUnc	Unc
		COLLINS / ALLEN : First year of issue - 1914						
94	68a	a. Small blue serif serials. Only Z prefix	110,000	145,000	185,000	240,000	315,000	395,000
95	68b	b. Medium black serif. Only Z prefix	110,000	145,000	185,000	240,000	315,000	395,000
		CERUTTY / COLLINS : First year of issue - 1924						
96	69a	a. Bold serials Suffix Z	35,000	65,000	120,000	185,000	265,000	330,000
97	69b	b. Medium serials Prefix Z	25,000	55,000	110,000	120,000	235,000	295,000

ONE THOUSAND DOLLARS

GOLD STANDARD : 1914 - 1924 215 x 143 mm

Predominantly orange. 137 x 76 to 137 x 78 mm

Reference # McD	Rks	Description	VG	Fine	VF	EF	aUnc	Unc
		COLLINS / ALLEN : Treasury issue - 1914						
98	70a	First year of issue Prefix 2A	95,000	175,000	225,000	375,000	800,000	950,000
		KELL / COLLINS : Note Issue Department - 1924						
99	70b	First year of issue	95,000	75,000	225,000	375,000	800,000	950,000

The above £1,000 note was introduced in 1914 to solve several financial issues that arise at the beginning of any World War. Uncertainty results in people hoarding gold and vast amounts of cash are required to build things to blow other things up. A banknote equivalent to a full year's average wage as expected to do the trick. Approximately 52,800 Collins/Allen £1,000 were put into circulation. They were available to the public until June, 1915. At that time, Denison Miller, Governor of the Commonwealth Bank advised Secretary of the Treasury Allen that there were 'enormous risks' arising from differences in colour, size and paper quality which offered little safeguard against forgery. Following this advice, the use of the notes was scaled back to bank to bank transactions. A census in 1921 revealed that several hundred notes were unaccounted for. By 1931, this number had fallen to 66. Most of the notes were destroyed in 1969 with just one unconfirmed report that in September, 1964, a £1000 note was donated to Reverend Sir Irving Benson of the Methodist Missions and was eventually sold to a Melbourne collector. For many years all surviving examples were thought to be crossed or perforated cancellations and restricted to museums and other institutions. However in 1998, Noble Numismatics offered a cancelled specimen with the serial number 2A 058383 in their Melbourne July 1998 sale. It sold for $94,000. The note is perforated with the word "Cancelled" twice and also four larger cancellation holes. It is graded as "good Very Fine" with thinning from gum attached at an earlier time. To date, no other examples have been identified.

UNISSUED SPECIMENS

KNOWN EXAMPLES IN PRIVATE HANDS

GEORGE V FIVE SHILLINGS - 1916

CERUTTY / COLLINS. 127mm x 70mm. Most destroyed in 1922. 4 known in private hands

The Five Shillings note was proposed during WWI when the price of silver rose rapidly. Treasury looked for an alternative to silver coin in circulation. The notes were printed in 1916 without any signatures. These were added some times later but there are no clear records to indicate just when this occurred. On February 5, 1920 the Treasurer of the Commonwealth Mr Watt, announced that passengers travelling overseas were only to take a maximum of £3 in Australian silver coins with them. It is interesting that this edict was initiated some four years after the notes were printed but they were not issued even though the price of silver and the shortage of coinage were so great. The Commonwealth Bank Act had included in it the authority to issue the Five Shilling notes. As it was, the notes were never issued even though some 1,020,000 were actually printed. This was due to the crisis point gradually passing and the price of silver falling over 70% between its peaks in 1920 to late in 1921. Burning in 1922 destroyed all but a handful of the notes printed.

HENRY PARKES FIFTY POUNDS - 1953?

CERUTTY / COLLINS. 186mm x 95mm. Most destroyed in 1958. 1 known in private hands

This privately owned note, which came from a European source, caused a sensation when it was first displayed to the numismatic fraternity at the Singapore International Coin Fair in February 1996. The note was signed by H.C. Coombs and Roland Wilson. The six-digit serial number was 000000 and did not include either a prefix or a suffix. Two years after being discovered, the note appeared as lot 4878 in Noble's Numismatic Sale 58 Part A held in Melbourne in July 1998. The note was passed in at after failing to reach its reserve of $100,000. Numismatic author, Mick Vort Ronald explanded on known information when writing in the May 1996 issue of the Australian Coin Review. In part he wrote: "In 1950 an Advisory Council wanted the portraits for a new design of the several denominations to be taken from a panel of early explorers. The G M proposed the portraits of General Monash to be put on the £20 note, Henry Parkes on the £50 note and Sir Edmund Barton on the £100 note. Preliminary designs of new £50 and £100 note fronts had been prepared by the Note Printing Branch staff but it was decided to wait until the Treasurer decided. On April 6, 1955 the Governor of the Commonwealth Bank received one machine-printed preliminary design of a completely new £50 note and four sketch designs of new £20 and £100 notes, both backs and fronts. By February 1958 Treasury had still not approved the reissue. In view of the generally negative reaction of the trading banks, it was then suggested that the obsolete high denomination notes be destroyed. This was later duly carried out with the approval of the Governor and Deputy Governor of the Bank."

GEORGE V ONE THOUSAND POUNDS

NO SIGNATURES. 186mm x 96mm. Most destroyed in 1969. 1 known in private hands

Records held in Reserve Bank of Australia Archives (formerly Commonwealth Bank of Australia Archives) show that in 1925 there were steel plates, copper line blocks and original copper plates for the new £1000 note in existence. The engravers were Perkins Bacon and Co. Ltd. By June 5, 1928 however, it was realised that the use of £1000 notes by banks was rapidly decreasing as the practice of central reserve banking was adopted. The board proposed not going to the expense of issuing a new design. £1000 notes of the Type One design were used by the Reserve Bank of Australia until June 1969 to facilitate internal transfers between the Note Issue Department and the banking section of their Sydney office. After that, because of changes in accounting procedures, £1000 notes were not needed internally and the notes were burned in late 1969.

MILLION NUMBERED NOTES

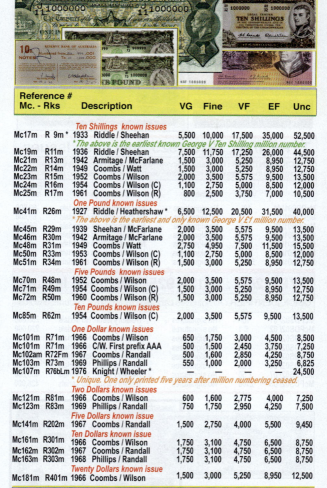

Reference # Mc.	Rks	Description	VG	Fine	VF	EF	Unc
		Ten Shillings known issues					
Mc17m	R 9m *	1933 Riddle / Sheehan	5,500	10,000	17,500	35,000	52,500
		** The above is the earliest known George V Ten Shilling million number.*					
Mc19m	R11m	1936 Riddle / Sheehan	7,500	11,750	17,250	26,000	44,500
Mc21m	R13m	1942 Armitage / McFarlane	1,500	3,000	5,250	8,950	12,750
Mc22m	R14m	1949 Coombs / Watt	1,500	3,000	5,250	8,950	12,750
Mc23m	R15m	1952 Coombs / Wilson	2,000	3,500	5,575	9,500	13,500
Mc24m	R16m	1954 Coombs / Wilson (C)	1,100	2,750	5,000	8,500	12,000
Mc25m	R17m	1961 Coombs / Wilson (R)	800	2,500	3,750	7,000	10,500
		One Pound known issues					
Mc41m	R26m	1927 Riddle / Heathershaw *	6,500	12,500	20,500	31,500	40,000
		** The above is the earliest and only known George V £1 million number.*					
Mc45m	R29m	1939 Sheehan / McFarlane	2,000	3,500	5,575	9,500	13,500
Mc46m	R30m	1942 Armitage / McFarlane	2,000	3,500	5,575	9,500	13,500
Mc48m	R31m	1949 Coombs / Watt	2,750	4,950	7,500	11,500	15,500
Mc50m	R33m	1953 Coombs / Wilson (C)	1,100	2,750	5,000	8,500	12,000
Mc51m	R34m	1961 Coombs / Wilson (R)	1,500	3,000	5,250	8,950	12,750
		Five Pounds known issues					
Mc70m	R48m	1952 Coombs / Wilson	2,000	3,500	5,575	9,500	13,500
Mc71m	R49m	1954 Coombs / Wilson (C)	1,500	3,000	5,250	8,950	12,750
Mc72m	R50m	1960 Coombs / Wilson (R)	1,500	3,000	5,250	8,950	12,750
		Ten Pounds known issues					
Mc85m	R62m	1954 Coombs / Wilson (C)	2,000	3,500	5,575	9,500	13,500
		One Dollar known issues					
Mc101m	R71m	1966 Coombs / Wilson	650	1,750	3,000	4,500	8,500
Mc101m	R71m	1966 C/W. First prefix AAA	500	1,500	2,450	3,750	7,250
Mc102am	R72Fm	1967 Coombs / Randall	500	1,600	2,850	4,250	8,750
Mc103m	R73m	1969 Phillips / Randall	550	1,000	2,000	3,250	6,825
Mc107m	R76bLm	1976 Knight / Wheeler *	—	—	—	—	24,500
		** Unique. One only printed five years after million numbering ceased.*					
		Two Dollars known issues					
Mc121m	R81m	1966 Coombs / Wilson	600	1,600	2,775	4,000	7,250
Mc123m	R83m	1969 Phillips / Randall	750	1,750	2,950	4,250	7,500
		Five Dollars known issue					
Mc141m	R202m	1967 Coombs / Randall	1,500	2,750	4,000	5,500	9,450
		Ten Dollars known issue					
Mc161m	R301m	1966 Coombs / Wilson	1,750	3,100	4,750	6,500	8,750
Mc162m	R302m	1967 Coombs / Randall	1,750	3,100	4,750	6,500	8,750
Mc163m	R303m	1968 Phillips / Randall	1,750	3,100	4,750	6,500	8,750
		Twenty Dollars known issue					
Mc181m	R401m	1966 Coombs / Wilson	1,500	3,000	5,250	8,950	12,500

Very few *Million Numbered Notes* have survived in each denomination. The hand numbering of notes with a million ceased after the Phillips / Randall signature of 1968 / 1969 with the exception of the 1976 issue of the Knight / Wheeler series. During this period *Note Printing Australia* embarked on an experiment to test the quality and durability of the quality of the paper. *(This series of "Test Notes" discussed in more detail in the One Dollar Section).* All the test notes had the prefix DBP and concluded with a unique *Million Numbered Note.*

RECENT SALES : The downturn in current values for this series have been sourced through auction catalogues and dealer pricelists. These notes do not come onto the market very often so even the price obtained for the first note listed below might be optomistic in today's market.
ONE POUND PAIR. Lot 465 at the International Auction Galleries Auction 73 held in March, 2011 featured a VF consecutive pair of Mc52, R34b banknotes that sold for $13,747 including commission.
TEN SHILLINGS SINGLE. Lot 3169 in Noble's sale 106, held in July 2014, a Ten Shilling note (1961 Mc25, R17) was described as having a vertical paper fold down the left side, otherwise virtually uncirculated. It sold for $6,960 against an estimate of $6,000.
ONE POUND SINGLE. Lot 3170 in the same Noble auction featured a One Pound note (1961 Mc52, R34b) which was described as having a centrefold but otherwise Uncirculated. It sold for $5,290 against an estimate of $5,290.

PRE DECIMAL SPECIMEN & TRIAL BANKNOTES

TYPE 1/ A : 1913-1925 Specimen Issues

QUICK IDENTIFIER : Previously unknown type. No serial numbers and single tiny perforation in the centre of the note. Some denominations have yet to be verified.

Ref. Mc	Face Value	Signatures	Description	Price as Issued
McPDS01/ 01	10/-	No signatures	No cancellations or serials	60,000
McPDS01/ 02	£ 1	No signatures	No cancellations or serials	60,000
McPDS01/ 03	£ 5	No signatures	No cancellations or serials	60,000
McPDS01/ 04	£ 10	No signatures	No cancellations or serials	60,000
McPDS01/ 05	£ 20	No signatures	No cancellations or serials	60,000
McPDS01/ 06	£ 50	No signatures	No cancellations or serials	60,000
McPDS01/ 07	£100	No signatures	No cancellations or serials	90,000

TYPE 2/ B : 1913-1925 Specimen Issues

QUICK IDENTIFIER : All notes are cancelled by two small perforated words

Ref. Mc	Face Value	Signatures	Description	Price as Issued
McPDS02/ 01	10/-	No signatures	Treasury issue. No serials	260,000
McPDS02/ 02	£ 1	No signatures	Treasury issue. No serials	270,000
McPDS02/ 03	£ 5	No signatures	Treasury issue. No serials	295,000
McPDS02/ 04	£ 10	No signatures	Treasury issue. No serials	325,000
McPDS02/ 05	£ 10	No signatures	Commonweath Bank issue	340,000
McPDS02/ 06	£ 20	No signatures	Treasury issue. No serials	390,000
McPDS02/ 07	£ 50	No signatures	Treasury issue. No serials	400,000
McPDS02/ 08	£100	No signatures	Treasury issue. No serials	425,000

TYPE 3/ C : 1913 Treasury Issues

QUICK IDENTIFIER : The word CANCELLED spelled out in large perforations. There are two minor types. The first shows CANCELLED punched out backwards and upside down on known £10 issues. Others have the word shown in the correct orientation when viewed from the front of the note. Has Collins/Allen signatures and serial numbers.

Ref. Mc	Face Value	Signatures	Description	Price as Issued
McPDS03/ 01	10/ -	Collins / Allen	Printed serial numbers	260,000
McPDS03/ 02	£ 1	Collins / Allen	Printed Red serial numbers	230,000
McPDS03/ 03	£ 5	Collins / Allen	Printed serial numbers	245,500
McPDS03/ 04	£ 10	Collins / Allen	Printed serial numbers	250,000
McPDS03/ 05	£ 20	Collins / Allen	Printed serial numbers	267,500
McPDS03/ 06	£ 50	Collins / Allen	Printed serial numbers	300,000
McPDS03/ 07	£100	Collins / Allen	Printed serial numbers	325,000
McPDS03/ 08	£1000	Collins / Allen	Printed serial numbers	325,000

PRE DECIMAL SPECIMEN & TRIAL BANKNOTES

TYPE 4/ D : 1918 Treasury Issue

QUICK IDENTIFIER : Similar to previous issue but with the addition of diagonal black lines forming a cross on both sides.

Ref. Mc	Face Value	Signatures	Description	Price as Issued
McPDS04/ 01	10/-	Cerutty / Collins	Cancelled & Diagonal lines	175,000
McPDS04/ 02	£ 1	Cerutty / Collins	Cancelled & Diagonal lines	175,000
McPDS04/ 03	£ 5	Cerutty / Collins	Cancelled & Diagonal lines	175,000
McPDS04/ 04	£ 10	Cerutty / Collins	Cancelled & Diagonal lines	175,000
McPDS04/ 05	£ 20	Cerutty / Collins	Cancelled & Diagonal lines	185,000
McPDS04/ 06	£ 50	Cerutty / Collins	Cancelled & Diagonal lines	210,000
McPDS04/ 07	£100	Collins / Allen	Cancelled & Diagonal lines	235,000

TYPE 5/ E : 1918 Treasury Issue

QUICK IDENTIFIER : This is a relatively new discovery and is similar to the previous Cerutty / Collins issues. However, instead of crossed diagonal lines, this issue has the same type of SPECIMEN overprint used for the first of the Queen Elizabeth II designs.

McPDS05/ 01	£ 50	Cerutty / Collins	SPECIMEN overprint in red	175,000
McPDS05/ 02	£ 100	Cerutty / Collins	SPECIMEN overprint in red	195,000

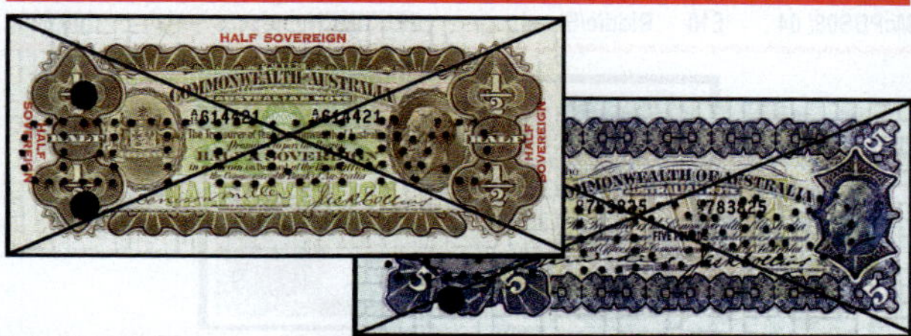

TYPE 6/F : "Harrison" Issue

QUICK IDENTIFIER : Has the addition of two or more large holes added to the other distinguishing features already mentioned in Type 3/C. The £1000 is unique in having four holes. Holed notes without the crossed lines are known in official archives.

McPDS06/ 01	10/-	Miller / Collins	Diagonal line & serials	140,000
McPDS06/ 01	£ 1	Miller / Collins	Diagonal line & serials	140,000
McPDS06/ 01	£ 5	Kell / Collins	Diagonal line & serials	147,500
McPDS06/ 01	£ 10	Kell / Collins	Diagonal line & serials	160,000
McPDS06/ 01	£1000	Kell / Collins	Diagonal line & serials	625,000

PRE DECIMAL SPECIMEN & TRIAL BANKNOTES

TYPE 7/ G : "ASH" Specimen Issue

QUICK IDENTIFIER [No image] : Design similar to 1933 Legal Tender issue. Has five large holes but missing diagonal crossed lines. Has serial numbers and signatures of Riddle/ Sheehan. Only the Ten Shilling note is known in official archives. None known in private hands. Unfortunately an image is not available at this stage.

Ref. Mc	Face Value	Signatures	Description	Price as Issued
McPDS07/ 01	10/-	Riddle/Sheehan	Five large holes with serials	No sales

TYPE 8/ H : "ASH" Specimen Issue

QUICK IDENTIFIER : Often referred to as the Edward VIII presentation notes as the issue included the watermarked profile of the then Prince of Wales. All four denominations of the first 1933 legal tender issues are known and all are lightly affixed to backing cards. Notes feature the word SPECIMEN instead of serial numbers. All notes signed Riddle/Sheehan. The 10/- and £1 notes are thought to be unique while there are three examples each of the £5 and £10 denominations.

Ref. Mc	Face Value	Signatures	Description	Price as Issued
McPDS08/ 01	10/-	Riddle/Sheehan	SPECIMEN replaces serial	145,000
McPDS08/ 02	£ 1	Riddle/Sheehan	SPECIMEN replaces serial	145,000
McPDS08/ 03	£ 5	Riddle/Sheehan	SPECIMEN replaces serial	110,000
McPDS08/ 04	£10	Riddle/Sheehan	SPECIMEN replaces serial	100,000

Ref. Mc	Face Value	Signatures	Description	Price as Issued
McPDS09/ 01	£ 1	Riddle/Sheehan	CANCELLED replaces serial	125,000

PRE DECIMAL SPECIMEN & TRIAL BANKNOTES

TYPE 10/J : KGV & KGVI Specimen Issues

17-ps/ 03	10/ -	Riddle/Sheehan	Geo V. Mc17. Brown	85,000
18-ps/ 01	10/ -	Riddle/Sheehan	Geo V. Mc18. Brown. O/P	85,000
19-ps/ 01	10/ -	Riddle/Sheehan	Geo V. Mc19. Orange	85,000
44-ps/ 03	£ 1	Riddle/Sheehan	Diagonal lines & serials	87,500
63-ps/ 02	£ 5	Riddle/Sheehan	Diagonal lines & serials	90,000
80-ps/ 02	£ 10	Riddle/Sheehan	Diagonal lines & serials	92,500
22-ps/ 01	10/ -	Coombs/Watt	Diagonal lines & serials	85,000
48-ps/ 01	£ 1	Coombs/Watt	Diagonal lines & serials	87,500
69-ps/ 01	£ 5	Coombs/Watt	Diagonal lines & serials	90,000
83-ps/ 01	£ 10	Coombs/Watt	Diagonal lines & serials	92,500

TYPE 11/K : Elizabeth II. 1953 - 1961 Issues

24ps/ 01	10/ -	Coombs /Wilson	Com/Bank SPECIMEN	57,500
50ps/ 01	£ 1	Coombs /Wilson	Com/Bank SPECIMEN	60,000
71ps/ 01	£ 5	Coombs /Wilson	Com/Bank SPECIMEN	62,500
85ps/ 01	£ 10	Coombs /Wilson	Com/Bank SPECIMEN	65,000
25/ps 01	10/ -	Coombs /Wilson	Reserve Bank. SPECIMEN	57,500
51/ps 01	£ 1	Coombs /Wilson	Reserve Bank. SPECIMEN	60,000
72/ps 01	£ 5	Coombs /Wilson	Reserve Bank. SPECIMEN	62,500
86/ps 01	£ 10	Coombs /Wilson	Reserve Bank. SPECIMEN	65,000

TYPE 12/L : Elizabeth II. 1953 - 1961 Issues

24-ps/ 02	10/ -	Coombs /Wilson	Comwth/Bank Diagonal lines	57,500
50-ps/ 02	£ 1	Coombs /Wilson	Comwth/Bank Diagonal lines	60,000
71-ps/ 02	£ 5	Coombs /Wilson	Comwth/Bank Diagonal lines	62,500
85-ps/ 02	£ 10	Coombs /Wilson	Comwth/Bank Diagonal lines	65,000
25-/ps 02	10/ -	Coombs /Wilson	Reserve Bank Diagonal lines	57,500
51-/ps 02	£ 1	Coombs /Wilson	Reserve Bank Diagonal lines	60,000
72-/ps 02	£ 5	Coombs /Wilson	Reserve Bank Diagonal lines	62,500
86-/ps 02	£ 10	Coombs /Wilson	Reserve Bank Diagonal lines	65,000

ONE DOLLAR

'COMMONWEALTH OF AUSTRALIA' HEADING

ELIZABETH II. PAPER ISSUE : 1966 TO 1974

Reference # McD	Rks	Description	Fine	VF	EF	aUnc	Unc
		COOMBS / WILSON - 1966					
101	71	General prefixes	5	10	20	40	100
101a	71F	AAA First prefix	275	450	950	1,350	1,950
101b	71L	AGE Last prefix	220	450	950	1,250	1,950
101s	71s	STAR General prefix	280	600	1,250	1,950	2,500
101sa	71sF	*Star* ZAA First prefix	325	750	1,500	2,250	2,750
101sb	71sL	*Star* ZAF Last prefix	400	900	1,900	2,500	3,250
		COOMBS / RANDALL - 1967					
102	72	General prefixes	85	200	450	550	1,100
102a	72F	AGE First prefix	200	350	675	995	1,500
102b	72L	AHY Last prefix	250	400	850	1,250	2,000
102s	72s	STAR General prefix	750	1,600	3,250	5,000	7,000
102sa	72sF	*Star* ZAF First prefix	850	1,750	3,750	6,750	8,750
102sb	72sL	*Star* ZAH Last prefix	950	2,275	4,200	7,500	9,500
		PHILLIPS / RANDALL - 1969					
103	73	General prefixes	4	9	15	35	80
103a	73F	AHY First prefix	210	350	775	1,200	1,950
103b	73L	BBE Last prefix	75	125	220	,300	425
103s	73s	STAR General prefix	265	575	1,150	1,850	2,300
103sa	73sF	*Star* ZAH First prefix	350	650	1,500	1,950	2,550
103sb	73sL	*Star* ZAQ Last prefix	395	800	1,850	2,250	2,750
		PHILLIPS / WHEELER - 1972					
104	74	General prefixes	4	9	15	35	85
104a	74F	BBF First prefix	75	125	220	275	400
104b	74L	BLG Last prefix	60	125	200	360	525

STAR NOTE DETAILS

Coombs / Wilson (Mc101s) : Serial number sequence ZAA 00001* to ZAF 35000*. A total of 535,000 star notes printed which offers a ratio of 1 star note to every 243 normal notes.

Coombs / Randall (Mc102s) : Serial number sequence ZAF 45001* to ZAH 17000*. A total of 172,000 star notes printed which offers a ratio of 1 star note to every 219 normal notes.

Phillips / Randall (Mc103s) : Serial number sequence ZAH 17001* to ZAQ 10000*. (Excludes prefixes ZAI, ZAO and ZAM). A total of 683,000 star notes printed which offers a ratio of 1 star note to every 438 normal notes.

ONE DOLLAR

LEGEND SHORTENED TO 'AUSTRALIA'

ELIZABETH II. PAPER ISSUE : 1974 TO 1982

Reference # McD	Rks	Description	Fine	VF	EF	aUnc	Unc
		PHILLIPS / WHEELER - 1974					
105	75	General prefixes	4	12	20	45	85
105a	75F	BLG First prefix	65	130	280	460	800
105b	75L	BYB Last prefix	50	95	180	300	600
		KNIGHT / WHEELER - 1976					
		• Centre Thread					
106	76a	General prefixes	4	9	17	25	50
106a	76aF	BYC First prefix	30	60	120	180	350
106b	76aL	CKE Last prefix	50	100	200	300	450
		TEST NOTE. DBP prefix					
		• Centre Thread					
107a	76bF	DBP 000001 - 500000	20	40	80	130	225
107b	76bL	DBP 500001 - 999999	20	40	80	130	225
		• Side Thread					
108	76c	General prefixes	4	7	12	19	30
108a	76cF	CGB First prefix ••	50	100	200	300	450
108b	76cL	CPJ Last prefix	30	50	100	145	235
		KNIGHT / STONE - 1979					
109	77	General prefixes	2	3	6	10	17
109a	77F	CPK First prefix	20	40	80	110	200
109b	77L	DGH Last prefix	25	40	80	110	200
		JOHNSTON / STONE - 1982					
110	78	General prefixes	1	2	3	4	7
110a	78F	DGJ First prefix	18	28	60	80	150
110b	78L	DPS Last prefix	4	9	15	35	65

DBP TEST NOTES

By 1976 $1 notes wore out in less than seven months which required Note Issue to produce over 100 million pieces a year. To cut costs it was decided to experiment with a more durable stock called "Double Fold" paper. 500,000 notes were produced using this heavy duty - but more expensive paper - while another 500,000 were printed from the "Single Fold" paper already in service. The idea was to issue a mixture of the two types from selected centres and compare their wear qualities. Although some of the notes were released in Hobart, the majority were sent in roughly equal amounts to banks in Perth and Brisbane - hence the easily identifiable prefix DBP. Notes numbered DBP 000001 to DBP 500000 were printed on the heavier "Double Fold" paper. Those numbered DBP 500001 to DBP 999999 were printed on "Single Fold" stock. When compared at the end of their useful life it was found the "Double Fold" paper was only marginally better and didn't warrant the extra expense.

TWO DOLLARS

'COMMONWEALTH OF AUSTRALIA' HEADING

ELIZABETH II. PAPER ISSUE : 1966 TO 1974

Reference # McD	Rks	Description	Fine	VF	EF	aUnc	Unc
		COOMBS / WILSON - 1966					
121	81	General prefixes	12	19	30	50	90
121a	81F	FAA First prefix	300	675	1,400	2,000	2,750
121b	81L	FKD Last prefix	250	500	1,000	1,500	2,200
121s	81s	STAR General prefix	325	750	1,500	2,200	3,250
121sa	81sF	*Star* ZFA First prefix	400	900	1,750	2,500	3,750
121sb	81sL	*Star* ZFH Last prefix	550	1,250	2,000	2,600	3,950
		COOMBS / RANDALL - 1967					
122	82	General prefixes	40	60	110	165	225
122a	82F	FKD First prefix	65	125	220	320	550
122b	82L	FPS Last prefix	60	120	200	300	525
122s	82s	STAR General prefix	750	1,450	3,000	4,000	6,000
122sa	82sF	*Star* ZFH First prefix	950	1,950	3,750	5,500	6,500
122sb	82sL	*Star* ZFK Last prefix	1,000	1,950	3,750	5,500	6,500
		PHILLIPS / RANDALL - 1968					
123	83	General prefixes	12	19	30	50	95
123a	83F	FPT First prefix	45	80	175	225	450
123b	83L	GRF Last prefix	55	95	175	225	450
123s	83s	STAR General prefix	325	700	1,600	2,250	3,500
123sa	83sF	*Star* ZFK First prefix	450	1,000	1,800	2,500	4,500
123sb	83sL	*Star* ZFS Last prefix	475	1,075	1,850	2,500	4,500
		PHILLIPS / WHEELER - 1972					
124	84	General prefixes	12	19	30	50	90
124a	84F	GRG First prefix	55	95	175	225	375
124b	84L	HBQ Last prefix	60	120	225	350	500

Coombs / Wilson (Mc121s) : Serial number sequence ZFA 00000* to ZFH 18999*. (Excludes notes issued between ZFH 15600* - 16000*; 16600* - 17000*; 17400* to 18000*). A total of 718,299 star notes were printed which offers a ratio of 1 star note to every 268 normal notes.
Coombs / Randall (Mc122s) : Serial number sequence ZFH 19001* to ZFK 89000*. (Excluding ZFI). A total of approximately 270,000 star notes printed which offers a ratio of 1 star note to every 281 normal notes.
Phillips / Randall (Mc123s) : Serial number sequence ZFK 89001* to ZFS 96107*. (Excluding ZFM, ZFO). A total of 607,107 star notes printed which offers a ratio of 1 star note to every 779 normal notes.
HBQ Last Prefix : Lot 1647 of Downies Sale 301 states that "of the one million notes produced with the HBQ prefix, just over half were of the 'CofA' variety, the remainder being 'Australia.'"

See their advertisement on pages 13

TWO DOLLARS

LEGEND SHORTENED TO 'AUSTRALIA'

ELIZABETH II. PAPER ISSUE : 1974 TO 1985

Reference # McD	Rks	Description	Fine	VF	EF	aUnc	Unc
		PHILLIPS / WHEELER - 1974					
125	85	General prefixes	12	19	30	50	90
125a	85F	HBQ First prefix	60	120	225	350	500
125b	85L	HLP Last prefix	60	95	200	325	475
		KNIGHT / WHEELER - 1976					
		• Centre Thread					
126	86a	General prefixes • Gothic serials	25	40	80	120	200
126a	86aF	HLQ First prefix	40	80	175	220	375
126b	86aL	HQV Last prefix ••	100	200	450	750	1,300
		• Centre thread					
127	86b	General prefixes • OCR-B serials	15	25	50	75	140
127a	86bF	HPU First prefix ••	65	100	200	275	425
127b	86bL	HUC Last prefix ••	75	100	150	250	450
		• Side thread					
128	86c	General prefixes • OCR-B serials	10	20	30	45	60
128a	86cF	HRZ First prefix ••	85	110	165	275	500
128b	86cL	JEY Last prefix ••	250	450	950	1,350	2,400
		KNIGHT / STONE - 1979					
129	87	General prefixes	3	6	10	18	28
129a	87F	JDX First prefix	35	40	80	120	200
129b	87L	KAJ Last prefix	50	100	200	275	425
		JOHNSTON / STONE - 1983					
130	88	General prefixes	3	6	10	18	25
130a	88F	JZH First prefix	30	40	80	120	175
130b	88L	KRP Last prefix	25	35	70	120	175
		JOHNSTON / FRASER - 1985					
131	89	General prefixes	2	3	4	6	9
131a	89F	KRQ First prefix	25	40	80	110	200
131b	89L	LQG Last prefix	4	15	25	40	80

•• Knight / Wheeler first and last Prefixes have yet to be confirmed

SERIAL NUMBER LETTERING

Two distinct serial number fonts were used in the printing process during the production of the now obsolete "paper" notes. The type of font can have a dramatic effect on the value of a note. The original "Gothic" style is shown (top) while the wider "OCR-B" style (Below) was introduced later for the $2, $5, $10, $20 and $50 issues. Both styles appear on some notes bearing the same signature and one style is usually rarer than the other. The OCR-B style, also known as ECMA-11, was also used exclusively on the paper $100.

SBU 227261

AAA 909142

FIVE DOLLARS

'COMMONWEALTH OF AUSTRALIA' HEADING

ELIZABETH II. PAPER ISSUE : 1967 TO 1974

Reference # McD.	Rks	Description	Fine	VF	EF	aUnc	Unc
		COOMBS / RANDALL - 1967 Legend reads "Commonwealth of Australia"					
141	202	General prefixes	45	80	155	245	325
141a	202F	NAA First prefix	200	345	625	950	1,550
141b	202L	NCS Last prefix	100	350	550	750	1,000
141s	202s	STAR General prefixes	950	1,750	3,300	5,000	7,500
141sa	202sF	*Star* ZNA First prefix	1,150	2,000	3,500	5,500	8,500
141sb	202sL	*Star* ZNC Last prefix	1,800	3,000	5,000	7,000	9,000
		PHILLIPS / RANDALL - 1969					
142	203	General prefixes	40	70	140	240	280
142a	203F	NCS First prefix	100	375	650	950	1,250
142b	203L	NGS Last prefix	70	300	450	625	850
142s	203s	STAR No general prefix	—	—	—	—	—
142sa	203sF	*Star* ZNC First prefix	1,250	1,750	3,250	8,500	16,500
142sb	203sL	*Star* ZND Last prefix	1,750	2,500	4,000	9,500	17,500
		PHILLIPS / WHEELER - 1972					
143	204	General prefixes	40	70	135	190	275
143a	204F	NGT First prefix	70	180	350	500	675
143b	204L	NKG Last prefix	100	250	450	600	800

STAR NOTE DETAILS

Coombs / Randall (McD141s) : Serial number sequence ZNA 00001* to ZNC 04000*. A total of 204,000 star notes printed which offers a ratio of 1 star note to every 831 normal notes.

Phillips / Randall (McD142s) : Serial number sequence ZNC 04001* to ZND 05619*. A total of 101,619 star notes printed which offers a ratio of 1 star note to every 283 normal notes.

"PAPER ISSUE" POSITION OF THE METALLIC THREAD

The difference between the "Centre" and "Side" threads. When the first decimal notes were issued the metallic thread was situated in the middle of the note. This resulted in the notes fraying in the central area from the constant folding. During the Knight / Wheeler signature combination (1976) the thread was moved to the left of centre. Both the "Centre" and "Side" thread variations are of interest to collectors and the position of the thread can often affect value dramatically.

FIVE DOLLARS

LEGEND SHORTENED TO 'AUSTRALIA'

ELIZABETH II. PAPER ISSUE : 1974 TO 1992

Reference # McD	Rks	Description	Fine	VF	EF	aUnc	Unc
		PHILLIPS / WHEELER - 1974					
144	205	General prefixes	38	70	135	175	250
144a	205F	NKG First prefix	90	250	400	550	750
144b	205L	NQT Last prefix	100	200	375	500	750
		KNIGHT / WHEELER - 1976					
		Centre Thread					
145	206a	General prefixes • Gothic serials	10	15	25	45	90
145a	206aF	NQU First prefix	40	120	180	250	330
145b	206aL	NVC Last prefix	50	175	275	375	525
		• Side Thread					
146	206b	General prefixes • Gothic serials	8	12	19	40	80
146a	206bF	NSZ First prefix	60	150	250	350	475
146b	206bL	NVC Last prefix	40	130	260	350	600
		•Side Thread					
147	206c	General prefixes • OCR-B seria	5	9	15	45	75
147a	206cF	NVD First prefix ••	40	110	220	300	525
147b	206cL	NYG Last prefix	110	250	450	550	875
		KNIGHT / STONE - 1979					
148	207	General prefixes	7	12	20	35	50
148a	207F	NXF First prefix	50	100	150	200	275
148b	207L	PDT Last prefix	45	100	150	200	275
		JOHNSTON / STONE - 1983					
149	208	General prefixes	7	12	20	35	50
149a	208F	PDU First prefix	35	100	150	200	275
149b	208L	PLG Last prefix	100	300	480	640	875
		JOHNSTON / FRASER - 1985					
150	209a	General prefixes • OCR-B serials	7	12	18	25	45
150a	209aF	PKF First prefix	35	90	130	180	250
150b	209aL	QFA Last prefix	28	100	150	200	270
151	209b	General prefixes • Gothic serials	5	9	15	45	65
151a	209bF	PXB First prefix	120	250	400	700	1,100
151b	209bL	QBJ Last prefix	35	100	150	200	275
		FRASER / HIGGINS - 1990					
152	212	General prefixes	7	12	17	25	40
152a	212F	QDF First prefix	30	100	150	200	275
152b	212L	QJR Last prefix	25	90	160	225	300
		FRASER / COLE - 1991					
153	213	General prefixes	6	9	12	18	25
153a	213F	QGX First prefix	35	100	150	200	275
153b	213L	QPG Last prefix	15	25	45	65	85

•• Knight / Wheeler first and last prefixes have yet to be confirmed

FIVE DOLLARS

FIRST POLYMER : LIGHTER COLOUR

ELIZABETH II : 1992 TO 1995

Reference # McD	Rks	Description	Fine	VF	EF	aUnc	Unc
		FRASER/ COLE - 1992					
		Medium to Dark Green serial numbers					
		Circulation issue. Without overprinted date					
301a	214	General prefixes Medium to Dark Green	6	9	16	25	45
301a/1	214F	AA00 First signature prefix Dark Green serial numbers	30	60	115	175	250
301a/2	214L	AB19 Last signature prefix Dark Green serial numbers	180	350	700	1,450	2,450
301b	214i	General prefixes Pale Green serial numbers	9	18	30	55	120
301b/1	214i	FAA00 First signature prefix [Pale Green serials]	80	150	275	400	775
301b/2	214i	LAB19 Last signature prefix [Pale Green serials]	180	350	700	1,550	2,250
		FRASER / EVANS - 1993					
		Medium to Dark Green serial numbers					
		Circulation issue, without overprinted date					
302a	216	1993 General Prefixes.	10	20	50	75	140
302a/1	216F	BA93 First signature prefix	9	18	30	55	110
302a/2	216L	EA93 Last 1993 dated prefix	9	18	30	55	110
		Pale Green serial numbers					
		Circulation issue, without overprinted date					
302b	216i	1993 General Prefixes	18	35	70	145	300
02b/1	216iF	BA93 First signature prefix	20	40	85	165	325
302b/2	216iL	EA93 Last 1993 dated prefix	20	40	85	165	350

Mc 301a/2. Judy also advises that the AB19 prefix was a specific last prefix as it was the end of consecutive numerical prefixes before the *Year Dated* notes were introduced in 1993. The only other polymer example was the Johnston / Fraser Bicentenary ten dollar note.
Mc 301b. Some numbers show a light green shading while others have a dark green (almost) black appearance. Discovered by dealer, Judy Shaw, the variation has even turned up in the same bundle of notes spread through a wide range of prefixes.
Mc 302a. This issue bucks the system with the general issue banknotes being rarer than either the first or last prefixes. This was the first issue to have a prefix combination that indicated the actual year of issue. This historic innovation was well publicised as was the final EA93 issue. Most collectors concentrated on the first and last prefixes as they had the reputation as being more valuable. This meant that *general* prefix notes were largely overlooked and were rarely put aside by collectors. The second important factor concerned the discovery of the Medium/Dark prefix colour variation which, in the main, were pale green. This variation was not discovered until some ten years after the issue was superseded. By then it was impossible to procure the variation at, or about, face value through the Reserve Bank, local banks or other sources. (See above footnote, Mc301b).

FIVE DOLLARS

SECOND POLYMER. RECOLOURED

ELIZABETH II : 1995 TO 2016

Reference # McD	Rks	Description	Fine	VF	EF	aUnc	Unc
		FRASER / EVANS - 1995					
		Recoloured Circulation issue. Without overprinted date					
		Wide orientation bands					
303a	217a	1995 General wide band	6	12	22	30	50
303a/1	217aF	AA95 First wide band prefix signature prefix	6	15	30	45	85
303a/2	217aL	KC95 Last wide band prefix	500	800	1,350	2,200	2,850
		Narrow orientation bands					
303b	217ai	1995 General narrow band prefix	6	15	30	50	90
303b/1	217aiF	HC95 First narrow band prefix	200	400	700	1,000	1,600
303b/2	217aiL	KC95 Last narrow band prefix	380	680	1,100	1,750	2,750
303c	217b	1996 General dated prefix	5	8	15	25	55
303c/1	217bF	BA96 First 1996 dated prefix	9	15	30	45	140
303c/2	217bL	EA96 Last signature prefix	8	12	20	40	120

BAND WIDTH : 1995 KC 95 PREFIX FRASER / EVANS

(Above) : WIDE [Normal] orientation bands. Has *four* diagonal white bands.

(Above) : NARROW orientation bands. Has *eight* diagonal white bands.

On April 24, 1995 the Reserve Bank introduced a more brightly coloured $5.00 polymer note to make it easier to distinguish it from the Ten Dollars note. At the same time the numeral "5" was made bolder and orientation bands were added on the top and bottom to assist in the sorting of large amounts.

McD 303a/1 : The first prefix number for the recoloured 1995 circulation issue began with AA. All subsequent circulation issues commenced with BA as its first prefix number. Subsequent AA prefixes (AA96) was confined to NCLT folder issues.

McD 303b: When the orientation bands were included in the redesigned note there were about seven wide lines included. A variety occurred (called the Thin or narrow bands) when artwork was used from an earlier proof of the note to make printing plates after a number of the existing printing plates were damaged. The Reserve Bank has advised that about 13,000,000 $5 notes out of a total of 95,000,000 $5 banknotes produced in 1995 exhibit the variation. The variety only occurs in the prefix HC95 to KC95. See illustrations above.

McD 303 & Mc 304 : 1996 dated notes exist with both the Fraser / Evans and Macfarlane / Evans signatures. Polymer banknote specialist, Trevor Wilkin reports that only about 115,000 Macfarlane / Evans notes for each signatures were printed.

McD 303b/1, 303b/2, 304a/2 & 304b/2. COMMENT REGARDING SCARCE PREFIXES (previously stated as unsighted notes). Prices for lower grades have been calculated by averaging documented sales. At the time of printing this catalogue, some of these banknotes have no recorded sales in higher grades. The prices listed here are estimations.

FIVE DOLLARS

SECOND POLYMER. RECOLOURED

ELIZABETH II : 1995 TO 2016

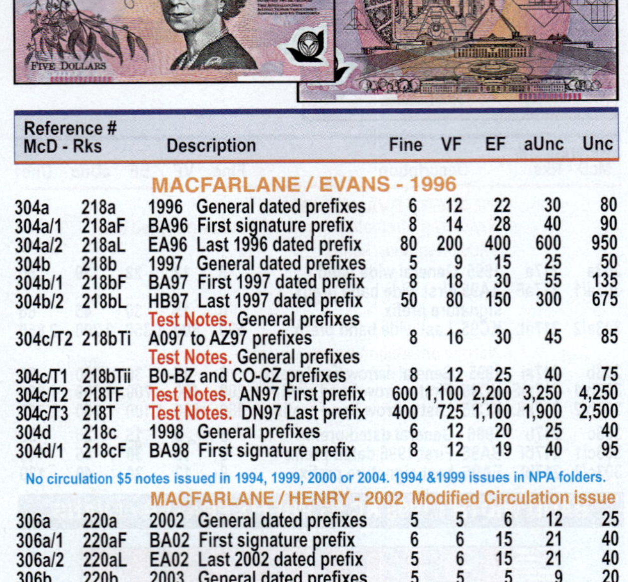

Reference # McD	Rks	Description	Fine	VF	EF	aUnc	Unc
		MACFARLANE / EVANS - 1996					
304a	218a	1996 General dated prefixes	6	12	22	30	80
304a/1	218aF	BA96 First signature prefix	8	14	28	40	90
304a/2	218aL	EA96 Last 1996 dated prefix	80	200	400	600	950
304b	218b	1997 General dated prefixes	5	9	15	25	50
304b/1	218bF	BA97 First 1997 dated prefix	8	18	30	55	135
304b/2	218bL	HB97 Last 1997 dated prefix	50	80	150	300	675
304c/T2	218bTi	Test Notes. General prefixes A097 to AZ97 prefixes	8	16	30	45	85
304c/T1	218bTii	Test Notes. General prefixes B0-BZ and CO-CZ prefixes	8	12	25	40	75
304c/T2	218TF	Test Notes. AN97 First prefix	600	1,100	2,200	3,250	4,250
304c/T3	218T	Test Notes. DN97 Last prefix	400	725	1,100	1,900	2,500
304d	218c	1998 General prefixes	6	12	20	25	40
304d/1	218cF	BA98 First signature prefix	8	12	19	40	95
		No circulation $5 notes issued in 1994, 1999, 2000 or 2004. 1994 &1999 issues in NPA folders.					
		MACFARLANE / HENRY - 2002 Modified Circulation issue					
306a	220a	2002 General dated prefixes	5	5	6	12	25
306a/1	220aF	BA02 First signature prefix	6	6	15	21	40
306a/2	220aL	EA02 Last 2002 dated prefix	5	6	15	21	40
306b	220b	2003 General dated prefixes	5	5	5	9	20
306b/1	220bF	BA03 First 2003 dated prefix	5	6	12	17	30
306b/2	220bL	EA03 Last 2003 dated prefix	5	5	9	18	35
306c	220c	2005 General dated prefixes	5	5	5	6	15
306c/1	220cF	BA05 First 2005 dated prefix	5	5	6	12	22
306c/2	220cL	KC05 Last 2005 dated prefix	5	5	8	30	50
306d	220d	2006 General dated prefixes	5	5	5	6	18
306d/1	220dF	BA06 First 2006 dated prefix	5	5	5	10	25
306d/2	220dL	HB06 Last signature prefix	5	5	5	10	25
		STEVENS / HENRY - First issued 2007					
307a	221a	2007 General dated prefixes	5	5	5	7	12
307a/1	221aF	BA07 First signature prefix	5	5	5	9	25
307a/2	221aL	HB07 Last 2007 dated prefix	5	5	5	9	25
307b	221b	2008 General dated prefixes	5	5	5	6	10
307b/1	221bF	BA08 First 2008 dated prefix	5	5	10	17	45
307b/2	221bL	HB08 Last signature prefix	5	5	8	30	55
		STEVENS / PARKINSON - First issued 2012					
308a	222a	2012 General dated prefixes	5	5	5	5	12
308a/1	222aF	BA12 First signature prefix	5	5	5	5	20
308a/2	222aL	EA12 Last 2012 dated prefix	5	5	5	9	20
308b	222b	2013 General dated prefixes	5	5	5	5	10
308b/1	222bF	BA13 First signature prefix	5	5	5	5	10
308b/2	222bL	EA13 Last 2013 dated prefix	5	5	5	5	10
308c	223c	2014 General dated prefixes	5	5	5	5	9
308c/1	223cF	BA14 First signature prefix	5	5	5	5	10
308c/2	223cL	EA14 Last 2014 dated prefix	5	5	5	5	10
308d	224d	2015 General dated prefixes	5	5	5	5	9
308d/1	224dF	BA15 First signature prefix	5	5	5	5	10
308d/2	224dL	EA15 Last signature prefix	15	25	60	135	250

2001 FIVE DOLLARS

FEDERATION ISSUE

MACFARLANE / EVANS. ONE YEAR TYPE

Reference # McD	Rks		Description	Fine	VF	EF	aUnc	Unc
			MACFARLANE / EVANS - 2001 • Circulation issue. No overprint date					
305a	219TN	2001	Special tender issue					
		AA01	000009 to AA01 000500	50	100	200	450	825
305b	219	2001	General dated prefixes	5	5	8	18	27
305b/1	219F	AA01	First Type prefix 000501 +	6	10	16	25	45
305b/2	219L	JD01	Last Type/Signature prefix	6	10	16	25	45

While Note Printing Australia (NPA) has conducted "highest bid Sale by Tender" offers to collectors before, this was the first time normal circulation notes without overprints or other special treatments were singled out for sale. In a circular sent out in March 2001, NPA invited collectors to bid for Uncirculated banknotes that had a serial number range from AA 01 000009 to 000500. The brochure indicated that the first eight numbers were retained for the Reserve Bank archives. The tender closed on Monday, May 21. The September 2001 issue of Noteworthy indicated that the highest tender was $1,275 with the lowest being $26. All notes sold.

POLYMER "TEST" BANKNOTES

FIVE & ONE HUNDRED DOLLAR ISSUES

In early 2002 banknote collector and author Scott de Young noticed that a 1997 dated Macfarlane/Evans $5 note was outside the published prefix sequences. The note in question had the prefix "AP97". The previously accepted range for this issue was BA97 to HB97 with "M" as the highest letter used as the second letter of the prefix. Independently, polymer banknote specialists Judy Shaw and Trevor Wilkin contacted the Reserve Bank and received a startling reply. The Bank confirmed the issue of a special printing *"to test a minor modification to one of the materials used in the opacifying inks."* In the case of the $5 polymer issue some 300,000 notes were produced with the prefixes running from AN97 to DN97. This would mean that there are only around 7500 of each prefix printed. *(See table below).* The inclusion of an "A" prefix letter is also interesting as it was not previously used for the 1996, 1997 or 1998 $5 re-coloured issues. The test was successful and rather than waste the special print-run it was decided to put the notes into general circulation. No special announcement to the public or the numismatic fraternity was forthcoming. Further correspondence with the Reserve Bank also confirmed that a similar "test issue" was produced in 1996 with the Fraser/Evans $100 notes. This special issue carried the prefix AN96 to CS96. *(See table at bottom).* The normal range of prefixes was from AA96 to JK96. Both the $5 and $100 Test notes have the letters "N" to "Z" as the second prefix. These had not previously appeared in the polymer series.

SHEET LAYOUT : $5 TEST NOTE ISSUE
1997 MACFARLANE / EVANS

AN97	AV97	BQ97	BY97	CT97
AO97	AW97	BR97	BZ97	CU97
AP97	AX97	BS97	CN97	CV97
AQ97	AY97	BT97	CO97	CW97
AR97	AZ97	BU97	CP97	CX97
AS97	BN97	BV97	CQ97	CY97
AT97	BO97	BW97	CR97	CZ97
AU97	BP97	BX97	CS97	DN97

SHEET LAYOUT : $100 TEST NOTE ISSUE
1996 FRASER / EVANS

AN96	AV96	BQ96	BY96
AO96	AW96	BR96	BZ96
AP96	AX96	BS96	CN96
AQ96	AY96	BT96	CO96
AR96	AZ96	BU96	CP96
AS96	BN96	BV96	CQ96
AT96	BO96	BW96	CR96
AU96	BP96	BX96	

2016 FIVE DOLLARS

NEXT GENERATION WATTLE SERIES

ELIZABETH II : 2016 TO PRESENT

Reference # McD	Rks	Description	Fine	VF	EF	aUnc	Unc
		STEVENS / FRASER - 2016					
		• Circulation issue. No date overprint					
		2016 Special tender issue					
315a	R224	AA16 000009 to AA01 000500	55	95	150	195	300
315b	R224	2016 General dated prefixes	5	5	8	18	8
315b/1	R224F	AA16 First Type prefix 000501 +	6	10	16	25	45
315b/2	R224L	EJ16 Last Type/ Signature prefix	6	10	16	25	45

For more general information about this new issue, turn to the NPA special First & Last section towards the end of this book.

TEN DOLLARS

'COMMONWEALTH OF AUSTRALIA' HEADING

ELIZABETH II. PAPER ISSUE : 1966 TO 1974

Reference # McD	Rks	Description	Fine	VF	EF	aUnc	Unc
		COOMBS / WILSON - 1966					
161	301	General prefixes	15	22	35	50	110
161a	301F	SAA First prefix	95	190	380	650	1,050
161b	301L	SDR Last prefix	165	500	800	1,350	2,000
161s	301s	STAR General prefixes	350	750	1,750	2,750	3,950
161sa	301sF	*Star* ZSA First prefix	400	900	2,600	4,500	5,500
161sb	301sL	*Star* ZSD Last prefix	550	1,100	2,750	5,000	6,000
		COOMBS / RANDALL - 1967					
162	302	General prefixes	100	200	400	700	950
162a	302F	SDR First prefix	130	400	800	1,150	1,700
162b	302L	SFR Last prefix	140	450	850	1,200	1,800
162s	302s	STAR No general prefixes	–	–	–	–	–
162sa	302sF	*Star* ZSD First prefix	850	1,950	5,000	8,000	12,500
162sb	302sL	*Star* ZSE Last prefix	850	1,950	5,000	8,000	12,500
		PHILLIPS / RANDALL - 1968					
163	303	General prefixes	20	40	70	120	180
163a	303F	SFR First prefix	50	230	350	500	675
163b	303L	STG Last prefix	45	160	300	400	550
163s	303s	STAR General prefixes	525	1,100	2,250	4,250	6,500
163sa	303sF	*Star* ZSF First prefix	600	1,500	2,750	4,750	7,250
163sb	303sL	*Star* ZSJ Last prefix	675	1,750	2,950	5,000	7,750
		PHILLIPS / WHEELER - 1972					
164	304	General prefixes	15	22	35	50	110
164a	304F	STH First prefix	40	130	200	270	385
164b	304L	TBB Last prefix	40	130	200	270	385

STAR NOTE DETAILS

Coombs / Wilson (McD161s) : Serial number sequence ZSA 00001* to ZSD 36000*. Approximately 333,000 star notes were printed which offers a ratio of 1 star note to every 232 normal notes. Final numbers uncertain as Coombs/Randall notes have been observed with numbers ZSD 33131* and 33132*.
Coombs / Randall (McD162s) : Serial number sequence ZSD 36001* to ZSE 10000*. (See above footnote). A total of approximately 167,000 star notes printed which offers a ratio of 1 star note to every 288 normal notes.
Phillips / Randall (McD163s) : Serial number sequence ZSF 00001* to ZSJ 48004*. A total of 348,004 star notes printed which offers a ratio of 1 star note to every 643 normal notes.

MISPRINTS AND ERROR NOTES

Banknote errors and misprints have not been featured in this guide. It is difficult to "catalogue" such errors as some may be regarded as unique, and so a pricing structure is impractical. It is generally felt that a local coin and banknote dealer will be able to give a more accurate value on the item after viewing it. You can also check recent auction results.

TEN DOLLARS

LEGEND SHORTENED TO 'AUSTRALIA'

ELIZABETH II. PAPER ISSUE : 1974 TO 1992

Reference # McD	Rks	Description	Fine	VF	EF	aUnc	Unc
		PHILLIPS / WHEELER - 1974					
165	305	General prefixes	30	60	90	175	275
165a	305F	TBC First prefix	70	135	260	375	575
165b	305L	TEL Last prefix	70	135	260	375	575
		KNIGHT / WHEELER - 1976. Gothic centre thread					
166	306a	General prefixes	35	60	120	170	250
166a	306aF	TEN First prefix	70	120	230	330	550
166b	306aL	TJV Last prefix	75	145	450	600	850
		• Gothic Side thread					
167	306b	General prefixes	15	22	35	50	100
167a	306bF	THU First prefix	45	85	165	225	400
167b	306bL	TPC Last prefix	40	75	170	250	400
		KNIGHT / STONE - 1979					
168	307a	General prefixes • Gothic serials	20	35	65	95	140
168a	307aF	TPD First prefix	40	85	180	220	375
168b	307aL	TTL Last prefix	40	85	180	220	375
169	307b	General prefixes • OCR-B serials	18	30	40	60	125
169a	307bF	TTN First prefix	40	85	180	220	375
169b	307bL	TXT Last prefix	40	85	180	220	375
		JOHNSTON / STONE - 1983					
170	308	General prefixes	15	22	35	50	100
170a	308F	TXU First prefix	35	75	150	200	325
170b	308L	UCC Last prefix	45	75	150	200	325
		JOHNSTON / FRASER - 1985					
171	309	General prefixes	12	18	25	35	50
171a	309F	UCD First prefix	45	60	90	150	310
171b	309L	MAC Last prefix	50	65	140	175	350
		FRASER / HIGGINS - 1990					
175	312	General prefixes	12	18	25	35	70
175a	312F	UYH First prefix	50	60	90	175	285
175b	312L	MHJ Last prefix	45	60	120	190	340
		FRASER / COLE - 1991. With Plate Letter					
176	313a	General prefixes	15	20	28	35	55
176a	313aF	MFQ First prefix	25	50	70	100	275
176b	313aL	MRR Last prefix	30	60	80	125	250
		• Without Plate Letter					
177	313b	General prefixes	16	22	30	40	65
177a	313bF	MNB First prefix. No plate letter	35	65	100	150	250
177b	313bL	MRR Last prefix	18	30	40	55	100

Please turn to the next page for information regarding the Plate Letter.

1988 TEN DOLLARS

BICENTENNARY ISSUE

JOHNSTON / EVANS. AUSTRALIA'S FIRST POLYMER

Reference # McD	Rks	Description	Fine	VF	EF	aUnc	Unc
		JOHNSTON / FRASER - ONE YEAR TYPE					
		Overprinted 26th January 1988. In blue Reserve Bank folder					
Mc$10GF 1		Prefixes AA00 - AA23	See collector folder section				
		First release. Withdrawn.					
173a	310a	1988 General prefixes	15	22	35	50	80
173a/1	310aF	AB10 First prefix. *(First release)*	110	225	430	675	1,000
173a/2	310aL	AB33 Last prefix. *(First release)*	250	550	875	1,250	2,200
		Second release. Issued late 1988					
		Circulation issue, without date.					
174b	310b	1988 General prefixes	15	18	25	35	60
174b/1	310bF	AB10 First prefix. *(Reissued)*	60	125	230	360	650
174b/2	310bL	AB57 Last prefix. *(Reissued)*	250	550	875	1,250	2,250

[McD173] : First release. Features a thin, smooth varnish over OVD. Prefix range from AB10 to AB33. Six digit serial number must commence with first two digits reading 93, 94 or 96 ie; AB12 **93**4568.
[McD174] : Second release. Features a thick, mottled varnish over OVD. Prefix numbers used for the first printing also used in the second issue.

THIS INFORMATION RELATES TO THE PAPER ISSUES ON THE PREVIOUS PAGE

PLATE IDENTIFICATION LETTERS (PIL) are very small letters found on each banknote of nearly all paper decimal notes issued. Although initially thought to be a security device, it seems that some markings were included to assist with quality control. The plate letters were on the intaglio printing plates. It is interesting to note that the prefix letters of a banknote run alphabetically and consecutively down (top to bottom) of a sheet. In contrast the plate letters run alphabetically and consecutively across the sheet (left to right).

PLATE IDENTIFICATION LETTERS were to be phased out by 1990 and prior to the introduction of polymer notes. Despite this, an interesting feature occurred during the latter part of the printing of the 1993 Fraser / Cole paper Ten Dollar note. Throughout bundles of the last print run there was a plate letter on every third note. To understand how this sequence works, it is necessary to have some knowledge of the production process. The machine used to print the notes had three intaglio plates on a circular drum and this printed three sheets for each revolution. If the plate prints 40 notes, as was the case with the ten dollar notes, then the machine would print 120 notes per revolution. In the case of the Fraser / Cole ten dollar issue, this is an important aspect as three consecutive notes reveal the full story. It would appear that during production, one of the three (post 1990) printing plates (with no plate identification) was damaged. It was replaced with a printing plate that was manufactured prior to 1990 and had the plate identification letter on it. This resulted in the final print run of the Fraser Cole ten dollar notes featuring a plate letter on every third note.

HOW TO LOCATE THE PLATE IDENTIFICATION LETTER. Hold a rule vertically from the "W" of B.W. Fraser (signature) and follow it up approximately 25 mm. If there is a plate letter it will be sighted on the outside of the left corner of a square in the intaglio design. As far as can be determined, all letters of the alphabet were used, except "I" and "W". When plate letters were used for the second time, a vertical line was printed before the letter but only two thirds of the letter height.

Thanks to Judy Shaw for suppling the above information.

TEN DOLLARS

ELIZABETH II. POLYMER ISSUE : 1993 TO PRESENT

[a] Blue Dobell

[b] Grey Dobell

Reference # McD	Rks		Description	Fine	VF	EF	aUnc	Unc
			FRASER / EVANS - 1993					
			Blue shading of Dobell Portrait					
			1993 Circulation issue. No date overprint					
401a	316a	1993	General prefixes	10	10	20	35	65
401a/1	316aF	AA93	First signature prefix	15	22	35	50	125
401a/2	316aL	KE93	Last 1993 prefix	60	120	250	550	1,100
			Grey shading of Dobell Portrait					
			1993 Circulation issue. No date overprint					
401b	316ia	1993	General prefixes	—	—	—		Not sighted
401b/1	316aiF	AA93	First signature	—	—	—		Not sighted
401b/2	316aiL	KE93	Last 1993 prefix	—	—	—		Not sighted
			Blue shading of Dobell Portrait					
			1994 Circulation issue. No date overprint					
401c	316b	1994	General prefixes	35	65	100	175	300
401c/1	316bF	AA94	First signature	40	85	160	300	1,000
401c/2	316bL	DF94	Last 1994 prefix	120	250	500	700	1,000
			Grey shading of Dobell Portrait					
			1994 Circulation issue. No date overprint					
401d	316bi	1994	General prefixes	30	60	90	150	280
401d/1	316biF	AA94	First signature	35	75	150	275	600
401d/2	316biL	DF94	Last signature prefix	120	250	500	675	1.200

No circulation $10 notes were issued in 1995 and 1996 (Fraser/Evans signature) 1999, 2000, 2001 and 2004. The 1995, 1996 and 1999 are available in collector folders

The above issues from 1993 and 1994 feature colour variations in the central part of the reverse of the note. This is particularly noticeable around the portrait of Dame Mary Gilmour as a young woman and the later controversial painting by Dobell. The colour variation ranges from a dark blue to a steel grey with subtle tones in between. Initially a dark blue ink was used that tended to smudge and cause a "wet ink transfer." *[See inset a]* This resulted in a mirror image of the number "10" appearing on the back of the note underneath the top left serial number and parts of the words "TEN DOLLARS" appearing below the serial number at bottom right. To rectify this situation, NPA experimented with various shades of blue to eliminate the problem. The very light blue shade finally adopted over the entire note led to the Dobell portrait of Dame Mary as an old lady appear to be steel grey. *[See inset b]*. This colour has been maintained to the present day. Most collectors are keen to obtain all colour variations and as some notes are scarcer than others, prices vary. Polymer expert Judy Shaw said that due to the random nature of adding prefixes on previously printed sheets, could mean that McD401a/2 may not exist.

401a/1, 401a/2, 401b/1 & 401b/2. COMMENT REGARDING SCARCE PREFIXES (previously stated as 'unsighted' notes). Prices for lower grades have been calculated by averaging documented sales. At the time of printing, some of these banknotes have no recorded sales in higher grades. This is not to say they do not exist in high grade but there is insufficient market information at this stage to determine a realistic price.

TEN DOLLARS

ELIZABETH II. POLYMER ISSUE : 1993 TO PRESENT

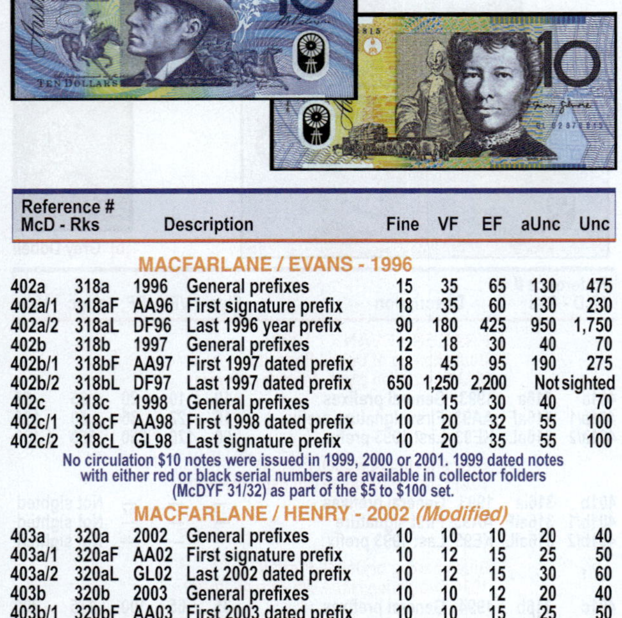

Reference # McD	Rks		Description	Fine	VF	EF	aUnc	Unc
			MACFARLANE / EVANS - 1996					
402a	318a	1996	General prefixes	15	35	65	130	475
402a/1	318aF	AA96	First signature prefix	18	35	60	130	230
402a/2	318aL	DF96	Last 1996 year prefix	90	180	425	950	1,750
402b	318b	1997	General prefixes	12	18	30	40	70
402b/1	318bF	AA97	First 1997 dated prefix	18	45	95	190	275
402b/2	318bL	DF97	Last 1997 dated prefix	650	1,250	2,200	Not sighted	
402c	318c	1998	General prefixes	10	15	30	40	70
402c/1	318cF	AA98	First 1998 dated prefix	10	20	32	55	100
402c/2	318cL	GL98	Last signature prefix	10	20	35	55	100
			No circulation $10 notes were issued in 1999, 2000 or 2001. 1999 dated notes with either red or black serial numbers are available in collector folders (McDYF 31/32) as part of the $5 to $100 set.					
			MACFARLANE / HENRY - 2002 *(Modified)*					
403a	320a	2002	General prefixes	10	10	10	20	40
403a/1	320aF	AA02	First signature prefix	10	12	15	25	50
403a/2	320aL	GL02	Last 2002 dated prefix	10	12	15	30	60
403b	320b	2003	General prefixes	10	10	12	20	40
403b/1	320bF	AA03	First 2003 dated prefix	10	10	15	25	50
403b/2	320bL	DF03	Last 2003 dated prefix	10	10	15	30	60
403c	320c	2006	General prefixes	10	10	10	12	30
403c/1	320cF	AA06	First 2006 dated prefix	10	10	12	20	45
403c/2	320cL	GL06	Last signature prefix	10	10	10	22	55
			STEVENS / HENRY - 2007					
404a	321a	2007	General prefixes	10	10	10	12	25
404a/1	321aF	AA07	First signature prefix	10	10	10	18	40
404a/2	321aL	GL07	Last 2007 dated prefix	10	10	10	18	40
404b	321b	2008	General prefixes	10	10	10	12	20
404b/1	321bF	AA08	First 2008 dated prefix	10	10	15	30	75
404b/2	321bL	DF08	Last signature prefix	10	10	30	55	110
			STEVENS / PARKINSON - 2012					
405a	322a	2012	General prefixes	10	10	10	10	18
405a/1	322aF	AA12	First signature prefix	10	10	10	10	30
405a/2	322aL	DF12	Last 2012 dated prefix	10	10	10	10	30
405b	322b	2013	General prefixes	10	10	10	10	15
405b/1	322bF	AA13	First 2013 dated prefix	10	10	10	10	20
405b/2	322bL	DF13	Last 2013 dated prefix	10	10	10	10	20
			No 2014 dated Ten Dollar banknotes were issued					
407a	322d	2015	General prefixes	10	10	10	10	20
407a/1	322dF	AA15	2015 dated prefix	10	10	10	10	70
407a/2	322dL	DF15	Last 2015 dated prefix	10	10	10	10	80

Mc403. Two design modifications were introduced with the Macfarlane/Henry series introduced in 2002. The first was to change the positioning of the signatories. On previous polymer issues, the Secretary to the Treasury appeared above that of the Governor of the Reserve Bank of Australia. This was reversed with this issue. For the first time the printed names of the portraits, with the exception of QEII, featured on the notes were included as part of the design.

TWENTY DOLLARS

'COMMONWEALTH OF AUSTRALIA' HEADING

ELIZABETH II. PAPER ISSUE : 1966 TO 1974

Reference # McD	Rks	Description	Fine	VF	EF	aUnc	Unc
		COOMBS / WILSON - 1966					
181	401	General prefixes	22	30	45	70	150
181a	401F	XAA First prefix	75	150	300	420	700
181b	401L	XBP Last prefix	80	200	325	400	600
		No star notes issued					
		COOMBS / RANDALL - 1967					
182	402	General prefixes	500	1,400	2,600	4,950	9,000
182a	402F	XBQ First prefix	620	1,500	3,000	5,500	10,000
182b	402L	XBS Last prefix	700	1,750	3,500	6,500	11,000
		No star notes issued					
		PHILLIPS / RANDALL - 1968					
183	403	General prefixes	45	100	200	275	350
183a	403F	XBS First prefix	100	250	400	550	775
183b	403L	XEU Last prefix	90	225	375	500	725
183s	403s	STAR ZXA prefix only	800	2,750	8,250	14,500	19,500
		PHIILLIPS / WHEELER - 1972					
184	404	General prefixes	50	110	225	330	500
184a	404F	XEV First prefix	110	250	400	550	825
184b	404L	XGY Last prefix	120	300	500	600	925

STAR NOTE DETAILS Phillips / Randall (Mc183s) : Serial number sequence ZXA 00001* to ZXA 62500*. A total of 62,500 star notes printed which offers a ratio of one star note to every 1,053 normal notes.

FIRST AND LAST PREFIX RARE ISSUES : Coombs / Randall (Mc182b) Of the one million Coombs / Randall notes issued with the XBS prefix, approximately 200,000 notes bore the Coombs / Randall imprint. *[See Downies Australian Auctions Sale 301. Lot 1683).*

INFORMATION BELOW FOR NEXT PAGE. FIRST & LAST PREFIXES

Phillips / Wheeler (McD185a) : The first prefix for the modified (Australia) issue was XGY. Of the one million notes with the XGY prefix, only approximately 40,000 of the 'Australia' notes were printed, the remainder being the 'Commonwealth of Australia' issue, exceedingly scarce in any condition. *[See Downies Sale 304. Lot 3356].*
Knight / Wheeler (McD186b R406aL). Gothic centre thread. It is now confirmed that the last prefix of centre thread notes is XSU. Approximately 650,000 examples were produced. *[Downie's Sale 301. Lot 1694].*
Johnston / Stone. (McD190a R408aF). First prefix VFV. Of the one million notes issued with this prefix, only approximately 330,000 were printed with the Johnston / Stone signatures. *[Downies Sale 302. Lot 2950].*
Johnston / Fraser. (McD191b R409aL). OCR-B typeface. Last prefix EYD. In the auction description it was recorded that only approximately 333,000 notes were issued with this prefix. *[Downies Sale 302. Lot 2951].*
Johnston / Fraser. (McD192b R409bL). Gothic typeface. The ENB prefix is the final one for this series. It is believed that no more than 137,000 notes carry the Gothic serials. This makes this issue one of the scarcest first or last prefixes paper issues possible in any denomination. *[Downies Sale 301. Lot 1704].*

TWENTY DOLLARS

ELIZABETH II. PAPER ISSUE : 1974 TO 1993

Reference # McD	Rks	Description	Fine	VF	EF	aUnc	Unc
		PHILLIPS / WHEELER - 1974					
185	405	General prefixes	48	100	210	320	500
185a	405F	XGY First prefix	400	750	1,275	1,700	2,350
185b	405L	XLH Last prefix	110	260	400	550	750
		KNIGHT / WHEELER - 1976 • Gothic Centre thread (70mm)					
186	406a	General prefixes	40	80	170	220	395
186a	406aF	XLJ First prefix	110	250	375	475	675
186b	406aL	XSU Last prefix	100	165	375	525	725
		KNIGHT / WHEELER • Gothic side thread (55mm)					
187	406b	General prefixes	55	115	245	380	500
187a	406bF	XQR First prefix	650	1,500	3,000	Not seen	
187b	406bL	XUZ Last prefix	120	300	475	550	800
		KNIGHT / STONE - 1979 • Gothic side thread (55mm)					
188	407a	General prefixes	28	45	80	125	225
188a	407aF	XVA First prefix	60	175	275	375	525
188b	407aL	VDQ Last prefix	70	250	425	550	775
		KNIGHT / STONE • OCR-B side thread					
189	407b	General prefixes	35	80	170	250	350
189a	407bF	VDR First prefix	100	450	850	1,250	1,750
189b	407bL	VGX Last prefix	110	250	400	550	750
		JOHNSTON / STONE • 1983 • OCR-B side thread					
190	408	General prefixes	25	45	80	125	240
190a	408aF	VFV First prefix	100	250	425	575	800
190b	408bL	VQK Last prefix	75	225	400	500	725
		JOHNSTON / FRASER - 1985 • OCR-B serials					
191	409a	General prefixes	18	25	40	65	135
191a	409aF	VQL First prefix	50	100	175	225	350
191b	409aL	EYD Last prefix	85	150	300	425	600
		JOHNSTON / FRASER - 1985 • Gothic serials					
192	409b	General prefixes	85	175	375	525	725
192a	409bF	EJY First prefix	65	250	600	850	1,200
192b	409bL	ENB Last prefix	225	525	950	1,300	1,850
		PHILLIPS / FRASER - 1989					
193	411	General prefixes	28	35	50	80	180
193a	411F	EVJ First prefix	60	150	275	350	550
193b	411L	EYD Last prefix	55	125	250	375	600
		FRASER / HIGGINS - 1990					
194	412	General prefixes	28	30	45	70	150
194a	412F	EYE First prefix	50	150	245	300	450
194b	412L	RKB Last prefix	60	150	275	350	550
		FRASER / COLE - 1991					
195	413	General prefixes	20	35	45	70	120
195a	413i	AAA prefix NPA issue	30	40	68	110	175
195b	413F	RHG First prefix	45	150	250	325	450
195c	413L	ABQ Last prefix	65	125	475	750	975
		FRASER / EVANS - 1993					
196	415	General prefixes	22	30	40	60	110
196a	415i	AAA prefix NPA issue	38	55	80	115	180
196b	415F	RZV First prefix	45	110	200	250	375
196c	415L	ADK Last prefix	28	38	50	65	135

TWENTY DOLLARS

ELIZABETH II. POLYMER ISSUE : 1994 TO PRESENT

Reference # McD	Rks		Description	Fine	VF	EF	aUnc	Unc
FRASER / EVANS - 1994 *Circulation issue. No overprinted date*								
501a	416a	1994	General dated prefixes	20	20	25	50	90
501a/1	416aF	AA94	First signature prefix	25	35	70	195	300
501a/2	416aL	PE94	Last 1994 dated prefix	1,250	2,500	4,000	n/a	n/a
501b	416b	1995	General dated prefixes	30	40	80	195	325
501b/1	416bF	AA95	First 1995 dated prefix	35	50	120	240	400
501b/2	416bL	DA95	Last 1995 dated prefix	525	900	1,850	2,700	4,000
501c	416c	1996	General dated prefixes	30	40	60	110	225
501c/1	416cF	AA96	First 1996 dated prefix	35	50	120	250	425
501c/2	416cL	DA96	Last signature prefix	50	80	195	450	750
MACFARLANE / EVANS - 1997 *Circulation issue. No overprinted date*								
502a	418a	1997	General dated prefixes	20	20	25	65	150
502a/1	418aF	AA97	First signature prefix	20	35	60	95	200
502a/2	418aL	GB97	Last 1997 dated prefix	50	80	175	500	975
502b	418b	1998	General dated prefixes	18	25	40	65	150
502b/1	418bF	AA98	First 1996 dated prefix	20	30	55	90	200
502b/2	418bL	DA98	Last signature prefix	25	60	95	225	475
MACFARLANE / HENRY - 2002 *(modified)*								
503a	420a	2002	General dated prefixes	20	20	30	40	75
503a/1	420aF	AA02	First signature prefix	20	20	30	45	85
503a/2	420aL	KM02	Last 2002 dated prefix	20	20	30	45	85
503b	420b	2003	General prefixes	20	20	25	35	70
503b/1	420bF	AA03	First 2003 dated prefix	20	20	30	45	85
503b/2	420bL	DA03	Last 2003 dated prefix	20	20	30	50	120
503c	420c	2005	General prefixes	20	20	20	25	55
503c/1	420cF	AA05	First 2005 dated prefix	20	20	20	30	70
503c/2	420cL	GB05	Last 2005 dated prefix	20	20	20	30	75
503d	420d	2006	General prefixes	20	20	20	24	55
503d/1	420dF	AA06	First 2006 dated prefix	20	20	20	34	70
503d/2	420dL	JC06	Last signature prefix	20	20	20	40	75
STEVENS / HENRY - 2007								
504a	421a	2007	General prefixes	20	20	20	20	40
504a/1	421aF	AA07	First signature prefix	20	20	20	25	65
504a/2	421aL	JC07	Last 2007 dated prefix	20	20	20	25	65
504b	421b	2008	General prefixes	20	20	20	20	40
504b/1	421bF	AA08	First 2008 dated prefix	20	20	20	27	100
504b/2	421bL	JC08	Last 2008 year prefix	20	20	20	27	100
504c	421c	2010	General prefixes	20	20	20	20	35
504c/1	421cF	AA10	First 2010 dated prefix	20	20	20	22	60
504c/2	421cL	DA10	Last signature prefix	20	20	20	22	60
STEVENS / PARKINSON - 2013								
505a	422a	2013	General prefixes	20	20	20	20	35
505a/1	422aF	AA13	First signature prefix	20	20	20	20	40
505a/2	422aL	DA13	Last 2013 dated prefix	20	20	20	20	40

No circulation $20 notes were issued in 1999, 2000 or 2001. 1999 dated notes are available in collector folders (McDYF 31/32) as part of the $5 to $100 set.

NB : These "AA" prices are for circulation notes and not for low numbered folder notes which feature a dated overprint. See chapter on *"Decimal (NCLT) Banknote Folders"* for details on special first release issues that includes overprinted issues.

FIFTY DOLLARS

ELIZABETH II. PAPER ISSUE : 1973 TO 1994

Reference # McD	Rks	Description	Fine	VF	EF	aUnc	Unc
		PHILLIPS / WHEELER - 1973					
201	505	General prefixes	85	130	225	300	385
201a	505F	YAA First prefix	260	420	825	1,000	1,500
201b	505L	YAU Last prefix	150	450	750	1,000	1,500
		KNIGHT / WHEELER - 1976 · *Centre thread (70mm)*					
202	506a	General prefixes	75	100	190	250	450
202a	506aF	YAV First prefix	125	250	400	600	900
202b	506aL	YBX Last prefix	110	240	375	575	850
		KNIGHT / WHEELER – *Side thread (55mm)*					
203	506b	General prefixes	75	100	190	250	295
203a	506bF	YAV First prefix ••	125	250	400	600	900
203b	506bL	YCZ Last prefix	110	240	375	575	850
		KNIGHT / STONE - 1979					
204	507	General prefixes	70	95	155	220	325
204a	507F	YDA First prefix	95	200	325	500	675
204b	507L	YHH Last prefix	95	190	300	450	625
		JOHNSTON / STONE - 1983					
205	508	General prefixes	75	100	165	235	300
205a	508F	YHU First prefix	95	225	350	500	700
205b	508L	YNS Last prefix	95	225	350	500	700
		JOHNSTON / FRASER - 1985. *Gothic serials*					
206	509a	General prefixes	75	120	180	235	300
206a	509aF	YNT First prefix	90	225	350	500	700
206b	509aL	YXH Last Gothic prefix	100	250	400	550	775
		JOHNSTON / FRASER - 1985. *OCR-B serials*					
207	509b	General prefixes	95	150	300	375	600
207a	509bF	YUE First prefix	140	375	600	800	1,100
207b	509bL	YXH Last prefix	175	475	750	1,000	1,450
		PHILLIPS / FRASER - 1989					
208	511	General prefixes	50	60	85	125	200
208a	511F	YXJ First Prefix	100	200	300	425	575
208b	511L	YYU Last Prefix	100	130	245	340	525
		FRASER / HIGGINS - 1990					
209	512	General prefixes	70	100	175	260	375
209a	512F	YYV First prefix	100	150	225	350	500
209b	512L	WDD Last prefix	100	150	225	350	500
		FRASER / COLE - 1991					
210	513	General prefixes	50	60	85	125	250
210a	513F	WBT First prefix	110	165	250	400	600
210b	513L	WQH Last prefix	100	150	225	350	500
		FRASER / EVANS - 1993					
211	515	General prefixes	55	65	100	135	200
211a	515F	WNY First prefix	110	200	350	450	625
211b	515L	FAB Last prefix	80	110	160	240	350
		• Note Printing Australia issue					
211c	515aF	FAA First prefix	60	80	130	180	325
211d	515bL	WZZ Last prefix	60	80	140	195	325

Fraser / Evans notes with FAA prefix (original Coombs/Wilson $2 first prefix) resulted from the $50 series running out of numbers.
McD202 & McD203 : K/ W first and last prefixes have yet to be confirmed.

FIFTY DOLLARS

ELIZABETH II. POLYMER ISSUE : 1995 TO PRESENT

Reference # McD	Rks		Description	Fine	VF	EF	aUnc	Unc
			FRASER / EVANS - 1995					
601	516a	1995	General dated prefixes	55	95	150	225	375
601a/1	516aF	AA95	First signature prefix	75	140	225	375	650
601a/2	516aL	VG95	Last 1995 dated prefix	100	195	525	950	4,500
601b	516b	1996	General dated prefixes	110	200	300	450	775
601b/1	516bF	AA96	First 1996 dated prefix	135	260	395	550	825
601b/2	516bL	DA96	Last signature prefix	125	225	350	1,250	2,550
			MACFARLANE / EVANS - 1997					
602a	518a	1997	General dated prefixes	50	50	70	145	275
602a/1	518aF	AA97	First signature prefix	55	70	175	325	495
602a/2	518aL	JC97	Last 1997 dated prefix	145	300	575	775	1,600
602b	518b	1998	General dated prefixes	50	60	70	160	300
602b/1	518bF	AA98	First 1998 dated prefix	65	95	160	250	450
602b/2	518bL	JC98	Last 1998 dated prefix	180	350	850	1,200	2,950
602c	518c	1999	General dated prefixes	50	50	70	125	240
602c/1	518cF	AA99	First 1999 dated prefix	60	70	110	195	350
602c/2	518cL	PE99	Last signature prefix	60	75	125	250	400

No circulation $50 notes were issued in 2000, 2001 or 2002. 1999 dated notes are available in collector folders (McDYF 31/32) as part of the $5 to $100 set.

Reference # McD	Rks		Description	Fine	VF	EF	aUnc	Unc
			MACFARLANE / HENRY - 2003 *(modified)*					
603a	520a	2003	General dated prefixes	50	50	60	95	160
603a/1	520aF	AA03	First signature prefix	50	50	70	110	225
603a/2	520aL	DA03	Last 2003 dated prefix	50	50	70	110	250
603b	520b	2004	General dated prefixes	50	50	55	75	180
603b/1	520bF	AA04	First 2004 dated prefix	50	65	70	100	180
603b/2	520bL	GB04	Last 2004 dated prefix	50	65	70	145	350
603c	520c	2005	General dated prefixes	50	50	50	60	120
603c/1	520cF	AA05	First 2005 dated prefix	50	50	55	75	135
603c/2	520cL	JC05	Last 2005 dated prefix	50	50	55	75	150
603d	520d	2006	General dated prefixes	50	50	50	60	120
603d/1	520dF	AA06	First 2006 dated prefix	50	50	50	75	175
603d/2	520dL	JC06	Last signature prefix	50	50	50	75	175
			STEVENS / HENRY - 2007					
604a	521a	2007	General dated prefixes	50	50	50	55	100
604a/1	521aF	AA07	First signature prefix	50	50	50	75	185
604a/2	521aL	DA07	Last 2007 dated prefix	50	50	50	60	185
604b	521b	2008	General dated prefixes	50	50	50	50	100
604b/1	521bF	AA08	First 2008 dated prefix	50	50	50	55	150
604b/2	521bL	MD08	Last 2008 dated prefix	50	50	50	55	160
604c	521c	2009	General dated prefixes	50	50	50	50	100
604c/1	521cF	AA09	First 2009 dated prefix	50	50	50	55	110
604c/2	521cL	SF09	Last 2009 dated prefix	50	50	50	55	120
604d	521d	2010	General dated prefixes	50	50	50	50	95
604d/1	521dF	AA10	First 2010 dated prefix	50	50	50	55	100
604d/2	521dL	GB10	Last year prefix	50	50	50	55	100
604e	521e	2011	General dated prefixes	50	50	50	50	90
604e/1	521eF	AA11	First 2011 dated prefix	50	50	50	55	95
604e/2	521eL	JC11	Last signature prefix	50	50	50	55	95

FIFTY DOLLARS

ELIZABETH II. POLYMER ISSUE : 1995 TO PRESENT

Reference # McD	Rks		Description	Fine	VF	EF	aUnc	Unc
			STEVENS / PARKINSON - 2012					
605a	522a	2012	General dated prefixes	50	50	50	50	75
605a/1	522aF	AA12	First signature prefix	50	50	50	55	90
605a/2	522aL	GB12	Last 2012 dated prefix	50	50	50	55	90
605b	522b	2013	General dated prefixes	50	50	50	50	80
605b/1	522bF	AA13	First signature prefix	50	50	50	55	90
605b/2	522bL	DB13	Last 2013 dated prefix	50	50	50	50	85
605c	522c	2014	General dated prefixes	50	50	50	50	80
605c/1	522cF	AA14	First signature prefix	50	50	50	55	90
605c/2	522cL	JC14	Last 2014 dated prefix	50	50	50	50	85

ONE HUNDRED DOLLARS

ELIZABETH II. PAPER ISSUE : 1984 TO 1996

Reference # McD	Rks	Description	Fine	VF	EF	aUnc	Unc
		JOHNSTON / STONE - 1984					
221 `	608	General prefixes	100	140	190	230	320
221a	608F	ZAA First prefix	160	225	375	575	695
221b	608L	ZCD Last prefix	250	450	750	1,000	1,450
		JOHNSTON / FRASER - 1985					
222	609	General prefixes	100	140	190	230	350
222a	609F	ZBC First prefix	150	225	375	550	825
222b	609L	ZFU Last prefix	150	250	400	600	850
		FRASER / HIGGINS - 1990					
223	612	General prefixes	120	140	190	230	325
223a	612F	ZEJ First prefix	150	225	375	550	825
223b	612L	ZJS Last prefix	275	600	1,100	1,450	1,950
		FRASER / COLE - 1991					
224	613	General prefixes	100	140	190	230	320
224a	613F	ZHG First prefix	150	250	350	500	725
224b	613L	ZLD Last prefix	135	175	245	300	375

ONE HUNDRED DOLLARS

ELIZABETH II. POLYMER ISSUE : 1996 TO PRESENT

Reference # McD	Rks	Description	Fine	VF	EF	aUnc	Unc
		FRASER / EVANS - 1996 : *Circulation issue. No overprinted date*					
701a	616	1996 General dated prefixes	100	100	140	195	350
701a/1	616F	AA96 First signature prefix	100	130	200	300	550
701a/2	616L	JK96 Last signature prefix	160	275	400	525	875
701bT	616T	Test Notes. General prefix	150	210	350	595	900
701bT/1	616TF	Test Notes. AN96 First prefix	95	195	400	1250	3,500
701bT/2	616TL	Test Notes. CS96 Last prefix	95	195	400	1250	3,500
		MACFARLANE / EVANS - 1998					
702a	618a	1998 General dated prefixes	100	100	125	150	450
702a/1	618aF	AA98 First signature prefix	125	170	250	395	700
702a/2	618aL	CF98 Last 1998 dated prefix	270	550	1,100	2,700	3,950
702b	618b	1999 General dated prefixes	100	100	100	155	240
702b/1	618bF	AA99 First 1999 dated prefix	100	100	140	195	300
702b/2	618bL	JK99 Last signature prefix	100	100	140	210	325
		STEVENS / HENRY - 2008					
703a	621a	2008 General dated prefixes	100	100	100	110	190
703a/1	621aF	AA08 First signature prefix	100	100	100	125	235
703a/2	621aL	EL08 Last 2008 dated prefix	100	100	110	125	23
703b	621b	2010 General dated prefixes	100	100	100	110	200
703b/1	621bF	AA10 First 2010 dated prefix	100	100	100	125	220
703b/2	621bL	EL10 Last signature prefix	100	100	110	125	22
703c	621c	2011 General dated prefixes	100	100	100	100	180
703c/1	621cF	AA11 First 2011 dated prefix	100	100	100	115	200
703c/2	621cL	EL11 Last signature prefix	100	100	110	115	200
		STEVENS / PARKINSON - 2013					
704a	622a	2013 General dated prefixes	100	100	100	100	125
704a/1	622aF	AA13 First signature prefix	100	100	100	100	145
704a/2	622aL	EL13 Last 2013 dated prefix	100	100	110	100	145
704b	622b	2014 General dated prefixes	100	100	100	100	135
704b/1	622bF	AA14 First signature prefix	100	100	100	100	145
704b/2	622bL	JK14 Last 2014 dated prefix	100	100	110	100	145

McD702a. Although the Macfarlane / Evans signature first appeared in 1997, no circulation $100 banknotes were produced in that year, apart from a small number being included in the "Decimal Dated Annual Issues/" The first issued prefix in this signature combination was the AA98.702b. This is the final Macfarlane / Evans combination as no $100 notes were produced in 2000, 2001, 2002 or 2003.

McD702a/2. COMMENT REGARDING SCARCE PREFIXES (previously stated as 'unsighted' notes). Prices for lower grades have been calculated by averaging documented sales. At the time of printing this catalogue, some of these banknotes have no recorded sales in higher grades. This is not to say they do not exist in high grade and the pricing here is an estimate of what they might sell for.

DECIMAL SPECIMEN NOTES

Specimen notes have no legal tender status but have been used world-wide by issuing authorities to give a clear representation of the design. They differ from normal circulation notes only in that they are overprinted with a description which invalidates them as currency. Some types have either no serial numbers or all zeros even though several hundred of the notes might have been produced. In Australia,specimen notes have been issued for presentation to VIPs as well as reference material for major banks, commercial agencies etc.

NB : As some of these notes were usually displayed in major banks, libraries etc by tacking them to a bulletin board, they are usually found with pinholes.

SPECIMEN TYPE ONE **SPECIMEN TYPE TWO**

1966 TYPE ONE SPECIMEN SERIES

LEGEND READS : 'COMMONWEALTH OF AUSTRALIA'

McDonald Reference No.	Description	EF	aUnc	Unc
McDS 1	ONE DOLLAR Coombs/ Wilson : AAA Prefix	3,250	4,000	4,750
McDS 2	TWO DOLLARS Coombs/ Wilson : FAA Prefix	3,500	4,250	5,000
McDS 3	FIVE DOLLARS Coombs/ Randall : NAA Prefix	3,250	4,000	4,750
McDS 4	TEN DOLLARS Coombs/ Wilson : SAA Prefix	3,250	4,000	4,750
McDS 5	TWENTY DOLLARS Coombs/ Wilson : XAA Prefix	3,500	4,250	5,000

The "Type One" specimen notes can be distinguished by the small oval in the watermarked area containing the wording "SPECIMEN". These notes come from 208 specially prepared books given to people involved in the decimal changeover. Two notes of each denomination (showing front and back) were lightly glued into a book containing details of the history and production notes. Initially the book contained only the 1966 $1, $2, $10 and $20 issues. Provision was made however for the $5 note introduced in 1967. Individual notes can be purchased as some books have been broken up.

1966 TYPE TWO SPECIMEN SERIES

LEGEND READS : 'COMMONWEALTH OF AUSTRALIA'

McDonald Reference No.	Description	EF	aUnc	Unc
McDS 6	ONE DOLLAR Coombs / Wilson - AAA 000000	4,500	5,750	7,000
McDS 7	TWO DOLLARS Coombs / Wilson - FAA 000000	4,500	5,750	7,000
McDS 8	FIVE DOLLARS Coombs / Randall - NAA 000000	4,500	5,750	7,000
McDS 9	TEN DOLLARS Coombs / Wilson - SAA 000000	5,000	6,250	7,500
McDS 10	TWENTY DOLLARS Coombs / Wilson - XAA 000000	5,000	6,250	7,500
McDS 11	ONE DOLLAR Phillips / Wheeler - BBF 000000	7,000	8,500	10,000
McDS 12	TWO DOLLARS Phillips / Wheeler - GRG 000000	6,000	7,500	9,000
McDS 13	FIVE DOLLARS Phillips / Wheeler - NGT 000000	6,000	7,500	9,000
McDS 14	TEN DOLLARS Phillips / Wheeler - STH 000000	7,500	9,000	10,500
McDS 15	TWENTY DOLLARS Phillips / Wheeler - XEV 000000	7,500	9,000	10,500

The "Type Two" specimens were issued individually rather than in book form although no reliable figures have been released by the Reserve Bank. Like Type One, the four original Coombs / Wilson denominations were issued in 1966 and the $5 note, containing the signature combination of Coombs / Randall, being released in 1967. Identified by the word "SPECIMEN" being printed diagonally several times in red ink on both sides of the note. It is believed that only two Phillips / Wheeler sets are available to collectors. A set was sold in 1989. McDS 12 and McDS 14 were unknown individually to collectors until one of each surfaced in the late 1990's. (See article in the April 1998 edition of the CAB Magazine).

DECIMAL SPECIMEN NOTES

McDonald Reference No.	LEGEND READS : 'AUSTRALIA' Description		EF	aUnc	Unc
1974 TYPE THREE SPECIMEN SERIES					
McDS 16	ONE DOLLAR	Phillips / Wheeler - BLG 000000	2,750	3,500	4,500
McDS 17a	TWO DOLLARS	Phillips / Wheeler - HBQ 000000	3,500	4,250	5,000
McDS 18	FIVE DOLLARS	Phillips / Wheeler - NKG 000000	3,500	4,250	5,000
McDS 19	TEN DOLLARS	Phillips / Wheeler - TBC 000000	3,500	4,250	5,000
McDS 20b	TWENTY DOLLARS	Phillips / Wheeler - XGY 000000	4,000	4,750	5,250
McDS 21	FIFTY DOLLARS	Phillips / Wheeler - YAA 000000	4,500	5,500	6,500
McDS 22	ONE DOLLAR	Johnston / Stone - DHY 000000	5,750	6,500	8,500
McDS 23	TWO DOLLARS	Johnston / Stone - KBL 000000	5,750	6,500	8,500
McDS 24	FIVE DOLLARS	Johnston / Stone - PFY 000000	5,750	6,500	8,500
McDS 25	TEN DOLLARS	Johnston / Stone - TYV 000000	5,750	6,500	8,500
McDS 26	TWENTY DOLLARS	Johnston / Stone - VGX 000000	5,500	6,750	8,250
McDS 27	FIFTY DOLLARS	Johnston / Stone - YJK 000000	6,000	7,500	8,750

The "Type Three" specimen series varies significantly from the previous two types in that they are individually numbered as well as having a serial number with all zeros. As well as the word "SPECIMEN" being printed twice on each side there is an added inscription stating "NO VALUE". This is the first specimen type issued with the revised legend reading "Australia" instead of "Commonwealth of Australia". The latter Johnston / Stone issues were the first to use the OCR-B font.

[a] An example of this note appeared as lot 3162 in Noble's sale 106 held in July 2013. it sold for $3,900 (inc commission) against an estimate of $3,000.

[b] An example of this note appeared as lot 3163 in Noble's sale 106 held in July 2013. it sold for $3,900 (inc commission) against an estimate of $5,000.

NB : The Specimen $1 and $50 notes are the only issue to have the OCR-B lettering. The circulation notes had Gothic lettering only.

1983 TYPE FOUR SPECIMEN SERIES

		EF	aUnc	Unc
	PAPER ISSUE			
Mc DS 28	HUNDRED DOLLARS Johnston / Fraser : ZAA 000000	5,250	7,500	10,000
	POLYMER ISSUE			
McDS 27	FIFTY DOLLARS Johnston/ Stone - YJK 000000	6,000	7,500	9,500
McDS 29	TEN DOLLARS [Bicentenary] Johnston/ Fraser- AA 00 000000	5,250	7,500	10,000
McDS 30	FIVE DOLLARS Fraser/ Cole - AA 00 000000	5,000	6,000	7,500
McDS 31	TEN DOLLARS Fraser/ Evans - AA 93 000000	5,000	6,000	7,500
McDS 32	TWENTY DOLLARS Fraser/ Evans - AA 94 000000	5,500	6,500	8,000
McDS 33	FIFTY DOLLARS Fraser/ Evans - AA 95 000000	6,000	7,500	9,500
McDS 33	HUNDRED DOLLARS Fraser/ Evans - AA 96 000000	6,000	7,500	9,500

Our first polymer banknote commemorated Australia's bicentenary in 1988. It also heralded a variation to the overprinting of specimen notes. "Type Four" specimens are similar to the previous three styles in that the serial numbers are all zeros and each note is individually numbered.

(a) An example appeared as lot 3164 in Noble's sale 106 held in July 2013. Still in its official folder, it sold for $9,600 (inc commission) against an estimate of $2,500.

NOTE PRINTNG AUSTRALIA ISSUE

ANNUAL DATED FOLDERS

Reference numbers - McDonald : Dated Yearly Folder = (McDYF)

In 1994, NPA began "dating" its banknotes by including the year of manufacture as part of the serial number. Following the two letter prefix, the first two digits of the serial number indicates the year followed by the normal six figure serial number. For example, a note with the serial number AA 94 000100 would mean that the note was issued in 1994. Sold in colourful folders at a premium, these special issues enabled enthusiasts to put together date sets in much the same way that collectors have saved yearly mint and proof coin sets. This low number collector folder series will also ensure that collectors will be able to obtain issues for all years. This is because it is possible that general circulation notes for some denominations will not be produced on a yearly basis due to the durability of the polymer note.

1994 Five Dollar folder design

1995 Five Dollar folder design

1994 TWO NOTE FOLDER SET

Mc Donald Reference No.	Description	Total Issued	Issue Price	Retail Average
McDYF 1	FIVE DOLLARS : Premium. Red serials Fraser /Evans AA94 000101- 001000	900	45	130
McDYF 2	FIVE DOLLARS : Deluxe. Green serials Fraser /Evans AA94 001001- 010000	9,000	15	90
McDYF 3	TEN DOLLARS : Premium. Red serials Fraser /Evans AA94 000101 - 001000	900	50	165
McDYF 4	TEN DOLLARS : Deluxe. Blue serials Fraser /Evans AA94 001001 - 010000	9,000	20	100

1995 THREE NOTE FOLDER SET

Mc Donald Reference No.	Description	Total Issued	Issue Price	Retail Average
McDYF 5	FIVE DOLLARS : Premium. Red serials Fraser /Evans AA95 000101- 001000	900	50	130
McDYF 6	FIVE DOLLARS : Deluxe. Black serials Fraser /Evans AA95 001001- 010000	9,000	15	90
McDYF 7	TEN DOLLARS : Premium. Red serials Fraser /Evans AA95 000101 - 001000	900	50	165
McDYF 8	TEN DOLLARS : Deluxe. Blue serials Fraser /Evans AA95 001001 - 010000	9,000	20	100
McDYF 9	TWENTY DOLLARS : Premium. Red serials Fraser /Evans AA95 000101 - 001000	900	85	185
McDYF 10	TWENTY DOLLARS : Deluxe. Black serials Fraser /Evans AA95 001001 - 007000	6,000	30	150

The set of number one premium $5, $10, & $20 folders was sold at a Noble Numismatics auction (Sydney) with the proceeds being presented to the Vooralla Society. The set of three folders raised a total of $3,000.

ANNUAL DATED FOLDERS : NPA

1996 Five Dollar folder design

1997 Ten Dollar folder design

1996 FOUR NOTE FOLDER SET

Mc Donald Reference No.	Description	Total Issued	Issue Price	Retail Average
McDYF 11	FIVE DOLLARS : Premium. Red serials Fraser /Evans AA96 000101- 001000	900	50	75
McDYF 12	FIVE DOLLARS : Deluxe. Black serials Fraser /Evans AA96 001001- 010000	9,000	15	40
McDYF 13	TEN DOLLARS : Premium. Red serials Fraser /Evans AA96 000101 - 001000	900	65	75
McDYF 14a	TEN DOLLARS : Deluxe. Blue serials Fraser /Evans AA96 001001 - 009000	9,000	20	110
McDYF 15	TWENTY DOLLARS : Premium. Red serial Fraser /Evans AA96 000101 - 001000	900	85	125
McDYF 16	TWENTY DOLLARS : Deluxe. Black serials Fraser /Evans AA96 001001 - 007000	6,000	30	150
McDYF 17	FIFTY DOLLARS : Premium. Red serials Fraser /Evans AA96 000101 - 001000	900	115	225
McDYF 18	FIFTY DOLLARS : Deluxe. Blue top serial Black bottom serial. AA96 001001 -005000	4,000	69	450

[a] Special NPA folders can be seen as a separate link associated with the collecting of decimal banknotes. However there is some crossover areas where 'diehard' collectors seek to obtain every type, date or variety. Some general circulation issues are hard to get and some special serial numbers, or year dates, are only available in folders, as general circulation notes were not printed. Examples include the Fraser / Evans ""AA96" $10, not issued for general circulation and the $5 notes as most circulation $5 notes started at "BA".

1997 FIVE NOTE FOLDER SET

Mc Donald Reference No.	Description	Total Issued	Issue Price	Retail Average
McDYF 19	FIVE DOLLARS : Premium. Red serials Macfarlane /Evans AA97 000101- 001000	900	50	75
McDYF 20	FIVE DOLLARS : Deluxe. Black serials Macfarlane /Evans AA97 001001- 010000	9,000	15	40
McDYF 21	TEN DOLLARS : Premium. Red serials Macfarlane /Evans AA97 000101 - 001000	900	65	70
McDYF 22	TEN DOLLARS : Deluxe. Blue serials Macfarlane /Evans AA97 001001 - 009000	9,000	15	100
McDYF 23	TWENTY DOLLARS : Premium. Red serials Macfarlane /Evans AA97 000101 - 001000	900	85	185
McDYF 24	TWENTY DOLLARS : Deluxe. Black serials Macfarlane /Evans AA97 001001 - 007000	6,000	30	150
McDYF 25	FIFTY DOLLARS : Premium. Red serials Macfarlane /Evans AA97 000101 - 001000	900	115	155
McDYF 26	FIFTY DOLLARS : Deluxe. Blue top serial Black bottom serial. AA97 001001 - 006000	5,000	60	80
McDYF 27	HUNDRED DOLLARS : Premium. Red serials Macfarlane /Evans AA97 000101 - 001000	900	115	135
McDYF28a	HUNDRED DOLLARS : Deluxe. Blue top serial Black bottom serial. AA97 001001 - 005000	4,000	69	80

The set of number one premium $5; $10; $20; $50 & $100 folders was sold at a Noble Numismatics auction with the proceeds being presented to Epping Hospital, Victoria. The set of five premium folders raised a total of $2,000.
[a] No general circulation Macfarlane / Evans $100 notes were issued in 1997. The above folder is the only way collectors can obtain this issue.

NOTE PRINTNG AUSTRALIA ISSUE

ANNUAL DATED FOLDERS

Reference numbers - McDonald : Dated Yearly Folder = (McDYF)

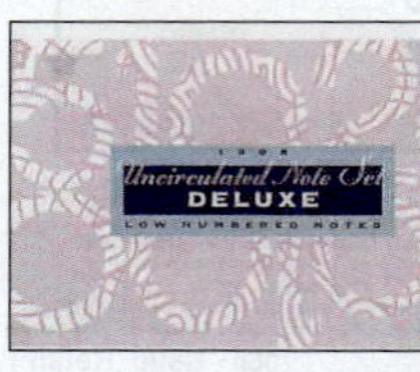

1998 ALL ISSUES IN ONE FOLDER : Macfarlane / Evans

Mc Donald Reference No.	Description	Total Issued	Issue Price	Retail Average
McDYF 29	**PREMIUM.** Red serials. Five notes in one folder. All matching numbers from AA98 000101 - 001000	900	480	690
McDYF 30	**DELUXE. Black serials.** Five notes in one folder. All matching numbers from AA98 001001 - 003000	2,000	285	425

For the first time since this series was started in 1994, Note Printing Australia offered the dated prefix issues in one folder instead of individually. All the notes in the folder shared the same serial numbers.

Lowest numbers : Uncirculated note sets contain the lowest numbered notes available to the public annually. The first 100 notes are kept in the NPA archives while those numbered from 000101 to 001000 have red serial numbers rather than the normal black serial numbers. In instances where a denomination is not printed within the year for normal circulation such folders are the only means by which a collector can obtain a "dated" issue. In 1997, for instance, the $100 note was not printed for general circulation and so the only way to obtain an AA97 dated $100 was by purchasing a folder. The 1996 (AA96) Fraser / Evans $10 is another example where no circulation notes were issued for circulation. Figures available may vary. The figures given in the "Total Issued" column are the official "Maximum" offered for sale by Note Printing Australia. In a number of cases, general interest among collectors did not meet the expected sales figures and all unsold folders were destroyed. Well - known banknote specialist, Judy Shaw believes that in some instances the wastage accounted for as much as half to two-thirds of some issues.

1999 ALL ISSUES IN ONE FOLDER : Macfarlane / Evans

Mc Donald Reference No.	Description	Total Issued	Issue Price	Retail Average
McDYF 31	**PREMIUM.** Red serials. Five notes in one folder. All matching numbers from AA99 000101 - 001000	900	480	795
McDYF 32	**DELUXE. Black serials.** Five notes in one folder. All matching numbers from AA99 001001 - 002200	1,200	325	550

For the second year running the annual dated prefix issues were housed in one folder. Previous issues were available individually. All the notes in the folder shared the same serial numbers.

Considering that the Deluxe Folders are far more common than the Premium Folders, the above pricing might be confusing to some collectors. Many of the most common folders have been broken up and kept or sold to collectors who specialise in prefixes.

FIRST & LAST FOLDERS

Reference Numbers - McDonald : First / Last Folder = (Mc F/LF)

Generally these are two banknote folders which contain one of the earliest serial numbered polymer banknotes and one of the last signature combinations of the paper issue. The rarer *(embossed)* folders usually also contain a paper banknote with the final prefix.

1992 $5 Folder

1993 $10 Folder

2016 $5 Folder

1992 : FIVE DOLLARS
TWO NOTE FOLDER : Fraser / Cole - Paper & Polymer

Mc Donald Reference No.	Description	Total Issued	Issue Price	Retail Average
Mc$5F/LF1	**Embossed Deluxe**. Polymer overprinted 7 July 1992. Front of folder embossed Paper note from the final print run	17,000	20	80
Mc$5F/LF2	**Standard Souvenir. [No embossing]** Polymer note overprinted 7 July 1992 and paper note from the final print run	30	19	75
Mc$5F/LF3	**Staff folder**	350	Gift	900

2016 : FIVE DOLLARS
FOLDER : Stevens / Fraser - New Wattle & Old Polymer

Mc Donald Reference No.	Description	Total Issued	Issue Price	Retail Average
Mc$5F/LF4	**Two Polymer Banknotes**. No overprint. Folder contains one superseded $5 note & one new 2016 'Wattle' issue. No special embossing, serial numbers or prefix.	tba	19.50	20
Mc$5F/LF5	**Single New Polymer banknote.** No special embossing, serial numbers or prefix.	tba	9.95	10

Compared to the many innovative and ground breaking issues found on surrounding pages, this issue was a disappointment to many collectors who had become accustomed to first day overprints, embossed covers, matching serial numbers etc. This was basically a nice folder stuffed with any nondescript banknote. Old time collectors of this series would all agree that such a thrown together offering wouldn't have happened during the watch of Alan Flint who masterminded the concept of all the NPA issues that spanned a full decade from 1988 onwards.

1993 : TEN DOLLARS
TWO NOTE FOLDER : Fraser / Cole [Paper] & Fraser / Evans [Polymer]

Mc Donald Reference No.	Description	Total Issued	Issue Price	Retail Average
Mc$10F/LF1	**First Day of Issue. Embossed Deluxe Folder.** Polymer note overprinted 1 November 1993. Black serials starting AA93 001001 to AA93 010000. Paper note. "MRR" last prefix	9,000	49	160
Mc$10F/LF1b	**ERROR** As above but date of issue imprint missing (See ACR April 1994)	*Ditto*	49	550
Mc$10F/LF2	**Standard Souvenir Folder** Polymer note overprinted 1 November 1993. Purple serials starting at AB93 000001 Paper note from the final printrun but not MRR.	40,000	36	80

FIRST & LAST FOLDERS

1994 : TWENTY DOLLARS
TWO NOTE FOLDER : Fraser / Evans - Paper & Polymer

Mc Donald Reference No.	Description	Total Issued	Issue Price	Retail Average
Mc$20F/LF1	**First Day of Issue. Embossed Deluxe Folder.** Polymer note overprinted 31 October 1994. Black serials starting at AA94 001001 to AA94 006000. Paper note. "ADK" last prefix	5,000	69	300
Mc$20F/LF2	**Standard Souvenir Folder. (No embossing).** Polymer note overprinted 31 October 1994. Black.serials starting at AB94 000001. Single polymer only. No paper issue included	25,000	36	75

1995 Fifty Dollars folder

1996 One Hundred Dollars folder

1995 : FIFTY DOLLARS
TWO NOTE FOLDER : Fraser / Evans - Paper & Polymer

Mc Donald Reference No.	Description	Total Issued	Issue Price	Retail Average
Mc$50F/LF1	**First Day of Issue. Embossed Deluxe Folder.** Polymer note overprinted 15 May 1995. Black serials starting at AA95 001001 to AA95 005000. Paper note. "FAB" last prefix	3,500	129	600
Mc$50F/LF2	**Standard Souvenir Folder. (No embossing).** Polymer note overprinted 4 October 1995. Black.serials starting at AB95 000001. Single polymer only. No paper issue included	7,000	66	290

1996 : ONE HUNDRED DOLLARS
Fraser / Evans - Paper & Polymer issue

Mc Donald Reference No.	Description	Total Issued	Issue Price	Retail Average
Mc$100F/LF1	**First Day of Issue. Embossed Deluxe Folder.** Polymer note overprinted 15 May 1996. Top brown and bottom green serials starting at AA96 001001 to AA96 003000. Paper note. "ZLD" last prefix	2,000	259	825
Mc$100F/LF2	**Standard Souvenir Folder. (No embossing).** Polymer note overprinted 15 May 1996. Brown / green serials starting at AB95 003001 to AA96 006000. Single polymer only in folder. No paper issue included	3,000	129	450

SPECIAL EVENT GENERAL FOLDERS

Reference numbers - McDonald : General Folder = (Mc GF)

The following folders are generally not part of an ongoing series but have been issued at random by NPA to commemorate a particular event. They range from one or more notes in a simple but colourful cardboard folder as distinct from the elaborate hardbound portfolios or the leather-bound issues. In most instances they are issues in their own right although in some cases hardbound "Premium" folders also exist. These are treated separately in a later section. As with all NPA collector products we have decided to present the issues by denomination rather than date of issue to make the series easier to understand. In many cases this has resulted in us having to assign new reference numbers to some of the issues.

TWO DOLLARS : LAST ISSUE

1988 - 1994 : Johnston / Fraser

Mc$2GF 1b. All issues in green folder

Mc $5GF 2 Premium 2 note folder

Mc Donald Reference No.	Description	Total Issued	Issue Price	Retail Average
Mc$2GF 1a	General issue in green folder, 1988	n/a	5	10
Mc$2GF 1b	NAA Hobart Fair (May 11 - 12, 1991)	500	8	30
Mc$2GF 1c	*NAA Melbourne Fair (July 13 -14, 1991)*	500	8	30
Mc$2GF 1d	NAA Sydney Fair (Nov. 16 - 17, 1991). LQG	500	8	95
Mc$2GF 1e	NAA Adelaide Fair (Sept 5 - 6, 1992)	500	8	30
Mc$2GF 1f	NAA Brisbane Fair (May 8 - 9, 1993)	500	8	30
Mc$2GF 1g	NAA Perth Fair (August 20 - 21, 1994)	500	8	30

Above issued to mark the withdrawal of the Two Dollar banknote.

First issued in 1988, the folder was resurrected some years later for special overprinted issues for coin and banknote fairs attended by staff of NPA. The notes issued at coin fairs can be distinguished by a map of the state featured on the cover of the folder as well as wording to indicate that only 500 special fair issues were issued. The Sydney Fair issue contained a $2 note with the final prefix number LQG.

FIVE DOLLARS : 'SIGNATURES'

1996 : Fraser / Evans & MacFarlane / Evans

	Premium Folders. Red serials			
Mc $5GF 1	Sold at auction	#001	Donated	850
Mc $5GF 2	FE96 000001 to FE96 001000 & ME96 000001 to ME96 001000	999	79	140
	Deluxe Folders. Black serials			
Mc $5GF 3	FE96 001001 to FE96 002500 & ME96 001001 to ME96 002500	1,500	39	100

The "Signatures" note folder contains two $5 notes with matching serial numbers. One note has the Fraser / Evans signature and the alpha prefix letters "FE". The other note features the Macfarlane / Evans signatures and has the alpha letters "ME". Neither prefixes were used for general circulation notes.
Mc$5GF1 : The number one folder was sold at a Noble Numismatic auction with the proceeds being presented to the Guide Dog Association of Australia. The premium set raised $780.

SPECIAL EVENT GENERAL FOLDERS

Reference numbers - McDonald : General Folder = (Mc GF)

HONG KONG HANDOVER

FIVE DOLLARS : 1997 MACFARLANE / EVANS

Mc Donald Reference No.	Description	Total Issued	Issue Price	Retail Average
Mc $5GF 4	Single polymer with HK prefix	8,000	18	95

The first Australian Banknote issued to commemorate an international event. Each note is printed with the unique red serial number combination of "HK" for Hong Kong and "97" for the year 1997. In presentation folder. All note serial numbers start with the numeral "9".

'FAMOUS FIVES' 30 YEARS

FIVE DOLLARS : 1997 MACFARLANE / EVANS

Mc Donald Reference No.	Description	Total Issued	Issue Price	Retail Average
	Premium Folders. Red serials			
Mc $5 GF 5	Sold at auction	001	Donated	850
Mc $5 GF 6	Three note set. Premium notes overprinted in red ink	999	85	150
	Deluxe Folders. Black serials			
Mc $5 GF 7	Three note set. Deluxe notes overprinted in black ink	1,500	45	100

Mc $5GF 5. The number one $5 Premium Signatures Note Folder was auctioned by Noble Numismatics, Sydney for charity. The three note folder was issued in both *"Premium"* and *"Deluxe"* form. The folder housed a $5 paper note from the final print run as well as a $5 EA93 *(last prefix)* old colour note. The third note features a $5 AA95 *(first prefix)* recoloured note. Each note featured a date of issue overprint. Details of the three notes are as follows.

(a) $5 Paper note - Fraser / Cole signatures. Final paper print run overprinted *"First issued May 1992"*.

(b) $5 Polymer note - Fraser / Evans signatures. Last prefix overprinted *"First issued 7 July 1992"*.

(c) $5 Polymer note - Fraser / Evans signatures. First prefix overprinted *"First issued 24 April 1995"*.

SPECIAL EVENT GENERAL FOLDERS

Reference numbers - McDonald : General Folder = (Mc GF)

CENTENARY OF FEDERATION

FIVE DOLLARS : 1997 MACFARLANE / EVANS

Mc Donald Reference No.	Description	Total Issued	Issue Price	Retail Average
	50 lowest numbers by tender			
Mc $5 GF 8	AA01 001001 to AA01 000050	**50**	**Tender**	**300**
	General Folder Issue			
Mc $5 GF 9	AA01 001051 to AA01 100000	**97,900**	**12.5**	**55**

When the polymer Centenary of Federation banknote was released on January 1, 2001, Note Printing Australia announced that 100,000 overprinted notes bearing the lowest serial numbers would be available to collectors at a premium. The overprint, in red ink, simply read "1901-2001." The first 50 folders, offering the lowest serial numbers, were offered through Tender 2/01 which closed on May 21, 2001. The highest bid was for $950 with the lowest bid being $90. All notes on offer were sold. The remaining folders were widely available through dealers as well as NPA's own mailing list.

FIRST POLYMER : BICENTENARY

TEN DOLLARS : 1988 JOHNSTON FRASER

Mc Donald Reference No.	Description	Total Issued	Issue Price	Retail Average
Mc $10GF 1	Polymer. Dated 26 January 1988. Prefixes AA01 - AA22	**800,000**	**14**	**65**
Mc $10GF 2	First prefix AA00	**Inc. above**	**14**	**320**
Mc $10GF 3	Last prefix AA23	**Inc. above**	**14**	**175**
Mc $10GF 4	Staff presentation folder Prefix AA00 0... Two notes (See below)	**499**	**Gift**	**1,100**

Australia's first polymer banknote. Issued to commemorate the 200th anniversary of European settlement.

The Staff Presentation notes (Mc $10GF 4) are housed in a different folder to the general commemorative blue folder. The Presentation folder is grey and opens up to reveal two consecutive numbered notes side by side. The serial numbers have the first prefix AA00 and the six digit serial numbers start with "0". As an example, a special Presentation note might have a serial number that reads AA00 012345.

SPECIAL EVENT GENERAL FOLDERS

Reference numbers - McDonald : General Folder = (Mc GF)

1988 Ten Years of Polymer Notes

1993 Commonwealth Currency 80th

TEN YEARS OF POLYMER TENS

TEN DOLLARS : 1998 JOHNSTON / FRASER & MACFARLANE / EVANS

Mc Donald Reference No.	Description	Total Issued	Issue Price	Retail Average
	Premium Folders. Red serials			
Mc $10GF 5	Two note folder. Number under 001001	1,000	85	175
	Deluxe Folders. Black serials			
Mc $10GF 6	Two note folder. Numbers over 001000	1,500	49	120

The above issue celebrates the tenth anniversary of Australia's leading role in polymer technology. The two-note folder contains an original randomly numbered bicentennial note of 1988 with the "AA" prefix along with a note from the current series. The red "Premium" serial numbers range from AB98 000001 to AB98 001000. The "Deluxe" black serial numbers range from AB98 001001 to AB98 002500. Normal circulating numbers are printed in blue ink. The 1988 note is overprinted "26 January 1988" while the current issue carries an overprint reading "26 January 1998."

80th ANNIVERSARY ISSUE

TWENTY DOLLARS : 1993 FRASER COLE

OVERPRINTED WITH SPECIAL SERIAL NUMBER FONT

Mc Donald Reference No.	Description	Total Issued	Issue Price	Retail Average
Mc $20GF 1a	First serial M000001 Raffled at Bris. Fair	1	—	1,500
Mc $20GF 1b	M000002 to M000500 Brisbane Fair	499	95	250
Mc $20GF 1c	M000501 to M003000 Brisbane Fair	2,500	49	150
Mc $20GF 1d	M003001 to M005500 Ballot	2,500	49	135

HAND DRAWN PENCIL PORTRAITS

TEN DOLLARS : 1998 : BANJO PATERSON & DAME MARY GILMORE

Mc Donald Reference No.	Description	Total Issued	Issue Price	Retail Average
Mc P - 1	Red serials unframed set of 2	1,500	75	120
Mc P - 2	Red serials framed set of 2	Inc above	185	220

Reference number : "McDonald Portraits" [McP]

These coloured pencil - drawn portrait prints are from the notes intricate key - line drawings as displayed on Australia's currency notes. The set comes complete with two genuine polymer $10 notes which have distinctive red serial numbers. Each pair featured serial numbers in the range of AA98 010001 to AA98 011500 for the $10 Paterson note and AB98 010001 to AB98 011500 for the Gilmore note. Due to a lack of interest among collectors the series was abandoned.

SPECIAL EVENT GENERAL FOLDERS

Reference numbers - McDonald : Vignettes = (Mc V-1)

BANKNOTE VIGNETTES

Mc Donald Reference No.		Description	Total Issued	Issue Price	Retail Average
Mc V-1	1989	Five Shilling Uniface Vignette	16,000	20	20
Mc V-2	1989	As above (Melbourne Fair issue)	3,300	20	20
Mc V-3	1990	Cook's Landing Vignette Folder	6,000	20	20
Mc V-4	1990	As above (Melbourne Fair issue)	4,000	20	20

When Note Printing Australia entered the collector market in 1989, its first product was a vignette of the reverse of the 1946 Five Shilling banknote. This issue was never issued for general circulation as originally planned. NPA used the actual paper stock still in storage for almost 50 years and the original printing plates to produce this unique product. In 1990, NPA followed up with a vignette similar to the George V One Pound banknote issued between 1923 to 1933.

BANKNOTES IN PERSPEX

BICENTENARY TEN DOLLAR POLYMER

1988 JOHNSTON / FRASER

Mc Donald Reference #	Description	Total Issued	Issue Price	Current Retail
Mc PX 1 - 1	NPA title deleted	150	50	120
Mc PX 1 - 2	With NPA title. 110mm high	250	50	100
Mc PX 1 - 3	With NPA title. 120mm high	550	50	100

FIVE DOLLAR PAPER ISSUE

1991 FRASER / HIGGINS

Mc PX 2 - 1	Only one official type	1,000	60	75

Privately issued copies of the above also exist. These sets are individually numbered while the official NPA issues are not. The NPA issues are reported to stand between 110 mm and 120 mm high. The privately issued perspex issues are believed to be 115 mm.

1995 : FIRST POLYMER $5 PORTFOLIO

COMBINED ORIGINAL AND NEW RECOLOURED $5 ISSUES

Reference numbers - McDonald : Portfolio = [Mc PT]

FRASER / COLE - FRASER / EVANS SIGNATURES

McDonald Reference #	Date	Total Issued	Description	Issue Price	Current Retail
Mc $5 PT 1	1995	900	Two note portfolio	195	300

1993 : FIRST POLYMER $10 PORTFOLIO

LAST 'PAPER' & FIRST POLYMER BANKNOTES

FRASER / COLE - FRASER / EVANS SIGNATURES

McDonald Reference #	Date	Total Issued	Description	Issue Price	Current Retail
Mc $10 PT 1	1993	900	Two note portfolio	295	350

1994 : FIRST POLYMER $20 PORTFOLIO

FRASER / EVANS SIGNATURES

McDonald Reference #	Date	Total Issued	Description	Issue Price	Current Retail
Mc $20 PT 1	1994	#001	Sold at auction	Donated	1,650
Mc $20 PT 2	1994	#100	Sold at auction	Donated	350
Mc $20 PT 3	1994	898	Two note portfolio	350	525

NOTE PRINTNG AUSTRALIA ISSUE

1995 : FIRST POLYMER $50 PORTFOLIO

LAST 'PAPER' & FIRST POLYMER BANKNOTES

Reference numbers - McDonald : Portfolio = (Mc PT)

FRASER / EVANS SIGNATURES

McDonald Reference #	Date	Total Issued	Description	Issue Price	Current Retail
Mc $50 PT 1	1995	#001	Sold at auction	Donated	1,350
Mc $50 PT 2	1995	#100	Sold at auction	Donated	350
Mc $50 PT 3	1995	898	Two note portfolio	350	600

1996 : FIRST POLYMER $100 PORTFOLIO

FRASER / CCLE - FRASER / EVANS SIGNATURES

McDonald Reference #	Date	Total Issued	Description	Issue Price	Current Retail
Mc $100 PT 1	1996	#001	Sold at auction	Donated	2,200
Mc $100 PT 2	1996	#002	Sold at auction	Donated	470
Mc $100 PT 3	1996	898	Two note portfolio	495	720

NPA & TELECOM PORTFOLIO - TYPE ONE

Reference numbers - McDonald : NPA / TELECOM Portfolio = (McN/TPT)

1995 CENTENARY OF WALTZING MALTIDA $10 PHONECARD & $10 BANKNOTE PORTFOLIO

FRASER / COLE - FRASER / EVANS SIGNATURES

McDonald Reference #	Date	Total Issued	Description	Issue Price	Current Retail
Mc $100 PT 1	1996	#001	Sold at auction	Donated	2,200
Mc $100 PT 2	1996	#002	Sold at auction	Donated	470
Mc $100 PT 3	1996	898	Two note portfolio	495	720

NPA & RAM PORTFOLIO - TYPE ONE

1988 FIRST FLEET BICENTENARY ALBUM

Reference numbers - McDonald : NPA / RAM Portfolio = (McN/RPT)

FRASER / COLE - FRASER / EVANS SIGNATURES

McDonald Reference #	Date	Total Issued	Description	Issue Price	Current Retail
McN/R PT 1	1988	20,000	Three Coins/ Three Notes	120	140
McN/R PT 2	1988	5,000	Coin Fair Issue	120	160

NPA & RAM PORTFOLIO - TYPE TWO

1997 SIR KINGSFORD SMITH COMMEMORATIVE SILVER $1 COIN & $20 "ADK" LAST PREFIX

Reference numbers - McDonald : NPA / RAM Portfolio = (McN/RPT)

FRASER / COLE - FRASER / EVANS SIGNATURES

McDonald Reference #	Date	Total Issued	Description	Issue Price	Current Retail
Mc N/R PT 3	1997	#0001	Sold at auction	Donated	670
Mc N/R PT 4	1997	3999	Silver $1/ ADK $20	129	225

The 1997 Kingsford Smith silver proof was unique to the set and not available through any other source.

NPA & RAM PORTFOLIO - TYPE THREE

1997 AUSTRALIAN COIN AND BANKNOTE COMPLETE CIRCULATION COLLECTION

Reference numbers - McDonald : NPA / RAM Portfolio = (McN/RPT)

FRASER / COLE - FRASER / EVANS SIGNATURES

McDonald Reference #	Date	Total Issued	Description	Issue Price	Current Retail
McN/R PT 5	1997a	#0001	Sold at auction	Donated	2,950
McN/R PT 6	1997	1,499	Set of notes and coins	395	700

[a] The number one Australian Note and Coin Collection was auctioned by Noble Numismatics at their November 1997 sale. It raised $2,700 for the Bone Marrow Donor Institute Inc. This combined effort between The Royal Australian Mint and Note Printing Australia contained a specially matched and numbered set of notes and a set of 1997 dated uncirculated coins. The complete range of banknotes from $5, $10, $20, $50 and $100 notes were combined with the 5¢, 10¢, 20¢, 50¢, $1 and $2 coins. It was the first time the two institutions have combined to offer their complete range of issues in the same package. The set of notes featured the unique prefix "ZZ97" with all serial numbers matching. The numbers ranged from 998500 to 999999. The number one portfolio contains the set of notes numbered ZZ97 999999. Each portfolio came with a hand numbered certificate of authenticity signed by the Managing Director of Note Printing Australia, R.L. Larkin.

NPA & RAM PORTFOLIO - TYPE FOUR

1998 AUSTRALIAN COIN AND BANKNOTE COMPLETE CIRCULATION COLLECTION

FRASER / COLE - FRASER / EVANS SIGNATURES

McDonald Reference #	Date	Total Issued	Description	Issue Price	Current Retail
McN/R PT 7	1998	1,000	Set of notes and coins	425	650

This second coin and banknote issue differed slightly from the 1997 issue in that proof coins were used rather than uncirculated specimens. The production run was also cut back from 1,500 to 1,000. The set featured a specially matched and numbered set of banknotes that incorporated the unique prefix "ZZ98". There was no 1999 currency set issued.

NPA & AUST. POST PORTFOLIO - TYPE 1

1993 EMINENT WOMEN
$10 BANKNOTE - PANE OF 25 STAMPS

Reference numbers - McDonald : NPA / AP Portfolio = (McN/APT)

1993 [a] Eminent Women showing stamps

1995 [b] Hargrave Centenary portfolio

[a] FRASER / COLE - FRASER / EVANS SIGNATURES

McDonald Reference #	Date	Total Issued	Description	Issue Price	Current Retail
Mc N/APT 1	1993	#0001	Sold at auction	Donated	1,650
Mc N/APT 2	1993	0499	Red serial numbers	175	170
Mc N/APT 3	1993	4500	Black serial numbers	95	130

NPA & AUST. POST PORTFOLIO - TYPE 2

1994 HARGRAVE CENTENARY
$20 BANKNOTE - PANE OF 25 STAMPS

[b] FRASER / COLE - FRASER / EVANS SIGNATURES

McDonald Reference #	Date	Total Issued	Description	Issue Price	Current Retail
Mc N/APT 4	1994	#0001	Sold at auction	Donated	2,200
Mc N/APT 5	1994	0999	Red serial numbers	175	185
Mc N/APT 6	1994	4000	Black serial numbers	95	150

NPA & AUST. POST PORTFOLIO - TYPE 3

1995 HOWARD FLOREY
$50 BANKNOTE - PANE OF 10 STAMPS

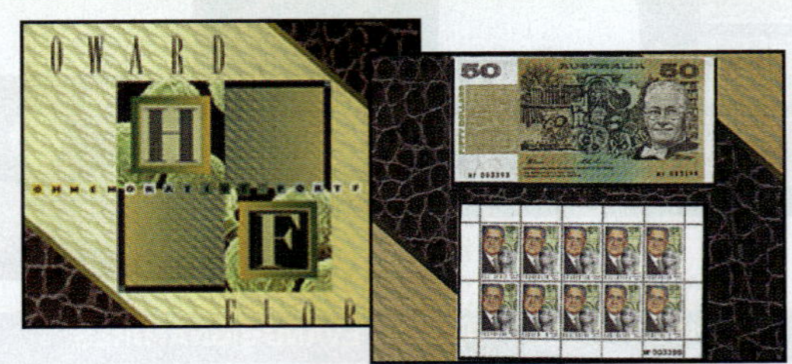

[c] FRASER / EVANS SIGNATURES

McDonald Reference #	Date	Total Issued	Description	Issue Price	Current Retail
McN/APT 7	1995	#0001	Sold at auction	Donated	1,650
McN/APT 8	1995	0999	Red serial numbers	199	175
McN/APT 9	1995	2500	Black serial numbers	129	170

NPA & AUST. POST PORTFOLIO - TYPE 4

1996 30 YEARS DECIMAL CURRENCY
$50 BANKNOTE - PANE OF 10 STAMPS

MACFARLANE / EVANS SIGNATURES

McDonald Reference #	Date	Total Issued	Description	Issue Price	Current Retail
McN/APT 10	1996	#0001	Sold at auction	Donated	975
McN/APT 11	1996	0999	Red serial numbers	95	145
McN/APT 12	1996	2000	Black serial numbers	49	120

NPA & AUST. POST PORTFOLIO - TYPE 5

1997 EMERGENCY SERVICES
$20 BANKNOTE - PANE OF 10 STAMPS

MACFARLANE / EVANS SIGNATURES

McDonald Reference #	Date	Total Issued	Description	Issue Price	Current Retail
McN/APT 13	1997	#0001	Sold at auction	Donated	995
McN/APT 14	1997	0999	Red serial numbers	145	200
McN/APT 15	1997	2000	Black serial numbers	85	165

NPA & AUST. POST PORTFOLIO - TYPE 6

1998 MARITIME HERITAGE
$20 POLYMER - PANE OF 10 STAMPS

FRASER / COLE - FRASER / EVANS SIGNATURES

McDonald Reference #	Date	Total Issued	Description	Issue Price	Current Retail
McN/APT 16	1997	#0001	Sold at auction	Donated	n/a
McN/APT 17	1997	0999	Premium red serials	135	200
McN/APT 18	1997	2000	Black serial numbers	75	165

UNCUTS : 1990 FIVE DOLLARS

FRASER / HIGGINS. Paper issue
Full & Half Sheets, blocks of four & pairs

Reference Numbers - McDonald : Uncut = (McU)

Mc Donald Reference No.	Description	Total Issued	Issue Price	Retail Average
Mc $5 U 1	Full sheet of 40	500 Sheets	500	795
Mc $5 U 2	Half sheet of 20	1,000 Sheets	250	400
Mc $5 U 3	Framed Block of 4	200 Blocks	75	275
Mc $5 U 4	Block of 4	3,800 Blocks	50	175
Mc $5 U 5 a	Pairs	4,000 Pairs	62.5	90

Prices are for "Centres" where applicable. Issues that feature a top or bottom selvedge may command a premium.

(a) Sold as two matching pairs through mail order only. The postage charge was part of the overall price. Actual cost of the two pairs was $50.

NB : These notes were issued loose and not in the familiar colourful folders introduced with later issues.

UNCUTS : 1992 FIVE DOLLARS

FRASER / COLE. Paper issue
Blocks of four & pairs

Mc Donald Reference No.	Description	Total Issued	Issue Price	Retail Average
Mc $5 U 6	Horizontal pairs (Melb)	3,000 Pairs	32.5	75
Mc $5 U 7	As above (Mailing List)	1,000 Pairs	32.5	75
Mc $5 U 8	Vertical Pairs (Adelaide)	1,500 Pairs	32.5	75
Mc $5 U 9	As above (Mailing List)	500 Pairs	32.5	75
Mc $5 U 10	Blocks of Four (Sydney)	1,500 Blocks	65	150
Mc $5 U 11	As above (Mailing List)	500 Blocks	65	150

Coin Fair issues come in a special dated folder. Also one of the banknotes in the fair issues was overprinted with the wording "25th Anniversary 1967 - 1992". Notes featured the prefix XXV, the Roman numerals for "25".

UNCUTS : 1993 FIVE DOLLARS

FRASER / COLE. Polymer issue
One Full Sheet. Auctioned for Charity. Later cut up

Mc Donald Reference No.	Description	Total Issued	Issue Price	Retail Average
Mc $5 U 12	Full sheet of 40 notes	Unique Sheet	Auction	Cut Up

[1] A full sheet with the serial number AA00 000000 was auctioned for charity by *Australian Associated Press Group Financial Markets* at a dinner held in Sydney. It raised $25,000. The $5 sheet was signed by Fraser and Cole. The sheet was later cut into one block of four; one pair and 34 single notes. The single notes were offered for sale at $2,500 each.

UNCUTS : 1996 FIVE DOLLARS

FRASER / EVANS. Recoloured Polymer issue
Blocks of four and pairs

Mc Donald Reference No.	Description	Total Issued	Issue Price	Retail Average
Mc $5 U 13 a	Block of 4. Red serials	001	Auction	2,500
Mc $5 U 14	Block of 4. Red serials	999	95	150
Mc $5 U 15 b	Block of 4. Black serials	2,200	65	140
Mc $5 U 16 c	Pairs. Red serials	001	Auction	1,400
Mc $5 U 17	Pairs. Red serials (Melb)	999	65	70
Mc $5 U 18 d	Pairs. Black serials	2,200	35	65

The above notes were taken from normal production sheets and featured the prefix range from BA 96 to EA 96.
[a] The number 000001 red block was auctioned and raised $2,200 including the buyer's commission at Downies Melbourne auction in February 1996. The proceeds were donated to the Malcolm Sargent Cancer Fund for Children in Australia.
[b] No specific numbers were set aside for the Sydney NAA Coin and Banknote Fair held on March 23 - 24, 1996. Leftover folders were added to the mailing list offering. There were no special features to distinguish those folders offered at the Fair and those sold later through the mail listing.
[c] The Number 000001 red pair was also auctioned by Downies' at their July 1996 auction where it raised $1,000 for the Australian Red Cross, Victoria.
[d] As was the case with the above mentioned Sydney NAA Fair, specific numbers were set aside for the Melbourne NAA Coin and Banknote Fair held on July 6 - 7, 1996. There were no special features to distinguish the folders offered at the Fair from those offered via the mail listing.

UNCUTS : 1997 FIVE DOLLARS

MACFARLANE / EVANS. Recoloured Polymer issue
Blocks of eight banknotes for Hong Kong Export

Mc Donald Reference No.	Description	Total Issued	Issue Price	Retail Average
Mc$5 U 19	Block of 8. "HK97". Red serials	5,000	180	550

This is the first Australian issue of banknotes ever produced to commemorate a foreign event i.e. the handover of Hong Kong to China. Note Printing Australia produced 5,000 sheets of *"Lucky eight"* Australian polymer $5 notes with specially printed red serial numbers prefixed "HK97". The first numeral of the serial number begins with the numeral "8". While mainly for overseas consumption, a small allocation was held back for Australian collectors.

UNCUTS : 1998 FIVE DOLLARS

MACFARLANE / EVANS. Recoloured Polymer issue
200 Full Sheets. Auctioned for Charity

Mc Donald Reference No.	Description	Total Issued	Issue Price	Retail Average
Mc $5 U 20	Uncut sheet of 40 notes	200	Tender	1,100

On March 31, 1998, NPA closed its tender for 200 specially numbered sheets of polymer five dollar notes. Each sheet of 40 notes has a face value of $200. The serial numbers range from AA98 005001 to DA98 005200. The numerical part of the serial number is the same for all notes on a given sheet.

UNCUTS : 2001 FIVE DOLLARS

UNIQUE FEDERATION ISSUE

MACFARLANE / EVANS. ONE YEAR TYPE ISSUE
Full Sheet of 40 notes and blocks of four

Mc Donald Reference No.	Description	Total Issued	Issue Price	Retail Average
Mc$5 U 21a	Full sheet of 40 notes	400	220	800
Mc$5 U 22	Block of 4. Black serials	1,500	69	120

The above notes were taken from normal production sheets and featured the prefix range from GD 01 to JD 01.

[a] The uncut full sheets of 40 notes were sold to collectors by tender. 400 sheets were offered but only 356 sheets were sold. In its Noteworthy Newsletter 37 issued in September 2001, Note Printing Australia advised that the highest bid was for $1,760. The lowest was $220. There was no explanation as to why 44 sheets were unsold or what happened to them.

UNCUTS : 1988 TEN DOLLARS

UNIQUE BICENTENNIAL POLYMER

JOHNSTON / FRASER. ONE YEAR TYPE ISSUE
Full & Half Sheets, Blocks & Strips of Four

Mc Donald Reference No.	Description	Total Issued	Issue Price	Retail Average
Mc $10 U - 1	Full sheet of 24	500 sheets	635/ 975	1,300
Mc $10 U - 2	Half sheet of 12	1,000 sheets	315/ 400	650
Mc $10 U - 3	Block of 4	1,373 blocks	99/ 125	350
Mc $10 U - 4	Strip of 4	1,673 strips	99/ 125	350

Prices are for "Centres"where applicable. Issues that feature a top or bottom selvedge may command a premium.

The 1988 plastic (polymer) note was Australia's first commemorative banknote and the first to be offered in uncut form. It was also the first banknote in the world to incorporate an "Optically Variable Device" (OVD). Developed in Australia, the OVD produces a varying rainbow pattern according to the viewing angle and is designed to deter counterfeiting. The Bicentennial plastic $10 note was issued in 1988 as a commemoration of the 200 years since the first British settlement. The front shows HMS "Sirius," the flagship of the "First Fleet" which arrived at Sydney Cove in 1788. The front of the note also features a scene of early Sydney and a group of people symbolising our national development from 1788 to 1988. The back shows items of Aboriginal culture. The OVD features a portrait of Captain James Cook. As well as the uncut version mentioned here, see elsewhere in this book for details on the presentation folder and the two types of normal circulation issues. The above notes were originally distributed to collectors in two ways. A small allocation was offered to selected staff of the Reserve Bank (now Note Printing Australia) while the majority were offered through a tender to dealers. This was won by M.R. Roberts of Sydney. The actual breakdown of the ratio eventually sold was recently made public through an Administrative Appeals Tribunal. Of the total 4,500 pieces produced, 80% (3,600 sheets, blocks or strips) went to tenderer, M.R. Roberts. The remaining 20% (900 pieces) was retained by the Reserve Bank and NPA. Collector, the late Harold Peake said that correspondence between himself and the issuing authority revealed that of the 900 pieces held back, a total of 531 sheets, strips or blocks were sold to senior bank staff. They paid $50 each for either blocks or strips; $150 each for half sheets and $300 each for full sheets. Mr Peake also said that the 531 pieces consisted of 44 full sheets; 44 half sheets; 127 blocks of four and 316 strips of four. This last figure meant that only 13 strips were originally left for collectors. However judging by the amount of material that was available in the market when the prices quickly rose, it is obvious that many of the lucky bank staff opted for a quick profit.

See their advertisement on page 453

UNCUTS : 1991 TEN DOLLARS

FRASER / COLE *(+ HIGGINS -ERROR)*. Paper Issue Blocks of Four and Pairs

FRASER / COLE - SIGNATURES

Mc Donald Reference No.	Description	Total Issued	Issue Price	Retail Average
Mc$10U 5 a	Hobart pairs (Fraser / Cole)	2,980	65	100
Mc$10U 6 b	Pairs (Fraser / Higgins)	20	65	2,150
Mc$10U 7	Pairs (Mailing list)	1,000	65	95
Mc$10U 8 c	Blocks of Four (Melbourne)	3,000	130	180
Mc$10U 9	Blocks of Four (Mailing list)	2,000	130	180
Mc$10U 10 d	Blocks of Four (Sydney)	3,000	130	180
	REPRINT VARIATIONS			
Mc$10U 11 e	(Similar Melb.Fair). Prefix MFQ, MFS, MFU,MFX. Serials 600106 - 600110	20	—	1,700
Mc$10U 12 f	(Similar Syd. Fair). Prefix MGS, MGU, MGX, MGZ. Serials 600100 - 600110	19	—	2,100
Mc$10U 13 g	Sydney Fair. Defective reprint. No plate numbers.	25/ 30	—	1,700
Mc$10U 14 h	Sydney Fair. Defective reprint. With plate numbers.	10/ 15	—	2.100
Mc$10U 15 i	Similar to Sydney Fair. Unique block printed twice	Unique	—	5,950

Prices are for "Centres" where applicable. Issues that feature a top or bottom selvedge may command a premium.

(a) Issued with a certificate at Hobart Coin Fair held on May 11 -12, 1991.
(b) Five sets of the Hobart Pairs with the serial numbers 600106 to 600110 were found to contain the superseded Fraser / Higgins signatures.
(c) Notes in a special folder overprinted with Fair details.
(d) As above but one note overprinted with Fair details.
(e) These notes originally had the error Fraser / Higgins signature from the same sheet from which the Hobart errors appeared. They also became a "replacement" issue when withdrawn and reprinted for the Melbourne Fair held from July 13 - 14, 1991.
(f) As above but Fraser / Higgins blocks reprinted for the Sydney Coin Fair held from November 16 - 17, 1991.
(g-h) Some Sydney blocks were sold with creases and other defects. NPA accepted the return of these blocks and sent replacements which varied slightly from the originals in the positioning of the "traffic light" and either with or without the security identification Plate Number. *(See Australian Accidental & More Banknotes by Harold Peake for more information).*
(i) This block with the serial number 600106 from the Sydney Fair is unique. Originally was reprinted from the Fraser / Higgins issue and again when returned as a defective issue from a disgruntled customer.

UNCUTS : 1994 TEN DOLLARS

FRASER / COLE. Paper Issue
300 Full Sheets. Sold through tender

Mc Donald Reference No.	Description	Total Issued	Issue Price	Retail Average
Mc$10 U 16	Full sheet of 40 Banknotes	300 Sheets	Tender	1,700

(1) Entire issue offered to collectors through tender. These tenders ranged from $829 to $3,100 according to a report in the June 1994 issue of the ACR.

UNCUTS : 1994 TEN DOLLARS

FRASER / COLE. Paper Issue
One Full Sheet. Auctioned for Charity. Later cut up

Mc Donald Reference No.	Description	Total Issued	Issue Price	Retail Average
Mc $10 U 17 a	Full Sheet of 45	Unique	Auction	Cut up

(a) A full sheet with the serial number AA93 000000 was auctioned for charity by Australian Associated Press Group Financial Markets at a dinner in Sydney on February 18, 1994. It raised $44,000. The $10 sheet was signed by Fraser and Cole. The sheet was later cut into one block of four; one pair and 39 single notes. The single notes were offered for sale at $1,950 each. As the notes are no longer in their original configuration as released by NPA, no value is given in this catalogue.

UNCUTS : 1997 TEN DOLLARS

MACFARLANE/ EVANS. Polymer Issue
Blocks of four and pairs

Mc Donald Reference No.	Description	Total Issued	Issue Price	Retail Average
Mc$10 U 18a	Blocks of 4. Red serials	#0,001	Auction	825
Mc$10 U 19	Blocks of 4. Red serials	0,999	125	180
Mc$10 U 20	Blocks of 4. Blue serials	1,600	95	175
Mc$10 U 21	Pairs. Red serials	1,000	95	110
Mc$10 U 22	Pairs. Blue serials	1,600	65	110

(a) The number one uncut Premium block was auctioned by Noble Numismatics where it raised $650 for the Australian Kidney Foundation.
(1) The entire blue serial issue of the blocks of four (called Deluxe Blocks) was overprinted with the wording "Released at the Coin, Note & Stamp Show, Sydney 21-23 March 1997."
(2) The entire blue serial issue of the pairs (called Deluxe Pairs) was overprinted with the wording "Released at the Coin, Note & Stamp Show Melbourne, 18 - 20 July 1997."
(3) Serial numbering for both blocks and pairs was in the range AA97 toDF97.

UNCUTS : 1999 TEN DOLLARS

MACFARLANE / EVANS. Polymer Issue
150 Full Sheets. Sold through tender

Mc Donald Reference No.	Description	Total Issued	Issue Price	Retail Average
Mc $10 U 23	Uncut sheet of 45 notes	150	Tender	2,750

On March 12, 1999 Note Printing Australia (NPA) closed its tender for 150 specially numbered full sheets of Australian polymer ten dollar notes. Each sheet consisted of 45 notes with a face value of $450. The serial numbers ranged from 010001 to 010150 and were printed consecutively.

UNCUTS : 1989 TWENTY DOLLARS

PHILLIPS / FRASER. Paper Issue
Strips of Ten Notes (2 x 5 configuration)

Mc Donald Reference No.	Description	Total Issued	Issue Price	Retail Average
Mc$20 U 1	Strip of 10 (2 x 5)	36 strips	500	3,100

UNCUTS : 1990 TWENTY DOLLARS

FRASER / HIGGINS. Paper Issue
One Full Sheet. Auctioned for Charity. Later cut up

Mc Donald Reference No.	Description	Total Issued	Issue Price	Retail Average
Mc$20 U 2 a	Full Sheet of 40 notes	Unique	Auction	Uncut

(a) Number 000001 was hand - signed by the signatories (Fraser / Higgins) and sold at a charity auction where it raised $38,000.

UNCUTS : 1993 TWENTY DOLLARS

FRASER / COLE. Paper Issue
Blocks of four and pairs

Mc Donald Reference No.	Description	Total Issued	Issue Price	Retail Average
Mc$20 U 3	Gold serials (Melb)	100 Pairs	98	600
Mc$20 U 4	Red serials (Melb)	1,400 Pairs	85	190
Mc$20 U 5	As above (Mailing list)	700 Pairs	85	190
Mc$20 U 6	Blocks of 4. Gold (Melb)	100 Blocks	165	1,200
Mc$20 U 7	Blocks of 4. Red (Melb)	450 Blocks	148	360
Mc$20 U 8	As above (Mailing list)	350 Blocks	148	335

[1] These uncut pairs and blocks of four incorporated a number of unique features. The notes feature a single letter prefix and gold coloured serial numbers on the first 100 pairs and blocks. The lowest numbered issues were released at the NAA Fair held in Melbourne on July 17 - 18, 1993.

UNCUTS : 1993 TWENTY DOLLARS

FRASER / COLE. Paper Issue
One Full Sheet. Auctioned for Charity. Later cut up

Mc Donald Reference No.	Description	Total Issued	Issue Price	Retail Average
Mc $20 U 9	Full Sheet of 40 notes	Unique	Auction	40,000

Sections of AA 94 000000 after being cut up for sale

UNCUTS : 1994 TWENTY DOLLARS

FRASER / EVANS. Paper Issue
One Full Sheet. Auctioned for Charity. Later cut up

Mc Donald Reference No.	Description	Total Issued	Issue Price	Retail Average
Mc $20 U 10	Full Sheet of 40 Banknotes	Unique sheet	Auction	Cut up

This unique polymer banknote sheet was auctioned at the annual AAP Group Financial Markets Charity Auction, held in Sydney where it raised $30,000. Each of the 40 notes in the sheet was numbered AA94 000000. The $20 sheet was signed by BW Fraser and EA Evans. The sheet was later cut into one block of four; one pair and 34 single notes. The single notes were offered for sale at $2,650 each. As the notes are no longer in their original configuration as released by NPA, no value is given here.

UNCUTS : 1995 TWENTY DOLLARS

FRASER / EVANS. Paper Issue
250 Full Sheets. Sold through tender

Mc Donald Reference No.	Description	Total Issued	Issue Price	Retail Average
Mc $20 U 11	Full Sheet of 40	250 sheets	Tender	3,200

On February 28, 1995, NPA closed its tender for 250 specially numbered sheets of Australian paper $20 notes from the final print run. The average tender was $1,454. The author was told by the buyer of sheet number one that he paid $5,300. Each sheet consisted of 40 notes with a face value of $800. The prefix range was ABR to ADK, the same as the last notes printed for general circulation. The numbers ranged from 000001 to 000250. The normal production process necessitates sheets of notes being numbered in descending order. During the final paper $20 print run, sheets of notes with alpha prefix letters ABR to ADK bore numbers 999999 descending to 611001. Therefore, the 250 sheets of notes for sale have been specially and consecutively numbered. The signature combination was B.W. Fraser and E.A. Evans. A certificate of authenticity with product number (the same as the serial number) was included with each sheet. Australia replaced its circulation paper $20 denomination with a new polymer note on October 31, 1994.

UNCUTS : 1998 TWENTY DOLLARS

MACFARLANE / EVANS. Polymer Issue
Blocks of four and pairs. Red & Black Prefixes

Mc Donald Reference No.	Description	Total Issued	Issue Price	Retail Average
Mc$20 U 12	Blocks of 4. Red serials	400	175	285
Mc$20 U 13	Blocks of 4. Black serials	800	135	250
Mc$20 U 14	Premium pairs. Red serials	400	135	140
Mc$20 U 15	Deluxe pairs. Black serials	800	95	130

Released in May 1998, both the red and black serial numbered blocks of four had prefixes ranging from AA98 to DA98. The 400 red serial numbered blocks had serial numbers from AA98 010001 to DA98 010050 while the black serial numbers ranged from AA98 010051 to DA98 010150. The pairs, released in July 1998, also used the prefix AA98 to DA98. The 400 red serials ranged from AA98 010151 to DA98 010170. The 800 black serials ranged from AA98 010171 to DA98 010210.

UNCUTS : 1989 FIFTY DOLLARS

PHILLIPS/ FRASER. Paper Issue. Blocks of four

Mc Donald Reference No.	Description	Total Issued	Issue Price	Retail Average
Mc $50 U 1	Block of four notes	72 blocks	500	2,125

UNCUTS : 1989 FIFTY DOLLARS

PHILLIPS/ FRASER. Paper Issue
One Full Sheet. Auctioned for Charity. Later cut up

Mc Donald Reference No.	Description	Total Issued	Issue Price	Retail Average
Mc $50 U 2 a	Full sheet of 32	Unique	—	—

(a) Number 000001 was printed but is still in NPA bank archives.

UNCUTS : 1994 FIFTY DOLLARS

FRASER / EVANS. Paper Issue
Blocks of four and pairs. Red & Black Serials

Mc Donald Reference No.	Description	Total Issued	Issue Price	Retail Average
Mc$50 U 3 a	Blocks. Red serials (Melb)	1	Auction	3,000
Mc$50 U 4 b	Blocks. Red serials (Melb)	249	350	750
Mc$50 U 5 c	Blocks. Black serials (Melb)	500	290	575
Mc$50 U 6	Blocks. Black serials (ballot)	250	290	575
Mc$50 U 7 d	Pairs. Red serials (Perth)	1	Auction	1,400
Mc$50 U 8 e	Pairs. Red serials (Perth)	249	250	375
Mc$50 U 9 f	Pairs. Black serials (Perth)	750	190	285
Mc$50 U 10	Pairs. Black serials (ballot)	500	190	285

The above notes had a single letter prefix with blocks featuring either A, B, C, D prefix with the pairs having an E or F prefix. The OCR-B typeface was used.
(a) Block number 000001 was auctioned by Noble Numismatics where it raised $2,600 for the Royal Childrens Hospital, Melbourne.
(b) A total of 249 red serial numbered blocks of four were sold at the NAA Melbourne Fair on July 16 - 17, 1994.
(c) A total of 500 black serial numbered blocks of four were sold at the NAA Melbourne Fair on July 16 - 17, 1994.
(d) Pair numbered 000001 was also auctioned and raised $1,100 for the Princess Margaret Childens' Hospital, Perth.
(e) A total of 249 red serial numbered pairs were sold at the NAA Perth Fair on August 20 - 21, 1994.
(f) A total of 750 black serial numbered pairs were sold at the NAA Perth Fair on August 20 - 21, 1994.

UNCUTS : 1996 FIFTY DOLLARS

FRASER / EVANS. Paper Issue
125 Full Sheets. Sold through tender

Mc Donald Reference No.	Description	Total Issued	Issue Price	Retail Average
Mc $50 U 11	Full sheet of 32	125 Sheets	Tender	3,700

[a] The entire production of this issue was offered to collectors through tender. The average tender was $2,376 according to a spokesperson from NPA. The highest bid was for over $20,000 for sheet number one. The notes carried the final paper prefixes WYR to the last prefix FAB and were numbered from 000001 to 000125

UNCUTS : 1996 FIFTY DOLLARS

FRASER / EVANS. Polymer Issue
One Full Sheet. Auctioned for Charity. Later cut up

Mc Donald Reference No.	Description	Total Issued	Issue Price	Retail Average
Mc $50 U 12	Full sheet of 32	Unique sheet	Auction	Cut up

UNCUT : ONE HUNDRED DOLLARS

1995 FRASER / COLE. Paper Issue
75 Full Sheets. Sold through tender

Mc Donald Reference No.	Description	Total Issued	Issue Price	Retail Average
Mc $100 U 9	Uncut sheet of 32	75 sheets	Tender	6,500

On February 28th, 1997, NPA closed its tender for 75 specially numbered sheets of Australian paper $100 notes from the final print run. Each sheet consisted of 32 notes with a face value of $3,200. As usual, the serial number prefix differs for each note on the sheet. The prefix range was ZJT to ZLD. The ZLD prefix was the same as the last notes printed for general circulation. The numbers ranged from 000001 to 000075. Australia replaced its paper $100 denomination with a new polymer note on May 15, 1996.

UNCUT : ONE HUNDRED DOLLARS

1997 FRASER / EVANS. Polymer Issue
One Full Sheet. Auctioned for Charity. Later cut up

Mc Donald Reference No.	Description	Total Issued	Issue Price	Retail Average
Mc $100 U 10	Uncut sheet of 32	Unique sheet	Auction	Cut up

The last of these unique polymer banknote sheets was auctioned at the AAP Group Financial Markets Charity Auction, held in Sydney on February 21, 1997. It was bought by Mark Duff of the Sydney Coin Exchange for $40,000. Each of the 32 notes in the sheet was numbered AA96 000000. The $100 sheet was signed by BW Fraser and EA Evans. The sheet was later cut into one block of four; one pair and 26 single notes. The single notes were offered for sale at $2,950 each. As the notes are no longer in their original configuration as released by NPA no value is given in this catalogue.

UNCUT : ONE HUNDRED DOLLARS

2000 MACFARLANE / EVANS. Polymer Issue
Blocks of Four and Pairs. Red & Black Serials

Mc Donald Reference No.	Description	Total Issued	Issue Price	Retail Average
Mc $100 U 11	Blocks of 4. Red serials	200	595	1,350
Mc $100 U 12	Blocks of 4. Black serials	280	495	1,000
Mc $100 U 13	Premium pairs. Red serials	200	540	775
Mc $100 U 14	Deluxe pairs. Black serials	280	430	675

The $100 blocks of four, the last in the polymer series, were released in March 2000 although they had serial numbers that identified them as being printed in 1999. They carried serial numbers in the range of AA99 to CF99. The 200 red serial numbered Premium sets range from AA99 010001 to CF99 010025 while the black serial numbers (Deluxe) went from AA99 010026 to CF99 010060. The pairs were released in September 2000 and also had the serial numbers with a "99" prefix. The 200 red Premium sets carried the serials AA99 010074 to CF99 010073. The 280 black numbered Deluxe pairs were numbered from AA99 010074 to CF99 010090.

NPA ARCHIVAL ALBUMS

1991 25TH ANNIVERSARY SET

Mc Donald Reference No.	Description	Total Issued	Issue Price	Retail Average
Mc AV 1	Set number one			15,500
Mc AV 2	Sets with serial numbers below 100			7,950
Mc AV 3	Sets with serial numbers above 100			6,250

One of the most spectacular presentations ever issued anywhere in the world, this leather bound, eight - note set was produced to mark the 25th anniversary of the introduction of decimal currency on February 14, 1966. The notes came from the archives at Note Printing Australia (NPA) and consisted of the last 800 ten shillings, one pound, five pounds and ten pounds issues coupled with the first issue of the one, two, ten and twenty dollar notes. Each of the notes featured a serial number of less than 1,000. All of the notes have the last three digits of the serial number in common while the ten shillings and five pounds notes have fully matching serial numbers. The notes were sold by public tender so it is impossible to determine an "issue price" as such. However it is generally known in the trade that set "Number One" went for $10,000. Following are general current prices. These prices are steadily rising as a growing number of sets are being broken up and the notes sold individually.

1994 TRIPLE ANNIVERSARY SET

Mc Donald Reference No.	Description	Total Issued	Issue Price	Retail Average
Mc TV 1	Set number one			11,000
Mc TV 1	Sets with serial numbers below 100			3,950
Mc TV 1	Sets with serial numbers above 100			3,750

Complementing the previous issue, this premium banknote set was issued in 1994. The 800 leather folders contained three banknotes that were reserved from the inital printing of the paper five dollars, fifty dollars and one hundred dollars denominations. Each set was individually numbered with each of the notes having fully matching serial numbers all under 1,000.

1996 : PRESENTATION SET OF AUSTRALIA'S POLYMER

FRASER / EVANS SIGNATURES. The issue price was $495.00.

Mc PP 1	Set number one	5,000
Mc PP 2	Sets with serial numbers below 100	1,100
Mc PP3	Sets with serial numbers above 100	900

UNCUTS : 1999 FIFTY DOLLARS

MACFARLANE / EVANS. Polymer Issue
Blocks of Four and Pairs. Red & Black Serials

Mc Donald Reference No.	Description	Total Issued	Issue Price	Retail Average
Mc $50 U 13	Blocks of 4. Red serials	200	395	700
Mc $50 U 14	Blocks of 4. Black serials	280	295	575
Mc $50 U 15	Premium pairs. Red serials	200	295	415
Mc $50 U 16	Deluxe pairs. Black serials	280	195	400

Released in May 1998, both the red and black serial numbered blocks of four had prefixes ranging from AA98 to DA98. The 200 red "Premium" blocks had serial numbers from AA98 010001 to DA98 010025 while the black serial numbers ranged from AA98 010051 to DA98 010150. The pairs, released in July 1998, also used the prefix AA98 to DA98. The 400 red serials ranged from AA98 010151 to DA98 010170. The 800 black serials ranged from AA98 010171 to DA98 010210.

UNCUT : ONE HUNDRED DOLLARS

1995 FRASER / COLE. Paper Issue
Blocks of Four and Pairs. Red & Black Serials

Mc Donald Reference No.	Description	Total Issued	Issue Price	Retail Average
Mc $100 U 1 a	Pairs. Red serials	1	Auction	2,200
Mc $100 U 2	Pairs. Red serials (ballot)	299	350	700
Mc $100 U 3	Pairs. Black serials (ballot)	350	295	575
Mc $100 U 4	Pairs. Black serials (Melb)	350	295	525
Mc $100 U 5 a	Blocks. Red serials	1	Auction	3,700
Mc $100 U 6	Blocks. Red serials (ballot)	150	595	1,200
Mc $100 U 7	Blocks. Black serials (ballot)	200	495	975
Mc $100 U 8	Blocks. Black serials (Melb)	300	495	950

The above notes featured a single letter OCR - B prefix with blocks featuring A, B, C, D prefix and the pairs having an E and F prefix. All folders were numbered to match the last four digits of the serial number. In a departure from the norm, the coveted low numbered notes were offered through the Note Printing Australia mailing list rather than the NAA Fair held in Melbourne from July 15 to 16, 1995.

(a) The number 000001 block and pair were auctioned through the Noble Numismatics Auction where they raised $2,800 and $1,500 respectively for the Astronomical Association. The Year 1995 celebrated the Centenary of the Sydney Branch of the British Astronomical Association (1895 - 1995). John Tebbutt, who appears on the $100 note, was the first president of the Sydney Chapter of the Association.